THE PENGUIN ANTHOLOGY OF

CANADIAN
HUMOUR

ALSO BY WILL FERGUSON

Happiness™

How to Be a Canadian
(with Ian Ferguson)

Canadian History for Dummies

Bastards and Boneheads

I Was a Teenage Katima-Victim!

The Hitchhiker's Guide to Japan

Why I Hate Canadians

Beauty Tips from Moose Jaw

Hitching Rides with Buddha: A Journey Across Japan

THE PENGUIN ANTHOLOGY OF

CANADIAN HUMOUR

Edited and with an Introduction by

WILL FERGUSON

VIKING
CANADA

VIKING CANADA

Published by the Penguin Group

Penguin Group (Canada), 90 Eglinton Avenue East, Suite 700, Toronto, Ontario, Canada
M4P 2Y3 (a division of Pearson Penguin Canada Inc.)

Penguin Group (USA) Inc., 375 Hudson Street, New York, New York 10014, U.S.A.
Penguin Books Ltd, 80 Strand, London WC2R 0RL, England
Penguin Ireland, 25 St Stephen's Green, Dublin 2, Ireland (a division of Penguin Books Ltd)
Penguin Group (Australia), 250 Camberwell Road, Camberwell, Victoria 3124, Australia
(a division of Pearson Australia Group Pty Ltd)
Penguin Books India Pvt Ltd, 11 Community Centre, Panchsheel Park, New Delhi – 110 017,
India
Penguin Group (NZ), cnr Airborne and Rosedale Roads, Albany, Auckland 1310, New Zealand
(a division of Pearson New Zealand Ltd)
Penguin Books (South Africa) (Pty) Ltd, 24 Sturdee Avenue, Rosebank, Johannesburg 2196,
South Africa

Penguin Books Ltd, Registered Offices: 80 Strand, London WC2R 0RL, England

First published 2006

1 2 3 4 5 6 7 8 9 10   (FR)

Selection and introductions copyright © Will Ferguson, 2006
The credits on pages 472–476 constitute an extension of this copyright page.

Publisher's note: Names, characters, places and incidents either are the product
of the authors' imaginations or are used fictitiously, and any resemblance
to actual persons living or dead, events, or locales is entirely coincidental.

Manufactured in Canada.

Library and Archives Canada Cataloguing in Publication data available upon request.

ISBN-10: 0-670-06443-2
ISBN-13: 978-0-670-06443-4

Visit the Penguin Group (Canada) website at **www.penguin.ca**

Special and corporate bulk purchase rates available; please see
www.penguin.ca/corporatesales or call 1-800-399-6858, ext. 477 or 474

To Effie, who read the proofs
and prepared the index

Contents

Introduction
by Will Ferguson

A nalyzing humour, it's been said, is an awful lot like dissecting a frog. You may learn something about anatomy, but the frog itself usually dies in the process.

Fortunately, I need not wield a scalpel here, for Stephen Leacock has already achieved the near impossible: he has defined the very essence of humour. And he did so without killing a single frog. The origins of humour, Leacock explained, "lie in the deeper contrasts offered by life itself; in the strange incongruity between our aspirations and our achievements."

It's there, in that *gap*—that gap between what we assume life will bring and how things actually turn out, between what we want and what we get, between our grand plans and high expectations and what is actually accomplished—it is there that humour is fostered, is born. Once you are aware of this principle, you recognize it everywhere. Certainly all of the pieces in this anthology—with the possible exception of James Martin, who's in a category all his own—draw upon this "strange incongruity," this discrepancy between the ideal world and the real.

Robertson Davies took it even further. A sense of humour, he noted, is more of a curse than a blessing. Life was easier, he felt, for those who went through their day-to-day existence without seeing the essential absurdity—the humour—underlying everything.

So. When perusing a collection such as this, it is important to take each author *on his or her own terms,* in his or her own voice. Whether you prefer folksy humour over urban grit (or vice versa), you should approach each selection for what it is: a distinct way of looking at the world, a distinct way of dealing with that gap.

From Ray Guy in St. John's to Jack Knox in Victoria, I have tried to throw as wide a net as possible. Some of the pieces gathered here are homespun and endearing. Others have a definite edge. Some are silly. Some are quite profound. Some are culled from alternative arts magazines, others from major literary works. All are distinctly Canadian in ways I can't quite put my finger on. It's like pornography; you know it when you see it—even if you can't come up with an exact definition. Sure, I have included hockey players and Mounties, and even a glimpse or two of the Rockies, but for the most part I have chosen pieces that resonate with me simply because they feel very Canadian.

I have included selections from some of our best-known authors: Mordecai Richler, Robertson Davies, Mavis Gallant, Douglas Coupland, Miriam Toews. But I've also included authors who, while perhaps not as well known, deserve to be much more widely read. Authors such as Ivan E. Coyote and Mariko Tamaki.

I tried to avoid obvious choices when I made my selections. As much as I love Roch Carrier's "The Hockey Sweater," it's an often-anthologized story, so I went instead with translator Sheila Fischman's delightful recommendation, "Titties Prayer." Similarly, although I'm a great fan of Robert Service and will prattle off a recitation of "The Cremation of Sam McGee" at the slightest provocation (I'm something of a philanthropist that way), I nevertheless wanted to avoid the predictable choice of "Dan McGrew" or the aforementioned "McGee," and went instead with a personal favourite, "The Ballad of Pious Pete."

This anthology is arranged alphabetically, by author, rather than along thematic or regional lines. Two reasons: First, I think collections such as these should be easy to use. Second, and more importantly, the focus must remain squarely on the authors. It is their own distinct, often skewed world views that are being celebrated here, not any overarching thesis of Canadian identity. The soothing conversational stylings of Stuart McLean couldn't be more unlike the wild exuberance of, say, Richard J. Needham. Yet both are assuredly Canadian. It's a Big Tent, this country.

If you do decide to read this book from start to finish in the order it is presented, be prepared to change gears wildly—an effect that can be enlivening or jarring depending on your point of view. The shift from Gary Lauten's gentle poke at married life to the sudden serrated edge of Dany Laferrière is particularly jolting, to name just one example. At other times, the alphabet throws out interesting rapports, such as the parallel between Thomas King's view of Indians in Canadian society and that of W.P. Kinsella's, both of which are oddly complementary.

But you aren't going to read this book in alphabetical order, from Bidini to White, are you? I didn't think so. So, to help you as you jump about, here are several through-lines you can follow. Sort of "mini-anthologies" embedded in the text:

- If you're interested in travel writing, you should start with Dave Bidini's hockey trip to Hong Kong and Paul Quarrington's search for God in the Galapagos, with Jacques Poulin's Volkswagen journey as a chaser.

- For comedic verse, there's the poetry of Bill Richardson and Robert Service, and the lyrics of Nancy White. (And for wonderfully *bad* comedic verse, there's Paul Hiebert.)

- For folk tales and fables, see Jacques Ferron's short stories and Antonine Maillet's *The Tale of Don L'Orignal,* which is very much in the tradition of Jonathan Swift.

- For social satire, with a slightly surreal touch, turn to M.A.C. Farrant's send-up of New Age "retreats," Zsuzsi Gartner's withering look at PowerPoint parents, and Erika Ritter's oddly poignant encounter with Barbie's bitter ex, Mr. Ken Doll.

- For parody—as opposed to satire—see Dan Needles's wonderful spoof of local history books; Paul Hiebert's devastating slam-dunk of literary criticism; Stephen Leacock's incisive guide to Shakespeare; and Bob Edwards's "transcript from a debate in the Canadian House of Commons."

- For quick, lighter reads, I have included a healthy selection from Canadian humour columnists. The newspaper column is an exacting art form, one with strict word counts requiring an economy of language and a single strong focus. You'll find Arthur Black on sailing, Chuck Brown on fixing a roof, Marsha Boulton on raising turkeys.

- Finally, there is a certain, unmistakably Canadian style of humour—playful, pithy, disarming, and at times touching—that can only be described as "Leacockian." You can see it Joey Slinger's advice on how to stay out of the gutter; in Brian O'Connell's visit from an imaginary friend; in Eric Nicol's experiences on Broadway; in *all* of Stuart Trueman's selections; and, of course, in the work of Stephen Leacock (who would, I'm sure, get a kick out of having his writing described as "Leacockian").

Regrets? Several. I was sorely limited in my choice of francophone writing. People would gush things like "What about Yvon Deschamps? You have to include Yvon Deschamps! He's hilarious." Deschamps, who famously described what Quebeckers really want as "*Un Québec indépendant dans un Canada uni!*" is indeed a sharp and witty fellow. I gladly would have included him if I could have found anything available in translation. (A good deal of French-Canadian literature is translated every year, but very little of it is humour. This may be part of the problem.)

The good news? The francophone writing that *is* included is very strong. Roch Carrier, Jacques Ferron, Dany Laferrière, Antonine Maillet, and Jacques Poulin provide some of the best pieces in this collection.

I desperately wanted to include a selection from Michel Tremblay's play *Les Belles Soeurs* (where fourteen women in a working-class Quebec neighbourhood gather in a kitchen to paste trading stamps into booklets for a contest), which would have dovetailed nicely with Tomson Highway's *The Rez Sisters* (a play about seven women from a Cree-Ojibway reserve in Ontario who are determined to beat the odds by travelling to Toronto to take part in—and the term is always given in caps—THE BIGGEST BINGO IN THE WORLD). But something happens when you lay down a play onto the page. It just sits there. It loses its vitality. Plays are meant to be heard, to be seen. They are not meant to be read in the way one might read a novel. So, to the poor typesetter who stayed up late resetting pages of text into proper play format, adjusting the margins and changing the indents—only to have it all taken out—I give a sincere and heartfelt, "Sorry, eh?"

Two other selections were also typeset and formatted before being yanked, with much anguish on my part. Yves Beauchemin's novel *Le Matou* (translated into English as *The Alley Cat*) and Edward Riche's novel *Rare Birds* defeated me. Both are terrifically funny books. Both were impossible to excerpt. I spent weeks wrestling with them, to no avail.

Beauchemin's *The Alley Cat* is a sprawling, satirical novel that has sold over one million copies worldwide and has been translated into fifteen languages. It's a Dickensian tale with multiple characters and interwoven storylines, and I never could figure out how to do it justice.

Riche's *Rare Birds,* set in Newfoundland and later adapted into a film, is the tale of a despondent chef, his relentlessly supportive neighbour, a mysterious and possibly sinister science experiment, a large bag of cocaine, and a grand hoax that quickly runs out of control. I tried again and again to excerpt this novel, isolating different aspects of the story, stringing disparate passages together with only a disingenuous ellipse between them—but no matter what I did, it ended up sounding like a thin-gruel *Reader's Digest* summary. (In a strange coincidence, both Riche's and Beauchemin's novels revolve around the inner workings of restaurants. So perhaps it was a mental block from my own days slinging hash as a line cook that kept tripping me up.)

When I read the final typeset pages, I came to the sad realization that these selections had to go. So, to fans of Tomson Highway, Michel Tremblay, Yves Beauchemin, and Edward Riche: You're right. They should have been included. But they weren't.

In a different vein, two other authors were removed at the last minute solely because neither the publisher nor myself could track down the owners of their estates. Maggie Grant and Robert Thomas Allen were both in the final Table of Contents, their pieces proofread and ready to go, but in both cases we could not locate the copyright holder and were thus unable to arrange permissions. This was especially surprising in the case of Allen, who was a very well-known humorist. He passed away in 1990, having won the

Leacock Medal for Humour *twice*. But, like Maggie Grant, he thwarted the best efforts of Google and our editorial sleuthing.

It was a long process. Oftentimes I would disappear behind towering stacks of books for days on end, reappearing only for air and the occasional Timbit tossed into my mouth from the top of the stairs by a worried spouse. "Why are you down there laughing like that? Alone?" I was dishevelled, unshaven—but happy. (Good therapy, that: editing humour books.) It's been fun and, if not exhaustive, it has certainly been exhausting.

I do hope you enjoy this collection of Canadian humour. If you have any queries, concerns, or corrections, I really don't want to hear about it. Errors and oversights should be ascribed to gremlins and late-night eye fatigue, not editorial intent. And please, please don't send me emails demanding to know "Why wasn't X or Y included? And what about Z? How can you *possibly* have an anthology that doesn't include Z???" Listen. X wasn't included because X isn't funny. Y wasn't included because I just plain don't like Y—she breathes through her nose when she eats and always adds sideways smiley faces at the end of her emails no matter how inappropriate. I mean, really. *"Our thoughts are with you in your time of loss :-)"* Who the hell does something like that? And don't even get me started about Z, that bastard.

Okay. So maybe editing a humour anthology is not the *best* form of therapy available. But reading one surely is. And that's where I shall leave it, while there is still life in the ol' amphibian yet. Happy reading!

—*Will Ferguson, en route to a nap*

THE PENGUIN ANTHOLOGY OF

CANADIAN
HUMOUR

Dave Bidini

What a great gig. Dave Bidini is Canada's hockey nomad, travelling
the globe in search of the game "in unlikely places." It's a quest that
has taken him from Mongolia to Siberia, from Transylvania to the
United Arab Emirates. The following is the opening chapter of
Bidini's freewheeling travel memoir *Tropic of Hockey,* which recounts
an early trip to Hong Kong—all for a game of shinny.

FROM *Tropic of Hockey*

Kris King Looks Terrible

I am going to China.

We've all been asked "So, what's new?" many times in our lives, but
it's almost never that you get to answer, "I am going to China." I am more
likely to respond, "Frig all. It's not like I'm going to China or anything." So
when I got the chance, I milked it. I was Marco Polo draped in robes, hand
held aloft, eyes to the sky: "I am going ... to *China*!" I liked saying it. I said
it lots. I might as well have walked around town with a *Guy Who Is Going to
China* sign around my neck.

Janet and I planned our trip based on the principle that, when we
dropped the name of the country and stated our purpose, people would have
to wobble on their heels in disbelief: "They play hockey there?" Of course,
there were other factors. Janet suggested that we stay clear of war zones, active
volcanoes, and places overrun by infestations or plague. I proposed that we
limit ourselves to nations regarded for their flush toilets.

"Well, that rules out about half the world," she said.

"The toilets can't be that bad, can they?" I asked.

"Ah, no. You bring toilet paper; you're fine."

"You bring what?"

"You'll be fine. Don't be a baby."

My apprehension over toilets was not just infantilism. I believe that if most men were asked to draw up plans for their dream bathroom, it would be located about fifty feet underground and have a steel-reinforced door. Maybe a stack of *Mad* magazines. Most of us could live there.

I was such a greenhorn when it came to prolonged, distant travel that I found even the process of making perfunctory arrangements for our trip exciting. I hadn't wandered but a mile from home when I started to feel the tingle of high adventure. That was my visit to the Tropical Disease Clinic. There I was shot full of a magic serum, which provided protection against yellow fever, diphtheria, and typhoid. The sense of adventure was fleeting, however, for I soon grew melancholy that I could no longer be stricken by such terrible diseases. Had I developed one of these horrible strains, I imagined the conversation in one of the city's taverns.

"Did you hear about Dave?" they'd ask.

"No. What?"

"He went to China and got yellow fever."

"Man, he's really living!"

There was a poster in the doctor's office identifying parasites found in developing countries. I remembered the Redmond O'Hanlon story about the parasite that slinks into the body through the penis and umbrellas inside one's intestines. This reminded me not to go swimming in China—and perhaps not anywhere ever again. I felt secure in the knowledge that this bug would not get within a country mile of my penis until I was struck by a rather phobic thought: What if that little fellow managed to stand up on the bowl with his hands arrowed and leap off the edge, only to shoot into me like that tiny submarine in *The Fantastic Voyage*? I explained this fear to Janet. "Don't be ridiculous," she said. "There's no such thing as a toilet bowl in China."

While I wrestled with the riddle of how toilets could apparently exist without toilet bowls, I left Janet to prepare herself for the Far East. My only pre-trip endeavour was to sort out my hockey bag. This was not the effortless job it may appear.

The challenge of lugging an equipment duffle around the world was daunting enough, let alone one sagging with wet socks, sweaty T-shirts, and used tape clods. As I cleaned it, I found the bottom to be too damp and malodorous to inflict upon the world; its foul stench could defeat all measures we'd take to comport ourselves like touring diplomats. I envisioned my gear being held at the border and searched by an unlucky customs official with a hanky pressed to his face, who would have no choice but to drag it out back against a wall and blast holes into its fetid body.

I bought a new hockey bag. It was the kind with pockets and flaps and a reinforced base that will not bow no matter how much swampy rink water you pour into it. I started packing it with a bar of soap, a pair of athletic underpants, and a shower towel. Janet had a good laugh at that one, as in all my years of recreational hockey, I have never once showered at the rink. If you understand anything about the leisure hockey community, you know that it is divided into those who shower and those who don't. For some, waving one's gherkin in front of other men is easy; they can tromp around naked in the company of others and not turn the slightest shade of red. But I find something disconcerting about a fellow who will stand unclothed in front of you and carry on a conversation as if he'd bumped into you at the frozen-food section of the supermarket. He could be Carl Sagan unveiling the secrets of the cosmos, yet I would absorb nothing. I find that the presence of one's dangling protuberance has the tendency to overshadow even the most profound thoughts. Perhaps this explains why dressing-room banter rarely touches upon science or mathematics. Really, it's hard enough to sell one's theory of the universe in a tweed suit, let alone with yer wanger hanging out.

In addition to hygiene products, I filled my bag with hockey tape, pucks, shoulder pads, pants, elbow pads, shin guards, helmet, skates, hockey socks, jockstrap, and garter belt. The bag bulged like a lumpy balloon, and looked as if a pinprick would send it flying. I had barely enough room in the side pocket to squeeze in my gummy, blue mouth guard, a recent purchase which, when fitted between my gums, made me feel like I was chewing on a child's bathtub toy. But I had a practical reason for bringing it. The last thing I wanted was to end up with a handful of my own teeth, strapped pale and bloodied into a dentist's chair in some fly-infested office in a strange land, although I must admit the notion of spending time in a foreign hospital seemed like the kind of episode that made one a true adventurer.

Janet's pre-trip preparation put me to shame: she signed up for Mandarin lessons. I was jealous until I realized I should be thankful that it had occurred to at least one of us that we'd be spending the next six weeks among people who spoke another language. She quickly mastered several key phrases, not the least significant being "My husband is a writer," which she repeated over and over, usually while staring into the toaster oven or riding her bike. This made me feel quite important until I learned that the word for writer was similar to those for table and chicken.

"You might have to get used to the fact that I'll be calling you a table chicken every now and then," Janet warned, before going on to say "My husband is a table chicken" over and over—perhaps with the intention of thrumming me into a catatonic state, making the phrase quite apt. I told her that it was fine to say, but hard to accept if you were the one being mistaken for either a table or a chicken.

"What if we order chicken in a restaurant and you use the word for writer by mistake?" I wondered.

"Maybe they'll bring us George Plimpton," she said.

I managed to learn one phrase in Mandarin: *Wo da bing xi*. In English, this means "I play ice hockey." Mandarin is a language based on tonal ups and downs that sound rather like a flautist running his fingers over the sound holes. While I am to linguistics what B.F. Skinner is to hip hop, still I found Mandarin fun to speak, and I understood why Janet was using it so much. After a while, *Wo da bing xi* was pretty much all I wanted to say, even though I realized the problem of knowing only one phrase in a land roughly three-quarters the size of Canada with, oh, forty times the people. For instance, should I have to tell an officer of the law of some kind of danger—say, a baby trapped inside a burning building—I wouldn't be much help if all I knew how to say was "I play ice hockey!"

"Wo da bing xi! Wo da bing xi!" I'd scream while gesturing at the flaming door. The cops would have no choice but to subdue me with a blunt club.

• • •

On the day we left for China—March 1, 1999—I arrived at the airport carrying my Winwell hockey bag and three Koho hockey sticks. Even though my lapsed physique made me look more like a Colonial League journeyman, armed with my own gear I still felt like a pro. I noticed other travellers squinting at me across the floor, trying to square my face with a hockey card. But it was an impossible composite, and I could hear them telling their friends later, "I saw the Leafs at the airport today. Kris King looks terrible."

We made our way to the departure gate, my hockey bag strapped to my back like a camel's hump. Janet was equipped with all the essentials of international transport—visas, passports, tickets, traveller's cheques, insurance, guide books, and toothpaste—and I with all the tools of athletic combat, plus two blank scribblers and a tape recorder.

No matter how thoroughly I prepare before going abroad, I find air travel hard. I enjoy it to an extent, but not without a deep-rooted fear that by hopping that little half-foot gap between passenger chute and airplane, I'm consigning myself to death at 30,000 feet. I could probably trace this fear back to the time I saw *Airport '77* at the drive-in. I still look for George Kennedy whenever I get on a plane, and if I don't find him, I know I'm all right. Fortunately, no one who ever travelled Air Korea looked anything like George Kennedy.

But the flight was uneventful, and we landed fifteen hours later at Hong Kong's new international airport, where we were met by a strange man in glasses. This wasn't quite the scene from a Bond caper that it sounds, because the stranger was a man with whom I was vaguely familiar. I'd written to Herb Shoveller—a journalist for the *London Free Press* who was on sabbatical in Hong Kong with his family—after reading his *National Post* article about hockey in Mongolia. He'd visited Ulan Bator in December 1998 with a

Chinese expatriate team for a round-robin tourney against a local Mongol club, and had talked about natural ice and players wearing newspaper pads. He talked of sitting in his hotel room watching CNN, then looking out his window to see men riding horses through the snow.

I told Herb, by email, that I was planning to visit his city for the Hong Kong Fives' Hockey Tournament, which I'd read about while researching Chinese hockey on the internet, and he offered to collect us on arrival.

We stayed with the Shovellers and their children, Aislin and Ben, in Repulse Bay, one of the island's toniest neighbourhoods. Their apartment complex—which included a Polo shop, a Japanese restaurant, and a cafe that sold a seventeen-dollar cup of coffee—was built on a hillside. It was designed to look like an enormous flag rippling in the wind, and it lorded over the bay. Remarkably, there was a seven-storey rectangular gap in the middle of the building so that the mythical Chinese dragon could pass through, should it decide to slither down from the mountains. A product of *feng shui,* the gap made the building look like a cyclops. Many Westerners who lived in Repulse Bay shook their heads when they talked of how *feng shui* had left the building with a divot the size of Peterborough, but this design feature had practical use beyond serving as the dragon's passageway. In a city of eight million, many of whom lived in grey apartment cubes, there was only one Repulse Bay, and "the building with the hole in it," was all you had to say for people to know exactly where to find you.

The Bay was patrolled twenty-four hours a day by security staff in white suits. They watched over the lush, manicured grounds where newlyweds posed for photos in formal wear rented from a nearby shop. Entire families could be found sitting tuxedoed and bejewelled on the lawn, scrutinized by an impassive sentinel lest someone pluck a clover. Jackie Chan had shot a film here; European diplomats peopled the ritzy apartments; and ex-pats who'd been shipped across the ocean by multinationals made it their home. This was not a place where you'd find Megadeth blasting from behind a window draped with the Confederate flag. It was as exclusive and self-important as Beverly Hills, and as lovely. I liked to stand on the white stone terrace with my hand on the balustrade looking over the South China Sea, imagining I was John Barrymore in a scarf staring into an eternity of sky and water. The terrace felt like a starting point—the tip of a latitude, the mouth of a trade route—and, ignoring the sound of sentries describing my appearance into their walkie-talkies, I was almost at peace.

• • •

After a full day's rest, we headed into town to find SkyRink, the home of the tournament.

The thought crossed my mind that SkyRink might not be anything close to what its name suggested. I almost expected to be disappointed since, these days, arena names make little sense. For instance, not only does the National Car Rental Center, home of the Florida Panthers, promise little in the way of aesthetics, you can't even rent a car there. Same with the horseless Saddledome in Calgary. And despite the nation's affection for the old Maple Leaf Gardens, there's probably more foliage growing on the Hoover Dam. These erroneous names aren't reserved only for the pro ranks, either. In Toronto, new hockey complexes are being called Ice Gardens, Ice Land, and Ice Palace, names better suited to the American south, where the word "ice" is required so that people don't show up in shorts clutching frozen cappuccinos. But in Canada, what does one expect to find in an arena? Beach volleyball? The Antiques Roadshow? A name like Ice Land is proof of how insidious the American lexicon is in Canada's game. I prefer rinks to be named after dead people— Ted Reeve, Jimmy Simpson, Max Bell. The names suggest a persona, a link to the past, the warmth of someone's den.

Judging by the nature of other arenas with *Sky* in their name, SkyRink did not hold much promise. SkyDome, the home of the Toronto Blue Jays, is fine if you enjoy the perils of sitting in a place where slabs of concrete have been known to come crashing down. In Edmonton, the Skyreach Centre is now the home of the Edmonton Oilers. The building used to be called Northlands Coliseum—a name that evokes hoarfrost and mulled wine and poplar trees—but the name was changed to Skyreach—which evokes nothing—when the local telephone company tossed a few million at the club, aping a trend that has besmirched more than a few stadia. The acquisition of naming rights is one of the scourges of modern sport. Candlestick Park in San Francisco was renamed 3Com Park after a software company, Jack Murphy Stadium in San Diego became QUALCOMM Stadium (software again), and Joe Robbie Stadium in Miami became Pro Player Stadium (you guessed it: men's underwear). Perhaps the most extreme example is the STAPLES Center, the home of the LA Kings. Until I heard the name, I hadn't realized how much hockey reminded me of the fast-paced world of office supplies.

The road out of the Bay was trimmed with long-armed trees cupping orange and pink blossoms like altar boys holding candles. The flowers hung in bunches over the road and whipped against the flank of the bus, which rushed along the winding road gripping the edge of the cliff. The bus tilted and tipped as it fought corners and, with each turn, small vistas of the city were revealed: knots of blue and white high-rises; the shimmering green track of the Happy Valley raceway; a whitewashed mansion with guard dogs and gold gates; a regatta of iron ships floating in the bay; the stone shelves of an old terraced graveyard rising over the city; and, at the bottom of a street of Victorian homes, a procession of checker-skirted schoolgirls.

We drove under one overpass, then another, and suddenly the city was very loud. The first few moments entering a strange city are always stage-directed by your senses. They're so inflamed by the newness of the environment that you find yourself thinking things like, "My God! That exhaust smells so wonderful and strange!" or "That garbage over there is just so darned colourful!" even as the locals are making choking sounds. While abroad, the senses refuse to be burdened by the mundane. They're wearing sombreros and drinking umbrella drinks and carrying on.

The bus let us off on Cheung Sha Wan Road in Kowloon market, renowned throughout the world as the hub of the pirated electronics underground. The market rattled at full pelt. Stereo salesmen had dragged their tallest sound systems to the edge of the sidewalk and were blasting Canto-Pop at ear-splitting volumes. There was junk everywhere. An electronics boneyard littered the sidewalk with hacked-apart eight-tracks and CB radios—not to mention the obligatory box of used LPs with the same unloved Seals and Crofts albums you'd find at home—laid out on old newspapers and blankets. Fruit vendors came at me bearing weird-looking apples. In narrow alleyways, goat carcasses and pig heads and groupers the size of cricket bats hung under vinyl canopies. A corner apothecary offered boxes of Leung Chi See Dog Pills, Ping On Ointment, Essence of Deer, and Atomic Enema in its window; next door a young man sat, legs crossed behind a row of typewriters with flowers stemmed through their print bars; wholesale clothing depots flooded three city blocks—Fancy Fashion, Funny Fashion, Top and Top Fashion, Bukky Fashion, and, of course, Fukky Fashion; shops tented in the middle of the street and lit by bare bulbs were festooned with cables, speaker wires, baskets of fuses, watches, and belt buckles; and a small pastry shop sold crates of sea prune, liquorice prune, and dried sour-cream prune, which young girls pressed into their mouths by the handful. The high clucking pitch of restaurant crowds filled the air.

I was in Parkdale no longer.

We stood in front of Dragon Centre mall, a huge building that loomed arms-crossed over the market. The entrance was filled with a circus of laughing children being scooped up by an escalator. We rode with them, upwards into the building behind a floor-to-ceiling glass façade. The ride was spectacular. We stared out at Kowloon across acres of high-rises pressed shoulder to shoulder, their sides thistled with television antennae. Laundry waved in a parade of coloured flags. Beyond that: smokestacks, the sea, the red horizon.

We floated higher.

Finally, on the eighth floor of the mall, I heard hockey—the honking of the score-clock, the bang of the puck against the boards, the referee's whistle, skates chopping snow. I smelled the chemicals of the ice and the Zamboni diesel, and then I saw it: a rink small enough to fit in your palm, a sprite's pond, a place for Tom Thumb, Gabby Boudreau. To best describe it I have to use a word not often associated with the greatest sporting stadia of our time: cute.

It was a play rink.

It was one-fifth the size of an NHL oval—18 metres by 42 metres, to be exact. Perhaps a homesick architect from Trois-Rivières had been left with a narrow concrete channel and decided to fill it with ice. It was maybe the width of three bowling lanes. I suspected that bigger puddles had been left by the monsoon. Every element of SkyRink was odd. Since it was eight storeys up inside a glass tower, you could look out and forecast the weather from the way the clouds rolled in off the South China Sea. There was a mezzanine with an arcade—pinball machines, toy cars, and robotic clowns—that cantilevered over the rink and filled the air with the sound of bells and horns and children crying out to each other. Between the mezzanine and the rink was a yellow roller coaster that was close enough to the ice that you could reach up with a hockey stick and tap it. It was a flame-tongued, turquoise dragon that hurtled over the ice at high speeds, a frightful spectacle for even the most steel-nerved goaltender. It seemed that SkyRink had been designed with the idea of marrying amusement-park folly to hockey, and while hockey has experimented with this theme before—San Jose's shark blimp and Anaheim's daredevil duck come to mind, as do the barrel jumping and dogsled races that were part of intermissions in the 1920s—at least those novelties were kept at a safe distance from the action. But at SkyRink, there was no barrier or railing to prevent someone in the arcade from pelting the players with eggs or worse, and it did nothing to allay my fears of being killed by a large metal lizard.

At both ends of the ice, loose white netting was strung up behind the goals. It reminded me of the mesh in those old Soviet rinks, which Team Canada used to complain about. The SkyRink netting served two purposes: to catch pucks and to act as a curtain for the dressing area, which lay just behind the end boards. It did neither job well. It whipped pucks back to the ice, and, like Cheryl Tiegs' macramé tank top, if you looked closely enough, you could see everything. Behind the netting, players freely changed in and out of their clothes. The scene was like something out of a rogue health club: fellows in towels strode to and from the bathrooms, the odd player revealing his bare ass and hairy stomach (or bare, hairy ass). This abundance of flesh did little to ease my fear of being naked before strangers, and while not every player flashed skin—some used a series of towels like semaphore flags to guard their parts—many treated the area like a Roman bath. Exhibitionists would dig SkyRink. I thought of that brazen Canadian couple who were caught love-making in the windows of the SkyDome Hotel. Here, you could press ham before eight million people.

SkyRink had a Zamboni. It was old and dented and looked as if it had stood in the way of a Matthew Barnaby shitfit. It had South China Ice Hockey League written in Chinese and English on the side and was driven by a young Chinese man in yellow sweats who was far too slender to bring any credibility to his job.

SkyRink had other credibility problems. Frankly, it didn't smell bad enough. Let's face it: hockey stinks. It's a bloated, heavy odour that you can poke with your finger. The first time I set foot in a rink after years away from the game, I rushed a hockey sock to my face to guard myself from the stench. Of course, after a few weeks in my equipment bag, the sock was well stewed and I was forced to wrap something else around my mouth. When I ran out of socks, I had to embrace the game's feral miasma.

But SkyRink smelled like jasmine (I should have been grateful, I know). The source of this fragrance was Kathy K's Pro Shop, which was stocked with a surprising complement of top-of-the-line hockey gear. Unlike many skate-sharpening depots—which tend to smell of plugged plumbing and are operated by large, unshaven men—Kathy K's carried the scent of blossoms, and if that wasn't strange enough, Kathy thanked you for your business and offered a bowl of candies by the cash register, allowing you to take to the ice chewing a gumball and spitting rainbow trails of purple, blue, and red.

There was also the food problem. And again, it wasn't so much a problem as, well, a treat. There was no snack bar at SkyRink, unless you counted the Jack in the Box, which I only ever saw used by ex-pats teary-eyed for the taste of grease. Instead, there was a food court opposite the rink, where women with faces carved by time spooned sea snails the size of silver dollars and braised aubergine and double-cooked pork onto plastic plates, the aroma of garlic and soya and sesame oil scenting the air. There were kiosks selling blackened grouper, lemon chicken, bean curd seared in garlic and peppers, sushi, and hot soup with prawns—not your typical hockey cuisine.

The crowd at SkyRink was also its own. It was mostly seniors who had wandered over from the food court (proving that, no matter where you go in the world, you'll find the same people hanging out in malls). It was a rare treat to skate along the boards and exchange glances with a group of old men who could have been extras in *The Last Emperor*. After a few days, I discovered that they appreciated pratfalls and gaffes rather than athletic grace and beauty. If someone scored an end-to-end goal, they'd get little reaction, but if they tripped over the net or were slew-footed or got slashed in the eye, the old men would laugh and pantomime their fall. The less able you were on your skates the more you were liked by the gallery; before the tournament ended, there was a real chance that I'd be a star.

Arthur Black

I think of Arthur Black as Canada's favourite uncle. A popular speaker, two-time winner of the Leacock Medal for Humour, and host of CBC Radio's *Basic Black* for almost twenty years, he lives in enviable idleness on Salt Spring Island in Canada's warm Pacific Northwest, where he continues to muse about life and pen columns, both funny and philosophical.

FROM *Flash Black*

Sailing, Sailing …

When it comes to sailing, sailing over the bounding main, I is not the b'y that built the boat, and I'se definitely not the b'y that sailed 'er. I've been a landlubber most of my life, living on solid ground, leagues away from any large bodies of water—unless you count the Grand River, which you shouldn't (average depth six inches). So I had a lot of nautical stuff to learn when I moved to an island in the Pacific a few years ago. And I decided it was high time I learned about sailing. Signed up for a three-day intensive course. Twenty-seven-foot sloop. Expert skipper. Couple of other greenhorns like myself.

One of the bonuses of sailing is that even before you get your sea legs, you learn a whole new language. Now, the words "port" and "starboard" I already knew, and "bow" and "stern" ("bow" being the pointy end). Heck, I even knew that the floor of the boat is called the deck. But when it came to the more arcane terms, I really didn't know the ropes.

Well, there now. You see what I mean? There are no ropes on a boat. They're called lines. Except when they're called sheets. Or shrouds. Or stays. Or halyards. Or a guy or a brace or a boomvang—those are all different ro—I mean, lines that you'll find on a … you know, boat. Except it's not a boat really either. It's a ship. See, the rule is that a ship *carries* boats. So the twenty-seven-footer I was on was a ship. Or specifically, a sloop. Or a ketch. Or a yawl. Or a catamaran/trimaran/galley/gondola/clipper/cutter/schooner/lateen/packet/trawler/sampan/smack—or a brigantine/barkentine/shipentine.

We'll call it the vessel.

And sails? You know sails? Forget sails. They are gennys or jibs or spinnakers. And the big guy? The main sail there? That's the *mainsl*. Get used to that too. Even words that you might recognize when written down, you won't recognize when the skipper bawls them at you. The main sail is *mainsl*. Leeward is *lured*. Bowline is *bowln*. Gunwale becomes *gunnel*. And forecastle is *fo'c'sle*.

On the other hand, the words "gudgeon" and "pintle" are pronounced exactly as they are spelled. I know that. What I don't know is what the hell a gudgeon and a pintle is. Or are.

Oh, it's an out-of-body experience bounding over the main for the first time. For one thing, you don't actually bound. You kind of ooze along. You know what the average speed of a sailboat is? Four knots. Four-and-a-bit miles an hour. You can walk that fast without breaking into a sweat. And the neat thing about walking is that you don't need the $30,000 yacht, the $800 depth finder, and the $250 Windjammer Hanson squall jacket. You want to walk down to the corner store—why, you just point your schnozz at the corner store and start shuffling towards it. Sailing isn't like that. You don't simply sail from A to B. You tack. Tacking is the polar opposite of the straight line. When you tack, the object is to cover as much ground (well, sea) as possible in your journey from where you are to where you're going.

You sail to the left (or port) until the skipper yells something unintelligible that sounds like "Helms alee," and then you sail to the right (or starboard). Eventually, the skipper hollers again, and you sail to the left for quite a spell. Then once more you sail to the right, all the time creeping up on your destination by the tiniest increments possible.

Now, if I've made sailing sound like a bewildering and ludicrously expensive way to spend your leisure time, then that's good. I might have saved you a lot of money and a shipload of grief. On the other hand, perhaps you're enchanted by the prospect of a pastime that consists of endless stretches of stupefying torpor punctuated by moments of stark terror. Perhaps you are one of those rare individuals with several thousand dollars you don't need, plus a supernaturally high tedium threshold. In that case, sailing might be for you.

I'll say one thing for sailing: it gives you a whole new respect and appreciation for those early mariners in their cockleshell boats. People like Giovanni Caboto and Jacques Cartier and Champlain …

And Columbus. We can't forget Columbus and his boats. Well, not boats—ships, really. Caravels, I think those were. Yeah, that's it. The three famous Columbus caravels: the *Gudgeon,* the *Pintle,* and the *Santa Maria.*

FROM *Black Tie and Tales*

Switch Those Pipes!

I've always had trouble with the bagpipes. What makes it extra troublesome is my genetic lineage. Near as I can figure, I come from a long line of Scottish Lowland sheep molesters. So my heart should quiver at the skirl o' the pipes.

Well, my heart doesn't. But my stomach does.

Bagpipes. Someone once described a gentleman as someone who knows how to play the bagpipes … but doesn't. And before my Meridian answering machine clogs up with collect calls placed by outraged MacMafiosi from Craigellachie, B.C., to Inverness, Nova Scotia, let me hasten to point out that the gentleman who made that observation was one Senator Allan MacEachen, a native Cape Bretoner, who could be counted on to know gentlemen—or a set of bagpipes when he saw them.

The bagpipes. A great caterwauling curse that's followed me all my life. When I was a kid, there was old Mr. Ritchie, down at the bottom of our street. Three or four times a year, Mr. Ritchie would retire to his cellar to commune with the spirits. A couple of Celtic saints named Haig and Haig.

After several hours, he would stagger into his yard, his chapped, knobby knees protruding from under a moth-eaten kilt. He would be carrying bagpipes, which he would then attempt to simultaneously strangle and blow up.

Mr. Ritchie wasn't a very good bagpiper. Or perhaps he was concert quality. That's the thing about bagpipes.

Later I moved to Thunder Bay for thirteen years. Thirteen mostly wonderful years. Except for the lunch hours, Monday to Friday. That's when the piper came out in a park near my radio station to scatter the pigeons and traumatize small children with his mutilation of "Road to the Isles."

People often ask me why I left Thunder Bay. Was it the winters? Was it the Mulroney filleting of CBC regional programming? The Siren call of that painted old hooker on the Humber, Hogtown?

Nah. It was mostly that godforsaken bagpiper in Patterson Park.

How clever of me, then, to leave all that and move to Fergus, Ontario. Fairrrrrrrgus. Whose main street is Saint Andrew, named after the patron saint of you know where. Whose emblem is the Scotch thistle! Fairrrrrrrrrgus. Home of the Highland Games, do ye ken. Where, each August, dozens and dozens and dozens and dozens of pipers pipe their Celtoid brains out.

Not without practice, of course. Contrary to the way they sound, the bagpipes require a lot of practice. Why, sometimes the pipers of Fergus don't even wait for the snow to melt before they get out there in their backyards and on the parade grounds, practising for the August Highland Games.

Bagpipes. When you think of it, we Scots have a lot to answer for. What have we given the world? Plaid. Porridge. Haggis.

And bagpipes.

But on the plus side of the ledger: single-malt Scotch. And Robbie Burns.

Even your tight-fisted Scot would have to allow that that's not a bad bargain.

Marsha Boulton

Marsha Boulton is the only person listed in the *Canadian Who's Who* with the occupation "Shepherd/Author." Boulton lives on a sheep farm in southern Ontario and is the creator of two very popular series of books: the wonderfully engaging Just a Minute collections of anecdotal Canadian history and her equally fun Letters from the Country series, which charts Boulton's transformation from "high heels to Wellington boots" and won her the Leacock Medal for Humour.

FROM *Letters from the Country Omnibus*

Talking Turkey

When I say grace over the Thanksgiving turkey, I always add my own private thanks that I did not have to grow the confounded bird.

I tried raising my own turkeys a few years ago, but once was enough. I was placing my spring order for day-old chicks and I noticed that the hatchery was also selling baby turkeys, so I ordered a dozen. With a hundred or so chickens ranging around the farm, I figured that a few turkeys could not do much harm.

My pal, Henry the Chicken Farmer, happened by the day I was installing the fluffy yellow chicks and the gawky, bald-headed baby turkeys in their pen. He laughed, called me Pilgrim, and told me he gets a real good chuckle out of young idiots from the city who haven't got the sense to just buy a Butterball when they crave a feed of turkey.

Henry then proceeded to offer me a quick course in turkey maladies and idiosyncrasies, along with some plain language talk about what he calls "the stupidest bird ever created."

First off, I quarantined my turkey poults. It seems turkeys and chickens just do not mix, and turkeys can give chickens a deadly disease called Blackhead. That meant building a new turkey pen, at a cost of about six store-bought, table-ready birds.

Chickens never impressed me as mental giants, but at least they have enough sense to eat and drink. I had to physically impel each baby turkey to the feed trough and provide the occasional refresher course in water drinking.

During the summer, the turkeys gobbled around in a pen next to the garden. They would flap their wings, but they weren't much for flying. About the best they could manage was a wild hopping gallop when they saw me coming with fresh carrot tops or corn cobs. All seemed right with the world, until we had a drenching rain.

The chickens were smart enough to run for the cover of their coop and perch on their roosts like sensible birds. The turkeys, however, stood in the middle of the field with their beaks upraised, swallowing the pouring rain. Two of them literally drowned themselves before I could herd them to safety. Another one had to take a spoonful of vodka before jump-starting to a sputtering revival.

While I was towel-drying the survivors, I began to wonder which of us had the smaller brain. Henry the Chicken Farmer told me he has seen flocks of 200 turkeys drown themselves in the rain. Great.

And turkeys are vicious. Chickens will occasionally rumble and rooster feathers will fly, but given enough space to range they tend to be fairly peaceable. The turkeys, however, literally pecked one of their own to death and tried to eat him!

"Cannibalism is just a phase they go through," advised Henry.

You would think that turkeys who could shred a fellow egg-mate into bits would be tough guys, but give them a few claps of thunder and watch them turn into total wimps. They would cower in a corner, piling on top of each other, and I had to wade through and separate them before they suffocated each other. A woman gets to feel a bit addled when she rides out a lightning storm making soothing gobbling sounds to a bunch of terrified adolescent turkeys.

If you live with turkeys long enough, you finally reach a point where you start asking basic questions such as, "Why do they exist?"

Consider the fact that the basic construction of a turkey is totally silly. The big white gobblers we devour at Thanksgiving are genetic hybrids of the original lean, dark-meated wild turkeys.

The fact is that not everyone wants a drumstick, so breeders have developed turkeys with a lot of breast meat. As a result, commercial turkeys cannot even reproduce without a helping hand. There is simply too much breast meat on a good breeding tom turkey for him to accomplish what nature intended, and the poor hen turkeys' legs were not designed to support heavy loads. So breeding hens must be artificially inseminated.

I found this out from my friend Susan, who spent one less than idyllic summer working as a "turkey jerker" at a big fowl breeding farm. Talk about a career opportunity. Ultimately, Susan became a blacksmith. She has strong arms.

The best time I ever had with my turkeys was stacking their plucked and vacuum-sealed torsos in the freezer. For once, they did not smell rude or gobble back at me.

From that day forward, I have stuck to raising chickens. When a turkey is called for, I do the simple thing. I make a pilgrimage to the supermarket and pluck a prime one out of the cooler.

Kiss a Pig for a Cause

If you want to raise money for anything in the country you need to get the local bankers on your side. Not because they are pillars of the community or persons of great charity but rather because they are generally and roundly despised.

Charitable groups, recreation committees, hospital boards and youth committees all suffer when farm commodity prices are low. The tightening of farmers' belts ripples through the community. Banks are generally the first to respond by reducing lines-of-credit, insisting on added security, or simply foreclosing.

So when a "dunking" game is featured at a fall fair, you can bet that the star attraction is going to be a banker. Dunking contraptions are fly-away chairs or bars set over large tanks of water. You pay a buck for a ball and try to hit the pie plate that releases the seating contraption and plops the subject into the water. Large crowds gather to observe this humiliation, and long lines form to risk a loonie on the chance of satisfaction. When a banker is scheduled, some joker is almost certain to dump a few bags of ice into the tank to add to the "vig."

During periods of killing interest rates, whole baseball teams stand in line to dump the banker. If you get a hot-shot, never-miss pitcher at the front of the line, it can be splish-splash-banker-takes-a-bath time for two solid hours. Teenage boys may get a kick out of dumping the Dairy Princess, but anyone old enough to have applied for a loan waits for a banker.

I gather that this was not always the case. There was a time a few generations ago when some rural bank managers inspired certain veneration. The bank earned the trust of farmers, and cash that once lived under the mattress went into the bank. In those days a banker might live out a lifetime serving the same clients, but in these times knowing the client too intimately is considered a disadvantage. The unseen evil known as "head office" makes sure that bank managers change every few seasons. This allows the banks to remove any notion of consistency. It also supplies a steady flow of fresh fodder for the dunking tank.

Communities are always trying to figure out new ways to raise money. A few years back, the idea of the duck race took hold. This involves selling bright yellow rubber duckies and letting them loose on the stretch of river that runs through most towns. Then someone decided that teddy bear picnics could be a grabber, and soon Bear Days were popping up everywhere. Such themes are worked to death, until another genteel idea springs forth. They work but, without revenge on a banker as the finale, they're about as exciting as watching bubbles rise in pancake batter.

Bingo is a main staple of fundraising. The most innovative variation on that theme is Cow Bingo. This involves a heifer and a controlled area that is divided into squares, which are sold by number. The heifer is fed and watered substantially, and let loose on the gridded plot. The game involves selecting the square where the first cow pie lands. Sometimes the judges have to wait for hours before they shout "bingo!" On the rare occasion when a banker is the winner, the local newspaper tries to run a picture of the winner beside the "deposit." Then, there is general praise for the acumen and aim of the heifer.

One contest that bankers always win is Kiss a Pig. In fact, if there is more than one financial institution in town, you can bet that those managers will place first, second, and third, relative to their general foreclosure rate. For the price of a loonie, the populace is invited to nominate and vote for the local person they would most like to see kiss a pig. Tax collectors, police chiefs, school principals, and dentists usually capture a fair share of the votes. But since there can be only one winner, it is the abused clients of the banks who dig the deepest.

"The nice thing about Rob is that he doesn't care who he kisses," said the swineherd, who offered his prize boar to buss the people's choice. Bank managers have been known to apply for transfers when confronting Rollo. Let's hope that automated tellers never take control of the world.

Max Braithwaite

Who knew that loneliness, isolation, and our vast prairie winters
could be so funny? Max Braithwaite's debut novel, *Why Shoot the
Teacher?*, was drawn from his experiences as a schoolteacher in
rural Saskatchewan in the 1930s. The book was turned into a very
successful movie, and although Braithwaite went on to write more
than two dozen books, he is still best remembered for his prairie
memoirs. The following is the title tale from Braithwaite's Leacock
Medal–winning work *The Night We Stole the Mountie's Car*.

FROM *The Night We Stole the Mountie's Car*

M ost people when they think of the Royal Canadian Mounted Police
think of a tall, beautiful figure in a trim uniform, or the musical ride,
or "they always get their man," or, if they're old enough, of Nelson Eddy
singing to Jeannette McDonald. I always think of dusty Ford V-8 cars,
bootleg whisky, and the night we stole Sir Percival Ardley's convertible.

During the Thirties the R.C.M.P. were the only police in rural
Saskatchewan. They were the town constable, the local sheriff, the captain of
detectives, the traffic cop, the highway patrol, the FBI, the chief of police all
rolled into one. They were kept busy during the depression helping to quell
riots, chasing bums—anybody who didn't have a job—off railway property,
keeping tabs on the communists who were trying to undermine our free
society. Depending on where you stood, the Mounties were respected,
revered, feared, or detested. As far as we were concerned, they were an important part of our social set.

Along with Sergeant Stoneman there were three constables in Wannego. They came and went even more frequently than schoolteachers and now and then there would be a romance with one of the local girls. The three I remember best I will call Nikochuk, McAdam, and Ardley. They were all single, all boarded at the hotel, and were all three excellent chaps. Well— practically all three.

Nikochuk was a friendly Ukrainian, who got along well with everybody. McAdam was a tall blond Scotsman with a great deal of boyish charm who liked to knit. He came to Wannego fresh from a three-year stint in the Arctic and he said that knitting was his way of putting in the time. If this were true, then half the Eskimo women in his territory must have been wearing woollen sweaters, for that was the only thing he ever knitted. They required a lot of fitting, those sweaters, and my best memory of McAdam is of him pulling a sweater on or off a well-rounded female torso and patting it here and there to check the fit.

McAdam could speak the Eskimo tongue, too. At least he could say a number of words that involved a great deal of lip-pursing, which he generously taught to the young ladies.

McAdam was a good source of material. He told me some lively incidents and I gleefully wrote them into short stories and sent them to editors, thinking that if there was anything they knew about Canada it was Mounties. But none of the stories sold and I realized later that I wasn't presenting the traditional Mountie—sharp profile, round hat, high boots, Sam Browne belt, sleek bay horse, and all—galloping across the plains, relentlessly following renegade Indians, never ceasing until he got his man. Mounties doing regular police work were to them "unrealistic."

One day when Aileen and Beryl were in Saskatoon and I was taking my meals in the hotel dining room, I was eating with Sandy McAdam when he said,

"Say, can you smell something?"

"Just this cheese omelette."

"No, I mean something else." He took a long sniff. "Yeah, it's still there."

I took a deep sniff. "You mean that sort of sour, putrid smell?"

"Correct. It's coming from my tunic. I've used everything I know on it, and I thought I'd got it all out. Evidently I didn't."

Then he told me this story.

For years the police at the Wannego detachment had been trying to get the goods on an old bootlegger named Anton Vrom. Vrom was a bachelor and lived in a dilapidated shack on a little knoll west of town. There were no real hills in the Wannego area, so that from the top of this knoll you could see about five miles of the dirt road leading to his place. Any car coming along that road could easily be spotted by Anton and by the time the police got there no evidence was to be found.

Each newcomer to the detachment was given the job of trying to catch old Anton. One tried driving up at night with no lights but ran into the ditch and had to walk back to town. Another borrowed a horse and tried coming across the fields, but prairie chickens and magpies that flew up at his approach warned the old rascal and all the Mountie got out of it was a sore backside.

Sandy McAdam had tried several times to catch Anton but had never made it. Invariably when he got to the shack the old man was sitting in his rickety chair beside his dirty table smoking a ragged cigarette and waiting for him. He'd grin his rotten-toothed grin and say, "Hello, Mr. Policeman. Nice of you to call."

But the Scots are a determined breed and Sandy refused to give up. There were more fights on the front street and more rotten home-brew in circulation which had the unmistakable stench of that produced by old Anton. Finally Sandy decided that he would walk out to Anton's place and catch him that way. He'd carry no light. In the Arctic he'd got pretty accustomed to travelling in the dark.

So he set out along the road, walking mostly in the ditch. Away off he could see the light of Anton's coal-oil lamp burning in the single room of the shack. It took him almost two hours to reach the yard. Then he had to be careful, for the wily old rascal had rigged up a system of wires attached to old rusty sleigh bells and strung them on sticks around the house. But he made it. Burst in the door and there, sure enough, was a bottle of rotgut sitting on the table.

The old man jumped for the bottle but Sandy got it first. "Oh no you don't!" He put the flat bottle into his huge tunic pocket and buttoned it shut.

"What you do?" the old man asked.

"I'm going to take you back to town—along with this evidence. Six ounces is all I need, so there'll be plenty here. Get your coat, it's chilly out."

The old man reached for his coat which was hanging near the stove. Beside the stove was a box full of wood and as Sandy took his eyes off him for a second the old man picked up a piece of stove-wood and smashed it against the tunic pocket, breaking the bottle.

But Sandy was quick, too. He unbuttoned his tunic, took it off, grabbed a water glass from the table, and squeezed the foul-smelling brew into it. He had just over the six ounces. I suppose you could say he got his man.

"The trouble is," Sandy told me, "now I can't get this damned stink out of my tunic. I've sent it to the cleaners but it's no good. What do they put in that stuff anyway?"

I got a letter back from the syndicate editor when I submitted this story, which I titled "Six Ounces of Evidence." He said that it was just an incident, not a story. To make a story it needed more conflict, possibly between the Mountie and his superior. Or perhaps I could bring a girl into it. I didn't know just where the girl would fit, there being no females on the force at the time, but I finally made this episode the key element in the Mountie getting a promotion and thereby being able to marry a girl. It didn't work. I liked it much better the first way.

Percy Ardley was an Englishman. He spoke with an English accent. He was cultured and refined and superior. I'm not sure that he was actually so superior come to think of it, as much as he made the rest of us blokes feel inferior. Especially in the eyes of our women. He made them discontented with their lot, for he had been everywhere, done everything and knew about art and music and the dance. The rest of us, having been born and raised in Saskatchewan, didn't know much about these things. Actually, I guess we were inferior.

Percy was nice about it though. He believed that it was part of his role in "the colonies" to elevate the natives. Civilize them. So he never hesitated to share his great fund of knowledge with us and to correct us when we made a gaff. This was particularly true when it came to tennis.

Tennis was our chief recreation in the spring, fall, and summer. Over in the fair grounds about a quarter of a mile from our house there was an old tennis court, all overgrown with weeds. A group of us got together and fixed it up. We scraped it level, got a load of shale and spread it around, got a new net and repaired the fence. I dug out a picture of this the other day, and I must admit it didn't look much—grass growing up through the shale around the edges, weeds all around, patched fence. But I can never remember it looking like that when we lived in Wannego. It was our summer recreation centre.

On Saturday we'd pack a lunch and walk over to the court in the morning, me carrying Beryl on my shoulders. She'd sit on a blanket or toddle after grasshoppers or play with her pup, Puddles. About six other couples would come along, too. There were Danny and Yvonne Beltier and Rick Tapley who worked on the railway and Ruth, one of the waitresses from the hotel, and whichever Mountie happened not to be on duty and Mary Simms, who worked in the bank. Mary was always the girl-friend of the current Mountie. She was thirtyish and friendly and very easy to be with. Vincent Denis and his wife and the DeSantes also played. It was a nice, friendly little group.

We'd take turns playing in an easy relaxed manner, and those who weren't playing sat on the sidelines in the blazing sun and watched and talked and fooled around. Nice.

That is, it was nice until Percy showed up. To begin with, he told us that we weren't playing tennis at all.

"I know," I admitted, "but we're trying."

"No, I don't mean that, old boy. This game is properly called lawn tennis."

"On this court?"

"No, you see, there are two games—Tennis and Lawn Tennis. Tennis is much the older game. Sometimes it is called Royal Tennis or, in the U.S., Court Tennis. It is an indoor game. This that you are playing is properly called Lawn Tennis although it is often played on a clay court."

I knew right then we were going to have trouble.

Then he walked about our court digging little holes in it with his heels and shaking his head.

"Who is the president of your club?" he asked.

"Oh we don't have any president," Mary Simms told him. "We just play."

"Well, I suppose that accounts for the wretched condition of your court." We all looked at it then, as though seeing it for the first time, and it certainly did look wretched.

"It's okay," I quipped. "We play a wretched brand of tennis, donchaknow."

This got a slight snicker from the others but Percy just turned on me and gave me that English look. I think that was the last funny I attempted in his presence.

"No," Percy proclaimed. "We'll have to get to work and put this court in shape. That's the first thing."

So, instead of playing, we worked. Under the direction of Percy we took up all the tapes and scraped and raked the surface until we had all the chickweed, dandelions, and grass out of it.

"Now we'll need new tapes," Percy told us. "Can't go putting those old tattered things down again."

But before we could raise money for new tapes we had to organize into a club. This we did, with proper parliamentary procedure under the direction of Percy. He wouldn't be president himself but he thought Danny Beltier should be because he was the only really permanent resident of the town amongst us all and, besides, through him we could get stuff wholesale. "You see the value of organization," Percy told us.

When we had all finished, the court did look better but it played a lot worse. Where we'd removed the weeds and grass was all soft now where once it had been hard. No matter how much we rolled it, we couldn't get it hard again.

There were other visual improvements, too. We had always played tennis in whatever we had—shorts, khaki pants, any old shirt with the sleeves rolled up. Didn't matter much. But the first day Percy appeared on the court carrying his two tennis racquets under his arm all that changed. He was a vision in white! Beautifully pressed white slacks, a white v-neck sweater, white tennis shoes, and a choice white eyeshade. He looked like something right out of an *Illustrated London News* story on Wimbledon, a fine trim yacht among coal barges, a sleek thoroughbred among farm horses.

Besides this, Percy had a car and none of the rest of us did. It was a cream-coloured convertible, I remember, and he loved it dearly. He kept it polished and shined as he did his belt and shoes, even scraped the grasshopper remains from the front grille. He'd drive up to the court, wheel around, stop, and, instead of opening the door and getting out like any decent person, he'd leap nimbly over the door and come smiling towards us.

"Here comes King Shit from Turd Island," Rick Tapley would whisper, but never loud enough for Ruthie to hear him.

For Percy was a great favourite with all the girls. He'd persuaded the club to go into debt for one of those round metal garden tables with a big umbrella, "Excellent for afternoon tea ..." and there they'd sit, Percy and the women.

We could hardly get any of them on the court any more. Afraid to muss up their nice white tennis ensembles. They much preferred to listen to Percy tell of his adventures in India, Australia, and South Africa and other places where the sun never sets.

"This is no good," Rick complained. "That damned Limey is buggering up the works. I'd rather be down at the poolroom."

This was serious. We had barely enough tennis players as it was and to lose one to the poolroom would be disastrous. As a matter of fact, I wasn't getting any fun out of tennis any more, either.

I was a smash-bang sort of tennis player. My first serve was powerful and cut across the net like a bullet. That is unless it hit the net, which it did about nineteen times out of twenty. Then my second serve was a nice gentle little thing that came over soft and easy and could be killed by any real tennis player. Until Percy showed up we hadn't any real tennis players to kill it.

In doubles I was a demon at the net. I'd stand right up close when my partner was serving and catch half our opponents' returns, twisting my racquet cleverly so that the ball came straight down and was impossible to get. The first time I did this against Percy, he said, "Our point?"

"What do you mean, your point?"

"Your racquet was over on our side of the net."

"Huh?"

"You see, old boy, you must keep to your own side. It's against the rules to reach over."

"But I always do it this way!"

"Then you always do it improperly. If you'd just stand back about a foot, now, there'd be no danger of an illegal procedure."

"A what?"

"A foul, old boy."

I was getting it at home, too. "Do you really think you should play tennis in those old blue denims?" Aileen suggested.

"Why in hell not?"

"Well, you must admit they're not very elegant. And another thing …"

"Another thing?"

"Throwing your tennis racquet when you lose a point."

"What's wrong with that? I've always done that."

"Well, it's really not very sportsmanlike."

"What difference does that make? This isn't Wimbledon, you know."

She laughed gaily. "I rather think not."

My wife—my own wife—talking like a bloody Englishman—or Englishwoman. It was too much. "Oh for Christ sake!" I blurted out.

"Please," she said, "don't be so crude. I don't see why you must swear all the time."

It was then I knew we were in real trouble. More and more often, one or another of the men had an excuse for not coming out to play tennis. It wasn't just that the women often didn't want to play—preferring to sit in the shade and talk—or that Percy always beat the pants off us. Even when he wasn't playing you could feel his eyes on you and it put you off your game. My percentage of successful first serves dropped from 5 percent to less than 1 percent; my backhand which had always been a bit weak became hopeless. I was about to give up the game.

I wrote a story about the whole situation. A screamingly funny story,

I thought, about an Englishman who had moved into a Saskatchewan small town and, to quote Rick Tapley, buggered up the works. It didn't sell, though; I suspect because it was written with too much emotion. Good humorous writing requires detachment. The writer must be far enough removed from the situation so that he can view it calmly in retrospect and not use words like "bastard" and "sonofabitch" in describing his people.

And then came the Tennis Club Ball.

This, too, was Percy's idea. He explained at one of our regular club meetings—we spent more time at meetings now than on the court—that the social proclivities of a club must not be overlooked. "Why," he said, "even in India, which is further from centres of culture and civilization than we now find ourselves, it is possible to maintain the amenities."

It was shortly after he made this statement that Rick Tapley began calling him Lord Percy, and the name stuck. We were surprised later to find that the people of the district with whom Percy had had dealings had been calling him that for months.

The ball was held in the hotel dining room, which Percy called the ballroom, and now that I think of it this was probably what caused all the trouble. Rick lived in a room in the hotel, as indeed did Lord Percy and Sandy McAdam. The ball was not restricted to members of the Tennis Club but tickets could be purchased by the general public for two dollars a couple. The high price, Percy explained, would keep out undesirable elements. It didn't work, though. All the same people came.

It's a funny thing about parties. I mean the way they develop. Sometimes everything goes along just fine with people drinking sensibly and everybody behaving themselves. At other times with the same people all hell will break loose. Maybe it has something to do with the ions in the air, or perhaps the little people become involved. Whatever the reason, where liquor is present you never know what will happen.

I remember such a catastrophe during the war when I was an officer aboard H.M.C.S. *Unicorn* in Saskatoon. *Unicorn* was not moored in the Saskatchewan River, although that body of water might have held a ship. No, she was moored at the corner of First Avenue and 24th Street and she was a converted garage.

It was the custom of the navy to call the training divisions "ships." The ratings, who had been recruited from the farms and towns of Saskatchewan, where the largest body of water most had seen was a slough, were obliged to say they were "going ashore" when they left the garage by a side entrance and "coming aboard" when they came back in.

What had once been the showroom had been converted into a wardroom where the officers drank and lounged about when they weren't working. Since we'd gone straight from the penury of the depression into the affluence of the navy, we weren't accustomed to having everything new and so the furniture of the wardrooms was made up of stuff the peacetime reserve officers had scrounged from here and there. It wasn't bad, but it wasn't opulent, either.

Also most of us weren't accustomed to drinking much, so when we got into the wardroom where all we had to do was call for drinks and the steward would come running with them, and then we didn't pay for them but just signed a chit—well, we sort of went a bit wild.

The first couple of commanding officers we had were local men who had been in the reserves for years and, like the rest of us, were products of the depression. Then they sent us a chap from Toronto by the name of Green who was, as they say in the navy, very pukka. He undertook to make real British sailors out of us, bring us up to scratch.

He was always urging us to refurnish the wardroom in the style befitting the navy. "This junk you have here …" he said with great contempt, "it looks like the lounge in the Elk's Lodge." But the wardroom committee demurred. Although the canteen fund was healthy, we couldn't get over our habit of not spending money. So despite his constant urgings we kept dragging our feet.

Then we had a wardroom dinner, complete with all the trimmings. That is, we began drinking well beforehand, drank heartily all through the meal, and continued drinking afterwards. Green introduced us to a custom which he said was very navy, although I've never heard of it since, called "Dogs of War." This was a simple little game in which the captain could call "dogs of war" on one of the junior officers and all the rest would leap on him and forcibly remove his trousers. Well, things went on in this motif of gay abandonment until somebody threw a cushion at somebody else and then everybody was throwing things.

It seems hard to credit, even now, but before we had finished we had completely demolished every piece of furniture in that room. Lamps were pitched out windows onto 24th Street, chairs were pulled apart, the dining room table broken up like matchwood, chesterfields torn asunder. Afterwards we refurnished the wardroom.

I tell this story to illustrate my point that where alcohol is involved anything can happen.

So it was with the Wannego Lawn Tennis Club Ball. All husbands had been warned by all wives that we'd better behave like gentlemen. And we did. There was a good turnout and the dancing was refined and nice and all went well. That is, during the dance all went well.

It was the custom in Saskatchewan then, and may still be for all I know, for people to drink in hotel rooms. I've consumed more liquor sitting on the edge of a bed or on the floor with my back propped up against a dresser in a room jammed with other drinkers than I've ever consumed in a proper tavern or lounge. So it was that we foregathered in Rick Tapley's room for this purpose, and along about midnight Rick said, "Let's get old Fancy Drawers Percy drunk."

This turned out to be more difficult than we thought. Not that Percy didn't drink. Percy would drink any given amount. But he never got even slightly drunk. He was one of those disgusting drinkers who become more steady the more they drink. They walk a little more carefully, talk a little more precisely, and don't swing from chandeliers.

So as Percy became more sedate and serious, we became more abandoned and carefree. At one point Rick and I were running through the dark, dingy corridors of the hotel, banging on the doors of travelling salesmen and shouting, "Take cover! The gophers are revolting!"

And then we'd pound each other on the back and laugh fit to kill. But no matter what we did we couldn't break through the reserve of Sir Percy.

And so we gave up. He had us and we knew it. Then about two o'clock in the morning I said I guessed it was time to go home and Rick said, "I'll drive you."

"Go on, you haven't got a car."

"I'll borrow Lord Percy's."

"Hey … do you think you'd better?"

"Sure, we're all friends together … members of the same tennis … excuse me, lawn tennis … club. Come on get Aileen and I'll drive you home."

So we went back to the room where Percy was beguiling the women with lies about his exploits in India and shh-ed at Aileen and Ruthie to come. Finally they came and, with a great deal of giggling and guffawing from Rick and me, we went down the stairs and out to the street where Percy's car was parked.

"Have you got a key?" I asked.

"This car doesn't have a key … just a switch. Besides, a policeman doesn't need to lock his car. Who's going to steal a policeman's car?"

Aileen said she didn't think we should do it and Ruthie agreed, but Rick and I just piled into the car.

It was a great joke, really, and we all laughed heartily at it. Rick fumbled with the switch and got the car going, turned on the lights, drove to the corner, and there right in front of the car was Percy. He'd got his tunic on and his big hat and he looked very stern. He had his big revolver in one hand. He held up the other and shouted, "Stop, in the name of the law."

Well this was the funniest thing we'd seen yet and we laughed much more heartily than before. In fact, we literally fell out of the car with laughing.

"You two are under arrest!" Percy shouted, and he was very red in the face.

"God, what an actor," I bellowed and held my sides.

"I'll take the women home. But you two stay here until I return," Percy said, and we laughed even harder.

So Percy drove Aileen and Ruthie home and when he got back Rick was climbing up the telephone pole in front of the hotel and singing "Shine On Harvest Moon." Percy drove up and got out his car. I snatched his big round hat off his head and threw it up to Rick who hung it on a peg. Then we both laughed so hard he nearly fell off the pole.

Things became pretty vague after that. The next thing I knew clearly was that Rick and I were in one of the cells in the town hall. My right arm was sore as though it had been twisted, and a very angry Englishman in a R.C.M.P. uniform was standing outside the cell saying things like car theft and resisting arrest and making a public nuisance. Before I toppled over on the hard bunk and went to sleep I remember thinking that this was a hell of a situation for a schoolteacher to be in.

The next thing I remember was waking up with a enormous headache. Not sick to the stomach or anything—just this head that felt as though a tractor had run over it. And Ernest Stoneman was unlocking the cell door.

"Are you okay?" he asked. "Can you make it home?"

"Think so. What happened?"

"Nothing. Forget it."

"Oh my God ... we took Ardley's car. We didn't steal it ... just borrowed it ..." Rick protested, feeling his way up from the hard bunk.

"I know. Damned fool thing to do with a guy like that. No sense of humour, these Englishmen. Take themselves too seriously."

I looked at Stoneman then and realized what a good guy he was. A good, tough, Saskatchewan guy. The kind you can trust. "Thanks," I said.

Not long after that Ardley was transferred out of the Wannego division and we resumed our weekend tennis.

It was nice. We'd go over when we felt like it and play as much as we wanted. I went back to throwing my racquet when I was mad and swearing and leaning over the net and doing all those things one doesn't do on a lawn tennis court. Nobody mentioned the club again. The president just kept forgetting to call meetings. We heard through Stoneman that Ardley had been sent to the Arctic. God help the Eskimos.

Chuck Brown

Chuck Brown lives in the border town of St. Stephen, New Brunswick, just a short hop-and-a-bridge away from the state of Maine. At twenty-seven, he was named editor of the venerable independent newspaper *The Saint Croix Courier,* and he is now a regular humour columnist for the *Telegraph-Journal,* although his original dream was to be a Canadian rap star. "But for the life of me," he says, "I couldn't find a decent rhyme for 'constable.'"

New Heights

You never know how you'll act just before you die until just before you die.

Lucky for me, I had a chance to experience the whole prelude to death thing without actually dying. My brush with death hit during a do-it-yourself project. Do-it-yourself projects are ideal for people who want to improve their homes, fix stuff, and get a general all around feeling of satisfaction from a job well done.

For me, do-it-yourself projects are evil necessities caused, in this case, by a leaking porch roof and a carpenter who said he's booked solid through Hanukkah.

So it was up to me to fix the roof—a superstructure, really, towering a good, oh, I'll say 10 feet high. After climbing a ladder to investigate I quickly discovered the main problem. I'm afraid of heights.

Actually, it's not so much the heights as what's waiting at the bottom of them that bothers me. The roof project's first job was to assess the real problem. Handypeople assess problems by looking at them from several angles and squinting. You have to pay particular attention to facial expressions. You're going for pensive or thoughtful, not totally clueless.

For a close-up examination, place a ladder leading up to the roof and test it by jiggling it two or three times. Climb to the roof and examine it more closely by touching and poking (the roof, I mean). Then find something to pry and some sort of a tool to pry it with. A shingle with a screwdriver, for example, or an acorn with a carpenter's square will work just fine. Say, "Hmmm" a lot when people are around.

Then it's on to the real work. I started spending my weekends and evenings on the roof and within two weeks or so I felt safe and secure enough to do things like open my eyes.

I've seen people working on roofs around town and they seem to have a technique where they just kind of, like, walk around and do the work. I've talked to some of these people about why they don't fall off the roof.

They tell me they don't even think about it, they just do their jobs.

I looked, realistically, at the height of my roof and determined, realistically, that a fall probably wouldn't kill me. But I also thought, realistically, of all the various ways I could land on the three-foot-high white picket fence below and realized, realistically, that I would probably prefer not to survive that landing.

So rather than scampering like a fearless and capable spider-monkey–like roofer, I spent most of my time working from a seated position. From this stance I managed to scrape away old shingles and pretty much tear the place apart.

On a few occasions, my shoelace snagged on nails sticking out of the roof. It made me think, wow, wouldn't it be something if I actually started falling and my shoelace got caught and that was the only thing that saved me. Then I started thinking, what if I started falling and something other than my shoelace got caught …

Not long after that, my fears of falling became reality. While moving across the roof, something called "roofing felt," which is a thick paper placed over the "roof wood" (which is a technical term for the wood on the roof), gave out from under my feet and sent me sliding down to my almost death.

My life didn't flash before my eyes as I slid. I was too busy thinking, "I can't die today! We rented *Princess Diaries II* and I haven't even seen it yet!"

And I swore. I was actually surprised by my choice of expletives. I was sure that in a life-or-death situation I'd go for something anatomical but instead I went almost completely biblical.

And it worked. The paper bunched under my feet and stopped me. Which was great except that I now had time enough to think, "Wow, the only thing holding me up right now is a crumpled bunch of paper."

After ever-so-gingerly plucking my fingernails out of the "roof wood" I carefully made my way to the far side of the roof and sat, refusing to move. I considered nailing my shoes in place until someone with a bucket truck or a helicopter could come get me.

As I sat, wondering why I wasn't impaled on a picket fence, I thought of the profound lesson learned—Hanukkah really isn't that far away.

Popping the Question

Today's important topic is one to which most of us can relate—guys who propose marriage by having the engagement ring delivered by a really cute kitty and the friends who mock them.

I have a friend (which I'll identify simply as "Jeff Dionne," but only because that's his actual name) who did just that. It was so romantic and so sweet and so thoughtful that when I heard about it for the first time I truly thought I was going to yarf on the spot (the spot being my friend's linoleum).

I asked him for details about how and why he proposed using a kitten and my friend looked deep into his heart to reply, "Shut up, Chuck."

The kitty proposal is one of those cultural turning points that will change the world of guys forever. It's like the first time a guy picked up his prom date in a limo and now every guy has to do it or risk being labelled "rational" or "sane."

It's like that time at the Zodiac Roller Rink when I was 12 and the DJ announced a "Moonlight Skate for couples only" and all the guys gathered to resume our ongoing debate about whether Darth Vader could beat up Jaws. But when we looked for input from our buddy Forbes, he was Moonlight Skating … with a girl!

After that, we all had to Moonlight Skate and soon after that we all had to Moonlight Skate … with girls!

Those early, awkward pairings were our first steps on the road to maturity. We became more self-aware and introspective and we demonstrated this by using hair mousse and sniffing our clothes before wearing them to school to make sure they didn't smell like wet goat. And now, thanks to my friend, Jeff Dionne, guys have to put a lot more thought (OK, thought) into how to propose marriage.

The days of guys popping the question the old-fashioned way—on stadium scoreboards—are gone. And guys can't just copy the kitten idea. They have to be different. And not just different like, using a gopher instead of a kitten different. Guys will have to come up with an Original Idea.

Creativity comes easily when guys are, say, trying to fix a leaky pipe so they don't have to call a plumber but not so easily when guys are, say, asking someone to join them in a binding union until one of them dies, or meets someone better in an internet chat room.

Unable to top my friend's kitty scheme, guys will turn anywhere for inspiration. Maybe even here.

And I have found a doozie. Propose by email. That's number 24 on a list of engagement ideas on the website Diamond Helpers.com

They are telling guys to email their bride-to-be a picture of a diamond along with the message, "Will you marry me?"

The site also suggests timing the delivery so you can see her reaction. I think it's an excellent idea, if by "reaction" they mean, "feelings of confusion, anger, dejection, more confusion then laughter through tears as she tells co-workers that the guy she thought she loved actually proposed in an email."

As impersonal as an email proposal is, I like it better than number 26 on the list—hide the ring in the butter dish. Or number 34, which I am not making up, train a parrot to say, "Will you marry me." I also found a story about a guy in Florida who created a fake lottery ticket, which his now-wife scratched to reveal a picture of a diamond ring and the message, "Will you marry me?"

Awww. Cue the gopher ...

Roch Carrier

If ever there were a truly archetypal Canadian story, it is
Roch Carrier's *The Hockey Sweater*, a tale of a young French
Canadian boy whose mother orders him a Montreal Canadiens
hockey jersey from the Eaton's catalogue only to be sent a Toronto
Maple Leafs sweater by mistake. The story is funny and sweet
and true, with a warmth and humour distinctly Carrier's.
The following selections are from the Leacock-winning collection
Prayers of a Very Wise Child, in which the seven-year-old narrator
prays for guidance in matters of the flesh and the weaknesses
thereof. The translation is by Sheila Fischman.

FROM *Prayers of a Very Wise Child*

Titties Prayer

God, I don't know if You, after You've eaten a meal, You lean back in
Your rocking chair and hibernate like our grandfather does. I wouldn't
want to bother You about a pair of titties—but I saw two of them: a pair of
two; two titties, I saw them, the whole thing, all round. I'm sorry if I woke
You up from Your nap, God. It's on account of those two titties. I came here
to confess that I saw two real live titties.

Before, I didn't know what titties were. Today I understood why they
never say the word on the radio. If you say it you want to see. It would be so
nice if You invented a kind of radio where people could see and hear at the
same time. Then we could look at titties.

Your priest never says that word—at least not in church he doesn't. He's a holy man but I bet he's seen titties, too. If I've seen two, Your priest could have seen just as many, or even more. Maybe two dozen. Or less. I'm seven years old and I've seen two titties. Your priest must be sixty-one or sixty-two or sixty-three. Seven into sixty-three gives what? Nine. Nine times seven years old. I'm seven and I've seen two titties. Nine times seven equals sixty-three. Nine times two titties equals eighteen titties equals nine pairs. Your priest must have seen nine pairs of titties. I could never see that many in my whole life. And maybe he's seen more, or less, because the priest sees Heaven when he gazes at the Earth.

Seeing titties is so impressive, it must be a sin. God, I confess that I saw titties, but to tell You the truth, as soon as I've finished my prayer, which will be short, I'm going to run back and sit in the same place, outside the general store, in case there's more titties on display. I'll come back afterwards and pray to You. Please God, let me see two more titties. Seven years times four titties times nine. When I'm sixty-three I'll have seen thirty-six titties. Eighteen pairs. Thank You God for inventing arithmetic.

Our mother has titties that I've never seen. Our father often goes out to the country to sell and buy. I don't know if he's even noticed that our mother has titties. Babies know. They're always squalling. When our mother can't stand it any more, she sighs and then she unbuttons her dress. After that she picks up the squaller, and what happens is like magic: the squaller disappears under a blanket. What do titties do to a baby? I guess that's a deep, dark secret.

I used to be a squalling baby too. And I used to cry and disappear under a blanket, but I don't remember a thing. God, why did You invent forgetting? I can remember the name of the capital of the Belgian Congo, but I can't remember our mother's titties.

Titties is a dirty word. When I hear it my cheeks go all red. I feel hot inside my ears and sometimes even at the bottom of my belly. Women never say that word. It's a man's word. You need dry ears to say it. Some children say it, too. Not girls though.

When girls hear it they shrug their shoulders and then they run away.

I say the word titties because I saw two of them. Seeing them, God, must be the same as not being wet behind the ears. Men always laugh after they say the word titties, as if it was the funniest thing in Your Creation.

At school, I took a really good look at the nun because, You see, the girls in my class are as flat as ironing boards. The nun wears so many dresses and slips and skirts and rosaries and veils you can't even tell if she's got titties underneath her bib. From what I hear, Your priest hasn't got a ding-dong under his soutane; maybe the nun hasn't got titties.

Learning about life isn't easy. I've been wondering for a long time how You made women's titties. Just wondering made me feel tickly, even in my ding-dong. When You were a little boy like me, God, You must have felt it too, didn't You?

I don't know why they make me learn the list of nouns that take "x" in the plural when I don't even know what a pair of titties is. You created the world in a really complicated way, God.

I'm going to tell You a story about titties. There was an unhappy widow that decided to die after her husband died. She took her dead husband's hunting rifle and she stuck the barrel two inches under her left titty because that's the side where the heart is. Then the unhappy woman pulled the trigger. A shot was fired. She didn't die. Two inches under her left titty, the bullet hit her knee.

Everybody in the general store laughed when they heard that story. So did I, even though I didn't understand it. I laughed as hard as a man. I was the last one to stop laughing. I told myself that one day I was going to see some real titties. I figured that titties aren't ordinary things like noses or ears or shoulder blades.

The Laframboise boy, the one with a finger cut off, said there's some titties that jump in the air. He knows a woman that got two black eyes from running too fast. Her titties punched her in the eyes like fists. He says you have to harness titties because if they aren't tied down really tight they jump around like colts leaving the stable in the spring. I've seen young colts snorting and frisking in the spring. I tried to understand how women could have two spring colts inside their dresses.

You don't seem to mind, God, that Your Creation is hard to understand. Why do You want titties to be a mystery? When I was a squalling baby I drank from the mystery. Why have You erased my memories like mistakes in my dictation book?

Today, You showed me a pair of titties. Right after the apparition I was all red from head to toe, as if I'd been dipped in red paint. Real titties! Two. I saw them both, one beside the other! They weren't hard, they didn't look as if they had bones. They were as soft as cream. I couldn't look at them for very long. They were hanging inside the neckline of the dress. The strong midday sun, full of fire, was drenching them in light. They weren't round like balls, they were long, but not like cucumbers. They were more like eggs, big eggs sliced in two. They didn't look as if they had a shell. They moved like Jello. And there's something at the end like chocolates. Now that I've seen them, God, I know what a sin is. My head was as dizzy as if I'd spun around a hundred times. Or more. I couldn't run because I couldn't walk: my legs felt as if they'd been cut off.

She saw me look. I could tell that she knew I was red. She didn't do up her blouse. I felt as if there were feathers tickling me all over my whole body from head to toe, and even inside my body, but it was mostly in my pants that the feathers were tickling, in a place I mustn't say because we're in Your church. But it's You that created that place so I'm going to tell You where it tickled: my ding-dong. I didn't like it. I can't wait to grow up. I won't feel that tickling any more.

I don't need to tell You how it happened, God, because it was You that made it happen. It was You that offered me titties in Your invisible hand.

Children who don't observe get bored. I spend whole days looking. I don't get bored because I learn. You can't get bored when you're learning. If I keep looking, I think I'll finally see You, God, even if You're invisible.

Every year there's a kind of Gypsies that come to the village. They come to sell little wicker tables or chairs. They come to tell the future or to sell magic medicines to cure diseases that Dr Robitaille can't do anything for. They don't seem to know anything about new cars. They always drive rusty, battered old jalopies with writing scrawled over them that's full of mistakes, like real ignoramuses. They know lots of secrets ordinary people wish they knew. Gypsies can pile at least twice as many people in their cars as ordinary people can. After our father piles the children and our mother in his Ford, we can't fit any more in. The Gypsies though, they can fit as many people in a car as in a bus.

Today it was a rusty panel truck that pulled up outside the general store. I was lying on my stomach in the grass. I was spying on life. There was rust all over, even on the brakes of the truck, and they screeched like a girl having a tooth pulled. And then the father Gypsy, with his long black hair and his pointed boots and a belt around his shirt instead of his pants, came to open the back door of his panel truck. The door didn't just open, it fell on the ground. The father Gypsy started kicking the door with his pointed boots. He was probably swearing but not in our language; it was in his language. God, do You understand cursing and swearing when they're in a foreign language?

A fat woman got down from the cab, carrying a suitcase, and barefoot, with dirty feet that haven't seen soap since last year, and a long skirt with bright colours and ruffles and pleats and ribbons. And a great big suitcase, like I already told You. Then I saw children get out, as many as if they were getting off a train: all sizes, all sexes, black hair, bare, dirty feet. All the girls had long skirts with ruffles, very long black hair and lots of necklaces that clinked, and squalling babies in their arms.

The last one arrived. She was tall. She had to bend over to get out. Then I saw, God! It was like lightning in your face. I saw those titties I told You about.

God, forgive my sin. Just confessing it is making me tickle again where I can't say. Forgive my tickle sin. Forgive my titties sin. Please God, let me see some others.

Thank You, God, for making titties appear to me. Now I understand one mystery in Your Creation.

Douglas Coupland

Douglas Coupland may have coined the term "Generation X," and he may have been on the cutting edge of the Microserf subculture, and he may indeed be a designer and artist of note, and a leading pop culture commentator who was once asked by Steven Spielberg to help envision a future world for the film *Minority Report,* but, by gum, he is still a Canadian—which is to say, he's a hoser just like the rest of us. And a very funny one, at that. The following short pieces are taken from Coupland's quirky coffee-table book *Souvenir of Canada.*

FROM *Souvenir of Canada*

Canuck?

Americans have pulled me aside on several occasions to ask, in the hushest of tones, "Is it, you know, *rude* to call Canadians Canucks?" When I say that it's perfectly fine, I get a disbelieving stare. So then I say, "There's even a hockey team called the Canucks," and only then do they relax. Yes, it's okay.

In a similar vein, on December 26 we have a holiday called Boxing Day. Whenever Americans ask what Boxing Day is—and I've been asked this maybe a dozen times—I tell them that it's the day after Christmas, and that there's no ritual of costumes or anything else attached to it—it's simply called Boxing Day. And the Americans always think that I made up the holiday on the spur of the moment.

Capitaine Crounche

Canadian companies frequently have names that function both as French and English names: … Rapidair … Canadair … VIA … Onex. When you're young, you don't know this, so more than a few times you wonder why Canadian names are so boring.

… Air Transat

… Alcan

… Inco

… Petro-Can

And then there are also products that not only have a different English and French name but also drastically different attitudes toward on-package hype. While the copy on each side of, say, a potato chip box, is given a mathematically equal amount of space, an English-language starburst will explain, "Chip-dilly-willy-icious!" while the French-language starburst will demurely state, "Bon Goût."

And then there are products whose name in French eclipses the product's English name. A salty snack food called Méli-Mélo comes to mind. In English, it's Bits & Bites … not the same.

Sometimes the French name is so bizarre and cool looking—Capitaine Crounche or Mistigri—Alley Cat—that you just have to accept the fact that Canada is, in some obtusely Star Trek manner, a parallel-universe country, with two variations existing alongside each other; and through the miracle of nationhood, we bounce back and forth between the two universes.

Cheeseheads

While I was collecting food items for a series of photos, I was struck by how odd it was that foods that felt intuitively "Canadian," when assembled together, looked more like camping trip provisions than actual groceries. The foods of France may be legendary, and American cuisine may be a joyous hash of Pop Art and military science, but Canadian food? A French newspaper once asked me to try to define Canadian food, and the best description I could come up with was, "It has to come from a box." I didn't mean this as a put-down or a put-up. It felt like the truth.

Canada is a cold and northern country. Aliens assessing the national diet would note that, from a biological standpoint, it is imperative that citizens live on concentrated forms of sugar, carbohydrate, fat, and salt. "Look, Zoltar! These Canadian beings prefer to stockpile their energy sources in cellulose units called 'boxes'—or if a box is unavailable, they use metal cylinders called 'cans.'"

Donuts ...

Baloney ...

Peanut butter ...

Bacon ...

Maple syrup ...

Beer ...

Potato chips ...

Canned beans ...

Processed cheese food products ...

My father has a cache of tinned food he takes with him every time he goes hunting or fishing. Part of his cache is this one can of baked beans that quite honestly must predate the moonwalk. The thought of it sitting in his cupboard at this very moment is disturbing on a deep level. It's just sitting there, but what's going on inside it—is it in permanent stasis? Is it breeding? Is it petrifying? Would eating it kill him?

Last year in Milwaukee, Wisconsin, I was in a gift shop and saw big yellow foam cheese wedges for sale—they were hats worn by locals to football games. It reminded me of driving up Interstate-5 from Seattle into Canada and seeing CHEESEHEADS GO HOME spray-painted on the highway overpasses, cheeseheads meaning Canadians who buy American cheese to cash in on lower U.S. cheese prices. Talk about a slur.

Cheese, in fact, plays a weirdly large dietary role in the lives of Canadians, who have a more intimate and intense relationship with Kraft food products than the citizens of any other country. This is not a shameless product plug—for some reason, Canadians and Kraft products have bonded the way Australians have bonded with Marmite, or the English with Heinz tinned spaghetti. In particular, Kraft macaroni and cheese, known simply as Kraft Dinner, is the biggie, probably because it so precisely laser-targets the favoured Canadian food groups: fat, sugar, starch, and salt. Most college students live on the stuff, and it's not the same as American Kraft Dinner—I've conducted a taste test and find there's something slightly chemical and off about the U.S. version. I invite you to take the taste test. I'd be happy to hear your conclusion.

Doug

An Austrian TV journalist was in Vancouver doing a piece last year, and I was there to help out. He said to me, "I hear that everybody in Canada is named Doug." I said, "Ha ha ha, that's just a media myth." And then the hired three-man crew arrived, and they were all named Doug, and suddenly there were four Dougs there, and I had to drink a glass of cold water to make sure that I wasn't dreaming, and in some intangible way it felt as if I were doing my national duty. I was then asked if Canada had a stereotypical girl's name. I had to think about it, but if we do, here it is: Kathy.

Hockey

The thing about hockey in Canada as opposed to hockey in other countries is that the sport percolates far deeper into our national soil and thus affects everything that grows in it. For instance, take my mother the hothouse flower. She visited my studio when a table hockey game was being prepped for a photo.

"Ooh! Table hockey—we used to have one just like that growing up."

"No way, really?" (Two sisters, no brothers—Winnipeg, circa 1948.)

"Oh yes. We'd put it on the dining room table and play it all winter. My sisters and I had such fun."

"You and your sisters played table hockey?"

"We loved it."

Last week my father was discussing a Russian player who'd sat out a year and as a result ended up being able to earn a salary in the tens of millions. I said it reminded me of a player who'd done something similar years before, but my mother by the sink cut in, "Oh no—that chap never made the big bucks. *He'd been concussed too often.*" This, from a woman who has honestly never watched a game of hockey in her life. How did she know about the overly concussed draft pick?

It's in the water.

My father and brother are into hockey pools in a big way. My brother is always "the admin guy," and over two decades has nursed the pools through the days of paper and pencil, into the world of Excel spreadsheets (which handle pools nicely) and then onto the internet. My dad has won big a few times, but my brother says this is because he always chooses the underdogs, and sometimes the underdogs make the playoffs, and once a team makes the playoffs it gets hot and takes off—which to me still seems like a perfectly reasonable way to win. To beginners, my brother offers the following advice: a) don't choose rookies; b) try not to draft with your heart [i.e., don't choose only Canadians or only Pisces or only lefties or whatever your category— you have to be Darwinian in your choices]; and c) don't drink during the selection process.

My other brother enjoys the fighting aspect of hockey games, and nothing puts a smile on his face faster than a VHS tape of *Best of Hockey Fights VII.* As an old boss of mine said, "A good rink is a red rink." Everyone fondly remembers the goalie who severed his artery on a goal post, lawn-sprinkling blood about the rink; the resulting ice posed a great challenge to the Zamboni operator.

Canadian winters are long. Life is hard and so is ice. Canadian teams playing within the NHL are, in effect, a microcosm of Canada's ongoing process of trying to remain a country—battling constantly not only against Americans but against other teams from within their own country. It's ugly and yet it's civil; and most tellingly, it's the one place where people still sing the national anthem.

Rye

Until I was twenty-six and toured a Scottish whisky distillery, I thought rye and whisky were the same thing. But they're not: rye is made from rye; whisky is made from malt. Rye is like this drink that only chain-smoking people over fifty-five drink, and the very word evokes the image of stale cigarette smoke bonding to the ice of a curling rink, the sight of the auditorium lights going from bright to dark, and perhaps the sound of Oldsmobiles out in the parking lot turning over their engines. Or another image: Boxing Day, melting grey snow outside, the sound of a hockey game playing too loudly on the TV while a seventy-one-year-old aunt in a fuchsia cardigan adorned with a sprig of holly enters the living room, carrying a tray of Triscuit crackers garnished with Vienna sausages and Kraft pimento cream cheese. "Jesus, get your feet off the table, why don't ya? We're not in the Legion. And pass me my smokes—the ones with the picture of the diseased lung on them." Rye is actually so fantastically out, it can only shortly become fantastically in. Don't forget the ginger ale.

Small Towns

A lot of Canadian literature deals with small town or rural life and/or the immigrant experience. Metropolitan novels with characters who don't discuss the family barn or their country of origin are nearly non-existent. CBC national radio also feeds this trend, with a hefty number of programs ending with a moral along the lines of *I think we all know there's a small town in each of us.*

The reason for this is simple: outside of a handful of largish cities, Canada is a nation of small towns, far more than most other industrialized countries. Many Canadians are only one generation away from the farm. I remember standing in the receiving line at my brother's wedding in Winnipeg. After shaking about the tenth hand missing umpteen digits, I asked one of the Winnipeg relatives what was the deal. The one-word answer? *Threshers.*

Everyone thinks small towns are folksy and cute—and mostly they are. But having visited relatives who live in small towns, I acknowledge that you sometimes need to substitute "bizarre" for folksy, and "scary" for cute. I don't always have a soft-focus view of small towns—there are too many of them in my ancestry to be totally comfortable.

… That Judy was bright as a dickens, but she never talked much after the night of the storm when they found Kenny's empty Chevelle in the middle of the canola field.

… Your great-grandfather had the four finest horses in the tri-county region—why, even the prime minister once looked out the window of a passing train and remarked, "Those are the four finest horses I've seen in the surrounding tri-county area!"

… Sure we told the RCMP it was just a stove fire, but everybody in the McGrath family lost their sense of smell that afternoon.

Obviously you need to remember that small towns now, and small towns back then, are different things altogether. Back then, they were prisons of sorts, the only escapes being religious orders or the military, which could be equally as freaky as the town you'd left behind. But now small towns have almost become lifestyle choices. People who live in northern Manitoba can get a dish and watch MTV Europe or most of the Asian and European stations. Hydro workers in deepest Labrador can trade aluminum futures in real time and then watch streaming video porn so hard-core that it's more a biological treatise than, uh, "casual entertainment."

So these days, if someone's working on the farm, it's likely they really enjoy doing it, as opposed to farm work being a life sentence handed to them at birth. Even still, the stories will undoubtedly go on forever.

… Well, you know, old Clem down by the poultry plant? It was never true he went off to Bermuda that winter like everybody said.

… Your great-great-grandmother really put that little mill town on the map. She could imitate every songbird on the North American continent minus Mexico!

Ivan E. Coyote

Born and raised in Whitehorse, and now living in Vancouver,
Ivan E. Coyote (the E is for Elizabeth; the blurring of genders,
intentional) is one of my favourite authors. "There Goes the Bride,"
presented here, is particularly outstanding, at once funny and
heartbreakingly sad. As a writer, Coyote always manages to strike
the perfect balance. Because this is a humour anthology, I have
chosen some of her lighter pieces. To get the full sweep of her
talent, you need to run out, right now, and buy her books
Close to Spider Man and *One Man's Trash*. Trust me on this.

FROM *One Man's Trash*

Clean and Sober

I t all started with the jam jars. My mom was in town visiting, digging in
my cupboards for mugs to pour us a cup of tea. She made that clicking
sound of disapproval with her tongue and raised an eyebrow at me.

"You, my dear, are thirty-one years old. Don't you think it's time you
stopped drinking out of jam jars?"

I jumped to my own domestic defence, pointing out that I actually
had six jam jars that matched.

"See, Mom? It's a full set." I said this with feeling, as though Martha
Stewart would be proud.

She shook her head. "We're taking you shopping."

•••

We returned the next afternoon with a sparkling array of drinking receptacles. It turns out there are different glasses for water and highballs and even little ones for juice. Who knew? Even more surprising was that I acquired all sixteen for less than the cost of six jars of organic raspberry compote.

Doing dishes became an exercise in household pride. I liked to see my newest additions shining in my cupboard in neat little rows, like glass soldiers ready to jump forth and fight thirst. It inspired me to throw a dinner party. Vodka and cranberry, anyone?

I felt so grown up.

I got matching tea towels next, and four coffee mugs the same colour as my teapot. This move precipitated the purchase of an actual kettle, because grown-ups don't boil water in a soup pot. Everybody knows that.

I was unstoppable. I bought an almost brand new carpet from a set sale to replace the old worn rug in my front room.

• • •

One spring day I came home to find a scratch-and-win lottery ticket in my mailbox. It looked like a bingo card and claimed that if I was one of the lucky few to scratch the right boxes, I could be the proud winner of a set of steak knives, a framed picture of a mallard duck, or a brand new twenty-four-inch colour television. Steak knives? What luck! I'm not fond of beef, but I could use them to cut up other things. I answered the skill-testing question and called the number right away. All I had to do was let a nice salesman come 'round to my house and demonstrate a new product. Then I could claim my prize.

In less than an hour he was at my back door, a guy in his early twenties, perspiring from hauling a remarkably large box up my back steps. His shirt was wrinkled and he had those little tassels on his brown dress shoes.

"I didn't win the duck picture, did I? What I'm hoping for is steak knives." I explained this to him as he unpacked a rather complicated looking vacuum cleaner. It was sleek and black, with ergonomic handles. I wondered if he worried about scratching the paint. I would.

"Impressive machine you got there, young man." I cleared my throat. "What is one of these things worth, if you don't mind me asking?"

"Well, without the hepa filter, and drape cleaning attachments, or the steam cleaning unit, about sixteen hundred dollars. The whole package will run you about three grand," he said without looking up.

I almost dropped my matching mug.

"Well, being as I am recently unemployed, I should probably tell you right now that the chances of my spending the bulk of my retirement savings on a vacuum cleaner are fairly slim," I said politely. I felt I should be honest.

He stopped assembling and stood up with a sigh. He suddenly looked older. "Can I borrow your phone?"

He dialed the number from memory. "Let me speak to Charlene." He held the phone between his chin and shoulder, and looked at his watch. "Charlene, it's Ricky. I'm in East Vancouver. I'm still in East Vancouver, Charlene. Do you think you could find it in your heart to get me a client who has a job? Uh-huh." He scribbled something down, and hung up.

"Nothing personal, you know. Charlene gets paid by how many houses she sends me to, but I only get paid by how many units I sell."

I nodded in sympathy. He began to pack up his box.

"I guess this means you're not going to vacuum my floor for me then?" I was pushing my luck. He knew it, I knew it.

"You're lucky I'm letting you keep the steak knives."

"Hey, I won those fair and square. I bingoed and answered the skill te—"

"Everybody wins, lady. That's the deal. I haven't seen any colour TVs, though. Just a whole lot of steak knives."

"What about duck pictures?"

He shook his head, took his vacuum, and left me thinking on my back porch.

The world was indeed a treacherous place, and I needed a new vacuum cleaner. I share my attic apartment with two dogs, the evidence of which could be seen collecting in corners and on carpets. Tumbleweeds of fur appear daily under the bed, an uphill battle any pet owner can attest to, one that had been bothering me more and more since the jam jar incident.

My hand-me-down Hoover had expired in a gasp of smoke a couple of months earlier, and I had been borrowing my neighbour's ever since. It was a geriatric drag-along model which wheezed and complained whenever I plugged it in. Every Sunday I feared might be its last. It made a high-pitched whining sound when it rolled over area rugs, and I would almost feel guilty for making it work so hard. It had one broken wheel and should have been retired from active service. It had done its time and dog hair seemed a little too much to ask.

• • •

It was the first time I ever read a flyer, and it worked. I bought a new vacuum, just like the one in the ad. I was too excited to read the manual, much less watch the instructional video. A brand new re-conditioned Phantom ThunderVac with dual cyclonic action and on-board attachments stood shining triumphantly in my hallway. It even had headlights. I finally understood those guys who wax their cars by hand every Saturday.

I called my mother long distance. "Mom, guess what? I got a brand new vacuum. I am the proud owner of a remarkable advance in household cleaning. I am about to change the way I feel about carpets by harnessing one of nature's most powerful forces. As soon as I install my patented cleaning wand."

"Good for you, honey. Maybe my allergies won't act up so much when I visit at Christmas."

"It has a hepa filter, Mom. Are you allergic to hepas? Because they won't trouble you any more. Not in my home.… I'll call you back in a bit."

I hadn't felt this kind of anticipation since I was twenty-one and had a bag of magic mushrooms and a long weekend ahead of me. I plugged it in, and both dogs leaped onto the bed for safety. Poor things. They just weren't used to the sound of this kind of raw power in our living room.

"It only hurts the first time," I said to my cowering Pomeranian, and set to work.

Minutes later, I sat down and surveyed my spotless living room. My dogs sniffed around, as if unsure they were in the same house. "Go ahead, shed your little heart out," I told my husky. "I'm not afraid of you any more." I wished I had taken before and after pictures.

The phone rang. "Hi, Mom. It looks amazing in here. I can hardly wait for my house to get dirty again, and I have you to thank. This whole thing started with the jam jars."

"What are you talking about?" It was my friend Michelle. "Are you okay? You haven't been taking too much NyQuil again, have you?"

"Sorry. I thought you were my mom calling back." I knew Michelle wouldn't understand about the ThunderVac. She hadn't turned thirty yet and still boiled water for tea in a soup pot. She wasn't ready to relate to this kind of advanced home improvement.

"Whatever, man, I just wanted to see if you were into going for a beer."

I wasn't. What I really wanted to do was be at home, at one with my new vacuum cleaner. Besides, I couldn't afford a beer. I was saving up for cutlery.

Mavis for Prime Minister

I work in the movie industry, in the props department. This means it is often my job to hunt down and purchase strange and obscure items, which often takes me to strange and obscure places. This day was like any other, and I found myself somewhere deep in the suburbs, seeking cheap pieces of foam to stuff into luggage for a scene we were shooting the next day at the train station.

There is a certain kind of woman, we all have met one or two: they waitress in truck stops, balance budgets in banks, answer phones at car rental places, take your tickets in airports, and today, charge you for three hundred pounds of foam in a warehouse somewhere next to a river you don't know the name of but wouldn't fish out of. These women are all, of course, unique and special, but I have noticed certain character traits they have in common. They are somebody's grandmother, the evidence of which is usually thumbtacked close to where they work. They smoke at their desks. They wear cardigans, and still call a shirt a blouse and a pair of pants slacks. They are not the highest paid employees, but chaos ensues if they call in sick for work, which they very rarely do. When they take their yearly trip to Reno or Vegas, no one can find anything, and productivity grinds to a halt. They are the only ones who know how to fix the photocopier or where to find the keys for any number of places. At home, they never run out of toilet paper and outlive their husbands by decades.

This particular woman's name was Mavis and for me it was love at first sight. Her voice was like sandpaper taking candle wax off an old oak table top, and she had me pegged right off the bat.

"You got a bed in the back of that piece of shit you call a van out there?" she asked, gesturing to the loading dock where two well-muscled lads were loading foam into my '72 Ford Clubwagon. "I thought as much. You need a piece of foam for it? Come with me, sweet pea, we'll fix you up."

She sold me a piece of four-inch-thick foam for twenty dollars, and instructed the boys to throw that in as well. She scoffed at me and shook her head when I told her I had been thinking of picking one up at Home Depot or something for a while now.

"What are you, made of money? You need foam, you come to me." That's another thing these women have in common. They always say things like "What am I, made of money?" or "I knew there was something funny about that guy right from the get-go," or "That's just how I am. Don't ask me to change."

I, for one, hope that she never does. The Mavises of the world keep things from falling apart.

As I started up my van, Mavis ground her cigarette out with the heel of her pump and winked at me. "There you go," she smiled, and nodded towards the back of my van. "Now she'll have something to rest her elbows on."

It was just as I suspected. Mavis doesn't miss a thing.

Stupid Man

I like the cheap produce, and the fresh flowers, and the Rice Dream (for guests), but mostly I shop there because of her attitude.

She single-handedly fights to fend off the stereotype of the docile, soft-spoken Chinese woman behind the counter. I see her on the front lines for everyone, heating up samosas and sliding packs of Player's Lights and setting an example for all of us.

I went in one night for cigarettes, and asked her how she was doing, more out of good manners than conversation, but she told me the truth; few ever do.

"I ask you now, what time is it? A quarter after nine o'clock? The only thing I ask my husband is for Tuesday nights I watch a—how do you say—Chinese soap opera? He is supposed to come here at eight o'clock, so where is he at? And where are my friends? Waiting outside my house maybe? I don't know, I am stuck here all night. And then some fucking guy, he just stole a whole box of Oreo cookie ice cream sandwiches, so I ask you, what kind of life is this?"

I took my cigarettes and left meekly. I was almost afraid to ask her how she was the next time I went in. When you ask someone how they are doing, you rarely expect them to actually tell you how they are doing.

A couple of weeks later I went in on a Friday night to pick up a few things for breakfast the next day. Never being one to shy away from the truth, I asked her, "How's it going?"

Her eyes flashed hard and sharp, and she snapped her answer back at me, her head jerking towards the back of the store: "Why don't you ask stupid man how am I doing?"

Her husband had his back turned towards us, quietly pricing cans of coconut milk; his wide shoulders slumped inward. I went to get some crackers and he met my eyes, nodded hello, and looked back down.

"What's up with her?" I asked him. "Good thing you can get a deal on flowers, huh?"

He smiled weakly, like January sun, and cleared his throat and spoke, quietly. "I was in the back, and I hear her scream that we're being robbed, so I come running out to see a tall, skinny, white man running out the door. I chase him up to Twelfth Avenue, and across the traffic and down past the Mohawk. I jumped him on the grass by the apartment, and he rolls over on his back and says: 'Don't hurt me don't hurt me I'm sorry, here is your orange juice, here take it back,' so I give him one kick in the ass and let him go. He runs away. I come back here and give her back the orange juice."

"And she's mad at you? She didn't even say thank you?"

He shakes his head like a wet husky and motions for us to lower our voices. "No, all she said is: 'Very good, there is my orange juice. Now where is my eight hundred and fifty dollars?' She didn't tell me he took the money from the till, too."

I managed to wait until I got in the car to start laughing at him. *Why don't you ask stupid man how I'm doing?* Not that robbery is funny at all. I myself lost all my CDs (again) the night before last; theft in the East End is never funny. None of us have insurance.

It's just that her husband is a black belt, could have killed the guy, and chose not to. He is a gentle man, great with produce, fresh flowers, sweet to his two daughters. Next time they get robbed, he should call in the heavy artillery. Next time he should send his wife.

FROM *Close to Spider Man*

There Goes the Bride

What can I say? Guess I'll start with what everyone else is saying. Congratulations. So you're all married up now. Weird, huh? Do you feel any different than you did an hour ago? I do. That could be the three scotches I had in a row, though, just to take the edge off.

Your father is freaking me out a bit. He seems rather thrilled to see me here. He's the one pouring me drinks, he keeps patting me on the back and saying "Good to see ya" like I was his long-lost ... whatever. He was never this friendly when his eldest used to sit on my face in her spare time. He still can't remember my name, but I wouldn't hold something like that against the guy, I always liked him, even if he is enjoying my position in this whole affair just a little too much.

I always cry at weddings, always have. 'Member when Laura got married in *Little House on the Prairie?* I lost it even then. I get this from my mom.

But I was trying not to today, seemed to me the ex-lover should remain dry-eyed, lest her feelings be misconstrued, but the truth is even the thought of all that true love and sickness and health and having and holding and all still sneaks past my cynicism somehow and pulls at some ancient believer in me, and I cry every time. Every time someone dares speak such lofty hopes aloud.

He seems like a nice guy, your ... husband. I was afraid he'd be an asshole and I'd hate him, or that I'd be an asshole and he'd hate me, but so far we both just smile at each other, more like teammates than adversaries, like we both know what it's like to step up to the plate when you're pitching.

Your friend—you know the one who never liked me so was always extra nice? She keeps putting her hand on my arm or my shoulder and asking, "So how *are* you?" like any minute now I'm bound to break down and confess to her my true feelings, unleashing the bitter testament of a lonely homosexual, but even if I were, lonely that is, I would never give her the pleasure. Instead I keep asking her if she has seen either of my dates, and finally I shake her hand off me and say, "I'm fine, for chrissakes. It's her wedding, not her funeral."

Oh, well. She was always looking for proof that I was, indeed, an asshole. I try to be helpful.

I was just helping myself to more food—I forgot how much food there is at these functions—and this cute little old Irish lady struck up an interesting conversation with me:

"Couldn't help but notice how much you're enjoying my broccoli cheese casserole there, dear."

"Did you make this?" I said. "This is some of the finest broccoli cheese casserole I've ever come across. I guess I should leave some for everybody else though, huh?"

She laughed and asked me if I played in your band, if that's where I knew you from.

"No, not exactly," I said.

"Did you work with her at the restaurant then?" she asked.

"No. No, I did not," I said.

"Down at the pub then, you work together down at the pub?"

"No, no we didn't work together down at the pub, either."

She looked puzzled, so I blurted it out. "We were lovers for a couple of years. That's how we know each other."

She didn't blink a wrinkled eye or skip a beat.

"So you take about a pound of broccoli and steam it, just a little, because you're going to bake it all for a while, once you've made your cheese sauce. You'll need some cream, not milk, and I find the older cheddar has more of a snap to it."

I laughed all the way out to the backyard, after one of your brothers rescued me and we all snuck out back to smoke a spliff.

I always liked your brothers. I see shadows of you in them sometimes, when they turn their faces just so; they feel like family, remind me of my cousins.

Your oldest brother was drunk, had his tie off already, and was feeling sentimental. "We always liked you the best, you know," he whispered, one arm slung around me, like it was a secret. "We thought you were the best of all of them."

Your little brother was stoned, self-reflective. "Ironic, eh?" he pondered. "She dumps you, to marry a guy in a kilt. Sorry, dude, no offence, but you know what I mean?"

You looked beautiful today, getting married. "She looks just radiant." Everyone kept saying it, and it's true. You did.

Your face alive with that kind of wide-eyed love that used to make even me wish that I could want that picket fence as much as you did. I could never believe like you could. We broke our hearts, you and I, figuring that one out.

But the truth is, I could never give you this. A wedding that makes your grandmother happy. What's it like? "Legitimate" love, I mean. The gifts and congratulations and tax relief, not to mention the relief in your father's face, what is that like?

Because I can't even imagine it, and reality provides that I probably won't ever be that blushing bride, and I don't quite cut the husband mustard, either. Motorcycles and non-monogamy, or a mortgage and a mini-van: I am old enough now to know that none of this is your fault, or even mine.

There will be no church bells for me, but I cannot bring myself to mourn the loss of something I never wanted. Toasters and linen and casserole dishes, and blessings bestowed when one does as our mothers did, I will never know, and you always had the option.

Did I mention how beautiful you look today? Happy and hopeful, what more could I wish for you? I mean, what more could I wish?

Herb Curtis

Herb Curtis is the author of The Brennen Siding Trilogy, a series of warm-hearted novels set in the all-but-mystical Miramichi Valley of eastern New Brunswick. Through his alter ego, Luther Corhern, an angler's guide at a local camp, Curtis narrates *Salmon Camp Chronicles,* which takes the form of a "fishing log." The following selections are from the *Chronicles.*

FROM *Luther Corhern's Salmon Camp Chronicles*

The Cure-All

My grandmother lived with us when I was a boy. She was a clean-living Baptist, and the rest of us were Anglicans. My grandmother thought that the Anglican organization was a bit too Catholic for her liking. We rarely crossed ourselves, but she had an idea that we were doing it behind her back. "You can't trust anyone but a Baptist," she used to say. She also always wanted to eat red meat on Friday. She suspected that the practice of eating fish on Friday was some sort of Catholic conspiracy, a plot to try and convert her. It didn't matter to her (or perhaps she just didn't realize) that nine out of ten Fridays we had nothing else in the house to eat but fish. On every other day of the week my grandmother would eat salmon, trout, mackerel, shad, smelts, whatever fish we could come up with, and enjoy it, even praise it, even thank the Lord for his generous bounty. But because she believed the Catholics would only eat fish on Friday, she would not.

"Eat fish on Friday? Next thing you'll have me kneeling in church! Bring on the beef!"

We were brought up on fish. If it were not for fish, I would probably not be sitting here writing. We ate fish, fished fish, smoked and salted fish, and showed other people where to fish. We bought our clothing with the money we collected for allowing people to fish our pool. We even used fish—salt herring—for medicinal purposes. I don't know what the ailment was, but I recall my mother putting salt herring on my sister Lena's feet to absorb the fever.

Several times a year the Baptist minister, Reverend Ralph Kamp, dropped in to visit my grandmother to assist her in trying to convert us Anglicans. "Big, fat, and good looking," was how my grandmother described him. I remember a few things about him, that he was indeed quite fat, wore dark-rimmed glasses, and a green and black checked suit. I remember, too, that he could ad lib the most profound and elegant prayers at the drop of a hat, and that he would never leave the premises without eating. He'd come in time for lunch, and if he missed lunch, he'd hang around for afternoon tea. Sometimes my mother would put the tea and cake on as soon as he arrived just to get rid of him, because if he didn't get his tea and cake, he'd stay for supper.

Back in 1958, we were exceptionally poor. My father was working in the woods for a contractor from Doaktown, but the snow was so deep and the weather so cold that he rarely reached any kind of a decent scale. He'd stay in a camp twenty-three miles up in the woods five nights of the week, come home on Friday evening, dirty and coughing kerosene and wood smoke from his lungs, and give a cheque to my mother, a cheque barely large enough to pay the hydro bill or buy the boots that I, or perhaps Lena, so desperately needed. My mother would spend all weekend washing his clothes, delousing him, and getting him ready for Sunday afternoon, when he climbed on the back of a truck with eight or ten other men for the cold and windy ride back into the woods. Because I was too little to do much, my father would spend his weekends splitting wood and cleaning the barn, pitching down hay from the mow, doing all he could to make life a bit easier for my mother.

It was after one of those weekends, on a Monday, that Reverend Kamp showed up.

Lena was sick in bed with a fever, the salt herring on her feet. My mother, perhaps afflicted with the same ailment as Lena, should have been in bed, too, but there were the fires to keep burning and the cattle, the hens, and now perhaps even a preacher to feed. Such were the demands on my mother that she allowed me to stay home from school that day, and though I was more often in her way than not, I helped her to the best of my ability.

We were in need of things, flour, eggs (the hens were not laying at that time of the year), sugar, salt, beans, soap, tea, Aspirin, basic things, but my mother was just too ill, and it was much too cold for her to attempt to walk the mile and a half to the nearest store. I was too young, my grandmother was too old, and Lena was up in her room with the salt herring on her feet. Not a pretty picture.

Reverend Kamp arrived at noon.

"And how's Mrs. Corhern today?" he asked my grandmother.

"I'm not too well, Reverend," she answered. "I have a sore back, corns on my feet, and, and, and look at the back of my hand, would ya?"

The Reverend looked at the bruise on the back of Grandmother's hand.

"Well well well," he commented.

"I hit that on something or other," she said. "Don't even remember doing it. Would you pray for me, dear Reverend Kamp? For me"—she gestured at my mother and me—"and them."

"Surely," said the Reverend and slid to his knees. So did my grand-mother, so did my mother, and so did I. It always puzzled me why Reverend Kamp kneeled to pray in our kitchen but thought it unnecessary to do so in church.

Reverend Kamp did not just pray. For the next hour, or what seemed like an hour, he preached an entire sermon. He asked the Lord to cure my grand-mother's many afflictions; he asked Him to bless poor Fred and Kate, little Luther and Lena, and encourage them to enter into the true faith, to accept the poor lost lambs into His flock. He asked for guidance into this frustrat-ing and complicated matter. Then he talked about the Premier of Quebec (I forget the issue) and an unnamed mayor of an unnamed town, who was thought to be perverted in some way or another, "best left unspoken, unuttered in the presence of innocent ears." He covered yields and bounties, icy roads, drinking, sins of the flesh and of the soul, saints and rakes, lambs and lions. Then, last but not least, he elaborately plunged into the subject of money and how so much more of it should be given to the church.

"Amen."

"Amen"

"Amen!"

"Amen."

The sweetest word in the world.

"Now," said my grandmother, "I think you should go up and speak with poor little Lena."

The look of horror on my mother's face told me that Lena's room had not been tidied up, that Lena was sick and perhaps sleeping, that Lena had salt herring on her feet.

"Oh, it would be my pleasure," said Reverend Kamp. "The poor lamb, yes, of course."

Well, it was unavoidable, there was nothing my mother could do but proclaim a hundred apologies for the state of Lena's room and lead the way up. My grandmother, Reverend Kamp, and I followed her up the creaking stairs to Lena's room. We found Lena pale and dishevelled. Her room smelled of Vicks, Sloan's, and salt herring.

We all knelt again, and Reverend Kamp went into his second sermon, shorter but no less elaborate than the first. I don't think poor Lena had a clue what was happening or what was being said. She looked about with clouded eyes, moaned now and again, and occasionally grinned, sighed, cooed, whimpered, and hacked.

Halfway through, my mother started to cry, and I saw the look of satisfaction and victory on the faces of my grandmother and Reverend Kamp. I suppose he was thinking that he had broken through, that he had finally penetrated the stubborn walls of my mother's cold and sinful heart. The funny thing about it was that I think my mother was so exhausted she would have encouraged and nourished the concept if only he would get up, shut up, and leave.

After the prayer, Reverend Kamp asked, "What's with the herring?"

My already sick and perspiring mother blushed and coughed into her hand. "Salt herring," she said. "On the feet like that. S'pose to be good for the fever."

"Indeed. Never heard of that."

"Oh, yes," my grandmother put in, "the only cure. Draws the fever, it does. Saved many a child, salt herring."

"Well, I'll be! I've heard of cod liver oil being good for you, but salt herring on the feet ..."

"Yes, yes. Bless us and save us, yes."

"Well, I'm sure she's going to be just fine," said Reverend Kamp, smiling down on Lena. "Keep her warm, give her Aspirin, she'll be fine."

Back downstairs in the kitchen, my mother said, "Well, Reverend, thanks for coming."

"My pleasure," said the Reverend and sat by the table. "The work of the Lord is my business. I make my rounds as often as I can."

I heard his belly growl.

So did my mother.

"You must be hungry," said my grandmother. "Fix the man something to eat, Kate."

"Oh, don't go to any trouble, dear woman. A cup of tea, perhaps. Maybe some little thing to eat, not much, mind you. Don't go to any trouble."

"Well, I didn't get to the store today," said my mother. "We're all out of tea, I'm afraid."

"Oh, well, that's quite all right. Anything at all."

"The store is a long way off, and it's so cold outside, too cold to walk, and I've not been feeling well."

"Well, don't you worry about it. I don't need tea. Anything at all for me. A glass of milk, perhaps, and a piece of cake or something. Don't worry about it. I'm not all that hungry. Anything at all."

"Fix the man something, Kate."

"Well, I suppose I could. I could peel a few potatoes and ... do you like salt herring, Reverend?"

The Reverend Kamp hesitated, then checked his watch.

The Craziest Dreams

B oys! I've been having bad nightmares lately! I get them every winter, but they've never been as scary as they are this year. They're what you might call recurring dreams, I guess. They have to do with the opposite sex and marriage.

I dream I meet up with the nicest little lady you ever laid your eyes on and we get married. I carry her across the threshold of my trailer. She's a woman with substance; a woman with money; she's tall and blonde and beautiful. She has eyes like Elizabeth Taylor's, and they gaze upon me with love and admiration. She rubs me in all the right places to make me feel whole, contented, warm inside. She cooks up a storm, plants flowers, cleans and organizes my trailer—everything from my fly boxes to my waders, from my golf balls to my three wood, from my chewing tobacco to my whittling knife are in their rightful places. I have to convert my junk shed into a closet to accommodate the suits and ties she buys me.

I like to plant things haphazardly, a clump of potatoes here, a beet patch there, a cucumber patch at one end of the trailer, and a radish bed where the barn used to be. But in my dreams, all that changes. In my dreams, everything is planted in neat, straight-as-an-arrow rows. In my dreams, even the fiddleheads in the gully grow in straight-as-an-arrow rows.

In my recurring nightmare, I get up in the morning and get all cleaned up before I have coffee and do the crossword puzzles, instead of the other way around. She kisses me before I go over the hill to fish and again when I get home. She kisses me after I eat and head out to the golf course and when I get home again. She kisses me after dinner as I head back to the river to fish until dark.

And when we go to bed at night, she ... well, I won't get into that.

Shad Nash almost got married once. He came within an inch, one little word of acquiring matrimonial bliss. "I asked a woman to marry me and she said no," he told me. "A close call."

Because of his experience, his close encounter, I thought I'd confide in him about my nightmares. Monday morning, I woke up in a sweat, and, soon as I got around to it, I drove over to Shad's place. I found him in the kitchen, playing the banjo.

I bared my soul to him.

"It's getting so I hate to go to bed at night," I told him. "What will I ever do?"

"It's not good, Lute," he said. "Not good at all. It sounds to me like you might need to see a shrink, a whatchamacallit, a psychiatrist." Here he plucked the strings of his banjo for effect.

"It's that bad, eh?"

"Oh, yes. There's no doubt in my mind. There's some pretty shady stuff swimming around in your head. You could be in serious trouble."

"What do you think a psychiatrist could do for me, Shad?"

"Lie. Psychiatrists mostly lie to you, to make you feel better."

"I could get a politician to do that."

"But you'd know the politician was lying. You need a psychiatrist, a good liar."

"Know any psychiatrists, Shad?"

"Well, you'd find one in Saint John, no doubt."

"That's a long drive, and he'd charge me a lot of money, wouldn't he?"

"You got that right. And you'd need an appointment. You might not get to see him until next summer."

"Bad time to be psychiatristing."

"Yeah, you'd better think of something else. How about Stan Tuney?"

"Stan Tuney!"

"Stan's the biggest liar I know. He can tell you anything at all, and half the time you can't help but believe him. Make a good psychiatrist, Stan would. And you don't ever need an appointment. Take a pint with ya and his door is always open."

"Hmm. Stan, eh?"

"Go see Stan."

So that evening I picked up a pint of Seagram's and over to Stan's I went.

"I have a problem, Stan," I confessed, and proceeded to tell him about my dreams.

"That's not a serious problem," he said. "Why are you letting a little dream bother you?"

"Well, it's not just the dreams," I said. "I could deal with the dreams if I could just stop thinking about them when I'm awake."

"Who's the woman in your dreams?"

"Nobody you know."

"Lotty?"

"No, not Lotty. If it was Lotty, I could handle it."

"In your dreams, does this woman want to fish with you?"

"No, not that I recall."

"Does she go golfing with you?"

"No, I don't think so."

"Well, it don't sound too bad."

"But it is bad, Stan. I'm sick, I tell ya. It's not natural for a man to think about getting married, is it?"

"Oh, come now, Lute! Don't be naive. Every man thinks of marriage now and again."

"They do?"

"Of course they do. It's perfectly natural."

"Then why does it bother me so much?"

"Because you're not putting it into perspective. You have to think about what's real and what's not. It has to do with ideals."

Stan Tuney, the master liar.

"Have a drink, Stan, and tell me more."

"Ideals are like … are like the hairline. They recede with middle age. Mid-life is what's happening to you, Lute. Amid the turmoil of mid-life a few dreams, ideals, regrets, fantasies are leaping out of your subconscious, like frogs from pond to pond. Don't worry about it. It'll only happen for a while, then reality will return."

"If I only knew what the reality was."

Stan yawned and scratched his belly. If I hadn't known him so well, I might have thought he was bored. But I know him very well. When Stan yawns and scratches his belly, it means he's thinking, fabricating, conjuring up new lies.

"Now, you say this girl in your dreams is young and pretty?"

"Yes, sir."

"And you say she's a great cook and neat and tidy, organized and loving, that in bed at night she …"

"Yes, all of that."

"Well, you're pretty much of a slob, right, Lute?"

"Well, I … a bit of a slob, I suppose."

"And you're not much to look at."

"I'm a … I suppose you're right."

"And you guide for a living."

"Correct."

"And you snore at night and make various other crude noises in the morning."

"Well …"

"You fish from sunrise to tee-off time and golf from tee-off time to evening fishing time, taking a break for bodily functions only."

"Pretty close."

"Well, there's the reality, Lute. This woman might exist in your dreams, but no woman in her right mind would have the likes of you around, not in her wildest dreams. And if there's any woman out there who would consider the likes of you, you can bet that she is crazier than the proverbial loon—in which case you'd be wise to stay clear of her."

"Thanks a lot, Stan. You're absolutely right. Thanks. You've made me feel so much better. Gave the old ego a boost, you did. Thanks a lot."

"Don't mention it, Luther, my boy. Go home and enjoy your dreams."

Taking Stan's advice, I went home. And I did dream about her, time and time again. Hell! I think I'm in love.

Good racket!

Robertson Davies

One of the joys of editing this anthology has been rediscovering the genius of Robertson Davies. I had forgotten how terrifically funny he could be. The selections here are from *Samuel Marchbanks' Almanack* and were chosen as one might assemble a sampler plate of hors d'oeuvres, both to whet the appetite and to give a sense of the full range available. The pieces include Marchbanks' horoscopes, letters to eccentric relatives, and even a plea on behalf of the Canadian Brotherhood of Snow Shovellers. Enjoy!

FROM *Samuel Marchbanks' Almanack*

Aries
(March 22 to April 20)

ARIES is the sign of the Ram, and those born under it are of robust physical health, strongly dominating disposition, and destined to be leaders. If you are not a leader now, explain this to your friends and employers, and show them that, if you are to make fullest use of your powers, you must be given your own way in everything. Once you have made this important adjustment to fate, you should enjoy a life of considerable happiness. Do not worry that you are not strongly intellectual; instinct is your best friend and you should never hesitate to act upon it, even when others counsel caution. People born under your sign often die violent deaths, so choose your friends carefully, and always look under the bed before retiring. Your sex-life may cause remark among the jealous: frown them down.

...

To Mrs. Gomeril Marchbanks ...

Dear Aunt Bathsheba:

Upon the whole I think you would be wrong to kill Uncle Gomeril. I recognize, of course, that mercy-killings are all the rage these days, and that any jury which knew him would probably compliment you on a good job well done, but there would be a lot of disagreeable publicity about the whole thing, and you don't know what sort of people you might have to meet before the affair blew over. Newspapermen, and such riff-raff.

Don't think that I have not given a lot of thought to Uncle Gomeril's condition. He has had acidity for years, and it seems to be getting worse. In fact, I think he is the sourest old man I have ever met. It would be a mercy to put him out of his misery, though the blow to the bicarbonate of soda industry might cause a sag in the stock-market. It is dreadful to have to watch him suffer, and it is even worse to hear him, but I suggest that you look upon this as a cross, and bear it as best you can. Mercy-killing, as a means of putting inconvenient people out of the way, has its attractions, but there is always the chance that there might be some crackpot on the jury who would ask toward whom the mercy was directed.

Therefore, dear aunt, I suggest that you order in another keg of soda, buy yourself a good book on Yoga, and put this tempting scheme out of your mind. The Marchbanks are a long-lived tribe, but it will get him at last.

Your affct. nephew,

Samuel.

...

Disingenuous Dedications Picked up a book, a new edition of a classic of fully a hundred years standing, and found that it had been dedicated, not by the author, but by the illustrator, to somebody called Alison. There were the words, "The illustrations in this volume are dedicated to Alison." I consider this impertinent. If one may dedicate the illustrations of a book, why not the binding? Why should not the paper manufacturers insert a note saying, "The genuine mashed pine parchment upon which this volume is printed is dedicated to Susan"? … The whole business of dedications is interesting. What does a dedication really mean? I have never heard of an author who made over the royalties on a book to the person to whom it was dedicated. The person to whom the dedication is addressed—the dedicatee, I suppose he should be called—has no control over what appears in the book. I shrewdly suspect that dedications are, in nine cases out of ten, attempts on the part of an author to seem generous without incurring any painful outlay of money. The saddest dedications are those which scholars make to their wives, as when the dedication of *A New Exegetical Consideration of Second Thessalonians* reads, "To Effie, who read the proofs and prepared the index."

• • •

Captive Audience Received a letter from a wretch who is obviously suffering from a bad case of Stenographer Fever. This disease, which is well known in business circles but unaccountably ignored by medical science, is a condition in which a man dictates letters to impress his stenographer, rather than the true recipient of his message. His letter becomes rhetorical and hectoring in tone. He tends to call his correspondent by name several times, thus;— "Now, Mr. Marchbanks, as you are no doubt well aware, it is not my custom to mince words with such a man as you, Mr. Marchbanks, seem to be …"— generally I deal with such letters by replying in this strain:—"Samuel Marchbanks has received your note. His answer is No." … No man, we are told, is a hero to his valet, but the world of business abounds with men who wish to be heroes to their stenographers and to this end they soar and bombinate, keeping an appreciative eye on the Captive Audience on the other side of the desk.

• • •

Prophecy consists of carefully bathing the inevitable in the eerie light of the impossible, and then being the first to announce it.

• • •

Babies and the Adult Male Across the street from my workroom window is an apartment which has a bay-window at my level; during the past few weeks a baby has been making regular appearances there, so that the doings in the street below may entertain it. I judge that it is a male baby, and it is a fine, large child, with a solemn and philosophical countenance. The baby views the street and I view the baby. I like babies, under special circumstances, and by a lucky chance the relationship between me and this particular baby perfectly fulfills all my conditions. I can see it, but I cannot hear it; I can admire its winning ways, and laugh indulgently when it topples over, but it is not near enough to wet me; when it wants anything, a pair of hands appear from behind it with the desired object. This is ideal, and I am thinking of putting this baby in my will. I believe that if the truth were known, my attitude toward this baby is that of most adult males; men like children, but they do not like them to be too close. Some barrier—as for instance a wide street, filled with traffic—between a man and a baby, acts as a powerful stimulant to affection between them.

FROM *My Letter Book*
To Samuel Marchbanks, esq.

Dear Mr. Marchbanks:

I write to enlist your support and membership in the Canadian Laudable Litter League which I am forming. Do you realize, sir, that every day thousands of pounds—nay, tons—of material of one sort and another which should be returned to the soil of our country is burned, or washed down our waterways to the sea, never to be recovered? Vital vitamins, irreplaceable minerals and animal and vegetable matter of all kinds is wasted in this way. The time has come to Call a Halt.

During the Summer I have been doing my bit to preserve what is Canada's for Canada. Whenever I have been on a picnic I have taken care to throw my hard-boiled eggshell back on the land, to preserve minerals. I have thrown my banana skins and other peelings into farmers' fields, to put vitamins back into the soil. When others have gathered up their waste paper, I have left it to blow where the wind listeth, for it came from the soil and should return whence it came.

Each member of the Laudable Litter League pledges himself never again to give his garbage to a wasteful urban collector, for burning; instead he takes it into the country (preferably in the dark of the moon, as this is the time approved by our hero, the late Rudolf Steiner) and throws it into the field of some farmer whose soil appears to be impoverished. This should be done by stealth, for the League seeks no credit for its good work.

Begging you to become an honorary L.L.D. (Laudable Litter Distributor) at once, I remain,

Yours literally,

Minerva Hawser.

FROM *My Files*

To Haubergeon Hydra, esq.

Dear Mr. Hydra:

I have been asked by several influential members of the Canadian Brotherhood of Snow Shovellers and Ploughmen to put their case to you as Pro. Tem. Sub-Re-Router of Labour, in order that you may draw it to the attention of the appropriate Minister. Here is our case in a nutshell:

(a) Some winters it snows a lot and we make money.

(b) Other winters it doesn't snow much and we don't make any money.

(c) We want a floor under snow. That is, in winter when the crop of snow is poor, we want the Government either to distribute false snow—salt, flour, Western wheat, or something of that sort—so that we can shovel it and make money, or—

(d) We want the Government to pay us for shovelling snow that isn't there, so we can make money.

You will see at once that this is in the latest economic trend and a good idea. See what you can do for us, like a good fellow, and some Christmas Santa may have something in his sack for a good Civil Servant.

Love and kisses from all us snowmen,

Samuel Marchbanks.

• • •

Fashion in Kisses To the movies, and as I sat through a double feature I was interested to observe that the audible kiss has come back into fashion. When the first talking pictures appeared, kisses were all of the silent variety; it was just about then that silent plumbing made its first appearance, and there may have been some connection. But now the shadow-folk of Hollywood kiss with a noise like a cow pulling its foot out of deep mud. In my younger days there were two types of kiss: the Romantic Kiss was for private use and was as silent as the grave; the Courtesy Kiss, bestowed upon aunts, cousins, and the like was noisy and wet, generally removing two square inches of mauve face powder. A visiting aunt, having been welcomed by two or three nephews, needed substantial repairs. The Romantic Kiss also involved closing the eyes, to indicate extreme depth of feeling, though it often occurred to me that if one cannot see what one is kissing, a pretty girl and a kid glove of good quality are completely indistinguishable.

• • •

To Amyas Pilgarlic, esq.

Dear Pil:

On Christmas Eve it is surely not indiscreet of me to confide the secrets of my Christmas List to you. As I told you earlier, I am giving Canadiana this year. Here is the list:

Uncle Fortunatus: an old drum, almost certainly used by troops in the 1837 rebellion. Both heads are gone, but can be easily replaced. All the decoration and regimental ornament have been worn, or rusted, away, but a skilful restorer could put them back again if we knew what they were.

Spiteful people say it is an old cheese-box, but I have the true collector's flair, and know it is a drum. Uncle will love it.

Brother Fairchild: an old Quebec heater, almost certainly the one around which the Fathers of Confederation sat when planning the future of this great Dominion. Who can say what historic spit may not cling to it? It is, in the truest sense, a shrine. As a stove, of course, it has seen its best days. Fairchild will be delighted.

Cousin Ghengis: a flag, used by a militia regiment which set out to quell the Riel Rebellion, but was detained in one of the bars in Toronto. It is a most interesting piece of work, which shows signs of having been an Orange Lodge banner before it was converted to its later purpose. It is rather stained with something which might be blood, though an analytical chemist says it still smells of whisky. Ghengis will be ecstatic.

Nephew Belial: a horn from Laura Secord's famous cow. When blown it emits a musty smell but no sound. Belial will be livid.

And as for you, my dear friend—but no; you must wait until tomorrow to see what I have sent you.

A Merry Christmas!

Sam.

Christmas Merrymaking
(a bonus for party-loving readers of the Almanack)

Nothing serves to break the ice at Christmas so effectively as a good-humoured hoax or imposture perpetrated by some quick-witted member of the company upon an unsuspecting fellow guest. You may play the coveted role of wit, and earn the gratitude of your hostess, by thoroughly mastering the following simple, but effective jests.

Showing him your fountain pen, induce a fellow-guest to wager that it will not write any colour he cares to name. When he says (for example) "Green," reveal nothing by your countenance but write the letters g-r-e-e-n upon a sheet of paper. Then appeal to the company at large as to whether you have not won your wager. His stupefaction will be very laughable. (If you are a lady, of course, you will wager half-a-dozen pairs of gloves rather than a sum of money.)

Another eminently "practical" joke is this: say to a fellow-guest (whom you have previously ascertained to be a philatelist) "Pardon me, sir (or if you are acquainted with him, "Colonel A," or "Judge B") but is it true that you collect stamps?" When he says "Yes," bring your right shoe smartly down upon his left instep (or *vice versa* if you happen to be left-handed), saying at the same time "Capital! Collect *this* one!" Whatever his feelings may be, the laughter of the company will certainly give him his cue to take this as a good joke upon himself, for no true gentleman wishes to be a spoilsport, embarrassing his hostess and clouding the delight of the company. (If a lady, be sure that you bring the *heel* of your shoe upon the instep of your "victim," as you may otherwise turn your ankle and be forced to send for your carriage.)

• • •

The Iniquity of Free Books There is a great rejoicing in some parts of Ontario because the provincial government has decided to give free schoolbooks to children, but I am not among the merrymakers. I am a writer of books myself, and any move which inculcates in children the idea that books are things which you get for nothing excites my implacable enmity. There are too many free books already, in public libraries and other institutions primarily designed to rob authors of their livelihood. A pox on the memory of Andrew Carnegie and his misplaced benevolence! There are in Canada, by actual count, 528 people who buy books for their own use; an author may count on these people buying a copy of any book he writes. There are 6,417,333 people who are on friendly terms with the 528, and they all borrow their copies of new books, read them, and then write to the author, pointing out typographical errors, plagiarisms from Holy Writ, faulty economics, and other blemishes. If the Ontario Government is going to teach children that books drop from Heaven, or are supplied from the public purse, like wheat subsidies, the profession of letters in Canada will drop below that of the night-soil removers.

...

To Dionysus Fishorn, esq.

Dear Mr. Fishorn:

No, I will not support your application for a Canada Council grant to enable you to write your novel. I know nothing about you, but I know a good deal about novels, and you are on the wrong track.

You say you want money to be "free of care" for a year, so that you can "create," and you speak of going to Mexico, to live cheaply and avoid distraction. Fishorn, I fear that your fictional abilities have spilled over from your work into your life. You see yourself in some lovely, unspoiled part of Mexico, where you will stroll out of your study onto the patio after a day's "creation," to gaze at the sunset and get into the cheap booze; your wife will admire you extravagantly and marvel that you ever condescended to marry such a workaday person as herself; the villagers will speak of you with awe as El Escritor, and will pump your beautiful servant Ramona for news of your wondrous doings; you will go down into the very depths of Hell in your creative frenzies, but you will emerge, scorched and ennobled, in time for publication, translation into all known languages, and the Nobel Prize.

Ah, Fishorn, would that it were so! But take the advice of an old hand; you won't write any better in Mexico than in Tin Cup, B.C., and unless you are wafted into a small, specially favoured group of the insane, you will never be free from care. So get to work, toiling in the bank or wherever it is by day, and serving the Triple Goddess at night and on weekends. Art is long, and grants are but yearly, so forget about them. A writer should not take hand-outs from anybody, even his country.

Benevolently but uncompromisingly,
Samuel Marchbanks.

• • •

To Waghorn Wittol, esq.

Dear Mr. Wittol:

It was a pleasure to encounter you at the theatre, but where was Mrs. Wittol? I thought I saw her with another gentleman, but very likely I was mistaken. I was much impressed by the melodrama in which a man shared with his wife the secret of a murder, and in which his wife contrived his death by a clever device. But you know, Wittol, I think that there is an even more exciting melodrama to be written about married life. What about a play in which a man and his wife, discovering that they are boring each other, set out on a race as to which can bore the other to death first?

Think of the scenes which such a drama could contain! The great scene in which the wife tells her husband the plot of a movie she has seen; he falls asleep, coma seems about to supervene until, with a tremendous effort, he rouses himself and retorts with a description of his bridge game at the club, recalling each hand in detail; she tumbles forward in her chair, and is seen to reach for the cyanide bottle. But no! She still has some fight left in her, and begins to read a letter from her mother, who is shuffle-board champion of St. Petersburg, Fla. You see the plan? A tournament of boredom! Hollywood would jump at it, but I think the Little Theatres ought to have it first.

My regards to Mrs. Wittol, when next you see her.

Samuel Marchbanks.

Bob Edwards

Bob Edwards arrived in the Canadian West in 1897 via a circuitous route from Scotland. A newspaperman, muckraker, boozehound, and tireless social crusader, Edwards eventually settled in Calgary, where his one-man newspaper operation, *The Eye Opener,* quickly gained international notoriety. Known for his barbed wit and scathing satire, Bob Edwards's fame spread as far as New York and London. His brilliantly comedic creations, such as Peter J. McGonigle (fictional editor of the equally fictitious Midnapore *Gazette,* who was constantly being thrown in and out of jail) and Albert Buzzard-Cholomondeley of Skookingham, England (exiled British remittance man and author of a series of increasingly elaborate letters home trying to inveigle funds from his gullible parents), stand with the best of Stephen Leacock and Mark Twain.

The following is a transcript of a House of Commons debate that could have been written yesterday, so accurate is its depiction of political accountability (and the lack thereof).

FROM *The Best of Bob Edwards*

"Now I know what a statesman is; he is a dead politician. We need more statesmen."

—Bob Edwards

...

Sample Debate in the Canadian House of Commons

Mr. John Herron (Alberta) moved the following resolution: That the circumstances attendant upon the murder of his mother-in-law by John T. Peterkins, inspector of swamp lands in Ungava, and subsequent disgraceful distribution of her body amongst the wolves of that country, and the continued retention of said official in office without investigation, reflects discredit upon the government and should receive the disapproval of this House.

Mr. Bourassa asked if the government intended to take any steps to remove from office John T. Peterkins, inspector of swamp lands in Ungava, who had recently become notorious through strangling his mother-in-law in her shack, cutting up her body into small chunks, filling them with strychnine, and setting them out as bait for wolves, on which there was a bounty of $1 a head. By these shocking means Peterkins had collected $545 from the government.

Hon. Frank Oliver: The honourable member has been misinformed as usual. It seems a pity that honourable members do not obtain more exact information on which to base their charge against the government. The number of pelts paid for by the government in this district was only 85, of which number Peterkins had a claim against 53. This money has not yet been paid over to the claimants, but the government sees no reason why Peterkins' claim should not be settled along with the rest. The territory of Ungava has for years been terrorized by large and ferocious bands of wolves, and the department considers that Mr. Peterkins has done the state no small service in ridding his district of the number of wild animals indicated.

Mr. Bourassa: Will the right honourable the minister of the interior inform the House whether or not the government proposes to retain Peterkins in the public service with this awful charge hanging over his head.

Hon. Frank Oliver: I cannot see whereof consists the "awful charge." No complaint has reached the department that Mr. Peterkins neglected the swamp lands of Ungava while sporadically engaged in trapping wolves. If it can be shown that the swamp lands were in any way neglected or allowed to fall into decay through lack of inspection, then the department may take steps to make further investigation into the matter. (Cheers.)

W.F. Maclean: That is not the point. The charge has been made that this government official, Peterkins, strangled his mother-in-law and fed her to the wolves. Surely such a monstrous piece of business should be looked into.

Sir Wilfrid Laurier: I must protest against the time of the House being frittered away in this manner. Mr. Peterkins' record as a swamp inspector is unrivalled in the annals of swamp lore. The Ungava swamps have thriven as they never throve before, under his inspection, and it does credit to his nobility of disposition that he devoted his leisure moments to the eradication of wild animals which had become a menace to the country. (Loud cheers.)

Mr. Bourassa: The right honourable premier begs the question. It has been proven beyond the shadow of a doubt that this man murdered his mother-in-law and threw her in sections to the wolves. What is the government going to do about it? Surely I am entitled to an answer to my question.

Hon. Frank Oliver: The department lays down no hard and fast rules as to what kind of bait shall be used in the case of wild animals on whose pelts a bounty is paid by the government. Ordinary meat is liable to be in a frozen condition at this time of the year, and poison administered through the medium of frozen meat takes longer to work on the vitals of a wolf. Even frozen hard it takes quite a while to melt after being swallowed, and the animal may stray for miles before the strychnine gets in its fine work, thus rendering impotent the work of the man who is out for the pelt. Fresh meat, when obtainable, is the most efficacious form of bait. Old trappers of the Hudson's Bay are unanimous in this opinion. Mr. Peterkins is one of the most zealous servants in the employ of the government and I certainly see no reason for his removal, as suggested by my honourable friend. I might mention that Ungava is a great lone land, and it is some-times hard to find a competent man to remain there for any lengthy period in the government service. However, I am happy to be in a position to inform the House that Mr. Peterkins is about to take himself another wife and will shortly marry into a prominent Esquimaux family.

M.S. McCarthy: Out of bait again?

W.F. Maclean: Wants some more fresh meat probably.

The Speaker: Order, order.

In concluding the debate, the premier asked the government members to vote down this frivolous resolution, as it involved an attack upon the government.

Upon a division being taken, Mr. Herron's resolution was defeated by a vote of ninety to forty-one.

The House then went into Committee of Ways and Means.

M.A.C. Farrant

Marion Farrant learned the power of initials at an early age, when
she first saw her name abbreviated with Roman numeral solidity.
She lives on Vancouver Island and is the critically acclaimed author
of absurdist fiction—sometimes referred to as "postmodern,"
though I'm not really sure what that means any more. I do
know she has a wickedly sharp sense of humour.

FROM *Darwin Alone in the Universe*

The Heartspeak Wellness Retreat

After the guests had left we did, you know, Feng Shui. We had this book,
Instant Feng Shui, that did away with the three thousand years it takes
to understand the practice and made it, well, instant. Feng Shui has to do
with energy flow and balance and harmony and it had just been discovered
in the West. It's the latest ancient thing. And this book, *Instant Feng Shui,*
boiled the practice down to a few handy how-to's which we appreciated,
being on the short side of a three-thousand-year-old tradition. The book had
a checklist called "Tips for Serenity" which was a kind of fast track to cosmic
understanding and this was another thing we appreciated.

Feng Shui is this ancient Asian practice, a very old practice, we understood, even more ancient than Moses or the Greeks. The most ancient
practice there is, practically ground zero as far as enduring, ancient practices
goes. More ancient than stone worship by the Druids which, when you think
about it, was really just a bunch of people in good-looking hooded robes
staring at boulders and getting cold at the sunrise.

So we consulted *Instant Feng Shui* after the guests had left their, you know, negative karma about the place, their critical, snotty comments and their foul moods making it difficult for us to sleep and generally carry on in the elevated, serene way we'd been so diligently practising.

The guests, a pair of hefty, middle-aged sisters from Winnipeg—nylon leisure suits, brush cuts—had rented the suite sight unseen from our ad in *Nature Now!* It was the first ad for our suite, renamed The Heartspeak Wellness Retreat— "Experience the life-enhancing calm ..."—and the sisters were our first guests.

On the second day of their three-week stay they began complaining. Where was the ozone-filtered water? What was Eco-friendly about a track house set in the suburban wilderness behind a strip mall? And where, they demanded, with three noisy preteens in residence, was the calm?

Soon after they began directing their malevolent energy towards us from below. We could actually feel it invading our sacred meditation time like a seeping mould. It took the form of chills and crankiness and black-hearted nastiness amongst the upstairs inhabitants—Jason and the boys, the household pets, myself. We could actually, you know, experience our perfect Now being contaminated. The sun may have shone for the time the guests were with us but their souls were imprisoned in a permanent thundercloud.

The dog's vicious dislike of the guests was their fault, of course; animals know and despise negative beings. Ditto for the droppings left by the cat on their kitchen floor. The suite's repeatedly overflowing toilet, the rips in the sheets, and the rock thrown through their bedroom window were further examples of the negative attracting the negative. About the broken window, we're certain it was not caused by one of our boys. More likely it was a message from a large, rock-hurling eagle and doesn't that speak volumes? Eagles, as everyone knows, are emissaries, ancient emissaries from the spirit world and they always make an appearance when negative forces are at the boil.

It's a blessing, I told Jason, that the guests paid for the rental in advance. It was an even greater blessing when they cut short their visit by ten days and moved to a motel in the city. Their names were Arlene and Bonnie and they left in a huff. I tried practising Tonglen while they loaded their rented Mazda. I tried practising Tonglen very hard. I stood on the front porch, screwed shut my eyes, breathed deeply, and concentrated on sending wave upon wave of loving kindness to those red-faced beings. Any time you encounter blood-boiling rage, Tonglen is the kindest thing you can do. Never give irritating paying guests a refund.

After they'd roared out of the driveway flinging gravel everywhere we meditated for thirty minutes. Then we consulted *Instant Feng Shui*. The book told us how to cleanse our home after unwelcome visitors have left. First you put two heavy stone jars on either side of the front door to usher in new beginnings. Then you light firecrackers. Set off firecrackers in the places where the offending guests have been. And this setting off of firecrackers made sense to us. Tiny explosions clearing the air, shaking things up, restoring harmony. Throw open the windows, the book advised, and light about two dozen firecrackers, mainly in doorways and in places where the guests have slept. And viola!, the book promised, clarity and peace restored.

But we encountered this big problem. It was mid-August and just try buying firecrackers in mid-August. There's some law against it. Some law that says you can only buy firecrackers during the last two weeks of October, for Halloween. So we wondered, what now? Because our need was pressing— bad karma headaches, pictures falling off the walls, general imbalance and disharmony in our home, the human and pet inhabitants gnawing on one another's tranquility.

So we built a bomb. Five bombs actually. Five little bombs trying, you know, to approximate firecracker size. But, of course, this was difficult. Jason and I visited Home Hardware for the raw ingredients, the dynamite and fuses and something to put the bomb-making materials into—tubing, we decided, plastic or metal tubing. And we encountered difficulty in the form of suspicious looks from the hardware store clerks who seemed to be thinking, you know, that we were dangerous, and while we'd certainly be the first to admit that there's plenty of things to be dangerous about these days, animal testing being a major scandal in our opinion and generally, the abuse and neglect of cats and dogs, well, this was not one of those times.

I said to Jason, after receiving a blast of ill wind from the pinch-mouthed clerk while purchasing bulk dynamite and filling out all those forms, I said, what we need to do right now, right here is Light Body. That's when you imagine, you know, a protective white light surrounding your body. So we did that. We said to the clerk, "Excuse us!" ran outside to the parking lot, got in our car, and practised Light Body. We got comfortable on the front seat—shoes off, lotus position—and took several deep abdominal breaths. We then visualized a protective white light emanating from the tips of our skulls and surrounding our bodies, top to bottom, side to side, like an egg.

When we returned to the hardware store inside our newly created, shimmering eggs everything was serene and delightful. In no time we completed our purchases.

Jason later said in affirmation, "You know, while I was practising Light Body it was amazing. A red light travelled all the way up from my perineum to my sixth Chakra where it became the most beautiful purple colour."

Jason, formerly in real estate, formerly called Gerald, followed his bliss last year and now does ear coning for a living. "I can't explain it," he's often said of his transformation. "But I felt this overwhelming call for ear wax and candles, for helping people with sinus irritation and tinnitus. I feel like I've got a Date with Destiny."

For a fee he'll also read your aura. So when he tells you he sees purple he means purple. Thanks to meditation, yoga, ozone therapy, touch point reflexology, zero-balancing, his Shamanic drumming circle, and a vegan diet, Jason's become a mild, pony-tailed, teddy bear of a man and all the women, his clients, just love "Ears by Jason."

He's funny, too, but in a joyful, non-judgmental way. When everyone started doing Random Acts of Kindness, Jason, for some reason, misunderstood the word "kindness," the way you can misread a headline and get a completely different meaning. He started doing Random Acts of Kinkiness and, for several days, handed out condoms and yellow nylon rope to complete strangers. While sharing with me the hostile reactions he'd received, I discovered his error.

"I don't understand it," he said, mystified. "Handing out all those condoms and ropes, I really believed I was touching people's hearts, rekindling our oneness, our kindred spirits. It felt wonderful."

What also felt wonderful was our successful practice of Feng Shui to rid our home of the bad karma left by the guests. Our homemade firecrackers, our mini-bombs, were each about the size of a Cuban cigar. For safety's sake, we made sure that each one had a fuse long enough to travel from inside the suite to the far end of the back yard. There, the boys and Jason and I gathered in a healing circle to ask for the Earth Goddess's blessing before lighting the fuses. And when those bombs exploded our relief was instant. Peace and harmony just came flooding back into our home like from an unleashed dam. We were so overjoyed we danced in spinning, you know, cosmic circles around the back yard—Jason and me, the boys, the dog.

The municipal firefighters, when they arrived with their sirens screaming, were amazed that there'd been so little damage—only one window broken and some incidental burn holes in the bedding. Otherwise there was just this pervasive, healing, sulphur-smelling smoke everywhere.

A month later that smell was still with us working its Feng Shui magic. That is, until we received a registered letter from Wisdom Inc., the company in Phoenix, Arizona, that was giving Jason and me our correspondence course in Enlightenment. It was the letter we'd been waiting for. Although we know we're supposed to live without fear or hope, we couldn't help feeling disappointed by the letter's contents.

We'd taken the course, completing all the chapters, writing the tests, pondering the red-inked replies, and redoing some of the questions, as required. We took it all very seriously. Then, when the final exam had been written, we filled out the application form for Graduate Postings, hoping for some exotic background in which to parade our newly awakened selves. Our passports were in order; we'd designated a Power of Attorney, and packed our bags. In short, we did everything that was required, including finding foster homes for the boys.

Now came the reply: Overseas posting denied. Candidates insufficiently evolved. Recommendation: Stay where you are. Take another course. Better luck next time.

We were stunned. We'd been posted to our own back yard.

Jason was momentarily, you know, livid. He'd been hoping to practise ear coning internationally. He started seeing red everywhere and not the good kind of red, either. "I'm forty-nine years old!" he cried. "I paid all that money to go through all those bleeding levels and I have to remain here?"

"Maybe it's a test," I said. "Some kind of ultimate test."

"What isn't ultimate?" he snapped.

"Exactly."

We unpacked our bags.

Temporarily for a nanosecond of my emptied Now state of mind, I was disillusioned. I was having misgivings about the Human Potential Movement and nearly changed my name from Ambika Crystal, Divine Bodywork Pet Counsellor, back to Debbie Thornbur, preparer of income tax returns.

Fortunately, *Instant Feng Shui* was on hand with its sage advice. "To promote happiness and prosperity and to hasten your journey along the path to Enlightenment," I read, perhaps a little too anxiously, "place a clear glass paperweight before a mirror in your hallway. At the exact same time each day stand before the mirror and place your hands on the paperweight. Now, with shoulders relaxed and head erect, gently smile at your reflection. Keep smiling for forty-five minutes. Do this for twenty-seven days."

This has now become my principal daily practice. While awaiting results, I've been writing in my "Vision Journal" as instructed by the knowing people at Wisdom Inc. Our first assignment for the new course is this: We are to imagine that the house we've lived in for eleven years with the boys, the dog and cat, and assorted possessions, is entirely New. We are to experience each moment with awakened eyes, as if the next moment after that will be one of blindness, deafness, and/or sudden, violent death.

This is what I wrote this morning:

Daybreak. Light frost. Sky along the strip mall washed pink and grey. Brush stroke of cloud stretching east to west. I, Ambika Crystal, a human Haiku in a velour dressing gown, am throwing toast crusts from an upstairs window to the scavenging crows in the back yard below. The cat sits beside me at the window, her jaws vibrating at the sight of the birds. Oh, get on with it, kill the bloody things, I want to scream. And scream.

Startled by what I had written, I raced back to the mirror. A double dose of Feng Shui should help.

Now I'm smiling. And for added measure, chanting "Ommmmm." Smiling and chanting at the same time is not as difficult as it sounds. Try this when the journey's just not moving along, you know, fast enough.

Ian Ferguson

Yes, he is my brother. And, yes, we once wrote a book together.
But if you think nepotism is behind his inclusion here, you'd be
wrong. Ian has an unimpeachable track record when it comes to
humour: he is the author of two books, both of which were
shortlisted for the Leacock Medal and one of which won it.
That's as close as you can get to batting a thousand.
The excerpt here is from *Village of the Small Houses,* a
fictionalized memoir about growing up in our hometown
of Fort Vermilion in the backwoods of northern Alberta.

FROM *Village of the Small Houses*

Moving Pictures

"I *don't know what to say."*
Fighting words. Not quite up there with "Just watch me" or "You
shall go no farther," but fighting words nonetheless. Those words were the
direct cause of the Great Fort Vermilion Movie Theatre Riot, an event that
lives on in the memories of participants to the point of legend.

Fort Vermilion may not have had a television signal or a radio station to
listen to on a consistent basis. We may not have had a sewer system, and
many of us lived in houses without electricity, let alone running water, but
we did have something that made us the envy of neighbouring communities.
We had something that filled the citizens of Buffalo Head Prairie, La Crete,
Tallcree, and Rocky Lane with jealousy. An attraction that brought them out
of their own homes and across badly maintained gravel and dirt roads into

the heart of Fort Vermilion. They came from far and wide every weekend, from Assumption, Meander River, Paddle Prairie, and Indian Cabins, and it was a source of considerable local pride that we had something they didn't. We had a movie theatre.

Now, this wasn't the kind of movie theatre you might find in other small towns. There was no lobby, no popcorn machine, and no soda fountain. The washrooms were located out back. The seats were wooden benches. The floor was dirt, with rough planks on top. The Fort Vermilion Movie Theatre was housed in a metal Quonset hut the government of Alberta had constructed or slapped up or thrown together as a temporary storage shed for road-building equipment. The road never got built, and the equipment was finally taken away to some other northern community where it wouldn't be used. Not building things was one of the biggest employment programs in the North; many people were seasonally employed to not build roads, not build hospitals and not build schools. Workers would drift from town to town, like nomads, depending on which MLA was pushing through which pet project in the legislature.

Fort Vermilion was in what was referred to as an "improvement district," which meant, theoretically, that lots of taxpayers' money was available to improve the district. The government down south would make a decision, and the next thing you knew, some duly elected representative would show up to make a stirring speech about how this bridge, library, or health centre would greatly improve everybody's life and make that particular town or district or reserve truly the Gateway to the North. This was a much sought-after designation, and half the communities that fell above the fifty-first parallel were aggressive in claiming it as their own. You can't drive more than a few hours north of Edmonton without running into several Gateways to the North. The towns of Peace River and Grimshaw, which are separated by a fifteen-minute drive, had a longstanding feud over the title, which was finally resolved when Grimshaw changed its designation to Gateway to Peace River on all the appropriate signage. Their original choice, Gateway to the Gateway of the North, was determined to be too confusing. Besides, it looked like a typographical error.

Most of the big capital projects were ignored or underfunded once the initial announcement had been made. Sometimes—and this is purely anecdotal; I certainly wouldn't want to malign the reputations of any of the fine elected officials of that era—the big project was revealed to have come about as a result of cronyism or influence-peddling. The North is full of projects that were started with great fanfare, shoddily and slowly developed, and never finished. Bridges were built to places where there were no roads, and roads were built where there were no people. Projects would peter out as funding became more and more scarce. Sometimes they were killed outright, when the government of the day decided it was time to give the province's taxpayers a break. Since most of the paying taxpayers lived down south, abandoning a project in a remote community was always deemed the most fiscally sound way to proceed. That's how it goes. Stop construction on a half-built senior citizens' complex in Calgary, and you might run into opposition. Taxpaying people, voters even, might complain. Do the same thing in a small northern village, and nobody says a word. And if they did, who would listen?

The upside to this system was that when the big projects were abandoned, stuff was sometimes left behind. The summer of 1975 was as good an example as any. In an attempt to support Fort Vermilion's non-existent tourism industry, a wooden boardwalk was being built along the riverbank. It was three-quarters finished when the plug was pulled. Somebody must have noticed that there were no tourists in town. Anyway, the construction workers had barely downed tools when the looting of the boardwalk began. Lloyd Loonskin and I went down to collect some wood—we had plans to build a tree house or a fort—but we were too late to pick up what we wanted. The workers had been given notice at 4:00 P.M., and they'd gone to pack up. By 4:15, the word had gotten out. By 4:30, the deconstruction was well under way.

The riverbank swarmed with families. Hammers and saws flew as the men ripped the boardwalk to pieces. Women and children scrambled up and down the embankment, transporting the detritus to waiting pickup trucks and wagons. The foreman of the construction crew, a large blond man with a perfect set of teeth who hailed from somewhere near Ponoka, came out on the street at about the same time Lloyd Loonskin and I arrived on the scene.

"Hey, partner," Lloyd Loonskin said, "look at that guy."

I turned around to take in the foreman. He was standing there mouth agape, eyes blinking furiously. I turned back to Lloyd Loonskin. "What about him?"

"That guy?" Lloyd Loonskin said. "He looks like he's gonna cry." Lloyd was smiling when he said it.

The rest of the construction crew slowly fanned out on the street behind their foreman. They didn't say a word. None of them even appeared to be breathing. The foreman ran one sunburned hand across his mouth, then he gave a little shrug, almost a shiver.

"Jeez," he said. "Jeez, you guys." He didn't seem to be talking to anyone in particular. "You could have at least waited until we left town."

Lloyd Loonskin gave him a benevolent smile. "Mister," he said, "if everybody waited, then all the good stuff would already be gone." Lloyd turned and gave me a look, as if to say, "See, I told you we should have got here earlier."

The Indians had fallen on that boardwalk as if it were a dying buffalo. They were devouring it, taking everything apart. And just like in a buffalo hunt, nothing went to waste, and nothing would be left behind. Glenn Lambert was building himself a work shed. He had plenty of lumber already, so he concentrated on the hardware. By some sort of unspoken agreement, he got first choice of any nail, screw, or bolt. Ted Carrier wanted to put a proper floor on his mother's house, so he went mainly after the prefinished waterproof slats along the railing. Bud Peyen staggered up the hill carrying an impossibly heavy load of pressure-treated posts. He gave me a grin as he passed by.

"Hey, little buddy, look at this. I got enough firewood for all winter." He continued on past the foreman and his crew, stopping to give them a polite nod of appreciation. Even after his accident, he was still relentlessly polite. "That's real good wood, fellas," he said. "Gonna burn nice and slow."

It must have looked fearful to those construction workers. It must have been a terrifying thing to see. The entire two and three-quarters miles of completed boardwalk was gone before the sun went down. The crew boarded their bus and crept out of town. The boardwalk was doomed from the start, anyway; it would have been wiped out in the first high water of the spring.

The Quonset hut that housed the Fort Vermilion Movie Theatre was also recycled. At one time the government had planned to build the Red Earth Road, a shortcut to Fort Vermilion from Edmonton that would have saved three or four hours. A winter-only forestry road already existed, but it was in such poor repair that no one would travel on it unless they were fleeing from the law or something of that significance. The paving for the Red Earth Road had started simultaneously at the north and south ends, the idea being to meet in the middle, but the money ran out after only ten miles or so on each side had been completed. To this day, they haven't finished putting down the asphalt. People travelling to the North for the first time will often look at their road maps and decide to go up the Red Earth Road to save a little time. Don't make this mistake yourself. Before the work on the Red Earth Road started, however, the road crew had erected a Quonset hut in Fort Vermilion to store their graders and earth-movers and other equipment. One year later all of that equipment was gone, and we had ourselves a movie theatre.

Ellen McAteer was the visionary who saw potential in the abandoned garage. She was a widow lady. Not a grass widow like so many of the women in town. Ellen McAteer's husband was actually dead. He had accepted a position with the school division but died shortly after arriving in Fort Vermilion. Ellen McAteer took to her bed for several months. Since she and her husband had been new in town, nobody bothered to see how she was doing, and by the time she emerged from her period of mourning she had gone a little crazy. The town decided she was, in the words of Bud Peyen, "bug-jack wack-adoo." Not that anybody held this against her. The town was full of people who would, in other communities, have been institutionalized. One more nut wasn't going to ruin anything.

Ellen McAteer got herself a job working at the post office. It kept her busy. That was a good thing, since she was a busybody. She wasn't an ugly woman by birth, but as she got older she became more and more nasty in appearance. Her face was composed entirely of sharp angles. Her eyes were watery and distrustful. Her skin was pallid and her hair colourless. She was the whitest white woman anybody had ever laid eyes on.

She terrified Bud Peyen, and on the rare occasion that he'd needed to see her in her professional capacity, he had always asked my father to come along for moral support.

"That woman scares me, Hank," Bud would say. "She's so damn pale."

Ellen McAteer was indeed a formidable presence. She served on every committee in town, and she never missed a meeting. She had deeply held religious beliefs, but had never managed to become friends with Father Litzler. He tolerated her as member of his congregation, but it was apparent that he couldn't stand her.

The Fort Vermilion Movie Theatre was, literally, the only show in town. After the road crew departed, Ellen McAteer purchased the abandoned equipment shed, hung a huge chunk of canvas across the back wall, and hired a couple of Mennonite boys to build seats and a projection booth. She didn't bother putting up a sign out front, or giving the town's first movie theatre a proper name. She simply called it the Fort Vermilion Movie Theatre. The rest of us called it "No Refunds."

Ellen McAteer would never give your money back, for any reason. Once the money went into the cash box, it stayed in the cash box. It didn't matter if the movie print was scratched, or if the movie shown was not the one promised, or if the reels got mixed up and shown in the wrong order, which was a fairly common occurrence. Any complaint, any request for reimbursement, any suggestion that you were owed something was met with a terse "No refunds." And that was that. You paid your money and you took your chances.

Ellen McAteer showed films on Friday and Saturday nights. The season was mainly spring and summer, since the building wasn't insulated and the only heat came from a wood stove at the back. Showtime was seven in the evening, unless people were late arriving; then the movie might start as late as eight or nine. It cost one dollar for adults and fifty cents for children. Stale bags of potato chips and room-temperature bottles of grape pop were available for a less than reasonable two bits.

There were no tickets. You simply waited until Ellen McAteer opened the doors and rushed inside to choose your seat. Grown-ups sat near the back and kids down near the front.

Just before starting the movie, Ellen McAteer would go up and down the aisles with her green metal cash box collecting admission. It was like church. If you timed it right, you could move up after she collected from the bench in front of you and avoid paying altogether. Ellen McAteer had to be momentarily distracted for this to work, and Lloyd Loonskin and I would take turns causing a mild disturbance. This was risky, however. If you got caught, you'd be banned from coming back for some appropriate amount of time. Worse, you'd be given a severe dressing-down that would delay the start of the movie and get you punched in the stomach by the other kids.

Once the money was safely in the cash box, Ellen McAteer would go up into her booth and start the film. She owned a single 16-mm projector, and between reels she would turn on the lights, rewind the reel you'd watched, thread the next reel into the projector, and then turn off the lights again. This would take ten to fifteen minutes, unless some kid slowed things down by buying some chips, definitely a stomach-punching offence. On average, it took three hours to see a feature. It's not like there was anything else to do. Besides, every time the lights came up, you could look around to see if anybody had changed seats or been caught kissing. Adults would visit, catch up on the news; it was a fairly sociable way to spend the evening. Smoking wasn't permitted while the movie was running, but grown-ups lit up in between acts, resulting in nicely diffused images by the time the show concluded.

The Fort Vermilion Movie Theatre was a gold mine for Ellen McAteer. Almost two hundred people could squeeze into the Quonset hut, and the place was usually filled to capacity for both the Friday and the Saturday shows. There was almost no overhead. No advertising was required. The metal cases carrying that week's film would come by truck from the bus depot in High Level and be dropped off at Stephen's General Store every Wednesday. By Thursday, the whole town would know what was playing on the weekend. Always careful to present entertainment with a good moral message, and mindful of the tastes of her audience, Ellen McAteer programmed a steady diet of cowboy movies and Elvis Presley musicals. Once she brought in an Elvis movie that was also a Western, and the demand was so great she had to add on extra screenings. None of the films she showed were first-run features. Many of them were in black and white, and the quality of the viewing experience was low. But it didn't matter. We had a movie theatre.

I can still remember the thrill of it all. The lights would go down, and we'd be somewhere else. Someplace better. Good guys and bad guys and action and excitement. We'd travel to places that none of us, not one of us, could ever hope to really see.

Even at fifty cents a ticket, the moving pictures were a luxury. We didn't get to go every weekend, and our mother could rarely afford to send my brothers and sisters and me as a group. We did, however, come up with a reasonable solution. Jobs were scarce enough for adults in Fort Vermilion, and there were even fewer ways for a kid to make money. If stealing wasn't an option, you were limited to hunting for beer bottles to redeem at Stephen's General Store. It wasn't the fastest way to make a buck. But if we combined our resources, we could usually raise enough cash to send one of us to the show. That person would then be responsible for filling everyone else in on what they'd missed.

We started off taking turns. My brother Dan had a fantastic memory, and he could describe the plots of movies in great detail. My brother Sean was the designated viewer for musicals, since he could not only tell us what had happened but be counted on to deliver perfect a cappella renditions of most of the songs. My talent lay in embellishment. I would come home and act out the entire movie, playing all of the characters, adding and deleting scenes or changing endings, always with an eye to making the movie as exciting as possible. Lloyd Loonskin was the first to pick up on this.

"Hey, partner, I seen that movie with you, and I don't remember Audie Murphy shooting two guys with one bullet."

"Yeah, but wouldn't it have been cool if he did?"

Word spread, and I would spend the week after seeing a show performing it for larger and larger audiences. I never outdrew Ellen McAteer, but my popularity got a boost. Lloyd Loonskin received a regular allowance from Gene Rogers now, but he stopped going to the movies every weekend. He would send me in his place every time I couldn't afford a ticket.

"I'd rather watch your movie than the one playing at the theatre," he said.

If I had known what Lloyd Loonskin went to the movies to escape, I like to believe I wouldn't have accepted his generosity.

It wasn't that difficult to improve on the movies Ellen McAteer showed at her theatre. Hoot Gibson seemed old-fashioned even to us. Elvis Presley was fine, although I wanted him to do more punching and less singing. My most interesting challenge was overcoming Ellen McAteer's censorship. Every Thursday afternoon, she would privately screen whatever movie had been dropped off, looking for profanity or lewd conduct. At the weekend shows, she would turn off the sound to blank out swearing, forcing us to lip-read desperately. During interactions that were the least bit sexual, she'd put her hand over the lens of the projector, leaving us to puzzle things out from the soundtrack.

My re-enactments left out nothing, another reason for their popularity. As it turns out, my versions were much racier than the content being censored. When I finally got around to renting *Nevada Trail* a few years ago, I was surprised to discover the love scene was extremely chaste. Not to brag or anything, but my version was an improvement.

God forbid we should see Elvis Presley kiss Ann-Margret, but we could watch John Wayne shoot a thousand Indians. We watched so many Indians get killed on screen it became annoying. I routinely changed the endings of the movies I'd seen, killing off all the cowboys when I acted them out. Then Ellen McAteer made the mistake of showing *Billy Jack*. Any Aboriginal person over the age of thirty-five can tell you where they saw this movie *and* quote it from memory. It was the first movie any of us had ever watched with an Indian as the hero. Not the bad guy. Not the sidekick. The hero. Sure, Tom Laughlin didn't look like a real Indian, but neither did those Italian or Jewish actors we were used to seeing play Aboriginals. *Billy Jack* was the all-time number-one box-office draw in Fort Vermilion. It played for six weekends in a row. Then Elvis returned. This time, however, nobody wanted to see him. The Duke followed. Same thing. People stayed away from the theatre. For the first time ever, it wasn't operating at capacity. Ellen McAteer was stunned. She sought help from a higher power.

"I don't know, Ellen. It's not my, uh, my problem," said Father Litzler. He went back to work on his beloved tractor.

"Yes, I can see how it would be a concern," said Constable Ledinski. "But I'm not sure what you want me to do about it."

"Maybe you should show *Billy Jack* again," I said. I was being sarcastic.

"Yeah," said Lloyd Loonskin, "bring back *Billy Jack*." He was completely serious.

Having apparently exhausted the advice available from the town's leading citizens, Ellen McAteer had cornered two of her best customers outside the post office to ask us our opinion.

"That's ridiculous," she said. "I can't keep showing the same movie over and over again."

"Why not?" Lloyd Loonskin asked.

"People will get bored and stop coming to my theatre."

"They're not coming now," I said.

"What did you say?"

"Nothing," I said.

"Indians!" That was Lloyd Loonskin, who sounded genuinely enthused. Mrs. McAteer turned her head to look at him. There weren't any flies on her, that's for sure. You could tell right away she knew what he was getting at.

"That's why everybody came to see *Billy Jack*," Lloyd said, getting more and more excited. "Because he was an Indian, and he could beat everybody up, and he wasn't scared of anybody." He smiled his lopsided smile at Ellen McAteer. "I bet if you showed another movie about Indians, everybody would turn up to see that."

Ellen McAteer put the word out that she was ordering in a special movie just for the Indians. And the half-breeds and the Metis. This time she even ran a few posters off on the Gestetner machine at St. Theresa's Hospital. The wording was simple; the posters simply said that she was proud to be presenting (or pleased to announce, I don't recall which) an all-Indian action film at the theatre on the upcoming weekend. People were dubious about whether there was such a film, but as the week wore on excitement started building, and Ellen McAteer drew a sold-out crowd for the Friday showing. The film was called *Red Gorge,* which was close enough to "redskin" to make everybody think that, if it wasn't exactly an all-Indian film, there was at least a strong possibility of some action, "gorge" being close enough to "gore." Lloyd Loonskin was convinced it was a film about Chief Dan George.

About half of the town had turned out for the movie. It took Ellen McAteer twice as long as usual to work her way through the crowd to collect her money. The lights went out. The title *Red Gorge* came up on the screen, which elicited a cheer from the crowd. The reels were in the right order. The cheer died down as the titles kept running. There was something terribly wrong. The actors' names were written in some foreign language. The first scene had an elephant in it, ridden by a man with a beard and a funny wrap-around hat. The elephant entered a courtyard, and there was another man waiting there. He was wearing an orange jumpsuit and standing by a fountain. The man looked right at the camera, right at us, then said something in a language none of us could understand. The bottom of the screen lit up with English subtitles. What the man in the orange jumpsuit had stated, apparently, was, "I don't know what to say." The bearded man on the top of the elephant replied, "You resemble a spider," possibly losing a little something in the translation. Then both men started to sing.

We were stunned into silence until the dancers came on screen and everybody figured out what was going on. The dancers were wearing saris. Just like Elisabeth Usman, Dr. Usman's wife. Elisabeth Usman was a large, jolly Danish woman adored by all. She had shocked most everybody when she wore her wedding sari to her first big do in town, but people got over it. This was different. Not only were people getting a musical when they'd been promised an action film, they were angry that Ellen McAteer, after living in Fort Vermilion for so long, couldn't tell the difference between a real Indian and someone from India.

It started fast. The first song wasn't even over when someone began stomping on the floor. Everyone else joined in. It wasn't loud, the way 200 people would sound stomping on linoleum or tile, but it was loud enough to make Ellen McAteer turn up the volume on the movie. Next, everybody started whistling. All at the same time, and all through their teeth. Then someone—I know for a fact that it was Lloyd Loonskin—started the chant.

"We want our money back, we want our money back, we want our money back."

Ellen McAteer turned the picture off, turned on the lights, and told everyone to go home.

"I'm going to call the police," she said. That was an empty threat, since "the police" consisted solely of Corporal Ledinski, and he was in the theatre watching the movie. He apparently had been hoping for a good Indian action film, too, because he stood up and faced her. Everybody stopped making noise.

"I'm right here, Ellen," Corporal Ledinski said, "and I want my money back, too."

Nobody cheered. Nobody applauded. We were too overwhelmed. We had won. The Great Fort Vermilion Movie Theatre Riot had succeeded. We had done the impossible. We got refunds.

Will Ferguson

When Penguin first approached me about editing this anthology, they asked if I could include something of my own, something that hadn't appeared before in other books. (Readers who feel that compilers of anthologies shouldn't include their own works in said collections should avert their gaze at this point.) The following article is about media "greenrooms," where guests wait until they are called out, one at a time, much like the entertainment at a Roman coliseum. It was first published in *The Globe and Mail,* and I include it here mainly because this story has since become something of an urban legend among publishers and publicists. If you've heard The Tale of the Author and the Blueberry Muffins, now you know the source. Just last fall, I was on tour again and I asked the publicist who was taking me around whether she'd had any bad experiences with previous authors. She said "No, not really, but," and her voice dropped, "I heard there was this one author who made the publicist *pick the blueberries out of his muffin ...*"

The Writer in the Greenroom

It seemed like a reasonable enough request.

"The blueberries," I said. "Can you pick them out of the muffin for me?"

The publicist, a focused and relentlessly well-organized young woman, blinked. We were in a van on our way to Kitchener-Waterloo, for a TV interview, and she had just driven through a Tim Hortons to pick up coffee and muffins for the road.

"Oh," she said. "I misunderstood. I thought you asked for blueberry. I can get you a plain muffin instead."

"No, no," I said. "I like blueberry muffins. I just don't like blueberries. Can you pick them out please?" I was on book tour, you see. Five cities. Nine days. It was my fourth tour in as many years, and I knew that the unwritten role of a publicist is to Indulge the Author, just as surely as the unwritten role of the author is to Torment the Publicist.

There are many ways to torment a publicist: You can show up late, you can refuse to do interviews, you can throw a hissy fit, you can make increasingly bizarre and petty demands. You can, in short, act like a prima donna. You can even demand that they pick the blueberries out of a muffin for you.

At first, book tours seem like a wonderful, all-expense-paid break from the solitary hunt-and-peck existence of writing. You jet into a different city every night. You get to raid the mini-bar, you can have wine with each and every meal, and you can order up room service for breakfast every single day—all on someone else's tab. But the $18 jars of mini-bar cashews get awfully tiresome after a while, and the novelty of free room service soon wears off. Damp toast and cold eggs. Long dull taxi rides from one airport to another. *If it's Monday, this must be Ottawa ...*

I'm not complaining. Most books don't get toured at all, and certainly in the precarious world of publishing, any author that gets sent on a cross-Canada national media whirl has no right to complain about anything. It's exhausting, but it's also deeply flattering. It never ceases to amaze me that an entire fleet of people, from publisher to publicist to marketing teams, are hard at work trying to sell your ideas—your *words*—to the general public. The only acceptable emotion any writer lucky enough to get toured should be allowed to demonstrate is, well, gratitude.

Ah, but writers are a notoriously prickly and insecure group, and there is something about running the gauntlet of interviews—two-minute wham-bam on-air hits followed by interminable call-in shows and ear-numbing phoners—that tends to bring out the very worst in people. And of course, when I say "people," I mean "me."

Long stretches of monotony punctuated by sudden self-conscious bursts of shameless self-promotion: It's not the most dignified way to reach an audience. Even then, you are jostling for position with other writers and snake charmers, with musicians and mountebanks and medical quacks, all hungry for a piece of the promo pie, all sparing with tight-lipped smiles in greenrooms across this great land of ours. The media is the master, and greenrooms are strange places, indeed.

After a while, they begin to blend into one another. The same guests seem to circulate, reappearing again and again with déjà-vu predictability. There is always a chef, oozing charm. There is always a singer, shellacked with bullet-proof hairspray. (Or a band: either Cape Breton fiddlers or faux-attitude urban hip-hop.) And there is always—*always*—a B-grade American actor who has some sort of role in some sort of upcoming made-for-TV movie.

Everyone fawns over the B-grade American actor, and the B-grade American actor always has a sour expression. Amid this odd microcosm, this one-room sociological experiment, sits a writer. He is in the corner, holding his book on his lap, as welcome as an insurance salesman at a cocktail soiree.

Some hosts have actually read your book—or at the very least have skimmed through it. They have Post-it Notes marking pages and index cards with questions. These hosts are almost always women. Others, mainly men, mainly guys, mainly radio talk-show hosts, are cheerfully—and completely—uninformed about who you are. They don't know and they don't care. When it comes time to interview you, they just flip over your book and read the bio directly from the backcover. "Welcome back. We are here today with ... where's the name? Let's see ... Wilf Erguson, author of—whoa!—*Bastards and Boneheads*. Where'd you get a title like that?"

This isn't necessarily a bad thing. After all, the hosts who haven't read your book are always the ones who praise it the most highly. ("Our guest today is the author of—what was it?—*Canadian Dummies for History*. No? Ah, close enough. Anyway, it's a great book! Very funny! Terrific! Fantastic!! I recommend it 110 percent!") Whenever you hear a radio host pouring effusive praise on a book, you can bet a week's wages that he hasn't even cracked its spine, let alone read the first page.

But no, it's not the interviews that grind you down when you are on a book tour. It's the waiting. The interviews are the highlights of the day. It's the "waiting-to-be-interviewed" part of it that's excruciating.

Here then, is my confession. Although I am always surprised—and genuinely appreciative—of any exposure that the media gives a touring author, I hate being the writer in the greenroom. I really do. I hate being the guy with the book. When you are the writer in the greenroom, you are always the least cool and most unhip person in the room. The chef is loud and gregarious and speaking in a staged Italian accent. The singer is flirty and radiant. The band is noisily scarfing down bagels with both hands. (I once watched in awe and admiration as the Barra MacNeils polished off an entire buffet just before heading out onstage, live, on a daytime talk show. Some of them were still chewing as they went out.) The B-grade American actor really *is* a prima donna—at least by Canadian media standards. But the writer?

It has been scientifically proven that the single most boring sentence in the English language is: "Mr. Jones will now speak about his book." When you're the writer in the greenroom, not even the singer will flirt with you. When you're the writer in the greenroom, the other guests' eyes glaze over when you tell them what you do. In fact, it got so bad that I took to lying whenever anyone asked.

"Why am I on the show? I invented a lethal dart-gun that can kill a cheetah from 140 paces."

"Really?" they say, eyes lighting up.

"Yes. And then I wrote a book about it."

"I see." Their eyes immediately begin glazing over.

This is where the publicist comes in. Among the many and varied responsibilities that fall upon him or her—media coordinator, chauffeur, troubleshooter—the publicist also acts as a sort of triage therapist, leaping in once the shooting stops to assuage wounds and stroke frail authorial egos. Which is to say, they lie an awful lot.

"You were wonderful," the publicist says as she whisks you from one disastrous TV interview to the next. "Don't worry about the nosebleed, you were fine. No one noticed."

Once, during a live interview at a campus radio station in Halifax, the host said, after a long, agonizing pause, "Well, I'm all out of questions." I ended up interviewing myself while the host flipped through a magazine. True story.

"You were fine," said the publicist afterwards. "You were fine."

Publicists collect author anecdotes the way Sicilians collect vendettas, and some writers clearly stand out. Everyone loved Timothy Findley, and everyone hated—well, never mind. My libel insurance has lapsed, so I won't pass on the juicier gossip.

Some authors—and one novelist in particular—are so nasty that the mere mention of their name causes teeth-grinding Pavlovian reactions among publicists. Some authors are infamous for being lewd, some for being petulant, some for being pouty. One is even renowned for his flatulence. Some authors treat publicists like personal servants, some treat them like confidants. One well-known female author, who wrote a children's book no less, took the publicist on a drunken pub crawl at the end of the day. "She was great," said the publicist. "But man, what a hangover."

I have no idea where I fit in. For all I know, publicists right now are sitting around a dim and dingy bar, drinking gin and muttering, "I had Will Ferguson last week. God, what a nightmare."

You see, I was just kidding about the blueberries. I was fooling around, pulling her leg. I was poking fun at the type of authors that publicists hate, but—incredibly—she took me seriously. Her face was set in diplomatic stone, but her eyes betrayed feelings of barely concealed contempt as she looked first at the muffin and then back at me.

"You want me to pick out the blueberries," she said. It was a statement, not a question.

"No, no," I said frantically. "I was only joking!"

"Oh," she said, her voice even and her gaze steady. "Very funny."

Later, once we were out on the highway and heading for the TV station, I asked the publicist what she would have done if I hadn't been kidding, if I had in fact been dead serious in my request.

"Well," she said, with a weary sigh. "I suppose I would have started picking."

· · ·

POSTSCRIPT: The day after this story ran in The Globe and Mail, *a FedEx package arrived at my front door from the publicist in question. Inside were a dozen blueberry muffins, a pair of tweezers, and a note that read: "Here you go, Will! Knock yourself out."*

Jacques Ferron

Jacques Ferron was many things: a diehard separatist, a formally trained medical doctor, a relentless prankster, and a renowned author. He was also co-founder of the Rhinoceros Party of Canada, which at its peak ran 121 candidates and included in its platform:

· repealing the Law of Gravity;
· declaring war on Belgium;
· moving the Rocky Mountains one metre west, as a make-work project;
· paving the Bay of Fundy (to provide more parking for Maritimers);
· making pop bottles Canada's official currency;
· turning Ste-Catherine Street in Montreal into the world's longest bowling alley;
· counting the Thousand Islands to make sure none are missing; and
· introducing British-style driving, on the left (to be phased in gradually over a five-year period, with large trucks and buses switching over in the first year, mid-sized cars the next, then smaller cars, and finally bicycles).

Ferron's humour is often slightly surreal, expressed in tall tales, modern fables, and political parables. The stories that follow were translated by Betty Bednarski.

FROM *Selected Tales of Jacques Ferron*

How the Old Man Died

There was a bone askew above his stomach; he was not sick, but the bone made him uncomfortable, stabbing him with every breath he took. He would have to stay quiet until the bone reset. After three or four weeks the wretched bone had not moved, the old man was going from bad to worse; they sent for the manipulator, but the manipulator, having felt him, refused to manipulate him, for by shifting the bone, he would at the same time have dislocated the nerve of the heart. The old man was done for. They sent for the priest.

"Old man," said the old woman to her husband, "maybe you're not very sick, but you're so old that you're dying."

"I'm dying?"

"Yes you're dying; what's to become of me?"

"And what about me?" asked the old man.

"You have nothing to worry about," replied the old woman, "all you have to do is lie back; the priest will take care of everything. Only you'll have to be polite; you'll fold your hands, look up, and think of the good Lord, if you can; if you can't, pretend to. And no funny business, do you understand!"

The old man was having difficulty breathing; he promised to behave. However, the arrival of his boys with their sanctimonious faces upset him in his resolve. His hands were already folded, he tried to separate them without being noticed, but the old lady had her eye on him; she fastened his wrists with a long rosary. Just then the priest arrived, concluded that there was no hope for the old man, and accordingly made haste to administer the last rites. After that he was at a loss to know what to do; it was not yet time to say the prayer for the dying.

"How are you feeling?" he asked the old man.

"Badly, thank you," replied he.

Badly, to be sure, but not badly enough to go under; now higher, now lower, he was still rising and falling with the swell. The priest, who was inclined to be squeamish, retired to the kitchen, accompanied by the women. The boys, who had stayed with their father, did not waste a moment: they removed his handcuffs. The old man raised his hand to them:

"Hi there, boys!"

"Hi there, Pa," they replied.

Short waves shook the man. This lasted an hour or more; then after the final wave came the final hour; the old man was at peace at last in his bed; the bone pained him no more; he was healed; he was about to die. The women had returned to his side, smothering seagull cries in their handkerchiefs. The priest was saying the prayer. It was too good, too good; it was too good to last.

"The pot," cried the dying man.

The priest stopped. The chamber pot was brought, but the old man pushed it away:

"Too late; I'll go on the other side."

And he died.

When they had put him in the coffin, clean-shaven and smartly dressed, he looked very distinguished. The old woman could not stop gazing at him, and tearfully she told him:

"Ah, old man, my old man, if only you'd always been like this, sensible, clean, quiet, how I'd have loved you, how happy we'd have been!"

She could talk all she liked, poor woman! The old man was not listening to her: he was in the kitchen laughing with his boys, laughing as much as one dare laugh at a wake.

The Parakeet

The departure of her eldest had never upset her, for she had always managed to replace them as she went along. But there came a year when she was no longer able, having, as it turned out, produced her lastborn the year before. This was the end of her family. The lastborn grew and, growing, nudged the rest, who, one after another, went their way.

"Soon they'll all have left."

"I hope so," said the old man.

The wife looked at this husband of hers and thought what a fool he was, what an old fool. What disconcerted her was that he had always been this way and that she loved him. He was of the opinion that as long as you'd done your duty by your children, and they weren't in poor health, they should be made to fend for themselves once they were of age—or sooner, in the case of the smartest ones; after that they didn't belong to the parents any more, but to the whole world, and to the good Lord; you had to let them go, and even, if necessary, show them the way.

"Even the lastborn?"

The lastborn was no different from the rest, for the old man was poor and hadn't the means to keep a single one. So in due course he, too, left, and the mother fell ill.

"Very well," said the old man, "but I'm warning you, old girl: if you die, I'll take a new wife."

He thought himself clever. She thought what a fool he was, what an old fool. What disconcerted her was that he had always been this way and that she loved him. She couldn't bring herself to leave him to another, and recovered. This changed nothing in the house, which was as sad as before. Even the old man was not happy.

Then, one day, they received from a daughter, who had never married, two parakeets in a white cage, birds the like of which had not been seen in the country, blue birds with masquerade beaks, which spent their time teasing, petting, nestling together to sleep, never tiring of love—two birds of paradise. As soon as they entered the house the sadness left it. The old couple were delighted. Soon the cage got in the way. They opened it, and the parakeets flew about the house. The only drawback—the holes pecked in walls and ceilings. The old man had a hard time repairing the damage, but he was only too happy to do it.

"Damned birds! I'll cut off their heads!"

The old woman looked at him and thought what a fool he was, what an old fool. What disconcerted her was that he had always been this way and that she loved him.

One winter afternoon, when the old man went out to fetch wood, one of the parakeets followed behind him and found itself burning in the icy air. Frantic, it flew straight for the sun. The old woman had rushed outside. Together on the doorstep, husband and wife watched as the bird fell, and they took it to be a sign that their own end was near. They went back inside. In the parakeet that lived on, the old man saw his bereaved wife, the old woman her widowed husband. Each was brokenhearted. Their last days were spent doting on the bird; by lavishing attention on it, they encouraged it to live. Each partner hoped in this way to lessen the other's pain.

Each morning, the old man would say to himself: this day will be my last. At his side, the old woman would think: this will be mine. After a time, however, they changed their chronology, instead of the last day, preferring to say the last week, then the last month. When a year had gone by, and they still hadn't died, they didn't know what to think. Above their heads, the blue parakeet, with which they had become one, hovered motionless, sardonic as an idol.

Mavis Gallant

Mavis Gallant is recognized as one of the masters of the short story. Though we don't immediately associate her with humour writing, in much of her work a definite sense of humour is at play, usually dry, often ironic. A Canadian living in Paris, Gallant's stories often deal with characters caught in transit between their point of origin and their final, sometimes undefined, destination. The following is from *Home Truths: Selected Canadian Stories*, which won the Governor General's Award for Fiction.

FROM *Home Truths*

With a Capital T

In wartime, in Montreal, I applied to work on a newspaper. Its name was *The Lantern*, and its motto, "My light shall shine," carried a Wesleyan ring of veracity and plain dealing. I chose it because I thought it was a place where I would be given a lot of different things to do. I said to the man who consented to see me, "But not the women's pages. Nothing like that." I was eighteen. He heard me out and suggested I come back at twenty-one, which was a soft way of getting rid of me. In the meantime I was to acquire experience; he did not say of what kind. On the stroke of twenty-one I returned and told my story to a different person. I was immediately accepted; I had expected to be. I still believed, then, that most people meant what they said. I supposed that the man I had seen that first time had left a memorandum in the files: "To whom it may concern—Three years from this date, Miss Linnet Muir will join the editorial staff." But after I'd been working for a short time I heard one of the editors say, "If it hadn't been for the god-damned war we would never have hired even one of the god-damned women," and so I knew.

In the meantime I had acquired experience by getting married. I was no longer a Miss Muir, but a Mrs. Blanchard. My husband was overseas. I had longed for emancipation and independence, but I was learning that women's autonomy is like a small inheritance paid out a penny at a time. In a journal I kept I scrupulously noted everything that came into my head about this, and about God, and about politics. I took it for granted that our victory over Fascism would be followed by a sunburst of revolution—I thought that was what the war was about. I wondered if going to work for the capitalist press was entirely moral. "Whatever happens," I wrote, "it will be the Truth, nothing half-hearted, the Truth with a Capital T."

The first thing I had to do was write what goes under the pictures. There is no trick to it. You just repeat what the picture has told you like this:

"Boy eats bun as bear looks on."

The reason why anything has to go under the picture at all is that a reader might wonder, "Is that a bear looking on?" It looks like a bear, but that is not enough reason for saying so. Pasted across the back of the photo you have been given is a strip of paper on which you can read: "Saskatoon, Sask. 23 Nov. Boy eats bun as bear looks on." Whoever composed this knows two things more than you do—a place and a time.

You have a space to fill in which the words must come out even. The space may be tight; in that case, you can remove "as" and substitute a comma, though that makes the kind of terse statement to which your reader is apt to reply, "So what?" Most of the time, the Truth with a Capital T is a matter of elongation: "Blond boy eats small bun as large bear looks on."

"Blond boy eats buttered bun …" is livelier, but unscrupulous. You have been given no information about the butter. "Boy eats bun as hungry bear looks on," has the beginnings of a plot, but it may inspire your reader to protest: "That boy must be a mean sort of kid if he won't share his food with a starving creature." Child-lovers, though less prone to fits of anguish than animal-lovers, may be distressed by the word "hungry" for a different reason, believing "boy" subject to attack from "bear." You must not lose your head and type, "Blond bear eats large boy as hungry bun looks on," because your reader may notice, and write a letter saying, "Some of you guys around there think you're pretty smart, don't you?" while another will try to enrich your caption with, "Re: your bun write-up, my wife has taken better pictures than that in the very area you mention."

At the back of your mind, because your mentors have placed it there, is an obstruction called "the policy factor." Your paper supports a political party. You try to discover what this party has had to say about buns and bears, how it intends to approach them in the future. Your editor, at golf with a member of parliament, will not want to have his game upset by: "It's not that I want to interfere but some of that bun stuff seems pretty negative to me." The young and vulnerable reporter would just as soon not pick up the phone to be told, "I'm ashamed of your defeatist attitude. Why, I knew your father! He must be spinning in his grave!" or, more effectively, "I'm telling you this for your own good—I think you're subversive without knowing it."

Negative, defeatist, and subversive are three of the things you have been cautioned not to be. The others are seditious, obscene, obscure, ironic, intellectual, and impulsive.

You gather up the photo and three pages of failed captions, and knock at the frosted glass of a senior door. You sit down and are given a view of boot soles. You say that the whole matter comes down to an ethical question concerning information and redundancy; unless "reader" is blotto, can't he see for himself that this is about a boy, a bun, and a bear?

Your senior person is in shirtsleeves, hands clasped behind his neck. He thinks this over, staring at the ceiling; swings his feet to the floor; reads your variations on the bear-and-bun theme; turns the photo upside-down. He tells you patiently, that it is not the business of "reader" to draw conclusions. Our subscribers are not dreamers or smart alecks; when they see a situation in a picture, they want that situation confirmed. He reminds you about negativism and obscuration; advises you to go sit in the library and acquire a sense of values by reading the back issues of *Life*.

The back numbers of *Life* are tatty and incomplete, owing to staff habits of tearing out whatever they wish to examine at leisure. A few captions, still intact, allow you to admire a contribution to pictorial journalism, the word "note":

"American flag flies over new post office. Note stars on flag."

"GI waves happily from captured Italian tank. Note helmet on head."

So, "Boy eats bun as bear looks on. Note fur on bear." All that can happen now will be a letter asking, "Are you sure it was a bun?"

Zsuzsi Gartner

I was tempted to say something like "Zsuzsi Gartner's writing is
as unusual and original as the spelling of her name!", but I figured
Gartner isn't that unusual a spelling. Raised in Calgary, based in
Vancouver, Zsuzsi Gartner is one damn fine talented writer.
Smart, quick, and unflinchingly funny, her prose ripples on the
page. The following is from Gartner's debut collection
of stories, *All the Anxious Girls on Earth*.

FROM *All the Anxious Girls on Earth*

Anxious Objects

The child has everything it could possibly want and now it comes to you,
this evening after the first day of junior kindergarten, and says, "I'd like
some pyjamas."

This child who already has a goldfish and rabbits (yet unnamed), a music
box with one of those tiny ballerinas that pop up and twirl slowly to *Swan
Lake,* a porcelain tea set bearing the likeness of that little Parisienne
Madeline, a skipping rope (yet unused), a horse (named Conan, after her
favourite late-night talk-show host), her own home page and internet
account, and an Air Miles card boasting 29,342 points; this child who has an
indoor speed-skating oval (which, you must admit, you and your wife have
tried out, once maybe, zipping along feeling like Hans Brinker and his love,
cheeks ruddy, hand in mitted hand, though only when the child wasn't
around as you would never encroach so aggressively upon the child's *space*);
this child who has a safety deposit box containing the following: a chunk of

the Berlin Wall, a swatch from the Shroud of Turin, and a signed, first-edition *Tropic of Cancer;* this child who has an older sister, stillborn, whom the child keeps in a jar of formaldehyde hidden away someplace known only to the child (although you suspect she has traded the former with a friend up the street for a Pocahontas poster, but, well, *kids will be kids*); this child of whom you still carry an ultrasound photograph in your wallet from the time before you even knew she would be a she (not that you *cared*), who is the glue that holds your marriage together, who is the indelible ink of your heart, who is now standing in front of you saying that *all* the other children at school have pyjamas.

You have, up until now, found it difficult, and largely unnecessary, to deny your child anything. Somewhere up there, invisible to the naked eye, orbits a man-made satellite named in her honour, and it wasn't cheap. Would that it were a planet. But *pyjamas?*

What kind of place is this school where children of all races and abilities learn together in harmony and yet claim to *all* have pyjamas? (Note: Find out who this Italian pedagogue Montessori really is and what kind of social experiment he or she is up to.) You might as well be sending the child to that public school down the block where syringes litter the schoolyard like space debris and twelve-year-old girls hanging around the sagging metal fence claim to be able to do outrageous things with their sturdy, black-licorice-stained lips.

Isn't there a point in a child's life, in your life together as parents and child, that you have to *lay down the law?*

"Pussywillow, kittycat, caramel corn, l'il Amy March, pigeon pie, Sailor Moon, apple-o'-my-eye," you say, carefully modulating your tone so as to spare the child any distress, "whatever do you need pyjamas for?"

Innocently, not aware that she's about to bring the whole sound structure of your Benzedrine-fuelled lives down upon your heads, she leans her face adorably to one side, folds both tiny hands together in a perfect simulacrum of prayer, and presses them alongside her tilted cheek.

"For sleeping," the child says.

And surely as if it were actually happening, the joists in the ceiling groan and the house shifts on its foundations. Plaster dust swirls down chalky and you struggle to see the child through the sudden whiteout, through this authentic, circa 1890s Manitoba snowstorm. The wind howls in your ears, your frostbitten toes and left hand will need amputating. In your arms there's an infant in a coarse saddle blanket who'll be stiff as a board soon, a blue boy. You've only completed grade five. Cows are all you've ever learned anything about, the only thing you're good at, and now they're stuck far out in the fields, the sky lowering down on them. You're Swedish, they won't let you forget. They (they, *them*) say you smell. It is your duty to brood. Your wife, dear God ... but right now all you can think, brain hot with jumbled coals, is, *read Dog, save my child.*

But the child is still standing there in front of you in the kitchen, bathed in halogen light, smiling sweetly, the corners of her mouth smudged chocolatey from an Energy Bar, saying, "For sleeping."

The chamber ensemble you've engaged to accompany all of the child's pronouncements stirs and launches into Schubert's string quartet in D minor, but you abruptly hold up the palm of your hand. The musicians move closer together, chairs squealing against the linoleum, and begin to mutter quietly among themselves, bows across their laps.

These other children *sleep?* When do they have time for ballet and kick-boxing, glass-blowing and oenology, snowboarding and target practice? And what about *citizenship*—staffing polling stations, canvassing door-to-door for the Vancouver Aquarium's new whale pool, and volunteering at St. Paul's Eating Disorders Clinic, not to mention all those guided tours to the sewage treatment plant on Annacis Island? How do they keep up? Can these children do a triple lutz? Can they even drive a four-by-four? Have they climbed K-2 yet (*without* oxygen)?

Upstairs, your wife is online, preregistering the child for an undergraduate year abroad at either the University of Strasbourg or the University of Kyoto (playing it safe, as neither of you, even after commissioning an exhaustive poll with a margin of sampling error of +/-3.5 percent, can predict with any degree of accuracy whether the next century belongs to the new Europe or the Pacific Rim). She is coolly oblivious to the drama unfolding down here in the kitchen. You seek to distract the child. "Let's check with mom, cherry popsicle. Meanwhile, why don't you practise some composition?" The child is currently undertaking the score for an *opéra bouffe* and appears to have a nice light touch. The chamber players, glancing over her shoulder at the computer screen, have more than once nodded their honest salt-and-pepper heads in approval.

She says she prefers to finish the chess game you started last week. You want to concentrate, give it your best shot, but the queen's knight, as you lower your hand to advance its pawn, flares its nostrils, snorting steam hot enough to scald your fingertips.

· · ·

Your wife descends half an hour later, looking marvellously thin and fingering the buttons on her blouse.

"Zöe," she says, sitting down on the bottom stair and calling to her daughter. Every day the child has a new name but none of them stick, no name ever seems *le nom juste*. Now you are at the end of the alphabet and must start again. Tomorrow the child will be Amelia or Agnes or Andrea or Aphrodite. And she will react accordingly, trying on the name like a new swimsuit, squirming a little—sometimes in discomfort, sometimes in delight. Tamara was one she liked, but it made her a touch too dreamy for your tastes. Other names make her sweat, like Debbie. "I feel fat," she had complained all day. And hadn't her inner thighs rubbed together a little, her tiny OshKosh corduroys singing like crickets when she walked?

Your wife unbuttons her blouse and the child settles herself into her mother's lap. The child has lost two of her milk teeth already and has grown a snaggletooth. So it was decided last month that braces were in order. The child's smile will be beautiful, but your wife's breasts are a mess of scrapes and hard-blooming bruises. You've discussed weaning the child, but not with any real conviction. You both know that nothing is as good for a child as mother's milk, and nothing is too good for the child. And besides, it keeps your wife's breasts large and the rest of her body thin, which pleases you both.

There was a time, not so long ago, when the space between the two of you was large and growing. At first the size of an audible sigh, then an

American-style football field, it became, over the course of a few years, a tundra of migrating caribou which, viewed from above through the window of a turbulent single-engine, resembled a swift, dirty river, but from up close thundered by so loud and hard your heart almost stopped. Now the space between you is the size and shape of one small child, a not unbridgeable distance. For there is always the child to consider. The things it would know. The things it might choose to imagine.

• • •

All night long, you and your wife discuss this pyjama thing in hushed tones, in hushed *Latvian* tones, as that is the only language, living or dead, that your child has yet to master. Unaware of what is at stake, the child has various feng shui manuals opened up on the living-room rug and is carefully rearranging the furniture in order to maximize the flow of positive *ch'i*. Every so often she implores you to help her drag the Eames chair or the Nienkämper couch to another location. She's so small and determined that it almost cracks you in two. The various objects, lined up on the mantel, look anxious.

The tired eyes of your wife are a holy purple—like the cloths draped over statues in churches at Easter—and tissue-paper thin. It's true that none of you have slept since the night the child was a giddy blue line in the home pregnancy kit—some four years, eleven months, twenty-three days, and six hours ago. A blue line wavering like a mirage that you and your wife regarded together as you sat on the cold edge of the tub and she on the toilet seat, both electrocuted with joy. It's true that you have pouches under your own eyes the size and heft of a kilo of coke and that the skin over your skull feels like Saran Wrap pulled tight and airless. Sometimes, sitting at your desk at work, you'll jerk violently as if breaking a fall, much like you used to do in your sleep, but you won't be sleeping. On the Burrard SkyTrain platform you've visualized jumping, a quick belly flop onto the tracks, just to relieve the pressure in your head. It's true that the child's eyes are so wide sometimes and so glassy that they look like they might just pop out and land in the soup.

The doorbell rings. Your wife yelps, even though the visit isn't unexpected. "I actually *yelped*," she says, forcing a laugh, because the child now looks worried. It's not all the moonlighting you both do that your wife minds, but this. Guys named Dougie and Chin coming to the back door with envelopes of money at 4:00 A.M. You get up, your knees popping stiffly, and go take the package out of the hall linen closet where it's shoved in behind the Christmas table runner, a porridge of guilt assembling in your gut. Your wife folds and unfolds the cuff of her blouse. The child is on tiptoes, reaching for the stars, her whole body vibrating like piano wire.

In the suburbs outside of Tokyo, just across the ocean, the next day's sun is already shining and schoolchildren rain from the sky, their smart little backpacks like parachutes that won't open. They spill off balconies like thread unspooling. They slip through your fingers. They land in your coffee, jangling your nerves.

The child is kneeling on the front windowsill when you get back, looking out into the darkness, silently working her way through the periodic table, her sweet milk breath misting the glass as she mouths the names of the chemicals. The chamber players play Prokofiev's string quartet no. 1 in B minor, music so discordant yet compelling it occurs to you that it could only have come to him in a sea-pitched dream. Your wife folds and unfolds the cuff of her blouse. The door of the hall closet is ajar.

The child turns her head and says, in a voice on tiptoes, vibrating like piano wire, "Radon, a radioactive, gaseous, chemical element formed, together with alpha rays, as a first product in the atomic disintegration of radium: symbol, Rn; at. wt., 222.00; at. no., 86; sp. gr., 973 g/1; melt pt., −71°C; boil. pt., −68° C."

The music folds and unfolds.

· · ·

Tomorrow, you and your wife just might send the child out with the nanny to find some pyjamas.

And tomorrow night, tomorrow night you might turn out the lights, and with your wife pressed to your stomach in one of your old T-shirts, sore breasts leaking, and with you naked because you're always so hot, and with your daughter in her new pyjamas (my jammies, she'll call them, already one step ahead of you), all three of you will close your eyes and try very hard to sleep. Just as a lark. To see what it's like.

A child, after all, must be resilient enough to take any curveball life throws at it. But a terrible fear stalks the neighbourhood of your heart, as you think you may be unleashing a force you can't control, some yet undiscovered monster.

Charles Gordon

Charles Gordon is a veteran newspaperman, recently retired from
the *Ottawa Citizen,* where he worked as a columnist, books editor,
and features writer. Gordon has explored the gentler side of Canada
in his books *At the Cottage* and *The Canada Trip.* He is also the
author of a tongue-in-cheek guide, *How to Be Not Too Bad,* which
has to be the ultimate title for a Canadian book. The following is
taken from Gordon's novel *The Grim Pig,* a splendidly satirical
send-up of the newspaper business—by someone who knows.

FROM *The Grim Pig*

The first thing they told me at the treatment centre was stop being cynical.
That would be a tough one, maybe even tougher than giving up the drink,
although giving up the drink seemed pretty hard at that particular time. Give
up the drink and give up being cynical.

Five years later and sober, I was sitting in a room full of newspaper guys
and trying not to be cynical, when the new editor walked in to address the
troops for the first time. Gladys Bushel from the lifestyles department actually stood up when the editor walked in, but the rest of us just sat there.
Newspaper guys—anything could happen and we would just sit there. If
Jesus arrived, we would just sit there. Some of us would criticize his clothes.
Nobody wears sandals any more. We pride ourselves that we have seen it all.

The new editor had on sandals, in fact, and grey socks, grey slacks, a
brown jacket, a green shirt that looked sort of Hawaiian, and a black tie, with
a big knot. Actually, it's just as well I'm not cynical any more, because I'm not

sure what a cynic would say about that, particularly the sandals. "Stylish," said my friend Davis, the business editor.

"Wait," I said.

"Sorry," she said, remembering negativity is not supposed to be good for me. She is very loyal to me, even though she knows I am bad for conversations at the big table in the cafeteria, which are snide and gossipy and cynical. At the big table, they try to be positive when I'm around, which makes the chatter sort of dry up. Sometimes Davis and I avoid that by going down the road to eat in the food court at the Grand Valley Mall. I like to think that makes people talk, but she says it doesn't.

The conference room of the *Grand Valley World-Beacon* is a big, squarish room, with windows. When announcements are made to the staff, which is hardly ever, they are made here. Otherwise, the room is made available free of charge for figure skating association annual meetings, rotisserie league drafts, and craft sales. Most of the big announcements, including Fred's appointment as the new editor, are made on the bulletin board in the newsroom. More and more frequently, they are made by email.

Now here was Fred, shuffling to the front of the room, head down, hands in his pockets, preoccupied. He stopped at the easel with the giant pad of paper on it and pulled a grease pencil out of his brown jacket. He scribbled something on the pad that we couldn't see because he was blocking it. Then he whirled to face us.

"Destiny," he said, his eyes flashing, or at least his glasses.

"DESTINNY," said the paper.

There was a muffled laugh from the back of the room where the entertainment department people were sitting. Bad spelling could amuse them. Davis raised an eyebrow at me. I pretended not to notice.

For most of us "destiny" was the first word we'd heard from Fred. In a week here, he had spoken to none of us. He kept his office dark, the blinds drawn. Occasionally strangers could be seen coming out: no one was ever seen going in.

Fred stopped to let the word sink in. It was a high-pitched word, the way it came out, surprisingly so, given Fred's size and reputation.

"Destiny," he said again. "That's what our readers want. They want to be connected with their destiny. They need a sense of how their lives intersect with the final things in our existence, the spirits that will accompany them on their next journeys, as well as the sprites and demons they meet in their everyday comings and goings."

"I told you he was a genius," whispered Lawrie Andrews, the sportswriter, from behind us.

"Mmmm," said Davis.

Fred paced a few paces. Then stopped in front of the easel. He turned and tore off the DESTINNY piece of paper, laying it carefully on a table.

Then he wrote another word and stepped aside.

"HELL-O," it said.

Davis nudged me. "Hyphenated?" she whispered.

"Maybe now," I whispered back.

"Hello," Fred said.

"Hello," said Alexei Ponomarev, the World-Beacon's Russian-born cartoonist, who was still finding his way around the language and didn't realize that Fred's hello was rhetorical, I think.

"Hello," said Dick Rivers, the Tri-Lakes Area's best-loved columnist.

Fred ignored them. "People sometimes tell me that I don't say hello enough," he went on. "I get caught up in my thoughts about making the human drama more compelling and forget to say hello. Please stop by my office, any of you, and say hello and I'll say hello to you. Being here for me, being able to give a new direction to this newspaper is really a …"

He paused, shook his head, paced, then stopped and looked out at us, as if waiting. I felt the first stirrings of a cynical thought. For a moment, the room was silent, then Gladys Bushel, who always broke the silences in these meetings, raised her hand. Fred smiled at her. It wasn't quite a smile, but his teeth showed.

"Fred," she said, "when you were talking a minute ago about sprites and demons, that was a metaphor, wasn't it?"

Fred waved his hand and showed his teeth again, then walked back to the easel. He picked up the grease pencil, paused, then put it down. Then he picked it up again and underlined HELL-O. Then he put it down again and turned toward us.

"Instead of sprites and demons, we give our readers the clichéd agenda story. How does that help them—all these thousands of words about school boards and hospital boards and Parliament and hockey teams? Meetings, meetings, meetings," he said and picked up the grease pencil.

"MEETINGS," he wrote, spelling it correctly.

"Good one," somebody muttered from the general direction of the entertainment department. Davis nudged me again. I stared straight ahead.

"Where is the adventure of everyday life?" Fred asked, staring out the window at the employee parking lot. We all stared out the window. Although we were barely into April, the snow was gone, and one of the assistant managing editors, the one that nobody knew what he did, was going home early again.

"People are wanting the adventure of daily life and we are giving them meetings. This won't do. We must challenge our readers, take them with us into exciting worlds of travel and romance and fine cloth."

Another hand went up. Fred pointed and showed his teeth.

"Fred," asked Pete Lester, one of the rewrite people, "do you think they'll be adding to the size of the parking lot? Because if you work an afternoon shift, like I used to do, by the time you get to the office …"

Fred waved his hand again and Pete stopped.

"What is your name?" he asked.

"Pete Lester."

Fred walked to the board and picked up the grease pencil. We held our breath. He folded over the last piece of paper and underlined the word "HELL-O" again.

"Hello, Pete," he said.

Pete nodded gravely.

"Pete," Fred continued, "we're going to embark on a great crusade together. What do you cover, Pete?"

"I do rewrite," Pete said. Fred turned the page and found the word "MEETINGS" then turned another page. "RERIGHT," he wrote.

"Actually," said Pete, "I do a lot of accidents—you know, bus plunges, some fender-benders."

Fred brightened. "bus plungers," he wrote.

"Now we're getting somewhere," he said. "Don't mind my spelling," he added, showing his teeth again. "There are so many more important things in life's daily adventure."

He paced again, staring at his sandals. "What do we think," he asked, looking up, "what do we think about when we think of bus plunges?"

There was a silence. The entertainment department was hushed. You could hear the squeak of the pen on Alexei Ponomarev's pad. Dick Rivers raised his hand but Fred ignored him.

"Buses," someone said at last.

"Good," said Fred. "What else?"

"Plungers?" said Lawrie Andrews.

Fred turned over a new sheet, looked back at us, and did that smilish thing with his teeth. "Words that sing," he said. "Words that sing. You all know the poet John Milton, I'm sure."

We all nodded and Fred wrote "john miltin" on the next sheet of paper.

"You remember how he wrote 'He who of those delights can judge, and spare / To interpose them oft, is not unwise.'"

We all nodded again, some of us a bit too quickly. Lawrie Andrews said: "How true." Davis made a muffled sound and I shook my head at her.

"That is what Milton was talking about—the bus plunges, great and small, that make up the adventure of our daily lives." He flipped back a sheet, underlined "bus plungers," then walked out of the room.

There was silence as we all waited for a moment to see if he was coming back, then a buzz of conversation. Davis and I stood up.

"Soooo," she said.

"Interesting start," I said. "Notice how he just started right in, without saying 'good morning' or anything?"

"Yes," Davis said. "What does that mean?"

"I don't know. I think it means he won't be like the others."

"And is that good?"

"It's different. Nobody said different was bad, necessarily."

• • •

The buzz carried down the hallway as we headed, past the publisher's office, past advertising and circulation, back to the newsroom.

"Did you hear something about cloth?"

"When was that?"

"It was after compelling human drama and just before avoiding the clichéd agenda story."

"I heard that, but I thought it was around the time of words that sing."

"No, words that sing was earlier, in the part about the adventure of everyday lives."

"I think he's a genius. Did you notice his eyes?"

"Never mind his eyes. What was that about cloth?"

"He didn't say cloth. He couldn't have said cloth. He must have said … what, sloth? Maybe it was avoiding sloth."

"Moth. Did he ever do stuff about moths when he was in Victoria?"

"No. There was a sixteen-part series about bats."

"This wasn't bats. It was cloth."

"Cloth? How could it be cloth? What's cloth got to do with newspaper stories?"

"His eyes were just flashing. Maybe we should do stories about cloth. Nobody's ever done stories about cloth. Maybe our readers need that and they haven't been telling us."

"It wasn't cloth. It couldn't have been. Broth?"

"Stories about soup. Didn't he win an award for that?"

"No, that was the thing on finger bowls."

"A sixteen-part series on finger bowls."

"Just twelve, I think."

"Goth."

"Froth."

"Moth."

"We already said that."

"Wrath."

"Huh?"

"Like the grapes of …"

"You don't pronounce it that way."

"I think he does. I hear we're going to have British spelling and put the Mr. and Mrs. back in the stories."

"Oh shit."

"We can't do that. Christ, we'll be running corrections every day about Ms. Jones is really Mrs. Jones and Mrs. Smith is really Miss Smith and the *World-Beacon* regrets the error."

"In Victoria, all the deskers had to learn the proper British titles for second reference."

"Great. The *World-Beacon* regrets that Sir Rodney is really Earl Rodney."

"Looks like we're getting British hyphenation too."

"Maybe it was cloth."

"Troth. That's it. The institution of marriage."

"I hear he's against marriage. There was a big campaign in the Lakehead. For weeks they ran articles about how marriage makes people more vulnerable to colds and gall bladder attacks."

"That's brilliant. See. We never do things like that. Just politics, politics, politics."

"Voth."

"What's Voth?"

"I don't know. I was just trying it. Woth. Yoth. Zoth. It has to be cloth."

"So we have a new editor who wants more news about cloth."

"Nothing wrong with fashion."

"I don't think that's what he meant."

• • •

I'm not too clear on all the history of the *World-Beacon*. To be truthful, there isn't the sense of reverence here about the institution that would make us all bone up on the *WB*'s glorious past. There was the *World* and there was the

Beacon, we all know that. They competed with each other late in the nineteenth century. One was Liberal and one was Conservative. They wrote completely one-sided stories about what crooks and brigands were on the other side, editorials denouncing the other paper's editorials as damnable lies, then they merged, it being good business to do so, and that was that. Thereafter, the *World-Beacon* supported the Liberals in some elections and the Tories in others. Whichever was best for Grand Valley, was the way the *World-Beacon* looked at it.

New technology has come to the *World-Beacon.* The composing room, where they used to bang the hot lead around, is almost gone now, because of the computers. There are a couple of guys left and every day they paste on the page numbers and the photographs. The rest of the page is done electronically by people like me. We move the stories around on our screens, make them fit, take out most of the typographical errors and some of the bad writing. Then we push a button and a little message comes up on the screen, saying, in effect, "Are you sure you want to do this?" I always stop there for a minute, impressed by the fact that whatever blame falls from this page will fall only upon me. Then I hit the RETURN key, signifying YES, and a few minutes later the entire page comes out of a machine in the composing room and either Orville or Smokey puts the page number on it.

For most of the century, the *World-Beacon* was just a newspaper like any other newspaper. It covered the war and the World Series and the devaluation of the dollar and the hemlines going up and down. It ran all the comic strips that weren't wrapped up by the big papers. We still have "Henry" and "Mandrake the Magician." Locally, the *WB* covered—very positively—decisions that were made by the railways. Those that resulted in hirings would boost Grand Valley's economy. Those that resulted in layoffs would increase the company's efficiency. We covered the tourist boat disaster of '57, when the *Miss Grand Valley* was hit by a waterskier at night and two people drowned. The waterskier herself miraculously survived to become a regular speaker at the service clubs, giving thanks for her life and the community's support and urging new laws against night waterskiing. Later, she would become our mayor and, soon after that, our ex-mayor.

We covered the Great Bypass Debate of '76, when it was decided that the Trans-Canada Highway would no longer go through the town. We covered—very positively—the arrival of the first suburban shopping mall in 1972. A few years later, we covered the various proposals brought forward by a number of consultants to revive the downtown area. We covered the fire that took down the Prince of Wales Hotel with miraculously no loss of life while it was up for sale in 1996.

We chronicled the rise of crime in the Tri-Lakes Area, including the first marijuana busts at the university, the dermatologist at the clinic who turned out to be a minor league outfielder from Kansas, and the sex scandal involving the suburban man who attempted to live off the avails of prostituting his wife, although, admittedly, she was not aware of it at the time. But he was kind of thinking out loud about it in the George Drew Room at the Prince of Wales one night and the police got wind of it and then the *World-Beacon* did, too.

By and large, the Tri-Lakes Area has been a peaceful place, although the *World-Beacon* would have you believe otherwise. The chief of police has accused us of exaggerating crime to sell newspapers, which he helps us to do when the police budget is up for consideration.

The name "Tri-Lakes Area" has not been around too long. The argument about the name is one of the first stories I remember from my time here. Somebody from the chamber of commerce went to the States on one of those highways meetings in the mid eighties and came back full of the need to give Grand Valley more of a name than it had. Every area is a tri-something down there and it looks enticing on the billboards, the chamber of commerce guy said. He was a buddy of our editor, two editors before Fred, and soon the *World-Beacon* was in on the act, editorially and in news coverage too, with interviews just about every day with local dignitaries—doctors, funeral directors, the member of Parliament and the coach of the junior hockey team, all of them saying that Grand Valley had gone long enough without receiving the recognition that was emblematic of being part of a Tri-Lakes Area.

There were a couple of people who protested, but they were the usual crowd, the Unitarian minister, a woman to boot, and some professors from the university, UGV. The Unitarian minister said Grand Valley shouldn't even be called Grand Valley, since there wasn't really a valley here, just a couple of lakes on one side and the hint of a hill on the other. Everybody figured it was a bit late to begin worrying about that. The professors pointed out that there were really twenty-three lakes in the Tri-Lakes Area, twenty-four if you counted one that was often called a pond, but was really quite large. They also noted that one of the lakes claimed as one of our tri was included in the Land of Eleven Lakes advertised by Small Portage, our rival city just fifty kilometres down the Trans-Canada.

I can remember the *WB*'s vigorous response because it ran the day after my first day at the paper and I was responsible for laying out the editorial page. The editor decided that the editorial, which he had written himself, deserved a special display and the task was given to me as someone who had worked at a big-city paper.

There would always be those timid and small-minded thinkers who quailed before visionary and courageous ideas, the editorial said. Such naysayers, not all of them Unitarians, the editorial scrupulously pointed out, sought refuge in technicalities, such as the alleged overlap in lakes between the Tri-Lakes Area and the adjacent Land of Eleven Lakes. The naysayers would quibble over the exact number of lakes in the area. But their real aim was to hold up the march of progress.

I decided to run this over four columns, instead of the usual two, illustrated by an aerial photograph of the three lakes. The library did have an aerial shot, but unfortunately there seemed to be nine lakes in it. I got some help in identifying the three relevant ones and it was not a difficult matter to crop out the others, which should have confused the issue if we had left them in.

Two problems remained. One was that there was a fourth lake right in the photo, in the midst of our three. Apparently the chamber of commerce could not figure out what to call an area with four lakes in it (Land of Four Lakes was clearly inadequate, given that there was a Land of Eleven next door) and Tri-Lakes just sounded better. Deciding which of the four not to include was simple enough; Wart Lake would not be a big tourist draw.

But there it was, right in the centre of the aerial photograph. To make matters worse, the aerial photograph, the only one in the *WB*'s library, had been taken during a time of heavy forest fires. I knew I would be getting off on the wrong foot if I ran, to illustrate the *WB*'s stirring advocacy of Tri-Lakes, a photograph of four lakes largely obscured by smoke. So I went to Charlie McPartland, the news editor. Charlie was an old-timer who had worked in Saint John, Montreal, Ottawa, Timmins, Winnipeg, Prince Albert, Winnipeg, Calgary, Vancouver, Victoria, and Brockville, never for very long at any one place. He had just come back from a late lunch at the Prince of Wales and was tidying up his desk in preparation for an early dinner at the Prince of Wales.

"There's lots of fuckin' lakes in the world," he said, then went back to his work.

That was true and it showed that he recognized in me a kindred spirit, a veteran newsman no longer unduly restrained by youthful idealism and thus unlikely to seek refuge in technicalities. I returned to the library and began digging through envelopes of photographs, each envelope labelled with the name of a country that might have lakes. Eventually I found what I was looking for in Switzerland—an aerial photograph of three shining lakes, surrounded by mountains. There were some goats in the middle, which wouldn't hurt, and a guy in short pants playing one of those long horns. The photo editor assured me that he could be manipulated in the photo department's computer and made to resemble grass.

The picture worked beautifully, enhancing the power of the editorial, and Grand Valley has been part of the Tri-Lakes Area ever since. My part in it was never overstated, which was fine with me, but it did help me develop a reputation in the *WB* newsroom as a real pro.

In my five years here, I've seen many major journalistic trends (all journalistic trends are called major, because they are reported by journalists). The trends started when television came and newspapers began to worry, for the first time, that there might not always be newspapers. So they tried various strategies, and called them philosophies.

One philosophy was to make newspapers more like television. Another was to make newspapers less like television. Given the way newspapers worked, it was never possible to tell whether a strategy was effective. At the same time as the intellectuals in the news department were making the newspaper less or more like television, the intellectuals in the promotion department were running a bingo in the paper for $5,000 and the intellectuals in the circulation department were raising the price of subscriptions. Even if we could tell what was happening, which was difficult, we could never tell why it was happening. So it made just as much sense to keep changing the paper.

When I arrived we were just on the tail end of entertaining people. All the stories were about celebrities and none of the stories was about political or social issues. There was lots of advice on what wines to drink and diagrams of the latest dance craze. Our reporters became celebrities and were photographed doing fun things, like whitewater rafting and playing trivia contests on machines in country music bars.

I was just getting comfortable with that, or at least resigned to it. In my fragile, newly sober state, I wasn't going to be the one to raise the possibility that we might be running a few more American starlet photos than was absolutely necessary for a Canadian town in which the railway was shutting down, lakefront property (even beside Wart Lake) was being snapped up by foreigners, and the provincial government was talking about shutting down our hospital and expanding the one in the Land of Eleven Lakes.

But I was getting used to it, when the chain that then owned the *WB* sent in a new publisher. The new publisher went to a cocktail party at the university and heard the dean of arts refer to the *World-Beacon* as the *Woeful Bacon*. The new publisher decided to make the *WB* less like television. That meant more serious. The trouble was that nobody, after all those years of covering the movie of the week, knew how to be serious. The senior editors went off for a weekend retreat to think about it, retreats just having come into fashion. After a weekend at the Prince of Wales, much of it spent in the George Drew Room, the senior editors decided to make the pictures smaller. The publisher hailed the retreat as an advance.

• • •

Cloth. That was the key. That's what he wanted. I didn't ask why. Tomorrow it might be snakes. But today it was cloth. I could give it to him.

• • •

The way a newspaper works these days, a lot of pages have to be filled the day before. The good stuff—murders, resignations, floods, bus plunges, and hockey games—gets in at the last minute, although the last minute gets earlier every year. Because of technological advances, the last minute is now 11:45 at night in Grand Valley, much earlier than before. There are still twenty or thirty pages that have to be filled the morning and afternoon before. Guys like me, deskers, we are called, or sometimes rim pigs, scour the wires for stuff to put on those pages. Then we stick them on an electronic representation of a page, find some pictures to illustrate them, write the headlines, and press the button. Bingo, a page.

The wires are from all over, the best papers and wire services in the world. Soft features—a new dance craze in Brazil—serious analysis—the effects on divorce rates of the new dance craze in Brazil—breaking news, columns, cricket scores, trends in volcano eruptions, recipes. And you would be surprised how much news there is about cloth, if you know where to find it.

And how to make it into news. The next Monday, working the inside World section pages, I found an Associated Press story about Edgar, a hurricane that might, but probably wouldn't, hit the coast of South Carolina. Half-hearted evacuation preparations were underway, a couple of merchants were nailing boards over their store windows, although they might have been doing it because they feared teenagers, not winds. A preacher in a suburban Unitarian church prayed publicly to the Supreme Being, If Any, for moderate winds. I looked up the encyclopedia online and confirmed that they grow cotton in South Carolina, rewrote the first two paragraphs, stuck it at the top of page C12 with a "Special to the *World-Beacon*" credit, and put a three-column headline on it: EDGAR THREATENS CLOTH PRODUCTION.

I was lucky, although South Carolina wasn't. Edgar grew in intensity, people packed their cars, and all the ministers started praying very hard. Every day, I produced headlines, bigger headlines, about how lives and cloth were at risk in the face of the deadly winds. By Thursday, the peril facing cloth was in the A section and so was I, recognized by the news editor as an expert on the subject.

It's true that the people of South Carolina were less aware of that specific danger, the threat to cloth, than the people of Grand Valley. The people of South Carolina were, according to the wire service accounts I edited, more concerned about trees falling on their cars, more worried about their houses flooding and their pets being carried away than they were about cloth.

But many other people were concerned, although they may not have known it in precisely that way. Using various newspaper databases and the internet, I was able to track down fashion experts and industrialists who had spoken favourably about the fabrics manufactured out of the crops that could conceivably be flattened by the hurricane. Without actually saying, in so many words, that they were speaking about the hurricane, I managed to insert some of those comments into the wire service accounts.

Thus, a story headlined WORLD HOLDS BREATH WHILE CLOTH FUTURE HANGS IN BALANCE was illustrated by photographs of a leading fashion designer and two supermodels, all of whom were quoted in the story, perhaps thinking at the time that they were referring to something else.

"We'd be doomed without cotton," one supermodel said, high up in a story on A5, beside a photograph of her not wearing much of it.

When Edgar hit the A section, it was noted in the newsroom that Fred was showing a specific interest in the subject. He would come out of his office late in the afternoon and stand behind me, saying nothing, but looking intently at the words on my computer screen. That would have been the time for the national editor to pick up the hint, but he was all wound up in some parliamentary thing. Davis noticed, though, dispatching Tony Frusculla, her eager rookie reporter, to gather concerned quotes from concerned members of the business community and the industry minister.

Tony was a gangly kid just out of community college, but he had nerve and knew how the game worked. He got himself a trip to Ottawa. "Is Canada prepared to assist with the looming cloth crisis?" the reporter shouted out at the minister, as she was climbing a staircase outside the House of Commons chamber.

The minister did what ministers do when they haven't the foggiest idea what the question means.

"We're giving the matter careful consideration," she said.

OTTAWA CONSIDERING CLOTH CRISIS ACTION, said Saturday's story, bumped from the business front onto page one by Fred's intervention. The re-election of the Communists in Russia was moved inside.

The next Monday, there was a note in my mailbox from Fred's secretary. Fred would like to see me at 10:30.

Ray Guy

Ray Guy is no starry-eyed romantic when it comes to Newfoundland. He once described his home province as the perfect setting for a spy drama, steeped as it was in "paranoia, xenophobia, and fog." For all that, Guy's love for Newfoundland is always in evidence, as is his distaste for pretensions and his unerring knack for cutting through the bullshit to get to the heart of the matter. Just for being able to claim Ray Guy as our own, for that alone, hooping Newfoundland into Confederation was a triumph for Canada.

FROM *Ray Guy's Best*

Ah, the Never Fading Charm of Bung Hole Tickle

I n the whole catalogue of charm-ridden Atlantic villages so celebrated in song, story, and regional magazine article, none stands closer to my own heart than Bung Hole Tickle on the wave-laved shores of G.D. Bay.

It was some years ago on one of those perfect late-June days that I stumbled upon this sequestered hamlet and the magic realism of that moment would have taxed the brush of a Pratt (Chris, not Mary) or of a Colville. Many times since I have found myself drawn back to Bung Hole Tickle and never has its soul-soothing tranquility failed to work its wonder on me. (Jet trails and asphalt highways have destroyed much of Newfoundland's precious, bucolic heritage yet B.H. Tickle clings to its isolation and is often confused by the postal service with such well-known centres of population here as Leading Tickles and Piper's Hole.)

It was the merciless big-city grind that first drove me blindly into that

G.D. Bay haven. For all its veneer of suave, swinging sophistication, St. John's can also be granite-hard on those who seek of life the kind, the gentle, the meaningful, the puerile. Early on that late-June day I'd had an argument with my hard-nosed city editor. He'd accused me of writing an article, in exchange for $20 and a bottle of Johnnie Walker, favourable to a shopping mall developer who'd proposed erecting over the Mary Queen of Peace Cemetery. I'd, in turn, explained to him that he was a dirty Mick and where else had he got that new chesterfield suite if not in return for all those editorials promoting the second Papist lieutenant-governor in succession ... an unspeakable breach of custom here.

And so it was that I still spat teeth and blood, not much mollified by the few quick knees I'd been able to get in, as my motor car crested a hill and I suddenly came face to face with that gem of rustic serenity known as Bung Hole Tickle.

Wheeling gulls scribed peace on the blue vault and white terns fluttered and dipped in the ultramarine cup below. I stopped my car and strolled over to a low roadside knoll the better to take it all in. Also, as it had been a three-hour drive, to let it all out. Just then, from a dozen feet below, came a voice. It belonged to a sun-blessed, tow-headed child of 10 or 12 years of age who sat on a rock playing intently with some toy or other in its lap.

"Arrr, go fugg 'ee self!" chirped the child in so pure an 18th-century Devonshire accent as it has been my privilege to hear in Newfoundland.

"And good day to you, too, my little man," I replied. "Tell me, do I see a village fête in progress down there in what is presumably your natal seat?"

The child repeated its earlier greeting and added several other archaic endearments. I wished the little tyke likewise and set off down the narrow road toward a green near the beach where the villagers had assembled in midsummer revelry.

Snatching up my Nikon I skipped from my motor and approached the tableau. An elderly lady with indifferent dental work was being in some way honoured. She reclined against a stout post while her neighbours laid tributes of kindling and dry brush at her feet.

Just then a rock a little larger than a gannet's egg glanced off my left temple and as I heard my windshield go a moment later I had the grace to blush. What business had I, a big-city slicker, to intrude on these simple folk unannounced and uninvited. Shamed, I drove quickly back up the hill even as smoke commenced to rise from their festal fire.

Yet, in the weeks and months ahead, my thoughts turned again and again to Bung Hole Tickle especially whenever the big-city grind threatened to get me down or the malevolence of the city editor weighed heavily upon me.

It was then I had the fortune to meet Professor Tory Archibald of the University, possibly the greatest authority on charm-ridden Atlantic villages we have.

From conversations with Dr. Archibald and with the great and good friends I made in Bung Hole Tickle as the strange bonds between it and me grew ever stronger, a full picture of that spikier Brigadoon emerged.

"Bung Hole, of course, from the orifice of a cask refers to the narrow entrance to that cove," explained Dr. Archibald, "whilst 'tickle,' a shallow, tide-rippled passage between island and mainland, would also apply here."

So far as is known, the first inhabitants, five brothers and a sister of the Sunks family of Poole, England, established the community in the mid-1700s. The records are sketchy. In some versions the Sunkses emigrated hastily after charges of sheep-stealing had been levelled; in others, deportation followed on rumours of interference with said livestock.

At any rate, the six Sunkses appeared to have lived, multiplied, and perished peacefully and uneventfully for the next 100 years or so in the little community they had carved from the wilderness. The first census of 1856 reports that 18 Sunks families and, inexplicably, three families named Boggs were domiciled in Bung Hole Tickle together with their goods, chattels, "manifold sheep of inferior quality and an lyttle black fellow captured off an American frigate."

"The genetic pool there has never been much larger than your average pudding basin," Dr. Archibald said, "but therein lies the charm of the place, don't you think?"

Not much else is recorded in the annals of Bung Hole Tickle until 1912 when a religious upheaval of sorts occurred. The little church is located on a bluff above the village so as to have a clear view of The Godsend Sunkers, a treacherous reef which has sent many a salvageable vessel to her doom.

In 1912, Bung Hole Tickle was under the pastoral charge of one Rev. Job Bales. When news of the *Titanic* disaster reached the village there were mutterings against Rev. Bales, and his theology was questioned. He later arrived in St. John's with both Achilles tendons cut and, after managing for some years a tattoo parlour on the seedier (if possible) end of Duckworth Street passed completely from the fabric of St. John's society.

"Arrr, bye, me grandpap told me'ee war droonk as per usual and fell agin' a brandy bottle," a village friend has told me. "Eee war no man of God. We had a puffitly good iceberg lyin' that same night not one mile off the Tickle yonder ... so where war she if Bales had good connection with He?"

Days come, days go, winters change to springs and springs to what passes for summers yet Bung Hole Tickle changes not. The womenfolk sit and gossip by their cottage doors in all seasons; the menfolk mull over the situation in Afghanistan or San Salvador and tend their sheep; the young ones are scarce.

For in the early years of the Smallwood era some overly-keen social worker convinced the menfolk that a vasectomy was part of the ritual connection with joining the Orange Lodge.

"A precious rustic backwater, no doubt about it," concludes the good Professor Archibald. "Still, we mustn't let Newfie chauvinism blind us here. Nova Scotia and New Brunswick boast as good or better having the advantage of the Scottish and the French influences, don't you see."

Nonetheless, it's Bung Hole Tickle for me, bye!

Our Climate Condemned Us to Canada

It was our climate that gave Newfoundland Confederation with Canada. Plus polka dot rabbits.

We're unlike most other places. Some days in June and in January are interchangeable. Winter lasts nine months followed by a milder spell which passes for the other three seasons. At least that's the way it is here in the southeast corner of the island. Nine months might seem like a harsh sentence. But what we mean by "winter" here is not a cut and dried thing. There's no head nor tail to it.

In other free Christian democracies you can set your calendar by the seasons. White Christmases are guaranteed. Promptly on the first day of spring the trees explode into leaf with a soft vegetable thunk. On midsummer's day, a heatwave arrives on time and at six minutes past four, September 21, every leaf unhitches itself simultaneously. Even in Newfoundland that's the sort of climate still being taught in the schools.

You get the same thing on calendars. Turn over to May and there's a picture of a maiden in national costume up to her armpits in tulips and apple blossoms in Ottawa or Vermont or Tweeney-Upon-Falstaff, Hants., Berks., Bucks., SW. 1, Eng. Press on to June and the summer heat is coming off the page in waves and the gin and quinine is being dispensed in the beeloud glades.

Here, however, the trees are just as bare on Coronation Day as they are at the Feast of the Circumcision while, on the other hand, there are shirt-sleeve days in February and icebergs in July. Incest and poor diet have long been put forward to explain Newfoundland politics and Newfoundland politicians but, to my own mind at least, not enough weight has been given to climate. It's hard to be a warm, meaningful, sincere, relevant human being like they have in the States when, for nine months of the year, you may step out the door on green grass in the morning and come back to supper with the snow halfway up to the windowledges.

There are not many places on God's great globe, either, where you'll find polka dot rabbits. Normal, well-adjusted bunnies are brown in summer and white in winter. Ours bounce around in a quandary. They settle for nine months of mottled indecisiveness. The Newfoundland human being is in much the same cleft stick as the Newfoundland rabbit. For nine months of the year you wouldn't, if in your right senses, bet a five cent piece on what you're going to see when you look out the window the next morning.

Our weather forecasters mumble a lot. On TV, they go at their maps like windmills in a force 10 gale, interspersing all sorts of swoops and arrows with pregnant lice representing the sun and when they're finished I'll challenge anyone to repeat what they've just said. It saves them from being kicked to death in public. High-speed gibberish is their only method of self-defence in a place where a balmy and tranquil sunset can give way to a night like that on which Lucy Grey was lost.

Nature itself is befuddled by Newfoundland weather. Former ministers and their brothers-in-law know enough and can afford to hump off to Florida and stay there for the duration. But robin red breasts, for instance, can't decide when to migrate. Some of them never do. There's been one in my front yard the year round. It takes one step south and two north and manages to look bilious and confused at the same time—rather like Joe Clark trying to grasp the rudiments of Sri Lanka's fiscal policies. It looks ruffled and vexatious, as if it had been sucked through a vacuum cleaner. So do the people passing on the sidewalk. Newfoundland winter is a nine-month Screech hangover.

Our politics suffer thereby. Had Joey Smallwood's fellow delegates to Canada not been children of the Newfoundland climate when they went to Ottawa in the spring of 1948, we might not be labouring as we are today under the handicap of televised Canadian football, P. Trudeau, and tinned B.C. salmon. Gordon Bradley, along with Smallwood and others, had been sent to Ottawa to make the final arrangements for Confederation. Gordon balked. Like our robin red breasts after Labour Day he was in two minds about the enterprise. But as chance would have it, the Newfoundland plenipotentiaries arrived in Ottawa in the midst of an early heat wave. Mr. Bradley was wearing that fleece-lined, cast-iron undergarment so necessary to survival in Newfoundland for much of the year. It was the custom among the older folk for the women to sew their men into these longjohns about the latter part of September and to cut them free again in early July.

In the heathenish malarial jungle of Ottawa in May, poor Gordon fell a victim to the heat and set his hand to those fatal terms of union on the promise that he be instantly whisked back to the blessed coolth of his natal isle. Our first Canadian senator, needless to say.

When it comes time to cut Canada adrift, let the deal be done in St. John's in May ... with the Ottawa chappies seated outside in their bathing drawers. It'd be all over in five minutes and they'd probably chuck in half Ontario as a going-away present.

Playing the Newf Goof for Mainland Media

"They tell me you're the funny guy around here," said the chap from CBC *National*, "so all I want from you is a short, snappy comment on each of the three political leaders." It isn't easy being a stock flutter in the regional pulse. Mainland newspaper and television "teams" divebomb you in relays demanding you make plain to them the mysterious east in 250 words or less, fuelled by a maximum of only two beers. These chaps are invariably harried. They have exactly a day and a half. Then it's off again to stuff northern Saskatchewan into a nutshell. A fogged-in airport is the constant hag that rides them.

Luckily they know just what it is they want: (1) an up-and-coming young leftish person destined to loom large in Newfoundland's future; (2) an up-and-coming young rightish person, likewise destined; (3) horny-handed fisherfolk in a picturesque village no more than 20 miles from St. John's airport; (4) a woman sociologist from the university, preferably one who rears goats and operates an airtight cast-iron wood-burning apparatus; (5) a populist buffoon who, with the fisherfolk, counterbalances the profundities of the two up-and-comings and the goat lady.

It seems straightforward. All our mainland press have to do is dash through the five categories and collect the standard offering from each. To make things even simpler, the same person holds office under each heading for a term of five years. Richard Cashin, the fisherman's union chap, occupies category Number One while Miller Ayre, a businessman and St. John's city councillor, fills Number Two. Number Three is staffed by three or four fishermen in Petty Harbour, a village conveniently near St. John's but which looks like Peggy's Cove, N.S. did when Peggy was still a maiden. In the fourth category, there are actually two women sociologists. They divide the burden, depending on whose goat herd is due to freshen. I have the honour to hold down the fifth posting myself with my term still a year and a half to run.

An easy 36 hours' work—or so you might think to pop off a plane, make the rounds, and head back to Toronto with the socio-economic essence of Newfoundland safely in the can. But in Newfoundland, alas, things are never that simple. A flat tire gets much flatter here than it does in central Canada and it's likely to stay flat for five hours longer. There are other hindrances. A Toronto reporter once told me he could encapsulate the whole of Manitoba and Northern Ontario in less time than it took him to do Newfoundland.

The CBC chap confided that those horny-handed, weather-beaten fisherfolk in Petty Harbour have become so professional they're almost useless. That's understandable. By now, they must have more camera time under their belts than most ACTRA members. The very gulls have learned to swoop past on cue. "I was tempted to tell them," sighed the CBC chap, "to drop their phoney Newfie act and show us something of their souls."

"Lucky you didn't," I said. "They might have misunderstood you and, instead of their souls, you could have had a haddock wrapped around your ears."

The script that category Number Three has by now honed to perfection is to the effect that "Far as we're concerned, bye, every one of them jeezly politicians in there to St. John's and up there in Ottawa should be in hell's fiery flames with their backs broke." But that's out of date now. What's wanted is less rustic pique and more salt-of-the-earth reassurances that This Great Nation of Ours stands firm even in the easternmost nooks; a script well-sprinkled with chunks of soul; a solid rehearsal in what the mainland media regard as a Newfie accent (thick enough to slice but just a notch this side of requiring subtitles); and an indoor set with stuffed kittiwakes on strings.

In fact, we all need to pull up our socks and get our acts together. We need a shared appointments secretary, a scale of fees, and a kiosk in St. John's airport. Those two young up-and-comings are often up and gone on holiday in the Antilles just when mainland media teams need them most desperately.

The lady sociologists spend too much time mucking around with their goats, the horny-handed weatherbeatens are still struggling with outdated scripts and the populist buffoon ... Ready for retirement. I knew it was high time to relinquish office when I saw the disappointment on the face of the CBC *National* fellow. All he wanted was a snappy comment on each of the three political leaders.

I couldn't come through. It was a poor excuse that I had a broken leg still a-mending, a six-month-old upstairs with a rising fever, a Block man at the kitchen table shaking his head over my income-tax returns, and the upshot of a recent Breathalyzer test still pending. The CBC was welcome to my blood but you couldn't see my merry old soul for bandages.

FROM *You May Know Them as Sea Urchins, Ma'am But You Said We Won*

A conversation with an older person who passed away in August 1943, out Home:

Do England still stand?

Oh, yes, sir. And our Sovereign sits yet at her castle at Windsor ... as they say.

Oh, they never had a boy, then, after.

No, sir. They never had a boy.

Well, we won, then.

Oh, yes, sir. We won. It was a bit ticklish in spots but we made it.

Um. And how was the fish last year? Much got?

Well, yes and no, sir. There was and there wasn't.

There was a good sign on the first of it but it dwindled off. But lobsters were plenty and a good price.

Is there many canning them now besides Manuel and Abby and Henry Alfred?

No, sir. They passed on, you know. They don't can them any more. The ice came last year.

Ice? Come in? Much?

More than was ever seen since back in your time, sir, they said.

I only seen it twice. No, three times. No, it was only twice I seen it. I think it was only twice. No difference. Did Billy last long?

Oh, yes, sir. He rallied after that and he was great and smart and only passed away, I think it was, the year before … no, in the summer … two years before Confederation. They put his pipe and a bottle of rum in the box along with him.

Eh, my son?

His pipe, sir, and a bottle. They put it in with him. It was his wish.

Confederation?

Yes, Confederation. Joined on to Canada. It was in 1949. April Fool's Day. You know, upalong. Canada. We were joined on.

You said we won.

But that was the war, sir. This was after. I can't mind too much about it. I was a boy then.

The Commission done it.

I don't think so, sir, altogether. I'm going by what I'm told. I believe we were more or less on our own again, then.

Then how many was there killed?

So far as I know, sir, there was no one killed. There was only a lot of talk all the time, and swearing. When it came about they put the flag down to half-mast but there was no one killed.

No one?

No, sir. No one … so far as I know.

No one.

The ground is sold, sir, but your house is still there and son John's. They rose the roof on it a long time ago, and they put the water in.

All the flakes are gone now, sir, and they got what they call a fish plant across from the Dock Garden below Uncle Walter's. They don't make fish at all, now, sir.

Do you mind Uncle Walter's saying, sir? "Things will rise and things will fall." I don't sir, but I hear them talk about it.

They say that you and Uncle Abby and Uncle Walter would have something to say if you could only see the television. Or, that's what they used to say first when the television came in.

That's what they said when the men was put on the moon, too. They said you and Uncle Abby and grandfather and them would have something to say about it if you were here now.

It must be hard to believe, sir, all these things. There was a vessel came in through the Bay to the Foxhead last year, sir, longer than The Great Eastern.

They have a thing down there for oil. All the people came down, you know, a few years back, to the Cove. There's nothing up on the Islands now. Wareham's left Harbour Buffett and I was up and saw the church falling down at Merasheen myself.

It must sound wonderful odd to you, sir, but I'm not telling any lies. What, sir?

There wasn't no one killed?

Paul Hiebert

Sarah Binks by Paul Hiebert is a small comedic gem. A fictional biography of an equally fictitious poet (or rather, "poetess"), it charts Sarah's rise to fame, her early influences, her (inevitably) tragic demise. Never mind that Miss Binks, "the Sweet Songstress of Saskatchewan," is an exquisitely bad poet: Hiebert never writes poems that are meant to be bad; he writes poems that are, quite clearly, *trying* to be good. Sarah tortures poetic meter, she invents words like "snoof" in order to force a rhyme with "hoof," she wrings meaning out of the most meaningless events, and she takes herself—as poets are wont to do—far too seriously. *Sarah Binks* is a terrific satire. It challenges romanticized images of stalwart settlers, sun-kissed farmers, noble Indians, hardy Swedes, and hardworking pioneers. But, above all, it pokes merciless fun at the academic pretensions of the literary world—right down to the footnotes and the petty jealousies. So a word of warning: If you are, by chance, a member of said academia, if you "deconstruct" poetry for a living or teach classes in literary criticism, you may not find this funny.

It will certainly feel uncomfortably familiar.

And for good reason.

FROM *Sarah Binks*

Hers was the pastoral simplicity of the plains, hers the gentle dust storm, the
dying calf, the long, somnolent afternoon of the drought summer. Give her a
field mouse, a grasshopper, or a jam pail of potato bugs and her poetry gushed
forth unbidden, uncalled-for, and unrestrained.—Paul Hiebert

From the Introduction

It is claimed by some writers that Sarah Binks sprang spontaneously from
Saskatchewan's alkaline soil, that she was an isolated genius such as the
ages have produced from time to time with no significance beyond her
unparalleled talent.

With this view the Author takes exception. Sarah Binks was the product
of her soil and her roots go deep. But more than that, she was an expression
of her environment and her age. Without Saskatchewan at its greatest, at its
golden age, Sarah would have been just another poetess. Sarah was the
daughter and the grand-daughter of a dirt farmer; she loved the soil and
much of Jacob Binks' passion for another quarter section flowed in her veins.
Her love for the paternal acres was a real love, she believed in the rotation of
crops, and in the fall, after the plowing was done, she spread the fertilizer
with a lavish hand.

Sarah Binks has raised her home province of Saskatchewan to its highest
prairie level. Unschooled, but unspoiled, this simple country girl has
captured in her net of poesy the flatness of that great province. Like a sylph
she wanders through its bluffs and coulees, across its haylands, its alkali flats,
its gumbo stretches, its gopher meadows;

Hark! Like a mellow fiddle moaning,
Through the reed-grass sighing,
Through a gnarled branch groaning,
Comes the Poet—
Sylph-like,
Gaunt-like,

Poeming—
And his eyes are stars,
And his mouth is foaming.

Thus, Sarah herself, in the divine frenzy. No wonder she is called the Sweet Songstress of Saskatchewan. Indeed she could be called much more. No other poet has so expressed the Saskatchewan soul. No other poet has caught in deathless lines so much of its elusive spirit, the baldness of its prairies, the alkalinity of its soil, the richness of its insect life.

Requiem for a Poetess

A plain shaft of composition stone with the simple inscription:

HERE LIES

SARAH BINKS

marks the last resting place of the Sweet Songstress of Saskatchewan. Below the inscription at the base of the shaft in smaller letters is carved the motto; ALONE, and above it in larger type:

THIS MONUMENT WAS ERECTED BY THE

CITIZENS OF THE MUNICIPALITY

OF NORTH WILLOWS

AND WAS UNVEILED ON JULY I, 1931

BY

THE HON. AUGUSTUS F. WINDHEAVER

IN THE PRESENCE OF

THE REEVE AND COUNCIL

Here follows the names of the reeve and councillors together with the names of a number of outstanding statesmen of the day. Truly a fitting tribute to so great a woman. And it is no less a tribute to the Province of Saskatchewan that on the occasion of the unveiling of this monument the register of names at the Commercial House at Willows should be at the same time the roster of the greatest of Saskatchewan's sons. The Hon. A.E. Windheaver writes of that occasion in a letter[1] to his committee;

> It was hot as hell! There was no making it by road and we could have arranged for a hot box to hold the 4.46 for half an hour, but it was no use. We had to stick it until everybody was through. I think I was wise to leave out the tariff in my speech. This Sarah seems to be something of a tin god around here.

Something of a god! The tribute of a great statesman to a great artist and a great woman.

Halfway between Oak Bluff and Quagmire in Saskatchewan lies the little town of North Willows. Its public buildings are unpretentious but pure in architectural style. A post office, two general stores, Charley Wong's restaurant and billiard parlour, two United churches, the Commercial House (Lib.), the Clarendon Hotel (Cons.), a drug store, a consolidated school, and eighteen filling stations, make up the east side of Railroad Avenue, its chief commercial street. On the west side Railway Avenue is taken up by the depot, the lumber yard, and four elevators. At right angles to Railway Avenue runs Post Office Street, so called because the post office was on this street before the last provincial election. It is, however, generally known simply as the Correction Line.

Business in Willows is not what it used to be. The Board of Trade meets every Thursday night above Charley Wong's, and the younger set of the town is beginning to give up auction bridge in favour of contract, but in spite of these signs of progress there has been little real growth for several years. The town is now in what is known as the dry belt. Once it boasted seven elevators; one was torn down and two were destroyed by fire and have not been rebuilt. But Willows has little need for commercial greatness. It lives in its glorious past, and to its shrine every year come hundreds who pause for a brief moment at the Clarendon Hotel or the Commercial House, or buy gasoline at the "Sarah Filling Station."

---

1. Private letter, now in possession of the Author.

If we follow Post Office Street, or the Correction Line, due east for half a mile to where it corrects we come to Willow View Cemetery where Sarah Binks' monument stands. From a distance it appears to rise in lonely grandeur. If we follow Post Office Street due west for a mile and a quarter from the town, we come to the North East Quarter of Section 37, Township 21, Range 9, West, the former home of Sarah Binks herself. Little remains of the old homestead. The house itself has been torn down by souvenir hunters, one of the barns leans drunkenly and the other is about to fall. Gophers play on the site of the little corral where Sarah kept the calf, wild roses grow where once were beans and potatoes. In the coulee, now dry, that ran behind the house, a meadowlark has built its nest. It may have been that Sarah, with the prophetic eye of the poetess, visualized this scene when, in her later years, she wrote those famous lines, now inscribed in bronze over the gateway of St. Midget's, entitled, *Ode to A Deserted Farm.*

> How changed and bleak the meadows lie
> And overgrown with hay,
> The fields of oats and barley
> Where the binder twined its way!
>
> With doors ajar the cottage stands
> Deserted on the hill—
> No welcome bark, no thudding hoof,
> And the voice of the pig is still.

The west was still the West in the days when Jacob and Agathea Binks first homesteaded the N.E. ¼ Sec. 37, Township 21, R. 9, W. To the east lay Oak Bluff, the end of the steel. To the west stretched the boundless prairies of the North West Territories, in which, to quote Sarah's own words, "The hand of man hath never trod." Here was the home of the coyote and the gopher, the antelope still flaunted his lack of tail to the western wind, and the pensive mosquito wandered unafraid.

...

Oh calf, that gambolled by my door,
Who made me rich who now am poor,
That licked my hand with milk bespread,
Oh calf, calf! Art dead, art dead?

Oh calf, I sit and languish, calf,
With sombre face, I cannot laugh,
Can I forget thy playful bunts?
Oh calf, calf, that loved me once!

With mildewed optics, deathlike, still,
My nights are damp, my days are chill,
I weep again with doleful sniff,
Oh calf, calf, so dead, so stiff.

Early Influences: Ole the Hired Hand

One may trace many influences which affected Sarah's work, influences great
and small which touched her here and there; Ole, Rover, William Greenglow,
Henry Welkin, Grandfather Thurnow, strong, masculine influences which
affected her outlook, touching her mind, and leaving their light and sometimes their shadow upon her poetry. But to Ole, cheerful hard-working Ole,
big of heart and feet, must go the honour of having been the first to put the
young Sarah upon the path of poesy. It is significant, even symbolical, that
just as years ago on the morning after Dominion Day, Ole himself was traced
for miles across the alkali flats that lie north of Willows, so to-day one traces
his splendid footprints across the dazzling pages of Saskatchewan literature.

Ole's other name is not known, or if it ever was known it has been
forgotten. He answered simply to the name of Ole. When, on the rare occasions a more formal address became necessary as when the extra mail order
catalogue arrived, it became, Ole, c/o J. Binks. Professor Ambush has
suggested that the name Ole may be a diminutive of Olafur or perhaps of

Oleander, but no diminutive can possibly apply. He was above all a big man such as the West is fond of producing. His feet found their way with difficulty through the trousers of his store suit, his shoulders were of gnarled oak, and his two hands swung at his sides like slabs of teak. He was noted for his great strength. He could haul the stoneboat with its two full water barrels from the coulee to the house, and when, as sometimes happened, a horse would straddle the barbed wire fence, he would assist it from its predicament by lifting one end or another as the circumstances required. He had an equine playfulness and would toss Mathilda, even when eighteen and already large for her age, from the ground to the hayloft with great ease and to her infinite delight.

But if Ole's strength was great, his good nature and cheerfulness were even greater. No one is known ever to have offended Ole. His mind had that simplicity and directness and that acceptance of the world which one associates with his race and occupation. He and Rover were inseparable; Ole shared his lunches in the field with Rover, and the latter shared his fleas at night with Ole. Both had a deep and abiding affection for Sarah.

Neither Rover nor Ole actually wrote any poetry, at least none has come down to us unless we accept the terse verses, often fragmentary and sometimes illustrated, which Ole was fond of writing upon the granaries and other small buildings with a piece of coal. (Two of these boards, one of doubtful authenticity, are known to exist in private collections of Binksiana.) But where both Ole's and Rover's chief influence upon Sarah's poetic talent lay, was that it was they who first taught her the singing quality of verse. Rover's voice had a deep and throbbing cadence with which he tended to experiment in metrical forms especially on moonlight nights. Grandfather Thurnow's remark, that, "At least he cuts it up into stove lengths," was at once a recognition of Rover's success and an appreciation of his talent. Ole's voice, on the other hand, was a high falsetto and tended to break. When it broke it took on a certain screeching quality, not altogether pleasant in itself, but particularly well adapted to the old Norse ballads and folk songs which he rendered with full pedal and with an abandon which aroused Sarah's boundless admiration. He translated these songs freely—almost too freely. But he planted the seeds of poesy in Sarah's heart, nor could Jacob Binks' frequent admonition to "Shut up, you dam' square-head!" prevent the seeds from sprouting.

Early Influences: Mathilda Schwantzhacker

Mathilda Schwantzhacker was the thirteenth daughter of Kurt Schwantzhacker who occupied the South East Quarter of Section 37, Township 21, Range 9, West. The Schwantzhackers and the Binks were therefore neighbours a half mile apart, and lived in reasonable amity except on those occasions when the horses strayed through the barbed wire or when Ole and Rover practised their duets. Kurt Schwantzhacker was a dirt farmer of the better class, independent to the point of obstinacy. His farm supported him in all things even to the extent of a species of wild rhubarb of which he harvested a small crop every year in the belief that it was tobacco. He believed in being self-sustaining and raised his own food, his clothing, and his help with the somewhat indifferent co-operation of his wife. The belief that the farm could satisfy every need was not shared, however, by the thirteen Schwantzhacker girls, and they accordingly welcomed Ole as an honoured guest. They paid frequent calls on Sarah, and when the thirteen Schwantzhacker sisters came calling on Sunday afternoon, carefully picking their way in single file across the pasture which separated the two farms, the resemblance to an ancient Druid procession was very close. Ole was always moved by this fine sight; some latent memory of his Viking ancestry must have stirred in his blood, but to Sarah the only really welcome visitor among the thirteen was Mathilda. She was by far the best looking of the thirteen, certainly she was the least cross-eyed; she was Sarah's own age, she had been her confidante at school, and above all she was the only one who showed any interest in and appreciation for poetry.

It was Mathilda who first introduced Sarah to German literature. Literature in any language did not occupy a particularly high place in the Schwantzhacker culture, but the sisters, although they spoke German, as they were anxious to have it understood, "only in the home," nevertheless still sang some of the folk songs of their parents' homeland, generally in chorus, and often, it is said, to drown out Rover and Ole. Sarah knew no

German but Mathilda taught her some of the songs, the words and melodies at least, without much regard for their meaning. But Sarah's mind was always awake to any poetic opportunity. She borrowed Kurt Schwantzhacker's dictionary and translated. Several of these translations have come down to us, but they have generally been omitted from the anthologies of Sarah's works as not being truly representative of Sarah and Saskatchewan and may, in fact, represent the combined efforts of Sarah and Mathilda. Her best known, and undoubtedly finest of these translations, are those of Heine's *Du Bist Wie Eine Blume*, and *Die Lorelei*. The former is an almost perfect translation....

DU BIST WIE EINE BLUME *(Transl.)*

You are like one flower,
So swell, so good, and clean,
I look you on and longing,
Slinks me the heart between:

Me is as if the hands I
On head yours put them should,
Praying that God you preserve,
So swell, so clean, and good.

But it must be confessed, even among her most ardent admirers that she is not at her best in a translation. She tends to be too literal, and in her efforts to preserve form and rhyme she loses, if not the actual content, at least some of the spirit of the original. Von Knödel,[2] in his study of these translations asserts that in her rendering of *Mit den Pfeil und Bogen,* etc. as;

With the file, and bending,
Come the gripes a-rending,

---

2. Von Knödel, *Geographic and Dietetic Influences upon Nordic Culture as Revealed in the Works of the Canadian Poetess, Mathilda Schwantzhacker.*—Doctor's Thesis, University of Kleinfurth.

she has lost not only the spirit but the form and content as well, but admits that she has improved on the original, for which, with a narrow nationalism he is inclined to give Mathilda the credit.

Sarah is certainly not at her best in translation, at least not from the German. What she might have done with translations from the Portuguese or the Greek, or the Hindustanee, as Professor Marrowfat suggests, we cannot say. Such statements as Marrowfat's, "Had Mathilda and her twelve sisters been Swahili girls such as I have seen in Africa, we might have another story to tell," belong to the field of idle speculation and not to literary criticism; certainly Professor Marrowfat's ethnological studies cannot be applied to comparative literature.

"The Athens of Saskatchewan"

The year 1926 marks the turning point in the hitherto uneventful life of Sarah Binks. In spite of her growing fame she had remained a simple and unspoiled country girl, but now she was to make her first contact with the great outside world. She took a trip to Regina.

Regina marks a definite break in Sarah's career; all her later work was profoundly affected by it. "It is from this trip that we may definitely date the great change which came over all her poems; it is as if from that moment she put aside childish things forever and blossomed forth into the woman she gave promise of being even as early as her birth."[3] But the change was not effected without great trial. From Willows to Regina is a big step, in her case it was to prove almost too big a step. She was overwhelmed, and for a while the voice of the Sweet Songstress is stilled. One hesitates to think of Sarah had she been taken as far as Winnipeg, and one shudders to think of her in Toronto. But the Regina which overwhelmed her with its vastness and confused her with its throngs was at the same time the Regina which gave her something which she had never had, and which was to lead her eventually to one of the highest awards which has ever been bestowed upon one of Saskatchewan's daughters, the Wheat Pool Medal.

---

3. Rosalind Drool— *"Great Lives and Great Loves"*—Bunnybooks Ltd.

Regina was at that time the Athens of Saskatchewan. At once the commercial as well as the literary and cultural centre of the province, it displayed a sophistication utterly alien to the mind of the untried country girl. Sarah's reactions were inevitable and might have been predicted; she felt crushed, inferior, her simple message lost in Regina's glitter, its allure. Fortunate indeed for the course of literature that Henry Welkin stood at her side in this hour, directed her thoughts, and showed her the real Regina behind its polish, its sophistication, and its long rows of box cars.

Literature owes much to Henry Welkin; it must forever stand to his credit that it was through his influence that Sarah was brought into contact with the great world of commerce and culture. Had it not been for his generosity in paying all her expenses to Regina, Sarah might never have left Willows, and consequently her poetry might never have reached its maturity. Even though the sudden change from the pastoral simplicity of Willows to the teeming marts of men brought about that crisis in Sarah's life, her "Dark Hour," and threatened for a while to extinguish the divine spark and leave her forever dumb, we would not have it otherwise. "The bed on which the poet sleeps," says Sarah in one of her poems "is not always a bed of roses." What then shall we say for a poetess like Sarah herself?

Henry Welkin, aesthete, patron of the arts and letters, and travelling salesman, has been described as a man of considerable personal charm. He was tall and his eyes, which were set closely together, and appeared even more so from his habit of intense mental concentration, gave him an appearance of thoughtfulness and dignity. He was a careful and discriminating dresser; on the occasion of his first meeting with Sarah he wore a suit of brown striped serge, tailored according to the fashion of the day with long sweeping lapels, fancy pockets with buttons, the coat tight at the waist, and the trousers of the style known as "peg" ending in a four-inch cuff. A collar of the very best quality celluloid, a green bow tie, and a mauve silk shirt worn without a vest the better to display its full richness, and high-toed button shoes to match the suit completed the costume. Evidently a man of taste and discernment....

The meeting of Sarah Binks and Henry Welkin took place in the Willows General store. The elder Binks, always a keen business man, had been holding his eggs for a rise, and had sent Sarah to town to inquire the price. She had, apparently, no other errands, or purchases to make if we except the usual pound of gum-drops for Grandfather Thurnow or the package of snuff for Ole. Her mind, for once free of the long list of groceries, condition powders, and insecticides, was therefore in that receptive condition which marks Sarah at her best. She felt, as she later related to Mathilda, "a poem coming on." And when the figure of Henry Welkin, who had followed her across the street from Charlie Wong's, crossed her vision, she experienced at once that quickening of the spirit and that emotional response whereby the great have always recognized the great. No introductions were necessary; Henry Welkin, speaking with a confidence born of some inner feeling, said simply, "Hello Babe." Conventional words! Meaningless, or almost meaning-less from a thousand repetitions! But the soul of the poetess leaped into perfect understanding. That same evening Henry Welkin called at Sarah's home and two days later sold Jacob Binks another tooth-harrow.

There are those who would see in the quick ripening of the friendship between Sarah Binks and Henry Welkin, something more than the spiritual and intellectual coming together of two kindred souls. Miss Rosalind Drool, in particular, has developed this theme in her recent book, *Great Lives and Great Loves* in which she dwells at some considerable length on the possibility, and, in fact, probability of a romantic attachment having sprung up between the two. Something may be said for this point of view. Making due allowances for Miss Drool's tendency towards overemphasis, and her natural proclivity to take a vicarious and Freudian delight in incidents and experiences which she has not been privileged to enjoy, one may still admit that it would have been unnatural if these two, Henry Welkin and Sarah Binks, had not found in each other's personality some expression of their poetic faith. Sarah was never beautiful as beauty is counted, nevertheless, as Miss Drool repeatedly points out, she was by no means unattractive. She weighed at this time a hundred and thirty-four pounds, and her hair had been bleached by the Saskatchewan sun until it could almost be classified as blonde. Both eyes were blue, and her sensitive mouth revealed the winsomeness of her nature as well as the strength of her character. She was something of a hoyden, as who would not be under Ole's companionship, and felt most at ease when clothed in overalls and sweater, a costume which suited her personality in that here also she revealed the same grace and perfection of line which characterized her poetry.

We have seen that Henry Welkin, too, was not without that indefinable something. He may have appeared in Sarah's susceptible eyes a more glamorous figure than he actually was—certainly he shines more in the light of Sarah's effulgence than at Charlie Wong's—but he had youth and poise, and above all he brought to the young poetess something of the outside world. Moreover he knew farm machinery as few know their farm machinery. It would have been odd indeed if these two in their community of interests had failed to find at the same time a warm personal friendship. But it must always be emphasized that their chief interest lay in the world of art. The Author cannot stress this point too strongly.

It was during the interval between their meeting and the trip to Regina that Sarah wrote *Me and My Love and Me*. She had ample time to write. Henry was engaged in selling the elder Binks several more tooth-harrows, of which the farm already had a surplus but which both Jacob Binks and Ole loved to have around the yard and in the various fields. But it was not a period of great literary activity for Sarah. Only two poems have come down to us from this interval, but these two must be counted among the finest, not only of Saskatchewan, but of the whole of Western Canada. In *Me and My Love and Me*, Sarah expresses in tones at once lyrical and subdued, her inner harmony with life.

ME AND MY LOVE AND ME

Over the moor at dusk there fled
    The dismal clouds, and we,
Facing the rain, with might and main,
    Me and my love and me.

The sea-gull screamed, the reeds were bent,
    But hand-in-hand the three,
We hurried on—going against wind,
    Me and my love and me.

Thus the Sweet Songstress in her hour of happiness. But Sarah was not to sing again for many a long day; her joy, her exuberance, her delight in the simple things, in Rover, in Ole, in the perennial calf, all were swept away in the rush of events which followed.

We do not know for certain how long Sarah spent in Regina. Professor Marrowfat, who for once treats Sarah sympathetically, even enthusiastically, limits the period to two and a half weeks. Doctor Taj Mahal, always a stickler for exactitude, has made a careful study of the railroad time tables of that period, and comes to the conclusion that the visit could not have lasted over a week, whereas Miss Rosalind Drool stretches it out to a full three weeks. Taking into account the personal error to which even the most careful investigators are subject, we may safely conclude that two weeks represent the length of Sarah's visit. But what crowded weeks! In that interval Sarah and Henry Welkin visited all the places of interest. Twice they went to the opera. Again and again they rode on Regina's street car. The cafes, Chinatown, the Botanical Gardens, the Union Station—Henry Welkin was eager that his young protégée should drink life to the full. He took her to the aquarium and to the public library, and together they studied what fish and what manuscripts were available at these places. They made the rounds of the art galleries; they visited the parliament building and studied its geology. Nor was the world of commerce neglected; together they visited the department stores, the groceterias, the banks, the freight yards, and the big implement warehouse of the firm which Henry represented and which he was particularly anxious for her to see. Sarah drank it all in. She was eager and she had youth. But human nature, and especially a nature so human as Sarah's, can encompass only so much. From Willows to Regina was a far bigger step than she had anticipated.

Her Darkest Hour

Regina had been too much for Sarah. She went into a literary decline which lasted for months and from which even her nearest friends seemed unable to arouse her. It marks a sharp line between the two periods of her work which scholars generally refer to as Pre-Regina, and Post-Regina, or more simply, P.R. and P.R., respectively. Sarah herself refers to this period between the two P.R. periods as "My Dark Hour." For a while she wrote nothing, and where she writes at all she strikes the pessimistic note, sometimes even the macabre. What shall one say of *They Arose,* or *I Buried My Love at Dawn,* or even of *High on A Cliff*? There is something not entirely Saskatchewan in these verses, and the fragment,

> With grief engraven on my soul,
>   I cannot roll in glee,
> The robin's note is but a dirge,
>   The biscuit-bird grits me.

touches the subsoil of human depression. "It is more than her Dark Hour," cries Principal Pinhole in despairing tones, "it is Darkest Africa."

It is no mere coincidence that the manuscript of *Take Me Away* should be stained with tears, or what appears to be tears, and although later chemical analysis showed these to be butter and rhubarb jam, it does not alter the fact that in this period was her darkest moment....

> When I'm buried in a graveyard,
> And this feeble flame is snuffed,
> Will a spotted magpie murmur,
> Mutely sigh with ruff unfluffed?

Sarah is not only deeply despondent but seems to be suffering from a bad cold in the head.

• • •

Sarah would recover from this, her darkest hour, and in the P.R. period would reach new heights of her art, culminating with that staggering magna opus—a "square foot of poetry"—entitled Up from the Magma and Back Again. *Alas, Sarah's greatest triumph would be followed by her tragic demise, the events of which I will not relate here, for this anthology is meant to be one of whimsy, and I do not wish to cast too melancholy a pall over these pages.*—W.F.

Donald Jack

Donald Jack managed to pull off the equivalent of a hat trick in the world of Canadian humour, winning the Stephen Leacock Medal not once, not twice, but three times. Even more impressive, he won all three of his Leacock Medals on the strength of the same comedic character: Bartholomew Bandy, a Canadian WWI pilot who bounces across Europe and beyond, winning medals, escaping from German prison cells, crashing planes (often on top of his own officers), getting demoted—and just as quickly promoted—through the ranks, and smiling all the while. The picaresque tale of B. Bandy eventually ran through nine novels, with the hero even becoming a Hollywood stunt pilot at one point. The following is from *Me Bandy, You Cissie*, which won Donald Jack his third Leacock.

FROM *Me Bandy, You Cissie*

You know me, of course, with my famous face with its display of full frontal effrontery, but who, you may ask—though then again you may not—is this Cissie who shares the title of this latest volume of shocks, triumphs, and calamities? That is a very good question—assuming you have asked it.

Following my escape from Bolshevik Russia in 1920, I reported to the High Commissioner's Office in London, and was duly processed—their word for it, as if I were a piece of cheese—for onward transmission to my homeland. This included the provision of temporary papers, some pocket money, and a new uniform, that of a major general. (Some snotty buggers claim that I achieved such a rapid rise in the hierarchy mainly because certain persons were anxious to get rid of me, and were rewarding me not so much for services rendered the country so much as to ensure that I did not render any further services to them. But as everyone knows who has followed my career thus far, this is an unworthy slander based on envy, frustration, apoplectic fury, keen insight, and similar deficiency.)

Accordingly, I was booked on the first westbound ship from Southampton. I met Cissie Chaffington soon after she boarded the ship at Le Havre, for she was placed at the same table in the dining lounge, directly opposite me.

An exceedingly tall girl of twenty, she had just completed her first year at a finishing school in Lausanne. It had not quite finished her off, though. She was with us for only a few minutes before she upset a bottle of wine.

As luck would have it, the vinous fluid chuckled over the edge of the dining table, straight onto the lap of a Westmount socialite, who was wearing a white silk dinner gown—now claret-coloured, courtesy of St. Julien Léoville-Poyferré, class of '17.

The claret clashed horribly with her emeralds.

As if to make amends, Cissie stained her face claret-coloured as well. She looked so desperately crushed that the lady was forced to reassure her that it didn't matter—it was just an unsuitable old Paris gown she happened to have bought in an impulsive moment a couple of weeks ago.

Still, the lady remained sort of canted away from Cissie after that. Which was just as well, for barely a minute later, Cissie, who because of her position at the table was having difficulty in keeping her long legs neatly folded, tripped a steward.

As it happened, the steward was delivering a duck on a silver platter. He went flying without a licence, and in the process flung the dinner into some ornamental shrubbery. That was bad enough, but the shrubbery, which was spraying artistically from an earthenware tub, was right next to the ship's captain, who was presiding at the head of the adjoining table. The result was that the captain's equally white dress uniform was liberally spattered with orange sauce.

The poor crimson beanpole of a girl just sat there, paralyzed with shame, quite incapable of either fleeing or fluttering, apologizing, or even offering to sponge down the captain in his bathroom.

The captain looked at her, then laughed. "It's quite all right," he laughed. "Actually, the duck looks quite at home, sitting there on that branch. What?"

Everybody else avoided looking at Cissie. Instead, they all studied the duck in the shrubbery.

"Yes, it does look quite at home up there," another lady said tactfully.

"Ornamental, sort of," the diplomat said.

"Yes… as if it really belongs up there," his young wife said timidly, glancing quickly at Cissie's wretched head, then away again.

"Oh, I don't know," I said, "*I've* never seen a duck up in a tree before."

Everybody frowned at me, as if I were spoiling the harmony of the occasion.

"Ducks are usually to be found waddling about in the muck," I went on. "I know, because my Camel once flung me into a duck pond. In France, this was."

"A camel flung you into a duck pond?" snapped Sir Alfred Cake. He was an elderly gentleman with angry eyebrows.

"I didn't realize people rode camels in France," the diplomat's wife babbled. "I suppose they import them from Algeria, do they?"

"What were you doing to the camel to cause it to fling you into a duck pond?" Sir Alfred inquired, rapping the table with his fish fork.

"It was a Sopwith Camel."

"You must have been mistreating it, whatever species it was, to cause it to fling you into a duck pond," the old chap said censoriously.

"He means an aeroplane, Sir Alfred."

"What aeroplane? We were talking about ducks."

"Anyway, the point was that it flipped over and emptied me into the duck pond," I explained. "So you see I know about ducks?"

"Still think he must have been ill-treating the beast," Sir Alfred muttered, giving me an unfriendly look. He was obviously fond of animals.

"The duck up there could be of the *platyrhynchos* breed," a well informed source put in, gazing thoughtfully into the shrubbery. "They've been known to sit in trees." He turned to the steward, who was standing there looking a bit dazed. "Do you happen to know? Is it of the *platyrhynchos* type?"

"They just give it to me in the galley, sir. Somehow I didn't think to ask."

"H'm. Well, it obviously is, or that duck wouldn't be up there, would it? Assuming, of course, that it is a duck."

"Yes, sir, it says so on the menu."

"It could be a drake."

"Oh no, sir. Otherwise they'd've called it *Drake à l'orange.*"

"Strictly speaking, though the term *duck* is commonly applied to both sexes," the well-informed one said, perhaps a shade didactically, "the duck is in fact the female of the species."

"Perhaps we'd better examine it and see," the captain said heartily just as Cissie suddenly scraped her chair back, jumped up, and fled from the dining lounge.

As soon as she was out of sight, the captain's jovial look faded.

"Some finishing school she must have gone to," he muttered, flinging down his napkin and plucking mumpishly at his saucy nauticals. "Though I will admit she's certainly finished off my uniform."

Poor Cissie was so affected by her spectacular entry into Cunard society that she didn't appear again for the next three meals. The following night, when I saw her leaning on the rail, watching the porpoises cavorting in the moonlit wake, I went up to her to say a few comforting words.

"It's all right," I told her in a kindly way. "You can rejoin us at table now. Everybody's got their overalls on."

Somehow this didn't seem to make her feel any better, for she jerked around and looked at me out of huge black eyes in a stricken fashion. So I went on to tell her about the time I got into a similarly embarrassing situation in a *pension* near Amiens, when the proprietress thought I was the husband of a certain French lady, and I tried to explain that I wasn't, and I got so confused that when I was leaving the kitchen, I went through the wrong door and fell into the cellar.

All of which gave Cissie time to recover. Whereupon she turned and said coldly, "I don't know why you're telling me all this. I don't find it the least interesting. Now if you'll excuse me." And she turned to hunch over the rail again.

Pride or starvation finally brought her back into the dining room, but for another two days she hardly spoke a word, except to reply in defiant monosyllables, as if she were saying, "I don't care what you think of me. Just get on with your stupid chatter and leave me alone."

Of course, that was just a defence, to give us no excuse to snigger at her *gaucherie*. Still, I persisted in cultivating her, partly because she reminded me of Katherine when I first met her.

Even so, we were in mid-Atlantic before she began to respond. The turning point came one evening when we both happened to be late for dinner and had the table to ourselves. After one or two attempts at conversation, I'd given up and was cocooned in thought when she said abruptly, "I've always wanted to fly."

I started and dropped a spoonful of jelly onto the tablecloth.

I stared across at her. She had actually raised her head, though her eyes had not quite managed to rise above the brand-new wings on my brand-new tunic.

"Whenever I got the chance, I used to go along and watch our boys training," she said jerkily. "Places like Kelly Field."

"Did you?"

"I used to wish so much I was a boy and could join up and get away from home," she said in a rush, then stopped and subsided, blushing.

Before she could vanish back into her carapace, I started to drone on about learning to fly on Longhorns and Shorthorns, and about my first solo in the tricky Camel.

By the time I'd reached the part where I'd crash-landed on my battalion commander, she was actually listening unself-consciously and had raised her eyes to the level of my teeth.

Because she usually kept her head bowed, her abundant dark-chocolate hair usually concealed half her face. Now, as she swept it aside for a better view of my drivel, I was half expecting a thoroughly disagreeable frontispiece, moulded by years of peevishness and discontent; but good heavens, it was a really fine face, well worth revealing now that it was alive with interest and intelligence. Not a fashionable face, perhaps; bony and oblong rather than heart-shaped, with lips that were straight and thin rather than the shape that was now all the rage, the cupid's bow.

It was a pity her body was equally straight and thin, with no discernible bust and, the equator of her frock being at hip level, no discernible waist either. These features, or lack of them, together with her inability to flirt and her awkward height, explained why she had attracted so little attention from the unattached males on board.

From then on, whenever there was nobody else around, Cissie opened up like a flower after an untoward cold spell. She told me about her year in Lausanne and about her best friend, Margot, who had run off to Paris with an older man, and about her ambition to learn to fly, and about her boyfriend. She had broken off with him some months previously. Back in California he had seemed eloquent, talented, and amusing, but his letters to her in Switzerland had proved witless, insensitive, and remarkably illiterate—even for an arts student.

"Mine were probably just as dull," she conceded with a hesitant smile, "but at least I didn't dot my *i*'s with funny faces. I've always been crazy about good letter-writing. All my life I've been reading other people's letters. In books, I mean. You know, collections of love letters, the correspondence of Madame de Sévigné. Lord Byron. People like that ..."

She broke off, looking at me anxiously. "I suppose you think it was awful, my breaking off with him just because he couldn't write a good letter? I must sound an awful snob?"

"No, I quite understand. Rather than marry him, you'd prefer to live in syntax."

A few seconds later she darted a constrained glance at me through her hair. The poor girl didn't even have sufficient confidence in herself to wince.

During the voyage she mentioned her parents only once, so it was some time before I learned who her father was. While we were lurching up and down the promenade deck one morning—she preferred the windy side of the deck because it was usually deserted—she mentioned that her father had wanted a son rather than a daughter.

"As it turned out, he didn't even get much of a daughter," she said with a laugh, and immediately moved to the rail and hunched over it, to reduce herself to a more acceptable height.

She had already told me twice, as if admitting rather defiantly to a felony, that she was six feet two inches tall.

She stood there for a while, searching for something interesting to say. That afternoon she was wearing a calf-length polka-dot frock in blue and white, and a white felt helmet of a hat that was having difficulty in subduing her masses of dark hair. She looked rather touchingly absurd in that supposed-to-be close-fitting hat. Because of the pressure of her hair, it looked ready to fly up at any moment, like a champagne cork.

"You didn't come down for breakfast or lunch today," she managed at length.

"H'm? No, I haven't the energy to eat."

"Yes, I guess it is a bit rough today," she said, checking up on the sea, which was hardly more turbulent than a vat of Lyle's Golden Syrup.

"It's not that, Cissie," I said heartily. "It's just that I've been somewhat undernourished for a couple of years, and all this fodder they keep slapping in front of us is killing me. Morning broth, coffee and cookies, elevenses, lunch, brunch, tiffin, tea—they seem to feed you about every forty minutes on this ship."

She nodded uncertainly. She herself was obviously enjoying the gastro-nomic and potable largess, guzzling all the provender that was offered without its having the slightest effect on her abdominal convexity—much to the annoyance of the Westmount lady, who was having to let out her stays every forty minutes.

I leaned on the rail beside her and gazed across the ocean. It was early May, and gently unrolling waves were creating decorative feathery designs on the Prussian-blue surface. Near the horizon the sun was sewing a million sequins, while along the ship's side the rushing waters formed delicate spume patterns.

A moment later there was a splash from further forward, and three mouldy loaves washed past, followed by pieces of orange peel, cabbage leaves, and some intestines.

"You were captured by the Russians, weren't you?" she asked abruptly. "I guess it must have been pretty rough—the famine and everything."

"Oh, it wasn't all that bad," I said, looking resolutely at the horizon. "After I got out of sundry jails, I was allowed to roam around quite freely, after giving my word not to escape."

"Jails? More than one?"

"Oh yes. Including the CPU cells at Number Two Gorohovaya Onlitsa, where they kept executing me."

"Where they *what?*"

"It was just a secret-police tactic. They would bring you out of your cell and put you against the courtyard wall and offer you a blindfold and a final clay pipe—cigarettes were in short supply, you see. Then they would line up the firing squad and go through the ready, aim, fire procedure, but never actually firing. At least not in my case, though I was expecting at any moment to be converted into a colander."

"Golly!" Cissie whispered, cupping her chin in her hand and gazing at me wide-eyed.

"Before that I was in the Kresty Prison on the other side of Petrograd, and after that I was in the ... but you don't want to hear all this stuff."

"Yes, I do," she exclaimed. Then, solicitously: "Unless it's too painful to...?"

"Not really. A lot of it was quite funny."

"It sounds it."

"Well, if you really want to," I began. "Well ... after the CPU episode, I was put in the condemned cell in the Peter and Paul Fortress. After that I—"

"You were condemned to death?"

"M'm," I said, locking myself into the nearest brown study and thinking about that cell in the *Petropavolovskaya Krepost* ...

• • •

The cell was, I believe, the one that had been occupied by the author Maxim Gorki until the Bolsheviks released him in 1917, but he had left no messages for mankind on the walls—not even an amusing limerick.

I was quite surprised when I was first escorted into it. Told I was destined for solitary confinement in one of the notorious dungeons on the hexagon-shaped island in the Neva River, I'd expected some small Hagstoned cavity, with water trickling from every nook and with just enough headroom to accommodate an arthritic hobgoblin. Something like the Count of Monte Cristo's boudoir in the Chateau d'If.

But land sakes, it was quite spacious, especially in comparison with some of the Slav bedsitters I'd been in recently. It was clean and smooth, and with plenty of fresh air, and even had a small barred window overlooking a deserted courtyard. It had furniture, too: an iron bed and tickly mattress with at least half a dozen straws to grasp at.

Not that it was perfect, mind you. It was a trifle chilly, for one thing. A good inch of ice coated the inside of the little window. Still, that was only to be expected since it was the middle of winter. At least I think it was. I think it was February. But of course, it could have been March. Or even April 1919.

It was almost as silent as it was cold. Good Lord, it was silent. The jailers were under orders not to make a sound; though even had they caroused up and down the corridor outside with a dancing bear and a dozen wanton baggages, the noise would not have seeped through those walls.

In the same way, no distracting activity was allowed in the courtyard beyond the high window. Once, though, clinging to the bars and peering out above trembling biceps, I thought I once glimpsed an eerie sparkle, a dewy veil that might have been the ghost of some frustrated tsar. Unless it was just a shower of snow crystals dislodged from an onion dome. For the Cathedral of St. Peter and St. Paul was also part of the fortress, and mouldering handfuls of royalty were buried in there, under a theatrical grandeur of iconostasis and gold moulding and red jasper and green quartz. True to Russian tradition, along with the baroque opulence, the former govern-ment had added these dark cells that huddled around the courtyard.

The hush was part of the treatment, of course. You weren't supposed to hear anything except the blood rustling around your own arterial system. Every now and then you also got a high-pitched note in your ears, which was also unpleasant. The only way to drown it out was to add a low-pitched accompaniment. So I sang "Rock of Ages," and "Silent Night," and every other hymn I could remember, and also whispered Russian grammar lessons, to keep my brain from turning into a sewage plant.

I was there for months. Exactly how many there was no way of knowing as there was only the footrule of my beard to measure the time.

Though I cringed a good deal in the Peter and Paul Fortress because of the cold, the only time I felt like despairing was when I learned, somewhat belatedly, that the rest of the world was at peace. I got a bit upset then at the thought that while we were committing ourselves irrevocably to intervening in the Russian civil war in northern Russia, at precisely the same hour the guns on the Western Front, after four and a quarter years of demented barking, had finally been muzzled. For I had been captured during the Battle of Toulgas, on November 11, 1918.

I thought it was absolutely rotten, them ending the war without me. After all I'd done for the war effort, too. It just wasn't fair. I felt really left out of things. Everybody else was now at home, receiving victory parades, money, and civilian suits and settling by the home fires burning and getting jobs and meeting girls and buying new cars and everything. And here was I in the cold and darkness of a land where the prospect seemed to be leading from a repressive past to an oppressive future, where all civilized feeling seemed to have atrophied.

Usually, however, by the time that dawn had turned up the celestial gas mantle, I was up and singing softly again, and marching up and down to the rhythm of the wheedling Russian language, tottering miles on rag-wrapped feet; eight paces from door to window wall, eight paces back, with the occasional special treat of a transverse march from latrine hole to iron bedstead, making every second about-turn in the opposite direction, so as not to get dizzy.

Then one day I had my first visitor. And my last.

It was a uniformed GPU officer with a face carved out of Neva ice.

He looked slowly around the darkish space, disapprovingly, as if it were far too good for the likes of me. After almost a minute, he gestured abruptly.

"Come."

"Who?" I asked. "Me?"

I felt rather pleased at this answer. It proved that prison had not entirely rehabilitated me.

He looked at me, his eyes like a pair of bullets. He gave me a shove.

"Shut your muzzle. Go on."

Accompanied by the officer and two other uniformed GPU agents, I was driven in a *kibitka* (a sort of raffia basket on runners) across the frozen Neva River to the Nevsky Prospekt and then some distance up that splendid three-mile thoroughfare.

When I saw where they were taking me, I was badly shaken. It was up there on the side of the building in burned-out light bulbs: *Evropeievskaya Gastinitza.*

My God, was there to be no end to my sufferings? They were putting me up at a Russian hotel.

Thomas King

Thomas King was born in California to parents of Greek/German and Cherokee descent. He grew up in Sacramento and moved to Canada as an adult, where he's created a name for himself as a novelist, scriptwriter, and poet dealing with issues of Native identity and culture. The piece that follows is the title story from King's recent collection, *A Short History of Indians in Canada*. I have also included his poem "Coyote Sees the Prime Minister," which is probably the most succinct summation ever written about how our society grapples with the "Indian problem." (For more Native Canadian humour see the anthology *Me Funny*, edited by Drew Hayden Taylor.)

FROM *A Short History of Indians in Canada*

Can't sleep, Bob Haynie tells the doorman at the King Eddie. Can't sleep, can't sleep.

First time in Toronto? says the doorman.

Yes, says Bob.

Businessman?

Yes.

Looking for some excitement?

Yes.

Bay Street, sir, says the doorman.

• • •

Bob Haynie catches a cab to Bay Street at three in the morning. He loves the smell of concrete. He loves the look of city lights. He loves the sound of skyscrapers.

Bay Street.

Smack!

Bob looks up just in time to see a flock of Indians fly into the side of the building.

Smack! Smack!

Bob looks up just in time to get out of the way.

Whup!

An Indian hits the pavement in front of him.

Whup! Whup!

Two Indians hit the pavement behind him.

Holy Cow! shouts Bob, and he leaps out of the way of the falling Indians.

Whup! Whup! Whup!

Bob throws his hands over his head and dashes into the street. And is almost hit by a city truck.

Honk!

Two men jump out of the truck. Hi, I'm Bill. Hi, I'm Rudy.

Hi, I'm Bob.

Businessman? says Bill.

Yes.

First time in Toronto? says Rudy.

Yes.

Whup! Whup! Whup!

Look out! Bob shouts. There are Indians flying into the skyscrapers and falling on the sidewalk.

Whup!

Mohawk, says Bill.

Whup! Whup!

Couple of Cree over here, says Rudy.

Amazing, says Bob. How can you tell?

By the feathers, says Bill. We got a book.

It's our job, says Rudy.

Whup!

Bob looks around. What's this one? he says.

Holy! says Bill. Holy! says Rudy.

Check the book, says Bill. Just to be sure.

Flip, flip, flip.

Navajo!

Bill and Rudy put their arms around Bob. A Navajo! Don't normally see Navajos this far north. Don't normally see Navajos this far east.

Is she dead? says Bob

Nope, says Bill. Just stunned.

Most of them are just stunned, says Rudy.

Some people never see this, says Bill. One of nature's mysteries. A natural phenomenon.

They're nomadic you know, says Rudy. And migratory. Toronto's in the middle of the flyway, says Bill. The lights attract them.

Bob counts the bodies. Seventy-three. No. Seventy-four. What can I do to help?

Not much that anyone can do, says Bill. We tried turning off the lights in the buildings.

We tried broadcasting loud music from the roofs, says Rudy.

Rubber owls? asks Bob.

It's a real problem this time of the year, says Bill.

Whup! Whup! Whup!

Bill and Rudy pull green plastic bags out of their pockets and try to find the open ends.

The dead ones we bag, says Rudy.

The lives ones we tag, says Bill. Take them to the shelter. Nurse them back to health. Release them in the wild.

Amazing, says Bob.

A few wander off dazed and injured. If we don't find them right away, they don't stand a chance.

Amazing, says Bob.

You're one lucky guy, says Bill. In another couple of weeks, they'll be gone.

A family from Alberta came through last week and didn't even see an Ojibway, says Rudy.

Your first time in Toronto? says Bill.

It's a great town, says Bob. You're doing a great job.

Whup!

Don't worry, says Rudy. By the time the commuters show up, you'll never even know the Indians were here.

Bob catches a cab back to the King Eddie and shakes the doorman's hand. I saw the Indians, he says.

Thought you'd enjoy that, sir, says the doorman.

Thank you, says Bob. It was spectacular.

Not like the old days. The doorman sighs and looks up into the night. In the old days, when they came through, they would black out the entire sky.

Coyote Sees the Prime Minister

Coyote went east to see the
PRIME Minister.

I wouldn't make this up.

And the PRIME Minister was so HAPPY
to see Coyote
that he made HIM a member of cabinet.

Maybe you can HELP us solve the
Indian problem.

Sure, says that Coyote,
WHAT's the problem?

When Elwood tells this story, he
always LAUGHS and spoils
the ending.

W.P. Kinsella

W.P. Kinsella is the author of *Shoeless Joe,* which was adapted
into the acclaimed film *Field of Dreams* and gave the world the
koan-like expression "If you build it, he will come." Kinsella has
written about Japanese baseball star Ichiro Suzuki and Cree
artist Allan Sapp, and is the author of eight collections of short
stories set in and around the Hobbema Indian Reserve of central
Alberta, featuring the adventures and misadventures of aspiring
author Silas Ermineskin and his best friend, Frank Fencepost.
The following is from *The Fencepost Chronicles,* which won the
Leacock Medal for Humour in 1987 (back when computer
automation was still considered "the wave of the future").

FROM *The Fencepost Chronicles*

Indian Joe

I never forget the Christmas my sister Illianna got Indian Joe as a present.
Pa had left us the year before and Delores was just a baby. I remember
Delores peering over Ma's shoulder as we walk down the hill from our cabin
to Blue Quills Hall, where the Christmas party was.

There was a big, tall Christmas tree inside Blue Quills Hall. The place
smell smokey because the stove backed up. Each of us kids was given a
candy cane and a glass of lemonade. Everyone sat around with their coats
on acting shy.

Finally Santa Claus showed up. All but the littlest kids could tell it
was Sven Sonnegard, a mechanic at the Husky Service Station on the

highway. He still got his greasy, steel-toed work boots on below his Santa Claus suit.

There were galvanized garbage cans on the stage, each covered in green and red paper, each got a sheet of black construction paper taped to it, with BOY or GIRL and different age groups written on in chalk.

We got in a long line and when a kid got to the top of the stairs to the stage, he would sneak across toward Santa Claus, head down. If Sven Sonnegard could get the kid to tell its age, he'd reach in the right barrel for a present. If the kid wouldn't tell, Sven would guess; sometimes he'd even have to guess if it was a boy or girl. One garbage can say BABY, others 1–3, 4–6, 7–9, and so on.

My friend Frank Fencepost notice the presents get bigger as the kids get older. When it's our turn, Frank he walk right up to Santa Claus and say, "Hi, Sven, I'd like to buy a quart of home-brew."

"Shut up, Kid," Sven say out of the side of his mouth, but he also have a hard time keep from laughing. We all know Sven make his living bootleg-ging, mainly to Indians.

"How old are you?" Sven say to Frank.

We are supposed to be in the 7–9 group.

"Fifteen," say Frank, push out his skinny chest, look Sven right in the eye.

"You ain't a day over eight," say Sven–Santa Claus.

"He's small for his age," I say.

"That's right, he's small for eight."

"I seen Constable Greer down by the door," said Frank. "How many cases of home-brew you think he'd find in your truck if he looked?"

Sven reach in the BOY 13–15 barrel, pull out a big package.

"My twin brother is at home sick," say Frank.

Santa Claus reach out another package, a basketball, and he nearly knock Frank over he push it into his arms so hard.

"My brother's brother couldn't be here neither."

Sven load another present into Frank's arms.

The line-up behind us getting restless.

"And my cousin …"

"Move along," said Santa. "What a good boy you've been," and push Frank so he skid clear across the stage.

"How old are you, Sport?" he said to me.

"Thirteen," I said, swallowing hard.

"Sure you are." He reach in the BOY 7–9 barrel and give me a package turn out to be a peg-board game got half the wooden nubbins missing.

It was at this party Illianna was gived Indian Joe. Joe was a mechanical Indian, run by batteries. He was six or eight inches tall, sit on his haunches in front of a drum, with little drumsticks raised up ready to play. In Joe's lower back was a switch, and when it pressed down he play. H-H-H-Rap, Tap-Tap, go the drum. The toys we was given was all used, but Indian Joe was good as new and Illianna was real proud of him.

"He look something like Pa," Illianna say on the walk home. Her being older she remember Pa better than the rest of us. I never knew him to play the drum, or have black braids, or even a red shirt with green suspenders like Indian Joe.

After Illianna got her toy home she is kind of like a miser with her money when it come to sharing. She like him so much she take him to bed with her that first night.

• • •

All that happened about three years before Illianna go off to work in the city. By that time everybody but Illianna forgot about Indian Joe. No one even notice he is one of the things Illianna take to Calgary with her.

After she been in the city for a year or two my sister married herself to a white man name of Robert McGregor McVey. He is a big wheel in some company that loan out money. Me and my friends have caused McVey a certain amount of grief over the years. The first time I ever seen their new house, I discover that in their bedroom Illianna and Brother Bob have what's called a walk-in closet. On one of the shelves sat Indian Joe. He look smaller than I remember him, but except that one of the plastic feathers is gone from his war-bonnet, he is good as new. I remember thinking it is strange for Illianna to keep a toy like that, 'cause she been married for years and have her own little boy named Bobby.

Last week me and Frank went to Calgary for a day. We park the truck and start walking around.

"What should we do?" I ask Frank.

"Let's go in the lobby of a bank and watch people withdraw money from the machines," says Frank.

We watch the machines for a while.

Later, I seen a sign take me by surprise. In gold letters in the form of an arch, just like McDonald's, it say INTERCONTINENTAL LOAN CO. LTD., Robert M. McVey, Division Manager.

"Look at that," I say to Frank. "You figure that's Brother Bob?"

"Let's go inside and see," he says.

We walk inside, and boy, the place is just like a bank. There is secretaries everywhere, dressed fancy as models. Quiet music is playing and typewriters tick. Everywhere there is machines look like a cross between typewriters and televisions.

"Good afternoon, may I help you?" a lady say. She is tall, with long blond hair, dressed in a brown, scratchy-looking suit, remind me of a doormat.

"I'd like to borrow twenty dollars," says Frank, give her a big smile. "I pay you back tomorrow for sure. I even leave my friend here. You can sell him if I don't come back."

The girl try hard to be polite.

"I'm afraid we only make industrial loans," she say.

"How about if you loan me twenty dollars personally?" say Frank, and he look at her real sad, lift up one finger point to his cheek. As he does a tear squeeze out of his eye, roll onto his cheek and stop there. Frank seen an Indian on TV do that, that Indian was sad about white men cutting down trees or something.

"How do you do that?" the girl says.

"Come real close and I show you."

The girl does, then turn to another girl, and say, "Hey, Francine, come look at this."

"Maybe you've seen me on TV?" Frank saying.

Frank wipe the tears off his cheek, start the water flowing again.

"Excuse me," I say to a grey-haired lady, "is Mr. McVey in?"

"Whom should I say is calling?" she say, look right at me as if what she's asking ain't funny.

"Tell him his brother, Silas, is here."

She scowl, and I bet she is going to say something nasty to me when she remember that Brother Bob have an Indian wife. She push her face into a tiny smile and pick up a white telephone.

A few minutes later, Brother Bob, his cheeks all shiny, wearing a striped suit and vest, smell like he just bathed in shaving lotion, come out of a door labelled EXECUTIVE OFFICES.

He try to be friendly, but he is embarrassed to see me there. Bet he wishes he could dress me up in a suit like him and cut my hair.

"Why Silas," he say, "what a surprise!"

"I seen your name on the window."

Brother Bob stare around kind of nervous. Then his eyes light on Frank's back. Frank got five or six secretaries watching him cry. I notice he is also putting a stapler in his pocket.

"You *didn't* bring that Posthole with you?" Brother Bob yell.

"He's keepin' himself busy," I say. "You never even know he's here."

"Well, Silas, how would you like a tour of our business facilities?" he ask. "We've got straight state-of-the-art technology here. Everything is done by computer. I expect you'll be buying, or how is it you put it, creatively borrowing, a word processor to facilitate your writing procedures," and he give me a little chuckle.

"I facilitate my writing procedures with a felt pen and a Royal type-writer," I say. "I'm scared of these here computers."

"It's inevitable, Silas. People in the horse-and-buggy era were afraid of the horseless carriage. Now, even *you* drive a car ..."

It get pretty noisy across the room where Frank and the secretaries gathered around a big copier.

Brother Bob and me work our way over to them.

I guess Frank ain't ever seen a copying machine up close before. One of the secretaries show him how it work, and Frank put his hand down flat, push the button, and out come a piece of paper with a big, blue-black hand on it.

"Hey, I bet this here machine could copy food," cries Frank. "Silas," he yell, "run down to a restaurant and get a sandwich. I'll copy it enough times to feed the whole reserve." The secretaries all laugh. I notice a couple of them is already touching Frank.

"He doesn't really believe that, does he?" Brother Bob ask. "Well ..." I say. "Mad Etta teach him pretty strong medicine. If he was to copy a sandwich it just might come out real."

Brother Bob stare me up and down, but he don't have the nerve to call me a liar. He shoo all the secretaries back to their desks. Then he take both of us through a couple of metal doors, thick as the kind they have in warehouses, and into a room with no windows.

"This is our computer centre," he say, wave one of his small, pink hands at the rows and rows of blinking machines.

The sounds in the room is quite a bit like an arcade, except all the humans is quiet.

"You keep the money inside those machines?" ask Frank.

"Oh, no," say Brother Bob, "no money, but all our records are in there. We can establish the status of any loan account in the nation in less than 10 seconds. Here, let me show you ..." and he actually smile at us, looking kind of purplish under the artificial light.

As I look at Brother Bob, I wonder how Illianna feel about being married to a white man, and living in a white world. She seem to be happy, and says Bob and her have lots of friends. And she has her little boy Bobby. Still, no matter how I try, I can't "walk in her moccasins," as Mad Etta our medicine lady would say. I can't imagine not being with other Indians. It seem to me I'd get awful tired of always being on display, of answering dumb questions, of always being afraid I'd make a mistake.

Brother Bob poke away at the keys of a computer and a whole page of figures appear. "See," he says. I can tell by looking at Frank that he is just dying to touch one of these machines.

"Watch this," says Brother Bob. "This machine can speak too."

He push a button and the machine talk, sound like somebody under a foot of water with his nose plugged. But once I tune my ears to it, I can understand.

"Can you teach it to cuss?" ask Frank.

"I suppose I could, if I was so inclined," Brother Bob reply, but pretty coldly.

The steel door open and that grey-haired lady stick her head in. "Excuse me, Mr. McVey, but Zurich is on the line."

"I'll be right back," Brother Bob say to us, and trot away.

"Boy, this is just like a video arcade," yells Frank, move up to the word processor and poke a button or two. "Which one do I push to shoot down all those squiggley things?"

"I don't know if we should be touching these here machines," I say.

"Where's the coin slot?"

"Brother Bob own these machines. You don't have to pay to use them."

"Wow! Brother Bob is in heaven and I bet he don't even know it." Frank go from machine to machine, poke a button here and there.

"These ain't games …"

"But I bet they could be," and Frank whack a few more buttons.

"We better go," I say.

About that time, a red light, look like an ambulance flasher, high above the door, start flashing, and a bell, like a fire alarm, begin ringing.

"I think I got this one working," yells Frank.

It does look as if it's turning into a game. The red light flashes, the siren bongs, it is just like our favourite arcade in Wetaskiwin.

Just as Frank really starting to enjoy himself, Brother Bob come crashing through the door.

"Don't touch that machine any more," he yells. "Our entire loan records are in there. If it goes down …"

"I'm gonna blow these little green suckers away," yells Frank, pound the buttons the way a Russian pianist I seen on TV pound his piano.

"That's enough, Frank," I'm surprised to hear myself saying. I move toward him, intending to pull him away from the machine. Sometimes it seem to me Frank don't think enough before he act.

"Don't hit that button ..." scream Brother Bob. We both dive for Frank. The machine look like it making fireworks and is about to explode.

I hit Frank like he was carrying a football and we both roll under a table, scatter a couple of wastebaskets across the room. Brother Bob shut off the machine, wipe his forehead, stare at us with his eyes bugging out.

I'm not sure if what I've done is good or bad.

"Another five seconds and our entire financial records would have been destroyed. Some of it could never be replaced."

I don't think Brother Bob realize that I was helping him. Maybe that's just as well. He march us both out of the building as if we was under arrest.

"We sure is sorry, Brother Bob," we say, but he don't even tell us goodbye.

• • •

Outside, Frank decide to wait the hour until closing time. He arranged to meet two or more of them secretaries. I decide to visit Illianna.

"We stopped in to see Brother Bob," I tell her. "He sure is busy, might be real late getting home tonight." By the way Illianna look at me I know she don't want to hear any details.

We have coffee at her kitchen table and I play with Bobby for a while, then say I'd better get going. I bet Brother Bob still ain't in a mood to be apologized to.

"I've got a present for Ma's birthday," Illianna say, "you can take it back with you." She get up and walk to her bedroom and I follow. She walk into the big closet take a package wrapped in flowered paper off a shelf. The package was sitting right beside Indian Joe.

"You still got old Indian Joe," I say, act kind of surprised.

"I got my doll, too," Illianna says, move aside a blanket and sure enough there is her one-eyed, bald doll, what at one time had platinum-coloured hair. Illianna touch Indian Joe on the top of the head. "We been through a lot," she says, smile sad at me.

Indian Joe still sit behind his drum, wear green felt suspenders down the front of his red shirt. His black braids hang straight as sticks. His arms hold up in awkward half-circles, the little wood drumsticks forever poised.

"He sure does bring back a lot of memories," I say. I flip the switch in Indian Joe's back. "H-H-H-Rap, Tap-Tap …" go Indian Joe, which surprise me a lot. I didn't think batteries lasted for so many years.

"H-H-H-Rap, Tap-Tap," he go again, and, as I switch him off, I look at Illianna 'cause I hear her make a funny sound. My eyes catch her face just in time to see it falling in on itself. The tears flood out of her big, brown eyes.

I hold out my arms to her. She takes one step forward and clasp onto me real hard.

"Is there anything I can do?" I ask.

"No, everything's alright, Silas. Really, everything's alright."

"I know," I tell her, though I'm not sure I do. I think I can guess what she's feeling. For Illianna I bet it's one of those times when the past seems so far away—so permanently lost. I've had the feeling myself, a terrible sense of loss, like someone important has died. But then there's the worse feeling of not being able to name the person who'd died. It's a little like looking at your own grave.

I just hold her for a while as she cries into my shoulder. I believe her when she says everything's alright.

Then I hear Bobby come pounding in the back door. "Mom! Mom!" he calls.

Illianna pulls back, take a deep breath, wipes her eyes with her hands, wipes her hands on her jeans.

"Coming, honey," she says, and squeezes my hand as she turns away and walks out of the room, leaving me and Indian Joe staring at each other.

Jack Knox

Jack Knox is a humour columnist based in Victoria, B.C., where the flowers bloom in February and the sun fills the air like warm honey. But that's no reason to hate him. Among his career highlights, Knox lists "interviewing a porn star in the nude." (I'm assuming it was the porn star who was nude, not Jack. Though you never know...)

Chronology of a Crisis, Vancouver-Island Style

—*5:35 p.m.* Environment Canada predicts "two to five centimetres" of snow will fall on Victoria within a 24-hour period. TV weatherman reads the forecast on-air, turns white, and faints.

—*5:40 p.m.* Victoria Mayor Alan Lowe issues immediate appeal for federal assistance. Prime Minister Paul Martin promises to send in the army.

—*8:45 p.m.* Victorians begin queuing at tire stores, leaving vehicles in line overnight to be first served in morning.

—*10:15 p.m.* It turns out B.C.'s last army base, CFB Chilliwack, closed in 1998. Martin promises to send in navy instead.

—*10:20 p.m.* Navy announces deployment to San Diego and Hawaii for "security reasons."

—*6:22 a.m.* Temperature plunges. Word spreads that Saanich man found ice on windshield. Curious neighbours gather to watch him scrape it off with credit card. One motorist, a former Albertan, claims use of mysterious "defrost" switch on dashboard can aid in process.

—*8:15 a.m.* Terrified downtown skateboarders lose toques to menacing mob of balding, middle-aged men. "We tried to run," they say, "but those stupid baggy-assed pants made us fall down."

—*9:30 a.m.* Hardware stores sell both of their snow shovels. Islanders begin cobbling together implements made from kayak paddles, umbrellas, plywood, cookie sheets, and boogie boards.

—*10 a.m.* Golfers switch to orange balls. Beacon Hill Park cricket players, anxious not to repeat the ugly "snowblower incident" of the Blizzard of '96, switch to orange uniforms.

—*Noon.* Word of impending West Coast snowfall tops newscasts across Canada. Saskatoon hospitals report epidemic of sprained wrists related to viewers high-fiving one another.

—*1:20 p.m.* Elementary schools call in grief counsellors. Grief counsellors refuse to go, citing lack of snow tires.

—*2:30 p.m.* Rush hour begins an hour early as office workers come down with mysterious illness and bolt for home. Usual traffic snarl is compounded by large number of four-wheel-drives abandoned by side of road.

—*2:50 p.m.* Airplanes are grounded and ferries docked. No way to travel between Island and rest of the world. *Times Colonist* headline: *Mainland Cut Off From Civilization!*

—*3:22 p.m.* Prime Minister Martin announces Canada's DART rapid-response team can be on the ground "within six months."

"We can't leave Victoria to deal with 225 centimetres of snow on its own," he tells Lowe.

"Um, that's two-to-five centimetres, not two-two-five," replies the mayor.

The prime minister curses and hangs up.

—*3:33 p.m.* Provincial government responds to crisis by installing slot machines in homeless shelters.

—*4:10 p.m.* At behest of Provincial Emergency Program, authorities begin adding Prozac to drinking water.

—*4:15 p.m.* Fears of food shortage lead to alarming scenes of violence and looting. Grocery shoppers riot across the city, except in affluent Oak Bay, where residents hire caterers to do rioting for them.

—*4:30 p.m.* Bracing for the arrival of snow, the city is gripped by an eerie stillness reminiscent of Baghdad on the eve of the invasion. Searchlights comb darkening sky for first sign of precipitation.

—*4:48 p.m.* Panic ripples across region as word comes in that first flakes have fallen on Malahat. False alarm. "Flakes" turn out to be nothing more than anthrax spores released by terrorists. An uneasy calm returns to city.

—*5:40 p.m.* TV weatherman, shaking uncontrollably, tells viewers that snow warning has been extended. This weather pattern could go on for days. Mercury plummets to Calgary-in-August levels. Martial law is declared. Victoria-area politicians announce plans to establish emergency command centre aboard HMCS *Regina* ... once it reaches Oahu.

Canada (In Reverse)

I videotaped *Canada: A People's History* on CBC the other night. Came to the end and started watching it backwards. Here's what I learned.

Canada was born as a flourishing, cosmopolitan, industrialized country with two official languages, 30 million people, and 43 million land claims. It's difficult to believe that from such promising beginnings came the tumult, dissension, and decay that would later tear this nation apart.

Yet it didn't take long for the social upheaval to start. The oil crisis of the 1970s crippled the economy, creating a breeding ground for the radicals of the '60s. The prime minister was deposed in a popular uprising—Trudeaumania—in 1968, but this failed to stem the exodus of worried citizens. The population continued to decline. "*Ca-na-da, now we are 20 million*" lamented songwriter Bobby Gimby one year later.

In the 1950s, weary Canadians welcomed the return of stability. Life finally became ordered, prosperous—even dull. Although people enjoyed the material trappings of well-being, there was an emptiness to this soulless, suburban existence. A general *malaise* set in. There was a decline in social values.

This gave birth to a generation of angry, restless young men who, casting off the shackles of domestic ennui, set off in search of adventure. It wasn't pretty. They laid waste to Europe, wreaking such destruction that the Germans were forced to rise up and drive them out.

Shamed by their defeat and lacking in confidence, the young men came home with their tails between their legs, moving about the country aimlessly, refusing to work. This was called the Great Depression.

Eventually prosperity returned, and with it a sense of environmental responsibility. Gas-guzzling automobiles were abandoned in favour of trains, bicycles, and horses. Clearcuts were replanted. Pavement was ripped up.

Alas, as Canadians' spirits rose, so did their consumption of the same. The authorities brought in Prohibition, which, rather than fostering sobriety, stoked the fires of violence. Still seething after the defeat at the hands of the Germans, another generation of young men demanded a rematch. At least this time they confined the fighting to the trenches.

It was around this period that women, disgusted by the testosterone-driven political process, chose to stop voting. Indeed, millions of people, disillusioned by Canada's propensity for bellicosity, chose to move to Europe. With them gone, there was no need for a railroad, so they tore it up. Pierre Berton wept.

French-English tensions, never far from the surface, came to a head on July 1, 1867. Declaring "Rene Levesque was right," Quebec seceded. In fact, the entire country broke apart in a manner that echoed the collapse of the Soviet Union.

And yet, like battling brothers who forget their quarrel when threatened by another family, Canadians joined ranks behind chocolate heiress Laura Secord and took on the Americans in the War of 1812. Taking a cue from the expulsion of Japanese-Canadians in the 1940s, the government subsequently deported a group of enemy aliens known as the United Empire Loyalists.

Spurred by a couple of legacies of the Trudeau years—official bilingualism, Katimavik—the French and English attempted a *rapprochement,* moving in together at Quebec City in 1759. Unfortunately, the English couldn't figure out what "rapprochement" meant and, fearing that it had something to do with eating horse meat, decided to go back to Britain. The redcoats, led by General Bernard Wolfe, secretly gathered on the Plains of Abraham and snuck down the cliffs in the middle of the night, silently boarding their ships and making their getaway before the French knew they were gone.

Lonely without their English friends, the French hung on as long as they could. They tried to eke out a living by importing furs from the Paris fashion houses and selling them to the Natives, but it didn't work out. Gradually their numbers dwindled.

By the 1500s, Jacques Cartier had launched a full-scale evacuation of Europeans. In a scene eerily reminiscent of the last helicopter leaving Saigon in 1975, John Cabot weighed anchor and set sail for the continent in 1497.

"Thank God they've gone," said the Natives. "We thought they'd never leave."

Dany Laferrière

Haitian-born Montreal author Dany Laferrière made a lot of people uncomfortable with his debut novel, *Comment faire l'amour avec un Nègre sans se fatiguer* (which was translated into English as *How to Make Love to a Negro*—the coda "without getting tired" having been discreetly dropped). The book was a huge hit nonetheless and was made into an equally successful feature film. With caustic humour, Laferrière addresses issues of race and sexuality full force—and without flinching. The translations that follow are by David Homel.

FROM *Why Must a Black Writer Write About Sex?*
How to Be Famous Without Getting Tired

T he title of my first novel made me famous. People who never read the book, especially those who had no intention of reading it, can quote you the title. It took me five minutes to come up with it. Three years to write the book. If only I'd known ... Forget about those hundreds of scribbled pages; all I needed were ten little words: How to Make Love to a Negro without Getting Tired.

The different reactions to the title would make a case study in themselves.

• • •

1. A cocktail party in Outremont, a tony Montreal suburb.
"Are you the one who wrote the novel with that title?"
"I'm afraid so."

"Why do you say that? It's wonderful! You're so gifted!"

"Thank you."

(Should I make my move or not?)

She looked at me with a silly smile on her lips. Her husband smiled, too. They were art collectors who owned a clothing-store chain.

"My husband hasn't read the book, but your title really made him laugh, I can tell you that." She laughed, too. "It's hilarious!"

"We sell lingerie in some of our stores in smaller cities." The man looked vaguely embarrassed. "I was telling my wife that your title would be great in our catalogue."

"Don't listen to him," his wife, a voluptuous redhead, interrupted. "All he thinks about is business."

"Not at all," I said. "I think it's a good idea."

She laughed noisily and clapped her hands, which seemed to be her nervous tic.

"You'd actually do it! That's great! And best of all, he's not pretentious! You know, I absolutely must see you again."

"Now, listen," the husband said, slipping into his hardheaded business-man's voice. "We'll try it out in the spring catalogue. If it works, we'll sign a contract. I'm not racist, you understand, but I have to wait and see how the clientele reacts. But don't worry, I'm almost sure it'll work."

"What are you talking about? Of course it'll work."

She smiled at me as if we were already accomplices.

"It'll be an honour for us to have your name in our catalogue."

The husband led his wife off to the bar.

"Don't forget, we absolutely have to see each other. I insist …"

And she blew me a kiss.

• • •

2. In Madrid, a young feminist challenged me.

"I changed a word in your title. Do you want to know what it is?"

"Of course."

"How to make love to a Negro without getting *him* tired."

• • •

3. At the Leeds Film Festival, in England, this is what I told a girl who wanted to know why I chose a title like that.

"Young lady, if it weren't for that title, you probably wouldn't be here tonight."

The hall broke up.

• • •

4. In New York City, at the premiere of the film that was made from the novel, a girl (another one!) came up to me.

"Are you the author of that book?"

"Yes."

"Aren't you ashamed of using a title like that?"

She threw her glass of wine in my face.

• • •

5. In London, England, a very tall, very thin man put a drink into my hand.

"I've just finished a novel. My publisher tells me it will be a terrible success, but he doesn't like my title."

"Publishers are like that."

"My book is the first one, I believe," he said, smiling, "that speaks of a white man's attraction for black men."

"I see ..."

"According to my publisher, it's going to create a tremendous scandal. I have a favour to ask of you." His voice dropped. "It's very personal ... Naturally, you're free to say no."

Good Lord! I thought to myself, he's going to ask me to fellate him, right here, in the pub. These Englishmen are something else!

"May I borrow your title?"

"What?"

He smiled broadly.

"What do you think? It's never been done before—at least, never with the author's permission. My publisher says that if you agree, it's legally feasible. Your title is the only one that fits my subject. I've racked my brains, believe me, but all I find is your title."

"If mine is the only one, then take it. But I'm warning you, it'll bring you misery. It's not the kind of title you can get rid of easily."

"How to Make Love to a Negro without Getting Tired, by John Ferguson. My publisher will be absolutely overjoyed. You know, my publisher is a personal friend of Salman Rushdie's."

• • •

6. In Paris, a young woman who saw the lighter side of life told me over a glass of wine at the Café de Flore, "I bought your book, you know, but not to read it. I put it on my bedside table; it scares off pretenders."

• • •

7. A young white man in Chicago found the title offensive. A young black man in Los Angeles found it racist. A young Montreal woman found it sexist. *Jackpot!*

• • •

8. In Toronto, a woman was reading the book in a bus when she noticed that everyone was looking at her strangely.

"I didn't realize that people could read the title on the cover."

"And?"

"I've never been so embarrassed in my life."

• • •

9. In Tokyo, the title was completely changed because, as the Japanese distributor told me, "We don't have words like that in Japanese."

• • •

10. In Rome, a thin woman, just skin and bones, heading towards sixty, the contessa type, whispered in my ear.

"You'll never guess where I tattooed your title ..."

"I give up."

"That's what I thought," she said mysteriously, then slipped into the crowd of party-goers at the Duchessa Bocconcini's villa.

How the hell could she have put a title that long on such a small body?

• • •

11. In Port-au-Prince, a very demanding friend told me, "The title's the only good thing about your book."

• • •

12. In Brussels, an African writer practically screamed at me, "Mark my words, brother, in three weeks no one will even remember your book!"

• • •

13. In Antwerp, the translator improved on the title which became, in Dutch, *How to Make Love to a Negro without Turning Black.*

• • •

14. In the United States, all the major daily papers censored the title. *The New York Times,* the *Washington Post,* the *Miami Herald,* the *Los Angeles Times,* the *Chicago Tribune,* the *Daily News,* the *Boston Globe,* the *New York Post.* Every last one.

I was asked to change the title. I told them it was up to America to change.

• • •

15. In San Francisco, everyone liked the title. But that's San Francisco.

• • •

16. In Sydney, Australia, a straightforward young woman challenged me to prove the veracity of my title.

There are days like that.

• • •

17. In Stockholm, a young blonde (what a coincidence!) introduced me to her black lover.

"Ask Seko," she laughed, "who gets tired first."

"Seko, no doubt," I said.

Seko laughed a giant Guinean laugh.

"How to make love to two Negroes without getting tired," she murmured with night in her eyes.

Seko stopped laughing.

• • •

18. In Amsterdam, a young white South African woman demanded an answer to this painful question.

"How *do* you make love to a Negro without getting tired?"

"Let him do all the work."

• • •

19. All around the world, everyone asks me the same question. Why did you choose that title? Well, why not? One thing's for sure: I never want to hear about it again. I've overdosed on it. Nowadays, it makes me sick.

I'm going to tell you how it got started, once and for all. Bouba thought it up. I remember, we were walking down the rue Saint-Denis, in Montreal. It was raining. A summer rain. And Bouba said, as if in a dream, very slowly, "How to make love to a Negro when it's raining and you have nothing better to do." His title was too long, but it was funnier.

My first novel. The gods could at least have waited for the third before hitting on me. The first shot. Bull's-eye. Not even the first novel. The first novel's *title*.

FROM *How to Make Love to a Negro*

Must I Tell Her That a Slum Is Not a Salon?

M iz Literature comes sweeping in with an enormous bouquet of peonies. I'm still in bed with Bukowski. The window is closed. A line of sunlight cuts the page in half lengthwise.

I read lying down with a pillow between my shoulder blades and my head slightly raised. Stiff neck guaranteed. Unfortunately, it's my favourite position. Usually I read early in the morning before it gets too hot, when I'm not likely to be disturbed. The building emanates an aura of calm. My neighbours, retired for the most part, are not yet awake. In an hour or two it'll be the breakfast routine, the whistling of the pipes, the tap of toothbrushes, and the smell of bacon.

I watch Miz Literature move through the shadows. It looks like she's wearing a yellow dress with a white collar. And ballerina shoes. I picture her dressing with care, putting on perfume (just a soupçon!) and her bra (she has small breasts) so she can go do dishes for a Negro in a filthy apartment on St. Denis near the Carré St. Louis. Skid row. Miz Literature comes from a good family, she has a bright future, upright values, a solid education, perfect mastery of Elizabethan poetry, she belongs to a feminist literary club at McGill—the McGill Witches—whose mission is to restore the reputation of unjustly neglected poetesses. This year they are publishing a luxury edition of Emily Dickinson with ink drawings by Valery Miller. So what's going on here? You could hold a gun to her head and she wouldn't do the tenth of what she does here for a white guy. Miz Literature is writing her PhD thesis on Christine de Pisan. Which is no mean feat. So what the hell is she doing in this filthy slum? And don't blame Cupid. If she were madly in love with a McGill guy he'd never ask her to do the tenth of what she does here, spontaneously, freely, and graciously.

"Why do the dishes now?"

"Am I disturbing you?"

"Not really."

"You're reading! Oh, I'm sorry."

And believe it or not, she really is sorry. Reading is sacred in her book. Besides, a black with a book denotes the triumph of Judeo-Christian civilization! Proof that those bloody crusades really did have some value. True, Europe did pillage Africa but this black is reading a book.

"There, I finished."

She puts the clean dishes away carefully. A real jewel. Her only shortcoming is that she'll go to any length to make this room pleasant. Confer an Outremont touch to it. Every time she comes she brings something new. Pretty soon, in a few months, we'll be crushed under the weight of rare vases, engravings, bedside lamps, and all that crap you can buy in those snobby boutiques on Laurier Street. McGill people are taught to decorate their environment. Look what I've gotten myself into! All right, I can understand that part. But I don't get why she's doing it here in this slum. Must I tell her that a slum is not a salon? Maybe it's part of her double life. By day a WASP princess; by night slave to a Negro. That could be exciting. Suspense guaranteed because with Negroes you never know. Let's just eat her up right now, yum-yum, with a little salt and pepper. I can see the headlines in *La Presse*.

THE TALK OF THE TOWN—

"DID YOU HEAR? TWO BLACKS ATE A MCGILL CO-ED."

"HOW DID THEY DISCOVER THE CRIME?"

"THE POLICE FOUND HER ARM IN THE REFRIGERATOR."

"OH, GOOD LORD! IS THAT THE NEW IMMIGRATION POLICY?
IMPORTING CANNIBALS?"

"I SUPPOSE THEY RAPED HER FIRST, WHILE THEY WERE AT IT?"

"WE'LL NEVER KNOW, THEY ATE EVERYTHING."

"OH, GOOD LORD."

Miz Literature climbs into my bed. I put the book down at the foot of the bed, next to the bottle of wine, then bring her down to my level. Europe has paid her debt to Africa.

Gary Lautens

Here is a simple truth: writing domestic humour *seems* easy. Deceptively so. You don't need to venture afar; you just jot down the daily goings-on of your own household. A lot of writers think they can do it; very few can pull it off. In the 1980s, Gary Lautens was the acknowledged master of domestic humour, winning two Leacock Medals and a loyal readership for his tales of the Lautens Family: his loving but eccentric wife, their three children, and their assorted pets.

FROM *Take My Family ... Please!*

Dig Those Bones

The other morning my son announced that he would like to go to the museum and see dinosaur bones and some of the other items which his kindergarten teacher told him were on display.

"Why don't you turn on the television and watch cartoons," I suggested. "Popeye's Playhouse is on now."

"I don't like Popeye," he whined. "I want to go to the museum."

"It's too cold," I said, rattling my newspaper and sinking a little deeper into my easy chair.

"I'll wear my pyjamas under my pants," he offered.

"They don't have a TV at the museum," I warned.

"I don't like TV," he stated sullenly.

"You can even watch one of those shows which gives you nightmares," I bargained, figuring he could never resist that bit of cheese.

"I want to go to the museum," he replied.

"Why don't you wrestle your sister or crayon on the walls like any normal five-year-old kid?" I wanted to know.

"I'm going to tell my teacher you wouldn't take me to the museum," he threatened.

That was the clincher. On a Saturday morning when it's cold and windy the last thing I need is a museum. But I'm not going to take the chance of getting a bad reputation with any kindergarten teacher.

"Let's stop for something to warm us up," I suggested as we walked into the museum. "They have a swell coffee shop in the basement. You can have …"

"I want to see all the guns and swords," he reported, heading straight ahead.

I trailed along as he marched from one exhibit to another. "This one has eight barrels," he would say. Or, "Did they use swords when you were young, Daddy?"

"These exhibits are all pretty much the same," I pointed out. "I think we can skip the rest of …"

"No. I want to see them all," he insisted.

So we trooped from one aisle to another until I suggested that, perhaps, I could wait for him at the door.

"I need you to read to me," he stated, scuttling that plan.

"Don't you have to go to the bathroom?" I asked after we had knocked off a couple of rooms and about ten million exhibits.

"No," he said. "What's up the stairs?"

I told him it was mostly a storage area and not worth looking at. However, he wanted to see for himself.

"You're wrong, Daddy," he said joyfully as he hit the second floor and spotted some dinosaur bones fastened together with wire.

"They must have changed things," I grumbled.

We walked through that wing of the building and saw some stuffed animals and paraded past an array of fish and snakes and then paused at the stairway where I had to hold him out over the railing so he could see the top and bottom of the totem pole.

"I'll bet you could use a nice, cold drink and a piece of chocolate cake," I tempted.

"Let's go up to the next floor," he answered.

So we saw Chinese exhibits, Greek exhibits, Egyptian exhibits, and young schoolchildren giggling at the statues.

The best thing I saw was the elevator which, however, we didn't use.

"We had better sit down," I said. "I don't want to tire you out. Your mother might get mad at me."

"I'm not tired," he unfortunately revealed. However, I finally convinced him he should stop for something to eat so that he wouldn't wind up looking like that mummy he stared at so intently in the wooden box.

"Let's take the stairs down to the cafeteria," he suggested. "We can race."

During lunch he said he would like to hurry because there was plenty of museum we hadn't seen yet—like the Indian stuff in the basement.

That's when I put my foot down.

"We're going to go to the show this afternoon and see a Disney movie whether you like it or not. And we're going to sit through the whole thing," I instructed.

So that explains why that little boy I was pulling by the hand out of the museum was crying. I just hope he doesn't blab to his kindergarten teacher.

One Christmas Card Coming Up

Every year in December we go through what is known as picture time at our house. It's sort of like World War Three but without rules.

The tradition started years ago when my wife and I thought it would be a good idea to have a Christmas card featuring our children and dog. It would be folksy, we agreed. And, since we didn't intend to be explicit about the children's faith, nobody could take religious offence.

However, there was one problem: we didn't have any children or dog.

I was all for renting but my wife figured it would be cheaper in the long run to have our own.

So I wound up having these three kids and a St. Bernard dog (my wife can do anything if she puts her mind to it) on my hands.

For 364 days in the year they cost me money but on the 365th they have their one duty to perform: they pose for our Christmas card.

Well, yesterday was it.

For some unknown reason we never get the same photographer twice. In fact, last year the one we had never even came back for his hat.

All we want is a simple picture of three sweet kids and a lovable 195-pound dog smiling in the Christmas spirit.

I can't think of anything easier than that.

But it never quite works out that way.

I assembled the cast and converged on the rec room to find the floor littered with laundry.

"What are the sheets doing all over the bar stools?" I asked.

"They're supposed to be there," my wife replied.

"Why?"

"To look like snow," my wife explained. "Could you tell they're bar stools covered with sheets?"

"Never in a million years," I said. "It looks exactly like snow."

"Should we put the children on a toboggan and have it pulled by the dog?" my wife asked. "I could bend a coat-hanger and make it look like a pair of antlers."

"Sounds swell," I encouraged.

"You don't think it looks a little phony, do you?" she wanted to know.

"Don't be silly. I would never guess that it's a dog pulling a toboggan across a rec room floor past some bar stools covered with white sheets," I said. "If I didn't know better I'd swear I was looking in on a scene in the Laurentians."

My wife seemed pleased with that.

"Stephen!" she ordered. "Stop crossing your eyes." And then she added to me, "Do you think we should dress them like elves?"

I said it was fine by me. "Everything's fine just as long as we hurry."

The photographer, meanwhile, was setting up his lights and trying to keep out of reach of the dog who was going around smelling everybody's breath to see what they had enjoyed for dinner.

"Didn't you give the dog a tranquilizer?" I asked.

"No, I thought you had," my wife said.

"He's just a little excited," I explained to the photographer who was trying to get his camera bag out of the dog's mouth without much success. "C'mon, boy. Give us the bag."

"Jane! Stop punching your brother," my wife interrupted. "You'll make him blink for the picture."

We finally got the camera bag and the kids took their place and our "reindeer" gave a big yawn.

"Smile!" the photographer pleaded.

I made faces.

My wife waved toys.

It was swell except that nothing happened. One of the elves had pulled the floodlight cord out of the wall socket and was trying to screw it into his sister's ear.

There's no point going into all of the details. Within ninety minutes, or so, we had our picture and the photographer gratefully retrieved his camera bag and left. Next year I think I'll handle it differently.

I'll mail out the kids and the dog directly and not bother with a photograph.

Stephen Leacock

Stephen Leacock, the greatest humorist Canada has ever produced, deserves an anthology all his own. Fortunately, he already has it: *The Penguin Stephen Leacock* (25th Anniversary Edition), selected and introduced by none other than Robertson Davies, which contains a grand swath of Leacock's best work, including extended excerpts from *Sunshine Sketches of a Little Town* (wherein Leacock implodes the myths of small-town Canada) and *Arcadian Adventures with the Idle Rich* (which is practically a template for how to write social satire). With Robertson Davies picking up the slack, I had a much less daunting assignment making my own Leacockian selections. I picked some of Leacock's lesser-known but equally polished pieces, which don't usually appear in anthologies. (*Note:* Stephen Leacock wrote two essays with the title "We Have with Us Tonight." The one included here is the lesser known of the two.)

FROM *Literary Lapses*

A Model Dialogue

In which is shown how the drawing-room juggler may be permanently cured of his card trick.

The drawing-room juggler, having slyly got hold of the pack of cards at the end of the game of whist, says:

"Ever see any card tricks? Here's rather a good one; pick a card."

"Thank you, I don't want a card."

"No, but just pick one, any one you like, and I'll tell which one you pick."

"You'll tell who?"

"No, no; I mean, I'll know which it is, don't you see? Go on now, pick a card."

"Any one I like?"

"Yes."

"Any colour at all?"

"Yes, yes."

"Any suit?"

"Oh, yes; do go on."

"Well, let me see, I'll—pick—the—ace—of—spades."

"Great Caesar! I mean you are to pull a card out of the pack."

"Oh, to pull it out of the pack! Now I understand. Hand me the pack. All right—I've got it."

"Have you picked one?"

"Yes, it's the three of hearts. Did you know it?"

"Hang it! Don't tell me like that. You spoil the thing. Here, try again. Pick a card."

"All right, I've got it."

"Put it back in the pack. Thanks. (Shuffle, shuffle, shuffle—flip)— There, is that it?" (triumphantly).

"I don't know. I lost sight of it."

"Lost sight of it! Confound it, you have to look at it and see what it is."

"Oh, you want me to look at the front of it!"

"Why, of course! Now then, pick a card."

"All right. I've picked it. Go ahead." (Shuffle, shuffle, shuffle—flip.)

"Say, confound you, did you put that card back in the pack?"

"Why, no. I kept it."

"Holy Moses! Listen. Pick—a—card—just one—look at it—see what it is—then put it back—do you understand?"

"Oh, perfectly. Only I don't see how you are ever going to do it. You must be awfully clever."

(Shuffle, shuffle, shuffle—flip.)

"There you are; that's your card, now, isn't it?" (This is the supreme moment.)

"NO. THAT IS NOT MY CARD." (This is a flat lie, but Heaven will pardon you for it.)

"Not that card ! ! ! ! Say—just hold on a second. Here, now, watch what you're at this time. I can do this cursed thing, mind you, every time. I've done it on father, on mother, and on every one that's ever come round our place. Pick a card. (Shuffle, shuffle, shuffle—flip, bang.) There, that's your card."

"NO. I AM SORRY. THAT IS NOT MY CARD. But won't you try it again? Please do. Perhaps you are a little excited—I'm afraid I was rather stupid. Won't you go and sit quietly by yourself on the back verandah for half an hour and then try? You have to go home? Oh, I'm so sorry. It must be such an awfully clever little trick. Good night!"

FROM *Winnowed Wisdom*

Leacock's "Outlines of Everything"

Volume One—The Outline of Shakespeare

*D*esigned to make Research Students in Fifteen Minutes. A Ph.D. degree granted immediately after reading it.

Life of Shakespeare. We do not know when Shaksper was born nor where he was born. But he is dead.

From internal evidence taken off his works after his death we know that he followed for a time the profession of a lawyer, a sailor, and a scrivener and he was also an actor, a bartender, and an ostler. His wide experience of men and manners was probably gained while a bartender. (Compare: *Henry V,* Act V, Scene 2. "*Say now, gentlemen, what shalt yours be?*")

But the technical knowledge which is evident upon every page shows also the intellectual training of a lawyer. (Compare: *Macbeth,* Act VI,

Scene 4. *"What is there in it for me?"*) At the same time we are reminded by many passages of Shakspere's intimate knowledge of the sea. (*Romeo and Juliet.* Act VIII, Scene 14. *"How is her head now, nurse?"*)

We know, from his use of English, that Shagsper had no college education.

. . .

His Probable Probabilities

As an actor Shicksper, according to the current legend, was of no great talent. He is said to have acted the part of a ghost and he also probably took parts as *Enter a citizen, a Tucket sounds, a Dog barks, or a Bell is heard within.* (Note. We ourselves also have been a Tucket, a Bell, a Dog, and so forth in our college dramatics days. Ed.)

In regard to the personality of Shakespere, or what we might call in the language of the day Shakespere the Man, we cannot do better than to quote the following excellent analysis done, we think, by Professor Gilbert Murray, though we believe that Brander Matthews helped him a little on the side.

"Shakespere was probably a genial man who probably liked his friends and probably spent a good deal of time in probable social intercourse. He was probably good tempered and easy going with very likely a bad temper. We know that he drank (Compare: *Titus Andronicus,* Act I, Scene I. *"What's there to drink?"*), but most likely not to excess. (Compare: *King Lear,* Act II, Scene I. *"Stop!"* and see also *Macbeth,* Act X, Scene 20. *"Hold! Enough!"*) Shakespere was probably fond of children and most likely of dogs, but we don't know how he stood on porcupines.

"We imagine Shakespeare sitting among his cronies in Mitre Tavern, joining in the chorus of their probable songs, and draining a probable glass of ale, or at times falling into reverie in which the majestic pageant of Julius Caesar passes across his brooding mind."

To this excellent analysis we will only add. We can also imagine him sitting anywhere else we like—that in fact is the chief charm of Shakesperian criticism.

The one certain thing which we know about Shakespere is that in his will he left his second best bed to his wife.

Since the death of S. his native town—either Stratford upon Avon or somewhere else—has become a hallowed spot for the educated tourist. It is strange to stand today in the quiet street of the little town and to think that here Shakespeare actually lived—either here or elsewhere—and that England's noblest bard once mused among these willows—or others.

• • •

Works of Shakespeare

Our first mention must be of the Sonnets, written probably, according to Professor Matthews, during Shakesbur's life and not after his death. There is a haunting beauty about these sonnets which prevents us from remembering what they are about. But for the busy man of today it is enough to mention, "Drink to Me Only With Thine Eyes," "Rock Me to Sleep Mother," "Hark, Hark the Dogs do Bark." Oh, yes, quite enough. It will get past him every time.

• • •

The Historical Plays

Among the greatest of Shakespeare's achievements are his historical plays,— Henry I, Henry II, Henry III, Henry IV, Henry V, Henry VI, Henry VII, and Henry VIII. It is thought that Shakespeare was engaged on a play dealing with Henry IX when he died. It is said to have been his opinion that having struck a good thing he had better stay with it.

There is doubt as to authorship of part, or all, of some of these historical plays. In the case of Henry V, for example, it is held by the best critics that the opening scene (100 lines) was done by Ben Jonson. Then Shakespeare wrote 200 lines (all but half a line in the middle) which undoubtedly is Marlowe's.

Then Jonson, with a little help from Fletcher, wrote 100 lines. After that Shakespear, Massinger, and Marlowe put in 10 lines each. But from this point the authorship is confused, each sticking in what he could.

But we ourselves are under no misapprehension as to what is Shakespeare's and what is not. There is a touch which we recognize every time. When we see the real Shakespeare, we know it. Thus, whenever it says

"A Tucket Sounds, Enter Gloucester with Hoboes," we know that Shakespeare, and only Shakespeare, could have thought of that. In fact Shakespeare could bring in things that were all his own, such as:— *"Enter Cambridge followed by An Axe." "Enter Oxford followed by a Link."* His lesser collaborators could never get the same niceness of touch. Thus, when we read, "Enter the Earl of Richmond followed by a pup," we realize that it is poor work.

Another way in which we are able to test whether or not a historical play is from Shakespeare's own pen is by the mode of address used by the characters. They are made to call one another by place designations instead of by their real names. "What says our brother France?" or "Well, Belgium, how looks it to you?" "Speak on, good Burgundy, our ears are yours." We ourselves have tried to imitate this but could never quite get it; our attempt to call our friends "Apartment B, the Grosvenor," and to say "Go to it, the Marlborough, Top Floor No. 6" has practically ended in failure.

• • •

The Great Tragedies

Every educated person should carry in his mind an outline idea of the greatest of Shakespeare's tragedies. This outline when reduced to what is actually remembered by playgoers and students is not difficult to acquire. Sample:

Hamlet. Hamlet, Prince of Denmark, lived among priceless scenery and was all dressed in black velvet. He was deeply melancholy. Either because he was mad, or because he was not, Hamlet killed his uncle and destroyed various other people whose names one does not recall.

The shock of this drove Ophelia to drown herself, but oddly enough when she threw herself in the water she floated, and went down the river singing and shouting. In the end Hamlet killed Laertes and himself, and others leaped into his grave until it was quite full when the play ends. People who possess this accurate recollection rightly consider themselves superior to others.

• • •

Shakespeare and Comparative Literature

Modern scholarship has added greatly to the interest in Shakespeare's work by investigating the sources from which he took his plays. It appears that in practically all cases they were old stuff already. Hamlet quite evidently can be traced to an old Babylonian play called *Humlid* and this itself is perhaps only a version of a Hindoo tragedy, *The Life of William Johnson.*

The play of Lear was very likely taken by S. from the old Chinese drama of *Li-Po,* while Macbeth, under the skilled investigation of modern scholars, shows distinct traces of a Scottish origin.

In effect, Shakespeare, instead of sitting down and making up a play out of his head, appears to have rummaged among sagas, myths, legends, archives, and folklore, much of which must have taken him years to find.

• • •

Personal Appearance

In person Shakespeare is generally represented as having a pointed beard and bobbed hair, with a bald forehead, large wide eyes, a salient nose, a retreating chin, and a general expression of vacuity, verging on imbecility.

• • •

Summary

The following characteristics of Shakespeare's work should be memorized— majesty, sublimity, grace, harmony, altitude, also scope, range, reach, together with grasp, comprehension, force and light, heat and power.

Conclusion: Shakespeare is a very good writer.

FROM *Too Much College*

We Have with Us Tonight

P ublic speaking is more or less of an ordeal even for those who have to undertake it constantly. Worse than all is speaking at a dinner, because you have to wait your turn and feel it coming for hours. Next time you are at a public dinner notice the men at the head table who sit and eat celery by the bunch and never stop. Those are the men who are going to speak.

I don't say that trained speakers are nervous. No. They wish the chairman would announce that the rest of the meeting is cancelled because of smallpox, or that the hotel would catch fire, or that there would be an earthquake. But they're not nervous.

But if speaking is an ordeal to *them,* what it is to those who have never spoken. Some men go through life and never have to speak; they rise to wealth and standing with the fear of it in the background—fear, with an element of temptation.

Such a one was my senior acquaintance of long ago, Mr. Gritterly—no harm to name him—general manager of the Toronto banks. He had just retired, without even speaking in public, when a Bankers' Three Days Convention came to town and they invited Mr. Gritterly to speak at the dinner.

He accepted, hung in the wind, flew round the flame—and finally, on the opening day, sent a note that he was called out of town for the evening.

I saw him round the hotel next morning. He was telling me how sorry he was to have missed the opportunity. He told me a lot of things he could have said about branch banking. He said, too, that he would like to have had a sly joke, very good-natured of course, about the American Treasury system. It was too bad, he said, he'd been called out of town. He had even intended, just in an offhand way, to get off one or two quotations from Shakespeare (he had them in his pocket). One read—"I know a bank whereon a wild thyme grows—" Gritterly thought that would get a laugh, eh? Too bad, he said, that he couldn't get that off.

"But, Mr. Gritterly," I said, "you're making a mistake. They didn't have the dinner last night. The trains were so late they only had the inaugural address. The dinner's tonight. You'll probably get an invitation—"

And as I spoke a boy brought it to him on a tray.

"So you see you'll be able to tell them about branch banking."

"Yes," said Mr. Gritterly, "yes."

"And the jokes about the U.S. Treasury."

"Yes," said Mr. Gritterly, "quite so."

All day Gritterly was round the hotel pulling the little bits of Shakespeare out of his pocket.

But the thing beat him.

In due course at the dinner the chairman announced: "I regret very much that Mr. Gritterly will not be able to speak. His speech, of which he gave me an outline, would have been a great treat. Unfortunately he had to leave tonight"—the chairman consulted his notes—"for Japan. With your permission I will take on myself to cable our representatives and I am sure they'll be glad to get up a dinner for Mr. Gritterly at Tokyo."

Gritterly got the invitation on board ship and went right on to Hong Kong. The bankers there received a cable and organized a lunch. Gritterly had gone on to Singapore but the bankers followed him up, and he left for Calcutta. They lost him somewhere in Tibet. He may have entered the monastery there. For many people that would be preferable to speaking.

FROM *Nonsense Novels*

Soaked in Seaweed: or Upset in the Ocean

(An Old-Fashioned Sea Story)

It was in August in 1867 that I stepped on board the deck of the *Saucy Sally*, lying in dock at Gravesend, to fill the berth of second mate.

Let me first say a word about myself.

I was a tall, handsome young fellow, squarely and powerfully built, bronzed by the sun and the moon (and even copper-coloured in spots from the effect of the stars), and with a face in which honesty, intelligence, and exceptional brain power were combined with Christianity, simplicity, and modesty.

As I stepped on the deck I could not help a slight feeling of triumph, as I caught sight of my sailor-like features reflected in a tar-barrel that stood beside the mast, while a little later I could scarcely repress a sense of gratification as I noticed them reflected again in a bucket of bilge water.

"Welcome on board, Mr Blowhard," called out Captain Bilge, stepping out of the binnacle and shaking hands across the taffrail.

I saw before me a fine sailor-like man of from thirty to sixty, clean-shaven, except for an enormous pair of whiskers, a heavy beard, and a thick moustache, powerful in build, and carrying his beam well aft, in a pair of broad duck trousers across the back of which there would have been room to write a history of the British Navy.

Beside him were the first and third mates, both of them being quiet men of poor stature, who looked at Captain Bilge with what seemed to me an apprehensive expression in their eyes.

The vessel was on the eve of departure. Her deck presented that scene of bustle and alacrity dear to the sailor's heart. Men were busy nailing up the masts, hanging the bowsprit over the side, varnishing the lee-scuppers, and pouring hot tar down the companionway.

Captain Bilge, with a megaphone to his lips, kept calling out to the men in his rough sailor fashion:

"Now, then, don't over-exert yourselves, gentlemen. Remember, please, that we have plenty of time. Keep out of the sun as much as you can. Step carefully in the rigging there, Jones; I fear it's just a little high for you. Tut, tut, Williams, don't get yourself so dirty with that tar, you won't look fit to be seen."

I stood leaning over the gaff of the mainsail and thinking—yes, thinking, dear reader, of my mother. I hope that you will think none the less of me for that. Whenever things look dark, I lean up against something and think of Mother. If they get positively black, I stand on one leg and think of Father. After that I can face anything.

Did I think, too, of another, younger than Mother and fairer than Father? Yes, I did. "Bear up, darling," I had whispered as she nestled her head beneath my oilskins and kicked out backwards with one heel in the agony of her girlish grief, "in five years the voyage will be over, and after three more like it, I shall come back with money enough to buy a second-hand fishing-net and settle down on shore."

Meantime the ship's preparations were complete. The masts were all in position, the sails nailed up, and men with axes were busily chopping away the gangway.

"All ready?" called the Captain.

"Aye, aye, sir."

"Then hoist the anchor in board and send a man down with the key to open the bar."

Opening the bar! the last sad rite of departure. How often in my voyages have I seen it; the little group of men soon to be exiled from their home, standing about with saddened faces, waiting to see the man with the key open the bar—held there by some strange fascination.

• • •

Next morning with a fair wind astern we had buzzed around the corner of England and were running down the Channel.

I know no finer sight, for those who have never seen it, than the English Channel. It is the highway of the world. Ships of all nations are passing up and down, Dutch, Scotch, Venezuelan, and even American.

Chinese junks rush to and fro. Warships, motor yachts, icebergs, and lumber rafts are everywhere. If I add to this fact that so thick a fog hangs over it that it is entirely hidden from sight, my readers can form some idea of the majesty of the scene.

• • •

We had now been three days at sea. My first seasickness was wearing off, and I thought less of Father.

On the third morning Captain Bilge descended to my cabin.

"Mr Blowhard," he said, "I must ask you to stand double watches."

"What is the matter?" I inquired.

"The two other mates have fallen overboard," he said uneasily and avoiding my eye.

I contented myself with saying "Very good, sir," but I could not help thinking it a trifle odd that both the mates should have fallen overboard in the same night.

Surely there was some mystery in this.

Two mornings later the Captain appeared at the breakfast table with the same shifting and uneasy look in his eye.

"Anything wrong, sir?" I asked.

"Yes," he answered, trying to appear at ease and twisting a fried egg to and fro between his fingers with such nervous force as almost to break it in two—"I regret to say that we have lost the bosun."

"The bosun!" I cried.

"Yes," said Captain Bilge more quietly, "he is overboard. I blame myself for it, partly. It was early this morning. I was holding him up in my arms to look at an iceberg and, quite accidentally I assure you, I dropped him overboard."

"Captain Bilge," I asked, "have you taken any steps to recover him?"

"Not as yet," he replied uneasily.

I looked at him fixedly, but said nothing.

Ten days passed.

The mystery thickened. On Thursday two men of the starboard watch were reported missing. On Friday the carpenter's assistant disappeared. On the night of Saturday a circumstance occurred which, slight as it was, gave me some clue as to what was happening.

As I stood at the wheel about midnight, I saw the Captain approach in the darkness carrying the cabin boy by the hind leg. The lad was a bright little fellow, whose merry disposition had already endeared him to me, and I watched with some interest to see what the Captain would do to him. Arrived at the stern of the vessel, Captain Bilge looked cautiously around a moment and then dropped the boy into the sea. For a brief instant the lad's head appeared in the phosphorus of the waves. The Captain threw a boot at him, sighed deeply, and went below.

Here then was the key to the mystery! The Captain was throwing the crew overboard. Next morning we met at breakfast as usual.

"Poor little Williams has fallen overboard," said the Captain, seizing a strip of ship's bacon and tearing at it with his teeth as if he almost meant to eat it.

"Captain," I said, greatly excited, stabbing at a ship's loaf in my agitation with such ferocity as almost to drive my knife into it, "you threw that boy overboard!"

"I did," said Captain Bilge, grown suddenly quiet, "I threw them all over and intend to throw the rest. Listen, Blowhard, you are young, ambitious, and trustworthy. I will confide in you."

Perfectly calm now, he stepped to a locker, rummaged in it a moment, and drew out a faded piece of yellow parchment, which he spread on the table. It was a map or chart. In the centre of it was a circle. In the middle of the circle was a small dot and a letter T, while at one side of the map was a letter N, and against it on the other side a letter S.

"What is this?" I asked.

"Can you not guess ?" queried Captain Bilge. "It is a desert island."

"Ah!" I rejoined with a sudden flash of intuition, "and N is for North and S is for South."

"Blowhard," said the Captain, striking the table with such force as to cause a loaf of ship's bread to bounce up and down three or four times, "you've struck it. That part of it had not yet occurred to me."

"And the letter T?" I asked.

"The treasure, the buried treasure," said the Captain, and turning the map over he read from the back of it, "The point T indicates the spot where the treasure is buried under the sand; it consists of half a million Spanish dollars, and is buried in a brown leather dress-suit case."

"And where is the island?" I inquired, mad with excitement.

"That I do not know," said the Captain. "I intend to sail up and down the parallels of latitude until I find it."

"And meantime?"

"Meantime, the first thing to do is to reduce the number of the crew so as to have fewer hands to divide among. Come, come," he added in a burst of frankness which made me love the man in spite of his shortcomings, "will you join me in this? We'll throw them all over, keeping the cook to the last, dig up the treasure, and be rich for the rest of our lives."

Reader, do you blame me if I said yes? I was young, ardent, ambitious, full of bright hopes and boyish enthusiasm.

"Captain Bilge," I said, putting my hand in his, "I am yours."

"Good," he said. "Now go forward to the forecastle and get an idea what the men are thinking."

I went forward to the men's quarters—a plain room in the front of the ship, with only a rough carpet on the floor, a few simple armchairs, writing-desks, spittoons of a plain pattern, and small brass beds with blue-and-green screens. It was Sunday morning, and the men were mostly sitting about in their dressing-gowns.

They rose as I entered and curtseyed.

"Sir," said Tompkins, the bosun's mate, "I think it my duty to tell you that there is a great deal of dissatisfaction among the men."

Several of the men nodded.

"They don't like the way the men keep going overboard," he continued, his voice rising to a tone of uncontrolled passion. "It is positively absurd, sir, and if you will allow me to say so, the men are far from pleased."

"Tompkins," I said sternly, "you must understand that my position will not allow me to listen to mutinous language of this sort."

I returned to the Captain. "I think the men mean mutiny," I said.

"Good," said Captain Bilge, rubbing his hands, "that will get rid of a lot of them, and of course," he added musingly, looking out of the broad old-fashioned porthole at the stern of the cabin, at the heaving waves of the South Atlantic, "I am expecting pirates at any time, and that will take out quite a few of them. However"—and here he pressed the bell for a cabin-boy—"kindly ask Mr Tompkins to step this way."

"Tompkins," said the Captain as the bosun's mate entered, "be good enough to stand on the locker and stick your head through the stern port-hole, and tell me what you think of the weather."

"Aye, aye, sir," replied the tar with a simplicity which caused us to exchange a quiet smile.

Tompkins stood on the locker and put his head and shoulders out of the port.

Taking a leg each we pushed him through. We heard him plump into the sea.

"Tompkins was easy," said Captain Bilge. "Excuse me as I enter his death in the log."

"Yes," he continued presently, "it will be a great help if they mutiny. I suppose they will, sooner or later. It's customary to do so. But I shall take no step to precipitate it until we have first fallen in with pirates. I am expecting them in these latitudes at any time. Meantime, Mr Blowhard," he said, rising, "if you can continue to drop overboard one or two more each week, I shall feel extremely grateful."

Three days later we rounded the Cape of Good Hope and entered upon the inky waters of the Indian Ocean. Our course lay now in zigzags and, the weather being favourable, we sailed up and down at a furious rate over a sea as calm as glass.

On the fourth day a pirate ship appeared. Reader, I do not know if you have ever seen a pirate ship. The sight was one to appall the stoutest heart. The entire ship was painted black, a black flag hung at the masthead, the sails were black, and on the deck people dressed all in black walked up and down arm-in-arm. The words "Pirate Ship" were painted in white letters on the bow. At the sight of it our crew were visibly cowed. It was a spectacle that would have cowed a dog.

The two ships were brought side by side. They were then lashed tightly together with bag string and binder twine, and a gang plank laid between them. In a moment the pirates swarmed upon our deck, rolling their eyes, gnashing their teeth, and filing their nails.

Then the fight began. It lasted two hours—with fifteen minutes off for lunch. It was awful. The men grappled with one another, kicked one another from behind, slapped one another across the face, and in many cases completely lost their temper and tried to bite one another. I noticed one gigantic fellow brandishing a knotted towel, and striking right and left among our men, until Captain Bilge rushed at him and struck him flat across the mouth with a banana skin.

At the end of two hours, by mutual consent, the fight was declared a draw. The points standing at sixty-one and a half against sixty-two.

The ships were unlashed, and with three cheers from each crew, were headed on their way.

"Now, then," said the Captain to me aside, "let us see how many of the crew are sufficiently exhausted to be thrown overboard."

He went below. In a few minutes he reappeared, his face deadly pale. "Blowhard," he said, "the ship is sinking. One of the pirates (sheer accident, of course, I blame no one) has kicked a hole in the side. Let us sound the well."

We put our ear to the ship's well. It sounded like water.

The men were put to the pumps and worked with the frenzied effort which only those who have been drowned in a sinking ship can understand.

At six P.M. the well marked one half an inch of water, at nightfall three-quarters of an inch, and at daybreak, after a night of unremitting toil, seven-eighths of an inch.

By noon of the next day the water had risen to fifteen-sixteenths of an inch, and on the next night the sounding showed thirty-one thirty-seconds of an inch of water in the hold. The situation was desperate. At this rate of increase few, if any, could tell where it would rise to in a few days.

That night the Captain called me to his cabin. He had a book of mathematical tables in front of him, and great sheets of vulgar fractions littered the floor on all sides.

"The ship is bound to sink," he said, "in fact, Blowhard, she is sinking. I can prove it. It may be six months or it may take years, but if she goes on like this, sink she must. There is nothing for it but to abandon her."

That night, in the dead of darkness, while the crew were busy at the pumps, the Captain and I built a raft.

Unobserved we cut down the masts, chopped them into suitable lengths, laid them crosswise in a pile and lashed them tightly together with bootlaces.

Hastily we threw on board a couple of boxes of food and bottles of drink-ing fluid, a sextant, a cronometer, a gas-meter, a bicycle pump, and a few other scientific instruments. Then taking advantage of a roll in the motion of the ship, we launched the raft, lowered ourselves upon a line, and under cover of the heavy dark of a tropical night, we paddled away from the doomed vessel.

The break of day found us a tiny speck on the Indian Ocean. We looked about as big as this (.).

In the morning, after dressing, and shaving as best we could, we opened our box of food and drink.

Then came the awful horror of our situation.

One by one the Captain took from the box the square blue tins of canned beef which it contained. We counted fifty-two in all. Anxiously and with drawn faces we watched until the last can was lifted from the box. A single thought was in our minds. When the end came the Captain stood up on the raft with wild eyes staring at the sky.

"The can-opener!" he shrieked. "Just Heaven, the can-opener." He fell prostrate.

Meantime, with trembling hands, I opened the box of bottles. It contained lager beer bottles, each with a patent tin top. One by one I took them out. There were fifty-two in all. As I withdrew the last one and saw the empty box before me, I shrieked out, "The thing! the thing! oh, merciful Heaven! The thing you open them with!"

I fell prostrate upon the Captain.

We awoke to find ourselves still a mere speck upon the ocean. We felt even smaller than before.

Over us was the burnished copper sky of the tropics. The heavy, leaden sea lapped the sides of the raft. All about us was a litter of corn beef cans and lager beer bottles. Our sufferings in the ensuing days were indescribable. We beat and thumped at the cans with our fists. Even at the risk of spoiling the tins for ever we hammered them fiercely against the raft. We stamped on them, bit at them, and swore at them. We pulled and clawed at the bottles with our hands, and chipped and knocked them against the cans, regardless even of breaking the glass and ruining the bottles.

It was futile.

Then day after day we sat in moody silence, gnawed with hunger, with nothing to read, nothing to smoke, and practically nothing to talk about.

On the tenth day the Captain broke silence.

"Get ready the lots, Blowhard," he said. "It's got to come to that."

"Yes," I answered drearily, "we're getting thinner every day."

Then, with the awful prospect of cannibalism before us, we drew lots.

I prepared the lots and held them to the Captain. He drew the longer one.

"Which does that mean," he asked, trembling between hope and despair. "Do I win?"

"No, Bilge," I said sadly, "you lose."

But I mustn't dwell on the days that followed—the long quiet days of lazy dreaming on the raft, during which I slowly built up my strength, which had been shattered by privation. They were days, dear reader, of deep and quiet peace, and yet I cannot recall them without shedding a tear for the brave man who made them what they were.

It was on the fifth day after that I was awakened from a sound sleep by the bumping of the raft against the shore. I had eaten perhaps overheartily, and had not observed the vicinity of land.

Before me was an island, the circular shape of which, with its low, sandy shore, recalled at once its identity.

"The treasure island!" I cried. "At last I am rewarded for all my heroism."

In a fever of haste I rushed to the centre of the island. What was the sight that confronted me? A great hollow scooped in the sand, an empty dress-suit case lying beside it, and on a ship's plank driven deep into the sand, the legend, "Saucy Sally, October, 1867." So! the miscreants had made good the vessel, headed it for the island of whose existence they must have learned from the chart we so carelessly left upon the cabin table, and had plundered poor Bilge and me of our well-earned treasure!

Sick with the sense of human ingratitude I sank upon the sand.

The island became my home.

There I eked out a miserable existence, feeding on sand and gravel and dressing myself in cactus plants. Years passed. Eating sand and mud slowly undermined my robust constitution. I fell ill. I died. I buried myself.

Would that others who write sea stories would do as much.

Antonine Maillet

Antonine Maillet, from the Acadian region of New Brunswick, is
the celebrated author of *La Sagouine,* which features an elderly
washerwoman who appears on stage, speaking in heavy dialect
about the poverty and defiant pride that has shaped her life. As
cultural heroine, *La Sagouine* stands in stark contrast to the
romanticized view of Acadians presented by Longfellow's
Evangeline. The following is from Maillet's wonderful fable
The Tale of Don L'Orignal, which is very much in the Swiftian
tradition and won the Governor General's Award for French
Literature. The translation here is by Barbara Godard.

FROM *The Tale of Don L'Orignal*

Concerning the strange birth of a little island destined to be great

On the shores of the country right next to yours where I still live, in
front of a village whose name I've forgotten how to spell, there arose
one fine morning in the middle of the ocean a sort of yellow blob that looked
just like a golden whale.

Such a phenomenon had never occurred before so close to their country.
As soon as the alarm was given, the mainlanders hurried to the shore and
spent the morning there deep in contemplation. Then at noon, the mayor
shivered, tossed her feathered bun, and proclaimed her profoundest thoughts
to the assembled town.

"It's an island of hay," she said.

The barber, the milliner, the merchant, the schoolmaster, the banker, the nursing sister, and the older children instantly relaxed, and their rapture faded away.

"It's only an island," passed from mouth to mouth, "an island of hay."

And each returned to his business or way of life, leaving the island of hay to the sea that had brought it into the world.

However, oceans that give birth to islands don't take them back until they've done their time and fulfilled their destiny, gambolling and splashing about, and spattering nearby shores too, if they don't watch out. This is what the island of hay did. Its neighbours had underestimated how deep and solid it was.

Thus the people of the mainland turned their eyes and attention away from the island, too eager to plant, hoe, pick, gather, produce, and market to concern themselves with a tiny little island of hay. And so it was able to shoot up and flower in peace, ignored and forsaken by all continents.

But one night, the lighthouse keeper directed his searchlight at the island and felt something crawl under his shirt. In the hay at the end of his spyglass, he had just caught sight of a whole species of jumping, flying, biting creatures on feet, strangely resembling a population of fleas. The island of hay was inhabited, occupied by the most execrable and contagious race that any civilized neighbour (made respectable by centuries of culture) could ever have feared.

The island of hay was an island of fleas.

The keeper lost no time. He went down the one hundred and thirty-two steps of the lighthouse without counting. Short of breath, his faith shaken, he roused the sleeping village from the repose of the just. In less than an hour, the best minds of the town (cultivated by the mayor, barber, milliner, merchant, schoolmaster, banker, and nursing sister) surrounded the breathless, pale face of the keeper. And there in the square, on a starless and moonless night, the inhabitants of the mainland learned that the island of hay was an island of fleas. And they resolved, that night, to destroy it.

To anyone who has never set his mind to such a task, the destruction of an island might seem like child's play, just a matter of sending it back where it came from—in this case to the bottom of the sea. Since it had already grown too big for a single kick or blow to sink it, the barber proposed to cut it first into little pieces, then give each district of the town its slice of island to set upon and finish off. The milliner found this method shameful and pernicious and suggested instead a powerful insecticide, capable of reducing the very roots of life to cinders, drying up the island so it would float away over foreign seas and run aground some day at the other end of the world. The merchant expressed the opinion that they should sell it to a neighbouring country and, to this end, at once began to proclaim the discovery of a new world.

"Terra incognita," uttered the schoolmaster.

But the mayor remained deaf to all this considered advice, continuing to gnaw on the lace of her high collar.

The banker proposed that they destroy the fleas but save the island, since all empty land is valuable real estate which one could exploit or inhabit. The nursing sister fell in with this position, on the condition, however, that the fleas not be harmed.

Meanwhile, seeing that the deliberations were going on so long (many suns could have risen and set since the discovery of the island and many moons since the finding of the fleas), the keeper had climbed back up the one hundred and thirty-two steps of his lighthouse. And it was there, at the point where the sky, land, and water meet, that he saw the sun rise one fine day on the extraordinary and unforeseeable event which is the subject of this very true story. Flea Island was peopled with men, women, children, dogs, cats, and rabbits. An entire species had landed on the island or had risen up through the hay or had somehow evolved from the fleas. However it happened, a people had been born, had built their shacks and dug wells there. They were there, standing upright, feet dug into the soft soil of the island, chests thrust forward, and brows lashed by the four winds.

Concerning the kingdom of Flea Island, where, in those days, reigned the noble and formidable Don l'Orignal

The little island rapidly grew in importance. For nothing is peopled as quickly as an isolated, barren land, neglected by everyone, since good lands remain by right the lot of the upper class, that uncommon and scattered species so scrupulously called the elite. Thus, in less time than it would take to establish a respectable family on the firm soil of the mainland, the soft soil of the island had engendered a nation.

The citizens of the mainland never knew how life had been organized over there, when a government had been formed or laws established. But they learned from the keeper that a coronation had certainly taken place, since Flea Island had become a kingdom. Indeed, every evening the light-housekeeper could follow the ceremony taking place around a shack slightly taller than the others. In front of this shack a horned colossus, bearded and hairy, was enthroned on a stump.

Don l'Orignal wore fake horns at the four corners of his fur hat, just to show that he was king. But the beard and the hair were his own. He put buckskin on his shoulders and pigskin boots on his feet. Dressed in this manner, Don l'Orignal ruled over Flea Island as king and over his house as the father of an only son. This son almost never slept under his father's roof. Not that Don l'Orignal had tyrannized his son, the hard and fearless knight, Noume, but the valorous Noume had many chicks to pluck those nights.

The inhabitants of Flea Island needed only to cross half an ocean to land on the mainland, and, for this reason, the mainland felt constantly threatened.

"Their island looks like a soldier's boot," said the barber.

"Like a battleship," said the milliner.

But neither the milliner nor the baker had ever seen a war. They only talked about it because they had read the history of the Boer War which sat on the top shelf of the municipal library. For three and a half months they had discussed the book, arguing about everything—the style, the ideas, the thesis, the language, the style, the thesis, the chapter divisions, the composition, the ideas, the language, the words—agreeing on one point: the Negroes were barbarians who had to be put in their place.

"One day they'll have to be put in their place," said the mayor to the lighthouse keeper, one night when she had voluntarily climbed up to keep watch for a short time.

Faced with this quiet resolution, such as had won Napoleon his empire in Europe, the keeper bared his four fangs like a good watchdog, ready to devour the whole island at a single word from his legitimate sovereign. However, that night the mayor said no more, keeping all these things in her heart.

Concerning the conversation the Flea Islanders had one day around a keg of molasses

One day, La Sagouine reported to the king of her island with her eyes glowering and her claws showing.

"Well?" she said.

And the whole assembly grew silent. Michel-Archange and Citrouille looked down at the ground, and the bums stared at the sky. On this day it was all pocked with tiny clouds that looked like many ancient gods, come there to applaud the entertaining spectacle which was about to unfold below.

Then Michel-Archange shook the mane covering his eyes and began this beautiful speech, which deserves to be told in full.

"That's how she be, then. There we was, all four of us, me, the bums, and Citrouille. We beached the dory and cast anchor. Then we started climbin the rock on all fours, no sweat. First to see us was the keeper. I know that cause just as we's passin under his tower the sunuvabitch lets go his lamp and one of his what the hells. So we took off. Nobody seen us in the streets. We slips behind them barns and fish sheds. Slips so good one of the bums leaves three parts of his shirt caught in a window. Then we goes off to the store. We brushes our duds, straightens our backs, opens up the door and there's the four of us facin the mayor, the milliner, the barber, the banker, and the storeman hidin behind the counter. Seems like the lighthouse keeper didn't waste no time. All them bigwigs in the country was lyin waitin fer us like a ecumulical council."

"Skunks," said La Sagouine.

"Pigs," added La Sainte.

But neither of these noble beasts was sufficient to incarnate the women's rage at the enemy's base treachery. And the noble Sagouine spat on the ground three times.

Then they learned how the merchant, under the intimidating eye of the mayor and her escort, had refused to sell a keg of molasses to the delegation from Flea Island.

"And the fire took, first just glowin embers, pfff pfft ... then a real good forest fire, pshpshpsh! Before ya knows it, the place'd burned down. Pffftpfft ... pshpshpsh! We opens our eyes and there's nobody there but me, the bums, and Citrouille. Everybody'd beat the hell outa there."

"Cept the storeman, scared stiff as a board," added a bum.

"So there ya got it," concluded Archange.

At this strategic moment in the discussion, Don l'Orignal stretched out his left leg, raised an eyebrow, and snorted. Then, lifting his sceptre shaped like a spruce branch up to the sun to impose silence, he solemnly uttered, "Godalmightyhellfire!"

And all the assembled people understood by this speech from the throne that the die was cast.

So they threw themselves body and soul into an illuminating debate worthy of the most august House of Commons. Hair stood on end, feet beat the ground, and fists drew fantastic arabesques in the sky.

"First of all the mayor," said La Sagouine, "then the milliner, then the barber, then the storekeeper ..."

"Then it's all them pretty girls in the village."

"Don't touch them girls. Us men'll look after the milliners and the barbers ourselves. Leave them pretty girls fer Citrouille."

Citrouille leaped at Michel Archange, but Don l'Orignal raised his sceptre and separated them.

"No fightin while the sun's up."

"Bejeezus! That got him! Just maybe I said somethin true?"

"These days," l'Orignal began again, "anythin a man can stuff into his thick skull he can bury in his guts."

"Still ya gotta see if a guy that's always sneakin round that country over there's got any guts."

"Everybody has his day, Michel-Archange. I remember yers. That happened on this side of the fence."

"Damn right. On this here side of the fence. I walk in my own shit, lemme tell ya, not in other people's."

"Cause their shit don't stink so much," ventured Citrouille.

"Not when they stuff it down yer mug. Tarnation!"

La Sagouine stood up then, shook her rump, and launched her most fiercesome challenge at the sky.

"I'm gonna get to the bottom on it, I'm tellin ya. I'm gonna learn the long and the short on it."

"Don't trust nobody."

"Holy bread ain't fer slaves."

"Ain't a place in the sun fer everybody."

"Bejeezus!"

"Prrrt!"

"That's what makes big shots."

"Bad weeds grows fast."

"Mary Mother of God fer Christ sake."

"Tarnation!"

"Every pot's got his cover."

"The only pot you'll cover's the one ya sits on."

"Jeezus Christ Godalmighty, shut up!"

"Like they says, he who gives to the Lord lends to the poor."

"Yeah!"

"Shut up!"

"Bejeezus!"

"Cheep-cheep! Devil's pointed chin, silver mouth, nose, quack-quack ..."

"Godalmightyhellfire!"

Thus ended the first political skirmish which opposed Flea Island to the mainland. The Estates-General dispersed, happy to have done their duty in saving the nation.

Concerning the strange apparition seen on the sea by the citizens of the mainland

Unfortunately for him, the lighthouse keeper had abandoned his tower to the angels' watch while he paid a fleeting visit to his wine barrel.

For the rest of his life the poor keeper would bewail that fatal minute which almost cost his country its peace and tranquility. For it was precisely that very minute which the mayor, in the company of her faithful lieutenants, chose to reconnoitre by the tower. Fixing her nose to the spyglass, what a sight the brave woman beheld in the direction of Flea Island! A red glow emerged from the water as if the very depths of the sea were on fire.

"The ghost ship," cried the barber.

And all the brave civil servants and members of the mainland parliament shuddered at what these words presaged.

For a century and a half now, the inhabitants of the shores of my country have periodically glimpsed the strange phenomenon of a ship in flames drifting on the horizon with sinister slowness. It was an enormous sailing ship, rigged with masts and ropes where busy sailors climbed up and down. The entire vessel and its crew were ablaze with a fire that lit up the whole sky.

"The fire of bad weather," howled the milliner.

This ghost ship had never failed to appear the day before a great storm, and it was a very foolhardy fisherman who would ignore this dark warning from the other world! For there was no doubt left in any mind as to the origin and nature of the phenomenon: the ghost ship came from hell.

The villagers told how this ominous sailboat was none other than an old vessel from the colonial period, which (according to some) had engaged in shady trade or which (according to others) had been guilty of abducting a young half-breed girl. In any case, an Indian mother, a bit of a witch by trade, had cast a spell on the unfortunate ship. The devils had carried out the spell to the letter. That same evening, the boat burned at sea, triggering one of the most terrible storms ever seen on this side of the ocean. And ever since, the same boat was doomed to repeat its tragic journey on the eve of every storm.

Try as they might to convince themselves that this ominous fate was well deserved, that illegal trade never pays, and that all base sins are punished sooner or later, the inhabitants of the coast remained no less terrified at each vision.

And so that evening heaven bestowed its dire warning once again on the mayor and her staff. For if the devil himself should appear before the noble gathering, it could only be a warning from heaven. But what did heaven want from them? That was the question.

"A ghost is still a ghost," said the barber reflectively.

"That depends," corrected the merchant.

"Depends on what?" asked the schoolmaster.

"That depends on its constitution," answered the nursing sister.

And the banker assented.

For some time they remained spellbound by the immense sea stretched out at the foot of the tower. The barber continued. "Just the same, the flaming ship is a ghost."

But the banker answered, "However, a ghost is ordinarily a man."

Then the merchant explained, "Ordinarily. But a ghost is never ordinary."

And everybody stopped talking. For the ship with all its rigging aflame had just sunk to the bottom of the sea once more.

The mayor, who had not thrown her weighty opinion into this altercation, turned the spyglass in the direction of Flea Island and saw a makeshift camp on its left bank. There was Sir Noume with his troops, bivouacking, battling, and buffooning around the remains of a great fire.

Concerning the famine which raged on the island and the second expedition of Flea Islanders to capture the keg of molasses

Don l'Orignal secretly dispatched Lady Sagouine to his son Noume with the order to report next day to the royal palace, where the best minds in the kingdom were to discuss the serious events of the day. La Sagouine acquitted her mission with her usual speed and passion and brought Noume back the same evening.

"Yer father sent me fer ya," she flung at him on arriving in the camp.

Leaving his troops under Michel-Archange, Noume was accompanied by half a dozen of his bold followers: Citrouille, Boy à Polyte, Soldat-Bidoche, and the bums. These parliamentarians followed La

Sagouine all along the coast as she told them about the subject at issue in the debate.

All night the leaders of the country argued the question of the island's safety, threatened as it was by the most fearful famine ever recorded in the annals of the country. Some maintained that the sea was to blame since it no longer provided cod; others that the cod were to blame for devouring the herrings' eggs. Some blamed the herrings' eggs themselves. Still others blamed the dredgers for emptying the sea of its herring and cod at one and the same time. But all were agreed on one point: no matter where the trouble came from, it had to be put right.

"Christ, we can't just start layin them herrin eggs," complained La Sainte.

"Hell, I knows some as'll never lay nothin else," added Boy à Polyte.

But before fighting broke out, l'Orignal nipped it in the bud.

"Shut up, godalmightyhellfire! Neither yer shoutin nor yer eggs'll get us dinner."

There was only one solution left for the economists of Flea Island: if they have no bread, let them eat cake. The keg of molasses the merchant in town refused to sell them must be captured at any cost. And the discussion turned to molasses.

Don l'Orignal turned to the elders of the kingdom, who were sitting peacefully chewing their tobacco around an earthenware spittoon. They didn't stir immediately. Then the eldest moved his dog-like ear, chewed three times on his quid, and said in an even but serious voice, "Before his late death my late father grabbed a case of salt cod to feed his family that was starvin to death. God forgive him."

And all the other grey heads responded to this contribution with more energetic chewing.

Then Citrouille came and said, "That ain't the way things is. Let's go work fer our food. And if them fish a just stopped runnin, let's sign on across the way and earn them kegs of molasses."

Poor Citrouille had scarcely finished his sentence when Boy à Polyte and Soldat-Bidoche and the bums jumped on him to explain syllogistically that the mainlanders didn't sell to the islanders; that the islands could starve to death without raising an eyebrow on the mainland; that men of goodwill had all died in the flood; and that, if God is dead, anything is permitted. Citrouille wasn't so sure about the role of God and the flood in this matter, but he felt that in a single sentence he had exhausted the very fount of his argument, so he kept quiet.

On principle, the debate continued for several hours, but the whole assembly knew from the moment of the elders' intervention that the gauntlet had been cast and that they would march on the capital.

Noume informed Michel-Archange who assembled the troops.

Wherein the author of this so true, so veritable, so veracious tale reveals his sources and exposes his methods in order to prove his complete objectivity

T he tale of the final battle waged on Flea Island appears in no chronicle, no archives, nor in any part of the Pamphilian memoirs. And, curiously, in the national annals of the mainland, no torn page is to be found for that date when, according to all conjectures, these lamentable events took place. Therefore this historical campaign has simply been wrapped in silence for reasons I cannot fathom.

In order to tell you the rest of the History of the Fleas, I have only been able to refer to secondary sources and auxiliary sciences such as archeology, numismatics, heraldry, epigraphy, and sigillaria, and these disciplines have indeed provided me with an abundance of documents. In this way, beginning with five holes of a button collected many years afterward on the charred sand of the island, I was able to reconstitute the complete button, deduce from this button the shape of the buttonhole, then the sort of material in which this buttonhole had been cut, and so on until I reconstituted the complete costume, which could only belong to the barber—the only one, moreover, who wore buttons with five holes.

A reader thus informed about all the care a historian takes to gather together the sparse pieces from a past buried in memories and sands can only bow before such an effort at objectivity. This reader, nevertheless, might yet have doubts about the chronicler's impartiality, for he might interpret real facts erroneously.

In order to meet this objection, I will tell you immediately that a paternal grandmother of the said chronicler was the daughter-in-law of a third cousin of the godfather of a lateral descendant of the great-grandson of a Flea man, and that after this confession, he had no intention of denying his ancestry. However, if all this isn't enough for you, I shall add that the younger son of an aunt by marriage of the son-in-law of the grandmother of a first cousin of the Fleas was a friend of the family when he was a child. At that time, he had more than one opportunity to show his interest in this nation.

After that, I am counting on the confidence and goodwill of the reader, who will gladly read the rest of this controversial story into which the author has put his soul, his fortune, and the name he bears.

James Martin

Montreal-based author and editor James Martin (whose one condition on being included in this anthology was that I use the phrase "devastatingly handsome" in his intro) first gained a cult following with his "Mr. Smutty" column, which ran for years in Calgary's alternative arts paper *Fast Forward*. Although not devastatingly handsome, Martin is one of the most talented humorists I have ever come across. His inventive and exuberant style constantly pushes the boundaries of what language can do. If I had to name the heir apparent to Richard J. Needham, it would be James Martin.

Chow, Hounds

Other countries make me laugh. *Hard.* I mean, one minute those people are out there speaking some crazy "language," the next minute they're wearing wacky "clothing," or engaging in zany "customs." I was cooling my heels at the doctor's office the other a.m. (waiting to get a catheter installed) (nothing's wrong, I just hate leaving the couch when my soaps are on), killing time by flipping thru a vintage *Nat'l Geographic,* and man-o-man was it cracking me up! I mean, seeing the stunts people pull over in their homelands … gawdalmighty, I think I would've whizzed m'pants, had I not already done so on the bus-ride over. (Damn anaesthetic.) My doctor was all like, "Son, can I get you some medicine?" (He sometimes slips me whatever leftovers are kicking around the office.) And I was like, "No thank you, doctor, for I have discovered *laughter* is in fact the best medicine." And he was like, "Yes, this is true. For thousands of years, doctors have been involved in a vast conspiracy to conceal this shocking truth and save our jobs." And I was like, "Since you offered, maybe I'll take a few Tylenol 3s."

I'm particularly tickled by what foreigners will eat when they think the rest of us aren't watching. Like over in South K_r__, where they eat dogs. Breakfast, lunch, dinner, snacks: mmmmm-mmmm, those dogeaters sure love eating dogs. I mean, how figged-up is *that?* I'll tell you: it's figged-up *beyond all repair,* that's how figged-up it is. Of course, it is perfectly accept-able to eat *certain* animals (chickens, turkeys, pigs, sheep, lambs, cows, geese, emus, lobsters, bison, Cornish game hens, hybrid "beefalos," and even baby cows—i.e. "veal"), but *other* animals (dogs) are just no-way-man. For e.g., it's perfectly normal for a strapping youngish N.American lad like myself to enjoy a hearty helping of, say, *ostrich*—not so if I were to chow down on a dachs-hund. For starters, I'd have to eat at least *four* of those little guys (and that's only if I'm vaguely peckish), so it's just not good value. Secondly, unlike poultry and swine, dogs are filthy little jerks. Correction: filthy little *genital-licking* jerks. R'member that old joke about why does a dog lick its unmentionables? Sure, there's an element of showmanship to the deed, but the main reason is simple: b/c they don't want people to eat them. And so we shouldn't.

But someone's always gotta be different. In this case, good ol' South K_r__. In a ballsy attempt to turn the world's anti-dogeating frown upside-down, scooby-snackers concocted a goodwill academic named "Dr. Dogmeat" to spread the culinary gospel and entice tourists into sampling "The *Other,* Other White Meat, The One That Licked Its Genitals Right Up Until It Gasped Its Final Breath." The plan called for Dr. Dogmeat to hand out recipes (incl. comfort-food classics like "Body Preservation Stew") (for real!), and to promote 5-star puppy-chow restaurants. Dog activists, howev, cornered Dr. Dogmeat whilst on his daily rounds, repeatedly smacking him on the nose w/ rolled-up newspapers. Later, they tied him up in the backyard and went to the movies. "We're lucky we didn't send that guy home in a doggie-bag," quipped one unnamed protester. "Hey, I just made a funny!" His friends all agreed it was "a good one."

In other South K_r__ news, a local brewery has concocted a novel new way to get drunk as a skunk: chewable liquor. Inspired by the fave euphemism "barley sandwich," the new product combines all the brain-cell-killing goodness of alcohol w/ the creepy texture of gelatin. "We think our invention will put the fun back into intoxication," said a spokesperson too hosed to remember his own name. He added children will enjoy the product's "wiggly neat shapes," and parents will appreciate its mind-numbing properties. "Best of all," he added, "it's a great way to kill the taste of dog genitals."

White Christmas

Perhaps you will find yerself on an aeroplane this holiday season, winging home for some family-sized squabbling and lightly-camouflaged contempt. Or it could be that yer embarking for sunnier climes, taking a well-deserved holiday on the curved spines of a broken people. (Don't get me wrong, I'm totally cool w/ it.) Both activities can be easily combined into some beach-blanket bickering, making the locals long for the good ol' days of Cortez & Columbus.

Speaking of travelling by air, don't you hate it when you've got an aisle seat and the guy next to you gets up, like, 200 times to squeeze past to the restroom, and then the plane crashes for entirely unrelated reasons? A qwik show of hands: is everyone w/ me on that one? How about when you try to pack a gun (just for fun), but the metal detector trips you up? Couldn't you just curl up & die when that happens? And who hasn't lived thru the embarrassment of having yr bowels sucked out by an over-amped airplane toilet? It's like I'm reading yr mind, innit? Or when you & a chum slip off to join the "Mile High Club," but instead of the washroom door, you mistakenly open an emergency exit and find yerselves enjoying *coitus impactus*? Quel drag!

(These sharply-drawn observations, plus 207 more of equal or more poignancy can be found in my new chapbook, *Li'l Jimmy's Pukebag Follies: 211 Sharply-Drawn Observations from the Belly of the Iron Bird.* It makes a perfect stocking stuffer, and even better kindling.)

Now, let us pause to reflect upon other people's misfortune. Such as, oh I don't know how about, the merry olde chumps on board a recent late-nite

LA–NYC flight. It seems that one passenger got the bright ideer to smuggle a glass bottle fulla liquid cocaine inside her carry-on. All you barristers familiar w/ Murphy's Law will have already guessed the punchline: glass breaks, cabin fills w/ cocaine aroma. The foul odour caused coughing and burning eyeballs. (That is, the people were coughing & their eyes were burning—the eyeballs themselves weren't coughing, altho I'd pay good coin to see such a thing.) The conditions were worsened by the fact nobody knew how to use those little masks that drop down from the overhead compartment, the ones that always remind me of hats for chimps. "I told you to put down that magazine and listen!" shrieked the head steward, who retaliated by popping a Sandra Bullock movie into the inflight VCR, then locking herself in the can. Sev'ral concerned passengers tapped on the door, but none could find out when the meal was being served.

Once the plane landed safely, a passenger was heard to remark, "Dude, when they said it was a red-eye, this isn't what I expected." The young man's colloquial candour really broke the tension. "As a habitual marijuana user," he added, "I am also hungry for more of those packaged peanuts." Again, more laughter.

"My parents always warned me that grass would lead to harder drugs," he continued, provoking scattered guffaws.

"Like, come fly the friendly skies. No no no, wait ... come *fry* the friendly skies!" Only the pilot laughed at that one, and it was really more of a throat-clearing thing.

"Eight miles high, man!" Crickets chirped, and the young man was escorted off the premises by armed guards.

Later still, the owner of the offending fluid claimed it wasn't liquid cocaine, but a homemade remedy for her grandmother, who has been suffering from acute sobriety. Police later raided the grandmother's cottage, where they were shocked to find a timberland wolf dressed in the elderly woman's nightgown. "In all my years on the force, this is the weirdest thing I've ever seen," said an arresting officer. He paused with great drama, chewing his lower lip. "Actually, now that I think about it, I've seen this exact thing once before so it's really not so weird after all."

Smuggler's Blues

As a certificate-holding specialist, I am often "called in" to give my professional opinion on matters most tricky. Summer is my busiest time, and it's not unusual to find me adjudicating a pie-eating contest in the a.m., testifying at a Napster hearing during lunch, and settling a neighbourly dispute over property boundaries during the afternoon. All I ask for in return is some milk of human kindness to pour over my cereal. Plus an unchecked expense account.

There is, howev, one matter that's sure to rear its oversized head no matter where I am. I could be heaping praise on a jar of award-winning preserves, or rescuing an exotic pet from a garage roof, or conducting surprise inspections of sidewalk lemonade stands (if you only knew what goes on behind kitchen doors, you'd just as soon suckle a fire hydrant)—no matter where I am, someone asks me the inevitable question: "Kind sir, pray tell what is the diff between monkeys and apes?"

Experience has taught me the common mind cannot readily grasp scientific nitty-gritty, so I instead give a stock reply: "Much like the difference between espresso and drip coffee, monkeys and apes differ in matters of *concentration*. Specifically, *entertainment* concentration. In other words, that which would req an entire *planet* of apes is easily achieved by a mere *barrel* of monkeys." I often prescribe an enlightening at-home experiment w/ which to illustrate this point.

All of which brings us to today's shocking revelation: flying in the face of longheld beliefs, scientists have now concluded that a suitcase of monkeys is *less fun* than a barrel filled w/ same. A man was recently detained at the Mad__d airport, after his luggage was discovered to contain three pint-size monkeys (alive). Incredibly, the man had successfully cleared inspections in both Bol_v_a and Fl_r_da, neither of which smiles upon such monkeyshinery. Mad__d officials were not so sloppy, but the man avoided arrest by agreeing to a battery of interviews with scientists specializing in all things monkey.

Ever since Chas. Darwin shocked the scientific community w/ his groundbreaking report entitled *Our Funny Ancestors* (later retitled *Origin of the Species* by a dour publisher), it has been widely held that monkeys in any concentration are equally fun. Much in the way that esoteric units such as inches rose to public prominence, the "barrel" became the standard measure of monkey-fun—that said, literature is full of references to satchels, valises, and old yoghurt containers full of fun-bearing monkeys. Scholars have long read such deviations w/ equal weighting. Not so, says the man collared at the Mad__d airport.

The smuggler reveals that, altho he was v. fond of the critters (for the record: two capuchins and one squirrel monkey), the whole "suitcase incident" was not much fun. "I've smuggled monkeys in barrels before," he wrote in a notarized statement, "and that was just a riot. Especially the time I used an old oil barrel—it greased those rascals up somethin' good. Snugglies and fanny-packs, also really fun. But that suitcase ... sweet mother of pearl ... that wasn't no fun at all."

In other animal news, there are an estimated 9 rats for ev'ry resident of N. York City. Faced w/ this disturbing figure, the city is toying w/ the ideer of using birth control. "If we can reduce our population by one, maybe two million people," said an unidentified city hall employee, "we stand a good chance of having at least 12 rats for ev'ry New Yorker." When asked if controlling rat births would perhaps be a more effective solution, the man screamed "Viva the revolution!" and scurried into a drainpipe.

(Police later identified the so-called "city official" as a mole planted by the rats. This confusing metaphor has since been euthanized, and order once again restored.)

Dead Abby

Namesakes: gifts that keep on giving (good), but don't require penicillin (even better). O! to live on long after this too-soft flesh has melted like so much ... uh, *flesh* that, errrr, somehow *melted,* I guess. Similes have never been my strongpoint (writing 'em is as difficult as building something that's widely acknowledged to be difficult to build—times 10!), but that doesn't change how I feel about namesakes. Why, just last summer some of the neighbourhood kids thoughtfully named some artwork after me (it was a mixed-media portrait, brick & spraypaint, of a bucktooth'd fellow w/ index finger jammed so far up one nostril that he's smelling burned toast—a touch derivative of Basquiat, but not w/o crude charm) and I must confess to being flattered.

Dream scenario: to have a monkey named after me. It doesn't have to be a whole species, just one monkey would do me fine. I can envision it all so clearly: me & my namesake monkey, dressed in identical outfits, out for our daily constitutional. We'd be inseparable, like that "My Buddy" doll they used to sell, the one where I misheard the TV jingle as "My buttocks / My buttocks / Wherever I go / They go." (Talk about stating the physically obvious, esp. that grammatically lousy bit about "My buttocks & me / Like to climb up a tree.") Local shopkeepers would be all "Heyheyhey! Lookin' good, you two!" and we'd be all "Up yours, from the two of us!" but they'd know we were only jesting. Jollygood backslappery would ensue. It'd be just like the opening credits of *King of Kensington,* only more like *King of Kensington & His Monkey Which Is Also Named King of Kensington* except I wouldn't blame people if they still called it *King of Kensington,* for short.

Prince Bernhard of the N_th_rl_nds is one lucky SOB, for he now has his v. own species of namesake monkey. Just discovered in the Brazilian Amazon, the bernhardi monkey is an exciting addition to monkey encyclopedias b/c of its groovy orange sideburns. Royal insiders, howev, report the Prince is none-too-happy about the honour. "I sport no such flaming burnsides," the ingrate is alleged to have shrieked. "Why am I being mocked so? This monkey & I could not be more dissimilar!" Then he scampered atop a tall bookshelf, where he ate half a peach and fell asleep.

Guess some people don't crave immortality. (And not just the ones w/ unfortunate handles, like Assy O'Asscrack or Reeker von Stinxsomuch IV.) Just ask … the late A.Landers, whose last will/testament prohibits a replacement advice columnist from assuming her byline post-mortem. OK, you can't v. well ask her *per se* (hot Ouija action being sketchy at best)—altho, due to foresight & stockpiling, she'll continue to *answer questions from beyond the grave* in coming weeks. Creepy. Call me a stick/mud, but the idea of channelling advice from dead people simply doesn't cut the mustard gas. History backs me up: it didn't work so hot for Hamlet, so I doubt "Should Know Better in Savannah" or "Ankle Fetish in Anchorage" will fare much better. And won't "I'm Soaking In It" be kinda freaked out to read *a corpse's thoughts* on adult bedwetting? I sure would, and I *hardly ever* wet the bed. We're essentially being haunted, w/ ol' AL's spectre coming 'round each morning to rattle her chains & dispense advice on gift-giving etiquette. I s'ppose, as far as ghostly declarations go, I'd rather hear "Don't sweat the small stuff" over "Get out of this house or die." But, after all is said/done, I'd hafta say—wait for it!—that corpses are better dead than read.

Almost Famous Second-Last Words

I've never paid my hydro bill. Ever. And so, w/ my electricity (a.k.a. "magic fire") minutes from being 86'd, I must "bust some ass," so to speak. I'm honestly not sure who speaks like that, nor do I really know what "bust some ass" actually means, but this is all inconsequential to the task at hand: filling this page, pronto. I've got 10 minutes, max.

So: Hullo word-count, my old friend, I've come to pad you w/ filler once again. I initially thought I'd rely on my loyal standby, *The Monkey Time Daily News & Report On Monkeys*. (Ask for it at yr newsstand. The Sunday edition features a special section about monkeys that is esp. riveting.) I flipped thru those familiar pages, hoping/praying a spicy headline would kickstart the ol' Muse. (She's been sleeping an awful lot lately. Malaria? Morphine?) But alas, *these* are the kinda lousy, 2-bit, good-for-nada headlines I found: "Monkeys & Feces: Nothing Funny Here, Folks." "Monkey Climbs Tree, Falls Asleep." "Monkey To Droopy Diaper: You're Not Going Anywhere, Pal." "Leading Evolutionists Fear Monkeys Becoming Less Funny By The Generation." "Monkeys Invade Village In Dull Fashion, Mayor Declares State of Emergency Boredom." Sure, parroting those headlines helped me pick off 35, maybe 40 words, but t'ain't much help now, izzit?

Fortunately, I've just discovered that I am, as a matter of fact, *wise*. Just like those three kings following yonder star, the ones who tried to smoke that rubber cigar. (Man alive, sometimes wise people do the stupidest shit. Such is our prerogative, I s'ppose.) This revelation hit me whilst engaged in a dicey bit of home improvement. I thought I'd "pull a Proust" (*not* a fraternity frosh ritual) & cover my bedroom in corkboard & then tack up notes for a ground-breaking, sweeping study cutting to the v. essence of something-or-other. But I gave up after covering one-and-a-half walls. (Don't laugh, that stuff is *heavy*.) Then, b/c I'm feeling misty b/c this is t*he penultimate Mr. Smutty ever,* I tacked up ev'ry last column I've ever written. It was a beyootiful sight, kinda like when Dad would measure you against the kitchen doorjamb, marking the year's growth w/ yet another pencil mark. (Except in this case, it's like the kid developed osteoporosis at age 3, and turned positively microscopic come kindergarten.) Where was I? Oh yeah: I'm wise. So I'm re-reading all those old brittle clippings and, as the clever aphorisms piled up like a mass of dilated veins in swollen tissue (pardon the cliché), I realized that I'm one wise guy. I never would've guessed it (friends have even been wagering to the contrary for years), but there it was in blk & wht. Even better: what finer way to run out today's word-count than by rehashing some old *boner mots?* Now *that's* wise. You may wish to tattoo these on yr person (like buddy in *Memento*) so's you don't forget 'em. Happy first day of the rest of, etc.

Why can't we all be friends? Oh, now I remember: it's because you're an ass.

Love means never having to say "I resent how you've ruined my life."

If you see the Buddha on the road, kill him. I hate that fucking guy.

Are we done yet? Not a pearl of wisdom, I just want to know if I can stop typing—the lights are starting to flicker & I'm scared. No? Darn.

Happiness is a warm puppy. Unhappiness is the warm puddle he left in yr bed while you were at work.

When Life hands you lemons, kick Life right in the cherries & then ask Life how it likes them apples.

Stuart McLean

Stuart McLean has done something few authors ever manage to do: He has created his own world, a small but richly inhabited neighbourhood in Toronto, one revolving around the everyday lives of Dave and Morley and their children, neighbours, and friends. This is the world of The Vinyl Cafe, as it appears on radio, on stage, and in books. When I was compiling this anthology, my wife wanted to know, "Which Stuart McLean story are you going to include? The one with the toaster? Make sure you put in the one with the toaster." And here it is.

FROM *Vinyl Cafe Unplugged*

Odd Jobs

It was on a Saturday afternoon in September, five years ago, that Dave and Morley sat in their backyard and had one of those conversations that married couples have from time to time, about where they had been and where they were going. It was during that conversation that they decided, once again, that they would, without fail, start saving money. They agreed to put away two hundred dollars a month in an account they would never touch, never, not ever. And for the last five years they have been doing that, making those monthly deposits—to their own amazement, without missing one month. They did, however, miss one step because it seemed so self-evident, they never hammered out *why* they were saving. This was not a problem when they were beginning and there was no money in the account, but after five years Dave and Morley had accumulated a significant nest egg, and nest eggs have a habit of hatching.

What had hatched in Dave's mind was a duck-egg-blue 1969 Austin-Healey 3000, with a cream scallop inlet, a red leather interior, fifty-two-spoke wire wheels, and Lucas fog lights mounted on a shiny chrome bar.

Ted Bescher, a retired schoolteacher who lives across the lane from Dave and Morley, owns a bright yellow TR6 that Dave has admired ever since Ted, and his car, moved into the neighbourhood. Ted's car hardly ever leaves the garage, but it is there calling out to Dave whenever he walks by. And sometime after his forty-fifth birthday Dave realized that under certain circumstances, just to be able to say that you owned an Austin-Healey would make your world a better place. He wouldn't *have* to drive it. In fact, he wasn't entirely sure he *could* drive an Austin-Healey without worrying what people were saying behind his back. But just to have one in his garage would make life better.

Morley, of course, had *her* own plans for the money, which had nothing to do with little blue cars. When Morley thought about the savings account she imagined a new second-floor bathroom, where there would always be clean towels and a dry toilet seat.

These were not things they talked about, however, until one summer morning when they were eating breakfast, and Morley looked at the toaster and said, "It would work so much better if we could plug it in at the table. So we wouldn't have to get up and walk across the kitchen every time someone wanted toast."

It was just an idle thought, but it struck her as a good one. She considered it for a moment and said, "Maybe we should take some of the money from the savings account and get someone to put in another outlet."

This sent a chill through Dave's heart.

The next morning, a Saturday morning, Dave was sitting alone at the breakfast table looking at the toaster on the other side of the kitchen. He was thinking, *I should install the outlet myself.* It had nothing to do with toast. It was a defensive manoeuvre. It had everything to do with the Austin-Healey.

Morley was already at work—they were opening a new play. As she left, she said she wouldn't be back until after the curtain came down.

The kids were still asleep—Dave wouldn't see *them* for hours. Sometime in July their body clocks had slipped into the Pacific time zone. Dave had the whole day stretched out before him like a white line running down the centre of a highway. How complicated could it be for an old roadie to run some wires through a wall and install an outlet?

The more he thought about it the more he liked the idea. What he liked best of all was that he would get to knock holes in the kitchen wall. It felt good just *thinking* about that. Without thinking about it any further, without letting coffee or the morning paper waylay him, Dave fetched a hammer from the basement. He returned to the kitchen and stared at the bare white wall beside the table, tapping the hammer anxiously on his thigh.

Like a Spanish conquistador sealing the fate of his troops by burning his ship as soon his last man stepped on shore, Dave raised the hammer over his head and swung it at the wall with all his might. *Hiii-yah.*

The hammer sank into the plaster with a pleasing crack. Dave pulled it out. *Take no prisoners! No turning back!* Three more whacks, and he was staring at a hole the size of a cantaloupe.

What a glorious feeling of destructive accomplishment. Not as good perhaps as changing the oil of a small blue Austin-Healey, but good nevertheless. Dave gave the edges of his hole a few prods with the butt of the hammer and bits of plaster flaked onto the floor. Then he reluctantly put the hammer down. He went upstairs to look for the big *Reader's Digest Book of Home Repairs* to see where he should find the wire that he was going to run to his hole. To his new outlet. It would have to come from somewhere.

He rooted around the bedroom for a while and decided he must have lent the book to a neighbour. He went downstairs and stared at his hole and decided to clean it up a bit. By the time he had finished tinkering, the hole was more symmetrical, neater, and considerably larger. More the size of a pizza than a melon. A largish pizza, thought Dave.

He wondered if Jim Scoffield had his repair book. He didn't really need it, but it would be good to see what the *Reader's Digest* had to say before he went too far. He glanced at the kitchen clock. Jim was the kind of neighbour you visited rather than phoned.

"I don't have your book," said Jim, "but I have a new mallet. I can't believe you started without me. Let me get it."

Jim and Dave stared at the hole where Dave wanted to put the new outlet.

"Where's the wire going to come from?" asked Jim.

"That's what I was wondering," said Dave.

Jim pointed at a light switch by the back door. "There'd be wire over there we could patch into," he said.

Then he smiled. "Of course, we'll have to punch a hole in the wall to pick it up."

He was fiddling with his new mallet.

"Be my guest," said Dave.

"Are you sure?" said Jim, moving towards the back wall, not waiting for the answer.

Two satisfying swings and Jim was through the plaster. Dave pushed forward to peer into the hole. Jim pushed him back. "Maybe," said Jim, "I should tidy that up a bit."

There *were* wires there. In fact, when Jim stepped back and they both peeked in his hole, wires were about all they *could* see—all sorts of wires. Black shiny wires, grey cloth-covered wires, wires snaking through the wall like ...

"Like spaghetti," said Jim.

"We're not wanting for wire," said Dave.

Jim pointed at a grey wire running through a porcelain insulator.

"Knob and tube," said Jim. "I didn't think that stuff was legal any more."

"Those aren't live," said Dave. "I had an electrician in to replace all that a couple of years ago."

Dave reached into the hole with his screwdriver and jiggled the old wire. There was a sudden puff of smoke. Dave gasped and the right side of his body jerked spastically. A deep alien-like moan rolled out of him as the screwdriver flew across the kitchen, end over end like a tomahawk, ricocheting off the kitchen sink and disappearing through the window.

There was a moment of stunned silence. Jim and Dave both stared at the broken window as shards of glass tinkled to the floor.

"Could you do that again?" said Jim. "I especially enjoyed the way the chip of porcelain from the sink followed the screwdriver through the window."

A minute later Bert Turlington was standing on the stoop. He had Dave's screwdriver in his hand. "This yours?" he asked, standing a little close, talking a little loud.

Dave nodded. Yes.

"Are you out of your mind?" said Bert, even louder now.

Dave shrugged his shoulders. No.

"I opened the back door," said Bert, "and this is flying across my yard like …"

"A tomahawk?" said Dave helpfully.

"It stuck in the door frame about a foot from my head," said Bert.

"We're moving some wires," said Dave. "I got a shock."

"You're moving wires?" says Bert, stepping back, his fists unclenching, his voice softening. "I got a new drill for my birthday. One of the cordless ones. Maybe I should bring it over."

Something inexplicable happens when a man picks up a tool to do home repairs. Some force, as yet undescribed by science, but nevertheless well known to women, is set loose. It's a force that lures men away from their families and the things they are supposed to be doing to the place where hammers are being swung.

Maybe the act of a hammer moving through the air sets off a cosmic thrumming only men can hear. Or maybe when a man picks up a screwdriver, he releases an odour only men with tools can smell—a musty, yeasty sort of smell, with a hint of leather and WD40. Men in their backyards raking leaves and men in their basements listening to ball games on portable radios are seized by this odour the way the urge to migrate seizes lesser species. Suddenly they're thinking, *I don't belong here any more. I belong in another place. I should be doing something else, and I should take my coping saw with me just in case.*

Men can sense when a wall is coming down, and they can't help the fact that they have to be there to watch it fall, or better yet, help push it over.

It has been argued that the fall of the Berlin Wall had nothing whatso-ever to do with the collapse of communism: it was just a weekend project that got out of control—thousands of German guys satisfying their undeni-able urge to fix things up.

• • •

Carl Lowbeer, himself of German descent, was the next neighbour to arrive at Dave's house on this Saturday morning.

He burst through the front door without knocking. Dave and Jim looked up to see him standing in the kitchen.

"Hi," said Carl, trying to slow himself down, trying to act nonchalant.

"Need any help?"

He was carrying a bright yellow thing about the size of an electric drill (except more dangerous-looking). It looked like a cross between an Uzi and a woodpecker. It was his reciprocal saw.

Carl got the saw last Christmas. It is his pride and joy. But there are only so many holes a man can cut in his own house before he is told to stop. The saw spent most of the summer on Carl's worktable in the basement—calling to him.

At the end of August, when Carl's wife, Gerta, went downstairs with a load of laundry and found him cutting random holes in a sheet of plywood, she took the saw away from him. She said he could have it back if he stood in front of the house on Saturday mornings with a sign around his neck that read *Need Holes Cut?*

By noon there were seven men in Dave's kitchen. Two of them friends of Jim Scoffield's whom Dave had never met—guys with tools.

Carl was in the living room, huddled on the sofa beside Bert Turlington. Bert was demonstrating his new electric drill. The drill had more gears than a Maserati. Bert was revving the motor and explaining what it could do. He handed the drill to Carl, who didn't expect it to be so light.

"Oops," said Carl, holding it too close to Morley's Brazilian hardwood coffee table. The drill skitted across the table leaving a long white streak in the dark finish, such as a skater might leave on a freshly flooded rink.

"That's okay—don't worry, don't worry," said Bert, spitting on the table and rubbing the gouge with the palm of his hand. "I have something at home that will cover that."

Things were lurching along at about the same pace in the kitchen. There were now a series of twelve melon-sized holes punched in the kitchen wall at two-foot intervals, leading from the light switch by the back door to the hole where Dave intended to install the plug for the toaster.

Twelve holes and seven busy men.

Jim and Dave were routering putty out of the broken window. Phil Harrison was sucking up plaster dust with Carl Lowbeer's Shop Vac. The two men Dave didn't know were racing a pair of belt sanders along a couple of two by fours they had set on the floor. Everyone was productively occupied—except for Carl Lowbeer, who was sitting at the kitchen table, morosely cradling his unused reciprocal saw and watching the belt sanders shudder along.

Counting Bert Turlington's electric drill, there were, at noon on that Saturday, six power tools operating in Dave's house.

And noon on Saturday was the moment when Sam arrived downstairs, rubbing his eyes, taking in the chaos of his kitchen, and asking the most reasonable question.

"What's for breakfast?"

"Toast," said Dave. He said this without turning the router off or even turning around. Sam stared at his father's back for a moment, then shrugged and dropped a couple of slices of bread in the toaster. As soon as he pushed the handle down, the toaster began a loud and peculiar buzzing. No one could hear it over the din of the tools. Except Sam, who said, "What's that?"

No one heard Sam either.

Then the lights went out.

And the tools died.

In the sudden silence someone, perhaps Bert Turlington, said, "Do you smell that?"

It was an elusive odour, but it was there.

Somewhere.

"I think it's coming from behind this wall," said Jim Scoffield.

"*This* wall," said Carl Lowbeer.

Sam watched the men, some of them bent over at the waist, some standing on their toes, all of them sniffing the walls, the ceiling, the cupboards.

And then there was smoke hanging in the air like wisps of fog.

Someone said, "We overloaded the wires. The wires are burning—cut the wall open over here."

And Carl Lowbeer jumped up and said, "My saw works on batteries." And he lurched towards the wall, revving his reciprocal saw in front of him. Before anyone could stop him, Carl had cut a hole in the wall the size of a loaf of bread.

"Not there," said Bert Turlington. "Here."

"Coming. Coming," said Carl, moving around the kitchen like a mass murderer. He cut a second hole five feet down the wall.

Sam's eyes were as wide as saucers.

"I've got a fire extinguisher in the truck," said one of the men Dave didn't know.

They found the remnants of the fire with the third hole. A mouse nest leaning against the overheated wires. It had burned itself out. The man with the fire extinguisher gave it a blast.

"Just in case," he said.

At twelve-fifteen Dave took stock of what they had accomplished: the broken window, the chipped sink, fifteen holes, the sodden plaster where they had used the extinguisher.

Arnie Schellenberger looked at Dave and said, "Uh, Dave, when's Morley coming home?"

Dave said, "Not until tonight, not until ten, eleven."

Arnie said, "There's an electrician I know from the plant. He might come over. If you did the window he could do the wiring and we could patch the holes by—" he looked at his wrist "—ten?"

The electrician, Ted—black jeans, black jeans jacket, earring—arrived at five. He looked around the kitchen and pointed at the knob-and-tube wiring and crossed his arms.

"I can't repair that. It's the law. Whatever you've exposed I have to replace."

He looked at the expression of horror on Dave's face.

"You need this done tonight. Right?"

Dave nodded.

The electrician looked around, "You guys got a reciprocal saw?"

Carl Lowbeer's hand shot into the air like a schoolchild's. "I do. I do," he said way too fast and about an octave too high. Everyone turned and stared at him. Carl looked down and said it again, this time slower and a register lower. "I do," he said.

The electrician pointed at the back wall of Dave's kitchen. "We're going to pop out the drywall," he said. "Take the wall down to the studs. That way I can get at everything at once."

Dave was frowning.

"It's the fastest way," said the electrician.

He looked at Carl.

"Cut around the top by the ceiling and along the baseboard. We'll pop it out, nice and simple."

Carl was beaming.

He was about to sink the saw into the wall when the electrician held up his arm.

"You guys turned the electricity off. Right?"

Everybody stopped and looked at each other.

• • •

Morley came home soon after nine.

When she turned onto their street, she noticed her house looked strangely dark.

She pulled into the driveway and parked the car and gathered an armful of junk, her purse, a sweater, some files. She headed towards the back door. She was exhausted. She dropped a file and stooped to pick it up. It was only then that she noticed the warm glow of candles flickering through the back window. She felt a wave of affection wash over her.

Dave had made a romantic meal.

She had barely eaten all day. She was smiling as she opened the back door. She put her purse down and called, "Hello." She stopped dead in her tracks.

Sometimes you are confronted by things that are so far from what you expect that your brain is unable to process what it is looking at. There is a momentary disconnect between what you think you are looking at and what you are actually looking at. Morley looked around her kitchen. There were candles everywhere. And flashlights and snake lights. And men. There were four men in the kitchen. All of them on their hands and knees.

The four strangers on their hands and knees were staring at her the way a family of raccoons might stare at her from the back deck. She thought, *This is not my house. This is not my kitchen. This is a frat house. This is a fraternity party.*

As her eyes adjusted to the light, she took in more details. The men were holding tools. There was a pile of pizza boxes on the floor. And an empty case of beer. Sam, her son Sam, was sprawled beside the pizza boxes. Asleep. What was he doing in a frat house? This couldn't be her kitchen—two of the walls were missing. She looked at the men again.

One of them stood up.

"Hi. I'm Ted," he said, "the electrician. We'll have this cleared up in just a minute or two."

And then she saw Dave, her husband, crawling towards her. He stopped about ten feet away. "Hi," he said.

He waved his arm around the room—at the broken window, the holes in the wall, the back wall that had completely disappeared—and he said, "We're fixing the toaster."

This *was* her kitchen.

Morley's mouth opened, but no words came out. It closed, then it opened again. She *seemed* to be trying to say something. Dave nodded, trying to encourage her, as if they were playing charades. Her mouth kept opening and closing, opening and closing, but no sound came out.

Then without saying anything—not one word—Morley turned around and walked out of the house. She got in her car and backed out of the drive-way.

Dave said, "She'll be back in a minute."

Bert said, "I think I should be going."

Carl said, "Me too."

Dave said, "Maybe if we could just get the power on before she comes back."

Morley wasn't back in a minute. She wasn't back for nearly an hour.

When she did return, she walked across the kitchen and opened the freezer door. About a cup of water trickled onto the floor. She let out a muffled sob.

Dave helped her empty the freezer. They deposited plastic bags of food in an assortment of neighbourhood fridges. "They're all within easy walking distance," Dave pointed out helpfully.

When they had finished unloading the fridge, Morley went into the living room and met Jim Scoffield's two friends. They were still sitting at her coffee table. They had a naphtha gas camping lantern resting on the arm of a chair and were playing cards in its garish light. When Morley came in the room, one of the men looked up and said, "Are there any subs left?"

• • •

The renovation took six weeks to finish.

Dave worked on it alone until the middle of the next week. He recon-nected the electricity on Tuesday, but when Morley came home she got a shock when she tried to open the refrigerator, which, unfortunately, was the first thing she tried to do. So he shut the power off again and rechecked everything and turned it on the next morning. Everything seemed to be working fine until Sam came home from school and showed them how he could turn the microwave on with the TV remote.

There was a thunderstorm that night. Morley became increasingly agitated with each lightning flash. She had read stories about women washing dishes at the kitchen sink and WHAMMO! they get hit by lightning. Cows, golfers, people in boats—why not her kitchen? She didn't trust the wiring.

They called an electrician to finish the job: a methodical and trustworthy man. It was the electrician who spotted the lead pipes running into the upstairs bathroom, and he said, "If you want to have them replaced you might as well do it while you have the walls down."

So they had the plumbers in and had the entire upstairs bathroom redone, and downstairs, where the back wall was, Morley had one of those bay windows put in, which is something she has always wanted. She has a herb garden going in the window space.

It was six difficult weeks and they had to get a new vacuum because the old one got clogged with plaster dust, but the upstairs bathroom is lovely and so is the bay window with the plants in it.

Dave was admiring the plants two weeks later, standing in front of the window and looking out into the yard, enjoying the new view. You can just see the alley over the back fence. He was standing there staring out the new window and into the alley when Ted Bescher drove by in his TR6.

But it *is* a beautiful window ... and Dave likes it, especially in the evening when the light is soft. In the morning too, especially Saturday mornings, when the kids are still in bed. It's lovely to sit in the kitchen together— the sun drifting down on the coriander, Morley and Dave sipping coffee and reading the paper. They were sitting there one Saturday morning in October, two months after the renovation was finished, when Morley stood up and walked over to the counter to make some toast. She turned and smiled at Dave and said, "Don't you think it would work better if we could plug it in at the table? So we wouldn't have to get up and walk across the kitchen every time someone wanted toast?"

Richard J. Needham

Richard J. Needham may not loom as large as Stephen Leacock in the imagination of Canadians, but he's still—far and away—one of the funniest writers Canada has ever produced. He writes at full gallop, and his books *The Garden of Needham* and the Leacock-winning *Needham's Inferno,* written at the height of the swingin' sixties, are as funny today as when they were first published.

FROM *Needham's Inferno*

Help, Help, a Heffalump!

Does he exist? How would I know? Sure, I'm the editor; sure, I have to clear his column; but I've never laid eyes on him. All I know is that it comes in every day. There are difficulties with it, to be sure—I'll tell you about those later—but it invariably arrives.

I used to have theories about him, or her—have you thought of that angle? I had it figured out once that he was a retired clergyman, living in Truth-or-Consequences, New Mexico. Or perhaps a little old lady, spinning out her remaining years in a cottage at Clappison's Corners. I considered the possibility that the column was written by a syndicate of Norwegian trolls, like the ones in *Peer Gynt.*

But now I've given up. All the theories make sense, and none of them does. Let me exemplify. You saw this morning's one. All right, it came all the way from Peking—by rickshaw, if you please—and was written on the back of an American laundry ticket. You saw the one the day before. It came over the teleprinter from Chichen Itzá. In Greek.

That meant he was peeved at us over something—a misplaced comma, let's say, in some previous column—but not really angry. When he's angry, he files in Urdu or Swahili, McLuhan or Maori. Once, when he was really furious, he wrote the column in Diefenbaker; it took the entire staff of Berlitz to decipher it.

The ways he transmits it! Once upon a midnight dreary, while I pondered weak and weary, wondering which of the editorial writers to fire next, I heard a strange rapping at the window. When I opened it, in came this damn raven, and perched himself on the bust of Mackenzie King which you'll notice just above my office door. Well, the raven demanded a stenographer be brought in, and then quoth the usual 800 words for the bottom right-hand corner. "Nevermore!" he shrieked as we threw him out.

I realized afterwards what the "nevermore" meant—that we'd never get it that way again. And that's true enough, it's always different. There was the time the Toronto Harbour Commission reported this enormous whale swimming up to Pier 24. We all rushed down thinking we might behold our elusive columnist. But no; when the whale opened its mouth, a hand came out and threw an envelope on the dock. The hand went back inside and the whale swam away, flicking its tail as contemptuously as Moby Dick.

I remember the day his column was very late—five minutes to deadline. Then a girl came rushing into my office—skinny to the point of emaciation. After making me close the door, she took off all her things. Yes, you're right. He'd written the column on an empty stomach. The day after that, a plane flew low over my house in East Toronto, and two great objects came crashing through the roof. Yes, tablets of stone.

Then there was the editorial conference. We were sitting around having jollies about Section 129 of the British North America Act, when three fingers appeared out of nowhere and started writing in blood-red letters on the wall. "Mene, mene, tekel, upharsin," it began, "which means, being translated, death to the editor"—and went on from there all the way down to the broadloom. A pretty bill that made for us! But nothing compared to the time it appeared in the blue prairie sky, 20,000 feet above Lethbridge.

I couldn't begin to tell you all the ways—carved on a tree in High Park, engraved on the head of a pin, signalled with flags from a flotilla in the lake, laboriously spelled out by a circus elephant which came up in the freight elevator. One wintry day, I noticed this queer, rhythmic clanking—yes, he was sending it through the radiators in Morse code. Then there was the 200-foot totem pole that arrived from B.C. some place—did you ever try to find a Haida Indian in Toronto?

I don't know: I sometimes think it's more trouble than it's worth. Look out of the window now, and you'll see what I mean. You don't ordinarily find one squirrel coming up the side of the building, let alone several dozen—and each with a fortune cookie between its teeth. Guess who'll have to sort it all out—praying it isn't in Sanskrit or maybe Australian....

A Tiger in His Thanks

There I was in my office, quietly drinking coffee and gnawing on a Danish pastry (name of Gerda Knudsen), when the secretary came in and said: "The man you hate, loathe, despise, and abominate most in the world wishes to see you; to wit, Dietrich Doppelganger, editor of *The Goat and Snail.*" I replied, "Tell him to go and expropriate himself."

As she insisted, I unleashed a string of Erse curses, stuffed Miss Copenhagen 1907 into a filing cabinet, and went in to see Mimico's contribution to the world of arts and letters. D.D. closely resembles Thomas Hobbes's description of human existence in a state of nature—solitary, nasty, brutish, and short. When he pollutes the waters of Lake Simcoe with his presence, he is often mistaken for a snapping turtle.

There's no sense treating someone like this with kid gloves, so I strode in wearing kid gloves, my scarlet matador's cape, and a brown paper bag on my head. With D.D., one must go in shouting, so I shrieked like an uprooted mandrake: "What the hell do you want? Your hairpiece is on crooked. Aren't you late for your Arthur Murray dance lesson?"

He started a bit, and that pleased me. For all his bluster, D.D. is quite neurotic. You should see the way his hand trembles when I burst into tears; or come into his office on hands and knees, shaking my head from side to side; or throw myself on the floor and start biting the Bigelow; or accuse him of having me followed by pterodactyls.

Controlling himself with an obvious effort, he said: "Well, R.J., with Thanksgiving Day coming up we thought you might write an appropriate column for the occasion—something, well, you know, reflective and moralistic; but of course in your own imitable style."

"Get your mind up out of the gutter," I snapped. "I'll write about sex and booze as usual." He blanched, and I pursued my advantage. "If I'm thankful for anything, D.D., it's that I've had to put up with you only in the eventide of my life. Everything about you is phony; even your teeth, which appear to be false, are real. You tell people you are going to Winnipeg so they will think you are really going to Montreal, when all the time you are going to Winnipeg. You are a liar and a prefabricator."

Thoroughly unnerved by this time, D.D. drummed his twelve fingers on the desk, and said quietly: "There are other things to be thankful for, R.J. For example, I have just approved your Western Canada expense account. Tell me, merely as a matter of curiosity, is it possible—even in a first-class hotel— to spend $37.85 on breakfast?" I looked him straight in his beady little eyes: "Airline hostesses have to eat, too, you know."

He nodded: "And how did you manage, during three hours in Winnipeg, to spend $187 on what you list merely as Etc.?" What a creep! It took five minutes to explain to him that what with inflation, Chinese wheat deals, and all the rest, the price of Etc. is now higher in Western Canada than anywhere else in the world. But still worth it, still worth it.

When he'd swallowed this, he said: "You've something else to be thankful for—the typewriter we gave you last week. You no longer have to hammer out your column on tablets of stone." I had him there: "That typewriter, as you describe it, was last used to send front-line dispatches from the Battle of Austerlitz. All the keys are functioning with the unfortunate exception of a, e, i, o, and u, the result being that my columns are comprehensible only to Toronto's Polish community."

D.D. quickly changed tack. "You could be thankful for the liberty we afford you, allowing you to use your office for teach-ins, preach-ins, screech-ins, drink-ins, gamble-ins, and lately, so I've observed, romance-ins. We hired an extra janitor to remove your discarded demi-tasses, demijohns, and demi-mondaines. We allow you to walk around the newsroom with a placard saying 'Locked In.' We give you space for your lifelong campaign against atheism, lump sugar, inter-office memoranda, and twin beds."

I just sat there looking bored. "Is it true," I asked, "that behind your external façade there's an internal one?" D.D. frowned: "You appear to be rather uncooperative." I answered: "The reason I appear to be uncooperative is that I am. However, I'll consider the matter as I take my afternoon stroll across the harbour." D.D. flared up: "In the circumstances, I'd just as soon you didn't write a piece for Thanksgiving."

That did it, of course; I went straight to my office, wrote a Thanksgiving piece, took it to him, and threw it contemptuously across his desk. He was gabbling away into the telephone: "Okay then, Mike. I'll check it out with Lyndon and Harold, then we'll try it on Leonid." I broke in: "Most impressive, D.D., but may I point out to you that the phone isn't connected?"

He blushed furiously, and slammed it down on the receiver as I went off cackling to myself. I climbed into my desk drawer, assumed the foetal position, and closed it shut. Drifting off to sleep, I reflected that I do, perhaps, have something to be thankful for. Give me the tools, and I will finish the slob.

The Wickedest Man in Old T.O.

Most people are rotten in parts (said the man at the bar) but I am rotten all the way through. Don't blame me for it; place the blame, if such there must be, on my upbringing. Yes, I am the product of an intact home at Bella Bella, B.C. My father was firm and kindly, my mother gentle and virtuous, my brothers and sisters polite and affectionate. Our household overflowed with love, with comradeship, with the smell of fresh-baked apple pie. No wonder I grew up to be so vile.

There was something more and perhaps even worse; I sought recognition of my evil nature, I wished to shock and disgust people; so after dynamiting my home, I came to Toronto with a diabolic ambition; I wanted to be the wickedest man in old T.O. Yes, I knew there was stiff competition; the number and size of the churches told me that; but I had confidence in my shortcomings.

The first thing I did on arriving was to consult a noted Torontologist who masquerades under the name of Rudolph J. Needleberry. I found him sitting on the grass at Queen's Park, surrounded by a snicker of shopworn shopgirls, who yawned and cut their toenails as he read to them from the collected speeches of George Drew. "Sir," I said, "I wish to become the wickedest man in old T.O. In order to achieve this distinction, I am prepared to lie, cheat, steal, conspire, and connive. I am ready to exploit the poor, to devour widows' houses, and to take from him which hath not even that which he hath."

"My dear fellow," he replied, "if you hope to become the wickedest man in old T.O., you are going the wrong way about it. Lying, cheating, stealing, exploitation of the poor, and all such are taken in this community as marks of success, and even of virtue; especially when you have passed the first $500,000. If you rob and cheat enough people, they'll name parks and streets after you, and possibly honour you with a statue. If you truly wish to scandalize Torontonians, to arouse their deepest hatred and revulsion, you must engage in what they consider the real sins—drinking, gambling, and frolicking with the fair. Take two of these girls to lunch at The Captain's Table and you'll have made a good start."

Grasping at this advice, I took girls out to dinner, to lunch, and not infrequently to breakfast; I held their hands on the street, bought flowers for them, and patted them on the Summerhill subway station. I drank my way through the whole LCBO list from Acadian Signature (103B) to William Younger's Double Century Ale (1123). I played bingo, bought sweepstakes tickets, and, finding there was a bookmaker on every block, bet on races as far away as the Flemington track in Melbourne, Australia.

Mr. Needleberry was right. My infamy grew; people shuddered and spat and crossed themselves at my approach; I was well on the way to being known as the Beast of Bay Street. Then disaster struck. A ticket I had bought on the Irish Sweepstakes turned out to be the lucky one; my name and face appeared on the front page of Toronto's newspapers with the information that I had won $187 million tax-free.

At this, I suddenly became popular. I was invited to join clubs, to run for public office, to sit on boards of directors of companies, to grace the governing bodies of hospitals and universities. Clergymen who had hitherto avoided me came to tell me of worthy causes I could assist. Business typhoons sought my counsel, Rotarians pleaded with me to address them, and society matrons with unmarried daughters asked me to dinner parties. I was flatteringly profiled in the Canadian edition of the famous news magazine *Lavender and Old Luce*.

I didn't give up. There was still one last desperate step, one means by which I might yet achieve my aim of becoming the wickedest man in old T.O. I rented a plane, took it up, and dropped bombs indiscriminately on the heart of the city. The authorities were waiting for me when I landed; now I've got to face the consequences of my action; and that's why I'm sitting here drinking double brandies (Bisquit Dubouche, 230B). In precisely one hour, I must present myself at City Hall, there to be awarded a medal for what the papers describe as my generous and imaginative contribution to Toronto's midtown redevelopment.

Two Hearts in Toronto Time

My name is Jack B. Quick. Like most other people in Toronto, I came here from some place else—to wit, Dog Pound, Alberta. And like most other people in Toronto, I ran into various troubles with the opposite sex.

My first experience was when I dialed a number, and a girl with a marvellously throaty voice said to me: "I'm sorry, the number you have just reached is not in service. Yes, I think I could learn to care." Immensely intrigued, I dialed another number, and she told me: "The present temperature in Toronto is 28 degrees. No, I don't have any serious attachments." Mad with desire by now, I dialed yet another number, and she murmured: "Our feature picture tonight is *Sunset in St. Petersburg,* starring Doris Day, and it begins at 8:30. It's a lousy show, frankly, and why don't you take me to the Sentry Box instead?"

I made frantic efforts to identify her, but discovered in the end that she didn't exist. I had fallen in love with a recorded announcement. To dispel my grief, I went on a mad round of cocktail parties, meeting at one of them an enchanting brunette, who told me: "I would like to see you again, and here is my phone number, but I may as well warn you that romancewise I am a flop from Flopsville." We associated for a while, and one day at lunch I told her: "That's not true what you said to me. You are by no means a flop romancewise, but on the contrary a smashing success."

Great tears started welling in her eyes, rolling down her cheeks, and splashing into her chicken pot pie. "That does it!" she sobbed. "Not only am I a flop romancewise, but you've started lying to me." Anxious to redeem the situation (she made $72 a week after taxes) I quickly back-tracked: "All right, I withdraw that remark. You really are a flop from Flopsville romancewise."

She picked up the ketchup bottle, and smashed it over my head. I was taken to hospital, where the ugly story soon got about—"He told some poor girl she was a flop romancewise. Serves him right." I was an outcast, a pariah, and the nurses came into my room and jammed enormous needles into me as a matter of principle. But in the room next to mine was a lively girl from Windsor, Ontario, and she will now take up the story:

My name is Sal Volatile, and I came to Toronto looking for a first-class man. I soon found out there weren't any, so I decided to settle for a second-class man, but discovered they were all spoken for. Moving on to the third-class men, I found they were all under analysis. The fourth-class men were—well, you know. The fifth-class men, I discovered, were all alcoholics. I knew then I would have to take a sixth-class man, and that was fair enough because of my awful failing.

I am a slob. At any given moment, my bed is unmade, there's a ring around my bathtub, and stockings hanging out of every bureau drawer. My kitchen sink presents a spectacular mélange of dirty dishes, used tea bags, cigarette butts, and coffee grounds. My bathroom sink is so full of undone laundry that I have to wash and brush my teeth at the office. As for my personal attire, my mother was always saying to me: "Sally, for heaven's sake, sew on that shoulder strap; you might be hit by a streetcar and taken to hospital, and then what would people think?"

Well, you know what happened. As I prowled about T.O. looking for a sixth-class man, I was in fact hit by a streetcar and taken to hospital, where it was immediately noticed that my underwear was held together with safety pins, paper clips, and wire staples. I was an outcast, a pariah, and the nurses came into my room and sneered at me as a matter of principle. When I found that the man in the next room, to wit Jack B. Quick, was in the same sort of disgrace, we got together, fell in love, and decided to wed. But there was an obstacle still to overcome.

Since we existed only in the imagination of a wicked newspaper columnist named Rudolph J. Needleberry, we had to get his approval; and we knew this would be difficult, because he likes to bring his people to horrible endings. He said to Jack: "You can't get married. I was planning to have you arrested at the Exhibition for exhibitionism, and sentenced to 187 years as a galley slave on the Island ferries." He said to me: "You can't get married. The fate I had planned for you was to perish in a pile-up on the Macdonald-Cartier-Disraeli-Parnell-Bismarck-Garibaldi-Kossuth-Kosciusko-Shevchenko Freeway."

Finally, our tears overcame him. "All right," he said, "but you'll have to live in Don Mills, make $10,000 a year, and spend $15,000. You must also promise me that you will never have any secrets from each other; and that once a week you will have a long, serious, forthright discussion on what is right and what is wrong with your marriage." This seemed reasonable to us, so we thanked him and wandered off hand-in-hand into the sunset. Behind us, as we left, we heard him laughing to himself like a hyena.

Dan Needles

Dan Needles is best known as the creator of the popular Wingfield Farm plays. *With Axe and Flask: The History of Persephone Township* (pronounced "purse-phone," if you please) is Needles's Leacock Medal–winning spoof of local history books, in which a narrator seeks to revise and update a volume written previously by his grandfather, one Dr. D.J. Goulding. As someone who has waded through more such history books than is healthy, I can testify to Needles's bull's-eye wit. You don't need to know early Ontario history to enjoy *Axe and Flask,* but the more you do know, the funnier it gets.

FROM *With Axe and Flask*

V isitors from abroad remark how similar the highland landscape of Persephone is to some parts of Afghanistan.

A distinctive feature of the highlands is the drumlin, a type of hill created by the retreat of a glacier. It is an oval-shaped mound of boulder clay that looks a bit like a snowdrift and covers an area roughly the size of a city block. It has an abrupt southern slope and a northern slope that is more gradual. Each drumlin will support up to two sheep at a time, provided the sheep are fond of Scotch thistles. The north slope is the last surface to lose its cover of snow in the springtime and the first to be hit by frost in the fall. Farmers usually drive off the sharp end of a drumlin at some point in their careers, suffering permanent injury. Cedar fence posts rot quickly in its sand, which is why most drumlin fences lie flat on the ground, making them useless for restricting the movement of livestock.

A geologist who was trying to explain why the life expectancy of the Irish had not kept pace with the general advances in Europe over the preceding five hundred years first identified the drumlin in Northern Ireland in 1866.* His research indicated that drumlins were part of the problem. When the Irish moved to Canada they instinctively moved to the nearest drumlin, cleared it of all trees, and settled down to the hand-to-mouth existence they were accustomed to. Many of Persephone's families can trace their origins to a particular set of drumlins for which they feel a fierce and inexplicable affection. For example, you might hear one of them say, "I'm assessed for a hundred acres, but I've got nearly twice that. It's all up on its edge and the cows can pasture both sides."

Drumlin farmers are proud, clannish, and contemptuous of anyone who farms in the "flats" of the Petunia and Pine River Valleys. Most of them limp. They firmly believe that farmers who grow crops in topsoil are cheating. Anybody can do that. It takes great skill to coax a crop of spring grain out of the north slope of a drumlin, as they are happy to remind anyone who slips into a booth in the Red Hen Restaurant in Larkspur today. In modern times, the highest and best use of a drumlin appears to be a golf course.

If you look at a climate and soil map for southern Ontario, you will see a small circular zone marked 4a. This area encloses the highlands of the township, giving it a climate and growing conditions very much like the south of France during July and August. For the rest of the year it is more like Churchill, Manitoba.

• • •

However cold the winters may have been, it is also clear that the summers could be brutally hot.† The fossil record shows evidence of mussels cooked

---

*The reader may be interested to consult the work of P. McBride, "Which Came First: the Irish or the Drumlin?" *Royal Geographic Conference Proceedings*, Vol. 27 (1870). I am informed by reliable sources that it is a fascinating essay.

†There is other evidence of high heat and humidity. Étienne Brûlé, the notorious French explorer, guide, and early *coureur de bois*, came to an untimely end because of excessively high temperatures at a Huron banquet he attended in 1633.

in their own shells, and tree rings during certain periods are closer together than the eyeballs of a Ministry of Transportation truck inspector, which indicates that at times trees almost stopped growing entirely. Today the last serious frosts occur in early June, and freezing temperatures do not resume until the second week of September. Annual rainfall varies between zero and fifty inches. Much of this precipitation comes in the form of snow. Fifty-year storms occur about once every three or four years, and tornado sightings have been recorded at least once every season since 1834. According to my grandfather: "The residents of Persephone never lack for a subject of conversation as long as the weather presents such opportunities for diversity and astonishment."

The prevailing winds in Persephone blow steadily enough that when they stop, cattle fall over. The Westerlies sweep in off the lake at high speed and collide with the drumlins of the highlands, the first and only obstruction they have encountered on the trip east from Winnipeg. Botanists have identified a local subspecies of conifer that locals call the Persephone pine. It has branches only on the east side.

The winds gave housebound pioneer women of the area the peculiar glassy-eyed stare that is recorded in many old photographs. Like the mistral in Provence and the Santa Ana in California, the Persephone Westerlies have inspired much poetry, but none of it has been published.* The wind was used successfully as a legal defence in the murder trial of the Widow McClay (*R. v. McClay*, 1923). After three months of listening to the windows rattle in the northwest gales, her husband greeted her at the dinner hour with the question, "Say, did you feel that breeze out there?" She bludgeoned him to death with a chunk of cordwood. Mrs. McClay was granted an absolute discharge on the condition that she move into town.

Despite the challenges of wind and winter, an assortment of hardy flora and fauna can be observed in Persephone. The flower on the township coat of arms is the pretty columbine, an exotic drooping plant of

---

* Probably because of its excessive dependence on profanity. For example: "Every day, from off the Bay the———wind doth Blow, / And what the———a man's to do, I———do not know …"—Anon.

crimson and yellow that grows everywhere in Persephone and the neighbouring townships. It is an ancient symbol of peace. It is also a stimulant with powerful narcotic properties. Plantings of columbine can now be found throughout the area.

Most indigenous tree species except the Persephone pine were cleared off in the days of early settlement and were replaced during the reforestation effort of the 1930s with spruce, pine, cedar, chokecherries, and dogwood. Not many houses are built out of dogwood these days (although some farmers up in the highlands still repair fences with grapevines and large burdocks), and the lumber industry is pretty much extinct. However, the eastern slope of Pipesmoke Mountain and the Pine and Petunia River Valleys have been designated by the United Nations as a World Biosphere Reserve. Many exotic and significant plant and animal species can be found here, including the zebra mussel, the purple loosestrife, the lamprey eel, the stinging nettle, poison oak, and the Rift rattlesnake, which is basically harmless if you're within ten minutes of a hospital.

In the second week of my stay in Larkspur I found myself trapped in yet another confab with the reeve and his entourage in a haze of bacon and cigarette smoke in the Red Hen Restaurant. After a decent interval I excused myself and went outside for a stroll along the Pine. The sun came out and some raucous red-winged blackbirds scolded me from the scrubby saplings that grow along the riverbank. As I made my way along the fishing path that follows the river, the birds were replaced by two large flies that circled my head, trying to take a piece out of my ear. I headed uphill to escape them along a little lane that winds up the side of Hall's Hill. After a vigorous climb I reached the summit and was rewarded with an impressive view of the lake away to the north and, in the distance, the great Hawk Island with her little Hatchling Islands in a row behind her in the blue-green water. But I'd walked long enough. It was time to return to the reeve in his smoke-filled den.

I was about to turn back down the path when I heard voices. I noticed a group of middle-aged types in Bermuda shorts a little way off, just sitting down to a picnic lunch on the crest of the hill. One of them was a pleasant red-haired woman about my age with an outdoor freshness about her. She mopped her freckled brow with a napkin from their hamper and explained that they were a band of volunteers with the Watershed Biological Trust who were releasing Rift rattlesnakes back into the wild in an attempt to reestablish a small core population of this indigenous species. According to the geodetic survey, she informed me, Hall's Hill is the second-highest point in southern Ontario. I would have stayed for lunch, but I wasn't sure which hamper had the snakes in it.

• • •

In the seventeenth century, the slope below Pipesmoke Mountain was the home of the Petun Indians, sometimes called the Tobacco Nation of the Huron people. The Petuns spent their days hunting, fishing, growing their own smoking material, and cultivating the three sisters: corn, squash, and runner beans. Nearly five hundred years later, the residents of Persephone Township still hunt and fish through the area. They too grow their own smoking material and, if weather permits, they do a little farming on the side.

The first contact between Europeans and the indigenous population did not take place until 1615, when Étienne Brûlé guided his old friend Samuel de Champlain to the land of the Petuns.* That summer, several of

---

* It is becoming increasingly obvious to present-day historians that Champlain was lost pretty much from the day he left his veranda in Brouage on the coast of Brittany, France, in 1603 until Christmas Day in 1635, when he died in Quebec City. He left six volumes of travel notes that contain only one reference to any recognizable physical landform west of Montreal, that being the Lachine Rapids, which had been marked on a map previously by Jacques Cartier, who believed he had found the Yangtze River. Historians say there is some evidence that Champlain spent the winter of 1615–16 in Persephone Township, but then again it could have been the area near what is now Chatham, Ontario, or the Finger Lakes district in New York State. By this time, he had long since thrown away his astrolabe and compass and was running bare-assed through the forest with his Indian friends. He did emerge from time to time over the next decade to ask for money from home, or to report some fresh quarrel he had started with the tribes to the south.

Champlain handed down to us very detailed accounts of his life with the people he called Indians, who clearly enjoyed his company and were happy to take him anywhere he wanted to go, which wasn't anywhere in particular. His employers often wrote to him asking for news of gold, northwest passages, fountains of youth, and so

Champlain's men drowned when a canoe overturned in the rapids of the Ottawa River, a tragic moment that was turned to great advantage by this ingenious explorer. Champlain noted that his Indian guides popped to the surface and were rescued, which prompted him to order his men to dispense with the conventional fifty-pound steel breastplate and helmet, the leather jerkin, and steel-toed boots in favour of doeskin underpants and primitive life preservers made of short cedar planks and rawhide. Not only did this innovation result in a remarkable increase in life expectancy, it proved to be an enormous relief to the French in coping with the brutal summer heat that Champlain frequently complained of in his journal. In another bold move, Champlain also banned horses from his canoes after this expedition, which cut travelling time even further.

Pipesmoke Mountain gained its name from the tobacco haze that hung over its ridges in the dead of late summer in the time of the Jesuits. Father Gauloise, writing in the *Jesuit Relation* of 1643, mentions "the delicate play of sunlight and cloud along the hills on the western horizon, presenting a hazy aura, which is pleasing to the eye but is offensive to the nostrils." The cleric was coming into contact for the first time with a tribe who had a serious smoking habit. The name Petun comes from the Huron word meaning "short of breath," and the Petun word Nottawasaga means "land of the morning cough."

Champlain was much taken with the area and named it Huronie, or Huronia, in honour of his guides, the Hurons, then acting as middlemen between the French and other tribes of what is now southern Ontario. In his blundering Eurocentric white male way, he failed to realize that the area already had a name, which was Petunia. The misapprehension continued for two more centuries and was only partially corrected with the naming of Port Petunia in 1852, which by that time carried the later Ojibway name of Oh-ke-won-do-say-mee (translation: "Why do you want to live down there with all those bugs?"). Then it was the Ojibway's turn to be offended.

---

forth, but they went to their graves without satisfaction. It is an ironic footnote to his career that Champlain's grave and headstone have been misplaced. In death, as in life, his whereabouts are unknown.

In spite of some grumbling about the names, the Indian tribes coexisted quite peacefully. The Jesuit mission among the Petun met with limited success. After thirty years living among the Native people, Father Gauloise could not document a single case of a successful Christian conversion. In 1649, the Iroquois passed a non-smoking bylaw, which upset the Petun nation and triggered the Tobacco Wars. The Iroquois drove the Petuns, the Hurons, and the French missionaries out of the area altogether, and a Dark Age began that lasted for more than a century.

Although the Jesuits recounted stories of savage battles between the Iroquois and the Petuns, with great loss of life on both sides, these are not first-hand accounts and cannot be relied on. One theory holds that the Jesuits were witnessing the quarter-final playoffs of the regional lacrosse season and didn't realize that the people being carried off the field were having fun and would probably recover from their injuries.

You have to remember the wide gulf that existed between these two great cultures, the European and the North American, the barriers of language and custom, theology and morality. Some of the Jesuit accounts of these "battles" were written by the *abbé* back in Quebec City four hundred miles away, and only after the bones of several of his missionaries had been delivered in a basket, with a birchbark note saying, "Please return the basket." This goes a long way towards explaining why one incident of 1649 in the village of Etharita is described in the *Jesuit Relations* by a certain Father Gitane as "a bloody massacre by the Iroquois" but comes down to us in the oral tradition of the Iroquois nation merely as "a solid hitting game."

• • •

It is at this point in his chronicle that my grandfather introduces the first of the big names of Persephone's early years, Captain Charles Augustus Fortescue, who later came to be known as the Champlain of Hillhurst County.* Were it not for Captain Fortescue's exploits, Persephone Township would look very different today. When you compare it with the

* Hillhurst County includes the three townships Fortescue surveyed in the 1830s, Persephone, Demeter, and Pluto.

orderly grid pattern of the townships around it, you'll see what I mean. Persephone sits on a 30-degree tilt compared with the normal inclination of its neighbours, and its borders and roads do not line up with those of any of the surrounding townships. It would appear that this peculiarity represents a bold attempt by Fortescue to survey the area without reference to any previous surveyor's mark.*

For my purposes, namely the post-contact saga of Persephone, Captain Fortescue enters the record in 1831, the year he secured a commission to survey the area around the mouth of the Petunia River on Georgian Bay to prepare it for settlement. Given Fortescue's crowded curriculum vitae, which included distinguished service under the Duke of Wellington during the Peninsular War and a significant contribution to General Isaac Brock's victory at the Battle of Queenston Heights, it must have seemed to his employer, the commissioner of Crown lands at York, that he was just the man for the job of bringing order to an unkempt wilderness. Time and again in his long and event-filled career, Fortescue had proved to be a man who understood the value of a straight line.†

---

* This is known in surveyors' language as "an uncontrolled traverse from an unknown point, performed by a deviant while disoriented."

† Charles Augustus Fortescue did not live to write his autobiography, but he was a man of opportunity who had risen from humble origins in his native Cornwall, where he was born in 1791. His parents ran a lighthouse near Penzance but were so poor they could seldom afford to light the lamp. However, they were able to eke out a living clearing shipwreck debris from the shore. Charles tired of this arduous work and at the age of fourteen joined the British army. By 1808 he was serving in the Peninsular War against Napoleon. Military documents of the period state merely that he was either a cook or a cook's assistant. But Fortescue's later campaign literature in his race for a seat in the provincial legislature sheds considerably more light on a remarkable military career. Perhaps through modesty, he did not see fit to reveal until then that he had risen rapidly through the ranks on merit alone to become first a sergeant, then a lieutenant, and finally lieutenant general. He would have been a general except that the post was already filled by Arthur Wellesley, who was about to become the Duke of Wellington. So Fortescue had to content himself with being acting general while Wellington was in town. Together Wellington and Fortescue defeated many of Napoleon's finest marshals and enjoyed many happy times together. After a particularly clever thumping of Massena at the battle of Torres

Fortescue's commission was simple: "Lay out the Persephone farms in lots of One Hundred Acres, each lot to be located by Astronomical Course and Variation." For this work, he was to be paid 15 shillings; his chief chain-bearer 5 shillings; seven axemen 3 shillings each; and three strong backs to do the heavy lifting, 2 shillings each. He selected as his chief chain-bearer an old friend from the mess tents of Fort York, Terence Lynch, and for the rest of the crew he drew a sieve through the taverns on Yonge Street.

In the only photograph of Captain Fortescue that survives, taken for his campaign for elected office in 1860, we see a man with the stamp of Wellington on him. He has the high forehead, beak nose, and thrust chin, but something about the eyes is wrong. They seem to focus about a

---

Vedras in 1810, Wellington began calling Fortescue "my beloved Charles," and Fortescue took to teasing Wellington as "Old Iron Pants." A remarkable accomplishment for a lad of nineteen, and difficult to believe, were it not for the fact that we have the authority of Fortescue's own account to verify it.

It was during the Peninsular War that Fortescue discovered his lifelong love of charting unknown territory, especially during an attack by the enemy. He seems to have been able to think more strategically away from the sound of the guns. Throwing away his rifle and knapsack, he would take to the woods armed with nothing but a compass and a canteen. Eventually he would emerge, much to the surprise of the enemy, who, having tired of chasing him, then fell an easy prey to the disciplined British square, an infantry defensive position.

A grateful king and country dispatched Fortescue across the ocean to Kingston Harbour on Lake Ontario with a contingent of prisoners of war and deserters to help fight the new enemy, the Americans, in the War of 1812. Fortescue asked to be returned to the ranks to pursue his first love, the feeding of his brother officers in the army mess tent. From there he took ship for the fledgling town of York, there to join a small contingent of British regulars led by General Isaac Brock. Shortly after that he found himself at the foot of Queenston Heights, just as the American army began crossing the Niagara River to invade Canada. Seeing so many of the enemy massed on the opposite side of the river, Fortescue instinctively reverted to his Peninsular War tactics and again took to the woods. This time he shed his rifle and knapsack and unbuckled his sword, which allowed him to make better time than ever. The Indians who tried to follow him were amazed at his speed and agility and christened him "Runs with Rabbits" in a traditional ceremony, some time after the battle, at which they returned his sword to him.

The route Fortescue took between Niagara and Fort York was so straight that it was later adopted as a road by the military and later still by the provincial roads department as the Queen Elizabeth Way.

thousand yards beyond the camera, producing an unsettling effect. Perhaps Dr. Goulding comes closest to explaining the personality of this man when he quotes several comments from elderly residents who knew Fortescue and remembered his "rabbit-like energy" and "firefly enthusiasms." Grandfather drew the conclusion that Fortescue was "quite mad."

• • •

Surveyors were often paid in land, and some eventually settled on their acreages to become farmers. But the real profits came from their manipulation of land purchases and the inside information they possessed about the choicest parcels. Fortescue was no farmer; his ambition was to secure fresh survey contracts and an appointment as a locator, the person who guided prospective pioneers into the township to their land grants.

A handful of government administrators, army officers, and clerics—known in the colony as the Family Compact—controlled all matters of settlement in Upper Canada in this period.* Every appointment went through the lieutenant-governor's office and passed under the sharp eye of the Reverend John Strachan, the leader of the Church of England in Upper Canada and the *eminence grise* in the vice-regal chambers.

I have reason to believe that Fortescue went to Strachan and persuaded him to support his applications in return for advice about which lands should be designated for the church under the clergy reserves system.† One-seventh of all new lands were set aside for the church. Strachan's son-in-law was the co-commissioner of the privately held Canada Company, then busy purchasing large tracts of the Ontario wilderness from the government and selling lots to settlers. With Fortescue looking over his shoulder and giving advice, Strachan would have had a distinct advantage in selecting the best lands for the church and for his son-in-law, which is exactly what happened. Strachan

---

* Control of the provincial government has been considerably streamlined since that time. Decision-making now rests in the hands of about three people: the premier, his speechwriter, and his pollster.

† Fortescue's estate included a single place setting of Strachan's silverware, which indicates he had dinner with the cleric about this time.

also seems to have recommended Fortescue as a locator for the Crown. And it was Fortescue who resurrected Sir James Yeo's imaginary escape route, the line on the Admiralty map that led into the heart of Persephone to Larkspur.

By the spring of 1832, Captain Fortescue and his crew were once again cutting their way into the bush, this time striking west from Kempenfeldt, having been awarded the contract to survey and build the New Military Road along Yeo's planned route. At the end of the year, they reached the Petunia River, where they began construction of a pontoon bridge. The next spring, Fortescue climbed a rudimentary wooden tower built for this purpose and took a sighting on the granite cliff he had seen at close range the previous spring, now clearly visible in the distance. Then he ordered his crew off into the bush to mark the trail west.

"The virgin forest now parted," writes Dr. Goulding, "Persephone lay soft and verdant and ready for her next assignation with history."

Eric Nicol

The grand old man of Canadian humour, Eric Nicol is a three-time winner of the Leacock Medal for Humour with a body of work that spans six decades, beginning with his debut work, *Sense and Nonsense,* in 1947. To give you some idea of the scope of Eric Nicol's remarkable career, I have included excerpts from *A Scar Is Born,* his 1967 account of taking a play to Broadway, followed by excerpts from his most recent work, *Old Is In,* which was published in 2004 when he was eighty-five years old.

from *A Scar Is Born*

T*he postmistress weighed the bulky package of playscript I was mailing to New York, affixed a customs sticker, and asked: "What is the value of the enclosure?"*

Having considered this for a moment, I said: "It's either worth a half a million or it's worth nothing. It's a stage play."

"I'll put 'No commercial value,'" said the postmistress.

...

The chubby, well-dressed gentleman who had boarded the jet at Toronto, and taken the seat beside mine, sighed as the stewardess brought him his Bloody Mary.

"It combines nourishment with sedation," he explained to me, fracturing the delicate silence that had constituted our relationship. There were only ten minutes more till landing time at Kennedy Airport, a tolerable period for conversation with the hayseed abutting him.

"You're a New Yorker?" I said.

He accepted the tribute gracefully.

"I flew up to Toronto this morning," he said, "for the CBC cocktail party in honour of Lorne Greene, an old and very dear friend of mine."

"You flew all the way to Toronto for a cocktail party?" I exclaimed, and I think it pleased him, in a quiet way. I said: "Lorne Greene has done all right for himself, hasn't he? I remember when—"

"He is a great talent and always has been." The crisp yet solemn tone made me feel that I had desecrated a monument. I observed a two-minute silence out of respect for Lorne Greene's talent. Then I ventured:

"Are you in show business?"

"Peripherally."

I had gone too far. Prying. I let him vampirize his Bloody Mary, hoping he might ask me why I was flying to New York. (Author of a play opening on Broadway, by God. I guess that matches being an old and very dear friend of the entire Cartwright family.)

The New Yorker did not ask. Instead he peered into the night sky and sighed:

"I've missed the helicopter connection from Kennedy to downtown New York. I'll have to take a taxi."

"I'm taking the airport bus," I said, deciding I might as well be totally loathsome. "I wonder if you would recommend a hotel in New York. I was thinking of staying at the Algonquin."

A small frisson of affront passed through the portly frame. He glanced at me for the first time, taking in the unprepossessing aspect that the flight from Vancouver had rendered even more wrinkled than usual.

"The Algonquin is a very nice theatrical hotel," he informed me. "If I were you I'd try some place like the Crassmore—a commercial hotel with reasonable rates."

"That sounds fine," I said, hating it already.

"And it's close to the garment workers' district," he said, with another visual sweep of my carbuncled trousers.

"I'd like to be handy," I conceded. (Why doesn't he ask me why I'm staying at the hotel? So much tact—it's boorish.) "I'm looking forward to seeing some New York theatre."

"All the old burlesque houses have gone, practically," he cautioned. "But you'll find plenty of nudie films. The Forty-second Street area is saturated with them."

"I love a good nudie film," I said, aching for him to choke on his Bloody Mary.

The plane subsided onto Kennedy Airport. My fellow passenger showed remarkable agility, for his size, in vanishing before I might present the horror of sharing his taxi.

Bloody Maryland, I am here.

. . .

I know why I am always the last person to be waited on in a restaurant. I know why cab drivers ignore me in the crowd hailing taxis, till I am standing alone with my baggage and the great empty night. It has something to do with my animal magnetism. Either I've got too much of it or not enough. I prefer to think that it is the former. I don't have any trouble attracting drunks. I have top priority with dogs in heat. But what baffles me is how the conveyor belt that delivers airline baggage to the waiting passengers knows which one is mine and holds it till the last.

The actual order of arrival from the chute is: 78 assorted pieces of luggage, then a wicker hamper, then nothing, and more nothing, and finally the brown suitcase and portable typewriter from which I was separated in an earlier life.

Anxiety plus New York in August equals perspiration in the quantity dreaded by researchers in the labs of deodorant manufacturers. Picking up my chattels, I know that I am not nice to be near. I walk out of the terminal building, and three aircraft are trying to take off at once—I know why. I wanted to make a good impression on New York, but my pores are open, my mouth is open, and I'm not sure about my fly.

The airline bus accepts me, after a swarthy individual has taken my baggage and thrown it under the wheels. The bus waits a long time, in case any other stragglers show up. A drunk boards the bus, and sits beside me. We wait for the dog in heat. He must have missed the flight. Uttering a curse in Spanish that apparently covers us all, the bus driver hurls the bus into gear and we career towards the island of Manhattan.

It is nearly midnight, and the bus driver drives as one who knows that if he does not get home to the garage before the hour strikes, his bus changes back into an overripe rutabaga.

The rules of the highway are simple: the smaller vehicle yields to the larger. We have the right-of-way so long as we do not converge with a missile-carrier.

The bus plunges into a tunnel, white tile whizzing past like an endless, frenzied comfort station. We are cast out of the pipe as by some cosmic plunger, draining into narrow alleys and the bus terminal. Manhattan is mine, but there is no one on hand to make the presentation.

•••

One thing I have learned from the read-through is that the playwright should be careful with his stage directions in the script:

HARRY: *Yes.* (*NODS HIS HEAD*)

The actor does not like this kind of stage direction because he prefers to interpret the word "Yes" himself. He is unlikely to nod anything but his head, and even if he could nod his feet he would sooner work the business out unassisted by the author.

Another kind of stage direction that is not a good idea, I've learned, is the kind that puts too much demand on the actor's ability to convey something. I mean the stage direction that goes:

(*Marcia puts down the telephone. In her eyes we see that she is contemplating suicide. In her right eye, she's thinking of shooting herself. In her left eye, poison. She tilts her head sideways, and we know that she has suddenly remembered her childhood, those happy days in the Pittsburgh dry cleaner's where she worked as a sponger. She clasps her hands together. Has she found the strength to go on? No. Her ears indicate that she hasn't. From the way she ripples her lips we gather that ...*)

And so on. I am told that it is partly because of stage directions like these that actors and directors have in recent years been putting on plays that do not require a playwright. Called a "happening" or "instant theatre," what they are actually is an escape from author's stage directions, which rot the actor's socks.

George Bernard Shaw wrote whole pages of stage directions, and directors hate him for it. They still do his plays, but they much prefer Shakespeare, whose plays have endured mainly because when Romeo enters, all Shakespeare writes is "Enter Romeo." He left it to the director to decide whether Romeo should walk on, run on, swing in on a rope, crawl forth on his stomach, or do a soft-shoe shuffle.

Directors are immensely grateful for this kind of leeway in their creative contribution to a production. Old Bill, having been an actor himself, knew what he was about when he went easy on the brackets. A dramatist can parenthesize himself to death.

On the first day of rehearsals the director of my play told the cast to draw a line through all the stage directions in the script. I think he was trying to tell me something.

• • •

Blocking is when the director shows the actors where he wants them to move on the stage during the course of the play. I have found it interesting, as the author of the play, to watch how the director has blocked the scenes. As I had visualized it, the actors would each stand in the same spot, and deliver my lines, and the roof would cave in. Just a simple, one-two-three kind of thing.

But no. It is astonishing how busy actors become once the director gets hold of them. I get the impression he believes that the more physical animation accompanying my lines, the better. I am braced to find, when I return to rehearsals, that a trapeze has been added to the library setting and the cast are making their entrances on motorcycles.

But the blocking is done. The specific reason that the director has shown me the door—a move not indicated in the stage directions—is that today he is going to tell the actors what the play is about. That he should have to tell them what the play is about may strike you as funny. Indeed, I got a chuckle out of it myself, ha-ha. But apparently actors need this guidance lest the fact escape them that the play is a comedy. If even one actor interprets his part as King Lear, the play loses something.

I rather wish I could be there, though, to learn for myself what the play is about. That I wrote the play gives me no credentials whatever. Any director will tell you that the author is the last person in the world to whom to turn for explanation of what the play means.

I hate to admit it, but I think they could have put on the play without me. Right from the beginning, I am the father of the child, of no further use after the act of conception. Once the labour pains begin, my presence is mere protocol unless there are complications, such as difficulty in the delivery of a line. It is no hell sitting in your hotel room all day muttering "Push! Push!"

• • •

The first preview leaves the audience—as one of my betters has said— completely underwhelmed. Our lighting man comments: "Laugh? I thought I'd never start." Before the last of the audience has cleared the aisle, producer and director descend upon me, faces as grim as a wet weekend in Walla Walla. However non grata the playwright's presence during rehearsal, once the performance is for real he recovers his popularity with a swiftness beyond the dreams of Scope.

• • •

I am taking my own notes during the preview performances. For this purpose I have brought with me from Vancouver a flashlight pen, a pitiful attention to detail in the same class with General Custer's packing his fishing rod before setting out for the Little Big Horn.

I could take an ordinary flashlight into the audience with me, but I have found that the theatregoers mistake you for an usher and turn ugly if you refuse to give them programs and show them to their seats. It can add up to a very tiring evening for the author, and I also got into trouble with the theatre attendants' union.

Alternatively, the playwright can hold a tape recorder on his lap, during a performance, and dictate notes to that. I tried it once, but it disturbed the people sitting around me to hear muttered comments like "Move that footstool" and "Kill that bloody worklight!" An umbrella brought down over your head affects the quality of the recordings.

The flashlight pen eliminated these hazards. Unfortunately, mine was made in Japan, by the Sunny Light Luminous Pen Company, and the assembly instructions have that polite yet enigmatic mien we associate with the Orient.

"When you change the battery turn the part B anti-clockwise to remove and replace a new battery." (Replace a *new* battery?)

"When you change ink refill or pencil please turn the head of an ink refill and the part E anti-clockwise to remove it."

I have the feeling I shall never change the ink refill. I just hope the supply holds out in the original refill.

The cast of the play do not, I think, share this hope. During rehearsals my note-taking, signalled by the little light going on in the orchestra, to them means that I am going to cut lines. And one thing an actor hates worse than hives where he can't scratch is to have one of his lines cut. He never assumes that the line is cut because it was no good in the first place. No matter how bad a line is, once he has learned it an actor believes that he can make it glow with such an effulgence as never was on land or sea.

It is his adopted child. Misshapen and dull though it is, he has learned to love each line with the kind of devotion that is lavished only on what makes a role plumper. What an actor fears most is emaciation of the part, which is of course greater than the whole.

In these circumstances, when my little flashlight pen lights up in the darkness, a ripple of anguish passes over the stage. The fairy-like glimmer is a Tinkerbell in reverse—everyone in the cast wishes that her light would go out and stay out. If applause would do it, they would bring the house down.

Should my playwriting be similarly extinguished, the investment in the flashlight pen is by no means lost. The Sunny Light Luminous Pen Company lists other careers available to pen owners: "Policemen, Doctors, Waitresses, Pilots, Taxi Drivers, Photographers, Stewardesses." All I need to do is turn anti-clockwise....

• • •

Eric Nicol's play "A Minor Adjustment" opened in New York on Friday, October 6, 1967. It closed on Saturday, October 7, 1967. "I arrived in New York as a nobody," he recalled. "But I left it as a complete nonentity."

FROM *Old Is In*

Actuarial Discrimination

No question: women age better than men. Their face develops a better class of wrinkle. Life has given old ladies laugh lines and old men exit lines.

Old men commit suicide more often than old women. Well, actually, they commit suicide only once, but it seems like more.

Why is this? How do women manage to age graciously, while men hang on grimly to the illusion that the expanding bald spot is temporary, caused by a surge of testosterone?

When we say "There's no fool like an old fool," we're talking Tom, Dick, and Harry, not Tess, Deb, and Hilda. Women mature like French wine and cheese, while men age more like meatloaf.

Women enjoy each other's society more as they get older, while men continue to eye one another as rivals in some endeavour that escapes their mind. When you visit a rest home you see the women residents sitting around together, verbally dismembering relatives, while each old guy sits alone outside in his wheelchair, trying to figure out an escape route.

Say "old hermit" and we automatically think of a guy with years of attitude. Old women are too sociable to avoid company unless their hearing aid is on the blink.

If, out in the woods, we see the sign "trespassers will be shot," we know that the property owner is an old man whose only remaining meaningful relationship is with a double-barrelled shotgun.

Thus all the evidence indicates that women accept the aging process, whereas men still see it as an unnatural affliction, probably caused by their earlier contact with females.

Pets for the Mature Masochist

Very often the senior has lost the marriage partner, as a result of death, divorce, or simply leaving the spouse alone in a wilderness area. Most commonly it is the wife who is now a widow and needing something to clean up after. This is why we see so many old ladies out walking small, short-hair male dogs on a leash. They are compensating for the lost hubby, but with a companion that doesn't shed or leave the seat up.

There is controversy over whether, with time, a person's dog comes to resemble the owner, or the other way around. What *is* demonstrable is that the larger the widow, the smaller the dog. In contrast, old men prefer to be seen with a big dog, in case the promenade turns violent. But the pet's food bill deters most seniors from owning a mastiff, let alone a horse.

For the lone senior who is allergic to the outdoors the ideal companion is of course a cat. A cat doesn't need to be walked, getting plenty of exercise climbing curtains or going on long, territorial hikes that strengthen the owner's relationship with the SPCA. The only other caveat with a cat is that the cat has never got over being considered sacred by the ancient Egyptians. Thus the senior must accept the feline's viewing him or her as a potential human sacrifice. It is one way for a person to feel wanted, though less so than a pound of liver.

As for supporting a parrot as a pet, only the wealthy senior can afford the cost of even a previously owned bird. Which may also have an intimidating vocabulary ("Eff off, matey!") unsuitable for visitors and some family members.

A canary is a more practical pet, especially if you are living in a coal mine, or other social housing. A budgie, however, can be a major disappointment when you realize that it is not normal for the bird to sleep on its back.

What about a poisonous snake? A great conversation piece, winning respect from neighbours, but hard to kennel. Also, you have to suspect the motive of the family member who surprises you with the Christmas gift of a boa constrictor.

As for other reptiles, such as turtles or tortoises, disappointment lies in expecting to have a pet that moves more slowly than you do. A motivated turtle can hustle its hump at a surprising pace, so that the senior joins the hare in being humbled by a shellful of wrinkles.

Finally, there are fish. The home aquarium is perfect for the senior who wants a pet that is likely to predecease him. The average domestic goldfish has a life expectancy of about two hours, or as long as needed to fetch it from the pet shop, whichever comes first.

It may be possible to become emotionally attached to a goldfish, but it will have to be a rush job.

The point is: everyone—and this includes older folk—needs to feel needed by some living entity as a reason to get out of bed in the morning. Unless a person has led an entirely self-centred life, she or he has to water something, clean its litter box, or just talk to the rubber plant about its for God's sake shaping up.

Home to Rust

A *home*. Something the old person dreads being put in. She, or especially he, resolves to use all of his or her remaining strength to hang onto their present home's doorknob, as caring family members try to drag the resident off to the Last Resort.

One of the advantages of a federal penitentiary over a rest home is that the inmate doesn't have to pay for his lodging. And of course there is a good chance that the inmate will one day walk out of the facility. Without being pursued by bloody-minded caregivers.

Running away from home is harder after age ninety. Yet a person will use all his remaining cunning to break out of stir and find his way back to his old home, whose new owner will have to beat him off with a broom.

This happens though the *retirement home* offers luxury incarceration. The elderly resident may even have a clear view of a golf course, used by younger people still able to pick up a golf ball without triggering a Code Red.

Actually life in a nursing home is not as bad as we anticipate, provided that the staff are liberal in administering narcotic tranquilizers. The difference between the outward signs of being senile and being stoned is mercifully slight after age eighty-five. Going to pot is the best trip available.

Still, most elderly people would prefer to die in the comfort of their own home. It is usually a family member who becomes unduly concerned about incompetence, such as the oldster's accusing the letter carrier of being an agent of a Middle Eastern terrorist organization, or Grandpa's trying to prune the cat, or his repeatedly phoning 911 to report a suspicious hydrant.

Sooner or later Gramps must yield to relatives or other picky authorities who insist that he fold his oxygen tent and totter into an institution. Chaining oneself to the bed will not deter grim kin.

So, is the oldster advised to accept his fate graciously? With a smile? "I'll treat this as a new adventure in living! A chance to make new friends! To explore the outer space of my soul!" Hell, no. The conscript should make the family feel as guilty as possible, while having to be physically removed by conservation officers.

You have enough rigid parts without adding the stiff upper lip.

Brian O'Connell

Some people have the phrase "codger" thrust upon them;
some resent it, some deny it, but there are some who revel in it.
Such is the case of Brian O'Connell of Antigonish, Nova Scotia,
who in his twilight years said he "looks back on his life as
one long, bitter battle with ill-health, poverty, and the
semi-colon …" You thought Maritimers were happy to see
us when we popped by for a visit? Now you know.

FROM *Magnets and Meatloaf*

Walter

There are a very, very few of us who, in the early days of childhood, did not have an imaginary playmate.

By age nine the imaginary friend had usually departed. If you were still conversing with him or her around age twenty the guys in the white coats came and took you away.

In the case of males there were some rather strict requirements for this friendly phantom. He had to be smaller, skinnier, and stupider than you so that you could beat up on him and generally overshadow him in all areas. He had to be prepared to accept all responsibility for bad conduct; to do what he was told without complaint.

Mine was named Walter and he led an awful life. He was blamed for a multiplicity of crimes but nobody believed me when I said it was Walter who was stealing cookies (cake, fudge, candy, etc.). They scoffed when I insisted it was Walter who was shooting at my sisters' legs with a pellet gun from under the veranda. I got the lickings anyway and naturally, I beat up on Walter. Pass it on!

But by and large he was good company. We went a lot of places together and despite my vastly superior talents, we hit it off fairly well.

Somewhere, long about grade four I sent him to the store to borrow some ice cream wafers and he never returned again in his entirety. Occasionally I saw him in the distance, but he was a stranger. We didn't speak at all and then one day he was gone completely. I don't know where; maybe he joined the navy or went to live in The Little House on the Prairie. It was someplace romantic, I'm sure.

Well, sir, you can imagine my astonishment when he showed up the other day while I was shaving. The sight of him made me sick. He didn't look a day over twenty-one. He was fit and trim, athletic looking, had all his hair and teeth and not a sign of a liver spot.

He stood there laughing at me.

"Go away, Walter," I told him. "I don't need you any more."

Walter shook his head in disgust. "Look at you," he said. "You're a sight. You look like a pot-bellied old man."

"Walter, that's what I am, a pot-bellied old man!"

"Absolutely no need of it," said Walter. "Look at me, if you had stuck with me, you might look like this today."

"Walter, if I had hung onto you I'd be locked up by now."

"You should be locked up, you're a sight."

"Do me a favour, Walter, go away. I'm too old for you."

"I'm going, but I owe you a thing or two, and I always pay my debts."

"Forget it, Walt, you don't owe me a thing."

"Ah, but I do," said Walter, and he walked over and punched me in the mouth. Fortunately I had laid the razor down or I would have cut my throat.

When I had fully recovered, he was gone, forever, I hope.

There is, of course, a moral to this memoir. Don't look in your mirror except when absolutely necessary. Walter, or Sally, or Becky or Bubu, Butch or Mannie, or whoever, may be waiting there for you.

Hub of the World

D eep in my flat chest I chuckle bronchially when I read that this or that
place is the centre of the universe; that on a certain corner in a certain
city ultimately everybody will pass.

I know where the centre of the universe is really located. I live smack dab
in the middle of it. Antigonish is the hospitality capital of the world and the
month of July—Highland Games time—is when it all reaches the peak.

Only a few of you oldtimers will remember Waltham McQuaig. He lived
here in relative obscurity but in his own circle of relatives, numbering 1300,
he was highly regarded.

He held the all-time record for hospitality locally. In a single week he
logged 118 guests spread thickly through the house and housed in nine trail-
ers and three tents pegged into the lawns and flower beds.

Unfortunately, Waltham was not robust and the effort killed him. He
died standing up en route to the front door to welcome yet another guest.
They buried him that way; with his right hand extended in warm greeting.
It posed some problems, that hand sticking up in the middle of the wake.
Some of his women relatives wanted to fill it with carnations but one of the
more literate members recalled that the pineapple is an ancient symbol of
hospitality. The McQuaigs were always big on culture. They voted for the
fruit.

So there he rested peacefully. The first time all summer he hadn't been
relegated to a camp cot; holding his pineapple high.

The innkeepers guild never would believe that Waltham housed and fed
all those people for nothing. They hated his guts and picketed the funeral. It
took place the same day as the Highland Games parade and caused considerable confusion. Some of the tourists wrote home that the flowers were
lovely but they couldn't find the pipe bands.

There is, of course, a popular myth that all Antigonishers are extraordi-
narily rich with lavish homes in the country. What really happens is this. The
visitors take over the homes in town and the natives move deep into the bush.
Somebody from the university recently got a grant of $39.50 to do a paper

on this phenomenon. It is entitled "The Hospitality Inspired Interior Rural Mass Migration In Northeastern Nova Scotia."

That brings up the case of Moody Stutz. Moody got upset by the summer influx and built himself a tree house in the Keppoch area. Every July 1 when his vacation came up, Moody, his wife and two kids, climbed twenty-five feet into the house and pulled the ladder up. Moody used to sit on the landing with a shot gun. Unfortunately, in 1969, he shot two distant cousins who tried to effect an entry by swinging through the trees. His sentence was, of course, quite light, and every summer they let him out to vacation in the tree house. But they won't give him back his gun.

Personally, I learned to cope long ago. I am an early riser and because, in summer, every foot of floor space is littered with sleeping people, I slip quietly from the house. I used to make a cup of tea first but I kept stepping on the faces of kids asleep on the kitchen floor. Now I sally forth without sustenance.

Attired in my snappy dark brown polo pyjamas and my golden judo robe, I stroll through the neighbourhood until the house quakes. I hesitate to use the word "wakes" or "rouses" because it hardly describes a small army coming to life.

Even my retreat is fraught with danger. The other morning two kids from the hockey school, en route to early practice, got fired up at the sight of my judo robe and, shouting some kung fu gibberish, they tossed me in the swamp twice.

The second time I stayed there. It was quiet and the bulrushes were fairly soft. It was damp and smelly but I was magnificently alone.

I plan to go there every morning now. All summer long.

Noreen Olson

I first discovered the writings of Noreen Olson while I was working in Japan, which is odd, considering she lives on a farm in the foothills of Alberta. In *The School Bus Doesn't Stop Here Any More*, Olson writes about the small joys and odd contradictions of life on a rural route, and she does so with unwavering honesty and good humour. It was one of Olson's earlier collections that turned up in Japan; it included "An Alternative to Farming," a funny and sharply pointed piece, included here.

FROM *The School Bus Doesn't Stop Here Any More*
Running the Combine

Julien, my husband's brother, was here for part of the harvest last year; and of course until school started the kids were able to help, but Julien had to go home to Ottawa, the kids started university, and the crew dwindled to one farmer and one unskilled labourer. It speaks well for the strength of our marriage that the farmer and his unskilled assistant still occupy the same bed.

It started out friendly enough. Ralph let me run the combine because the cab is air conditioned and because I don't back up well with the big truck. He made one round with me and explained the power takeoff, the correct gear to use, how to stop and start the elevators and augers, and at what height to maintain the pickup.

"It's all pretty simple and straightforward," he said, and (these are his exact words), "Watch that the grain auger is working, that floppy thing is going round and round, and stuff is coming out the back."

He drove off to a distant granary. I moved all the proper levers and the combine roared into action. I watched the grain auger, the floppy thing, and the stuff coming out the back. I watched so closely that several times I nearly missed picking up the swath and then I came to a corner and had to concentrate all my efforts on that. When the corner was safely negotiated, I checked the auger, the floppy thing, and stuff coming out the back. They seemed fine, but what was this tremendous heap of swath tumbling and growing ahead of the table? And why were all the little wheels and belts chattering so horribly, like two thousand sets of those wind-up false teeth? It was terrible. I shut off everything and sat there shaking.

"You have plugged the auger!" Ralph yelled "When you saw it starting to pile up, why didn't you stop?"

"You didn't tell me I had to watch this end too," I yelled back.

"I shouldn't have to tell you every little thing."

"If it's such a little thing, then why are you having such a big fit?"

The next few rounds were uneventful, then another funny noise began to bother me. It was not a chattering teeth sound, it was a grinding, pounding sound, but the auger was working, the floppy thing flopping, stuff coming out the back, and no big piles in front of the pickup. Oh no, the pickup! It was dragging terribly, and clods of dirt were being swallowed by the big corkscrew thing. I hit the lever and the whole table rose about nine feet in the air. I missed fifteen feet of swath, hit the lever again and resumed plowing, overcorrected and rose above the swath. I stopped the machine and adjusted the table height.

"I don't know why I didn't think of this myself," my husband said through clenched teeth. "Fall plowing and combining in one operation."

Late one night as we sat together over corned beef sandwiches and tea, he forgave me for plugging the machine and for ruining the pickup belt.

"Explain to me about the twenty feet of swath you missed in the southwest corner," he said.

"There was a mother grouse in there who must have had a late hatch. The babies couldn't run very fast and I think they were hiding in that piece of swath."

He nodded understandingly. "And how about the big piece on top of the hill?"

"Did you know that you can see the mountains from up there? When the sun shines through the clouds and individual beams fan out onto the mountains, I almost expect to hear a pronouncement from God. I'm afraid I was imagining what the pronouncement might be and I got off track a little. I meant to go back for it, but I couldn't find it."

"Ah yes," he sighed. "That explains the aimless wandering, which was going to be my next question."

"Actually," I told him, "I thought everything went very well. During that whole time, the auger worked, the floppy thing flopped and a lot of stuff came out the back."

An Alternative to Farming

When I first heard about the federal government's latest scheme to benefit the agriculture industry I was puzzled and skeptical. Under the proposed Rural Transition Program, federal funds would pay economically depressed farmers to, "relocate and retrain," so that they might "find an alternative to farming," and "explore differing life styles."

From where to where would they relocate? From west to east? From east to north? From fresh air family farm to smoggy city slum? What will the retrained farmer do? If he finds an alternative to farming will that alternative be one that he can live with? And as for "exploring different life styles," that could mean anything. Welfare is a different life style, so is begging, starving, picking pockets, staying with your in-laws, and visiting the food bank.

"You are being overly pessimistic," my husband observed. "Versatile as farmers are they should be wonderful candidates for retraining. The ones who went broke could become agricultural economists. They could teach from experience as in, 'don't do what I did, which was listen to the bankers and agricultural economists.'"

I could see that he was warming to the subject.

"Dalton Camp is the new adviser to the prime minister," he told me, "at a salary of $100,000 a year. Dalton could be replaced by four farmers at $25,000 each. Farmers have been telling the prime minister where to go and what to do for years but no one has ever offered to pay them for it."

"How about training farmers as football coaches," I suggested. "They are capable of handling large dumb animals under adverse weather conditions and they don't expect job security."

"Lawyers," Ralph contributed, "they could write more poorly worded and obscure laws and then appoint other farmers to judicial inquiries to study and implement the new rules."

"Hey," I added, "that suggests a whole new field, task forces on everything, ten to a task force and subjects could include land use, pollution, global warming, pornography, graffiti, TV violence, rural high speed internet, interest rates, CEO salaries, day care, paroles, and a financial system that allows food to be destroyed in one area while people are starving in another. Task Force heads could unionize, ratify contracts, establish tenure, and meet with a bargaining committee formed by other retrained farmers. The whole thing is self regenerating, it could go on forever!!"

"Farmers could take their rightful place in the scientific world," Ralph said, "for years we have been unwittingly testing chemicals for the herbicide, pesticide, and fertilizer manufacturers. Now maybe they can retrain farmers to take the place of those poor rabbits, rats, and monkeys. Greenpeace and the animal rights groups would be pleased."

Ideas were coming fast now.

"Weather forecasters," Ralph said. "Farmers guess wrong most of the time, they would fit right in with professional meteorologists."

"Rock stars," I yelled, "they are used to the sound of heavy metal."

"Counters of migratory birds," Ralph offered.

"Grasshopper stompers," I cried.

Our eldest son had been observing all this nonsense and now I asked him if he had any suggestions. "To tell you the truth," Mark said quietly, "I don't think it's a humorous subject."

Neither do we son, neither do we.

Patricia Pearson

Ah, yes, the joys and delights of impending parenthood.
The glow of pregnancy, the warmth that comes from knowing
you are nurturing a life within you, the bloated, swollen breasts
and the cracked, aching nipples. Oh, if only men could
experience such joys. *(Whew!)* In *Playing House,* Patricia Pearson
takes us on a romp through modern motherhood, beginning
with her discovery of the good news.

FROM *Playing House*

New life announces itself as a mystery that a mother cannot solve. Something happens, a certain gear-shifting in the body that she notes, but makes no sense of. Especially if she isn't planning to be pregnant. I shall offer myself as an example. I did not have a basal thermometer handy on my bureau, or any recall as to when I last had my period. I was not expecting to read *What to Expect When You're Expecting.* I was barely even in a relationship, with a man about whom I knew little. I was simply going about my business, enjoying early spring in New York City, when all of a sudden I woke up in the clean morning sunshine to find that my breasts had inflated like dinghies and were heavier than my head.

Late for work, I fiddled with my bra straps irritably, to no avail. They had all the supportive power of Scotch tape. I searched through the clothes on the floor of my one-room apartment and dragged on a shirt taut with Lycra, then I cupped my breasts in my hands as I stepped gingerly down the four flights of stairs of my walk-up, arranging my arms just so—as I entered the brisk-stepping crowds on Sixth Avenue—so that I could look like I was clutching myself in vexed contemplation over the Great Issues of the Day, as opposed to holding my tits up.

My first assumption was that I had a bad bout of PMS, so I dosed myself with evening primrose oil. We were wrapping up our April issue at *The Pithy Review,* heading into the inevitable panic of magazine production. There were last-minute changes, troubles with ad placement, authors to placate after pompous sentences were slashed from their essays, an editor-in-chief who rendered himself inaccessible behind closed doors in a pointed sulk. It happened every month, as if none of us possessed a short-term memory.

I had, myself, a rant to scribble for the back page, which I'd put off until the last minute, and a half-finished play to complete by the first of April. There was a letter to be sent to the editor of *The New York Times* about the treatment of carriage horses in Central Park, and postcards home to be mailed, lists of ideas, Post-it notes about people to meet, cocktails and beet chips to consume at the Temple Bar.

Life in a city as opportunistic and exuberant as New York always felt busy, even if nothing got done. It was the whirl of the place, the sense of movement that mattered to me, and I grounded myself with small certitudes: I am here. I pay my rent. I like my friends. I have a membership to MOMA. God, when I think about it now, what a slender ledge of a life I was comfortably sitting on then.

On Good Friday, I was in Rizzoli's bookstore contemplating the new Sylvia Plath biography when I realized that my nipples were so sensitive that I couldn't turn around quickly without crying out. For a few days, I donned the softest fabrics I could find in my closet—an old cashmere sweater my mother had given me to coddle myself through a documentary on Kurds, a silk blouse, and double-wired bra to ineffectually brace me for dance lessons—and still I walked around going, "Ow, ow, ow," as if I'd fallen into a patch of nettles.

Perplexed, I peered at myself in my small bathroom mirror, which entailed leaning over sideways while standing on the worn enamel sides of my tub, effectively looming into the circular looking-glass from stage left. My breasts looked more or less the same as always. My nipples seemed darker, and even bigger, somehow, but I hardly ever looked at my breasts. I liked my waist and my rear end, but in truth my breasts grew in a bit droopy from the outset, with the nipples too low on the orbs, as if Mother Nature stuck them on during a game of pin the tail on the donkey. I had a tendency to fling my arms above my head like the Venus de Milo whenever lovers were afoot, in order to lift the nipples to a more acceptable position. It took a bit of work, this manoeuvre, especially when I had to walk across the room to answer the phone. But worth it, you know, for not revealing everything your nakedness actually offers to say.

I'd been arm lifting quite a bit of late, because of a fellow named Calvin Puddie. No. Pudhee. Or no, that doesn't look right—I think it could be Puhdey. In any event, it's some sort of French-Canadian name, or more specifically Acadian, as in the French who emigrated to eastern Canada, and otherwise to Louisiana.

"That strikes me as a rather stark pair of choices," I told Calvin on our second date. "Either they opted for the frozen, craggy coast of Cape Breton and slogged away in coal mines, or they got to do Mardi Gras? A or B?"

"Well, it's a bit more complicated than that," he said lightly. But being a rather laconic man, he chose not to elaborate.

I knew that Calvin's father was a coal miner, and that he himself had been aiming no higher than a job as a janitor at the local veterans' hall when someone pointed out that he was musically gifted and ought to pursue it. This inspired him to head to Halifax to study music, after which he moved to Toronto, and from there, at some point, to New York. He worked as a jazz musician, living off the avails of his art, which was the annual salary equivalent of two Smarties and a piece of string.

We met at a bar called the Knitting Factory, where a band was playing Indonesian gamelan music. It was something a friend had dragged me to, and that friend bumped into Calvin, whom he knew through a mutual friend, who was a friend of other friends. So various friends gathered, and obediently listened to the occasional *ping* followed by half an hour of murderous silence, as is the tradition in gamelan music, and my friend from work said, "Frannie, that guy over there is also Canadian."

Therefore you must meet him, because you are of the same nationality.

So, after several vodka tonics, I did, and he was funny, if quiet. Very, very quiet, really, bordering on mute. He sat there in an old fedora with his hands placidly in his lap, gazing around inscrutably, tapping his brogues on the floor as if absently filling in rhythmic gaps for the musicians on stage.

He reminded me of Canada in small, distinct ways. His self-effacement was familiar, and he understood certain expatriate secrets, such as where Alberta was and how it felt to be treated like a doofus in Manhattan for being Canadian, as if we were a nation of cheerful, unimportant people with Down's syndrome.

He also had a talent for sly ridicule, which I happily discovered before I left the premises and forgot all about him. There was a novelist in our party who had had too many favourable notices in *The Paris Review* to keep his head low. He began droning on at length about anthropology and American Indians, whom he'd researched for an upcoming novel called *Whiskey Lament.* With his chin up and tilted in faux-reflectiveness, ennobled by his whitey-pants guilt, he waxed eloquent about Big Bear and Running River and Dances With Wolves, until I waned, bored senseless. I wanted to leave and began to pull on the sleeves of my jacket, tugging futilely until I realized that one of them was inside out. Calvin had been watching me, and tipped his fedora up an inch: "Calling it a night, Struggles With Coat?"

We began hanging out. Not really dating, as such, but meandering through the city in comfortable silences and chuckling at store signs, such as the one he pointed out in Chinatown that advertised BEAUTY. RICE. AIDS.

"Beauty you have," he offered to me gallantly, "AIDS you don't wish to acquire. But it would be my pleasure, madam, to buy you your own sack of rice."

• • •

One night, after draining all the alcohol in my apartment, he came over to my narrow single bed and climbed in beside me. I kicked and shooed sleepily, "No." I pressed my face into his collarbone. He hugged me and lay still: never mind. But you know how it is, how eventually your loneliness strips you. After a few more walks, more films, more lunches on Sunday, he began to sleep over, to warm me with his unassuming presence. He understood the rules of courtship in our generation: touch without faith, suppress all expressions of hope as bad manners. Do what we're doing, pretend that we're not.

And then this puzzling something happened. This highly unexpected mischief with my breasts.

. . .

After a lengthy exam in the bathroom mirror, I switched off the light and wondered, in awesome testimony to the power of denial, if I'd simultaneously developed eczema and put on weight.

"Do you think I'm fat?" I asked Calvin, when we talked on the phone that night. We were having one of those sweet, aimless conversations you get to have when you're newly interested in somebody and have nothing important to discuss.

"No," he said, amused. (This sort of question has a charm half-life of about two weeks. After that, the man tends to interrupt tersely when you're partway through the sentence. "Do you think I'm f—" "Late. Gotta go.")

For now, he was still thinking: *Silly, charming girl.* So I basked in his permission to pose worried little queries.

"I think my breasts have gained weight."

"All right, just lower them carefully onto the scales from a sitting position and then advise them on their diet."

"What if I weighed four hundred pounds, would you leave me?"

"Yes." He said this wryly, just playing along.

"What if I left you? Not when I weighed four hundred pounds, but this month, what if I left you?"

"I'd join the foreign legion."

How romantic! How untrue!

The next day I barfed into a sweater display at the Gap. Surely I should have known it wasn't the seafood bisque I had just eaten at the Time Café?

Seafood generally agreed with me, as did pinot grigio, three espressos, and a couple of bites of gingerbread. Indeed, I felt fine when I ducked into the Gap on my way back to work on West Broadway, and was just investigating a new pair of jeans, thinking to myself that it would be a vast improvement in my ability to be fashionable if flared pants did not begin their flare at precisely the height I have to hem them, when all at once my mouth began to water and I broke into a sweat. My stomach lurched, I darted frantically toward nowhere in particular and ran headlong into the sweaters, which I proceeded to ruin in one commodious heave.

Shocked, I raised my head slowly from my dripping hand and dared to peer around the store. Is everyone staring at me? Why yes, they are! The sales-clerk was a few feet away, frozen in midstride, regarding me with the wide-eyed solemnity of Agent Scully encountering an alien.

Oh. I'm so sorry.

"You wouldn't have a napkin or a Kleenex, by any chance?"

How about a mop?

I cleared my throat as discreetly as I could, and went off to commit suicide in the fitting room.

• • •

What this meant about my life—including my ability to ever fit into any of the ten sweaters I had to purchase (*you vomit, you pay*) from the white-lipped clerk—remained stubbornly opaque to me. In novels and films, women always seem to discover they are pregnant by feeling faint and having to quickly sit down with the blush draining out of their cheeks. It was romantic, suggesting fragility and need of a gentleman's rescue. That was my notion.

This was not that.

"Do not, under any circumstances, go near the seafood bisque at the Time Café," I therefore told my friend Marina when I got back to the office. "Of course you wouldn't, since you're a vegan," I added. "But warn your friends. You will not believe what I just did."

Marina was going to be the star of my one-woman play, but in the mean-time she acted as the receptionist at *The Pithy Review*, a job she attended to with a grim, self-loathing competence. She was smart enough to be the editor-in-chief. But she didn't have the résumé, having flung herself like a June bug at the lights of Broadway for ten years after majoring in theatre in college. Her valiant theatrical ambition got her one gig as an understudy in an off-Broadway play that collapsed after opening night. Now here she was, at thirty-five, with nothing on paper to prove her quick and literate mind. She was a fine-boned, green-eyed beauty, but her expression most days was one of deep exasperation.

I had just finished my barf-in-the-Gap yarn when the Great Editor himself padded into the reception area with a Marlboro dangling from his lips. He was, as usual, in his stocking feet, since his wood-panelled office lined with books was more his home than home itself, and of course there were all sorts of rumours about that. But he was otherwise elegantly turned out in a dark green suit and pale gold tie, having gone out to lunch with the director Anthony Minghella.

"Marina," he rumbled in his bass voice, not quite looking at her while he sheepishly held up an apple, "when you have a moment, there are bits of white wax on my apple that I can't seem to rub off. Perhaps you'd do a better job …"

Marina glared at him. "Just stick it in my *in box*."

The Editor actually did so, to our vast bemusement, and then turned his sidelong attention to me. "Frannie, I gather the Joyce Carol Oates story has come in, so I'd like you to have a look today if you can. I don't want to inadvertently repeat any of her metaphors in my own essay." I nodded obediently and he padded off silently, trailing smoke.

"Do I smell like vomit?" I asked Marina.

"Not yet," she replied, and turned to attend to the complaining phone.

I headed down to my cubicle—a washroom-sized space with a desk and an off-kilter chair—and began to flip through the Oates manuscript, rolling my pencil contentedly back and forth between two fingers. I love editing. I love the precision of it, and the focus. It stills me. I enter the minds of the finest thinkers of our time as if through a secret passage and polish their thoughts. Clarifying a concept here, querying a word there. I consider myself a craftswoman, or even a sculptress. I can't think my way out of a cab for having to calculate the tip, but I can edit. Yes I can! Sometimes, when I'm drunk, I proclaim that I am the power behind the throne, like William Shawn at *The New Yorker*. A founder of intellectual empires. A leader of sock-footed men. *En garde!* We are musing!

When I'm standing in line at a shop, I confine myself to fuming about the businessmen ahead of me, and imagine bursting out—*rat-a-tat*—like The Lone Semantic: "*Psychologize* is not a fucking word!"

The afternoon slipped by as I contemplated the sequence of sentences, every now and then reaching down to rustle my hand in a potato-chip bag, until I realized that I'd eaten the whole lot. I poked my head into the next cubicle and mooched some blue corn chips. Then I resumed, snacking and editing and snacking long into the quiet night.

The next morning, I was heading up West Broadway to work when I suddenly got blown over sideways by a thunderous clamour in my head to eat a bowl of mashed potatoes.

"Eat mashed potatoes with grav*y right now.*"

I looked around, unsure where the voice had come from. Not me, surely? I'd never had the faintest interest in mashed potatoes with gravy.

And now look. What's this? I'm storming into a diner and waving away the proffered menu—"Nope, thanks, know what I want."

I wanted to go on a gobbling spree all over Manhattan. After several days of this, I realized that I had to talk to myself in that mirror. Leaning sideways, staring sternly into my own brown eyes, I said: *Look here, Frannie, you're running about with a feverish lust for gravied mashed potatoes, preferably accompanied by a tuna salad sandwich. And a Rice Krispies square. And a packet of almonds. And chocolate milk. And another Rice Krispies square. And some peas.*

Jolly Green Giant. Love of my life, fire of my loins …

You can't, by any chance, be pregnant?

Laurence J. Peter

Humour is no less humour for being true. Canadian-born
Laurence J. Peter gave the world one of the most incisive concepts
ever put forward in the study of hierarchies, both corporate and
bureaucratic: his justly celebrated "Peter Principle," which states
that in any hierarchy people tend to rise to their level of incompe-
tency. F'r instance, an able—albeit uninspired—finance minister
who, say, is elevated to the rank of prime minister … with
predictably disastrous results. It's the Peter Principle in action.

FROM *The Peter Principle*

Chapter 1

> *"I begin to smell a rat."*—M. De Cervantes

When I was a boy I was taught that the men upstairs knew what
they were doing. I was told, "Peter, the more you know, the
further you go." So I stayed in school until I graduated from college and
then went forth into the world clutching firmly these ideas and my new
teaching certificate. During the first year of teaching I was upset to find
that a number of teachers, school principals, supervisors, and superintend-
ents appeared to be unaware of their professional responsibilities and
incompetent in executing their duties. For example my principal's main
concerns were that all window shades be at the same level, that classrooms
should be quiet, and that no one step on or near the rose beds. The superintendent's main concerns were that no minority group, no matter how
fanatical, should ever be offended and that all official forms be submitted

on time. The children's education appeared farthest from the administrator's mind.

At first I thought this was a special weakness of the school system in which I taught so I applied for certification in another province. I filled out the special forms, enclosed the required documents, and complied willingly with all the red tape. Several weeks later, back came my application and all the documents!

No, there was nothing wrong with my credentials; the forms were correctly filled out; an official departmental stamp showed that they had been received in good order. But an accompanying letter said, "The new regulations require that such forms cannot be accepted by the Department of Education unless they have been registered at the Post Office to ensure safe delivery. Will you please remail the forms to the Department, making sure to register them this time?"

I began to suspect that the local school system did not have a monopoly on incompetence.

As I looked further afield, I saw that every organization contained a number of persons who could not do their jobs.

A Universal Phenomenon
Occupational incompetence is everywhere. Have you noticed it? Probably we all have noticed it.

We see indecisive politicians posing as resolute statesmen and the "authoritative source" who blames his misinformation on "situational imponderables." Limitless are the public servants who are indolent and insolent; military commanders whose behavioural timidity belies their dreadnaught rhetoric, and governors whose innate servility prevents their actually governing. In our sophistication, we virtually shrug aside the immoral cleric, corrupt judge, incoherent attorney, author who cannot write, and English teacher who cannot spell. At universities we see proclamations authored by administrators whose own office communications are hopelessly muddled; and droning lectures from inaudible or incomprehensible instructors.

Seeing incompetence at all levels of every hierarchy—political, legal, educational, and industrial—I hypothesized that the cause was some inherent feature of the rules governing the placement of employees. Thus began my serious study of the ways in which employees move upward through a hierarchy, and of what happens to them after promotion.

For my scientific data hundreds of case histories were collected. Here are three typical examples.

Municipal Government File, Case No. 17 J.S. Minion* was a maintenance foreman in the public works department of Excelsior City. He was a favourite of the senior officials at City Hall. They all praised his unfailing affability.

"I like Minion," said the superintendent of works. "He has good judgment and is always pleasant and agreeable."

This behaviour was appropriate for Minion's position: he was not supposed to make policy, so he had no need to disagree with his superiors.

The superintendent of works retired and Minion succeeded him. Minion continued to agree with everyone. He passed to his foreman every suggestion that came from above. The resulting conflicts in policy, and the continual changing of plans, soon demoralized the department. Complaints poured in from the Mayor and other officials, from taxpayers and from the maintenance-workers' union.

Minion still says "Yes" to everyone, and carries messages briskly back and forth between his superiors and his subordinates. Nominally a superintendent, he actually does the work of a messenger. The maintenance department regularly exceeds its budget, yet fails to fulfill its program of work. In short, Minion, a competent foreman, became an incompetent superintendent.

Service Industries File, Case No. 3 E. Tinker was exceptionally zealous and intelligent as an apprentice at G. Reece Auto Repair Inc., and soon rose to journeyman mechanic. In this job he showed outstanding ability in diagnosing obscure faults, and endless patience in correcting them. He was promoted to foreman of the repair shop.

But here his love of things mechanical and his perfectionism become liabilities. He will undertake any job that he thinks looks interesting, no

---

* Some names have been changed, in order to protect the guilty.

matter how busy the shop may be. "We'll work it in somehow," he says.

He will not let a job go until he is fully satisfied with it.

He meddles constantly. He is seldom to be found at his desk. He is usually up to his elbows in a dismantled motor and while the man who should be doing the work stands watching, other workmen sit around waiting to be assigned new tasks. As a result the shop is always overcrowded with work, always in a muddle, and delivery times are often missed.

Tinker cannot understand that the average customer cares little about perfection—he wants his car back on time! He cannot understand that most of his men are less interested in motors than in their paychecks. So Tinker cannot get on with his customers or with his subordinates. He was a competent mechanic, but is now an incompetent foreman.

Military File, Case No. 8 Consider the case of the late renowned General A. Goodwin. His hearty, informal manner, his racy style of speech, his scorn for petty regulations, and his undoubted personal bravery made him the idol of his men. He led them to many well-deserved victories.

When Goodwin was promoted to field marshal he had to deal, not with ordinary soldiers, but with politicians and allied generalissimos.

He would not conform to the necessary protocol. He could not turn his tongue to the conventional courtesies and flatteries. He quarrelled with all the dignitaries and took to lying for days at a time, drunk and sulking, in his trailer. The conduct of the war slipped out of his hands into those of his subordinates. He had been promoted to a position that he was incompetent to fill.

An Important Clue! In time I saw that all such cases had a common feature. The employee had been promoted from a position of competence to a position of incompetence. I saw that, sooner or later, this could happen to every employee in every hierarchy.

Hypothetical Case File, Case No. 1 Suppose you own a pill-rolling factory, Perfect Pill Incorporated. Your foreman pill roller dies of a perforated ulcer. You need a replacement. You naturally look among your rank-and-file pill rollers.

Miss Oval, Mrs. Cylinder, Mr. Ellipse, and Mr. Cube all show various degrees of incompetence. They will naturally be ineligible for promotion. You will choose—other things being equal—your most competent pill roller, Mr. Sphere, and promote him to foreman.

Now suppose Mr. Sphere proves competent as foreman. Later, when your general foreman, Legree, moves up to Works Manager, Sphere will be eligible to take his place.

If, on the other hand, Sphere is an incompetent foreman, he will get no more promotion. He has reached what I call his "level of incompetence." He will stay there till the end of his career.

Some employees, like Ellipse and Cube, reach a level of incompetence in the lowest grade and are never promoted. Some, like Sphere (assuming he is not a satisfactory foreman), reach it after one promotion.

E. Tinker, the automobile repair-shop foreman, reached his level of incompetence on the third stage of the hierarchy. General Goodwin reached his level of incompetence at the very top of the hierarchy.

So my analysis of hundreds of cases of occupational incompetence led me on to formulate *The Peter Principle:*

In a Hierarchy Every Employee Tends
to Rise to His Level of Incompetence

A New Science! Having formulated the Principle, I discovered that I had inadvertently founded a new science, hierarchiology, the study of hierarchies.

The term "hierarchy" was originally used to describe the system of church government by priests graded into ranks. The contemporary meaning includes any organization whose members or employees are arranged in order of rank, grade, or class.

Hierarchiology, although a relatively recent discipline, appears to have great applicability to the fields of public and private administration.

This Means You! My Principle is the key to an understanding of all hierarchal systems, and therefore to an understanding of the whole structure of civilization. A few eccentrics try to avoid getting involved with hierarchies,

318   The Penguin Anthology of Canadian Humour

but everyone in business, industry, trade-unionism, politics, government, the armed forces, religion, and education is so involved. All of them are controlled by the Peter Principle.

Many of them, to be sure, may win a promotion or two, moving from one level of competence to a higher level of competence. But competence in that new position qualifies them for still another promotion. For each individual, for you, for me, the final promotion is from a level of competence to a level of incompetence.

So, given enough time—and assuming the existence of enough ranks in the hierarchy—each employee rises to, and remains at, his level of incompetence. Peter's Corollary states:

In time, every post tends to be occupied by an employee who is incompetent to carry out its duties.

Who Turns the Wheels? You will rarely find, of course, a system in which *every* employee has reached his level of incompetence. In most instances, something is being done to further the ostensible purposes for which the hierarchy exists.

Work is accomplished by those employees who have not yet reached their level of incompetence.

John Porteous

If you've ever purchased an authentic Maritime lobster trap from an authentic sun-creased Maritime fisherman—or looked with awe upon the clean, clear waters of the Fundy—you may want to skip this next part. In his book *They Choke Herring, Don't They?* columnist and broadcaster John Porteous of Saint John, New Brunswick, sets forth his proposals for new Maritime souvenirs, local world records, and the fine art of fleecing tourists.

FROM *They Choke Herring, Don't They?*

Trapping the Tourist Dollar

Are the tourists gone? They can't hear? Okay ... it's safe to talk! Well, folks, we did it again!!! More tourists than ever before, and did they spend money!

But the best of all, by my unofficial reckoning, they took back with them at least 38,427 lobster traps, making an all-time record in the selling of worthless, weatherbeaten wood at an average of $20 a square foot!

Oh, I tell you fellow Maritimers I'm proud, and you can be truly proud of this year's lobster trap rip-off! Those cars with Ontario and Quebec licence plates with their genuine lobster traps tied on the roof brought a tear to my eye as they passed by, because each and every one represented badly needed revenue for our native manufacturers. This winter, recreation rooms in Oshawa and Willowdale and in St. Lambert and Town of Mount Royal will be LOUSY with New Brunswick lobster traps, incapable of trapping a lobster of course, but perfectly capable of getting us fiscally even with those smart aleck Upper Canadians.

And of course while peddling these wooden artifacts takes a lot of skill and practice, especially to maintain a straight face, let's not forget the men who *make* these fool things. Some down east craftsmen have been known to take as long as ten minutes to rap one of these jewels together, and then often have to deliver them to the roadside lobster trap "traps" as well, often gaining a return of only 4 or 5 hundred percent on their labour and materials!

Next season it's hoped the Provincial government will set up a lobster trap marketing board aimed at stabilizing prices, quality, and selling techniques and providing technical advice such as proper ways of weathering the wooden strips and pre-rusting of wire.

As for me, time was when I planned to retire and write a bestselling novel. But this summer has shown me the real way to make money in the Maritimes. Just bring me about 15,000 square feet of good dry lumber, 10,000 yards of rusty wire, and some used cotton netting. Now … bring on the suckers … I mean TOURISTS!

Among My Souvenirs

We need souvenirs that truly reflect the Maritimes, and I've been thinking of a few items that would really please people.

First of all, how about a series of postcards that really show the things people see in their travels? Included could be a close-up shot of a squashed porcupine on the road, and a dimensional view of one of the really large potholes that are such a fun feature of our highways.

People love little bottles of things to put on their mantle piece, and what better gift to take back to Pointe Claire or Don Mills or Brookline than a genuine vial of tidal sludge taken from one of our Maritime bays or inlets. Just like those snowstorm paperweights you used to see, the owners of these bottles could stir them up occasionally, watching the guck settle slowly to the bottom again.

We have our celebrities in the Maritimes, and these people could be involved in producing valid souvenirs as well. Up in Baie Ste. Anne, N.B., retired boxer Yvone Durelle could receive visitors who would ask him how it was he lost his last fight with Archie Moore. Yvone could then punch out the visitor (gently) and then sell him a certificate suitable for framing which read "I got a punch in the mouth from Yvone Durelle." A terrific item for hanging over the mantle back home.

An item that's popular with tourists are those gag books that say things like "All I know about politics, by Joe Clark." The Maritimes could produce these novelties, which when you open them, turn out to be filled with blank pages. Some suitable titles would be: "Night Life in Georgetown, P.E.I.," "Enthusiastic Comments About Moncton's Tidal Bore," and "Who's Who in Digby, N.S." Other blank books could be "Digest of Wisdom from Maritime Politicians" and "What Ottawa Thinks of the Atlantic Provinces."

Tourism authorities of the Provinces often hand out plastic litter bags to visitors, but as one can readily see by glancing at the roadsides of the region, these don't always do the job. Why not kill two birds with one stone by packing small quantities of litter and garbage from the sides of the highways and selling them as souvenirs. Visitors could then take home a genuine reminder of their stay with us, and would help in the cleanup at the same time.

Guinness in the Maritimes?

One of the bestselling books on the shelves is the *Guinness Book of Records,* a collection of trivia which includes the "firsts," "greatests," and "bests" in everything from mountain climbing to taffy pulling.

It seems to me a lot of Maritimers should be candidates for inclusion in the Guinness Book, and here are some of my suggestions:

Everyone knows that breaking into closed-up summer cottages is a favourite winter pastime in the Maritimes, and in this category, the Malcontent Brothers of Shubenacadie Falls, N.S., appear to be shoo-ins. Between them, Harley and Farley Malcontent have vandalized a total of 341 furnished cottages, 57 hunting camps, and an assortment of lean-to's. They credit their record to "one hell of a fast snowmobile and a CB radio that tunes in the Mounties frequency."

In the entertainment area, Buster "Tinhorn" McGinley of Moncton, N.B., is believed to hold the Maritimes record for failure to tip beverage-room waiters. Buster has been drinking at the same place for 27 years and has never been known to tip anyone who served him, although he did advise one waiter "Don't eat the food here," which he claims is a very good tip indeed. Buster's finest moment came in 1968 when he found a Bulgarian five-drachma coin on the street, and after ascertaining its total worthlessness, left it on the table after finishing his beer.

The record for the most boring dates ever endured is said to be held by a Georgetown, P.E.I., girl, Cora Conviviality. Cora works for the Provincial Government, and between last fall and the first day of summer, dated the entire male portion of the P.E.I. Civil Service. As a result of this experience, Cora is planning to enter a Convent, even though she is a Presbyterian.

Cheating American tourists on their U.S. dollars is an entrenched Maritime custom, and in this category, Mr. Clifford Hatrack of West Pubnico, N.S., is thought to be without peer. Mr. Hatrack never gives Americans their premium at his No-Tell Motel but last year, he actually charged tourists 10% on their money, explaining it was a "special foreign currency surcharge."

And finally, the *Guinness Book of Records* is very big on gastronomic feats, and in this category, who better to represent the Maritimes than Helmut Switchkey of Shelburne, N.S.? On March 15, 1977, Mr. Switchkey ate 43 tins of Kippered Snacks at one sitting. He was forced to abandon an attempt to beat his own record when he began to be followed by twelve huge cats.

There they are, folks ... the Maritime candidates for the *Guinness Book of Records.*

Jacques Poulin

A Québécois author with an Anglo name; a Metis girl of indomitable spirit that he meets along the way; and an aging Volkswagen van: Jacques Poulin brings together one of the great love triangles of modern Canadian literature in his novel *Volkswagen Blues*. When "Jack" sets off for the Gaspé to find his missing brother, he picks up a hitchhiker nicknamed La Grande Sauterelle, and what began as a small familial quest soon becomes an epic journey into the heart of a continent—a modern retelling of the *voyageur* legend. The translation that follows is by Sheila Fischman.

FROM *Volkswagen Blues*

On Being a Great Writer

Jack Waterman was not very pleased with himself as a writer. He didn't like himself very much in general (he thought he was too thin and too old and too withdrawn), but what he hated about himself more than anything was his way of working. He had always had an image of the ideal writer, and he was utterly unlike that model. He ranked himself with those whom he called "the industrious class": patient and persistent but bereft of inspiration or even impulses, he went to work at the same time every day and, thanks to methodical and dogged work habits, managed to turn out his daily page.

Here is what he imagined the ideal writer to be like and the terms in which he talked about him:

• • •

One fine evening, the ideal writer is sitting in the back room of the Sainte-Angèle Bar, when all at once he gets an idea for a novel. He hasn't written a novel for two years perhaps, and that night, as he sips a Tia Maria with friends in a bar in Old Quebec this idea comes to him out of the blue.

The idea is far-ranging, yet precise, with two very clear-cut characters, the plot, the tone—even the first sentence!

He says excuse me and goes up to the bar. He borrows a pen from the barmaid. He writes the first sentence on a paper napkin. But then the second sentence comes to him, and he writes it on the other side of the napkin. It's longer than the first one, but it, too, is all thought out, and he has no trouble writing it; and the tone is exactly right.

Just as the writer is about to go back to his friends, a third sentence comes to him, but there's no room left on the napkin. He's afraid he'll forget it, and he repeats it in his head several times. He senses it going away.... He has a terrible memory. He rummages in his pockets, looking for a scrap of paper, but he finds nothing, so finally he writes the sentence in abbreviated form on a matchbook that's lying on the bar.

He leaves the Sainte-Angèle, waving a vague goodbye to his friends. One of them catches up with him on the street.

"Anything wrong? Don't you feel well?"

The writer shakes his head.

"Shall I take you home?" asks the friend.

He nods.

The friend has him get in his car and drives him home. He asks if he needs anything.

"Five writing pads."

"*Five* pads?"

"Yes, five!" he says impatiently.

"Lined or unlined?"

The question sounds like the stupidest thing he has ever heard. He glares at his friend, who says nothing more and leaves at once.

The writer sets to work.

He begins by transcribing the first three sentences onto an old pad and all three stand up; they are well constructed, and at the end of the third comes another, then another. The ideas are jostling one another in his head; they come faster and faster, and he wonders if he will be able to keep up to the rhythm. Then he takes a sheet of paper and jots down, as they occur to him, the ideas that will be useful later. And then he goes back to his writing. It's pleasant and comforting to have ideas in reserve. He writes with a sort of feverish pleasure. Words and sentences come easily, and the source seems inexhaustible. He has the impression that someone is dictating what he has to write. He feels very good. He is writing at full speed, and he is living intensely ....

....

The sound of a voice nearby makes him start.

His friend has come back.

The writer didn't hear the door … Nor did he understand what the other man said, but he found some writing pads.… That's it, he said something like, "I had to go all the way to Lower Town. Lippen's Drugstore."

"Thank you," he said. "Now please go away."

"I'm going to sleep here," says the friend.

"Leave me alone!"

"Listen, it's four a.m.!"

"SCREW OFF!"

The friend gets the point. He leaves. He doesn't look very happy, but he goes. Just before he shuts the door, the writer says, "Tell Marie not to come tomorrow."

"Okay."

"Or the day after, either! Tell her not to disturb me."

His friend goes out and he starts writing again.

To immerse himself in the atmosphere again, he rereads the previous page, and at once the words start coming! His friends the words are there when he needs them. They arrive *en masse,* pushing one another to make room. He is very glad to see them, and he writes like a madman, a maniac.

He no longer knows what time it is, whether it is day or night. His characters argue, they act, they make decisions, and he has a strong sense that he is
a spectator in this story and that his role consists of describing as faithfully as
possible the action that is taking place before his eyes. The characters know
precisely where they are going and they take him along with them into a New
World ....

....

Fog.

Everything is white.

He hears a far-off voice: "Jack! Jack Waterman!"

A face is bending over him. Marie.

"Bonjour," she says.

The walls are white. He is in a bed.

He tries to get up but cannot. He can hardly move his head. He is very
tired.

"Everything's fine," says Marie. "Don't move."

She takes his hand and raises it gently so he can see: a transparent plastic
tube is attached to the back of his hand; beside the bed, a flask of serum is
hanging from a stand.

A nurse comes into the room and busies herself taking his blood pressure.

"Glad to see you back with us!" she says, smiling.

He makes an effort to ask what has happened, but no sound emerges
from his mouth. And suddenly he remembers: THE NOVEL! THE SHEETS OF
PAPER SCATTERED OVER THE TABLE AND FLOOR ... then a great black space....

"Stay calm," says the nurse.

"Wait a minute," says Marie.

She opens a drawer in the little chest beside his bed and takes out a
binder. A very big one.

"Don't talk," says the nurse. "You've been unconscious for three days and
you mustn't tire yourself. Understand?"

He nods and looks at Marie, because he needs to know. She is bending over
him, holding the manuscript against her chest and looking intently at him.

She says, "The writing's hard to decipher, especially at the end, but ..."

There are tears in her eyes when she says, "It's the most beautiful story I've ever read!"

...

On the Love of a Good Van

The man was very fond of the old Volks.

When he'd bought it, the year he'd won a literary prize, the Volks was already four years old and pitted with rust. He had rebuilt almost the entire underside of the body, using sheets of galvanized metal that he had cut, bent, and rivetted in place, then he had repainted the vehicle with antirust paint. The thick metal and the heavy rivets made the minibus look like an armoured truck. Under the new metal, however, the rust continued to do its work, as you could see whenever the Volks drove out of a parking space: it left a fine powdering of rust on the ground.

From old bills he found in the glove compartment when he was cleaning up, Jack learned that the Volks had been purchased in Germany; it had driven around Europe and crossed the Atlantic on a freighter, then it had travelled along the east coast, from the Maritime provinces to southern Florida. In the bottom of the baggage compartment were some shells and coloured stones. The cupboard behind the seat had an odour of cheap perfume, which sometimes drifted into the vehicle at night when it was hot and humid. And here and there, on the walls or inside the doors of the plywood cupboard, were all sorts of graffiti; a mysterious inscription in German, under the sun visor on the driver's side, read: *Die Sprache ist das Haus des Seins.*

Probably on account of its age, the Volks had its peculiar habits. The seat belts, for example: once they were buckled it was very hard to unfasten them, and you had the impression that the Volks was reluctant to let people go. The same with the windshield wipers: they would stop when you turned the button but then all of a sudden, as if they were afraid they'd forgotten something, they would start up again and make one more pass before they stopped for good. But the foremost characteristic of the minibus was that it very much disliked being hurried. Until it was warmed up in the morning it preferred to travel at a reduced speed. It hated, under any circumstances, to be pushed beyond its cruising speed, which was one hundred kilometres an hour, and the impatient driver who exceeded that limit could expect all sorts of protests: the visor would suddenly drop and block his view, or the roof would come undone and threaten to lift off, or suspicious sounds would be heard from the motor or the gears.

The old Volks had travelled 195,000 kilometres in its lifetime, and it wanted respect for its age, its experience, and its odd little ways.

• • •

On Western Hospitality

"We're going to stop at the ranch," said the girl.

They had crossed a desert region; for two days they had seen nothing but gloomy, grey expanses that made them think of lunar landscapes.

And they hadn't talked to anyone except campground and service-station attendants. "How are you today?" and "Have a nice day!": those were the only words they had exchanged with the local population during those long days.

That was why, as soon as there was greenery to be seen again, they decided to "go looking for someone to talk to." It was La Grande Sauterelle's idea. More precisely, she wanted to make an expedition to a ranch.

"All right," said Jack, who was driving. "It may be our last chance before California. I've never been on a ranch."

"Me neither," she said. "Maybe they'll invite us to have something to eat and then we'll go for a horseback ride!"

"Apparently Westerners are very hospitable. I read that in the literature on Nevada."

"So did I."

They had also read something about the large ranches found in the northern part of the state. It even said there were Basque shepherds and flocks of sheep. They looked over the fields all around them, but they saw nothing. No cows or horses or sheep.

"There aren't even any houses by the roadside," said Jack. "It's as if we're still in the desert."

"Maybe the houses are set back, far from the road," said the girl. "Know what I think?"

"What?"

"I think we should turn onto the first private road we see. I'm sure that any private road will take us straight to a rancher's house."

"We can try," said the man, his voice betraying a certain apprehension.

They drove another twenty kilometres before they spotted a dirt road that started at the Interstate and disappeared far away toward the north. There was a fence, but it was open and there was a sign that read:

NO TRESPASSING

"It sounds like a bad translation of *trépasser*," said Jack. "Forbidden to depart this life," he snickered, steering the old Volks onto the private road. "We'll tell them we're looking for a shortcut to Carson City. That's Kit Carson's town."

"They're bound to believe us," said the girl. "Especially because the road goes north and Carson City's to the south...."

"Sorry."

"It doesn't matter," she laughed. "We'll think of something."

"Sure."

They weren't going to let some insignificant details stand in their way. Nothing could diminish their pleasure at the prospect of being entertained on a Nevada ranch.

The ranchers would say: "Quebec in Canada? Oh, long way from home!" And then they'd invite them inside, where it was cooler, for a drink. And they'd say that their neighbour had a son who was working in Canada. "*Ah, oui*? Is that so? Whereabouts, if you don't mind my asking?" "Calgary, he's in the oil business!" "Very interesting, but Calgary's in the West, you know, whereas Quebec ..." "Is that so?" And they had another neighbour who had a daughter working in Halifax? Well, it's true Halifax is in the East, but you know, Quebec actually isn't that far east: it's somewhere between the two. See what I mean? Get the picture?

And Jack would nudge the girl with his elbow to tell her it wasn't polite to say "get the picture" to their hosts, but the ranchers would be broad-minded and wouldn't take offence at a small breach of etiquette. They would invite the visitors from Quebec to take a horseback ride around the ranch and give the cowboys a hand as they rounded up the cattle in the corral, if they weren't too tired. Then they'd invite the visitors to eat with them, because *as a matter of fact* they had prepared a huge barbecue that very night. All their neighbours within a hundred-kilometre radius were coming over to eat and celebrate with them.

Jack and La Grande Sauterelle were having a lively conversation about the size of the T-bones they were going to eat at the giant barbecue when suddenly they saw the rancher's house at the end of the road.

It was a large two-storey frame house with a very wide veranda on which, from a distance, they could see chairs and a table.

They didn't see any people.

They saw trees, a swing under the trees, an old tire hanging on a rope from a branch, but no children.

Absolutely nobody.

Jack stopped the Volks in front of the steps that went up to the front door. He opened the car door....

As his foot touched the ground a police dog pounced on him. He had just enough time to get back in the minibus.

Immediately two other police dogs emerged from under the veranda and hurled themselves at the Volks, barking furiously. The three huge dogs, drooling, lips curled, fangs threatening, ran around the old Volks, leaping up at the windows. One of them—the one that had appeared first—lunged at Jack. He put his front paws on the windowframe, stuck his head inside, and clamped his jaws shut, just missing the man's left arm; his teeth snapped on the air because Jack had instinctively flung himself to the right.

The man and the girl rolled up the two windows, closed the air vents and locked the doors.

The dogs were German shepherds. They were tan and black. They kept circling the Volks and barking, and from time to time they jumped up, trying to attack the passengers.

The black cat, hiding under a seat, gave a muffled growl.

Jack started the engine and drove slowly away from the rancher's house. The three dogs accompanied the Volkswagen for several minutes, then wheeled together as if someone had called them. Jack looked in the rearview mirror, but he didn't see anyone at the house. They drove along in silence for a while.

Then the girl asked, "Want me to drive?"

"It's okay," he said. "Thanks."

At the end of the dirt road they got back on Interstate 80 and the black cat came out of its hiding place.

"Our expedition wasn't a success!" said the man.

"We'll try again another time," said the girl calmly.

"It's true, not all people are dogs," he said.

The girl gave him an odd look.

He realized his slip and corrected himself: "I meant, not all people have dogs."

Paul Quarrington

Fans of Paul Quarrington may question my choice of
selection when it comes to Mr. Quarrington. To which I say,
"Tough nuts. This is my anthology. Go edit your own." Well, no.
It's true that Paul Quarrington won both the Leacock Medal for
Humour *and* the Governor General's Award for his fiction, but
his non-fiction is just as strong. The following is from
The Boy on the Back of the Turtle, a travel memoir.

FROM *The Boy on the Back of the Turtle*

On March twenty-fifth of the year nineteen hundred and ninety-six,
with my spirit made dull and muzzy by so long spent ashore, I
embarked upon a voyage of the Encantadas, the storied, shrouded archipelago that lies some six hundred miles to the west of the southern Americas.
For companionship upon my travels I had with me my daughter Carson,
aged seven years, and my father Bruce, ten times that. The sun, punctual and
prompt upon the equatorial line, was withdrawing behind the globe as we
first stepped onto our vessel, the mighty *Corinthian,* not five years out of the
wrightyard but no less worthy for that. It had been our design to set to sea
by midday, but we had been made behind time by some hopeless dickwads—
oops. Well, I would never have lasted the whole book anyway. I had hoped
to break a paragraph before descending into the vulgate, but there you go.

Delayed we had been, unaccountably, forced to sit in a departure lounge
in the Quito airport for some five hours, staring at the craft from SAN airline
that sat idly on the tarmac. Rumour had it that the machine needed mechan-

ical attention, but we saw no grease-covered fly-boys ministering to it. My father sat with his large fingers curled around his armrests, nodding in and out of sleep. My daughter worked on her journal, inscribing the single word "bored" over and over again. I read from the small library of books I was carting with me: *A Traveller's Guide to the Galápagos Islands, Field Guide to Birds of the Galápagos, Darwin's Islands: A Natural History of the Galápagos,* and a small dog-chewed paperback edition of *The Origin of Species.* That last book assumes some importance in these pages, so allow me to remind you: it was written by Charles Darwin (1809–1892), who, sailing aboard a "coffin-brig" named the H.M.S. *Beagle,* visited the Galápagos Islands in 1835. He saw something there that caused him to give voice to the Theory of Evolution by Means of Natural Selection. This in turn caused people to squabble savagely. That squabbling has bothered me throughout my life; I heard it even as a small child, angry adult voices muted behind closed doors and thick walls.

So when, many months ago, the Publisher asked what I had in mind to follow a very modest success (significantly, a book about a fishing trip where no fish were caught), my answer was quick. "The Galápagos."

The Publisher is a man of boyish enthusiasms. Almost any place name would have elicited some reaction, but this one caused his head to snap upwards, his eyes to widen with wonder. Mind you, we were both holding wine glasses at the time. "Yes," he enthused. "Why?"

"Well …" I couldn't tell him the truth, which involved Dr. Moody and a makeshift movie theatre. I couldn't tell the Publisher that visiting the Galápagos Islands was, in effect, the Prime Directive. It wouldn't have been at all professional, for one thing, to claim that I had been somehow "programmed" to visit the archipelago. I am by nature a private man, even with more wine inside than is absolutely necessary, so I sighed and started upon the road to something not quite as near the truth. "My father is a psychologist, a professor," I told the Publisher. "He is an academic. And, for my whole life, he has told me about Charles Darwin. He is a huge Charles Darwin fan."

"Yes!" the Publisher enthused. "Why?"

Good question. It was not always easy to read a moral or a lesson in some of the stories my father told me. Like this one: Darwin was fascinated with worms. Of course, Darwin was fascinated with every living thing, but he had his favourites and passions, worms being one of them. And in his tiny poop cabin on the *Beagle,* he devised and built an earth-filled drawer beneath his berth. Charles would wake up in the middle of the night, lean over, and pull out the drawer so that he could watch the nocturnal activity of the worms. That is a story my father told me. I have reasons to doubt that the story is true—for example, there would be no light in the tiny poop cabin, and the story lacks a certain credibility when we picture Darwin fumbling with a lantern just to aid whimsical worm-inspection—but that is hardly the point. What did my father mean for me to learn from it? So I put to the Publisher that my aim was to answer just that sort of question. Darwin and the Galápagos had become connected with the issue of *fatherhood.* Therefore, I wanted to take with me my elder daughter (the other was then too wee), and I would use the experience as an opportunity to meditate on the joys and mysteries of paternity. Most publishers would bolt in terror, but not this one, who considers the subject of fatherhood underrepresented on the book-shelves. He sipped his wine and appeared thoughtful.

I didn't mention to the Publisher that I'd tried a few dry practice runs, meditation-wise, sitting up in my office with a furrowed brow, the fusty air filled with appropriately brooding music, Bruckner, Brahms, and Mahler. I hadn't really been able to generate much. Still, I wasn't worried. All this would change in the Galápagos. Cruising about the Encantadas, I would be granted an Insight. After all, the one granted to Charles Darwin is one of the great Insights, perhaps the greatest ever. It was an Insight—as opposed to a discovery, or a creation—because the Theory of Evolution by Means of Natural Selection had always been lying in plain sight. As Darwin's great defender and advocate Thomas Huxley (1825–1895) remarked, very famously, "How extremely stupid not to have thought of that."

There's competition on the Insight front, no doubt. Archimedes shout-ing "Eureka!" for example, although I'm sure whoever was in charge of cleaning that particular bathroom floor wandered away muttering, "*Eureka,* your fat ass. It happens every time you take a bath." Or Einstein and his $E=mc^2$, although I don't think that was properly an "Insight," I think it was something Albert and his wife Mileva hashed out over breakfast.

No, the Great Insight was had by Charles Darwin—admittedly some years after he had visited the Galápagos—and set down in *The Origin of Species*.[1]

So, I elaborated to the Publisher—wine lapping over the top of the stemware—if Charles Darwin could be smacked about the head by the Great Insight, then surely I, while not a particularly observant or intelligent fellow, well—you know. Fish have been caught on empty hooks before.

This is what I told the Publisher. He seemed convinced.

• • •

My father, my daughter, and I were labelled, there at the San Christóbel airport, actually and physically labelled. We all wore little stickers that said *Corinthian*. There were others with *Corinthian* labels; a few middle-aged, well-heeled couples, two young women travelling together, a couple of singleton young males, and a trembling clutch of old people. No children as far as we could see, which was a little unfortunate, although I had stopped far short of promising Carson that there would be playmates aboard the ship. I had reason to suspect there wouldn't be. Ingrid the travel agent had placed a call, sitting behind her desk in downtown Toronto, securing her cigarette between her lips to free her hands, punching at her telephone with power and accuracy. "Hello, Julio," she said, the name coming from deep down in her throat, rolling across her tongue with authentic Spanish curves. "Could you do me a favour?" She bid Julio to check the guest register for the *Corinthian*, which he did only on the condition, I gather, that he report nothing other than passengers who had declared themselves to be children. There were none. Ingrid cradled the phone and resumed her cigarette smoking. "Mind you," she suggested, "there could still be children. They're just not recorded as children."

---

1. "I think I have found out (here's presumption!) the simple way by which species become exquisitely adapted to various ends."

I nodded, but was rightfully unconvinced. So I made no promises to Carson that she would have friends and playmates. She is a social creature, my daughter is, ever eager to be in company. "Can I bring a friend?" is a constant refrain with her.

Indeed, that was one of the driving forces behind the trip, at least, one of the more practical purposes, to establish a friendship, a *chumminess,* with my daughter, because many times I've said, "Hey, Carson, let's you and I go out to a ballgame, a movie, the museum, whatever," only to have her demand, "Can I bring a friend?"

"Well, you know, I thought it would be fun, just the two of us."

Carson's constant response is to allow little creases to inform her features, just enough to warp her face with doubt and concern for my sanity. *Why would that be fun?*

So, as I say, I had guaranteed no other children, and was even relieved that there were none. Because this, by god, was going to be fun.

Meanwhile, a host of healthy young people, wearing tight blue shorts and white golf shirts that said *Corinthian,* corralled everyone with the proper label and pushed us over into one corner of the outdoor airport. More paperwork was done. We were then ushered onto a bus, an ancient white beast of a bus, and driven down to the sea.

The sun was sinking.

· · ·

Here's the story I didn't tell the Publisher:

When I was thirteen years of age, I received permission to go to the Ex by myself. The Ex being the Canadian National Exhibition, an annual phenomenon here in Toronto, an outsized version of Ontario agricultural fairs. It consists of many old buildings, long resident near the grey Lake, each dedicated to some sphere of human endeavour. There is the Agricultural Building, for example, which didn't (and doesn't today) smell at all nicely. There is a Better Living Building, where, for many decades now, they have predicted upcoming boons and benisons, few of which have materialized. The builders and stockers did accurately predict the advent of the vibrating chair thirty-odd years ago, several examples of which adorned the ground floor. This made the Better Living Building a mecca for the tired and weary. The Ex consists largely of the midway, a garish avenue of carnival amusements. There are whirligigs, humbugs, and tawdry diversions. When I was a lad, there was even a Freak Show, where I saw a family with flippers instead of arms, a man with green and scaly skin, people variously tiny and huge, and a Rubber Man. (The first time I saw the Rubber Man, I was eight or nine years old and pressed up to the apron. The Rubber Man opened his act by grabbing his forefinger and bending it until it lay flat against the back of his hand. I took hold of my own finger and pushed, trying to gauge the pain involved. Surprisingly—to both me and the Rubber Man—my finger folded backwards obediently. I didn't pursue this career opportunity, which is just as well, because my finger stiffened in my twenties, and I would have been a washed-up carnival freak very early in life.)

The Better Living Building lay at the far end of the midway, and people who'd survived the traverse gathered there to settle into the vibrating chairs. On that day in late August, when I was thirteen years of age, I entered the Better Living Building only to find all of the vibrating chairs occupied. Children and old people languished in the Naugahyde comfort. None showed any inclination to move and many were fast asleep. This is what sent me outside again, through the nearest exit.

I was sweaty and exhausted. My journey through the midway had been long and arduous, consisting of a stop at the Freak Show, multiple turns on the Flyer and the Wild Mouse, several Belgian waffles with slabs of ice cream sandwiched between them. I had thrown and gambled away most of my money and had only managed to win a single minute plastic gewgaw. I won this by letting a thin man with the history of the world tattoo'd upon his face attempt to guess my weight. He was unsuccessful, lowballing by many pounds, but I suspect he was merely being kind, any more accurate assessment of my weight likely to wound and insult. For I was a pudge of a boy, bespectacled and pimply.

Attending the Ex alone was a badge of maturation and independence, even though our parents' reluctance to allow it was a little ill-thought. *No,*

338 The Penguin Anthology of Canadian Humour

don't go to that place by yourself, where you will be quieted by fear and cowed into obeisance of the public laws; go instead in packs and hordes, so that you may be the very instruments of violence and mayhem. My friends often claimed that going alone increased their chances of picking up girls, but this was an audacious and preposterous statement for the coolest of them, so I never even attempted it. Mostly I wanted to go alone so that I could travel at my own pace (my friends didn't stop to eat as often as I did) and pursue my own interests (they didn't much like the Freak Show; I tended to make a beeline for it).

It was an extremely hot mid-afternoon and I was spent. I mostly wanted to go home, although this would have been a humiliating defeat, because it was customary to remain at the Ex until closing at 10:00 P.M.

Now, I knew my way around the Ex as well as any young man, keying not only on the common landmarks—the Shell Tower, for example—but several more idiosyncratic ones. (The Belgian waffle stand figured large.) But I'd left the Better Living Building through the handiest exit, impatient and frustrated, and I found myself somewhere foreign. There was a building immediately before me, one I'd never seen before, a strange edifice that seemed to have been transported from Victorian England. There was a cobblestone pathway surrounding it, bordered by gas lamps that burned even in the day. The building was corniced and friezed, much more complicated architecturally than the rest of the Ex, which was tendered in the no-nonsense Presbyterian style so admired in Ontario.

This was, if memory serves (and it doesn't, often, I just thought you should know), the Boosey & Hawkes Museum of Brass and Woodwinds. Or something like that. I dutifully entered, being the first clarinetist for the school band, the Concertmaster, which brought me honour much like that accorded Torquemada, Chief Inquisitor. So I entered, made a quick revolution of the exhibits and found myself back outside.

Beside the main door, huge and wooden and thrown open invitingly, was a smaller one, painted a dull red. I noticed a sign suspended above it, swaying and creaking in the breeze. It announced, "The Moody Theatre of Nature." (I actually think it may have been "Moodie," but I have decided to go with the former spelling. This isn't to avoid possible legal entanglements, it just seems a much more apt rendering.) What actually caught my attention, I'll confess, was another sign creaking in tandem with this one. It read, "AIR CONDITIONED."

I pushed open the door and mounted a shadowed staircase. In years to come, I was to enter many squalid dens and squats; I won't go into the details, but my point is, for gloomy forbiddenness this staircase remains a clear winner. At the top were shadows of a deeper hue. I stepped gingerly, half-expecting the final riser to give way to nothingness. But then there was a sudden illumination and Dr. Moody was addressing me. "The world of nature," he announced, "is wondrous and astounding."

Dr. Moody's image was being projected onto a screen, or at least a plastic groundsheet or something that had been pressed into service as a screen. He was a fleshy man, possessed of an unnatural healthiness. Across a face that was tanned the colour of mahogany spread a dazzling smile. What dazzled about the smile was not so much the whiteness (although it was indeed angelic and incandescent) as the energy and earnestness with which the smile was fashioned. You and I would probably have a hard time coming up with such a smile, certainly on our own. We might manage with advanced intoxicants, or a group of our closest friends adhering to specific and complicated instructions, but we couldn't manage what Dr. Moody did, to flash this smile perpetually, for no apparent reason. Dr. Moody affected the dress of an insurance salesman: a sober suit, a white shirt, a tie knotted so rightly that it shot colour into his jowls. Despite the fact that he seemed to be situated in an office, Moody tramped and kicked about the place as though hiking through the Alps, although he'd periodically place a buttock gingerly on the edge of the desk, fold his hands, and bend over slightly to address the camera with especial import. This is what he did as I entered what I shall graciously call the theatre. Dr. Moody placed a ham on the edge of his desk, smiled at the camera lens (making the unseen operator pull back abruptly), and said, "Suppose I were to find a pocket watch on a deserted beach ..."

I took a seat in the back row. This is indicative of a congenital demureness, because the place was deserted. Dr. Moody continued talking about this watch he'd found, or supposed that he had, but I didn't really pay attention, basking blissfully in the shower of cold air leaking from the vent above. Then there was music, gushing with peppy grandeur, and the titles went and came. Because I'd walked in on the end of one film, you see, and now watched another from the beginning. "The world of nature is wondrous and astounding," Dr. Moody assured me.

But I didn't have to take his word for it. Dr. Moody had film footage, which he introduced (he'd changed clothes for this second film, altering the tone of his suit and tie, although his face was no less woody, his smile undiminished) and then seemed to watch for himself, turning his head to the right as though the world of nature existed just beyond the edge of the movie screen.

I certainly cannot remember all that I saw that day. I spent the rest of the afternoon and that evening there, until the Exhibition's closing. People entered the darkened room during this time, drawn, like me, by the siren call of air conditioning, but few stayed longer than ten minutes, twenty minutes tops. Twenty minutes was the approximate length of one of Dr. Moody's films, and no one other than myself stayed for a second.

The films had a sameness. After Dr. Moody's proclamation—the words would change, but the "wondrous and astounding" theme was restated again and again—there would be a short documentary. Dr. Moody had obviously gathered these up from disparate sources. Some were grainy, and the hands that held the camera trembled. In others the images were crystal clear, and obviously made with much more sophisticated equipment, lenses that roamed and zoomed everywhere. Many of the documentarians favoured time-lapse photography, and any number of wondrous and astounding flowers exploded out of the earth and struggled toward heaven. Then these films would end abruptly. Or Moody would appear and turn toward the camera, away from all the wonder. "Suppose I were walking along a deserted beach," he'd say, hiking a cheek over the lip of his desk, folding large hands over his crotch, "and I found a pocket watch. Suppose I'd never seen a pocket watch before. Now, I might be able to convince myself that this watch was simply a happenstance amalgam of molecules, that they had aligned themselves this way by purest chance. But how then would I explain the beauty and functionality of the pocket watch? No, the simplest logic would tell me that someone had *made* it. So it is with the wonders of nature ...”

I'm sure you are beginning to see Dr. Moody's point. You are likewise beginning to understand why no one stayed for more than the one film, because Dr. Moody was the ordained representative of some Christian sect (I forget which, perhaps the Church of Jesus Christ, Naturalist) and his true desire was not to educate, rather to convert. His success rate must have been rather low, I think. Most evangelists have figured out that the easiest targets are the downtrodden and twisted, people with lives so unblessed that organized religion becomes the last refuge and sanctuary. The evangelists are on television late at night only partly because the rates are low. Late at night is when the Truly Wretched are sitting there on their sofas, blue-eyed and unthinking, a bottle of their favourite poisonous beverage clutched in both hands. Dr. Moody was out to convert others of his ilk, the Perpetually Beaming, but others of his ilk were not in attendance at the Exhibition. So the closest he got to a spiritual transformation was the chubby little thirteen-year-old sitting in the back row.

• • •

In the pocket-watch speech, Dr. Moody was, in fact, paraphrasing William Paley and his seminal work *Natural Theology, or, Evidences of the Existence and Attributes of the Deity, Collected from the Appearances of Nature,* published in 1802, many years before anyone thought that books needed snappy titles. (I suppose Moody was not paraphrasing so much as stealing, but that's all right, as Paley had borrowed much of this watch business from a Dutch philosopher named Bernard Nieuwentyt.) William Paley is very elaborate in the analogy, much more so than Dr. Moody, making a leisurely appraisal of the timepiece. “We next observe a flexible chain,” he writes, “artifically wrought for the sake of flexure, communicating the action of the spring from the box to the fusee.” Paley then asks the reader to consider an eye; is it any less complicated, is there any less evidence of contrivance? He comes to the same place as Dr. Moody, that there is an obvious intelligence, “adequate,” as Paley puts it, “to the appearances which we wish to account for.” And both men, Moody and Paley, turn their eyes

Heavenward. "Upon the whole," concludes *Natural Theology,* "after all the schemes and struggles of a reluctant philosophy, the necessary resort is to a Deity. The marks of *design* are too strong to be gotten over. Design must have had a designer. That designer must have been a person. That person is God."

• • •

I bought it.

I walked away from the Museum of Brass and Woodwinds with the argument folded neatly and tucked into my breast. I had been struggling with questions of *belief* since early childhood—not with the actual belief itself, because I'd long accepted God as my Father Who Art in Heaven—but with a justification for it. This (what I've since learned is referred to in theological circles as the "Argument from Design") was just what I needed. I became a whiz in high-school science classes, and when dissecting frogs would often step back and take a blissful look skyward. I didn't go so far as to study natural sciences in university, concentrating instead on Beer Consumption and the Intricacies of 9-5-2. But I read about nature, I was an inveterate visitor of zoos and museums, and certainly, most certainly, whilst powering through the television channels, I could be stopped in an instant by the image of a bird or insect. And thus I remained convinced of God's existence.

Shortly after the birth of our first daughter, my wife and I were lying in bed (the infant cradled at our feet) fretting anxiously and watching television. I had possession of the channel changer, which I rarely relinquish, and was traipsing through the frequencies when an image caused my hand to relax, my thumb to leave the button. A pile of black rubble rose out of the water. Huge turtles and lizards romped upon it. "The Galápagos," I said, with the authority of personal recognition. I somehow have always been able to recognize the Encantadas. "You know," I said, "when Carson is seven years old, I think I'm going to take her there."

"Why?" yawned my wife.

I shrugged. "I don't know." And I didn't, at least, I wouldn't have been able to give it voice. But the answer has since made itself clear: *To introduce her to God.*

• • •

We huddled in the Zodiac, shoulder to shoulder, twenty people, strangers to me, except of course for my father and my daughter. My father sat with one hand on his hat. He had a brand-new Panama, the largest he could find, although that was still a little small for his skull. My daughter likewise had a new Panama—they actually come from Ecuador, you see—although hers was oversized. She, too, was forced to raise an arm and paste the thing down, setting the brim a-flapping in the evening sea breeze.

Our little boat snaked through the bay, which was full of yachts and fishing vessels. Beyond all these other ships, silhouetted against the darkening sky, sat the *Corinthian.* It was easily the biggest craft in the harbour (it is actually the second largest ship cruising the archipelago) and seemed capable of riding the roughest waters. It looked to me like a warship, oversized and ironclad. The weathervane above the fo'c's'le spun around at quite a clip.[2] A pelican did its best to rest upon it, a study in blissful self-denial, because every gust threatened to hurtle the bird from its perch.

The bird was reluctant to give up its roost, treacherous as it was, because competition for resting places was fierce. Flying creatures, black slashes against the departing sun, filled the welkin with fluid design. Creation was abundantly evident in this empyrean; I could almost sense His hand at work. I nudged my daughter in the side with my elbow.

She yawned.

---

2. It may not have actually been the fo'c's'le, but how often do you get a chance to use a word with three apostrophes in it?

David Rakoff

David Rakoff is an ex-pat Canadian who has lived for many years in New York without succumbing to cynicism, without becoming even the slightest bit jaded. An essential humanity is at work in his humour, even when he's dealing with situations that all but cry out for cynicism. I flatter us (undeservingly, I am sure) by thinking of this as an essentially Canadian characteristic. The following is from Rakoff's debut collection of essays, *Fraud*.

FROM *Fraud*

Before and After Science

King Constantine II, the deposed monarch of Greece, was passionate about my French vanilla root beer floats. The French vanilla was definitely one of our better flavours; we charged five cents more per scoop. It was completely reasonable that this crowned head of Europe, with his highly developed taste for the finer things, would insist upon nothing less and insist upon no one but me to make them. This is my boxing Hemingway, my wooing Josephine Baker in a swan-shaped bed.

Not every ice-cream parlour in Toronto in the summer of 1982 came equipped with lapsed royalty. But Athos and Melina, the married couple who owned the shop where I worked, were old friends of the king. He spent his time at the front table, chatting with them in Greek, reminiscing about the good times, back when he was still ensconced in happy figurehead-hood, and when Athos and Melina were clearly at the tippy top of Athenian society, he a drug company executive, she a noted scientist in the perfume industry.

They remembered fondly those halcyon days before Constantine's reign, however titular, was effectively ended by an outbreak of democracy. Before he threw his lot in with the slim ranks of perpetually tanned do-little European ex-royals, that shallow band of frivolous hemophiliacs who live out their days reading the yachting news, roaming the world, and dressing for dinner.

Athos and Melina had not been quite as leisurely in their travels. The sense one got was that this was a couple on the lam for some reason. From Athens they had fled to the Sudan, where they continued their rarefied lifestyle and where, a few years later, the volatile politics of that region would send them into flight yet again. Landing them in Toronto, exhausted and vaguely punch drunk, the stunned franchisees of a well-known ice-cream parlour that trafficked in an ersatz Barbary Coast saloon chic of faux Tiffany lamps, frosted mirrors, and wrought-iron chairs. It was an aesthetic so relentless and so forced in its attempt to evoke those bygone days in the City by the Bay that it even went so far as to name its biggest and most vulgar sundae after a civic disaster where thousands upon thousands of San Franciscans were killed. *I know a special birthday boy. Will you be having the Earthquake?*

Imagine, if you will, the queen of France who, instead of succumbing to the decapitory charms of the guillotine, is safely spirited away from France to England, along with other fortunate aristocrats. Now resettled, she runs a fish-and-chips stand in Brighton, where daily the tiny golden ship perched in the frothy waves of her high, powdered wig regularly topples into the deep-fat fryer. This will give you a sense of how profoundly strange was Athos and Melina's presence in our midst.

Athos looked like a latter-day Jean-Paul Belmondo, a formerly handsome man whose features have gone rubbery and heavy with age. He wore dress shirts and socks of the thinnest material I had ever seen. It would be years later before I would recognize these garments of dragonfly wings as the haberdashery of choice of the strip club bouncer, the penny-ante henchman, and the double-breasted thug. But to me, at that time, they indicated only his good breeding. He was, for the most part, a surly, taciturn man, constantly trying to bilk us out of our near minimum wages by pretending to suddenly understand less English than he actually did. But despite his gruff manner, Y chromosome, and ultimate control of our salaries, it was no secret who was truly in charge: Melina. Formidable, fire-hydrant-size Melina. If *she* had ever decided to withhold our payment, she would never have resorted to falsely broken English. She would have simply told us outright, and nobody, not the Royal Canadian Mounted Police, nobody, could have gotten our money out of her. I adored her. She was smart as a whip, was possessed of an appreciative and often bawdy sense of humour, and sounded not a little bit like Peter Lorre. She was also prone to moods so changeable— from borderline-inappropriate affection to homicidal seething rage in mere seconds—that one gave up trying to guess her mental state and surrendered to the hurricane of emotion that was Melina. Sometimes she simply abandoned decorum, as when wondering aloud, the store full of people, "Why do the blacks always order the rum raisin? Tell me. Is it the rum?" Or she might take a sudden dislike to a customer she found stupid: "Madam. You see before you two tubs of ice cream. One is brown and one is purple. There are two nameplates on the glass in front of them. So tell me, madam, HOW IS IT POSSIBLE THAT ONLY ONE OF THESE FLAVOURS IN FRONT OF YOU WOULD BE NAMED CHOCOLATE FUDGE BROWNIE BLACKBERRY SHERBET?!? Hmmm? Use your head, madam, please."

While Melina might have yelled at customers with impunity, I have no recollection of her yelling at Athos. In fact, I can barely remember them conversing at all beyond their talks with His Majesty. If you hadn't known that they were actually married, you might never have guessed it. I thought this chilly estrangement, like Athos's shirts, was more evidence of some aristocratic world beyond my comprehension.

Actually, Athos and Melina were not aristocrats. They were meritocrats. Their position in that world of Levantine glamour from which they had been lately cast out was earned by dint of study, expertise, and labour. They definitely knew the meaning of hard work. If anything, it was this new realm of pineapple syrup and rainbow jimmies that was not up to the challenge of them.

Take, for example, the light fare that was served in back. Sandwiches, potato skins, fried mozzarella sticks, and the like, all meant to be prepared according to the strict specifications of a menu book put out by number crunchers. A food service manual full of directives about the height from which pancake batter should be poured, the optimum diameter of said pancake, the respective number of slices of processed poultry in the turkey club, versus the sandwich, versus the platter, and so on. Food as utilitarian and unimaginative as that served from the galley of a 747. Most franchisees left their kitchens in the lugubrious but sufficiently capable hands of a bunch of pot smokers who, a decade later, would find gainful, bleary-eyed employment at Kinko's.

Not, however, Athos and Melina. To oversee things, they hired Benoît, an Alsatian of mercurial and easily affronted disposition who arrived each day with a leather carrying case of his own carbon-bladed kitchen knives. Many was the customer who ducked in order to avoid an enraged Benoît, who would emerge regularly from the kitchen, clutching an eleven-inch Sabatier in his wildly gesticulating fist, to scream at Melina over one of her cost-cutting measures or a difference of opinion over the finer points of the spicy Buffalo wings with blue cheese dip. *"J'en ai marre de ce bordel! Je ne peux pas faire la cuisine comme ça!"* Even holding weaponry, he was the unarmed party, thoroughly outmatched by the unmovable force that was Melina. A non-native speaker, she could still out-French him, her words flying like tracer bullets from her mouth. After a few minutes of Gallic fireworks, Benoît would return to the back, bested, seething with rage.

Despite Benoît's pyrotechnics of temperament, the kitchen was still a haven for all of us. As anyone who's ever worked in an ice-cream parlour can tell you, two things end up happening really quickly: you get sick of ice cream almost immediately, and soon thereafter you fall in love with the nitrous oxide used to make the whipped cream. You Heart Whippets. This ardour eventually cools when you realize that it's been weeks since you've been able to subtract simple sums, use an adjective correctly, or spell your own last name. But at the first bloom of narcotic romance, you merely wonder where whippets have been all your life.

We were frequently joined in our daily worship at the nozzle by Melina and Athos's son, Nick. I was desperate to be Nick. In 1982 I was sporting pegged trousers so tight at the ankles that by day's end my feet were numb. I was trying valiantly to look alternative, eccentric, Devo. With my hair in a short-back-and-sides 'do with a long and floppy New Romantic quiff on top, framing a face of such poorly concealed sweetness and naiveté, I looked about as threatening and alternative as a baby poodle—as complicated as one of the ice-cream cones I spent my days scooping.

But Nick! Nick had perfected that epoch's brand of sullen anomie, with his eyelids at the perpetual half-mast of weary disdain, his two-tone spiky hair and tapered jeans. If the front of the store was Athos and Melina's putative living room, where they didn't feel the need to talk to each other except in the presence of company, then the kitchen in back was Nick's domain, where they almost never ventured. The teenage bedroom of one's dreams, namely, one with a working refrigerator, a six-foot-tall tank of pressurized mind-altering gas, and a gaggle of stoners to laugh at everything you say.

Aside from working the register occasionally, Nick slouched about curating the music, a seemingly constant running loop of *Big Science* by Laurie Anderson, giving special play to its hit song, "O Superman," with its obligato of metronomic, aspirating laughter. But his true pride and joy was his self-published magazine, *Before & After Science*. This was years prior to the term *'zine* and the widespread use of computers. Like most every homegrown publication from the Punk/New Wave heyday of the early 1980s, *Before & After Science* was a samizdat, cut-and-paste affair of snippets of William Burroughs, Sex Pistols lyrics, black-and-white checkerboard backgrounds, lots of ransom note typography, old cheesecake photographs of women in bullet bras, and the ubiquitous image of that Ska Everyman: the porkpie-hatted Teddy Boy, limbs akimbo in a crazy running dance. *Before & After Science* was available for sale at the front of the store at a cost of five dollars for the premiere—and what was to regrettably be the only—issue.

Still, the pile of magazines provided a welcome counterpoint to the saccharine boosterism that invaded the store that summer. It was dubbed the Summer of *Annie* by proclamation of the Head Office, in honour of the release of the musical film adaptation of the Broadway show. Franchisees had been encouraged to invest in *Annie* ice cream, a special tie-in flavour.

Annie ice cream was a noxious combination of strawberry and marshmallow of such a vile and diabetic coma-inducing nature that it was too cloying even for its target market of little girls, a demographic not known for its sophisticated palate. Seven- and eight-year-old angels would skip into the store, all pigtails and horse love, and the scales would fall from their eyes as they spied the pink and white of the tubs of *Annie,* seeing them for what they were: blatant marketing; a pernicious inducement to submit to the patriarchy. These apple-cheeked youngsters became suddenly hardened and cynical. They took up smoking right there on line, laughing bitterly like baby Piafs, derisively ordering Futility Shakes and double scoops of Alienation Chip.

Available, along with the ice cream, and stacked into a doomed, unpurchased pyramid, were the *Annie* glasses. Drinking glasses emblazoned with the movie's logo and the likeness of Aileen Quinn, the little girl chosen in a nationwide search to portray the plucky, iris- and pupil-deprived orphan. Sales of these would benefit local charities. Even this altruism was not enough to move a single tumbler. Melina employed her usual insinuating tricks.

"Are you wearing Anaïs Anaïs, madam?" she would coo. "Ah yes, it's a lovely fragrance. I was one of the chemists who created it in Paris.... Yes, thank you so much. Can I interest you in one of our *Annie* glasses? Of course, it's for charity.... No? That's perfectly fine. I thank you, madam. Good day."

Wheeling around the instant the door closed, she would hiss at us, "Did you *see* the jewels dripping off of that woman, and she could not even buy one *Annie* glass. This is a film directed by John Huston, the man who made *The Maltese Falcon.* What is wrong with you people?"

We just laughed at her, imitating her anger behind her back. What I could not have known, at age seventeen, was that Melina's rages had nothing to do with a lack of appreciation for cinematic auteurism. I was too young to smell in the shop air the definite tang of flop sweat. That smell of exertion at keeping away the wolves of failure. It must have seemed so foolproof to them: an American ice-cream parlour ... and so close to America! And how perfect, too, that summer's thematic undercurrent: the unloved cartoon urchin with her little mongrel, delivered from abandonment and privation to a life of love and untold riches. What a tale of the New World, what fortunate augury under which to begin one's life fresh, for the third time. Nick's magazine might almost have been the story of their family. Before and After Science. "Before" was their tenure in the reliable field of chemistry, where something as ethereal as fragrance—even a fragrance so indescribably heady and complex that its mysteries could be approximated only with images of women lying by swimming pools as shadows of airplanes passed up and across phallic architecture—could be created through the sober logic of a recipe. "After" was this random, anarchic world of business. A world that was failing them—a mapless, unchartable landscape. Looking back, I can see in the pendulum swings of affect the desperation of a woman running out of ground beneath her feet where she could resettle and start over yet again.

• • •

A year later, away at college, I would be sent a small newspaper item, the untold story made only sadder by the clinical dispassion of the clipping. A precipitous disappearance, no forwarding address, thousands of dollars in loans and bills outstanding, a shuttered store with no plans to reopen, a sheriff's department notice of seizure taped to the window.

I often imagine them on an airplane. Athos sleeps. Nick tampers with the smoke detector in the bathroom so he can light up. And there is Melina's face at the small round window. Shielding her eyes against the glass, she stares out into the night, past the blinking wing lights, past the Western edge of the continent, out over the ocean, scanning the horizon for the next piece of dry land.

Bill Richardson

If posterity has any damn sense, it will recognize Bill Richardson's novel *Waiting for Gertrude* as the classic it is. The premise alone is as inventive and original as they come. In Père-Lachaise cemetery of Paris, the graveyard's illustrious inhabitants—Jim Morrison, Oscar Wilde, Alice B. Toklas, Marcel Proust, Isadora Duncan, Chopin, and their ilk—have been reborn as feral cats. Told through a series of letters written by various cats, and interspersed with passages of brilliantly comedic verse, *Waiting for Gertrude* manages to be a romance, a fantasy, a literary satire, and a gothic mystery all at once. I have selected some of the poetry, as penned by the feline La Fontaine, followed by an open letter from the now-catty Maria Callas—though I do fear I have done a disservice to Richardson's novel by taking these passages out of their original context. Nevertheless, enjoy!

FROM *Waiting for Gertrude*

La Fontaine's Versified Walking Tour: Welcome

Welcome, cats. I offer thanks—
Tabby, ginger, Persian, Manx,
Tortoiseshell and coal-vein black,
Plump of belly, sleek of back,
Eyes of copper, eyes of green,
Randy tom and preening queen—
Welcome, stray and purest bred,
To this playground of the dead,
Welcome to this yard of bones.
Please turn off all pagers, phones,
Render mute whatever might
Rend our sacred, silent night.

Excellent. Now let's be sure,
As we start this guided tour,
Creeping forth on velvet paws,
Everyone has come because
They've a hunger they must sate
Here among the late and great.
If you tag along with me,
Having paid a modest fee,
You shall, for this evening, bide
Where Parisian greats who died
Came to rest, not knowing that
They would be reborn as cats.

Sages wise have often taught,
When the body starts to rot,
That the soul from flesh is pried,
Then is changed, transmogrified.
And they're right. It happens thus:
Shortly, and with little fuss,
When one's breath has finally failed,
One appears again, be-tailed.
Some will bellow, "That's absurd!
First interred and then be-furred?"
But it's true. Hence, I was born
La Fontaine in feline form.

What, one wonders, would they say,
Bernhardt, Balzac, or Bizet,
Had they known the final score:
Two legs one day, next day four?
How would they have laid their bets,
Chopin, Callas, or Colette,
Had they known their future role
Would entail a taste for vole?
Would they weep or would they laugh,
Proust and Poulenc and Piaf,
At the thought of eating mouse?
Would they grin? Or would they grouse?

Oscar Wilde, Seurat, Molière:
Check the roster, all are there,
Deepening their catlike ways
On the grounds of Père-Lachaise.
Celebrity's a shiny lure,
You shall meet some on this tour—
All save Gertrude. I'm afraid
That *grande dame* has been delayed.
Gertrude who? Why, Gertrude Stein.
Poor Miss Toklas! How she pines,
Exiled from her land of bliss,
Aching for her husband's kiss.

Questions? Yes, there, on the right.
Ah. You wonder if the night
Is riskless, safe, hazard-free?
This, I cannot guarantee.
By and large, though, not to fret,
Not one tourist's perished yet.
Should the Lizard King arise,
Caution then I might advise.
Ready, then? Fine. Let's begin.
Welcome, cats! Cats, welcome in.

La Fontaine's Versified Walking Tour: Maria Callas

When Death decides it's come your turn,
You have to opt for earth or urn.
Maria Callas, when she died,
Said no to "buried," yes to "fried";
No casket grand with brassy hinge,
It's over when the singer's singed.
Her loved ones came to pick her up,
They took Maria—half a cup—
And housed her, feeling rather glum,
Within the columbarium.

Soon, student pranksters, on a spree,
Connived to set Maria free,
They planned the heist, they named the day,
They stole the ash, then stole away.
A gendarme, acting on a tip,
Restored the cinders to the crypt.
Maria's kin, inclined to nix
All future sophomoric tricks,
Yanked the rug from young collegians,
Scattered her on the Aegean.

In her blue, refulgent cloister,
La Divina feeds the oysters.
Free of ballast, safe from malice,
Au revoir, Maria Callas.
That is, goodbye to human flesh:
A cat skin is her soul's new cache.
She's black and white and grey and tan,
And oh, the voice! "Sing!" plead her fans.
They beg in vain, in vain beseech,
For divas e'er stay out of reach.

Interview: Maria Callas Sends a Form Letter

November 12

To Whom It May Concern:

I am in receipt of your letter dated _____ requesting an interview for your ( ) magazine ( ) newspaper ( ) radio show ( ) television program. While I am grateful for your interest in my career, I fear I must decline your kind invitation. Life is simply too short. In the few lines that follow, you will find every answer to every question I would willingly have entertained had a face-to-face encounter been possible. You have my express permission to use this in whole or in part, to represent it as your original work, and to attach to it your byline, without fear of calumny or reprisal from this quarter.

M.C.

Q: Madame Callas, what was your reaction when you discovered that you had been reborn as a cat?

A: Initially, surprise, of course. Why would one expect otherwise? It is nothing one would think to ask for, after all, and then so much is so vastly different from what one has previously known. Perspective. Instinct. Longing. The sudden urge to hold one's foot to one's mouth and suck on it, and the easy flexibility that makes such carnal indulgences a possibility. It's all quite unanticipated, as you can readily imagine. However, astonishment soon gives way to willing acquiescence. And why would it not? If there's one thing one learns from a life in the opera, it's that destiny will not be denied.

When the Fates have you in their sights, you may just as well open your arms wide in a gesture of welcoming embrace and make yourself a conspicuous target. Concealment is useless, for they are relentless; the Fates, I mean. Eventually, they will track you down. When you accept that this is your lot and that this is the hand you have been dealt, you require neither explanation nor consolation. You merely accede to the fact that this life, like any other, is nothing more or less than a costume party: *un ballo in maschera,* as Verdi would have it. Did you ever see my Amalia, by the way? I can recommend my 1957 *La Scala* performance, Gianandrea Gavazzeni conducting.

Q: I know that recording. I adore it.

A: Of course you do. Who could cavil at perfection?

Q: Do I understand that you have no regrets about your present situation?

A: None. *Je ne regrette rien.*

Q: I take it that you are acquainted with Madame Piaf?

A: Everyone knows Edith. She's the most sought-after laundress in Père-Lachaise. Her mangling is above reproach.

Q: She cleans rather than sings?

A: Her art, like my own, was as much incantatory as it was musical. Her true talent, in that other place, that other time, was to cut through the dross, the encumbrances, to reveal to her audience the unsullied heart of matter. In other words, she was endowed with the ability to cleanse and make pure. She still is. Her gift remains intact. All that has changed is the medium of its delivery. In her singing days, she used her voice to reverse the flow of blood from the head to the heart. Now that she has come to live at Père-Lachaise, she knows how to reverse the effects of bloodstains on sheets. Both skills are priceless, and they grow from the same root.

Q: Do you often have blood on your sheets?

A: Young man, that is a foolish question coming from one who claims to know about opera. Does the word "tubercular" mean nothing to you? Have you any idea how many consumptive heroines I have had thrust upon me? How many Violettas I have had to wrestle to the ground? Bloodstained sheets are the least of it.

Q: So, unlike Piaf, you continue to sing.

A: I could not do otherwise.

Q: Are there roles that are particularly well-suited to your present circumstances?

A: Tosca, most especially. I can throw myself from the parapet and land on my feet without risk of injury. And then the audience is always mightily impressed when I leap right back up again for an encore. Up and down, up and down. Why, I could go up and down all night and hardly break a sweat.

Q: So rumour has it. Would you care to comment on reports linking you romantically to Mr. Morrison?

A: Ha! Why not just come right out and ask if I'm bearing his love child? One hears that, too! From what polluted well are these lunatic speculations drawn? The only way to deal with such excremental musings is to bury them in the sand. Which now I do. There. See? They are gone.

Q: Nonetheless, several reliable sources report seeing Mr. Morrison with his teeth sunk deeply into your neck.

A: Quite. Mr. Morrison, who is skilled in first aid, was assisting me to remove a small fishbone that had become lodged in my craw. I am fortunate he happened to be passing by at just that moment. Otherwise, surgery would surely have been required. Who knows what deleterious effect a tracheotomy would have had on my instrument? Mr. Morrison was most generous and most efficient. His was a very welcome interference.

Q: Still, it must have been painful. Every report has it that you were howling.

A: Young man, that was not howling. That was my Salome.

Q: I do beg your pardon.

A: As well you might. Are we done now?

Q: Nearly. Latterly, many operatic singers have been forging collaborations with pop stars. Do you think that you and Mr. Morrison might undertake such a partnership?

A: Oh, my goodness! Can you imagine Mr. Morrison singing "E Lucevan Le Stelle"?

Q: It would be sauce for the gander after your recent performance of "Come on Baby, Light My Fire," would it not?

A: Why, look at that clock. I believe it is time for you to go. Goodbye, young man.

Q: But—

A: Young man, goodbye.

Mordecai Richler

Name an award and Richler has won it; name a laurel and he has received it: *two* Governor General's, the Giller, the Commonwealth Prize, the Leacock Medal for Humour. His writing is rooted in Montreal's St. Urbain Street, in the Jewish enclave of a French Canadian city dominated by Anglo money. It is a world rich with humour, conflict, and personality—a world where ambition matters, family is everything, and poverty is all in how you look at it. The following is from Mordecai Richler's memoir, *The Street*.

FROM *The Street*

"Why do you want to go to university?" the student counsellor asked me.

Without thinking, I replied, "I'm going to be a doctor, I suppose."

A doctor.

One St. Urbain Street day cribs and diapers were cruelly withdrawn and the next we were scrubbed and carted off to kindergarten. Though we didn't know it, we were already in pre-med school. School starting age was six, but fiercely competitive mothers would drag protesting four-year-olds to the registration desk and say, "He's short for his age."

"Birth certificate, please?"

"Lost in a fire."

On St. Urbain Street, a head start was all. Our mothers read us stories from *Life* about pimply astigmatic fourteen-year-olds who had already graduated from Harvard or who were confounding the professors at M.I.T.

Reading *Tip-Top Comics* or listening to *The Green Hornet* on the radio was as good as asking for a whack on the head, sometimes administered with a rolled-up copy of *The Canadian Jewish Eagle,* as if that in itself would be nourishing. We were not supposed to memorize baseball batting averages or dirty limericks. We were expected to improve our Word Power with the *Reader's Digest* and find inspiration in Paul de Kruif's medical biographies. If we didn't make doctors, we were supposed to at least squeeze into dentistry. School marks didn't count as much as rank. One wintry day I came home, nostrils clinging together and ears burning cold, proud of my report. "I came rank two, Maw."

"And who came rank one, may I ask?"

Mrs. Klinger's boy, alas. Already the phone was ringing. "Yes, yes," my mother said to Mrs. Klinger, "congratulations, and what does the eye doctor say about your Riva, poor kid, to have a complex at her age, will they be able to straighten them ..."

Parochial school was a mixed pleasure. The old, underpaid men who taught us Hebrew tended to be surly, impatient. Ear-twisters and knuckle-rappers. They didn't like children. But the girls who handled the English-language part of our studies were charming, bracingly modern, and concerned about our future. They told us about *El Campesino,* how John Steinbeck wrote the truth, and read Sacco's speech to the court aloud to us. If one of the younger, unmarried teachers started out the morning looking weary we assured each other that she had done it the night before. Maybe with a soldier. Bareback.

From parochial school, I went on to a place I call Fletcher's Field High in the stories and memoirs that follow. Fletcher's Field High was under the jurisdiction of the Montreal Protestant School Board, but had a student body that was nevertheless almost a hundred percent Jewish. The school became something of a legend in our area. Everybody, it seemed, had passed through FFHS. Canada's most famous gambler. An atom bomb spy. Boys who went off to fight in the Spanish Civil War. Miracle-making doctors and silver-tongued lawyers. Boxers. Fighters for Israel. All of whom were instructed, as I was, to be staunch and bold, to play the man, and, above all, to

Strive hard and work.

With your heart in the doing.

Up play the game,

As you learned it at Fletcher's.

Again and again we led Quebec province in the junior matriculation results. This was galling to the communists amongst us who held we were the same as everyone else, but to the many more who knew that for all seasons there was nothing like a Yiddish boy, it was an annual cause for celebration. Our class at FFHS, Room 41, was one of the few to boast a true Gentile, an authentic white Protestant. Yugoslavs and Bulgarians, who were as foxy as we were, their potato-filled mothers sitting just as rigid in their corsets at school concerts, fathers equally prone to natty straw hats and cursing in the mother-tongue, did not count. Our very own WASP's name was Whelan, and he was no less than perfect. Actually blond, with real blue eyes, and a tendency to sit with his mouth hanging open. A natural hockey player, a born first-baseman. Envious students came from other classrooms to look him over and put questions to him. Whelan, as to be expected, was not excessively bright, but he gave Room 41 a certain tone, some badly needed glamour, and in order to keep him with us as we progressed from grade to grade, we wrote essays for him and slipped him answers at examination time. We were enormously proud of Whelan.

Among our young school masters, most of them returned war veterans, there were a number of truly dedicated men as well as some sour and brutish ones, like Shaw, who strapped twelve of us one afternoon, ten on each hand, because we wouldn't say who had farted while his back was turned. The foibles of older teachers were well-known to us, because so many aunts, uncles, cousins, and elder brothers had preceded us at FFHS. There was, for instance, one master who initiated first year students with a standing joke. "Do you know how the Jews make an 's'?"

"No, Sir."

Then he would make an "s" on the blackboard and draw two strokes through it. The dollar sign.

• • •

In 1953, on the first Sunday after my return to Montreal from a two year stay in Europe, I went to my grandmother's house on Jeanne Mance Street.

A Yiddish newspaper fluttering on her massive lap, black bootlaces unravelled, my grandmother was ensconced in a kitchen chair on the balcony, seemingly rooted there, attended by sons and daughters, fortified by grandchildren. "How is it for the Jews in Europe?" she asked me.

A direct question from an old lady with a wart turned like a screw in her cheek and in an instant I was shorn of all my desperately acquired sophistication; my *New Statesman* outlook, my shaky knowledge of wines and European capitals; the life I had made for myself beyond the ghetto.

"I don't know," I said, my shame mixed with resentment at being reclaimed so quickly. "I didn't meet many."

Leaning against their shiny new cars, yawning on the balcony steps with hands thrust into their trouser pockets or munching watermelon, pinging seeds into saucers, my uncles reproached me for not having been to Israel. But their questions about Europe were less poignant than my grandmother's. Had I seen the Folies Bergères? The changing of the guards? My uncles had become Canadians.

Canada, from the beginning, was second-best. It made us nearly Americans.

My grandfather, like so many others, ventured to Canada by steerage from a Gallician *shtetl,* in 1904, following hard on the outbreak of the Russo-Japanese War and the singularly vile pogrom in Kishinev, which was instigated by the militant anti-Semite P.A. Krushevan, editor of *Znamya (The Banner),* who four months later was the first to publish in Russia the *Minutes of the Meeting of the World Union of Freemasons and Elders of Zion,* which he called *Programme for World Conquest by the Jews.*

My grandfather, I was astonished to discover many years later, had actually had a train ticket to Chicago in his pocket. Canada was not a choice, but an accident. On board ship my grandfather encountered a follower of the same hasidic rabbi; the man had a train ticket to Montreal, but relatives in Chicago. My grandfather knew somebody's cousin in Toronto, also in Canada, he was informed. So the two men swapped train tickets on deck one morning.

On arrival in Montreal my grandfather acquired a peddler's licence and a small loan from the Baron de Hirsch Institute and dug in not far from the Main Street in what was to become a ghetto. Here, as in the real America, the immigrants worked under appalling conditions in sweatshops. They rented halls over poolrooms and grocery stores to meet and form burial societies and create *shuls*. They sent to the old country for younger brothers and cousins left behind, for rabbis and brides. Slowly, unfalteringly, the immigrants began to struggle up a ladder of streets, from one where you had to leave your garbage outside your front door to another where you actually had a rear lane as well as a back yard where corn and tomatoes were usually grown; from the three rooms over the fruit store or tailor shop to your own cold-water flat. A street with trees.

Our street was called St. Urbain. French for Urban. Actually there have been eight popes named Urban; but ours was the first. Urban 1. He was also the only one to have been canonized.

St. Urbain ultimately led to routes 11 and 18, and all day and night big refrigeration trucks and peddlers in rattling chevvies and sometimes tourists used to pass, hurtling to and from northern Quebec, Ontario, and New York State. Occasionally the truckers and peddlers would pull up at Tansky's for a bite.

"Montreal's a fine town," they'd say. "Wide open."

Unfailingly, one of the truckers would reply, "It's the Gay Paree of North America."

But if the trucker or peddler was from Toronto, he would add, ingratiatingly, "The only good thing about Toronto is the road to Montreal. Isn't that so?"

The regulars at Tansky's felt it was a good omen that the truckers and peddlers sometimes stopped there. "They know the best places," Segal said.

Some of the truckers had tattoos on their arms, others chewed tobacco or rolled their own cigarettes with Old Chum. The regulars would whisper about them in Yiddish.

"I wonder how long *that* one's been out of prison?"

"The one with all the holes in his face smells like he hasn't changed his underwear since God knows when."

The truckers struck matches against the seat of their shiny trousers or by flicking them with a thumbnail. They could spit on the floor with such a splash of assurance that it was the regulars who ended up feeling like intruders in Tansky's Cigar & Soda.

"I'll bet you the one with the ears can't count to twenty without taking his shoes off."

"But you don't understand," Takifman, nodding, sucking mournfully on an inverted pipe, would reassure them. "Statistics prove they're happier than we are. They care their kids should go to the McGill? They have one every nine months regular as clock-work. Why? For the family allowance cheque."

When the regulars carried on like that, belittling the bigger, more masculine men, Tansky would regard them reproachfully. He would put out delicate little feelers to the truckers. His brothers, the French Canadians. Vanquished, oppressed.

Peering over the rim of his glasses, Tansky would say, "Isn't it a shame about the strikers in Granby?" Or looking up from his newspaper, pausing to wet a thumb, he'd try, "And what about our brothers the blacks?"

Then he would settle back and wait.

If one of the truckers replied, "It's shit, everything's shit," and the other sneered, "I try to mind my own business, buster," Tansky's shaggy grey head would drop and he would have to be reminded to add mustard and relish to the hamburgers. But if the truckers were responsive or, more likely, shrewd, if one said, "It's the system," and the other, "Maybe after the war things will be different," they would earn heaping plates of french fried potatoes and complimentary refills of coffee.

"It's one hell of a life," one of the truckers might say and Tansky would reply fervently, "We can change it. It's up to the people."

Even in winter the regulars used to risk the wind and ice to slip outside and stamp up and down around the enormous trailer trucks, reminding each other that they too could have been millionaires today, fabled philanthropists, sought-after community leaders, if only, during prohibition, they too had been willing to bootleg, running booze over the border in trucks like these.

Another opportunity missed.

Looking in here, landing a little slap there, the regulars always stopped to give the tires a melancholy kick.

"You should have what one of these babies burns in gas in one night."

"Ach. It's no life for a family man."

It was different with the peddlers. Most of them were, as Miller put it, members of the tribe. Even if a man was so stupid, such a *putz,* that he couldn't tell from their faces or if—like Tansky, perhaps—he indignantly held that there was no such thing as a Jewish face, he still knew because before the peddlers even sat down for a coffee they generally phoned home and looked to see if Tansky sold pennants or toys to take back as a memento for the kids. They didn't waste time, either. They zipped through their order book as they ate, biting their pencils, adding, subtracting, muttering to themselves, and if they were carrying an item that Tansky might feasibly use they tried to push a sale right there. If not, they would offer the regulars cut-rates on suits or kitchen ware. Some of the peddlers were kidders and carried come-ons with them to entice the French Canadian hicks in Ste Jerome and Trois-Rivières, Tadoussac and Restigouche. Hold a key chain socket to your eye and see a naked cutie wiggle. Pour seltzer into a tumbler with a print of a girl on the side and watch her panties peel off.

Segal told all the peddlers the same joke, ruining it, as he did all his stories, by revealing the punch-line first. "Do you know the one," he'd say, "that goes Bloomberg's dead?"

"No. Well, I don't think so."

So Segal, quaking with laughter, would plunge into the story about this traveller, one of ours, a man called Bloomberg, who had a cock bigger than a Coorsh's salami. Built stronger than Farber the iceman's horse, let me tell you. He went from town to town, selling bolts of cloth, seconds, and banging *shiksas* (nuns included) on the cot in the back of his van, until the day he died. Another salesman, Motka Frish, was also in this godforsaken mining town in Labrador when he died. Motka hurried to the mortuary where the legendary Bloomberg lay on a slab and sliced off his cock, his unbelievably large member, to bring home and show to his wife, because otherwise, he thought, she would never believe a man could be so well hung. He returns home, unwraps the cock, and before he can get a word out, his wife has a peek and begins to pull her hair and wail. "Bloomberg's dead," she howls. "Bloomberg's dead."

Afterwards, still spilling with laughter, Segal would ask, "Heard any hot ones yourself lately?"

Takifman was another one who always had a word with the peddlers. "How is it," he would ask, already tearful, "for the Jews in Valleyfield?"

Or if the peddler had just come from Albany it was, "I hear the mayor there is an anti-Semite."

"Aren't they all?"

"Not LaGuardia. LaGuardia of New York is A-1."

The peddlers would usually ask for a couple of dollars in silver and retreat to the phone booth for a while before they left.

Tansky's beat-up brown phone booth was an institution in our neighbourhood. Many who didn't have phones of their own used it to summon the doctor. "I'd rather pay a nickel here than be indebted to that cockroach downstairs for the rest of my life." Others needed the booth if they had a surreptitious little deal to transact or if it was the sabbath and they couldn't use their own phones because they had a father from the stone ages. If you had a party line you didn't dare use the phone in your own house to call the free loan society or the exterminator. Boys who wanted privacy used the phone to call their girl friends, though the regulars were particularly hard on them.

Between two and four in the afternoon the horse players held a monopoly on the phone. One of them, Sonny Markowitz, got an incoming call daily at three. Nat always took it for him. "Good afternoon," he'd say "Morrow Real Estate. Mr. Morrow. One moment, please."

Markowitz would grab the receiver, his manner breathless. "Glad you called, honey. But I've got an important client with me right now. Yes, doll. You bet. Soon as I can. *Hasta la vista.*"

Anxious callers had long ago picked the paint off one wall of the booth. Others had scratched obscenities into the exposed zinc. Somebody who had been unable to get a date with Molly had used a key to cut MOLLY BANGS into the wall. Underneath, Manny had written ME TOO, adding his phone number. Doodles tended toward the expansively pornographic, they were boastful too, and most of the graffiti was obvious. KILROY WAS HERE. OPEN UP A SECOND FRONT. PERLMAN'S A SHVANTZ.

After each fight with Joey, Sadie swept in sobbing, hysterical, her house-coat fluttering. She never bothered to lower her voice. "It's happened again, Maw. No, he wasn't wearing anything. He wouldn't. Sure I told him what the doctor said. *I told him.* He said what are you, the B'nai Jacob Synagogue, I can't come in without wearing a hat? How do I know? I'm telling you, Maw, he's a beast, I want to come home to you. *That's not true.* I couldn't stop him if I wanted to. Yes, I washed before Seymour. A lot of good it does. All right, Maw. I'll tell him."

Sugarman never shuffled into Tansky's without first trying the slot in the booth to see if anyone had left a nickel behind. The regulars seldom paid for a call. They would dial their homes or businesses, ring twice, hang up, and wait for the return call.

Tansky's was not the only store of its sort on St. Urbain. Immediately across the street was Myerson's.

Myerson had put in cushions for the card players, he sold some items cheaper than Tansky, but he was considered to be a sour type, a regular snake, and so he did not do too well. He had his regulars, it's true, and there was some drifting to and fro between the stores out of pique, but if a trucker or a peddler stopped at Myerson's it was an accident.

Myerson had a tendency to stand outside, sweeping up with vicious strokes, and hollering at the men as they filed into Tansky's. "Hey, why don't you come over here for once? I won't bite you. Blood poisoning I don't need."

Myerson's rage fed on the refugees who began to settle on St. Urbain during the war years. "If they come in it's for a street direction," he'd say, "or if it's for a coke they want a dozen glasses with." He wasn't kind to kids. "You know what you are," he was fond of saying, "your father's mistake."

If we came in to collect on empty bottles, he'd say, "We don't deal in stolen goods here. Try Tansky's."

We enjoyed the excitement of the passing peddlers and truckers on St. Urbain—it was, as Sugarman said, an education—but we also had our traffic accidents. Once a boy was killed. An only son. Another time an old man. But complain, complain, we could not get them to install traffic lights on our corner.

"When one of ours is killed by a car they care? It saves them some dirty work."

But Tansky insisted it wasn't anti-Semitism. Ours was a working-class area. That's why we didn't count.

St. Urbain was one of five working-class ghetto streets between the Main and Park Avenue.

To a middle-class stranger, it's true, the five streets would have seemed interchangeable. On each corner a cigar store, grocery, and a fruit man. Outside staircases everywhere. Winding ones, wooden ones, rusty and risky ones. An endless repetition of precious peeling balconies and waste lots making the occasional gap here and there. But, as we boys knew, each street between the Main and Park Avenue represented subtle differences in income. No two cold-water flats were alike and no two stores were the same either. Best Fruit gypped on weight but Smiley's didn't give credit.

Of the five streets, St. Urbain was the best. Those on the streets below, the out-of-breath ones, the borrowers, the *yentas,* flea-carriers, and rent-skippers, *goniffs* from Galicia, couldn't afford a day in the country or tinned fruit for dessert on the High Holidays. They accepted parcels from charity matrons (Outremont bitches) on Passover, and went uninvited to bar-mitzvahs and weddings to carry off cakes, bottles, and chicken legs. Their English was not as good as ours. In fact, they were not yet Canadians. *Greeners,* that's what they were. On the streets above, you got the ambitious ones. The schemers and the hat-tippers. The *pusherkes.*

Among the wonders of St. Urbain, our St. Urbain, there was a man who ran for alderman on a one-plank platform—provincial speed cops were anti-Semites. There was a semi-pro whore, Cross-Eyed Yetta, and a gifted cripple,

Pomerantz, who had had a poem published in *transition* before he shrivelled and died at the age of twenty-seven. There were two men who had served with the Mackenzie-Paps in the Spanish Civil War and a girl who had met Danny Kaye in the Catskills. A boy nobody remembered who went on to become a professor at M.I.T. Dicky Rubin who married a *shiksa* in the Unitarian Church. A Boxer who once made the *Ring* magazine ratings. Lazar of Best Grade Fruit who raked in twenty-five hundred dollars for being knocked down by a No. 43 streetcar. Herscovitch's nephew Larry who went to prison for yielding military secrets to Russia. A woman who actually called herself a divorcée. A man, A.D.'s father, who was bad luck to have in your house. And more, many more. St. Urbain was, I suppose, somewhat similar to ghetto streets in New York and Chicago. There were a number of crucial differences, however. We were Canadians, therefore we had a King. We also had "pea-soups," that is to say, French Canadians, in the neighbourhood. While the King never actually stopped on St. Urbain, he did pass a few streets above on his visit to Canada just before the war. We were turned out of school to wave at him on our first unscheduled holiday, as I recall it, since Buster Crabbe, the Tarzan of his day, had spoken to us on Canada Youth Day.

"He looks to me *eppes,* a little pasty," Mrs. Takifman said.

My friends and I used to set pennies down on the tracks to be flattened by passing freight trains. Later, we would con the rich kids in Outremont, telling them that the Royal Train had gone over the pennies. We got a nickel each for them.

Earlier, the Prince of Wales came to Canada. He appeared at a Mizrachi meeting and my mother became one of thousands upon thousands who actually shook hands with him. When he abdicated the throne, she revealed, "Even then you could tell he was a romantic man. You could see it in his eyes."

"He has two," my father said, "just like me."

"Sure. That's right. You sacrifice a throne for a lady's love. It kills you to even give up a seat on the streetcar."

A St. Urbain street lady, Mrs. Miller of Miller's Home Bakery, made an enormous *chaleh,* the biggest loaf we had ever seen, and sent it to

Buckingham Palace in time for Princess Elizabeth's birthday. A thank you note came from the Palace and Mrs. Miller's picture was in all the newspapers. "For local distribution," she told reporters, "we also bake knishes and cater for quality weddings."

• • •

St. Urbain, we felt was inviolable. Among us we numbered the rank-one scholars in the province, gifted artists, medical students, and everywhere you looked decent, God-fearing people. It was a little embarrassing admittedly, when Mrs. Boxer, the *meshugena,* wandered the streets in her nightgown singing Jesus Loves Me. Our landlords, by and large, were rotten types. Polacks, Bulgarians, and other trash were beginning to move in here and there. When that sweet young man from CHFD's "Vox Pop" asked Ginsburg, didn't he think Canada ought to have a flag of her own, he shouldn't have come back with, you do what you like, *we* already have a flag. Not on the radio, anyway. Sugarman's boy, Stanley, it's true, had had to do six months at Ste. Vincent de Paul for buying stolen goods, but all the time he was there he refused to eat non-kosher food. We had our faults on St. Urbain, but nobody could find anything truly important to criticize.

Then one black, thundering day there was an article about our street in *Time* magazine. For several years we had been electing communists to represent us at Ottawa and in the provincial legislature. Our M.P. was arrested. An atomic spy. *Time,* investigating the man's background in depth, described St. Urbain, our St. Urbain, as the Hell's Kitchen of Montreal. It brought up old election scandals and strikes and went into the housing question and concluded that this was the climate in which communism flourished.

The offending magazine was passed from hand to hand.

"What's 'squalor'?"

"Shmutz."

"We're dirty? In my house you could eat off the floor."

"We're not poor. I can walk into any delicatessen in town, you name it, and order whatever my little heart desires."

"In our house there's always plenty for *shabbus*. I should show you my butcher's bills you'd die."

"This write-up's crazy. An insult."

"Slander, you mean. We ought to get Lubin to take the case."

"Ignoramous. You don't bring in ambulance chasers to fight a case like this. You need one of theirs, a big-shot."

"What about Rosenberg? He's a K.C."

"Yeah, and everybody knows exactly how he got it. We would need a goy."

"Oh, here he comes. Takifman, the fanatic. Okay, we've got the Torah. You try it for collateral at the Bank of Canada."

"For shame," Takifman said, appalled.

"Listen here, *Time* is a magazine of current affairs. The Torah is an old story. They are discussing here economics."

"The Torah is nothing to laugh."

"But you are, Takifman."

"A Jew is never poor," Takifman insisted. "Broke? Sometimes. Going through hard times? Maybe. In a strange country? Always. But poor, never."

Tansky threw his dishrag on the counter. "We are the same as everybody else," he shouted.

"What the hell!"

"Now listen, you listen here, with Chief Rabbi Takifman I don't agree, but the same—"

"You know what, Tansky. You can stuff that where the monkey put his fingers."

Sugarman finished reading the article. "What are you all so excited about?" he asked. "Can't you see this magazine is full of advertisements?"

Everybody turned to look at him.

"According to my son, and he ought to know, these magazines are all under the heel of the big advertisers. They say whatever the advertisers want."

"So you mean it's the advertisers who say we're poor and dirty?"

"You win the sixty-four dollars."

"*Why*, smart-guy?"

"Why? Did I say I know everything? All I said was that according to my son it is the advertisers who—"

"Jews and artists are never poor," Takifman persisted. "How could they be?"

"We are the same as everybody else," Tansky shouted. "Idiots!"

"A Jew is never poor. It would be impossible."

Erika Ritter

Playwright, novelist, broadcaster, and social commentator, Erika Ritter is one of the grand dames of Canadian humour. (We can still say "dames," right?) In *The Great Big Book of Guys,* Ritter takes the reader on an anthropological and alphabetical tour of the various types of men she has known, everything from "Amigos" and "Bad Boys," all the way to "Zealots." It's a journey that is often funny, sometimes poignant, and always thought provoking. The following is from her encounter with a fellow named Ken. As in "doll."

FROM *The Great Big Book of Guys*

Ken Dolls

It was back in 1999 that this story begins, but the details are as clear as if it happened yesterday. Late at night, when I was on my way home from work, something prompted me to turn down a street I don't usually take and stop in for a drink at a place I'd never even noticed before.

A real hole-in-the-wall this bar was, where they apparently didn't care whom they served, because some of the clientele looked decidedly underage. Yet familiar. In one corner, I thought I spotted several Cabbage Patch dolls, although in the general darkness, it was hard to be sure. But the drinks they were giggling over were *not* Shirley Temples. That much I knew for certain.

Meanwhile, Tickle Me Elmo was becoming a little truculent with the barman, who'd evidently cut him off—and not, I sensed, for the first time. A family of Trolls took turns dangling each other by their hot pink hair from the mirror behind the bar, much to their own amusement, if nobody else's.

Even My Little Pony was in evidence, lapping something out of a bucket that definitely did not smell like water.

My God, I exclaimed to myself. It's like an outtake from *Toy Story* in here, a place where all the forgotten toys have gone—in this case, to do some forgetting of their own.

No sooner had I formed the thought than I caught sight of a slim, attractive young man, somewhat vacant in expression and not even a foot tall, trying unsuccessfully to bend his moulded plastic elbow as he sat at the bar, belting back straight Scotch. Surely, it couldn't be.... And yet, I felt sickeningly sure that it was. Very tentatively, I approached and sat down beside him.

"Excuse me," I said. "But aren't you Ken? Barbie's boyfriend?"

Without turning his head (though it *was* movable) he continued to drink relentlessly. "I used to be."

"*Used* to be Ken?"

He attempted to twist his lips into a sardonic grimace, but as they were merely painted on, the effect was somewhat diminished. "That's right. Now I'm nobody. If you don't believe me, ask Barbie. Mind you, she may be too busy to answer. Seeing as this is her big day and all."

"What big—?" I started to ask, before recalling I had recently read a promotional piece about Barbie. "Oh, isn't today Barbie's birthday or something?"

At that, Ken laughed. "Or something? That's rich. Barbie's fortieth birthday is only the media event of the century, that's all. This morning, she rang the opening bell at the New York Stock Exchange. All the traders wore vests of Barbie Pink in her honour. And she was togged out as Working Woman Barbie with laptop, cellphone, and CD-ROM, each sold separately. At this very moment, at the Waldorf Astoria hotel, there's a Barbie Ball going on, and the U.S. Postal Service has issued a Barbie stamp. Her birthday or something? I'll say."

As Ken recited this bitter catalogue of kudos to Barbie, a Betsy Wetsy doll close enough to overhear shed a real tear. I felt moved to sympathy myself. Who wouldn't be? A night of unparalleled triumph for his girlfriend, and yet where was Ken? Drowning his sorrows in an anonymous bar, lost and all alone.

"Not that I'm entirely alone," he continued, as though reading my unspoken thought. "Sometimes G.I. Joe drops by on his way home from the rifle range, or Raggedy Andy manages to shake his better half and stop in to hoist a few and reminisce about the good old days, when we boy toys were hot."

Hot? I couldn't speak to G.I. Joe, but God knows I'd never thought of *my* old Raggedy Andy doll as particularly hot. Nor had I thought of him much at all, except as an inescapable adjunct to Raggedy Anne—who was, after all, the main event, with her little appliquéd heart and its embroidered "I Love You" motto. Raggedy Anne had Raggedy Andy the way the Queen had Prince Philip: an official escort for public engagements who knew his place, a few paces behind.

Much, in fact, as Ken had always functioned in Barbie's life, for all of the thirty-eight years he'd known her by the time her fortieth birthday rolled around, on that fateful March night in 1999, when I ran across him in a nameless bar, drinking regret and resentment to their bitter dregs. After all, by the age of forty, Barbie had already had something like seventy-five careers, from Astronaut Barbie, to Barbie the Dentist, to Medic Sergeant Barbie, to Barbie the Vet. Ken, meanwhile, had had … what? A camper van, some scuba-diving gear, tennis clothes, a Hawaiian shirt, and a few pairs of bathing trunks. Ken, in other words, had never been dressed for success—only for fun.

"Barbie may not get to make as many of her own choices as you think," I suggested. "For all you know, it's a marketing thing on Mattel's part, putting her forward as Working Woman Barbie on her birthday, all corporate and independent and—"

"And uncaring and cold and rich," Ken concluded. "I, meanwhile, don't even have a decent place to live in." He gestured to the barkeep for another round. "You should see it; it's a shoebox."

Poor Ken. I could tell he meant it really *was* a shoebox. By contrast, it was impossible not to recall Barbie luxuriating in her very own Winnebago,

or in a well-appointed poolside cabana, or in any of the many other glamorous dwellings she'd acquired over the past forty years.

Once again, even as the thought formed, Ken seemed able to intercept
it. "So there it is: How could I ever expect a successful career type like
Working Woman Barbie to lower her standards to the level of my current
life?" As he ran his hands despairingly through his hair, I was at least glad for
him that it was made of moulded painted plastic that could tolerate such
treatment without looking disreputably tousled. Otherwise, though ... not
much uptick in being Ken, standing stiff-armed and rigid behind the same
woman for so many years, only to wind up cast away in a shoebox at the
bottom of some dark closet like a worn-out pair of Hush Puppies.

"She ... she still might change her mind," I persisted, but without much
conviction. "It's a woman's prerogative, after all. Even a working woman, like
Barbie."

"Not a chance. Not at this stage. It's too late for her to settle down and
slip into the background and let me be the breadwinner."

I saw his point. Breadwinner Ken? In all his incarnations over the years,
what had he ever done, except to relax and smile, and lounge and smile, and
play and ... smile?

"Besides," he continued glumly, "if I know Mattel, they're already
coming up with new versions of Barbie for her twilight years that'll also
exclude me: Peri-menopausal Barbie, Elder Stateswoman Barbie, Raging
Granny Barbie ..."

What could I say to that? As I left him in the bar, droning on to whoever
would listen, I reflected more intensely than I ever had before on the world
of toys he came from—perhaps the only world in which dolls were so clearly
favoured over guys that a dumb blond chick like Barbie could wind up feted
on Wall Street while her discarded male companion bought rounds of drinks
he probably couldn't afford for every other second banana fallen to obscurity
from the top of the Toyland tree.

And yet, I further pondered all the long way home, why *should* poor Ken
be perceived as such a laughable loser, instead of as a progressive prototype of
self-assured New-Age masculinity? After all, the same egalitarian impulses

that had brought Alan Alda and others of his gentle ilk into prominence in the Seventies and Eighties had undoubtedly inspired Mattel to keep Ken smilingly self-effacing in the background, while Barbie increasingly expressed her independence as a woman of travel, of adventure, and, eventually, of business. At the same time as life-sized men were being encouraged to cook, to clean, to commiserate, and to cry, ten-inch-tall Ken was playing the part of a similarly supportive spouse in whatever new domestic drama starred Barbie, her retinue of female associates, and her apparently endless parade of work- or pleasure-related accoutrements, costumes, and cars.

By the time I was unlocking my front door, however, and preparing to head off to bed, I was beginning to look at the whole question of the benign Background Man in a slightly different light. Perhaps what had happened to Ken, on his miniature scale was no different than the gradual decline and fall of the sensitive New-Age human guy from a revolutionary male role model in the 1970s and 80s to a contemptible wimp by century's end.

It was, after all, 1999. Who any longer respected men who could cry? The grunting club-wielding hunter type seemed back in vogue—TV remote in one hand, can of brewski in the other, and an endless string of derisive cracks about his wife's shopaholic habits on his lips to be dispensed at intervals between burps and guffaws and swigs of beer. Small wonder Barbie's real-life counterparts—similarly evolved from Malibu beach-bunnies into independent women of substance—had chosen, just as Barbie had, to go it alone, leaving behind the soft-centred Kens of their acquaintance as they walked onto Wall Street to face the bulls and the bears—and the boors—by themselves.

I felt sorry for Ken, I have to say. In fact, I may even have shed a furtive tear or two of my own for that small, broken vinyl figure on a barstool I'd last seen drowning his he-man-sized sorrows with the other lost boy toys.

But as it turned out, I had kissed off Ken too quickly. For lo and behold, only a couple of years later, what did I discover in my email inbox but an invitation issued by Mattel to an event headlining him as the guest of honour? It was true. While the evening would also feature yet another unveiling of Barbie in yet another incarnation, this time she was slated to be a mere female sidekick to Ken—who was depicted on the invitation suavely decked out as Agent 007.

My God, I thought. Could it be that Ken, the perpetual second banana, has suddenly slipped one over on Emma Peel?

Yes, it apparently could. When I arrived at the event, there was Ken, holding court in satin lapels. It's no exaggeration to say he left the invited audience both shaken and stirred by the impression he made as the self-satisfied Bond. Barbie, meanwhile, deferentially held up the rear, while a garter held one of her inevitable cellphones, right next to her stockinged thigh.

So much for Ken's dire, slightly drunken predictions of a life of continued second-string schlepper status. So much for my own tacit concurrence with his pessimistic view of himself as a guy doomed in a world where dolls held sway. What on earth had moved Mattel to promote shrinking-violet Ken at brash Barbie's expense? And yet … surely toy companies do their research. For all I know, recent surveys of pre-selected preteen Barbie-doll fans have begun to show that little girls of the twenty-first century have grown sick of Barbie at centre stage, and long to see Ken in the starring role—preferably as an unreconstructed man's man, like James Bond.

I would certainly have taken these matters up with Ken, had he given me the chance. But so caught up was he in demonstrating the many ingenious features of his fleet of cars and cunning array of concealed weaponry that he didn't even seem to remember he and I had ever met, let alone recall my sympathetic concern for his situation.

Under the circumstances, I saw little point in asking him if he'd heard anything lately from Raggedy Andy, or whether his old friend G.I. Joe was finding himself similarly in hot demand again, in a Toyland seemingly so newly charged with testosterone. Instead, I merely excused myself from Ken and sidled over to the open bar to lay hands on a couple of Pink Ladies, just in case poor Barbie might be looking for a chance to bend a friendly female ear.

But before I got anywhere close to the bar I spotted Barbie, earnestly involved in conversation with her best friend Midge, who'd come to the event, I could only assume, as moral support. Well, good. If ever Barbie needed someone on her side, this was the night. Without giving much more thought to the matter than that, I betook myself home.

How much time elapsed before Ken—and by extension, Barbie—came back into my consciousness yet again? Six months, a year at most. It was a chilly winter morning—I do recall that—and I'd just settled down to breakfast with the paper, when a banner headline leaped out at me: "Barbie and Ken Call It Quits."

There was no mistaking the couple in the photo smiling fixedly for the camera though it was clear their hearts weren't in it.

"After forty-three years as the world's prettiest pair," ran the lead paragraph, "the perfect plastic couple is breaking up." Barbie and Ken, it seemed, had appointed a spokesman from Mattel to explain their situation to the world. It was the vice-president of marketing.

"Like other celebrity couples," he was quoted, "their Hollywood romance has come to an end. Though Barbie and Ken will remain friends."

For some reason, I was staggered by this news. Even more surprised than when I'd first encountered Ken, sloshed and sloppy in that neighbourhood bar, and certainly more startled than I'd been by his glitzy resurrection as 007.

Numbly, I continued to read what the vice-president had to say about the separation, including his sly suggestion that Barbie may have been pressing Ken too hard to take her to the altar in one of her many, many bridal ensembles.

Oh, Lord, I thought, I should never have left her without a word of comfort at that awful 007 do. I'll bet that might-as-well-be-married idea originated with Midge, desperate to see herself in the Maid of Honour outfit, as well as angry at Ken for letting Barbie get relegated to second banana without the cushion of matrimony to fall back on.

It was early in the day, far too early for a drink. Still, I needed something to steady my nerves. I thought of that hole-in-the-wall downtown where I'd first met Ken. It seemed like the right place to go. Nobody in my regular life—that is, nobody who came more than halfway up my calf—would be likely to offer anything but a chuckle, as they paged past the news about

Mattel's two biggest stars headed for Quitsville. Whereas down at the bar, I might find G.I. Joe or even a Cabbage Patch kid or two, in for an eye-opener and a commiserative chat about the Barbie–Ken debacle.

When I got there, the place looked empty, and even dingier than I remembered. But I tried the door, and was surprised that it opened. Inside, it seemed much the same, except for the absence of clientele. Nobody at the bar, nobody at all, except … Ken, nursing a Scotch.

"Ken!" I said. "What are you doing back here?"

He didn't even bother to turn around. "What does it look like I'm doing?"

"But why? The way the newspapers tell it—"

"—I'm the one who busted up with Barbie? I'm the one who backed away from permanent commitment, right?"

As my eyes adjusted to the low light, I began to see how dreadful he looked: pale under his plastic tan, his unblinking eyes bloodshot, his clothes stained and dishevelled.

"Ken, that bespoke James Bond outfit you had, your new career, Barbie as your smiling sidekick. What on earth has happened to all of it?"

"Oh, that!" Despite his perpetual smile, Ken managed a laugh entirely devoid of mirth. "I can't believe I didn't see it coming for miles. I mean, hey, it's Mattel, right? Since when is anything about me *actually* about me?"

"You mean that big promotional 007 event, with you in the spotlight, and Barbie bringing up the rear…?"

"Nothing but a way of getting Barbie's dander up so she'd dump me and they could stick me back in my shoebox, once and for all."

"I'm sorry, I'm afraid I don't get why Mattel would go to the trouble of bringing you out of obscurity, building that Bond campaign around you, simply to piss off Barbie."

"Because Barbie, for all her tough vinyl finish, is a softie at heart, that's why. And as conventional as they come. You think it was her own idea to freeze me out, back in '99 when that turning-forty marketing frenzy went on? Nah. Mattel talked her into it. But not for long. Eventually, Barbie started asking questions. "Where's Ken? How can I turn my back on a guy

I've been dating since 1961? Why do I have so many bridal outfits, when I'm too busy changing careers to ever settle down?"

"Ah," I said. "So that vice-president from Mattel was telling the truth: Barbie really does want to tie the knot."

"Of course she does." Ken was helping himself to Scotch right from the bottle now. "Conventional as they come, just like I said. Only Mattel … they've seen how this same-sex marriage thing is taking off. They see little girls being raised to believe in sisters like Rosie O'Donnell and Ellen DeGeneres doing it for themselves …"

"You mean … Mattel is trying to turn Barbie gay?"

"Figure it out. Who did she end up huddling with that night of the 007 launch?"

"Well, Midge. But since Midge is Barbie's very best friend, I …" The penny finally hit the floor. "Oh Ken, come on! You're not suggesting that—"

"Barbie and Midge? Why not? Look at it from the marketing point of view: Twice as many engagement diamonds, twice as many bridal gowns, twice as many going-away outfits, twice as many trousseaus and bridal bouquets—all sold separately."

It made a certain kind of ludicrous sense. Still, the way Ken was knocking back the booze, how could I be sure he really had—had ever had—any real idea of what he was talking about?

"Ken, you've got to lay off the Scotch."

"Why?" he snorted. "Because martinis are 007's drink?"

Suddenly, I felt tired. Not only bored with Ken and his drunken self-pity, but exhausted by the entire world from which he'd sprung, with its synthetic values, false smiles, and small-minded behaviour. Before I even realized I'd made up my mind to leave, I was halfway to the door.

"So long, Ken."

For the first time since I arrived, he turned from his drink to look directly at me. "Where are you going?"

"As far away as I need to get, to find something *real*. Someplace where people stand tall, are able to bend a little, and care about changing the world instead of their careers and their clothes every five minutes!"

It was a pretty speech, but I didn't stick around to wait for Ken to applaud. I headed off without a backward look, and as I hurried home I vowed never to find my way back to that dreary little dive again.

Yet, by the time I got home, I'd begun to feel, in spite of myself, sorry once more for that poor, polystyrene creature on his barstool—as well as for Barbie and even Midge. None of them, I believed, was to blame for their cynical exploitation by Mattel. In fact, the manufacturer deserved an angry email from me to that effect.

But when I logged on to the Barbie.com website, what did I discover? Barbie wasn't about to make same-sex history by wedding Midge after all. Instead, what Mattel now had in store for her was a brand new boyfriend named Blaine, chosen to replace Ken—so the site said—by more than two million fans worldwide! And what a replacement: Blaine was Australian, enjoyed muscle shirts, hanging ten on his surfboard, and scarfing chili dogs. Worst of all, he boasted sunstreaked, rooted Saran hair, unlike Ken's rigidly moulded mane.

Oh well, then. Mattel I might fight, but two million fans? I clicked off the Barbie.com website and resolved once and for all to get on with a larger life. As I'd told Ken, there had to be something bigger out there, for those of us flexible enough to get out of our own little box, and grasp opportunity with our two prehensile hands.

Robert W. Service

Scotland's loss, Canada's gain. In 1904, a bank teller and amateur "versifier" by the name of Robert Service was transferred to the Yukon region, first to a CIBC branch in Whitehorse and then to the one in Dawson City. It was at a time when the ghosts of the great Klondike Gold Rush were still very much in evidence, and in the Land of the Midnight Sun, Robert Service discovered a vein of pure poetic ore. Although he's best known for his ballads "The Cremation of Sam McGee" and "The Shooting of Dan McGrew," I've included one of his lesser-known but equally wonderful works, "The Ballad of Pious Pete."

FROM *Best Tales of the Yukon*

The Ballad of Pious Pete

"The North has got him"—Yukonism

I tried to refine that neighbour of mine,
    honest to God, I did.
  I grieved for his fate, and early and late
    I watched over him like a kid.
I gave him excuse, I bore his abuse
    in every way that I could.
  I swore to prevail; I camped on his trail;
    I plotted and planned for his good.
By day and by night I strove in men's sight
    to gather him into the fold,
  With precept and prayer, with hope and despair;
    in hunger and hardship and cold.
I followed him into Gehennas of sin,
    I sat where the sirens sit;
  In the shade of the Pole, for the sake of his soul,
    I strove with the powers of the Pit.
I shadowed him down to the scrofulous town;
    I dragged him from dissolute brawls;
  But I killed the galoot when he started to shoot
    electricity into my walls.

God knows what I did, that he'd seek to be rid
    of one who would save him from shame.
God knows what I bore that night when he swore
    and bade me make tracks from his claim.
I started to tell of the horrors of Hell,
    when sudden his eyes lit like coals;

And "Chuck it," says he, "don't persecute me
    with your cant and your saving of souls."
I'll swear I was mild as I'd be with a child,
    but he called me the son of a slut;
And, grabbing his gun with a leap and a run,
    he threatened my face with the butt.
So what could I do (I leave it to you)?
    With curses he harried me forth;
Then he was alone, and I was alone,
    and over us menaced the North.

Our cabins were near; I could see, I could hear;
    but between us there rippled the creek;
And all summer through, with a rancour that grew,
    he would pass me and never would speak.
Then a shuddery breath like the coming of Death
    crept down from the peaks far away.
The water was still; the twilight was chill;
    the sky was a tatter of grey.
Swift came the Big Cold, and opal and gold
    the lights of the witches arose;
The frost-tyrant clinched, and the valley was cinched
    by the stark and cadaverous snows.
The trees were like lace where the star-beams could chase,
    each leaf was a jewel agleam.
The soft white hush lapped the Northland and wrapped
    us round in a crystalline dream;
So still I could hear quite loud in my ear
    the swish of the pinions of time;
So bright I could see, as plain as could be,
    the wings of God's angels ashine.

As I read in the Book I would oftentimes look
      to that cabin just over the creek.
Ah me, it was sad and evil and bad,
      two neighbours who never would speak!
I knew that full well like a devil in Hell
      he was hatching out, early and late,
  A system to bear through the frost-spangled air
      the warm, crimson waves of his hate.
I only could peer and shudder and fear—
      'twas ever so ghastly and still;
  But I knew over there in his lonely despair
      he was plotting me terrible ill.
I knew that he nursed a malice accurst,
      like the blast of a winnowing flame;
  I pleaded aloud for a shield, for a shroud—
      Oh, God! then calamity came.

Mad? If I'm mad, then you too are mad;
      but it's all in the point of view.
  If you'd look at them things gallivantin' on wings,
      all purple and green and blue;
If you'd noticed them twist, as they mounted and hissed
      like scorpions dim in the dark;
  If you'd seen them rebound with a horrible sound,
      and spitefully spitting a spark;
If you'd watched *It* with dread, as it hissed by your bed,
      that thing with the feelers that crawls—
  You'd have settled the brute that attempted to shoot
      electricity into your walls.

Oh, some, they were blue, and they slithered right through;
    they were silent and squashy and round;
  And some, they were green; they were wriggly and lean;
    they writhed with so hateful a sound.
My blood seemed to freeze; I fell on my knees;
    my face was a white splash of dread.
  Oh, the Green and the Blue, they were gruesome to view;
    but the worst of them all were the Red.
They came through the door, they came through the floor,
    they came through the moss-creviced logs.
  They were savage and dire; they were whiskered with fire;
    they bickered like malamute dogs.
They ravined in rings like iniquitous things;
    they gulped down the Green and the Blue.
  I crinkled with fear whene'er they drew near,
    and nearer and nearer they drew.

And then came the crown of Horror's grim crown,
    the monster so loathsomely red.
  Each eye was a pin that shot out and in,
    as, squid-like, it oozed to my bed.
So softly it crept with feelers that swept
    and quivered like fine copper wire;
  Its belly was white with a sulphurous light,
    its jaws were a-drooling with fire.
It came and it came; I could breathe of its flame,
    but never a wink could I look.
  I thrust in its maw the Fount of the Law;
    I fended it off with the Book.
I was weak—oh, so weak—but I thrilled at its shriek,
    as wildly it fled in the night;
  And deathlike I lay till the dawn of the day.
    (Was ever so welcome the light?)

I loaded my gun at the rise of the sun;
      to his cabin so softly I slunk.
   My neighbour was there in the frost-freighted air,
      all wrapped in a robe in his bunk.
It muffled his moans; it outlined his bones,
      as feebly he twisted about;
   His gums were so black, and his lips seemed to crack,
      and his teeth all were loosening out.
'Twas a death's head that peered through the tangle of beard;
      'twas a face I will never forget;
   Sunk eyes full of woe, and they troubled me so
      with their pleadings and anguish; and yet
As I rested my gaze in a misty amaze
      on the scurvy-degenerate wreck,
   I thought of the Things with the dragon-fly wings,
      then laid I my gun on his neck.
He gave out a cry that was faint as a sigh,
      like a perishing malamute,
   And he says unto me, "I'm converted," says he;
      "for Christ's sake, Peter, don't shoot!"

They're taking me out with an escort about,
      and under a sergeant's care;
   I am humbled indeed, for I'm 'cuffed to a Swede
      who thinks he's a millionaire.
But it's all Gospel true what I'm telling to you—
      up there where the Shadow falls—
   That I settled Sam Noot when he started to shoot
      electricity into my walls.

Sandra Shamas

Sandra Shamas came roaring onto the Canadian stage with her
one-woman show *My Boyfriend's Back and There's Gonna Be
Laundry*. This turned into a very successful trilogy, ending with
Wedding Bell Hell. And then, one day, her world caved in. Shamas's
marriage collapsed, unexpectedly, and she fled the city to
a property she owned in the country. The following is from
the raw and funny memoir that followed, *Wit's End*. (Sherry,
who appears in this excerpt, is her neighbour.)

FROM *Wit's End*

I named the farm "Wit's End," because that's where I was. You know, I felt
like I was being banished from my whole life; anything that I had
worked for, put any kind of investment in, was absolutely gone from my
sight. My relationship was gone, my work was gone, and my city-world was
gone. I was the only thing left standing, and I could barely recognize myself.

I said to Sherry, "Sherry, women don't live alone on farms, Sherry, they
just don't!"

She said, "Well, you know what, honey, I don't think you have a choice."

I said, "But what if there's a medical emergency?"

She said, "Well, if it's any consolation, they can land a helicopter in your
front yard."

Now, the farm itself is a house, and a barn, and the house and the barn
sit on a piece of property that is one hundred and twenty-three acres. The
fifty that are around the house and barn are presently in hay, the middle fifty

are hardwood forest, mostly maple, and the bottom twenty-three acres hold a twelve-acre lake that's thirty-five feet deep. It's pretty where I live.

Somebody asked me, "Did you purchase a rural property because you were raised in a rural landscape?"

I said, "No, I was raised in a lunar landscape." Which is Sudbury, Ontario, 1960-anything. Inco, that fine corporate citizen, basically smelted anything green off the fuckin' face of that place.

When I was a kid I remember my dad telling a story once at supper, that if the paint on your vehicle was bubbling because of the shit that was falling out of the sky, then you could call Inco and they would take your vehicle and repaint it for you. There's that nasty pollution problem taken care of, there you go. And then they got so much pressure from the environmentalists, they built the Super Stack, and started painting cars in Parry Sound.

No, I wasn't raised in Nature. I hardly knew what my own nature was.

So I moved out to the farm. The very first thing I noticed is how quiet it is. It is skull-crushingly quiet. It is so quiet, all you can hear is the bullshit in your own head! And I had no shortage of it. It was like tuning a short-wave radio from hell.

Like, you're tuning, and you hit the who-do-you-think-you-are channel. Then you keep tuning, until you hit the what-the-hell-do-you-think-you're-doing channel, or my favourite, the no-one's-ever-going-to-love-you channel. Shut the fuck up!

The second thing I noticed, pretty much the same day, is how dark it gets at night. It is *so* dark. They are serious about black. It's like a black I've never even seen, it's like a puddingy, thicky, puddingy black; it's like so fuckin' black, okay, when it went black, it turned every window in the house into a mirror! Walking through the house that night, I suddenly saw someone following me. And I screamed! It was just my reflection, but that's no way to get to the kitchen, let me tell you.

And last, but not least—if you hear a sound, something *makes it*. So my ears were the size of an elephant's. I'm getting ready to go to bed, I'm on the second floor of my house, and if you look off into the distance, against the road, you can see the silhouette of the Group of Seven trees. Group of Seven trees look like this: all their limbs are on one side. Hydro makes them. Yeah. It's a perfectly good tree and then Hydro comes along, lops off all the limbs on one side, making them Group of Seven trees.

I'm getting ready to go to bed, so I get into bed, and I start tucking my ears in with me, and I'm propped up, 'cause there's no fuckin' way I'm lying down! And as I'm lying there, and it's so black, I think of that expression,

"It was so dark you couldn't see your hand in front of your face," and I'm experimenting with it, and I boink myself in the eye.

Ow!

Now I have one eye closed—like it matters.

So as I'm lying there, or propped up there, more or less, I hear a terrible screeching, choking sound.

I bring up the big Rolodex of sounds:

Choo choo?

No.

Piano?

No.

Sound of something losing its life?

Yeah.

I make the choice at that moment not to run out and save it. Because while something is dying, something else is *dining*.

This is the sound of Nature shopping, apparently.

And it takes forever for something to die. It was going on and on and on. Finally, and I never thought I'd hear *me* say, "Fuckin' die, already!"

So I'm lying there in the black, and it's the perfect moment to start The Movie of My Life!

So there it goes, every memory, every nine years' worth of memories, every look, every glance, every word, every touch, every la la la, la la la la, and I would watch, I would cry, and then I'd fall asleep.

And then, I'd wake up like I'd been touched by electricity.

Jolt awake! Stare into black.

Feverish, "Where am I?"

Revelation. "I'm on the farm," and cry 'til I fall asleep.

Jolt awake, "Where am I?"

"Oh, I'm on the farm."

That went on for months.

I was looking good!

I had no idea how bad it was until I got my driver's licence photograph.
When I looked at the photo, I was shocked.

I said, "This woman has been set on fire and put out with an axe!" Man.
I still have it as a happy memento of those times.

• • •

Now, I had never made my own home. I'd never made a home for myself. I
had taken all of my talent and my enthusiasm and my ability and put it into
the "We," for "Us, Our," and when it came time for "Me" making my own
home, I found myself strangely still, like inert, almost, and I realized that I
will work harder and longer and more cheerfully on the behalf of others than
I will work on my own, that I will happily do for others the very things that
I need to do for myself.

And when I understood this, I was saddened by it. I thought, this is
pathetic. I mean, I am not even on my own side.

And I thought, "Sandra, if you are not on your own side, who is? And,
who wants to be on the side of somebody who isn't on their own side?"

Having never made my own home, I simply let the environment dictate
to me. I would wake up when it got light, I would make coffee, I would sit
at the kitchen table, and I would look at the fields. When it got dark, I'd go
to bed. I would wake up when it got light, I would make coffee, and I would
sit … and if it got cold, I'd go over to the heat register and turn it up. When
I got tired of standing near the heat register, I'd sit down, eat two Fig
Newtons. When it got dark, I'd go to bed.

The farm is on a piece of land called the Escarpment, and the
Escarpment used to be an ancient sea, and I found little fossils in the garden,
sea shells embedded in sandstone, and I put them on the windowsill in front
of me. And I remember one day looking out, and looking at the fields, and
looking at these sea shells, and how extraordinary the thought was that this

was all once under water, and how long ago that was, and I thought, geez, that's amazing, and as I looked up, I felt as if the land was looking back and laughing at me. Laughing at me, going:

"Hey! Hey you, human in the window! Yeah, you! Are you sad? Awwwwww … Hey, you see that little sea shell in front of you? It was sad, too. Then it died!"

In that moment I understood that the land is infinite, it is eternal, and I am a snap of the fingers to the land. In the timescape of the land, I am maybe half a snap; we are all a snap of the fingers to the land. I thought, "Oh, my God, I'm finite! I had no idea." I thought, you know, "If I've got a limited amount of time, I'd better get my shit together."

So I called the septic man. You want to know about shit, go to the top.

I'm on a septic system, and I didn't know where it was. I mean, I was just flushing with the hope that it was going away from the house. And it's under ground, of course, so it all looks the same, the lawn, it all looks the same, grass looks like bug looks like twig, I don't know. So I invited him to come on the land and he came, and we were walking around the house and talking and walking, and suddenly he stops and goes:

"Whoa whoa whoa whoa … there she is, right there." And he digs into the dirt with the toe of his boot.

That's how men point in the country, by the way.

I said, "That's who right where?"

He said, "That's where the opening for your septic system is, right there!"

I said, "How do you know that?"

He said, "Cleaned 'er out myself, three year ago."

"You are a god to me," I said. "Listen, is it going to be enough for me?"

He said, "You could put a family of five on that one."

I said, "You know, that's good news, 'cause I'm doing a fig thing right now."

So I found out where my septic bed was. I didn't plant a Buick there or anything. I ordered a wood stove, and I had it installed in the kitchen. From the name "wood" stove, I got some wood delivered, and they delivered the wood in the yard next to the stump. Now, it was just a stump before, but suddenly with the wood next to it, I realized, "Oho ho ho! This is where they split the wood." Hello. I thought, you know, I can split wood. I'm kind of a Dr. Quinn, medicine woman, I can split wood. So I went out and I bought a splitting axe, which is basically a sharpened anvil on a stick.

Okay, I realized now I should've got the instructional video. Wood comes in tubes called "logs." If you want to split a log, you take a log and then you put it on the stump on its end, and let it go. It should stay. If it doesn't, just shimmy it around until it does, then let it go. It should stay. This could take hours. If it got dark, I'd go in. Start fresh in the morning. Finally I got one to stand on its own.

Okay, now, I have seen men split wood, only on TV. They swagger as they walk towards the log, then there's the full-arm extension, lifting the axe over the head, and then the hands come together as the axe actually hits the wood, and then splits it.

There's no fucking way I could do that. The first time I lifted the axe over my head, it continued until it rested on the ground behind me, pinning me in a back bend. So, I decided I'd just choke up on it, and planted the axe in the log, and then I couldn't get it out. That was the day I decided to burn them whole! You put in enough paper, shit burns. Who's going to come by? The Wood Police? I don't think so.

Now, to get to my house, you have to go up a very big hill. I call it "The Widowmaker." It's like a two-tiered event, this thing, and well, that fall was very, very cold, and it rained, and froze quickly and I only had the half-ton with two-wheel drive. I backed down that hill so many times, thinking, "Oh, we're not even into winter yet. How am I going to get up to the house?"

And so I went down the road and talked to Sherry's husband, Bill.

I said, "Bill, what am I going to do? Should I just go out and buy something four-wheel drive? 'Cause I can."

He says, "No, no." He kicks the tire. "That's a good truck! You just need some weight in the back. Get yourself some cement block."

I said, "Ah, phew! Thanks, Bill. Of course. Cement block. Let's go get some cement block."

Where do you get cement block? Oh, I know? I'll surf the web. Ce-men-t Bl-ock. No website. Under construction. So I got it into my head it had to be square, and heavy. So I was at Home Hardware, and I noticed they have bags of sand, and they were square, and heavy. So I bought ten sixty-six-pound bags of sand.

I know now it is too much. I didn't know. I was going with the half-ton truck, so that's how much you have to put in the back.

Anyway, I buy all this sand and then they give me the receipt, and they said at the cash, "Okay, drive around into the yard at the back and pick up the sand."

So I drive around the back, and in the yard is this really little guy. He's like, a young guy, his coat's wide open, it's freezing outside, and he's not old enough to wear gloves, apparently, so he shoves his fists up into his sleeves. He's got no scarf. His neck's all red. He's freezing out there.

So I go over and I say, "Hi. Listen, here's my receipt, I bought some sand." He says, "Yeah, it's right there," gesturing with one of his handless arms. Uh-huh.

I look at the sand, I look at the truck. I look at the sand. I look at the truck. I look at the sand and I realize there's no way I can lift six-hundred-and-sixty pounds of sand. I decide to use my feminine wiles, and I say, in my best girly voice:

"Um, excuse me, could you help me? Could you put them in there, 'cause I'm not very strong."

Suddenly, he's a man of action. He went, "Sure."

Okay, in my life, I have never done the jiggly thing to get a guy to do something for me. I always thought it was too manipulative to do that. I'm here to tell you, it works like a fuckin' charm. Apparently, all you have to do is pretend you're mostly cartilage. Yeah. I think it's the bones men fear. Course, I could have popped a wheelie now with the truck, I had so much fuckin' sand in the back. We are not going to even discuss the fine gas mileage I got that year.

• • •

I knew it was time for me to be with my own kind, so I took Ladies' Adult
Skate. I can skate! I just can't stop. So every Sunday I would show up at the
Memorial Arena at one o'clock for Ladies' Adult Skate. I was the oldest
woman there at thirty-eight, and the only one in the arena who had never
had a child. That included the gay men, do you understand? They were all
crowded around me going:

"So you, you, so you never had a child?"

"Not to my knowledge. I think I'd remember something like that."

And I had to ask myself why I never had children, really. And the truth
is, whatever prompts a woman to want children never happened to me. I
never got the call.

Maybe I got the call, and I was out.

I took a pottery course. I made two bowls: $127.50. The cats eat out of
them. Oh, nothing's too good for my cats! Oh, and I was invited to join a
garden club. I'm a gardener; I gardened in Toronto. One of the reasons to buy
the farm was so I could blow my brains out gardening. But, man, you have
no idea how big an acre is until you see the size of your spade. I gardened in
downtown Toronto, when I lived there, and gardening in Toronto is not like
gardening anywhere on the planet, certainly not the kind of gardening you're
ever going to see on *Martha Stewart:*

"When I'm picking used condoms out of *my* front yard, I like to use a
long barbecue tong. It's a good thing. Let's re-use those syringes, and make
a festive wreath for the door."

So I was privileged to be asked to join this garden club, and I got to meet
some women in my neighbourhood, and I was invited into their homes,
these beautiful homes, to see what they've done with their country homes.
Their gardens were magnificent. I mean, these women have forgotten more
about gardening than I will ever know, and they're also the baking-est gals
you'll ever meet. Oh, man, they bake your head right off. "Bring me your
head, I'll bake it off." And it was at garden club I was introduced to bars, or
squares—you know, sweet squares, with names. The first ones I encountered
were "Hello Dollies." Do you know? I did not know. I don't know, it's a
square, and it's square, and I'm at the garden club, at the buffet, with the

coffee and the three-tiered plate thing. Yeah, you know it, right, with the different offerings on every tier?

So, I'm standing there, and the hostess says, "Sandra, have you tried the Hello Dollies?"

And she gestures to the plate, and I take one, and eat it. "Okay ... *Hello Dolly!* Shit. These are good."

I spread my arms out on either side, keeping the other women away, and proceeded to eat the rest of them.

The other one is "Sex-in-a-Pan." Yeah? For those of you who do not know: pan, shortbread bottom, and then layers of sweet thing, sweet thing, sweet thing, sweet thing, sweet thing, and then white sweet thing on top. "Sex-in-a-Pan."

She came into garden club, looking like a librarian, a little dress with a little scarf tied to the side of her neck, her hair in a bun, holding the pan, and she said, "Sandra, have you tried the Sex-in-a-Pan?"

"Well, I shouldn't." I almost climbed into her lap.

I was told later by an Anglican minister's wife that you can make it with or without nuts.

It was at garden club that I had the good luck of meeting a woman in my neighbourhood named Audrey. Audrey is in her middle eighties, and is a force of nature. She is an astonishment. And as a way of greeting me to the community, she invited me to her home. I was so honoured, really, and so I went there for tea and scones. It was so great.

We sat down, and she says, "Now, Sandra, how do you like living in the country? So quiet. So private."

I nod.

She said, "Oh, but you know, dear, I'm worried for you, I'm worried that you'll be lonesome. So, my recommendation is to accept *all* invitations. Oh, because you never know, dear. They may not come around again."

You got that right.

So whatever came my way, I was there!

"Highland Fling in Fergus?! What time's the caber toss?"

"Monster-Mudder Truck Rally?! Pick me up at five!"

That February I was invited to the Millcroft Inn, for the "How to Attract Butterflies to Your Garden" seminar. When I got there, I met all the other fabulous women in my neighbourhood, and once we figured out how to attract butterflies to our gardens, we figured out how to attract alcohol to our table!

So now I was starting to know folk, and I'd see them on the road, and I'd wave.

• • •

That spring I got a phone call from my neighbour, Natalie. She's eight years old. Natalie called, and she said, "Would you please be the Assistant Coach for our girls' soccer team?"

I said, "Put your mother on."

I said, "What's the story?"

She said, "Well, they need an Assistant Coach."

I said, "You know, I've never played soccer. I've never played a team sport, honestly. I'm not a team player. Hello."

She said, "Sandra, it's just Assistant Coach. All you have to know is how to cut an orange."

Accept all invitations!

"Put me down! I'll buy oranges, I'll practise at home!"

Within three days of that call I got a phone call from the league. Due to the magic of attrition, I have become a Coach.

"No no no no, no no no no no ... 'cause the Coach *knows* something! I know *nothing*!"

She says, "Oh, for heaven's sakes, they're girls under eight, just have fun!" Click!

So, I meet my team. They're eight years old, and astonishing. They're all sucking on their hair, or trying to, and I meet them, and I say, "Guys, c'mere, okay, listen, honest and for true, I do not know how to play soccer. I have never played soccer, and the only reason I'm a coach is I'm taller, and I drive. Does anybody here know how to play soccer?"

Sadie puts up her hand.

I go, "Yeah, Sadie."

She goes, "Like, 'cause we're only eight, there's just half a field, and there's three forwards, and three defence, and there's a goalie."

"Okay. How are we with that? Good, then let's have lunch."

So that summer I coached girls-under-eight soccer on a platform of Poise and Congeniality.

Standing on the sidelines, cigarette in a holder, with a slight British accent, yelling, "Run, babies, run! Danielle! Fab earrings! Play forward for a while, darling."

At the end of the summer, we weren't at the top, but we were not at the bottom. They were an excellent little team. The guy who coached the top team, he was a mess! He would yell at his team the whole time.

And all the tendons in his neck were sticking out; he looked like he was going to stroke out at any second. He scared me.

"Babies, come to me quickly. We're playing that maniac again. I say we forfeit and go to Dairy Queen."

It was one of the best summers of my life.

Antanas Sileika

The immigrant experience figures prominently in the story of
Canada, and nowhere quite as exquisitely as in *Buying on Time,*
Antanas Sileika's collection of linked stories about a family of
Displaced Persons (DPs, as they are known) who have settled,
somewhat incongruously, in the suburbs of Toronto in the
1950s. Sileika's world of Lithuanian immigrants in Weston,
Ontario, has been compared favourably to Mordecai Richler's
St. Urbain Street, and justly so. Both authors cut to the core of
family, community, and the collision of cultures.

FROM *Buying on Time*

Going Native

S tan was a DP like my father, like the rest of us, but the outhouse in
our back yard had made even him laugh. Not the outhouse itself,
although it was the only one in the subdivision growing up in the old
orchards, but the neat squares of newspaper my father had us stack beside
the seat.

"You such fucking DP," Stan said to my father, and he held his sides as
he laughed like a character out of a cartoon. Stan only swore when he spoke
English, a language that didn't really count.

My father went out and bought two rolls of toilet paper, but for half a
year we used them only as decoration, like twin flower vases. Stan's advice on
toilet paper and anything else in this foreign land was reliable. As for what
the locals advised, one could never be sure.

"A fool is always dangerous," my father told me, "but a foreign fool is worse. You can't tell if he's an idiot or simply a foreigner."

Mr Taylor was the only real Canadian we knew in the dawn of our subdivision, and we watched him as if we were anthropologists trying to fathom the local customs.

Mr Taylor was a special kind of Canadian, an "English." They were the only kind who really counted, and observation of them could pay a dividend. Mr Taylor was our English, the one who lived across the street and whose habits could be observed at will. We were astonished that he stayed in his dress shirt and tie as he read the evening paper in a lawn chair in his back yard. The lawn chair was just as astonishing. Who else but an English would spend good money on a chair that could only be used outside?

My father spat on the ground at this foolishness, but my mother sighed.

"These English are just like Germans," she said. She meant not like us, not DP. We belonged on the evolutionary tree with the Italians, Poles, and Ukrainians. Our knuckles still scraped the earth.

"He's a banker," my mother told us, and the word was heavy with meaning. It explained how he lived in a house that not only had proper brick walls and a roof, but a lawn as well.

Our street had half a dozen other houses on it, but none of the rest were finished. People dug the foundations and laid the basement blocks. Then they waited and saved. When a little money came in, they bought beams and joists and studs. Then they waited some more. The Taylors stood out because a contractor had built their house from start to finish. We stood out too. We moved in before the above-ground walls went up.

"You want us to live underground?" my mother had asked. "Like moles? Like worms?"

"No," my father said, "like foxes."

One day we had even woken to the smell of tar, and gone out to see that Mr Taylor was having his driveway paved.

My father snorted at this. It was 1953. Our street was still covered with gravel, and if a man had money, he laid crushed stones on his driveway. Everybody else had twin ruts in their yards. Asphalt was as unlikely as a skyscraper in the new suburb-to-be, where the apple trees from the old farm orchards still stood in rows all around us, their sad fruit unpicked. But Gerry and I were filled with envy. A paved driveway was a sign of sophistication— something so fine we never knew it was possible until we saw it.

"What a game of hockey you could play on this," Gerry said to me one Thursday evening when we knew the banker and his wife were out shopping, and we knelt on the pavement to feel the smoothness with the palms of our hands. "You could shoot a ball from one end of the driveway to the other, and it would almost score by itself. A ball on pavement moves faster than a puck on ice. My science teacher told me that." I listened and I palmed the smooth pavement and the vision in Gerry's mind was seeded in mine.

When I wasn't hating him, I admired my older brother Gerry. He sensed the openings in this country faster than the rest of us, and he slipped through them. If we were quick enough, we could slip in behind him. Even on the ice, he could out-skate the other fast ones, and leave only the half-heard whisper of "asshole" in their ears. The goalies feared him most, because the *Life* magazines stuffed in their socks did nothing to save their shins from the sting of his flying puck.

But to Mr Taylor, he was only a boy, and a suspect boy at that. The kind of boy who was sure to have matches in his pocket, if not a stolen cigarette as well.

When Mr Taylor crossed the street to speak to my father, we felt naked. We'd watched him carefully, but never guessed he might notice us.

"Your cat," said Mr Taylor to my father, "has been running across my lawn."

My father glanced down at Gerry and me to see if he had understood the English correctly. Gerry shrugged.

My father pondered the words. The relationship between our cat and Mr Taylor's lawn was impossibly remote to him. What could the one have to do with the other? My father sucked on his empty pipe, and the sickening sputter of nicotine resin in the stem was the only sound. Clearly there was a problem, or this English would not be there, standing in his shirt and tie in the ruts by our subterranean home. My father strained to imagine the problem.

"It shits on lawn?"

Gerry and I were mortified. The colour rose in Mr Taylor's face as well, for in 1953, a man did not speak that way, not out in front of his house. Gerry and I knew it, but my father did not.

"No, no," Mr Taylor said. "That is not what I meant."

"It pisses on flowers?"

"It merely walks. I do not want your cat to walk on my lawn."

It was all that Mr Taylor could admit to without uttering the same sort of vulgarities as his neighbour. My father would never understand terms such as *defecate* or *urinate*. Mr Taylor's linguistic squeamishness had backed him into a corner.

My father sucked on his pipe and thought some more. He had negotiated with Red Army commissars and saved his sister-in-law from a Nazi labour battalion, but he had never heard an accusation such as this. This had to be an eccentricity. Banker or not, Mr Taylor was an idiot.

"I fix," my father said.

Mr Taylor would have been happy to leave it at that, to take his victory against the foreigner and return to his evening paper, but my father gestured for him to stay where he was, and then went down the steps to our underground house.

He came out with the cat in his hand. He did not cradle the cat, for my father had come from a farm, and cradling was only for women or citified men. He carried the cat by a handful of skin behind its head, and he held it out to Mr Taylor.

"I told cat not walk on lawn, but it doesn't listen. Bad cat. You tell it."

The cat hung in the air, its legs splayed and tense, but its face calm and inscrutable.

Mr Taylor's lips pursed.

"Really. If cat walks on lawn again, you can kill it."

Mr Taylor stepped out of our ruts and onto the gravel street, and he strode back to his own home.

"I can kill it for you if you want. Tell me and I will do it!" He shouted at Mr Taylor's back, but Mr Taylor's back continued to recede.

That had been in the summer, but the memory of it must have stuck in Mr Taylor's mind throughout the months as it became clear that our pit in the earth was not going to have a proper house on top of it before the winter snows fell. The memory of it must have galled him as it became clear that the outhouse was not going to come down either, and his revulsion must have grown when my mother brought home the baby in November.

One February morning we heard the muffled thump of a foot against the snow on the cellar door. This was a real distinction. We were the only family in Weston that had a door you knocked on with your feet.

I looked up at the building inspector from the bottom of the staircase, a dark figure against a blue so brilliant that it hurt my eyes. Gerry and I stood beside our father in case we had to translate for him. Only my mother hung back by the woodstove because Tom was on her breast and the cold was always slipping down the stairway like an eager cat.

It was the woodstove that gave us away in the first place. That and the outhouse. He never would have found us after a new snow if it weren't for the smoking pipe above us. After every snowfall, my father dug out the stove-pipe so the smoke could pass freely, and from a distance you could always see the plume rising out of the ground at the top of the hill like a vent out of hell.

We had no doubt that the man at the top of the stairwell, the town building inspector, had been called by Mr Taylor.

"Come in!" my father shouted heartily. "It is cold. My wife will make tea."

My father was desperate to get the man to sit at a table. There would be no trouble then, not if he could see the inside was clean and we had a baby as well. A cup of tea at best, or a couple of drinks and ten dollars at worst, would get rid of the problem. But the inspector would not come down the steps.

"The law says you can't live like this," the building inspector called down the stairwell as if he were looking down into the hold of a slave ship. "The roof doesn't have any pitch, and the snow could crush every one of you! Besides, it's not decent."

"Wait. My English bad."

This was another tactic in my father's strategy for life in a foreign land. He could deny he had understood anything, and an order not understood never existed in the first place.

"It's for your own good." We could not make out his face. He was like an angel at the top of the staircase, surrounded by painful blue light.

"We have baby," my father said expansively, as if showing off a new heifer. He motioned to my mother and she stepped closer into the cold air that came down the steps.

"The baby'd be the first to go when the roof collapses."

"Danger?"

"For the baby. Yes. You must move out for the sake of the baby."

"Then you take baby." My father took Tom from my mother's arms, and she did not complain, did not hesitate.

"You take baby and bring him back in April when snow gone. If you want, bring him back in September, after we have walls and roof."

A crunch of snow as the inspector left, and then a quick return.

"Are you Catholic?"

"What?"

"Your religion."

"Church of England."

The inspector slammed the door down on us.

• • •

How could my father have known there was a Catholic Children's Aid? An admission of religion would have brought them down on us. He was in seas only partially charted and, where he was ignorant of how to act, he navigated by dead reckoning.

Dead reckoning could be a problem. Sometimes it was dead wrong, and this time my mother was not sure my father had his bearings right.

"You were ready to give him the baby."

"So why did you hand him to me?"

"I thought you knew what you were doing."

"I do. He won't be back."

"But what if he does come back? What if they make us leave? We have no place to go."

"I know what I'm doing."

"Just like you said we'd have the roof on by the end of September."

"We ran out of money."

She knew that. She had calculated how many nails he would need, so there would be none left over—no extra money spent for nails that would lie uselessly in a box for years. She knew the butcher gave a free piece of liver if she bought a pound of bacon—double the savings because she could use the bacon drippings on our sandwiches instead of butter. She knew the matters of money very well—the cost of condensed milk for the baby and counting the tins of it on the shelf each day because Gerry might snatch one and suck it dry.

And this problem of money was not a new one for her, because even in the house where she had lived before the war, the men who came to cut the hay were paid in eggs or meat or beer and as little money as possible. She knew the value of money even from up in the tower of the white frame house that was gently sinking into the mud below. A shallow pit had to be dug so the front door could swing open. The problem of money had always been there. She was the one who had brought home fifteen cents' worth of lamp oil each day, so her father could read to them from Shakespeare for an hour.

They were sent to bed when there was still a little oil left in the lamp, and her father stayed up alone to read Voltaire in translation. He put the book behind others when the priest came to visit. Voltaire was their secret—they knew not to talk of the book—it was their father's weakness, like a need for liquor or pornography. He was enlightened enough to read Voltaire, but his Catholic heart demanded penance. Not to be paid to the priest, that fool. He paid for his vice by teaching Shakespeare to his daughters. They already learned German in school, so he was edifying them, arming them with another language. It never occurred to him that any other book was necessary for their English. If he could only afford to own one book, then he wanted it to be the best.

She memorized and repeated Hamlet's speech. The sisters spoke to one another in Shakespeare's English at the dinner table where their mother silently watched the servant girl dish out the mashed potatoes and listened to the foreign sounds, no more perturbed than a cat on a windowsill. Even their father had been self-taught. Father and daughters spoke to one another, innocent of the rules of English pronunciation.

And so years later, she became the English teacher in the DP camp in Hamburg, in the British zone, and when the English colonel came on an inspection visit, she was the one who had trained the children and had them repeat in a chorus:

> Now is the Winter of our discontent
> Made glorious summer by this son of York;
> And all the clouds that lower'd upon our house
> In the deep bosom of the ocean buried

But the English colonel heard the rhythmic beat of foreign vowels and consonants of what he guessed was some folk poem. It was only months and years later that my mother and her now dispersed English students were bewildered in front of immigration officers on the piers of Halifax and New York and Sydney as their words made no impression on officialdom, which scowled or smiled on them depending on their luck but which clearly understood nothing of the winter of their discontent.

Now my mother was marooned with her children in the underground dwelling, a victim of my father's dead reckoning. Yet he assured her that the way ahead of us was clear. We could go on confidently until spring, when there would be enough money for the walls and a roof. If only the inspector did not return, that emissary of the English Mr Taylor, that scuttler of our dreams. For the bank was only a hundred yards down the road from the town hall. To us, Mr Taylor and the inspector were practically the same man, and to make an ally of one would make an ally of the second.

"I'll bake them a Napoleon cake," my mother said, and my father approved the expenditure on two pounds of butter, two dozen eggs, flour, sugar, and vanilla.

"It would be cheaper to kill the cat. Then he'd be happy for sure."

Gerry and I looked at one another, panic stricken, but my mother just shook her head swiftly at us. It meant either that my father was joking or she wouldn't let him do it.

She chopped the butter into the flour with a knife.

"Don't let the butter get too warm, or it doesn't form into grains. There's another way of doing this whole thing, a method of folding over the pastry to make puffs. That's the way the French do it. After all, this is a French cake. But we have our own special way. We chop the butter into the flour until the pieces are the size of small peas."

"If we burned his house down, we'd be rid of him sooner."

Gerry was walking around the room, rocking Tom in his arms as my mother made the cake. He looked funny to me, his face all fierce and twisted and the baby in his arms. I laughed.

"Don't think I wouldn't do it."

"It's a brick house. How are you going to make it catch fire?"

"Toss a bottle of gasoline through the window."

"You'd be in jail in a minute."

"They'd never catch me. I'd go north into the woods."

"Stop that talk," my mother said. "You're beginning to sound like your father."

That shut us up.

"Roll out each leaf right on a round metal pan. Don't try to lift the rolled leaf from the counter onto the pan. It has to be thinner than a pie crust, and it'll break as you move it."

Our basement room was sweltering with the heat from the woodstove. Gerry and I were in our T-shirts.

"You have to be just as careful when you take the leaf out of the oven. It's supposed to be very thin. You need at least twelve of these leaves. If one does break, crumble it up and use it as a garnish on the very top layer."

"What are you telling us this for?" Gerry asked. "We're never going to bake cakes."

"I don't have any daughters."

"Well, I'm not going to be one for you."

"You look like one already with that baby in your arms," I said.

"You take him. Catch!"

"Toss that child and you will not be able to sit down for a week, I promise you."

Gerry scowled.

"Make a custard with sugar and a dozen egg yolks and a little milk," my mother said. "Make sure you let the custard cool. If you add butter to hot custard, it melts and separates. Beat the butter into the custard, and spread a little between each of the leaves."

"I said I'm never going to bake one of these."

"This is a Napoleon cake. Do you know who Napoleon was?"

"Yeah," Gerry answered, but he did not sound sure of himself.

"He was a French general who became the most warlike man France has ever known. He knew how to use artillery—big guns, and he marched across most of Europe. This cake is named for him."

"But I bet he didn't bake it himself."

"Don't be so sure. Napoleon was a man who knew all weapons."

After Gerry suggested we put a dead mouse in the middle of the cake, my mother selected me to take the gift across to the banker and his wife.

The beaten snow path to the road was slippery, and half an inch of water lay on the icy road. We were in the middle of a warm spell, and icicles hung off the eaves and the sound of running water came from under the snow. The cake was heavy, placed on a board covered with wax paper, and I had to hold it out in front of me with two hands.

Mrs Taylor answered the door.

My mother had made me rehearse the whole speech twice, about neighbours and friendliness and helping out, but I froze when I saw her in her perfection. Short hair, red lipstick (lipstick at home!), and a dress with short sleeves and cuffs and a blue-checked apron. She looked like she had stepped out of an ad in the household section of the Eaton's catalogue.

"You're beautiful!" I said, and then regretted it, and felt ashamed of the grey wool mittens that she could see holding up the cake. They were scratchy, like everything else I had to wear in the wintertime, but worse, they were wet and had a patch where I'd poked my finger through once and my mother had repaired it with pink thread. Pink thread and grey mittens came from across the road, in the basement where we lived, and I hoped then that we *would* be forced to move, because I couldn't bear the shame of being across the road from her.

Mrs Taylor laughed, and asked me what I had in my hands.

"A cake. We baked it for you."

Mr Taylor was behind her in a moment.

"We can't take that."

"Oh, Harvey, they're just trying to be nice."

"It might not be sanitary."

"Hush. Thank you, dear, and say thanks to your mother. Wait a minute." And she disappeared back into the house.

Mr Taylor stood there glowering at me. I looked down and away from him, and studied the lower walls of his house, where the concrete blocks came out from the ground to meet the bricks. I saw a step-shaped crack there, and I stared at it until Mrs Taylor came back.

"There's a piece of fudge for you and one for your brother. Now remember to thank your mother." I took the two pieces, each wrapped in a square of wax paper, and stuffed them into my pocket and went back home.

"Thank God for women," said my mother as she nursed Tom in the armchair.

"You say they had a crack in the basement wall?" my brother asked.

"Yeah."

"We could pour acid through there and it'd turn into gas. We could poison them."

"A boy exactly like his father."

The uncharacteristic February thaw kept up with much dripping of icicles and gurgling in ditches still covered with snow. Three days later, the temperature dropped to zero and the neighbourhood became a treacherously shiny surface. Gerry and I skated over the crust of ice that had formed on the snow in the abandoned fields beyond our subdivision. We skated down the long aisles between the drooping trees, kicking frozen apples with the toes of our skates. Gerry could always last longer than me, and he came in one night after dark, when the rest of us were already finishing our supper at the kitchen table. He was carrying a strange bundle of newspapers that he pulled apart before anyone could say a word. The Napoleon cake fell from the newspaper wrapping and clanged onto the floor like a piece of iron.

It was frozen from sitting outside. No piece had ever been cut from the cake.

"Where did you get that?" my father asked.

"It was wrapped up in newspapers in their garbage can. I thought you wouldn't believe me if I told you about it, so I dug it out and brought it home."

"Did they see you?" my father asked.

"They're out shopping."

"What do you think people will say about us if they find out you've been lifting the lids off garbage cans?" my mother began, but my father cut her off.

"He did the right thing. Now at least we know where we stand."

"I've got a plan, Dad," said Gerry, and my father turned to him to listen. Gerry had just earned the right to speak.

"There's a crack in their basement wall. Dave saw it. We get some kind of acid, you know, something poisonous, and we pour it through the crack, and then at night the fumes rise up through the house and kill them both."

My father sucked on his unlit pipe, and the nicotine in the stem made the sickening slurping sound.

"What crack?"

"The crack in their basement wall."

"Did you see it too?"

"Yeah, I checked. We could get this little pipe or something and do it at night. We'd just have to cover our tracks in the snow and nobody'd be the wiser."

"You say they are out shopping?"

"They go every Thursday."

"And you could show me this crack?"

Gerry couldn't believe my father was taking him seriously. He was getting more and more excited, stepping from side to side in the puddles from the melted snow on the concrete floor.

"Why are you letting him go on like that?" my mother asked. "He's morbid enough as it is."

"I want to see this hole," my father said, and he rose deliberately from his chair and carefully stuffed his pipe before going to put on his coat and hat.

Gerry looked back triumphantly at my mother and me before the two of them took the steps up and out of the cellar.

"Are they going to kill them?" I asked her.

"Nothing would surprise me from your father. Nothing at all."

"You mean he'd do it?"

"What?"

"Kill them."

"He can't even bear to prune a tree. He's all talk, talk, talk, and it all winds up being no more significant than farting in the bathtub."

I didn't like it when she spoke like that. She had told me again and again about the house with a tower, and her childhood there with a view over the fields and woods. A woman from a white house should not talk about farts.

That night, Gerry whispered to me in the bed.

"We're on," he said.

"You mean you're going to kill them?"

"Father smiled like a Cheshire Cat when I showed him the crack."

"What's a Cheshire?"

"It's a cat, stupid."

"So what's the difference between a cat and a Cheshire?"

"Clean out your ears during science class and you might learn something, like how to make poison."

I had visions of Mrs Taylor in her apron, falling to her knees in the kitchen as the poisonous fumes rose up. She'd be at the stove, frying fish sticks, and when she fell unconscious, the grease would catch fire, spread to the curtains, and soon she'd be surrounded by flames. Mr Taylor's cigarette would fall from his mouth as he was reading the newspaper. If I watched the house carefully, I could break through the door just at that moment and carry her out to the back yard. I thought about her size for a moment, and then decided I could drag her if I had to. By then it would be too late to save Mr Taylor, and when she woke from unconsciousness, she would wrap her arms around my shoulders and cry.

The imminent destruction of Mr Taylor was beginning to seem less appalling.

• • •

"I have to take Tom to the doctor for his shot," my mother said when Gerry and I came back from school. "Gerry, you come along too. I need to buy some things and you can carry them for me."

"Why can't Dave go?"

"You're stronger."

Gerry nodded sagely. He reminded me to peel the potatoes and put them on to boil.

I hated potatoes. My father bought them in hundred-pound bags in the fall, and by February the eyes were growing right through the burlap. I was picking potatoes out of the bag in the pantry under the steps when my father threw open the door above me and came down in his snow-covered boots.

There were no separate rooms in our cellar yet. I stayed where I was, the only real hiding-place, and watched him.

"Forget the potatoes and come with me, Dave. Hurry up."

It was frightening how much he sensed. I was afraid to think about him in case he smelled out my mutinous thoughts.

Mrs Taylor opened the door to the two of us. The pipe in my father's pocket was still smoking, and intermittent clouds escaped from around the pocket flap as if he had the Little Engine That Could puffing away inside. He held his hat in his hand and smiled with his yellow teeth. Mrs Taylor went to get her husband.

"Use your nose," my father whispered, "what do you smell?"

"Liver and onions."

"That's right," and he smiled as Mr Taylor came to the door.

"Big problem with house," my father said, pointing to the crack. "I see. I think, tell or not tell?"

"Yes, a crack, I see. I'll get the contractor to come around and patch it when the weather warms up. Thank you very much."

"No patch."

"I beg your pardon?"

"Three days warm, and already your footings shift. Bad foundation. When real spring comes, crack will open much more. Foundation move—walls move. Walls move—doors and windows break—roof shift. Very bad. Very expensive to fix. You tell contractor dig out everything. I check for you—make sure he do good job."

"And we just laid the lawn in the fall!" said Mrs Taylor from the screen door. "I wanted to put in a garden this spring."

We left them then, and walked back across the road to our cellar.

"Get the potatoes on. I'll make the soup."

He whistled tunelessly to himself. I couldn't understand what he was so happy about.

"The neighbours are taken care of," he said to my mother as soon as we sat down to dinner. He began to slurp on his soup, using a big European spoon, the size of a small ladle.

Gerry froze.

"You mean you did it without me?" Gerry asked.

"Of course. This was no business for a boy."

Gerry slammed his own spoon down on the table.

My father told the story.

"Like trying to pull a goat by its horns," my father said of Mr Taylor's reluctance to come outside. "He started to tell me his contractor would come back and do it, but I know a man who worked for that contractor. He's bankrupt. Mr Taylor is going to have to pay oh, I don't know, maybe six hundred dollars to have the job done, and he doesn't have the money."

"He told you that?"

"No, but we figured it out. Tell her, Dave."

"I don't know," I stammered.

"Sometimes I wonder what they teach you at school. What were they eating?"

"Liver and onions."

"What kind of liver?"

I stared at him blankly.

"Pork liver. That means they're broke. They spent all their money on asphalt and rolls of grass. He'll have to save to get his foundation fixed. It should take him a year or two to get the money. Unless the building inspector catches sight of it and makes him do it right away."

My mother put her hand on his arm and she began to laugh.

• • •

Gerry was glum at the rink that night, and got into two fights. On the way home, he finally said, "I don't like it. It's not a sure thing. If that inspector shows up at our house again, I'm going to do it myself."

We waited over the weeks that followed, as the first true thaw came in late March, and just as my father had said, the crack in Mr Taylor's basement wall grew wider.

By April, we had lumber and several squares of bricks stacked in the muddy back yard. My father whistled often and my mother took Tom out to be in the sun during the occasional warm day.

Only Gerry sulked that spring.

Joey Slinger

"My grandfather has told me stories," reminisces Joey Slinger, "of coming to this country to escape the oppressions of Europe and to carve a new life out of the untrammelled wilderness. They settled in what we now call Rosedale and he felled trees and squared the timbers and, with the help of his sons, painstakingly constructed a rough, twenty-three room mansion. They scraped a meagre existence out of the unforgiving Toronto Stock Exchange; slowly they tamed the savage bond market and ventured warily into speculation on railroad rights-of-way." You want funny? We've got funny. The following is from Joey Slinger's Leacock Medal–winning book *No Axe Too Small to Grind*, beginning with what has got to be one of the best author prefaces I've ever read.

FROM *No Axe Too Small to Grind*

Preface

This book was commissioned as a *Guide to Moral Fitness* and was to be illustrated with actual photographs of the author in a leotard doing the exercises he undertakes daily to improve his rectitude and tone up principles that have run to fat, but that idea got lost somewhere along the way. I don't know where. I might have left it on the subway. It's too bad, because it would have been a dandy book—just looking at the photographs makes me break out in an idealistic sweat, and I imagine the text would have been equally inspirational. That's how it is with a book, though. When you start off you never know what's going to become of it. It's all right for a reader. A reader can read the reviews and say, "Ah, so that's what this book is about," and know exactly what he's getting into, but the author doesn't have reviews to go by when he's writing. Every word he sets down is a step into the unknown. It's a foolish way to operate, when you think about it, like building a house and then pulling out the blueprint to see if what you ended up with bears any resemblance to what it was supposed to be. Book writing will never be on a solid footing until reviews are published first and given to authors who can then turn out their books accordingly. If there is ever a royal commission into book writing, and we're certainly due for one, that's what I will recommend.

With the *Guide to Moral Fitness* gone by the boards, the book then became a novel about a young boy growing up in a Fine Old Ontario Family, and his quest to become an ethnic. It was a blockbuster set against the sweeping panorama of the Battle of Jenkin's Ear and would have been a sure-fire bestseller if it had contained a plot and characters. But time was running out and there was no money in the kitty for a plot and characters. All we could afford was punctuation, and while some of it was first-rate, the publisher believed that an historical novel with an ethnic twist about the United Empire Loyalists that consisted only of punctuation was leaving too much to chance. People could read God knows what into it.

After that, the book was, briefly, a script for a television series on compost, a recipe for Veal Supreme, a sonnet cycle glorifying dairy price supports, and a home auto-repair manual. None of these was found to be satisfactory, especially the recipe for Veal Supreme, which, for some reason no one can figure out, called for six gallons of 4 Aces Sherry, a box of Alpha-Bits, and included the home address of Evelyn Kostelnyk in Estevan, Saskatchewan, who, it turns out, moved to North Battleford years ago. When she got married. It tasted dreadful.

All further plans had to be abandoned when the deadline ceased looming and roared through like a hurricane, leaving a trail of carnage and shattered dreams. It was all the survivors could do to assemble a collection of short pieces that had previously been published in *The Toronto Star,* although the newspaper denies it and will punch you in the nose if you press the point.

A word about facts: the facts in this book shouldn't be taken too literally, unless they happen to be accurate. And I have discovered, too late, it turns out, to do anything about it, that some people find some of these pieces humorous. That bothers me. There is nothing worse than writing a thoughtful piece about the perils besetting mankind and to discover someone laughing. What's so funny about the Organization of Petroleum Exporting Countries? Or the fact that Niagara Falls has jelled? If I had written anything funny about stuff like that, I'm sorry. I didn't know I was doing it. It is unconscious humour. Unconscious humour is the worst kind because you don't know it's happening and your inclination is to suggest that whoever is laughing seek professional counselling. Unconscious humour is when you're writing about another Russian wheat-crop failure and what comes out is about the Baptist with the wooden leg who met the nun with a chainsaw. You didn't intend for that to come out, it just came out. Don't go looking for anything like that here.

Listen, what I'm trying to get at is this: none of this stuff is supposed to be humorous. This is a serious book covering a full range of serious topics. If you want to laugh, fine. But it's your funeral....

Staying Out of the Gutter

Young people are always asking for my advice. My advice to them is always the same: don't end up in the gutter.

Look at what they wear in the gutter. It is not the latest styles. It is unfashionable and filthy, discarded garments out at the knee or elbow, whichever is the relevant joint. The shoes are split and must be stuffed with newspapers to keep out the damp. The laces are frequently broken and knotted and the little plastic things at the tips of the laces have disappeared, that is for certain. Nothing matches.

Look at what they eat in the gutter. It is not wholesome home-cooked meals. It is not junk food. It is trash. Fish innards, cantaloupe rinds, tea bags, and a lot of stuff that can no longer be easily classified apart from saying it is green, or very green, or green with orange spots, or mostly orange spots, and so on. That is variety, but variety alone will not sustain a body.

How do people end up in the gutter? The story of each person in the gutter is unique, but they can be broken down into two broad, general themes. (1) Did not tidy up after themselves despite entreaties and, occasionally, threats from parents. Came to express defiance through messiness, later sought solace in it. Finally drifted to the one place in town where they could always be assured of finding a mess. Or (2), are on the lam from heartbreak.

Opportunities for advancement in the gutter are meagre. From time to time some self-debased wretch is hired by a revivalist tent show. Every night he or she comes forward at an appointed moment (usually at a signal from the podium, a hankie dropped, a shrill chord on the steam calliope, a pistol fired, sometimes all three if several wretches are to come forward at once) to relate to the goggle-eyed audience how he or she fell upon wicked ways and ended up in that place whence he or she had so lately been retrieved.

This is not hard work but it is tedious and if there is one thing people in the gutter share it is a despair bred of tedium, so before long they quit and return to the gutter where they can achieve the same despair with less effort and their tedium is not threatened by a stampede from the bleachers as believers rush forward, having been swayed by their tale of degradation.

Is the gutter full of riff-raff? Not necessarily. The percentage of riff-raff in the gutter remains about the same as the percentage in the population at large, slightly lower than in professional groups, slightly higher than in poolrooms, roughly the same as among the idle rich, and, while the ratio is the same as among academics, there is a great deal less borrowing money and forgetting to pay it back, although since no one in the gutter ever has any money to lend, this latter point may be moot.

In any event, steer clear of the gutter if you're looking for a statement of man's basic nature asserting itself amid the shattered ethos of the once-grand urban experiment, especially if you are inclined to make sweeping generalizations. Which is all by way of saying that your chances of getting stabbed in the back by people in whom you have placed your trust is about the same in the gutter as anywhere else in society, so if you're going to get stabbed in the back, why not do it someplace warm and dry like a plush boardroom on Bay Street or the reading room of an exclusive club?

Avoid gutter language. Gutter language begets gutter thinking begets a gutter lifestyle begets the gutter itself. "Nucular" is an example of gutter language, as in "the impending nucular holocaust." Also the verb "to impact." It is perhaps unfair to say everyone who uses impact as a verb is destined to end up in the gutter, since that includes the entire advertising industry, but there is nothing fair about the gutter. And they may well end up there for other reasons.

Have people in the gutter lost all pride? Definitely. Oh, rarely you'll hear somebody from one gutter say to somebody from another, "My gutter is utterly depraved compared to yours," but usually they forget the subject of the conversation before the sentence is finished.

How to stay out of the gutter: emulate decent members of the community. Listen to their advice. Tidy up after yourself. Avoid heartbreak.

My Father's Pyjamas

My father's pyjamas moved in with me. My father came and stayed one night and after he left I found his pyjamas hanging on a hook on the back of the bathroom door. They are white pyjamas with a blue paisley design. They didn't seem in any hurry to leave.

Mine is a one-bedroom apartment in a building inhabited mainly by young people who spend most of their time in Old Vienna beer commercials. I would have thought my father's pyjamas would find their ways frivolous and noisy. Some of these young people are not great respecters of their parents' pyjamas. "They don't even wear pyjamas of their own," I told my father's pyjamas.

But they just hung there, unfazed by the suggestion that they were out of their element. I put them in the laundry. I thought of the philosophical irony: the child is father to the father's pyjamas. I took them out of the dryer, folded them, and put them in a drawer. And then I started to feel just awful.

"Comes a time in a life"—I debated with myself. "Comes a time in a life when pyjamas aren't much use to anybody any more. That's when, as it may be, they just get washed and folded and put away in a drawer.

"Oh, sometimes they get a bit of extra use as a duster or as a rag to polish shoes. But I couldn't let that happen to my father's pyjamas. The family wardrobe always had its pride. Even at its most threadbare, it was too proud to go into a rummage sale. It could always fend for itself. At the very least I have some responsibility for caring for my father's pyjamas.

"After all, flannelette is thicker than water."

I took them out of the drawer and put them on the couch beside me and we watched the news. I had to switch from the CBC news to Global, though, because my father's pyjamas are accustomed to watching Global. "That's all right," I said. "News is news."

When it was over, I spread my father's pyjamas out on the couch and went into the bedroom and climbed into bed.

I lay awake for ages. Sleep wouldn't come. All I could think of was my father's pyjamas on that narrow, lumpy couch. Finally I got up, took the pyjamas off the couch, put them in the bed, and tucked them in. "It's all right," I said. "You need a rest. A little discomfort doesn't bother me at all." I went and lay down on the couch.

Until my father's pyjamas came I hadn't realized how small the apartment was. Now it seemed that everywhere I turned they were there. Spread over a chair with the paper on their lap. Draped over the shower rail when I was in a rush to shower and get to the office. Listening to the radio when I wanted to play a record. Knotting and unknotting their ties disapprovingly while I explained why I was late getting home.

When in need of warm companionship it was my habit to drop by an Old Vienna beer commercial, sweet-talk a waif, and invite her back to my apartment for a little hanky-panky.

"What's that?" the waif hissed as we came in one night.

My father's pyjamas were seated at the table, a game of solitaire spread out before them. "Just my father's pyjamas," I explained. "Pay no attention to them."

In any case, I took them and hung them in the bathroom. It did no good. My whining entreaties were as much use as a candle trying to boil an iceberg. "I'm sorry," she said. "I just don't feel right, knowing your father's pyjamas are in there."

I sent her back to the beer commercial in a cab and brought my father's pyjamas out and settled them beside me. Together we watched Global news. "It's all right," I said. "Having my father's pyjamas is company enough. What need have I of transient, insincere relationships with women?"

But despite my best intentions, my father's pyjamas started to get on my nerves. I would raise my voice when I spoke to them. Sometimes when I went off to work I left them in a heap. Soon I wasn't coming home for meals. I stayed in bars until all hours and rolled home full of abuse for the lint they left everywhere.

One day I came home to find the Goodwill truck in front of the building and the Goodwill man coming out of my apartment with my father's pyjamas over his arm. "Ingrate," sneered the Goodwill man. My father's pyjamas didn't look back as they left.

Mariko Tamaki

What can you say about someone as funny and as fearless as
Mariko Tamaki? A performer, playwright, and author, Tamaki
delves deep into the urban world of poseurs, misfits, oddballs, and
artists—and she does so with panache and aplomb. So allow me
to simply state the obvious: Mariko Tamaki is one of the freshest
new voices to appear in a long, long while. The following is from
Fake I.D. and *True Lies: The Book of Bad Advice.*

FROM *Fake I.D.*

Sad Trees

"It's Tree Day," Matthew trills on the phone over the background
conversation of glassware being shelved and washed. "TREE DAY!"

Matthew is a movie buff, so he's coming off like Bill Murray in
Groundhog Day.

"Get your wheels and let's go! It's seven o'clock and the woods await us!"

There's a pause and mumbling in the background. "John says to wear
boots. It's going to be muddy."

As he's hanging up the phone, I can hear John laughing with glee in the
background.

Driving theatre homosexuals around is something I've been doing for
almost a year now, since last fall when I backed into the bike rack outside
a local playhouse. What started out as a string of "favours" to pay off a
bent back tire has blossomed into a part-time job. About the only down-
side, so far, are the latte cups and fancy biscotti wrappers I'm constantly

finding in the back seat.

Other than that, it's not a bad gig. I drive them where they want to go, they pay me. It's like being part school bus driver, part FedEx girl.

The fact that I got this job because of, rather than despite, my accident should tell you a little something about the people I'm working for. As a writer, I'm often seen by my straight friends as a flake, but my theatre friends think I'm a pillar of stability. It seems no one there is as much worried about my crappy parallel parking skills as they are thrilled to bits that I (a) can drive and (b) have a car.

It's damn interesting work a lot of the time because it's THEATRE. So, we could be picking up lights and speakers, or just about anything under the sun. To name a few: a cotton candy machine, a pair of unicycles, a parachute, and two giant foam lemons that we strapped to the top of the car with bungee cords and twine.

It's like a car commercial: "WHAT HAVE YOU DRIVEN IN YOUR HONDA LATELY?"

Today it's "sad trees."

They are for the set of Matthew's new play about these four art school students who commit suicide in a national park, *Smells Like Pine but Tastes Like Death*. Nickname: *Tasty*. John, the set designer, wants real trees for the set. I think they're going to hang them from the ceiling, or something.

Whatever, so long as they're not hanging them off my car, which already has a scratch in the roof from the suit of armour we crammed in the trunk in April for Matthew's other play, *A Suit of Armour for My Broken Heart*.

For such a chipper guy Matthew writes incredibly depressing plays. I suppose it would be worrisome if not for the fact that everyone's writing sad plays these days. Like it's some new thing, being sad, or, I suppose, being this sad. It could be that I wasn't paying attention before, that plays have always been sad, but it seems to me lately that even the funny plays I've seen have been kind of depressingly funny, like the movie *Beaches,* if *Beaches* had been written by a boy. My friend Rocky, who recently opted to grow a soul patch, says the heart is the new frontier of the millennia.

One of the results of this emphasis on sad theatre, aside from the enormous amount of drinking that happens after these plays, is that theatre set designers are specializing in rapid decay, sets of weather-beaten wood, planks banged with hammers and rocks to look old, then painted to look chipped. It's like what my mother did to ruin my living-room table at home using something called "crackle," which looks like dry skin—only on a grander scale. You spend three hours creating something and then eight hours fucking it up so that it looks decrepit.

There's a larger metaphor there but I won't get into it.

This tree-hunting trip is a bit of a lavish expense in the interest of artistic integrity. The trees could be ordered over the phone and delivered, but John and Matthew want to go to the tree farm to pick them out. They want to make sure that the trees chosen are especially morose, rather than, say, smug or just mildly disappointed with their station in life. Matthew, who also has a soul patch, spends the drive up to the tree farm sketching on a napkin, gesturing with his hands. He'd like five sad trees, all drooping towards the camp scene that will be constructed centre stage.

I'm supposed to have read the play but I haven't, so I say nothing, concentrating on the butts of the cars in front of me, which look like angry robotic faces with flashing red eyes.

John, who is from British Columbia, where everything is green and easygoing (and yet, inexplicably, he is not all that fun to be around), spends the entire car drive up to Milton bitching about how we're having to go outside the city to BUY a tree. Like, whatever. The very idea that trees in Toronto are so special that we can't just chop one down, he grumbles, periodically pulling at his blond dreads and making eye contact with me in the rearview mirror to further impose his point.

Last night John tried to organize a group to go to Eglinton Park and steal a tree, but no one would go.

Cowards.

I am trying to convince John that the city of Toronto does a tree count every night.

"Yeah, whatever."

"It's true, dude."

"Oh yeah. Who does a tree count?"

"The parking meter attendants."

"Shut up."

"It's true."

John pauses and looks at Matthew, who is scribbling ideas on his little notepad and does not glance up.

"Whatever," says John.

You gotta love those West Coast hippie arts types. So trusting.

"How would you even know something like that?"

Aha! "Oh please," I say, "do you think that the city would pay a bunch of people to check just on cars? Who cares about CARS?"

Matthew, who is not big on sarcasm, jabs John with his elbow. "Don't get her started."

The Milton 100 Acre Tree Farm is a fenced-in lot surrounded by white gravel and an army of concrete lawn statues. Inside the log cabin headquarters is a small shop of glazed outdoor knickknacks and, interestingly enough, clay toilet-paper holders, exaggerated snobbish butlers with their pants down holding toilet-paper rolls on their fingers, and farmers with signs on their overalls that say BORN IN A BARN? WASH YOUR HANDS!

We march straight to the sales desk and ring the little bell on the clay lily pad.

Moments later we have the rapt attention of Mary, the tanned duchess of the trees. Adjusting her heavy green MILTON 100! apron, she gives us a raised eyebrow. "Sad trees," she repeats, like she's misheard us.

We smile expectantly.

Matthew, who is dressed appropriately in red gingham and jeans, leans on the counter and says slowly but without any extra information, "Sad trees."

Looking away briefly to see where John is, he misses the clearly unimpressed look on Mary's face, like, *Who does this schmo think he is?*

It's moments like these that are indicative of the hazard of being an artist and hanging out with artists, who have a bad rap for being uninterpretable and/or unapologetically strange. If you hang out with artists enough, you know the rap is well deserved. The problem, I think, has something to do with the fact that artists spend such a large portion of their adolescence alienated by the world around them, a world that often doesn't appreciate poetry, say, or *Star Wars*. So when the artist grows up and discovers others who do appreciate art—their art—and all the art-speak that goes with it, they're so thrilled to have found this, their community, that they lose all interest in translating, or explaining, their artistic impulses to the rest of the world. Grad students are the same way.

That's my theory.

The effect of this rift on the artist's relation to the outside world plays out differently depending on what kind of artists they are; visual artists, because they are driven by a nonverbal medium, are virtually uncommunicative (even amongst themselves); writers are a bit better, although often pained by attempts at day-to-day socializing, preferring instead the cold comfort of journals, diaries, and intensely long emails.

Theatre artists are a wild card because they're so dramatic and attention craving, so even if they think you won't understand what they're saying, they have to say it big or, at least, with feeling.

Then again, I know a lot of artists who feel that what separates them from the rest of the world, what draws these curious stares and, sometimes, this confusion, is that they have an intuitive emotional sense of sorts, that draws them, creates a need in them, to really experience. Something non-artists often find hard to deal with. It's a distinguished stronger heart muscle of sorts, so I'm told, a third eye. An extra EMOTIONAL FEELING third eye....

As Matthew and Mary speak, John is off in a corner on one knee, stroking the nose of a concrete bear lawn ornament, staring into its unpainted white eyes.

"Bears are such noble creatures, hey?" he says.

How embarrassing.

Thank God Mary is game for a challenge. She rolls her eyes and directs us through the back door to the outside yard.

"My little tour guide car," she explains, pointing us to a golf cart parked by the door. "It's a big lot and everyone wants to pick out their trees personally, so we ride in this."

Matthew smiles.

"I'm driving, though, so no funny business."

No sweat. We scramble into the dusty golf cart, which is practically cemented into the scorched dirt, the wheels surrounded by a pie crust of baked mud. As we skid out of the lot there's a distinct ripping sound as the mud and rubber separate, and we're off.

As we take sharp turns, we feel like we're riding a tiny streetcar, an aggressively rugged woman driver at the wheel.

At first Mary, apparently at a loss, takes us to a field of very small trees. Walking around there makes us all feel powerful and gigantic, as our palms stretch down to graze the tips of the trees in the tiny forest.

"Not very sad, though," John finally says, "the fact that they're small."

Everyone looks at me because I'm short.

"What?!"

"No, of course not," Mary hastily agrees. "Maybe we need to look for something ... skinnier."

So we all jump back on the cart and hook a left to a series of taller, thinner pines, standoffishly situated to one side, by the fence. They don't look especially sad. Even to me.

Mary decides to take us over to the birch trees. "Maybe birches are sadder than pines," she suggests.

The birches, which are spaced farther apart than the other trees, do look lonely, with their pale white arms stretched up and out. If you step back they kind of look like they're reaching up to the sky, heads tilted back all the way so you can't see them.

John hops out of the cart and stands beside one of the trees for a while, wrapping both hands around the trunk.

Matthew looks startled. "What is he doing?"

"I think he's trying to talk to the tree."

"Hmmmmm," says Matthew, stroking his soul patch.

I read this book once that had a passage about how you can divine a lot of an area's history by cutting open a tree and reading the rings inside. It's called dendrochronology: the art of talking to trees by cutting them open. It's known as dendroclimatology if you're using the tree rings to deconstruct the climate of a certain place, like how much rain there was three years ago, or how much sun there was a decade before that. It's kind of curious, if you consider it: you have to kill the tree to read its insides, which is a high cost for reading into something or someone.

My friend Abi, who is not a tree lover but a deep thinker, has noted the enormous significance of this twist, a thing having to die so we can know it. I find it ironic that you're not even really learning about the tree itself, but killing the tree to find out about the world around it.

Now *that's* sad.

How come no one's writing plays about that?

John leans forward and pushes his head into the tree trunk, flattening his dreads against the white bark.

Mary, who has returned to her cart to sit sideways on the seat and stare at John along with the rest of us, is quiet and still. We're all a little stunned suddenly, like special-order concrete statues, lost in thought.

Personally, I'm half thinking about Halloween, have been on and off since Matthew called me two weeks ago and told me why he needed my car. Trees make me think of Halloween.

In my experience, almost every family has a thing that, for some reason, they will not buy. And the unwillingness to bend financially gets passed down from generation to generation. Matthew will not buy a car. My friend Katie would rather starve than buy canned soup. I come from a long line of kids whose parents wouldn't buy Halloween costumes, instead dressing us in theatric monstrosities that mom and dad lovingly created at home.

My father's reason was financial.

"I can MAKE you into a ghost," my father would say. "I'm not going to go buy you something for ONE NIGHT."

My mother's reasoning was more whimsical. "I don't even understand why you would consider BUYING something this important," she used to tell me every year when I begged for a plastic Wonder Woman costume pack from Shoppers Drug Mart.

When my father wasn't paying attention, my mother would sneak out and buy reams of fabric that she would later "find" in the basement, then spend hours at the sewing machine making me my Dream Costume.

Either that, or *her* dream costume, I was never sure which.

Every year I braved October 31st in one of my mother's homespun eyesores.

One year she made me a bubble.

"I don't WANT to be a bubble."

"You said you did."

"No, I didn't."

"Yes, you did," my mother said, zipping me into the Bubble. "Tell your dad if you have to pee and he'll unzip you."

Of course my friend Liam, whose father was a carpenter, had it even worse. At least my costumes weren't especially HEAVY. One year Liam got beaten up by a bunch of older kids while wearing the Boom Box costume his father had made him for Halloween. The costume was pretty cool actually, with silver matchboxes glued on as buttons and duct tape marking where the tape would go. It was also incredibly cumbersome, making it difficult to, say, escape a gang of twelve-year-old boys dressed as pirates. Possibly, if Liam had had any free limbs, he would have defended himself. Unfortunately he had to use both arms to hold up the heavy 4 by 1½ by 3-foot silver frame, or else he would fall down. Thank God his little brother, dressed as a break-dancer, was able to run and alert the authorities.

I remember the Boom Box because that same year my mother spent an outrageous sum making me into a Christmas Tree, complete with three tiers of heavy crinoline and wire that made it impossible to sit down.

I started to cry as soon as she put the star on top of my head, the very moment I realized the entire getup was not cool, as my mother had promised, but hideously ugly.

"I—I don't want to be a treeeee!"

Too late. I had to lean on the science board all through class and spend recess kneeling in a makeshift graveyard of ugly Halloween costumes with

Liam, the beat-up Boom Box, and two other kids dressed as pop cans. What kind of parent dresses their kid up as a Coke can? Honestly.

I stormed home after school and started to tear at my crinoline skirt in a blind third-grader rage. My father pointed out that if I ruined this costume I wouldn't be able to trick-or-treat at all.

Sometimes little girls have to buck up and be angry trees, he said.

· · ·

As I ruminate on past childhood events, John and Matthew are now throwing themselves into the tree search. John stands in front of Mary with one arm raised straight up, the other bent at the elbow so that his hand dangles just behind his head. Matthew reaches over and pushes John's spine so that his stomach sticks out.

It's tree charades and Mary isn't paying any attention, she's just staring at me with this desperate look on her face.

Oh dear.

"You know what?" I finally offer. "I think we need to think up a Plan B."

After a briefing between John and Matthew, who have finally taken Mary's toe tapping and engine revving as a sign that they are becoming less and less worth the effort, it is decided that what is really needed is a tree that they can *make* sad, which could really be *any* tree, preferably something not too pricey.

"Five that aren't too pricey," Matthew says.

This Mary can easily comply with. She tags five trees and zips us back to the head office.

"Hey," adds John, as Mary tallies the invoice, "would you throw in the bear for an extra $20?"

"Yes," Mary says, not looking up.

John grins.

Done and done.

For the rest of the drive home, with the giddy twins in the back sniffing their sleeves for the smell of pine, I'm in an explicably bad mood, suddenly not interested in the plans John has for *Tasty*. After all this talk of looking for sad trees, it now seems brutal to *make* a tree sad. Like we're going to buy a perfectly content tree and then take it outside and give it a beating, tell it we killed its puppy.

Matthew says he wants to strip the needles off a bunch of the branches, the nervous-cat method of tree saddening.

I tune out and turn up the radio, miffed because the tree-saddening all sounds a little morbid.

God, I think, turning onto Highway 401 to head home, who's the hippy-dippy now, huh?

Shakespeare said that all the world was a stage, but for a myriad of reasons, some uglier than others, some of us are more active and aware participants in this artistic farce than others.

FROM *True Lies: The Book of Bad Advice*

Dear Ms. Tamaki,
   On behalf of the Writers' Guild of Canada
   I'm afraid that I must officially request
   that you cease referring to yourself as a writer
   from this point forward.
   We have,
   at the request of several of your peers,
   done an informal investigation
   and discovered
   that you have had
   neither a disruptive childhood
   nor an ounce of artistic integrity.

   It was also revealed to us
   by a private source
   that you spent your grant money on shoes
   and chips at the 7/11

You have been heard
at recent gatherings
making fun of Margaret Atwood
and expressing an interest
in moving to the United States;
if you were an actor
this might be appropriate
but as a writer
this behaviour
borders on sacrilegious.
Move to Europe,
maybe,
but not the States.
I mean,
really.

We had hoped
that your homosexuality
and apparent disregard
for societal norms
would prove fruitful
but apparently
your apathy
and materialism
outweigh any potential these features might have offered.
Please return
your notebooks
(we know you have them stashed under your bed)
your air of superiority
and your caffeine addiction.
You can keep the computer
you only use it to surf the Web anyway.

We hope
you find some other way to serve your country
in another field
perhaps customer service
or family law.
We realize your prior plans
of becoming a marine biologist
are now out of the question
but are confident
you will find something else
to fill your time.

Yours sincerely,
The Writers' Guild of Canada

William J. Thomas

William J. Thomas is known for his writings on (a) dogs, (b) guys,
and (c) guys travelling with dogs. Which is to say, as a humorist,
Thomas has tapped into a wellspring of material: big dumb
friendly animals ruled by appetite and not particularly bright.
I'm speaking about the guys here. The dogs are almost as bad.

FROM *The Dog Rules (Damn Near Everything!)*

The Dog Rules: As They Apply to the Family Car

More and more I see cars and trucks travelling on public thoroughfares with what appears to be a dog in the driver's seat. I am utterly opposed to dogs driving cars because there's no doubt in my mind that they'd always be trying to bump off cats and making it look like an accident. Therefore …

Rule 1
Dogs are not allowed to travel in motorized vehicles. Period.

Rule 2
Okay, a seeing-eye dog is allowed to travel in a vehicle with its owner provided that the owner is not the operator of said vehicle.

Rule 3
Okay, in a medical emergency, a dog may be taken directly to and from a veterinary clinic in a moving vehicle.

Rule 4
Okay, if the family's out for a Sunday drive, on Sundays only, the dog can go along provided he sits in the back seat.

Rule 5
Okay, the dog can sit in the front seat on the passenger side provided there's no passenger in that seat. And if it's really hot, he can roll the window down, but not all the way.

Rule 6
Okay, the dog can hang out the side window like a misplaced hood ornament going 60 mph with tears and saliva spraying the passengers in the back seat.

Rule 7
The dog is never, repeat, *never* allowed to operate a moving vehicle. That would be insane.

Rule 8
Okay, the dog can sit on the driver's lap with his paws on the steering wheel, but he's not allowed to put his foot on the accelerator.

Rule 9
Okay, the dog can steer the car and work the pedals, but he's not allowed to drive at night or take the car out alone.

Rule 10
Okay, the dog can drive at night by himself, but not if he's been drinking. No way. That's against the law.

Miriam Toews

Miriam Toews grew up in the small Mennonite community of
Steinbach in southern Manitoba. Her childhood experiences
provided her with the subject and themes of her breakout novel,
A Complicated Kindness, nominated for the Giller and winner of
the Governor General's Award, which put Toews in the forefront
of Canadian fiction—and deservedly so. The following is from an
earlier novel, *A Boy of Good Breeding,* which demonstrates the
warmth and humour that is such a hallmark of her writing.

FROM *A Boy of Good Breeding*

Algren was Canada's smallest town. It really was. Canada's Smallest
Town. It said so on a big old billboard right outside the town limits
and Knute had checked with one of those government offices in the blue
pages and they said fifteen hundred is what you need for a town. And that's
what Algren had. If it had one less it would be a village and if it had just one
more it would be a bigger town. Like all the rest of the small towns. Being
the smallest was its claim to fame.

Knute had come to Algren, from the city of Winnipeg, to look after her
dad who'd had a heart attack. And to relieve her mom who said if she spent
one more day in the house she'd go insane.

She was twenty-four years old. Her mother, Dory, had intended her
name to be pronounced "Noot uh," but nobody got it so it became just
Knute, like "Noot." Even her mom had given up on the "uh" part but did
from time to time call her Knutie or sometimes, and she hated this, Knuter.

Knute had a daughter, Summer Feelin', and Summer Feelin' had a strange way of shaking when she was excited. She flapped her arms, and her fingers moved quickly as though she were typing to save her life, and sometimes her head went back and her mouth opened wide and sounds like *aaah* and *uh-uh-uh* came out of it.

When she first started doing it, Knute thought it was cute. Summer Feelin' looked like she'd lift right off the ground. But then Knute started worrying about it and decided to take her to a specialist, a pediatric neurologist. He did a number of tests, including an encephalogram. Summer Feelin' liked the wires and enjoyed the attention but told the doctor that flapping was just something she was born to do.

Eventually after all the results came in and the charts had been read and analyzed, he agreed with her. She was born to flap. There was no sign of strange electrical activity in her brain, no reason to do a CAT scan, and all accounts of her birth indicated no trauma had occurred, nothing untoward as she had made her way through Knute's birth canal and into this world.

Every night Knute lay down with Summer Feelin'. That was the time S.F. told Knute stories and let her in on her big plans and Knute could feel her daughter's body tremble with excitement. It quivered. It shook. It was out of her control. Knute would hold Summer Feelin' until she stopped shaking, maybe a twitch or two or a shudder, and fell asleep. The specialist said S.F.'s condition, which wasn't really a condition, was very rare but nothing to worry about. Then he'd added, in a thoughtful way, that the condition or lack of condition might be the precipitator to that rare phenomenon known as spontaneous combustion. So Knute worried, from time to time, about S.F. bursting into flames for no apparent reason. And that was the type of concern she couldn't really explain to people, even close friends, without them asking her if she needed a nap or what she'd been reading lately or just plain laughing at her.

• • •

March was the month that Knute and Summer Feelin' arrived in Algren. Tom had had a heart attack (or *his* heart attack as Dory called it) in

December. He'd been putting up the last decorations on the tree and BAM, it happened. He fell over, and because he was sort of clutching at the tree it fell on top of him. Ten days later, in the sterile intensive care ward of the hospital, nurses were still finding tiny pine needles in his hair and in the many creases of his skin. He picked up a nasty infection called septicemia in the hospital and, as a result, his lungs malfunctioned and he was put on a respirator. Of course, he couldn't talk, but in his more lucid, pain-free moments he could write. Sort of. All he ever wrote, in a barely legible scrawl either stretched out over the whole page or sometimes scrunched up in the bottom corner, was "How is the tree?" Or "Is the tree okay?" Or "Is the tree up?" Or "I'm sorry about the tree."

One day in the hospital Dory told him, "Tom, it's Christmas Day today. Merry Christmas, sweetheart."

His eyes were closed but he squeezed her hand. She said, "Do you remember Christmas, darling?"

And he opened his eyes and looked up at her and shook his head. Yet the next day, again, he wrote about the tree. He couldn't remember Christmas, but he knew a tree should, for some reason, be erected in his living room.

Gradually he could remember a bit more and he could spell "world" backwards and count by sevens and all those things they'd asked him to do in the hospital when he was off the respirator and out of intensive care, but still he had a strange scattered memory, like, for instance, he knew he must, absolutely *must,* shave every morning, but he was unsure why. He reminded Dory to check the battery in the smoke detector, but when she said, "Oh, Tom, what's the worst that can happen if our battery is dead for a day or two?" he didn't have an answer. So he was caught in a bind where he was committed to doing what he'd always done but he couldn't remember why he was doing it. His life, some might have said, had no purpose.

Neither did Knute's, really. Summer Feelin' was in a day care that she hated and Knute was working full time as a hostess in a busy downtown restaurant where everybody was used to seating themselves. She wasn't aggressive enough to say, "Hey, can't you read the sign? It says 'wait to be seated,'" and so, pretty much, she just stood there all day smiling and feeling stupid. From time to time she moved the sign right in front of the door, but people would walk into it and then move it back out of their way. Sometimes the waitresses got mad at her because she wasn't seating anybody in their sections or because everybody was sitting in their section and they were run off their feet trying to keep up with the orders. Then, for a while, Knute would try to keep people from walking past her and she'd say things like, "Please follow me," or "A table will be ready in a minute," or "How many of you are there?" Usually there would be two and when she asked how many of them there were, they'd look at each other like she was nuts, then they'd hold up two fingers or point at each other and say, "one, two," in a loud voice.

"Two!" Knute would say "okay, two, hmmm … two, you say," like she was trying to figure out how to seat twelve. Then she'd meander around and around the restaurant with them behind her, suggesting possible tables, and she'd say, "Oh I think, well, no, well, yes, okay, sure, right here is fine. Wherever you want really, I guess."

Her boss's wife and all the waitresses and the dishwasher and the two cooks kept telling him to fire her, but her boss kept giving her more chances. He told Knute she'd get the hang of it in a while, just get in their faces and make them wait. "They're like pigs at the trough," he said. "You gotta keep 'em under control."

On her first day Knute had actually managed to lead an old couple to a table. But somehow they got their wires crossed, and Knute pulled a chair away from the table just as the man was going to sit on it. In slow motion he fell to the ground while Knute and his wife stared, horrified. As he fell, he knocked over the fake flower arrangement and the vase shattered.

Knute's boss came running out and picked the old man up, cleaned up the glass, and told them lunch was on the house. Then he took Knute into the kitchen, made her a salami sandwich on a bagel, sat her down on a lettuce crate, and told her not to worry, not to worry, this was her first day, she'd work out the kinks. But she never did. Anyway, it was a lot better than pumping gas. The one time Knute tried that she accidentally filled up a motor home with gas—not the gas tank, but the interior of the motor home itself. She had stuck the nozzle into the water-spout hole instead of the gas tank hole. The woman driving the van hadn't noticed until she lit up a cigarette and her motor home exploded, partially, and her leg ended up needing plastic surgery. Her husband sued the gas station and won a bunch of money, of course. Knute was let go and told, by her supervisor, that she should get tested for brain damage.

On her way home from the restaurant, Knute would pick up Summer Feelin' and listen to her tell lies about the day care. How Esther, one of the workers, had punched her six times in the face, how Justin, one of the twins, had made her put her tongue on the cold swing set and it had stuck and they left her out there all alone all day, how a terrible man with purple skin and horse feet had come and killed seven of the kids.

"Summer Feelin'," Knute would say, "I know how much you hate it, but for now you have to try to find something good about it. It can't be that bad."

Knute was tired from standing around stupidly all day. But she felt she had to make it up to Summer Feelin', so for an hour or two before bedtime the two of them would play in the park or get an ice cream, maybe rent a movie or walk to the library. And that wore Knute out even more. Her favourite days were when Summer Feelin' would relax and they could just sit at their little table and talk. Summer Feelin' would tell her funny stories and shake with excitement and then, in the evening, they'd curl up together with Summer Feelin's soft head under Knute's chin. Knute would try not to fall asleep because that would mean that was it, the day. If she didn't fall asleep she'd get up very quietly and make herself a cup of coffee and phone Dory, collect, or her buddy Marilyn, who just lived a couple of blocks away but had a kid and so was housebound like her in the evenings. Sometimes Marilyn and Knute watched TV together over the phone.

When Dory called and suggested Knute and Summer Feelin' come back to Algren and live with her and Tom for a while, Knute felt like someone had just injected her with a warm, fast-acting tranquilizer. It felt like she had just put her head on a soft feather pillow and been told to go to sleep, everything would be fine. Dory made it sound like she needed Knute desperately to help with Tom, to protect her sanity, and it's true she did. But Dory also had a sense that Knute was tired, really tired. That all she was doing was spinning her wheels. It took Knute about fifteen minutes to quit her job, cancel Summer Feelin's spot at the day care, tell her landlord she was moving, and pack their stuff. When she told Summer Feelin' that she could kiss her awful day care goodbye, she flapped like crazy, and Knute had to put her in a nice, warm bath to calm her down. She told Marilyn she was going to her mom and dad's for a while and Marilyn asked if she could go, too. The next day Summer Feelin' and Knute were on the road.

Not for long, though, because Algren was only about forty miles away from Winnipeg. Knute and Summer Feelin' peered out the car windows at the clumps of dirt and piles of melting snow and S.F. said it reminded her of the moon.

When they got to the outskirts of Algren, which was really the same thing as the town, they saw Hosea Funk, the mayor, standing in a ditch of water with high waders, gazing soulfully at the billboard that said, Welcome to Algren, Canada's Smallest Town. Of course there's not a lot to be done when people die or when they're born. They come and go. They move away. They disappear. They *reappear*. But more or less, give or take a person or two, Algren was the reigning champ of small towns. Well, there was another famous thing about Algren but it wasn't as impressive (if you can call being a town whose population consistently hovers around fifteen hundred people *impressive*): Algren was also the original home of the Algren cockroach. The Algren cockroach was one of only three types of North American cock- roaches. Apparently it was first brought to Algren on a plant or a sack of potatoes or something a hundred years ago from Europe and the rest was history. In the encyclopedia under "cockroach" it listed the Algren cockroach and mentioned Algren as a small town in southern Manitoba. No mention of its being *the* smallest town in Canada, much to Hosea Funk's chagrin.

As they passed Hosea standing in the ditch, Knute honked her horn and waved. "Who's that?" S.F. asked.

"The mayor," said Knute. "He's an old friend of Grandpa's." The horn startled him out of his reverie and Hosea straightened his golf cap and started up the side of his ditch. He didn't wave back. He tugged for a second at the front of his jacket and then nodded his head, once. That's how the men in Algren greeted everyone, friend or foe.

...

When Knute and Summer Feelin' drove up to the house they could see Tom and Dory standing in the living room, staring out the picture window. Next to them were small bronze statues and clay busts that Tom had bought, and he and Dory seemed to blend in with these things. As soon as they saw Knute's beater pull up in the driveway, though, they came to life. Dory zipped to the front door and Tom smiled and waved. These days he stayed away from the doors when they were being opened. He couldn't afford to get a chill and get sick all over again. S.F. ran up to the picture window, flapping like crazy, and Tom gave her a high-five against the glass, smudging it up a bit. Dory came running out of the house saying, "Welcome, welcome, oh I'm sooooo glad you're both here." And she scooped up S.F. even though her heart wasn't in much better shape than Tom's and then, with her other free arm, wrapped herself around Knute. Tom beamed through the glass.

Dory had prepared a large meal. It consisted of boneless chicken breasts with a black bean sauce, steamed broccoli, slices of cucumbers, tomatoes, and carrots, brown rice, and a fruit salad. Knute could just barely pick out the grimace on Tom's face when he sat down at the table, rather ashamed and annoyed that all this dull stuff constituted a celebratory meal. And that it was all made especially for him and his fragile heart. He would have preferred a big piece of red meat with lots of salt, some potatoes and thick gravy, cheese sauce to accompany his steamed broccoli, great slabs of bread with real butter to soak up the gravy and juice from the meat, a large wedge of apple pie and ice cream, and four cups of coffee to wash it down.

But, of course, Tom couldn't eat steak every day, or maybe he could have and it wouldn't have made any difference. Who knows? Anyway, Knute could tell that Dory felt very good about herself when she prepared the chicken and steamed vegetables, and the fact that they had hardly any taste made S.F., at least, happy.

After lunch Tom did a bit of walking up and down the hall, S.F. went down to the basement to play with the toys, and Dory and Knute had a cryptic conversation about Tom.

"So?" said Knute, and jerked her head in the direction of Tom and the hallway.

"Well," said Dory "you know ..."

"Mmmmm ..."

And then Dory said, "One day at a time ..." and Knute nodded and said, "Yup ..."

They sat there and stared at their coffee cups for a bit and Dory added in a very hushed tone, "A bit more," she tapped at her chest, "these days."

Knute tapped her own chest. "Pain?" she asked.

Dory nodded and pursed her lips.

"Hmmm ... well, what does the doctor say?"

"OH TOM, YOU'RE DONE?" Tom had finished his walk and Dory had been timing him. He had walked for eight minutes. Dory was trying to be extremely upbeat about the eight minutes. "Well, Tom, yesterday it was only seven," and that sort of thing. Tom went over to the picture window and stood with his back to Dory and Knute. He punched his fist into his palm once and then after about thirty seconds he did it again. He slowly walked back to the couch and lay down with a heavy sigh.

• • •

After supper (of leftovers), Dory and Knute played Scrabble. For weeks Dory had been playing with "Marie," a phantom Scrabble opponent whom she had given her own middle name to. Knute asked Dory how she felt when "Marie" won, and she said, "Divided." Summer Feelin' had wandered over to the neighbours' house to play with the little girl, Madison, who lived there. Dory could never remember Madison's name. "Montana?" she'd say. "Manhattan?" Which got them onto the subject of names, and Dory wondered if Knute had, perhaps considered calling S.F. just "Summer" instead of "Summer Feelin'"? Knute knew Dory wasn't altogether enthusiastic about her granddaughter's name and she told her she'd think about it, although she wondered if Dory was really any authority on girls' names considering the choice she'd made when her own daughter was born.

"Summer," Dory said over and over. "If you say it enough times, you know, Knutie, you *get* that summer feeling. You don't have to actually *say* it. The Feelin' part becomes rather redundant, don't you think? Or maybe you could change the spelling of Feelin' to something, oh, I don't know, Irish, maybe like Phaelan, or ..."

Just then the doorbell rang. Tom woke up from his nap on the couch and Dory answered the door. A large man with a pale yellow golf cap tugged twice at the front of his coat before greeting Dory and stepping inside.

Tom was the first to speak. "Hosea Funk, c'mon in, c'mon in." And he nodded his head once, in the traditional male greeting, got up from the couch, and stood there in his polo pyjamas looking a bit like William Shatner in the *Enterprise* and smoothed down his hair, which had become mussed from lying down. Dory said she'd make a fresh pot of coffee and told Hosea to have a seat.

"Hose, do you remember our Knutie?" Dory asked him, putting her arm around Knute's shoulder and grinning. Hosea's thumb and index finger went for the front of his shirt, but then, through some act of will on his part, he adjusted his golf hat instead and replied, "Why sure, Dory, I remember Knutie." Everybody smiled and nodded and finally Hosea broke the awkward silence. "So, are you here for a visit, Knutie, or ..."

Knute was just about to answer when Dory said, "No, she and Summer Feelin' have moved back, for the time being."

"Oh, well," said Hosea, "that's great! Welcome back to Algren."

"Tha—" Knute was cut off by Hosea, who had suddenly sprung to life. "You still barrel-racin', Knute?"

Barrel-racing! thought Knute. The one time she had barrel-raced, badly, was in a 4-H rodeo and Hosea Funk had happened to be her timer. That was years ago, before he became the mayor. Back then he got involved in every event in town. If there was a parade, Hosea walked along throwing out candy to kids. If there was a flood, Hosea organized a sandbag crew. If the hockey team made it to the playoffs in the city, Hosea offered to drive. Once, at a fall supper in a church basement, he was given a trophy by the main street businesses and it said, Hosea Funk, Algren's Number One Booster.

"Nah, I've given it up," said Knute. And she kind of buckled her knees to look bowlegged and horsey. Hosea Funk nodded and Knute could tell he was thinking of something else to say. She waited. A few seconds more. There. This time he couldn't help it. His fingers went to his shirt and tugged, not twice but three times. He was ready to speak.

Morley Torgov

"I wanted to name the book 'Goodbye Soo, Fuck You,' but the publisher thought the use of 'Goodbye' in the title was too negative." Morley Torgov was referring to his father's ritual farewell as it appears at the start of *A Good Place to Come From*, his classic memoir about growing up Jewish in Sault Ste. Marie in the 1940s, which won Torgov the Stephen Leacock Medal for Humour. He won the Leacock again for his novel *The Outside Chance of Maximilian Glick*.

FROM *A Good Place to Come From*

It was four o'clock in the afternoon, a half hour before train time. "We better get going," my father said, snapping shut the locks on his brown valise. The businesslike tone of his voice, the sharp clicking of the locks, the firmness of his step as we walked toward the car—everything contributed to an air of determination. "It's only a two-minute drive to the station, what's the rush?" I asked. "Sure, that's right," he responded, "leave everything to the last minute, drive like a crazy fool, kill somebody, ruin a perfectly good brand new car, what do you care?" I shook my head in defeat. It was no use trying to convince him I cared.

Always, on the day my father was leaving for Toronto to buy goods for his store, there was this atmosphere of tension, this feeling of great commercial urgency: schedules to be met, judgments to be exercised (will this be a hot little item? … will this be a lemon?), deals to be made, money to be spent—all this to be accomplished in the garment-manufacturing jungle that was Spadina Avenue in those days. This time, however, my father was especially on edge. Earlier that day he had taken delivery of a new 1949 Pontiac sedan—his first new car since before the war. It was gleaming black with white sidewall tires; parallel chrome stripes ran along the centre of the hood and continued again over the trunk lid giving the car a sleek, sporty appearance. "Look how she sits, just like the Queen Mary," my father said as he rolled the car lovingly, almost tenderly, out of the dealer's garage on Tancred Street. We made our way home along Queen Street behind the proud prominent nose of the chrome Indian head mounted atop the grille. My father's touch at the wheel was delicate, as if he were driving a crystal chandelier. Suddenly, at the corner of Queen and Bruce, mere yards away from where his own garage waited with doors thrust open to receive the distinguished new guest, rain began to fall, a soft mid-May rain. "Ach, sonofabitch!" he hissed, switching on the wipers. "Rain! My goddam luck. There must be a devil in my life. That's all there is to it … a devil in my life."

That had been several hours ago. Now we were on our way to the C.P.R. station at the head of Pilgrim Street. It was my maiden voyage at the helm (he had handed me the key to the ignition as if it was the key to a great city) and I drove as the historic importance of the moment dictated—avoiding pot-holes and puddles, creeping warily through intersections, while my father sat nodding with approval. He smelled strongly of after-shave lotion, having shaved—as he always did when he was leaving for Toronto—only an hour before train time. "Got to look my best," he would explain, "just in case I run into a good-looking skirt between here and Sudbury." That pre-train shave was the only festive gesture in an otherwise solemn departure routine.

I drove, and we talked … or rather *he* talked.

"You'll remember to double-check the cash at the end of each day to make sure it's not short or over. What's the combination to the safe?"

"Left to forty, right to twenty-two, left again to fifteen, then right again to fifty."

"Good. Try not to forget it."

"Okay. I'll write the numbers down on a piece of paper—"

"*Schmeckle!* Somebody'll find it—"

"So what should I do for godsake?"

"Keep repeating it. Say it over to yourself a few times every day."

"I got a great idea," I said. "Maybe I'll say it before meals, like grace."

"That's right, smart-aleck, make fun. You'll see how funny it is some day when you come into the store and find the whole goddam place cleaned out … everything gone, stolen!"

I rattled off the magic numbers once again just to make him happy. He went on. "Remember to turn off the window lights at ten each night, don't waste electricity. You'll roll up the awning if it looks like rain but for Chrisake remember to put it down if it's sunny, it shouldn't fade the goods in the windows. And make sure you lock the garage good and tight before you go to bed. You never can tell these days who'll fool around with the car, there's so many strangers in town now. Oh yes, and stay off Wellington Street; they're putting down fresh tar on the road, the bastards, and it makes a mess of the tires."

"A person would think you're going to Europe," I said.

He sighed deeply. "Europe. I only wish to hell I was going to Europe. Anywhere but Toronto. Those whores on Spadina, I can see them now, dragging out one lousy *shmateh* after another, telling every lie in the book about how wonderful their crap is put together and how much they're selling to this one and to that one. Making phony promises. Gypsies, every one of 'em."

"So why do you stay in the ladies-wear business?" I asked.

"Why do I stay? Because there's a devil in my life. That's all there is to it."

As he said this, the car bounced into and out of a giant pot-hole. I grinned sheepishly. "Sorry."

"Why the hell don't you look where you're going?" he pleaded, wounded and bleeding there on the passenger side.

"I did look, honest to God—"

"If you looked, how … how could you possibly drive right into it?"

"I don't know. I guess there's a devil in my life, and that's all there is to it."

Staring straight ahead through the windshield, maintaining a sharp lookout for pot-holes, he sighed deeply again. "You see," he said quietly, "a university can give you an education—but it can't give you brains."

Rain began to fall again, pelting down into the face of the chrome Indian, drumming like war music against the black hood. We were almost at the intersection of Queen and Pilgrim, about to turn north to the station. "Look at this lousy town," he said moodily, "six months winter, six months rain. Sault Shtunk Marie. Same weather. Same sidewalks. Same buildings. Same faces day in, day out."

"You're just sore because it's raining on your car," I said, trying to sound cheerful. "Just think of this: if you'd stayed in Russia you wouldn't be driving a new Pontiac now, you'd be a slave to some dumb Siberian Cossack."

"What's the difference whose ass you kiss? In Russia it was a Cossack's, here it's some bitch-of-a-customer's ass. I dug a grave for myself in this town, that's all there is to it."

"So be happy," I suggested. "You're off to Toronto. A few days out of the grave."

"Every place is a grave. Russia was a grave. The Soo's a grave. Toronto's a grave. You see this car? It's a toy, that's all. It's a toy they give you to play with, to take your mind off all the crap you had to put up with to earn the toy. It means nothing. *Jesus Christ! Be careful.*"

I swung the car hard just in time to miss another giant pot-hole. "The sonsofbitches," my father said, referring to the local Works Department, "they got no respect for other people's property."

We stood on the platform waiting for the conductor's signal to board. "Every time I come here," my father said, "I think of the first time you went to Camp Borden with the Air Cadets—when was that, 1943?—and you told me on the way to the station I shouldn't kiss you goodbye in front of the other boys. When I drove away afterwards, I was so upset I wasn't sure should I laugh or cry. Now look at you. College boy. Big shit!"

I smiled and let him kiss me goodbye on the cheek.

He stood on the lowest step at the entrance to the Pullman coach, holding onto the handrail to steady himself as the train heaved and strained to overcome its own inertia. In a moment he would make the short farewell speech that he delivered always at the precise moment of the wheels' first forward motion, and that I had come to know so well.

Waving, he called out, as if pronouncing his blessing upon everyone gathered on the platform, "Goodbye Soo, fuck you."

Then he was gone.

Stuart Trueman

Journalist, folklorist, popular historian, and Leacock
Award–winning humorist, Stuart Trueman is also—and I note this
solely because it's such a fascinating aside—one of the original
discoverers of New Brunswick's famed Magnetic Hill. It happened
back in 1933, when Trueman was working at *The Telegraph-Journal*
in Saint John. Having heard rumours of a country lane near
Moncton where automobiles rolled *up*hill, Trueman set off in a
Ford roadster with his colleagues John Bruce and Jack Brayley to
try to find it. The rest, as they say, is a multi-million dollar
tourist attraction. As a humorist, Trueman's wit is crisp and clear
with a style that is very much in the Leacock tradition.

FROM *Life's Odd Moments*

Welcome, Neighbour!

As I am a very friendly person, I always like to make new neighbours feel
welcome as soon as they arrive. Strangers appreciate somebody
showing an interest in them.

When the Fiswells moved in next door last week I was right there,
smiling and nodding repeatedly at them from my veranda as they directed
the furniture movers. They just stared back; they still felt like strangers, you
see.

After supper I saw Mr. Fiswell lying back in a lawn chair with his eyes
shut. He seemed exhausted. I walked right over and said, "Having a little
nap?" He looked startled, and said yes, he was.

The trick in making friends, you see, is always to ask something that calls for a yes answer. It starts everything off on an agreeable note.

Bright and early next morning I saw Mr. Fiswell through his open bathroom window. "Having a shave?" I asked, smiling. He seemed to be taken aback, and said yes, he was. I couldn't blame him for jumping; he wouldn't find such friendliness everywhere.

Taking every opportunity to make him feel at home, I asked him in the next few days:

"Doing some reading?"

"Washing the car?"

"Watering the garden?"

"Mowing the lawn?"

"Putting up the clothesline?"

"Eating an apple?"

"Thinking about something?"

"Not feeling so well?"

He said yes in every case, of course, but he seemed the kind who has a hard time making friends. In fact, he talked less and less. I think he had a problem on his mind.

When I passed the Fiswells' kitchen window on the fourth day, they seemed to be having quite a fracas. Mr. Fiswell was shouting, "I've had all I can stand of it, I tell you—it's worse than Chinese water torture."

To pour oil on the troubled waters, I looked in and said, smiling, "Having a friendly little argument?"

Mr. Fiswell wheeled around, wild-eyed, and said rather tensely, with his lower teeth showing, "Why, no—we're rehearsing for a play. Do you want to buy a ticket, or have you seen it all?"

"Why, certainly, thank you," I said. "I'll take one."

Oddly enough, Mr. Fiswell didn't bring me the ticket. I suppose he got so preoccupied with all the work of moving again yesterday—they couldn't have been satisfied with the house—that he completely forgot it.

Well, I see a furniture truck has just finished moving the McCullochs in—they're the new tenants—and there's a man out front, who must be

Mr. McCulloch, raking the leaves. I must hurry right out and ask him if he's raking the leaves.

Fireman, Save That Cup!

Well, has our fire brigade ever been having fun competing for the J.W.F. Brownswatt, MP, District Trophy!

"My silver cup," Mr. Brownswatt said proudly, "is designed to stimulate friendly rivalry between the Millvale and Grasstown volunteer departments. Whichever arrives first at more fires this year will be the winner. And I trust that the property owners who benefit will remember their gratitude to me next election."

The MP's idea was sure a smart one. The friendly rivalry has increased like a house afire. A good illustration was the blaze last week in the old Barker dump, five miles from here.

Boy, was *that* a close one! Only by the merest stroke of good luck did we Millvale fellows escape a humiliating defeat.

It just happened that our deputy sub-chief, Dan Polker, sprinting down the highway to meet our fire truck, saw the Grasstown truck roaring up in the lead. Dan had the presence of mind to grab a pitchfork and pose as a farmer, directing them down the wrong road, or they'd have beaten us to it.

Due to the fact that our own truck broke down a moment later, a Grasstown undercover agent having put sand in the carburetor, we didn't get to the fire either.

But at least we'd earned a tie (one point); those Grasstown sneaks hadn't humbled us. In appreciation we unanimously elected good old Dan a full sub-chief. We heard later the dump burned up. The Barkers should have been more careful about it anyway.

Dan was the hero of another fire the very next day. When the Mercer sawdust pile started going up, our sub-chief acted in a flash. He phoned his cousin, near the mill, and offered the kids a quarter to stand out in the road and tell the Grasstown brigade the fire was already out.

This enabled us to pass them standing still—and you should have seen their faces when we doused them with high-velocity vapour spray! Unfortunately the next minute our front tires blew—I *knew* there was something suspicious about the "new county inspector" who visited our fire station the night before—but we Millvale boys aren't the kind to give in easily. We hoisted the truck across the road just in time to catch the Grasstown truck headlong. They won't soon forget the drenching they took from our hoses before they had a chance to regain their senses!

Altogether it was a wonderful day, and we elected Dan permanent chief. Oh yes—the sawdust pile. It burned up. It was no good anyway.

For some reason, the ratepayers of Millvale and Grasstown have since held an emergency meeting and decided to amalgamate the two brigades immediately. Mr. Brownswatt has announced he will offer his trophy instead for the prettiest garden in the county, and hopes the householders will remember their gratitude to him at an appropriate time.

Personally I think they're making a great mistake; they're taking away the healthy competitive spirit that's made our brigades what they are. Chief Dan Polker feels it's all a jealous move by Grasstown to prevent us from winning the cup.

"It would serve the property owners right," he says, "if we refused to put out any more of their old fires."

How We Made Mr. McQuill's Christmas Merrier

"Please tell me," said Inspector Hawkloft quietly, "any possible clues you can suggest concerning what happened to Sylvester J. McQuill."

Well (I told him), I don't imagine I can help you much, but here goes:

I always like to see people get enjoyment out of Christmas cards. That was one thing that stood out about Sylvester McQuill. He just *loved* Christmas cards! He'd start shopping for them in October, badgering Mr. Crumley the stationery store manager to get him something distinctive, something nobody else would be sending out.

"Yes," said Inspector Hawkloft, quietly making notes. "Please go on."

It was (I went on) two years ago that I first called at his boarding house on Christmas Eve. I shook hands with Mr. McQuill warmly and wished him a Merry Christmas.

But he shook his head. "You can't expect me to feel happy this Christmas," he said. "People don't like me."

He just brooded and wouldn't explain. But later his kindly old landlady, Mrs. Peabody, confided to me his bitter secret—he'd sent out eighty-nine cards and got back only seventy-three!

"Mr. McQuill refused to eat his supper," she said in great distress. "He just sat by the Christmas tree counting his cards over and over, trying to figure out who hadn't sent him any and why they should be mad at him. He's terribly angry with the postman for not bringing more, and simply furious with Mr. Crumley because two of the greetings he got were the same as he sent out—the 'Winter Hackmatack Forest' card."

Inspector Hawkloft broke in quietly, "I remember the occasion quite well. That was the Christmas Day Mr. McQuill phoned my house at six A.M. and demanded I investigate a postman who was suspected of keeping back some of his greeting cards. Please continue."

Well (I continued), on Christmas Eve the next year I took the precaution of phoning Mrs. Peabody before supper and asking her how the situation stood. The dear old soul was overjoyed! She could hardly wait for Mr. McQuill to arrive home and see all the cards—he'd got more this time than he sent out!

So I dropped in later and shook Mr. McQuill's hand warmly and wished him a Very Merry Christmas, because naturally I knew he'd feel enthusiastic about how popular he was.

But he shook his head glumly. "A lot of people are annoyed at me this Christmas," he said. "You see, I got 104 cards—but I only sent out ninety-two! What must the other twelve people be thinking of me?"

He fretted all evening. He was inconsolable. Poor Mrs. Peabody told me he was simply raging at the postman for bringing him so many cards. He was mad at Mr. Crumley too, for some reason.

Inspector Hawkloft observed quietly, "I remember the occasion quite well. That was the Christmas he woke me at five A.M. and insisted I arrest a

Mr. Crumley for false pretences because he had received six cards of the same kind Mr. Crumley sold him as exclusive—'Cherubs in a Snowfall,' I think it was. Kindly proceed."

Well (I proceeded), *this* Christmas I realized there was one thing I could do for the peace of mind of Mr. McQuill and his lovable old landlady: I could personally see that he got exactly as many cards as he sent out, *no more and no less.*

So I bought a dozen cards from Mr. Crumley—making sure, of course, they were different from the "Pixies Throwing Snowballs" card which Mr. McQuill had bought. I signed them with vague names like "Jack" and "Dick" and "Fred" and addressed them all to Mr. McQuill.

As Christmas approached, I kept in touch with Mrs. Peabody and the postman. Whenever cards for Mr. McQuill were arriving too thick and fast, she hid a few in the bookcase. Whenever they began to slump, she brought out the hidden cards and added some of the special ones I had given the postman to deliver. The idea was that Mr. McQuill would finally have an even hundred cards—the same number he had mailed.

"Yes," said Inspector Hawkloft quietly, "the case is becoming quite clear now. Please resume your story."

Well (I resumed), on Christmas Eve, which was tonight, I called in and shook Mr. McQuill's hand warmly and wished him a Joyously Merry Christmas, because I knew this time he would be delighted.

But he shook his head in despair.

"It's not such a Merry Christmas as you think," he said. "My cards are driving me crazy!"

I asked him why.

"Because," he said, "I sent out a hundred cards and I got a hundred back—but some of the people I sent to didn't send to me, and some of the people who sent to me I didn't send to, and as they just signed their first names I can't figure out who they are so I can get Mr. Crumley to open up his store and sell me enough cards to send back to them tonight, that is if I can get the postman to come and pick up the cards so they can be date-stamped before midnight—and when I *do* see

Crumley will I ever give *him* an earful, because I got *eight* 'Pixie Throwing Snowballs'—"

It was precisely at that moment (I said) when I drew out the revolver and shot him.

The *bang!* seemed strangely to echo more than once, which was explained when I noticed that dear sweet old Mrs. Peabody, across the room, also had a smoking revolver in her hand. Further, I may say, I perceived that the front window was shattered and a postman was walking down the street whistling merrily and tossing a revolver into an ash can. It was then, also, that Mr. Crumley stepped out beaming from behind the living-room drapes, pocketed a smoking revolver, and, remarking that he had just dropped in, apologized that he couldn't stay as he had to hurry home and prepare his house for "the Merriest Christmas yet."

It was not, you understand, Inspector, that any of us had anything against Mr. McQuill. It merely occurred to all of us that he would have a much happier Christmas if he didn't have the cards on his mind.

So as I said at the start, I don't think I can help you much. I really haven't the slightest idea who shot him. By the way, Inspector, how did you happen to reach the scene so quickly? It seemed no sooner did Mr. McQuill hit the floor a few moments ago than you climbed out of the hot-air vent.

"It was," Inspector Hawkloft said quietly, "pure coincidence." And, after jotting down in his notebook the words "committed by person or persons unknown," he quietly took a revolver from his pocket, blew through the chamber, sending a puff of blue smoke out the end of the barrel, replaced it in his pocket, said "A Merry Christmas to all," and strolled home with me for a cup of coffee and a sandwich.

Nancy White

Although this is a literary anthology, I thought I'd end it with a song. "Daughters of Feminists," by Canada's master troubadour Nancy White, takes us back full circle to the premise first put forward by Stephen Leacock, as presented in the Introduction: That humour lies in the gap between our aspirations and our achievements, between our dreams and our reality, between what we expect life will bring and how things actually turn out. It is from this gap, this small but profound gap, that humour—and tragedy—both spring.

Daughters of Feminists

Daughters of feminists
love to wear pink and white
short frilly dresses,
they speak of successes
with boys—
It annoys
their mom.
Daughters of feminists
won't put on jeans
or the precious construction boot
mama found cute,
ugly shoes
they refuse—
how come?

Daughters of feminists
think they'll get married
to some wealthy guy
who'll support them forever,
Daughters of feminists
don't bother voting at all,
Daughters of feminists
beg to wear lipstick
each day from the age of three,
Daughters of feminists
think that a princess
is what they are destined to be.

How do they get so girly?
How come they want a Barbie?
Why does it start so early?
Why, when we bring her up just like a fella,
Who does she idolize? Cinderella!

*Oh, honey, she's a doormat. You think when she marries that prince
he won't expect to run the entire castle? Think of all the rooms!
And he's always "on the road." And Snow White? Doing all the
housework for SEVEN GUYS in return for room and board?
This is no deal, darling. Think! Pensez!*

Daughters of feminists
bruise so easily,
Daughters of feminists hurt,
Daughters of feminists
curtsy and skip,
Daughters of feminists flirt,
They say "Please, mommy,
can I do the dishes?"

And "Let's make a pie for my brother!"
Are they sincere? Are they crazy?
Or are they just
Trying to stick it to mother?

How do they get so girly?
How come they want a Barbie?
Why does it start so early?

Daughters of feminists
love to wear pink and white
short frilly dresses
They speak of successes
with boys.

The Authors

DAVE BIDINI (1963). Writer and musician Dave Bidini published his first book in 1998, *On a Cold Road,* about what it's like to tour Canada as a rock and roll band. His other books include *Tropic of Hockey: My Search for the Game in Unlikely Places* (2000), *Baseballissimo: My Summer in the Italian Minor Leagues* (2004), *For Those About to Rock* (2004), and *The Best Game You Can Name* (2005).

ARTHUR BLACK (1943). Arthur Black was the host of CBC Radio's *Basic Black* for nineteen years. Now the host of *Weird Homes* and *Weird Wheels* on the Life Network, he is also a columnist for *FiftyPlus Magazine, The Victoria Times-Colonist,* and fifty-odd newspapers across the country. Two of his books, *Black in the Saddle Again* (1996) and *Black Ties and Tales* (2000), won the Stephen Leacock Medal.

MARSHA BOULTON (1952). Marsha Boulton is a journalist and author whose work has appeared in *Maclean's, Chatelaine,* and *Toronto Life* magazines. Her *Letters from the Country* (1995) was awarded the Stephen Leacock Medal and was followed by three more volumes. Her other works include *Just a Minute* (1994), a compendium of anecdotal Canadian history that was followed by two other volumes.

MAX BRAITHWAITE (1911–1995). Born in Nokomis, Saskatchewan, Max Braithwaite was one of Canada's most prolific freelance writers. He authored numerous books, articles, radio dramas, and screenplays. His best-known work is *Why Shoot the Teacher?* (1965), which was made into a film in 1979 and became part of a trilogy that includes *Never Sleep Three in a Bed* (1969) and *The Night We Stole the Mountie's Car* (1971), which was awarded the Stephen Leacock Medal.

CHUCK BROWN (1970). Born in Pickering, Ontario, Chuck Brown was the editor of the *Saint Croix Courier* in St. Stephen, New Brunswick, from 1997 to 2000, and is now a reporter and humour columnist with the New Brunswick *Telegraph-Journal.* An Atlantic Journalism Awards finalist in feature writing, he is also the co-author of *The Girlfriend's Guide to Football* (2001).

ROCH CARRIER (1937). Born in Sainte-Justine, Quebec, Roch Carrier's best-known work is *The Hockey Sweater* (1979), which drew on Carrier's childhood worship of Maurice Richard. This laid the foundation for Carrier's 2001 biography of the hockey player, *Our Life with the Rocket.* Other works include *Prayers of a Very Wise Child* (1991), which won the Stephen Leacock Medal, and *Prayers of a Young Man* (1999). He is currently Canada's National Librarian.

DOUGLAS COUPLAND (1961). One of Canada's most successful and best-known authors, Douglas Coupland grew up and lives in Vancouver. He is the author of *Generation X* (1991), *Microserfs* (1995), *Hey Nostradamus!* (2003), and *Eleanor Rigby* (2004), among many other novels. Coupland has also written non-fiction, including *Polaroids from the Dead* (1996), a photographic tour of Vancouver entitled *City of Glass* (2000), *Souvenir of Canada* (2002), and *Terry: The Life of Canadian Terry Fox* (2005).

IVAN E. COYOTE (1969). Ivan E. Coyote is a writer and member of the perform-ance collective Taste This, which collaborated on the award-winning book *Boys Like Her* (1998). Coyote's other books include two short story collections: *Close to Spider Man* (2000)—which won the Danuta Gleed Literary Award—and *One Man's Trash* (2002).

HERB CURTIS (1949). Born outside of Blackville, New Brunswick, on the Miramichi River, Herb Curtis is the author of many novels, including *The Americans Are Coming* (1989), *The Last Tasmanian* (1991), *The Lone Angler* (1993), and *The Silent Partner* (1996). Curtis was shortlisted for the Stephen Leacock Medal for his collection of short stories, *Luther Cohern's Salmon Camp Chronicles* (1999).

ROBERTSON DAVIES (1913–1995). Robertson Davies was one of Canada's most distinguished men of letters. As a novelist, he gained worldwide fame for his three trilogies: *The Salterton Trilogy, The Deptford Trilogy,* and *The Cornish Trilogy.* Davies was the first Canadian to be made an Honorary Member of the American Academy of Arts and Letters, and he received honorary degrees from twenty-six American, Canadian, and British universities.

BOB EDWARDS (1864–1922). Bob Edwards was born in Edinburgh, Scotland, and at the age of thirty-three arrived in Wetaskiwin, Alberta, to launch his newspaper, the *Free Lance.* From 1902 to 1922, he was the editor of the *Calgary Eye Opener,* earning him a reputation as one of Canada's most distinctive and irrepressible journalists. Often compared to Stephen Leacock and Mark Twain, his writings can be found in the collection *Irresponsible Freaks, Highball Guzzlers & Unabashed Grafters* (2004), as edited by James Martin, and in the recently reissued biography *Eye Opener Bob* by Grant MacEwan.

M.A.C. FARRANT (1947). Born in Sydney, Australia, and raised in Cordova Bay on Vancouver Island, M.A.C. Farrant is the author of many critically acclaimed books, among them *Sick Pigeon* (1991), which was shortlisted for the Commonwealth Writers Prize and the Ethel Wilson Fiction Prize; *Raw Material* (1993); *Girls Around the House* (1999); *Darwin Alone in the Universe* (2003); and a popular memoir, *My Turquoise Years* (2004), which was serialized on CBC Radio.

IAN FERGUSON (1959). Ian Ferguson is an award-winning playwright and humorist. In 2001, he co-authored *How to Be a Canadian* with his brother Will, which was shortlisted for the Stephen Leacock Medal and won the CBA Libris Award for best non-fiction book of the year. His memoir, *Village of the Small Houses*, was awarded the Stephen Leacock Medal in 2004.

WILL FERGUSON (1964). Will Ferguson is one of Canada's best-selling authors, with work that is published in twenty-six languages around the world. A two-time winner of the Leacock Medal for Humour—first for his novel *Happiness*™ (2001) and again for *Beauty Tips from Moose Jaw* (2004)—his most recent book is *Hitching Rides with Buddha: A Journey Across Japan* (2005).

JACQUES FERRON (1921–1985). Born in Louiseville, Quebec, Jacques Ferron was a playwright, novelist, essayist, and co-founder of the absurdist Rhinoceros Party. He was the author of *Tales from the Uncertain Country* (1972), *The Saint-Elias* (1975), and *Wild Roses* (1976), among others, and he was the winner of the Governor General's Award for Literature, the Prix France-Quebec, the Prix Duvernay, and the Prix David.

MAVIS GALLANT (1922). Mavis Gallant is one of the few Canadian authors whose works regularly appear in *The New Yorker*—many of her stories have appeared there first, and have subsequently been brought together in collections such as *Home Truths: Selected Canadian Stories* (1981), which was awarded the Governor General's Award for Literature. Other collections include *The Other Paris* (1956) and *The End of the World and Other Stories* (1974), and the novels *Green Water, Green Sky* (1969) and *A Fairly Good Time* (1970).

ZSUZSI GARTNER (1960). An award-winning journalist and fiction writer, Zsuzsi Gartner's collection of short fiction *All the Anxious Girls on Earth* (1999) was a finalist for the Danuta Gleed Award and the Ethel Wilson Fiction Prize. She has been nominated for numerous Western and National Magazine Awards for her fiction and non-fiction, most recently winning a Gold Award for feature writing in 2003.

CHARLES GORDON (1940). The author of five books, including *At the Cottage* (1989), *The Canada Trip* (1997), and *The Grim Pig* (2001), Charles Gordon has written for *National Lampoon, Canadian Forum, Cottage Life, Maclean's,* and, for thirty years, the *Ottawa Citizen.* He has won three National Magazine Awards and has been shortlisted three times for the Stephen Leacock Medal.

RAY GUY (1939). Journalist, playwright, and actor, Ray Guy was born in Come By Chance, Newfoundland, and began his career as a reporter at the St. John's *Evening Telegram.* Four collections of his columns have been published: *You May Know Them as Sea Urchins, Ma'am* (1975); *That Far Greater Bay* (1976), which was awarded the Stephen Leacock Medal; *Beneficial Vapors* (1981); and *Ray Guy's Best* (1987).

PAUL HIEBERT (1892–1987). Comedic poet Paul Hiebert was born in Pilot Mound, Manitoba, and was a professor of chemistry at the University of Manitoba for many years. His first book, *Sarah Binks* (1947), was awarded the Stephen Leacock Medal and was followed by a sequel, *Willows Revisited* (1967), and other comedic works.

DONALD JACK (1924–2003). Author Donald Jack was born in England and served in the Royal Air Force in the Second World War before coming to Canada in 1951. Known for his film and television scripts, and his plays, he is most widely remembered for *The Bandy Papers,* a series of comic novels that have gained three Stephen Leacock Awards.

THOMAS KING (1943). Thomas King is an award-winning novelist, short story writer, scriptwriter, and photographer. His first novel, *Medicine River* (1989), was shortlisted for the Commonwealth Writers Prize and was made into a CBC television movie. King's other novels and short story collections include *One Good Story, That One* (1993), *Green Grass, Running Water* (1993), *Truth and Bright Water* (1999), and *A Short History of Indians in Canada* (2005). In 2003, he received the National Aboriginal Achievement Award.

W.P. KINSELLA (1935). W.P. Kinsella was born in Edmonton, Alberta, and now lives in British Columbia. In 1977, he published his first collection of stories about the Ermineskin Reserve, *Dance Me Outside,* and has since published many other collections, including *Born Indian* (1981) and *The Fencepost Chronicles* (1986), which won the Stephen Leacock Medal. His novel *Shoeless Joe* (1982) was the basis for the Hollywood movie *Field of Dreams* and was awarded the Houghton Mifflin Literary Fellowship.

JACK KNOX (1958). A full-time news columnist for the *Victoria Times Colonist,* Jack Knox lives on Vancouver Island. A finalist for the 2005 Jack Webster Award for Feature Writing, his weekly humour piece, "Slightly Skewed," appears regularly in a variety of Canadian newspapers.

DANY LAFERRIÈRE (1953). Dany Laferrière was born in Port-au-Prince, Haiti, and went into exile in Canada in 1978. His first novel, *How to Make Love to a Negro* (1985), was published in English in 1987 and was made into a feature film. His other books include *Eroshima* (1991), *An Aroma of Coffee* (1993), *Dining with the Dictator* (1994), and *Why Must a Black Writer Write About Sex?* (1997).

GARY LAUTENS (1928–1992). Born in Thunder Bay, Ontario, Gary Lautens published four books in his lifetime, including *Take My Family … Please!* (1980) and *No Sex Please … We're Married* (1983), both of which were awarded the Stephen Leacock Medal. Two collections of his columns have been published posthumously: *Peace, Mrs. Packard and the Meaning of Life* (1993) and *The Best of Gary Lautens* (1995).

STEPHEN LEACOCK (1869–1944). Stephen Leacock is remembered as a humorist and the author of close to forty books of nonsense, starting with *Literary Lapses* (1910) and including *Nonsense Novels* (1911), *Sunshine Sketches of a Little Town* (1912), *Behind the Beyond* (1916), and *My Remarkable Uncle* (1942). In 1946, the Leacock Society decided to present a silver medal annually to the best book of humour published in Canada, and it has since become one of the world's most outstanding literary awards.

ANTONINE MAILLET (1929). Born in the Acadian community of Boutouche, New Brunswick, Antonine Maillet is the author of several books, including *Les Cordes-de-Bois* (1977); *The Tale of Don L'Orignal* (1972), which won the Governor General's Award; *Pelagie-la-Charrette* (1979), which won France's prestigious Prix Goncourt; and *La Sagouine* (1979), which has become a defining work in Acadian identity.

JAMES MARTIN (1970). From 1997 to 2002, James Martin wrote two hundred and eighty-three "Mr. Smutty" columns for Calgary's *Fast Forward Weekly*. He is the editor of *Irresponsible Freaks, Highball Guzzlers & Unabashed Grafters: A Bob Edwards Chrestomathy* (2004) and a non-practising librarian. Martin lives in Montreal, where he is collaborating on a screenplay that is/isn't entitled *Rule Beertonia.*

STUART McLEAN (1948). Host of CBC Radio's The Vinyl Cafe, Stuart McLean is an author and professor of broadcast journalism. His *Vinyl Cafe Unplugged* (2000) and *Home from the Vinyl Cafe* (1998) both won the Stephen Leacock Medal. *Welcome Home: Travels in Smalltown Canada* (1992) won the Canadian Authors Association Award for Non-fiction, and he has also written *Stories from the Vinyl Cafe* (1995) and *The Morningside World of Stuart McLean* (1989).

RICHARD J. NEEDHAM (1912–1996). Raised in India, Ireland, and England, Richard Needham was a celebrated humour columnist for *The Globe and Mail* for many years. He is the author of *Needham's Inferno* (1966), which won the Stephen Leacock Medal, and the equally funny and ribald follow-up, *The Garden of Needham* (1968).

DAN NEEDLES (1951). Columnist and playwright Dan Needles is the creator of the Wingfield Farm plays—full-length stage comedies that have filled theatres across North America. He wrote his first play, *Letter from Wingfield Farm,* in 1985, followed by *Wingfield's Progress* (1987), *Wingfield's Folly* (1990), *Wingfield Unbound* (1997), *Wingfield on Ice* (2001), and *Wingfield's Inferno* (2005). He won the Stephen Leacock Medal for *With Axe and Flask* (2002).

ERIC NICOL (1919). Eric Nicol is the author of more than thirty-five books, including *Say, Uncle: A Completely Uncalled-for History of the U.S.* (1961), *A Scar Is Born* (1968), *Anything for a Laugh: Memoirs* (1998), and *Old Is In: A Guide for Aging Boomers* (2004). Three of Nicol's books were awarded the Stephen Leacock Medal, and he was the first recipient of the B.C. Gas Lifetime Achievement Award for outstanding contribution to the literary arts in 1995.

BRIAN O'CONNELL (1916–1991). Brian O'Connell worked as a reporter, editor, and public relations director at St. Francis Xavier University. He was a columnist for the *Antigonish Casket* for twenty-five years and also wrote for the *Halifax Chronicle.* Brian O'Connell was the first news director for radio station CFRA in Ottawa, and is the author of the books *Magnets and Meatloaf* and *Say, Scribe.*

NOREEN OLSON (1935). Columnist for the *Didsbury Review* since 1980, Noreen Olson lives on a farm in southern Alberta and has self-published six very successful collections of her award-winning columns. She is the author of *The School Bus Doesn't Stop Here Any More* (2004), a look at life "on a rural route" that has been praised for its honesty and warm humour.

PATRICIA PEARSON (1964). Journalist and fiction writer Patricia Pearson has won two National Magazine Awards, a National Author's Award, and the Arthur Ellis Award for best true crime book for *When She Was Bad* (1997). Her first novel, *Playing House* (2003), was shortlisted for the Stephen Leacock Medal, and her other works include the novel *Believe Me* (2005) and a collection of essays, *Area Woman Blows Gasket* (2005).

LAURENCE J. PETER (1919–1990). With wide experience as a teacher, school psychologist, prison instructor, and university professor, Vancouver-born Laurence J. Peter was the celebrated author of several books, including *Prescriptive Teaching* (1965), *The Peter Principle* (1969), which coined a term that has since entered the public lexicon, and *Peter's Almanac* (1982).

JOHN PORTEOUS (1932–1995). Columnist and journalist John Porteous was also the voice of Miramichi pulp-cutter Ernie Freshet, a character who appeared regularly on New Brunswick radio telling stories in a staunch local dialect. Porteous wrote several radio plays for CBC and was the author of three humour collections: *They Choke Herring, Don't They?* (1980), *My Lobster Is Double Parked* (1981), and *Here's Your Chainsaw ... What's Your Hurry?* (1984).

JACQUES POULIN (1937). Jacques Poulin is the author of many novels, including *Volkswagen Blues* (1984), *Autumn Rounds* (1993), and *Wild Cat* (1998). He won the Governor General's Award for *Les grandes marées* in 1978, and in 2001 was presented with the Molson Prize by The Canada Council for the Arts.

PAUL QUARRINGTON (1953). Paul Quarrington is the author of many novels, including the highly acclaimed *Whale Music* (1989), which received the Governor General's Award for Fiction and was turned into a feature film. His 1989 work, *King Leary,* was awarded the Stephen Leacock Medal, and *Galveston* (2004) was shortlisted for The Giller Prize.

DAVID RAKOFF (1966). David Rakoff was born in Toronto and lives in New York City. He is a regular contributor to *Outside* and *The New York Times Magazine,* and has written for *GQ* and *Harper's Bazaar*. *Fraud* (2001) is Rakoff's first collection of autobiographical essays, followed by *Don't Get Too Comfortable* (2005).

BILL RICHARDSON (1955). Born in Winnipeg, Bill Richardson is a CBC Radio host and former children's librarian. He is the author of several books, including *Bachelor*

Brothers' Bed and Breakfast (1993), which was awarded the Stephen Leacock Medal; *Scorned & Beloved* (1997); *Oddball @ Large* (1998); *After Hamelin* (2000); and *Waiting for Gertrude* (2001), which was shortlisted for the Stephen Leacock Medal.

MORDECAI RICHLER (1931–2001). Mordecai Richler was born in Montreal, Quebec. His novels include *The Apprenticeship of Duddy Kravitz* (1969), *St. Urbain's Horseman* (1971), *Solomon Gursky Was Here* (1989), and *Barney's Version* (1997). Among his short story and essay collections are *The Street* (1969) and *Home Sweet Home: My Canadian Album* (1984). Richler is also the author of the children's book *Jacob Two-Two Meets the Hooded Fang* (1975), and among his many honours are two Governor General's Literary Awards, the Commonwealth Writers Prize, the Stephen Leacock Medal, and The Giller Prize.

ERIKA RITTER (1948). Born in Regina, Saskatchewan, Erika Ritter lives mainly in Toronto where she works as a playwright, radio dramatist, novelist, humorist, short fiction writer, and host of CBC Radio's *Ontario Morning*. Her published works include a number of plays, two collections of humour, *Urban Scrawl* (1984) and *Ritter in Residence* (1987), a novel entitled *The Hidden Life of Humans* (1997), and *The Great Big Book of Guys* (2004).

ROBERT W. SERVICE (1874–1958). Robert Service was a war correspondent for the *Toronto Star* and served as an intelligence officer in the Canadian Army in World War I. In 1907, Service published his first collection of poetry, *Songs of a Sourdough*, published in the United States as *The Spell of the Yukon, and Other Verses*. In 1909, Service published *Ballads of a Cheechako* and *The Trail of 98*, a novel about the Gold Rush.

SANDRA SHAMAS (1957). Sandra Shamas is best known for *A Trilogy of Performances* (1997), a collection of her three smash hit shows: *My Boyfriend's Back and There's Gonna Be Laundry, The Cycle Continues,* and *Wedding Bell Hell.* This collection was shortlisted for the Governor General's Award and the Stephen Leacock Medal, and in 2002 she published *Wit's End.*

ANTANAS SILEIKA (1953). Artistic Director of the Humber School for Writers, Antanas Sileika is a Toronto broadcaster and journalist, and author of *Dinner at the End of the World* (1994) and *Buying on Time* (1997), which was shortlisted for the Toronto Book Award and the Stephen Leacock Medal. In 2004, he published his novel *Woman in Bronze.*

JOEY SLINGER (1943). Toronto columnist Joey Slinger is the author of *No Axe Too Small to Grind* (1985), which won the Stephen Leacock Medal, *If It's a Jungle Out There, Why Do I Have to Mow the Lawn?* (1992), *Down and Dirty Birding* (1996), and *Punch Line* (2005).

MARIKO TAMAKI (1975). Mariko Tamaki is a Toronto writer and performer, and has appeared on CBC Radio's *This Morning,* at the Buddies in Bad Times Hysteria

Festival, and, more recently, at Calgary's Folkfest. Her first novel, *Cover Me* (2000), was followed by a short fiction collection, *True Lies: The Book of Bad Advice* (2002). Tamaki's second collection of short stories, *Fake I.D.,* was published in 2005.

WILLIAM J. THOMAS (1946). A nationally syndicated humour columnist, William J. Thomas lives on Sunset Bay in Wainfleet, Ontario. He is the author of many books, including *Guys: Not Real Bright and Damn Proud of It!* (1996), *The Dog Rules (Damn Near Everything!)* (2000), and *Never Hitchhike on the Road Less Travelled* (2002).

MIRIAM TOEWS (1964). Miriam Toews is the author of three novels: *Summer of My Amazing Luck* (1996), which was nominated for the Stephen Leacock Medal and won the John Hirsch Award; *A Boy of Good Breeding* (1998), which was named the McNally Robinson Book of the Year; and *A Complicated Kindness* (2004), winner of the Governor General's Award for Fiction and finalist for The Giller Prize.

MORLEY TORGOV (1927). Morley Torgov is the author of the Leacock-winning *A Good Place to Come From* (1974) as well as *The Abramsky Variations* (1977), *St. Farb's Day* (1990), *The Outside Chance of Maximilian Glick* (1982)—which also won the Stephen Leacock Medal—*The War to End All Wars* (1998), and *Stickler and Me* (2002). His work has been adapted to the stage and is performed regularly across North America.

STUART TRUEMAN (1911–1995). Newspaper man and author Stuart Trueman was born in Saint John, New Brunswick. Many of his pieces were published in Canadian and American magazines, including *The Saturday Evening Post* and *The Atlantic Advocate*. In 1969, his third book, *You're Only as Old as You Act* (1968), won the Stephen Leacock Medal, and in 1984 he published *Life's Odd Moments*.

NANCY WHITE (1944). Singer-songwriter Nancy White is best known for the topical songs she wrote for CBC Radio's *Sunday Morning* and for her CDs *Momnipotent: Songs for Weary Parents* (1990), *Pumping Irony* (1993), *Gaelic Envy* (1998), and *Stickers on Fruit* (2002). She is a co-author of the musical *Anne and Gilbert,* and she gives concerts.

Acknowledgments

I would like to thank the following people who were a great help when it came to compiling this anthology. They recommended many books and made excellent suggestions on authors to include and passages to consider: Michael Schellenberg, Sheila Fischman, Carolyn Swayze, Charles Gordon, Noreen Olson, Kirsten Olson, Don Denton, Jackie Ford, Mona Lutfy, Kirsten Van Ritzen, and especially my mom, Lorna Bell, who showed up at the house with boxes full of Canadian humour. It was a homecoming of sorts, for many of the books were ones I had grown up with, books by Max Braithwaite, Morley Torgov, Robertson Davies, Richard J. Needham, and many, many more. And finally, I would like to express my deep thanks and appreciation to everyone at Penguin Canada who helped put this book together: Andrea Crozier, Kalpna Patel, Beth McAuley, Christine Gambin, Janette Lush, Mary Opper, and Tracy Bordian. Well done!

MOONWALK

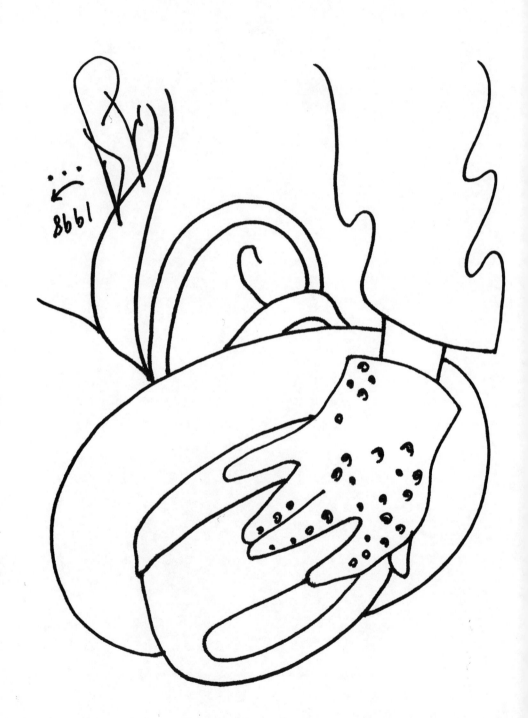

MOONWALK

By *Michael Jackson*

Harmony Books
New York

Library of Congress Cataloging-in-Publication Data
Jackson, Michael, 1958–2009
Moonwalk.
1. Jackson, Michael, 1958–2009.   2. Rock musicians—United States—Biography.
I. Title.
ML420.J175A3 1988 784.5'400924[B] 88-384
ISBN 978-0-307-71698-9

This book is dedicated to
F R E D   A S T A I R E

Michael Jackson was not an artist who comes along once in a decade, a generation, or a lifetime. He was an artist who comes along only once, period. I had the good fortune of meeting him when he was nine years old. Even then there was something so compelling about him that, frankly, I did not know what to make of it. How could this kid have that effect on me? It was an effect so potent that I would immediately discard my misgivings about being in business with "kid acts," and rush to create an environment for Michael and his brothers that would nurture and expand their talent.

Even then he had a knowingness about him. He knew he was special. He could dance and sing and act like anybody—he just wanted to do it better.

He was driven by his hunger to learn, to constantly top himself, to be the best. He was the consummate student. He studied the greats and became greater. He raised the bar and then BROKE the bar. His talent and creativity thrust him AND entertainment into the stratosphere.

Moonwalk was the first time he told his story in his own words, reflecting on his life, how he thought, how he felt about things. This book is a unique opportunity to get to know the real genius of Michael and how this young kid from Gary,

Indiana, propelled himself to become the biggest star in the world.

Moonwalk reveals so much of Michael's true self, but you have to read between the lines to really understand what he was all about. I must say, though, that he did have two personalities. Offstage he was shy, soft-spoken, and childlike. But when he took that stage in front of his screaming fans, he turned into another personality; a master, a "take no prisoners" showman. For him it was kill or be killed.

Besides being a creative master of writing, singing, producing, acting, and staging, he was also a thinker. And in order to protect himself, sometimes he created mental mechanisms—personalities—onstage, offstage, in boardrooms, in his deal making, business plans, and self-promotion. Brilliant? Right! Genius? Damn right. He made it all happen. His personality may have been contradictory, but his core was always pure, beautiful, and loving.

When Michael and his brothers Jackie, Jermaine, Tito, and Marlon auditioned for me at Motown in Detroit that July day in 1968, they blew us all away with their incredible talent. Little Michael's performance was way beyond his years. After singing and dancing like James Brown and Jackie Wilson, he sang a Smokey Robinson song called "Who's Loving You" with the sadness and passion of a man who had been living with the blues and heartbreak his whole life. I couldn't believe it. As great as Smokey sang it, Michael was better. I told Smokey, "Hey, man, I think he gotcha on that one." Smokey said, "Me

too." When Michael and his brothers performed it on the *Ed Sullivan Show*, there was no doubt that the rest of the world agreed.

I moved them out to California and they became part of the Gordy and Motown families. Those were great times— we swam, we joked, we played games, we rehearsed. I put together a songwriting team, and we came up with four hit records for them: "I Want You Back," "ABC," "The Love You Save," and "I'll Be There." The Jackson 5 was the only group in history to ever have their first four singles go to number one. We were thrilled—especially Michael. We had broken through a major barrier. For Michael, it was the inspiration to break all the rest. And he did.

We cast Michael with Diana Ross in a movie we produced called *The Wiz* and there he met legendary producer Quincy Jones. That collaboration yielded the greatest-selling album of all time, *Thriller*, along with *Off the Wall* and *Bad*.

By 1983 the Jacksons were no longer at Motown. However, the brothers reunited to perform on the television special *Motown 25: Yesterday, Today, Forever*. After a high-powered, dazzling medley of their songs, Michael took the stage alone and proceeded to make pop history. From the first beat of "Billie Jean" and the toss of his hat, I was mesmerized. But when he did his iconic moonwalk, I was shocked. It was magic. He soared into orbit . . . and never came down.

Though it ended way too soon, Michael's life was beautiful. Sure there were some sad times and maybe some question-

able decisions on his part, but Michael Jackson accomplished everything he dreamed of. Even at nine years old, his passion was to be the greatest entertainer in the world. He was willing to work hard and do whatever it took to become what he indeed was—the undisputed "King of Pop" the world over.

What kid wouldn't give his right arm to fulfill his wildest childhood dreams? Michael loved it all—every moment onstage, every moment in rehearsal. He loved creating what had never been done before. He loved giving all he had to his music and all he had to his fans.

I mean, Michael was awesome! Totally in charge. In fact the more I think and talk about Michael Jackson, the more I feel the "King of Pop" was not big enough for him. I think he was simply "The Greatest Entertainer That Ever Lived."

Berry Gordy
Founder of Motown
2009

What can one say about Michael Jackson? He is one of the world's most acclaimed entertainers, an innovative and exciting songwriter whose dancing seems to defy gravity and has been heralded by the likes of Fred Astaire and Gene Kelly.

His public is perhaps unaware of the extent of his dedication to his craft. Restless, seldom satisfied, he is a perfectionist who is constantly challenging himself.

To many people Michael Jackson seems an elusive personality, but to those who work with him, he is not. This talented artist is a sensitive man, warm, funny, and full of insight. Michael's book, *Moonwalk*, provides a startling glimpse of the artist at work and the artist in reflection.

—*Jacqueline Kennedy Onassis*

When I want to discover something, I begin by reading up everything that has been done along that line in the past —that's what all the books in the library are for. I see what has been accomplished at great labor and expense in the past. I gather the data of many thousands of experiments as a starting point and then I make thousands more. The three essentials to achieve anything worthwhile are, first, hard work; second, stick-to-it-iveness; third, common sense.

—Thomas Edison

When the real music comes to me—the music of the spheres, the music that surpasseth understanding—that has nothing to do with me 'cause I'm just the channel. The only joy for me is for it to be given to me and transcribe it. Like a medium. Those moments are what I live for.

—John Lennon

MOONWALK

CHAPTER

ONE

JUST KIDS
WITH A DREAM

've always wanted to be able to tell stories, you know, stories that came from my soul. I'd like to sit by a fire and tell people stories—make them see pictures, make them cry and laugh, take them *anywhere* emotionally with something as deceptively simple as words. I'd like to tell tales to move their souls and transform them. I've always wanted to be able to do that. Imagine how the great writers must feel, knowing they have that power. I sometimes feel I *could* do it. It's something I'd like to develop. In a way, songwriting uses the same skills, creates the emotional highs and lows, but the story is a sketch. It's quicksilver. There are very few books written on the art of storytelling, how to grip listeners, how to get

a group of people together and amuse them. No costumes, no makeup, no nothing, just you and your voice, and your powerful ability to take them anywhere, to transform their lives, if only for minutes.

As I begin to tell my story, I want to repeat what I usually say to people when they ask me about my earliest days with the Jackson 5: I was so little when we began to work on our music that I really don't remember much about it. Most people have the luxury of careers that start when they're old enough to know exactly what they're doing and why, but, of course, that wasn't true of me. They remember everything that happened to them, but I was only five years old. When you're a show business child, you really don't have the maturity to understand a great deal of what is going on around you. People make a lot of decisions concerning your life when you're out of the room. So here's what I remember. I remember singing at the top of my voice and dancing with real joy and working too hard for a child. Of course, there are many details I don't remember at all. I do remember the Jackson 5 really taking off when I was only eight or nine.

I was born in Gary, Indiana, on a late summer night in 1958, the seventh of my parents' nine children. My father, Joe Jackson, was born in Arkansas, and in 1949 he married my mother, Katherine Scruse, whose people came from

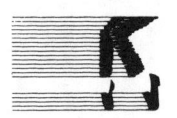

Imagine singing and dancing at this age.

Alabama. My sister Maureen was born the following year and had the tough job of being the oldest. Jackie, Tito, Jermaine, LaToya, and Marlon were all next in line. Randy and Janet came after me.

A part of my earliest memories is my father's job working in the steel mill. It was tough, mind-numbing work and he played music for escape. At the same time, my mother was working in a department store. Because of my father, and because of my mother's own love of music, we heard it all the time at home. My father and his brother had a group called the Falcons who were the local R&B band. My father played the guitar, as did his brother. They would do some of the great early rock 'n' roll and blues songs by Chuck Berry, Little Richard, Otis Redding, you name it. All those styles were amazing and each had an influence on Joe and on us, although we were too young to know it at the time. The Falcons practiced in the living room of our house in Gary, so I was raised on R&B. Since we were nine kids and my father's brother had eight of his own, our combined numbers made for a huge family. Music was what we did for entertainment and those times helped keep us together and kind of encouraged my father to be a family-oriented man. The Jackson 5 were born out of this tradition—we later became the Jacksons —and because of this training and musical tradition, I

moved out on my own and established a sound that is mine.

I remember my childhood as mostly work, even though I *loved* to sing. I wasn't *forced* into this business by stage parents the way Judy Garland was. I did it because I enjoyed it and because it was as natural to me as drawing a breath and exhaling it. I did it because I was *compelled* to do it, not by parents or family, but by my own inner life in the world of music.

There were times, let me make that clear, when I'd come home from school and I'd only have time to put my books down and get ready for the studio. Once there, I'd sing until late at night, until it was past my bedtime, really. There was a park across the street from the Motown studio, and I can remember looking at those kids playing games. I'd just stare at them in wonder—I couldn't imagine such freedom, such a carefree life—and wish more than anything that I had that kind of freedom, that I could walk away and be like them. So there were sad moments in my childhood. It's true for any child star. Elizabeth Taylor told me she felt the same way. When you're young and you're working, the world can seem awfully unfair. I wasn't forced to be little Michael the lead singer—I did it and I loved it—but it was hard work. If we were doing an album, for example, we'd go off to the studio after school

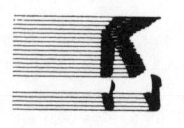

My father and my mother.

and I might or might not get a snack. Sometimes there just wasn't time. I'd come home, exhausted, and it'd be eleven or twelve and past time to go to bed.

So I very much identify with anyone who worked as a child. I know how they struggled, I know what they sacrificed. I also know what they learned. I've learned that it becomes more of a challenge as one gets older. I feel old for some reason. I really feel like an old soul, someone who's seen a lot and experienced a lot. Because of all the years I've clocked in, it's hard for me to accept that I am only twenty-nine. I've been in the business for twenty-four years. Sometimes I feel like I should be near the end of my life, turning eighty, with people patting me on the back. That's what comes from starting so young.

When I first performed with my brothers, we were known as the Jacksons. We would later become the Jackson 5. Still later, after we left Motown, we would reclaim the Jacksons name again.

Every one of my albums or the group's albums has been dedicated to our mother, Katherine Jackson, since we took over our own careers and began to produce our own music. My first memories are of her holding me and singing songs like "You Are My Sunshine" and "Cotton Fields." She sang to me and to my brothers and sisters often. Even though she had lived in Indiana for some

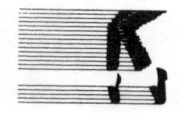

time, my mother grew up in Alabama, and in that part of the country it was just as common for black people to be raised with country and western music on the radio as it was for them to hear spirituals in church. She likes Willie Nelson to this day. She has always had a beautiful voice and I suppose I got my singing ability from my mother and, of course, from God.

Mom played the clarinet and the piano, which she taught my oldest sister, Maureen, whom we call Rebbie, to play, just as she'd teach my other older sister, LaToya. My mother knew, from an early age, that she would never perform the music she loved in front of others, not because she didn't have the talent and the ability, but because she was crippled by polio as a child. She got over the disease, but not without a permanent limp in her walk. She had to miss a great deal of school as a child, but she told us that she was lucky to recover at a time when many died from the disease. I remember how important it was to her that we got the sugar-cube vaccine. She even made us miss a youth club show one Saturday afternoon—*that's* how important it was in our family.

My mother knew her polio was not a curse but a test that God gave her to triumph over, and she instilled in me a love of Him that I will always have. She taught me that my talent for singing and dancing was as much God's

work as a beautiful sunset or a storm that left snow for children to play in. Despite all the time we spent rehearsing and traveling, Mom would find time to take me to the Kingdom Hall of the Jehovah's Witnesses, usually with Rebbie and LaToya.

Years later, after we had left Gary, we performed on "The Ed Sullivan Show," the live Sunday night variety show where America first saw the Beatles, Elvis, and Sly and the Family Stone. After the show, Mr. Sullivan complimented and thanked each of us; but I was thinking about what he had said to me *before* the show. I had been wandering around backstage, like the kid in the Pepsi commercial, and ran into Mr. Sullivan. He seemed glad to see me and shook my hand, but before he let it go he had a special message for me. It was 1970, a year when some of the best people in rock were losing their lives to drugs and alcohol. An older, wiser generation in show business was unprepared to lose its very young. Some people had already said that I reminded them of Frankie Lymon, a great young singer of the 1950s who lost his life that way. Ed Sullivan may have been thinking of all this when he told me, *"Never* forget where your talent came from, that your talent is a gift from God."

I was grateful for his kindness, but I could have told him that my mother had never let me forget. I never had

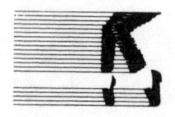

polio, which is a frightening thing for a dancer to think about, but I knew God had tested me and my brothers and sisters in other ways—our large family, our tiny house, the small amount of money we had to make ends meet, even the jealous kids in the neighborhood who threw rocks at our windows while we rehearsed, yelling that we'd never make it. When I think of my mother and our early years, I can tell you there are rewards that go far beyond money and public acclaim and awards.

My mother was a great provider. If she found out that one of us had an interest in something, she would encourage it if there was any possible way. If I developed an interest in movie stars, for instance, she'd come home with an armful of books about famous stars. Even with nine children she treated each of us like an only child. There isn't one of us who's ever forgotten what a hard worker and a great provider she was. It's an old story. Every child thinks *their* mother is the greatest mother in the world, but we Jacksons never lost that feeling. Because of Katherine's gentleness, warmth, and attention, I can't imagine what it must be like to grow up without a mother's love.

One thing I know about children is that if they don't get the love they need from their parents, they'll get it from someone else and cling to that person, a grandpar-

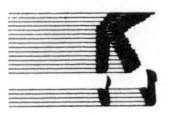

ent, anyone. We never had to look for anyone else with my mother around. The lessons she taught us were invaluable. Kindness, love, and consideration for other people headed her list. Don't hurt people. Never beg. Never freeload. Those were sins at our house. She always wanted us to *give,* but she never wanted us to ask or beg. That's the way she is.

I remember a good story about my mother that illustrates her nature. One day, back in Gary, when I was real little, this man knocked on everybody's door early in the morning. He was bleeding so badly you could see where he'd been around the neighborhood. No one would let him in. Finally he got to our door and he started banging and knocking. Mother let him in at once. Now, most people would have been too afraid to do that, but that's my mother. I can remember waking up and finding blood on our floor. I wish we could all be more like Mom.

The earliest memories I have of my father are of him coming home from the steel mill with a big bag of glazed doughnuts for all of us. My brothers and I could really eat back then and that bag would disappear with a snap of the fingers. He used to take us all to the merry-go-round in the park, but I was so young I don't remember that very well.

My father has always been something of a mystery to

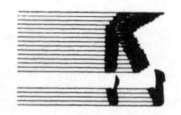

My mother and Janet in Indiana.

me and he knows it. One of the few things I regret most is never being able to have a real closeness with him. He built a shell around himself over the years and, once he stopped talking about our family business, he found it hard to relate to us. We'd all be together and he'd just leave the room. Even today it's hard for him to touch on father and son stuff because he's too embarrassed. When I see that he is, I become embarrassed, too.

My father did always protect us and that's no small feat. He always tried to make sure people didn't cheat us. He looked after our interests in the best ways. He might have made a few mistakes along the way, but he always thought he was doing what was right for his family. And, of course, most of what my father helped us accomplish was wonderful and unique, especially in regard to our relationships with companies and people in the business. I'd say we were among a fortunate few artists who walked away from a childhood in the business with anything substantial—money, real estate, other investments. My father set all these up for us. He looked out for both our interests and his. To this day I'm so thankful he didn't try to take all our money for himself the way so many parents of child stars have. Imagine stealing from your own children. My father never did anything like that. But I still don't know him, and that's sad for a son who hungers to

17

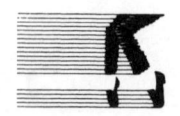

understand his own father. He's still a mystery man to me
and he may always be one.

What I got from my father wasn't necessarily God-given,
though the Bible says you reap what you sow. When we
were coming along, Dad said that in a different way, but
the message was just as clear: You could have all the talent
in the world, but if you didn't prepare and plan, it
wouldn't do you any good.

Joe Jackson had always loved singing and music as
much as my mother did, but he also knew there was a
world beyond Jackson Street. I wasn't old enough to remember his band, the Falcons, but they came over to our
house to rehearse on weekends. The music took them
away from their jobs at the steel mill, where Dad drove a
crane. The Falcons would play all over town, and in clubs
and colleges around northern Indiana and Chicago. At the
rehearsals at our house, Dad would bring his guitar out of
the closet and plug it into the amp he kept in the basement. Everyone would be set up and the music would
begin. He'd always loved rhythm and blues and that guitar was his pride and joy. The closet where the guitar was
kept was considered an almost sacred place. Needless to
say, it was off-limits to us kids. Dad didn't go to Kingdom
Hall with us, but both Mom and Dad knew that music was

a way of keeping our family together in a neighborhood where gangs recruited kids my brothers' ages. The three oldest boys would always have an excuse to be around when the Falcons came over. Dad let them think they were being given a special treat by being allowed to listen, but he was actually eager to have them there.

Tito watched everything that was going on with the greatest interest. He'd taken saxophone in school, but he could tell his hands were big enough to grab the chords and slip the riffs that my father played. It made sense that he'd catch on, because Tito looked so much like my father that we all expected him to share Dad's talents. The extent of the resemblance was scary as he got older. Maybe my father noticed Tito's zeal because he laid down rules for all my brothers: No one was to touch the guitar while he was out. Period.

Therefore, Jackie, Tito, and Jermaine were careful to see that Mom was in the kitchen when they "borrowed" the guitar. They were also careful not to make any noise while removing it. They would then go back to our room and put on the radio or the little portable record player so they could play along. Tito would hoist the guitar onto his belly as he sat on the bed and prop it up. He took turns with Jackie and Jermaine, and they'd all try the scales they were learning in school as well as try to figure out

19

how to get the "Green Onions" part they'd hear on the radio.

By now I was old enough to sneak in and watch if I promised not to tell. One day Mom finally caught them, and we were all worried. She scolded the boys, but said she wouldn't tell Dad as long as we were careful. She knew that guitar was keeping them from running with a bad crowd and maybe getting beat up, so she wasn't about to take away anything that kept them within arm's reach.

Of course, something had to give sooner or later, and one day a string broke. My brothers panicked. There wasn't time to get it repaired before Dad came home, and besides, none of us knew how to go about getting it fixed. My brothers never figured out what to do, so they put the guitar back in the closet and hoped fervently that my father would think it broke by itself. Of course, Dad didn't buy that, and he was furious. My sisters told me to stay out of it and keep a low profile. I heard Tito crying after Dad found out and I went to investigate, of course. Tito was on his bed crying when Dad came back and motioned for him to get up. Tito was scared, but my father just stood there, holding his favorite guitar. He gave Tito a hard, penetrating look and said, "Let me see what you can do."

My brother pulled himself together and started to play a few runs he had taught himself. When my father

saw how well Tito could play, he knew he'd obviously been practicing and he realized that Tito and the rest of us didn't treat his favorite guitar as if it were a toy. It became clear to him that what had happened had been only an accident. At this point my mother stepped in and voiced her enthusiasm for our musical ability. She told him that we boys had talent and he should listen to us. She kept pushing for us, so one day he began to listen and he liked what he heard. Tito, Jackie, and Jermaine started rehearsing together in earnest. A couple of years later, when I was about five, Mom pointed out to my father that I was a good singer and could play the bongos. I became a member of the group.

About then my father decided that what was happening in his family was serious. Gradually he began spending less time with the Falcons and more with us. We'd just woodshed together and he'd give us tips and teach us techniques on the guitar. Marlon and I weren't old enough to play, but we'd watch when my father rehearsed the older boys and we were learning when we watched. The ban on using Dad's guitar still held when he wasn't around, but my brothers loved using it when they could. The house on Jackson Street was bursting with music. Dad and Mom had paid for music lessons for Rebbie and Jackie when they were little kids, so they had a

21

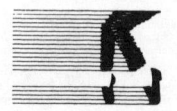

good background. The rest of us had music class and band
in the Gary schools, but no amount of practice was enough
to harness all that energy.

The Falcons were still earning money, however infre-
quent their gigs, and that extra money was important to
us. It was enough to keep food on the table for a growing
family but not enough to give us things that weren't necessary. Mom was working part-time at Sears, Dad was still
working the mill job, and no one was going hungry, but I
think, looking back, that things must have seemed like
one big dead end.

One day Dad was late coming home and Mom began
to get worried. By the time he arrived, she was ready to
give him a piece of her mind, something we boys didn't
mind witnessing once in a while just to see if he could take
it like he dished it out, but when he poked his head
through the door, he had a mischievous look on his face
and he was hiding something behind his back. We were all
shocked when he produced a gleaming red guitar, slightly
smaller than the one in the closet. We were all hoping this
meant we'd get the old one. But Dad said the new guitar
was Tito's. We gathered around to admire it, while Dad
told Tito he had to share it with anyone who would *practice*. We were not to take it to school to show it off. This

was a serious present and that day was a momentous occasion for the Jackson family.

Mom was happy for us, but she also knew her husband. She was more aware than we of the big ambitions and plans he had for us. He'd begun talking to her at night after we kids were asleep. He had dreams and those dreams didn't stop with one guitar. Pretty soon we were dealing with *equipment,* not just gifts. Jermaine got a bass and an amp. There were shakers for Jackie. Our bedroom and living room began to look like a music store. Sometimes I'd hear Mom and Dad fight when the subject of money was brought up, because all those instruments and accessories meant having to go without a little something we needed each week. Dad was persuasive, though, and he didn't miss a trick.

We even had microphones in the house. They seemed like a real luxury at the time, especially to a woman who was trying to stretch a very small budget, but I've come to realize that having those microphones in our house wasn't just an attempt to keep up with the Joneses or anyone else in amateur night competitions. They were there to help us prepare. I saw people at talent shows, who probably sounded great at home, clam up the moment they got in front of a microphone. Others started screaming their songs like they wanted to prove they didn't need the

23

mikes. They didn't have the advantage that we did—an advantage that only experience can give you. I think it probably made some people jealous because they could tell our expertise with the mikes gave us an edge. If that was true, we made so many sacrifices—in free time, schoolwork, and friends—that no one had the right to be jealous. We were becoming very good, but we were working like people twice our age.

While I was watching my older brothers, including Marlon on the bongo drums, Dad got a couple of young guys named Johnny Jackson and Randy Rancifer to play trap drums and organ. Motown would later claim they were our cousins, but that was just an embellishment from the P.R. people, who wanted to make us seem like one big family. We had become a real band! I was like a sponge, watching everyone, and trying to learn everything I could. I was totally absorbed when my brothers were rehearsing or playing at charity events or shopping centers. I was most fascinated when watching Jermaine because he was the singer at the time and he was a big brother to me—Marlon was too close to me in age for that. It was Jermaine who would walk me to kindergarten and whose clothes would be handed down to me. When he did something, I tried to imitate him. When I was successful at it, my brothers and Dad would laugh, but when I began

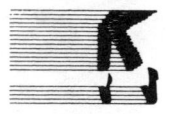

Johnny Jackson is playing the drums in this early publicity photograph.

singing, they listened. I was singing in a baby voice then and just imitating sounds. I was so young I didn't know what many of the words meant, but the more I sang, the better I got.

I always knew how to dance. I would watch Marlon's moves because Jermaine had the big bass to carry, but also because I could keep up with Marlon, who was only a year older than me. Soon I was doing most of the singing at home and preparing to join my brothers in public. Through our rehearsals, we were all becoming aware of our particular strengths and weaknesses as members of the group and the shift in responsibilities was happening naturally.

Our family's house in Gary was tiny, only three rooms really, but at the time it seemed much larger to me. When you're that young, the whole world seems so huge that a little room can seem four times its size. When we went back to Gary years later, we were all surprised at how tiny that house was. I had remembered it as being large, but you could take five steps from the front door and you'd be out the back. It was really no bigger than a garage, but when we lived there it seemed fine to us kids. You see things from such a different perspective when you're young.

Our school days in Gary are a blur for me. I vaguely

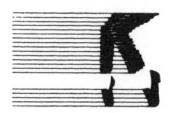

Returning home to our small house in Gary after our success. The welcome was overwhelming.

remember being dropped off in front of my school on the first day of kindergarten, and I clearly remember hating it. I didn't want my mother to leave me, naturally, and I didn't want to be there.

In time I adjusted, as all kids do, and I grew to love my teachers, especially the women. They were always very sweet to us and they just loved me. Those teachers were so wonderful; I'd be promoted from one grade to the next and they'd all cry and hug me and tell me how much they hated to see me leave their classes. I was so crazy about my teachers that I'd steal my mother's jewelry and give it to them as presents. They'd be very touched, but eventually my mother found out about it, and put an end to my generosity with her things. That urge that I had to give them something in return for all I was receiving was a measure of how much I loved them and that school.

One day, in the first grade, I participated in a program that was put on before the whole school. Everyone of us in each class had to do something, so I went home and discussed it with my parents. We decided I should wear black pants and a white shirt and sing "Climb Ev'ry Mountain" from *The Sound of Music.* When I finished that song, the reaction in the auditorium overwhelmed me. The applause was thunderous and people were smiling; some of them were standing. My teachers were crying

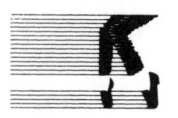

and I just couldn't believe it. I had made them all happy.
It was such a great feeling. I felt a little confused too,
because I didn't think I had done anything special. I was
just singing the way I sang at home every night. When
you're performing, you don't realize what you sound like
or how you're coming across. You just open your mouth
and sing.

Soon Dad was grooming us for talent contests. He was a
great trainer, and he spent a lot of money and time working with us. Talent is something that God gives to a person, but our father taught us how to cultivate it. I think we
also had a certain instinct for show business. We loved to
perform and we put everything we had into it. He'd sit at
home with us every day after school and rehearse us. We'd
perform for him and he'd critique us. If you messed up,
you got hit, sometimes with a belt, sometimes with a
switch. My father was real strict with us—real strict.
Marlon was the one who got in trouble all the time. On
the other hand, I'd get beaten for things that happened
mostly outside rehearsal. Dad would make me so mad and
hurt that I'd try to get back at him and get beaten all the
more. I'd take a shoe and throw it at him, or I'd just fight
back, swinging my fists. That's why I got it more than all
my brothers combined. I would fight back and my father

29

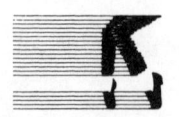

First Place Winners Of The Talent Search

THE JACKSON FIVE..... Youthful musical aggregation who were First Place winners of the Annual Talent Search held last Sunday at Gilroy Stadium. The well attended and entertaining affair was Emceed by WWCA's popular Disc Jockey, Jesse Coopwood, who is well known for keeping the public entertained with his capers via the mike. Cherry, assisting Coopwood with the group of "Winners" is shown left in the photo. Proceeds from the affair will go toward a scholarship fund.

One of the early talent shows where we won a trophy.

Practicing after school.

would kill me, just tear me up. Mother told me I'd fight back even when I was very little, but I don't remember that. I do remember running under tables to get away from him, and making him angrier. We had a turbulent relationship.

Most of the time, however, we just rehearsed. We *always* rehearsed. Sometimes, late at night, we'd have time to play games or play with our toys. There might be a game of hide-and-go-seek or we'd jump rope, but that was about it. The majority of our time was spent working. I clearly remember running into the house with my brothers when my father came home, because we'd be in big trouble if we weren't ready to start rehearsals on time.

31

Through all this, my mother was completely supportive. She had been the one who first recognized our talent and she continued to help us realize our potential. It's hard to imagine that we would have gotten where we did without her love and good humor. She worried about the stress we were under and the long hours of rehearsal, but we wanted to be the best we could be and we really loved music.

Music was important in Gary. We had our own radio stations and nightclubs, and there was no shortage of people who wanted to be on them. After Dad ran our Saturday

afternoon rehearsals, he'd go see a local show or even drive all the way to Chicago to see someone perform. He was always watching for things that could help us down the road. He'd come home and tell us what he'd seen and who was doing what. He kept up on all the latest stuff, whether it was a local theater that ran contests we could enter or a Cavalcade of Stars show with great acts whose clothes or moves we might adapt. Sometimes I wouldn't see Dad until I got back from Kingdom Hall on Sundays, but as soon as I ran into the house he'd be telling me what he'd seen the night before. He'd assure me I could dance on one leg like James Brown if I'd only try *this* step. There I'd be, fresh out of church, and back in show business.

We started collecting trophies with our act when I was six. Our lineup was set; the group featured me at second from the left, facing the audience, Jermaine on the wing next to me, and Jackie on my right. Tito and his guitar took stage right, with Marlon next to him. Jackie was getting tall and he towered over Marlon and me. We kept that setup for contest after contest and it worked well. While other groups we'd meet would fight among themselves and quit, we were becoming more polished and experienced. The people in Gary who came regularly to see the talent shows got to know us, so we would try to top ourselves and surprise them. We didn't want them to

begin to feel bored by our act. We knew change was always good, that it helped us grow, so we were never afraid of it.

Winning an amateur night or talent show in a ten-minute, two-song set took as much energy as a ninety-minute concert. I'm convinced that because there's no room for mistakes, your concentration burns you up inside more on one or two songs than it does when you have the luxury of twelve or fifteen in a set. These talent shows were our professional education. Sometimes we'd drive hundreds of miles to do one song or two and hope the crowd wouldn't be against us because we weren't local talent. We were competing against people of all ages and skills, from drill teams to comedians to other singers and dancers like us. We had to grab that audience and keep it. Nothing was left to chance, so clothes, shoes, hair, *everything* had to be the way Dad planned it. We really looked amazingly professional. After all this planning, if we performed the songs the way we rehearsed them, the awards would take care of themselves. This was true even when we were in the Wallace High part of town where the neighborhood had its own performers and cheering sections and we were challenging them right in their own backyards. Naturally, local performers always had their own very loyal fans, so whenever we went off our turf and

onto someone else's, it was very hard. When the master of ceremonies held his hand over our heads for the "applause meter," we wanted to make sure that the crowd knew we had given more than anyone else.

As players, Jermaine, Tito, and the rest of us were under tremendous pressure. Our manager was the kind who reminded us that James Brown would *fine* his Famous Flames if they missed a cue or bent a note during a performance. As lead singer, I felt I—more than the others—couldn't afford an "off night." I can remember being onstage at night after being sick in bed all day. It was hard to concentrate at those times, yet I knew all the things my brothers and I had to do so well that I could have performed the routines in my sleep. At times like that, I had to remind myself not to look in the crowd for someone I knew, or at the emcee, both of which can distract a young performer. We did songs that people knew from the radio or songs my father knew were already classics. If you messed up, you *heard* about it because the fans knew those songs and they knew how they were supposed to sound. If you were going to change an arrangement, it needed to sound *better* than the original.

We won the citywide talent show when I was eight with our version of the Temptations' song "My Girl." The contest was held just a few blocks away at Roosevelt High.

From Jermaine's opening bass notes and Tito's first guitar licks to all five of us singing the chorus, we had people on their feet for the whole song. Jermaine and I traded verses while Marlon and Jackie spun like tops. It was a wonderful feeling for all of us to pass that trophy, our biggest yet, back and forth between us. Eventually it was propped on the front seat like a baby and we drove home with Dad telling us, "When you do it like you did tonight they can't *not* give it to you."

We were now Gary city champions and Chicago was our next target because it was the area that offered the steadiest work and the best word of mouth for miles and miles. We began to plan our strategy in earnest. My father's group played the Chicago sound of Muddy Waters and Howlin' Wolf, but he was open-minded enough to see that the more upbeat, slicker sounds that appealed to us kids had a lot to offer. We were lucky because some people his age weren't that hip. In fact, we knew musicians who thought the sixties sound was beneath people their age, but not Dad. He recognized great singing when he heard it, even telling us that he saw the great doo-wop group from Gary, the Spaniels, when they were stars not that much older than we. When Smokey Robinson of the Miracles sang a song like "Tracks of My Tears" or "Ooo, Baby Baby," he'd be listening as hard as we were.

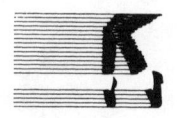

The sixties didn't leave Chicago behind musically. Great singers like the Impressions with Curtis Mayfield, Jerry Butler, Major Lance, and Tyrone Davis were playing all over the city at the same places we were. At this point my father was managing us full-time, with only a part-time shift at the mill. Mom had some doubts about the soundness of this decision, not because she didn't think we were good but because she didn't know anyone else who was spending the majority of his time trying to break his children into the music business. She was even less thrilled when Dad told her he had booked us as a regular act at Mr. Lucky's, a Gary nightspot. We were being forced to spend our weekends in Chicago and other places trying to win an ever-increasing number of amateur shows, and these trips were expensive, so the job at Mr. Lucky's was a way to make it all possible. Mom was surprised at the response we were getting and she was very pleased with the awards and the attention, but she worried about us a lot. She worried about me because of my age. "This is quite a life for a nine-year-old," she would say, staring intently at my father.

I don't know what my brothers and I expected, but the nightclub crowds weren't the same as the Roosevelt High crowds. We were playing between bad comedians, cocktail organists, and strippers. With my Witness up-

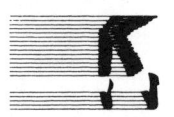

bringing, Mom was concerned that I was hanging out with the wrong people and getting introduced to things I'd be better off learning much later in life. She didn't have to worry; just one look at some of those strippers wasn't going to get me *that* interested in trouble—certainly not at nine years old! That was an awful way to live, though, and it made us all the more determined to move on up the circuit and as far away from that life as we could go.

Being at Mr. Lucky's meant that for the first time in our lives we had a whole show to do—five sets a night, six nights a week—and if Dad could get us something out of town for the seventh night, he was going to do it. We were working hard, but the bar crowds weren't bad to us. They liked James Brown and Sam and Dave just as much as we did and, besides, we were something extra that came free with the drinking and the carrying on, so they were surprised and cheerful. We even had some fun with them on one number, the Joe Tex song "Skinny Legs and All." We'd start the song and somewhere in the middle I'd go out into the audience, crawl under the tables, and pull up the ladies' skirts to look under. People would throw money as I scurried by, and when I began to dance, I'd scoop up all the dollars and coins that had hit the floor earlier and push them into the pockets of my jacket.

I wasn't really nervous when we began playing in

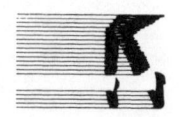

clubs because of all the experience I'd had with talent show audiences. I was always ready to go out and perform, you know, just *do* it—sing and dance and have some fun.

We worked in more than one club that had strippers in those days. I used to stand in the wings of this one place in Chicago and watch a lady whose name was Mary Rose. I must have been nine or ten. This girl would take off her clothes and her panties and throw them to the audience. The men would pick them up and sniff them and yell. My brothers and I would be watching all this, taking it in, and my father wouldn't mind. We were exposed to a lot doing that kind of circuit. In one place they had cut a little hole in the musicians' dressing room wall that also happened to act as a wall in the ladies' bathroom. You could peek through this hole, and I saw stuff I've never forgotten. Guys on that circuit were so wild, they did stuff like drilling little holes into the walls of the ladies' loo all the time. Of course, I'm sure that my brothers and I were fighting over who got to look through the hole. "Get outta the way, it's *my* turn!" Pushing each other away to make room for ourselves.

Later, when we did the Apollo Theater in New York, I saw something that really blew me away because I didn't know things like that existed. I had seen quite a few strippers, but that night this one girl with gorgeous eyelashes

and long hair came out and did her routine. She put on a *great* performance. All of a sudden, at the end, she took off her wig, pulled a pair of big oranges out of her bra, and revealed that she was a hard-faced guy under all that makeup. That blew me away. I was only a child and couldn't even conceive of anything like that. But I looked out at the theater audience and they were *going* for it, applauding wildly and cheering. I'm just a little kid, standing in the wings, watching this crazy stuff.

I was blown away.

As I said, I received quite an education as a child. More than most. Perhaps this freed me to concentrate on other aspects of my life as an adult.

39

One day, not long after we'd been doing successfully in Chicago clubs, Dad brought home a tape of some songs we'd never heard before. We were accustomed to doing popular stuff off the radio, so we were curious why he began playing these songs over and over again, just one guy singing none too well with some guitar chords in the background. Dad told us that the man on the tape wasn't really a performer but a songwriter who owned a recording studio in Gary. His name was Mr. Keith and he had given us a week to practice his songs to see if we could

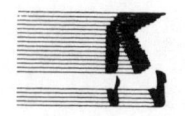

make a record out of them. Naturally, we were excited. We wanted to make a record, any record.

We worked strictly on the sound, ignoring the dancing routines we'd normally work up for a new song. It wasn't as much fun to do a song that none of us knew, but we were already professional enough to hide our disappointment and give it all we could. When we were ready and felt we had done our best with the material, Dad got us on tape after a few false starts and more than a few pep talks, of course. After a day or two of trying to figure out whether Mr. Keith liked the tape we had made for him, Dad suddenly appeared with more of his songs for us to learn for our first recording session.

Mr. Keith, like Dad, was a mill worker who loved music, only he was more into the recording and business end. His studio and label were called Steeltown. Looking back on all this, I realize Mr. Keith was just as excited as we were. His studio was downtown, and we went early one Saturday morning before "The Road Runner Show," my favorite show at the time. Mr. Keith met us at the door and opened the studio. He showed us a small glass booth with all kinds of equipment in it and explained what various tasks each performed. It didn't look like we'd have to lean over any more tape recorders, at least not in this studio. I put on some big metal headphones, which came

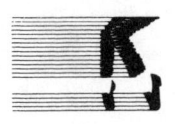

halfway down my neck, and tried to make myself look ready for anything.

As my brothers were figuring out where to plug in their instruments and stand, some backup singers and a horn section arrived. At first I assumed they were there to make a record after us. We were delighted and amazed when we found out they were there to record with us. We looked over at Dad, but he didn't change expression. He'd obviously known about it and approved. Even then people knew not to throw Dad surprises. We were told to listen to Mr. Keith, who would instruct us while we were in the booth. If we did as he said, the record would take care of itself.

After a few hours, we finished Mr. Keith's first song. Some of the backup singers and horn players hadn't made records either and found it difficult, but they also didn't have a perfectionist for a manager, so they weren't used to doing things over and over the way we were. It was at times like these that we realized how hard Dad worked to make us consummate professionals. We came back the next few Saturdays, putting the songs we'd rehearsed during the week into the can and taking home a new tape of Mr. Keith's each time. One Saturday, Dad even brought his guitar in to perform with us. It was the one and only time he ever recorded with us. After the records were

41

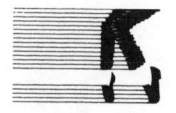

"Big Boy" was our first recorded song.

pressed, Mr. Keith gave us some copies so that we could sell them between sets and after shows. We knew that wasn't how the big groups did it, but everyone had to start someplace, and in those days, having a record with your group's name on it was quite something. We felt very fortunate.

That first Steeltown single, "Big Boy," had a mean bass line. It was a nice song about a kid who wanted to fall in love with some girl. Of course, in order to get the full picture, you have to imagine a skinny nine-year-old singing this song. The words said I didn't want to hear fairy tales any more, but in truth I was far too young to grasp the real meanings of most of the words in these songs. I just sang what they gave me.

When that record with its killer bass line began to get radio play in Gary, we became a big deal in our neighborhood. No one could believe we had our own record. *We* had a hard time believing it.

After that first Steeltown record, we began to aim for all the big talent shows in Chicago. Usually the other acts would look me over carefully when they met me, because I was so little, particularly the ones who went on after us. One day Jackie was cracking up, like someone had told him the funniest joke in the world. This wasn't a good sign right before a show, and I could tell Dad was worried he

was going to screw up onstage. Dad went over to say a word to him, but Jackie whispered something in his ear and soon Dad was holding his sides, laughing. I wanted to know the joke too. Dad said proudly that Jackie had overheard the headlining act talking among themselves. One guy said, "We'd better not let those Jackson 5 cut us tonight with that midget they've got."

I was upset at first because my feelings were hurt. I thought they were being mean. I couldn't help it that I was the shortest, but soon all the other brothers were cracking up too. Dad explained that they weren't laughing at me. He told me that I should be proud, the group was talking trash because they thought I was a grown-up posing as a child like one of the Munchkins in *The Wizard of Oz*. Dad said that if I had those slick guys talking like the neighborhood kids who gave us grief back in Gary, then we had Chicago on the run.

We still had some running of our own to do. After we played some pretty good clubs in Chicago, Dad signed us up for the Royal Theater amateur night competition in town. He had gone to see B. B. King at the Regal the night he made his famous live album. When Dad gave Tito that sharp red guitar years earlier, we had teased him by thinking of girls he could name his guitar after, like B. B. King's Lucille.

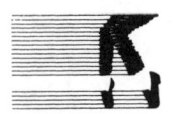

At the NAACP Image Awards.

Performing together in the early days.

We won that show for three straight weeks, with a new song every week to keep the regular members of the audience guessing. Some of the other performers complained that it was greedy for us to keep coming back, but they were after the same thing we were. There was a policy that if you won the amateur night three straight times, you'd be invited back to do a *paid* show for thousands of people, not dozens like the audiences we were playing to in bars. We got that opportunity and the show was headlined by Gladys Knight and the Pips, who were breaking in a new song no one knew called "I Heard It Through the Grapevine." It was a heady night.

After Chicago, we had one more big amateur show we really felt we needed to win: the Apollo Theater in New York City. A lot of Chicago people thought a win at the Apollo was just a good luck charm and nothing more, but Dad saw it as much more than that. He knew New York had a high caliber of talent just like Chicago and he knew there were more record people and professional musicians in New York than Chicago. If we could make it in New York, we could make it anywhere. That's what a win at the Apollo meant to us.

Chicago had sent a kind of scouting report on us to New York and our reputation was such that the Apollo entered us in the "Superdog" finals, even though we

hadn't been to any of the preliminary competitions. By this time, Gladys Knight had already talked to us about coming to Motown, as had Bobby Taylor, a member of the Vancouvers, with whom my father had become friendly. Dad had told them we'd be happy to audition for Motown, but that was in our future.

We got to the Apollo at 125th Street early enough to get a guided tour. We walked through the theater and stared at all of the pictures of the stars who'd played there, white as well as black. The manager concluded by showing us to the dressing room, but by then I had found pictures of all my favorites.

While my brothers and I were paying dues on the so-called "chitlin' circuit," opening for other acts, I carefully watched all the stars because I wanted to learn as much as I could. I'd stare at their feet, the way they held their arms, the way they gripped a microphone, trying to decipher what they were doing and why they were doing it. After studying James Brown from the wings, I knew every step, every grunt, every spin and turn. I have to say he would give a performance that would exhaust you, just wear you out emotionally. His whole physical presence, the fire coming out of his pores, would be phenomenal. You'd *feel* every bead of sweat on his face and you'd know what he was going through. I've never seen anybody per-

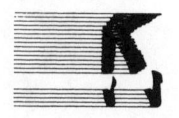

form like him. Unbelievable, really. When I watched somebody I liked, *I'd be there.* James Brown, Jackie Wilson, Sam and Dave, the O'Jays—they all used to really *work* an audience. I might have learned more from watching Jackie Wilson than from anyone or anything else. All of this was a very important part of my education.

We would stand offstage, behind the curtains, and watch everyone come off after performing and they'd be all sweaty. I'd just stand aside in awe and watch them walk by. And they would all wear these beautiful patent-leather shoes. My whole dream seemed to center on having a pair of patent-leather shoes. I remember being so heartbroken because they didn't make them in little boys' sizes. I'd go from store to store looking for patent-leather shoes and they'd say, "We don't make them that small." I was so sad because I wanted to have shoes that looked the way those stage shoes looked, polished and shining, turning red and orange when the lights hit them. Oh, how I wanted some patent-leather shoes like the ones Jackie Wilson wore.

Most of the time I'd be alone backstage. My brothers would be upstairs eating and talking and I'd be down in the wings, crouching real low, holding on to the dusty, smelly curtain and watching the show. I mean, I really did watch every step, every move, every twist, every turn,

every grind, every emotion, every light move. That was my education and my recreation. I was always there when I had free time. My father, my brothers, other musicians, they all knew where to find me. They would tease me about it, but I was so absorbed in what I was seeing, or in remembering what I had just seen, that I didn't care. I remember all those theaters: the Regal, the Uptown, the Apollo—too many to name. The talent that came out of those places is of mythical proportions. The greatest education in the world is watching the masters at work. You couldn't teach a person what I've learned just standing and watching. Some musicians—Springsteen and U2, for example—may feel they got their education from the streets. I'm a performer at heart. I got mine from the stage.

Jackie Wilson was on the wall at the Apollo. The photographer captured him with one leg up, twisted, but not out of position from catching the mike stand he'd just whipped back and forth. He could have been singing a sad lyric like "Lonely Teardrops," and yet he had that audience so bug-eyed with his dancing that no one could feel sad or lonely.

Sam and Dave's picture was down the corridor, next to an old big-band shot. Dad had become friendly with Sam Moore. I remember being happily amazed that he

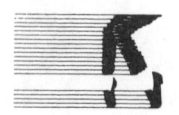

was nice to me when I met him for the first time. I had been singing his songs for so long that I thought he'd want to box my ears. And not far from them was "The King of Them All, Mr. Dynamite, Mr. Please Please Himself," James Brown. Before he came along, a singer was a singer and a dancer was a dancer. A singer might have danced and a dancer might have sung, but unless you were Fred Astaire or Gene Kelly, you probably did one better than the other, especially in a live performance. But he changed all that. No spotlight could keep up with him when he skidded across the stage—you had to *flood* it! I wanted to be that good.

We won the Apollo amateur night competition, and I felt like going back to those photos on the walls and thanking my "teachers." Dad was so happy he said he could have *flown* back to Gary that night. He was on top of the world and so were we. My brothers and I had gotten straight A's and we were hoping we might get to skip a "grade." I certainly sensed that we wouldn't be doing talent shows and strip joints much longer.

In the summer of 1968 we were introduced to the music of a family group that was going to change our sound and our lives. They didn't all have the same last name, they were black and white, men and women, and they were

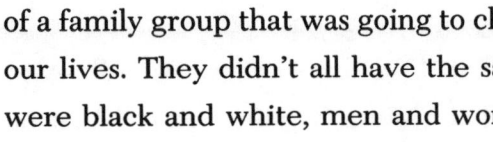

called Sly and the Family Stone. They had some amazing hits over the years, such as "Dance to the Music," "Stand," "Hot Fun in the Summertime." My brothers would point at me when they heard the line about the midget standing tall and by now I'd laugh along. We heard these songs all over the dial, even on the rock stations. They were a tremendous influence on all of us Jacksons and we owe them a lot.

After the Apollo, we kept playing with one eye on the map and one ear to the phone. Mom and Dad had a rule about no more than five minutes a call, but when we came back from the Apollo, even five minutes was too long. We had to keep the lines clear in case anyone from a record company wanted to get in touch with us. We lived in fear of having them get a busy signal. We wanted to hear from one record company in particular, and if they called, we wanted to answer.

While we waited, we found out that someone who had seen us at the Apollo had recommended us to "The David Frost Show" in New York City. We were going to be on TV! That was the biggest thrill we'd ever had. I told everyone at school, and told the ones who didn't believe me twice. We were going to drive out there in a few days. I was counting the hours. I had imagined the whole trip,

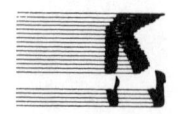

My love of hats began long before the days of "Billie Jean"

trying to figure out what the studio would be like and how it would be to look into a television camera.

I came home with the traveling homework my teacher had made up in advance. We had one more dress rehearsal and then we'd make a final song selection. I wondered which songs we'd be doing.

That afternoon, Dad said the trip to New York was canceled. We all stopped in our tracks and just stared at him.

We were shocked. I was ready to cry. We had been about to get our big break. How could they do this to us? What was going on? Why had Mr. Frost changed his mind? I was reeling and I think everyone else was, too. "I canceled it," my father announced calmly. Again we all stared at him, unable to speak. "Motown called." A chill ran down my spine.

I remember the days leading up to that trip with near-perfect clarity. I can see myself waiting outside Randy's first-grade classroom. It was Marlon's turn to walk him home, but we switched for today.

Randy's teacher wished me luck in Detroit, because Randy had told her we were going to Motown to audition. He was so excited that I had to remind myself that he didn't really know what Detroit was. All the family had

been talking about was Motown, and Randy didn't even know what a city was. The teacher told me he was looking for Motown on the globe in the classroom. She said that in her opinion we should do "You Don't Know Like I Know" the way she saw us do it at the Regal in Chicago when a bunch of teachers drove over to see us. I helped Randy put his coat on and politely agreed to keep it in mind— knowing that we couldn't do a Sam and Dave song at a Motown audition because they were on Stax, a rival label. Dad told us the companies were serious about that kind of stuff, so he wanted us to know there'd be no messing around when we got there. He looked at me and said he'd like to see his ten-year-old singer make it to eleven.

We left the Garrett Elementary School building for the short walk home, but we had to hurry. I remember getting anxious as a car swept by, then another. Randy took my hand, and we waved to the crossing guard. I knew LaToya would have to go out of her way tomorrow to take Randy to school because Marlon and I would be staying over in Detroit with the others.

The last time we played at the Fox Theater in Detroit, we left right after the show and got back to Gary at five o'clock in the morning. I slept in the car most of the way, so going to school that morning wasn't as bad as it might have been. But by the afternoon three o'clock rehearsal I

was dragging around like someone with lead weights for feet.

We could have left that night right after our set, since we were third on the bill, but that would have meant missing the headliner, Jackie Wilson. I'd seen him on other stages, but at the Fox he and his band were on a rising stage that moved up as he started his show. Tired as I was after school the next day, I remember trying some of those moves in rehearsal after practicing in front of a long mirror in the bathroom at school while the other kids looked on. My father was pleased and we incorporated those steps into one of my routines.

Just before Randy and I turned the corner onto Jackson Street, there was a big puddle. I looked for cars but there weren't any, so I let go of Randy's hand and jumped the puddle, catching on my toes so I could spin without getting the cuffs of my corduroys wet. I looked back at Randy, knowing that he wanted to do the things I did. He stepped back to get a running start, but I realized that it was a pretty big puddle, too big for him to cross without getting wet, so, being a big brother first and a dance teacher second, I caught him before he landed short and got wet.

Across the street the neighborhood kids were buying candy, and even some of the kids who were giving me a

hard time at school asked when we were going to Motown. I told them and bought candy for them and Randy, too, with my allowance. I didn't want Randy to feel bad about my going away.

As we approached the house I heard Marlon yell, "Someone shut that door!" The side of our VW minibus was wide open, and I shuddered, thinking about how cold it was going to be on the long ride up to Detroit. Marlon had beat us home and was already helping Jackie load the bus with our stuff. Jackie and Tito got home in plenty of time for once: They were supposed to have basketball practice, but the winter in Indiana had been nothing but slush and we were anxious to get a good start. Jackie was on the high school basketball team that year, and Dad liked to say that the next time we went to play in Indianapolis would be when Roosevelt went to the state championships. The Jackson 5 would play between the evening and morning games, and Jackie would sink the winning shot for the title. Dad liked to tease us, but you never knew what might happen with the Jacksons. He wanted us to be good at many things, not just music. I think maybe he got that drive from his father, who taught school. I know my teachers were never as hard on us as he was, and they were getting paid to be tough and demanding.

Mom came to the door and gave us the thermos and

the sandwiches she had packed. I remember her telling
me not to rip the dress shirt she had packed for me after
sewing it up the night before. Randy and I helped put
some things in the bus and then went back into the
kitchen, where Rebbie was keeping one eye on Dad's
supper and the other on little Janet, who was in the high
chair.

Rebbie's life was never easy as the oldest. We knew
that as soon as the Motown audition was over, we'd find
out if we had to move or not. If we did, she was going to
move South with her fiancé. She always ran things when
Mom was at night school finishing the high school diploma
she was denied because of her illness. I couldn't believe it
when Mom told us she was going to get her diploma. I
remember worrying that she'd have to go to school with
kids Jackie's or Tito's age and that they'd laugh at her. I
remember how she laughed when I told her this and how
she patiently explained that she'd be with other grown-
ups. It was interesting having a mother who did homework like the rest of us.

Loading up the bus was easier than usual. Normally
Ronnie and Johnny would have come to back us up, but
Motown's own musicians would be playing behind us, so
we were going alone. Jermaine was in our room finishing
some of his assignments when I walked in. I knew he

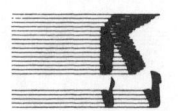

wanted to get them out of the way. He told me that we ought to take off for Motown by ourselves and leave Dad, since Jackie had taken driver's ed and was in possession of a set of keys. We both laughed, but deep down I couldn't imagine going without Dad. Even on the occasions when Mom led our after-school rehearsals because Dad hadn't come home from his shift on time, it was still like having him there because she acted as his eyes and ears. She always knew what had been good the night before and what had gotten sloppy today. Dad would pick it up from there at night. It seemed to me that they almost gave each other signals or something—Dad could always tell if we had been playing like we were supposed to by some invisible indication from Mom.

There was no long good-bye at the door when we left for Motown. Mom was used to our being away for days, and during school vacations. LaToya pouted a little because she wanted to go. She had only seen us in Chicago, and we had never been able to stay long enough in places like Boston or Phoenix to bring her back anything. I think our lives must have seemed pretty glamorous to her because she had to stay home and go to school. Rebbie had her hands full trying to put Janet to sleep, but she called good-bye and waved. I gave Randy a last pat on the head and we were off.

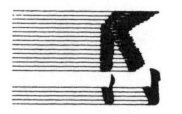

Dad and Jackie went over the map as we drove away, mostly out of habit, because we had been to Detroit before, of course. We passed Mr. Keith's recording studio downtown by City Hall as we made our way through town. We had done some demos at Mr. Keith's that Dad sent to Motown after the Steeltown record. The sun was going down when we hit the highway. Marlon announced that if we heard one of our records on WVON, it was going to bring us luck. We all nodded. Dad asked us if we remembered what WVON stood for as he nudged Jackie to keep quiet. I kept looking out the window, thinking about the possibilities that lay ahead, but Jermaine jumped in. "Voice of the Negro," he said. Soon we were calling roll all over the dial. "WGN—World's Greatest Newspaper." (The Chicago *Tribune* owned it.) "WLS—World's Largest Store." (Sears.) "WCFL . . ." We stopped, stumped. "Chicago Federation of Labor," Dad said, motioning for the thermos. We turned onto I-94, and the Gary station faded into a Kalamazoo station. We began flipping around, looking for Beatle music on CKLW from Windsor, Ontario, Canada.

I had always been a Monopoly fan at home, and there was something about driving to Motown that was a little like that game. In Monopoly you go around the board buying

things and making decisions; the "chitlin' circuit" of theaters where we played and won contests was kind of like a
Monopoly board full of possibilities and pitfalls. After all
the stops along the way, we finally landed at the Apollo
Theater in Harlem, which was definitely Park Place for
young performers like us. Now we were on our way up
Boardwalk, heading for Motown. Would we win the game
or slide past Go with a long board separating us from our
goal for another round?

There was something changing in me, and I could
feel it, even shivering in the minibus. For years we'd
make the drive over to Chicago wondering if we were
good enough to ever get out of Gary, and we were. Then
we took the drive to New York, certain that we'd fall off
the edge of the earth if we weren't good enough to make
it there. Even those nights in Philadelphia and Washington didn't reassure me enough to keep me from wondering if there wasn't someone or some group we didn't
know about in New York who could beat us. When we tore
it down at the Apollo, we finally felt that nothing could
stand in our way. We were going to Motown, and nothing
there was going to surprise us either. We were going to
surprise them, just like we always did.

Dad pulled the typewritten directions out of the
glove compartment and we pulled off the highway, pass-

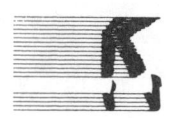

ing the Woodward Avenue exit. There weren't many people on the streets because it was a school night for everybody else.

Dad was a little nervous about whether our accommodations would be okay, which surprised me until I realized the Motown people had picked the hotel. We weren't used to having things done for us. We liked to be our own bosses. Dad had always been our booking agent, travel agent, and manager. When he wasn't taking care of the arrangements, Mom was. So it was no wonder that even Motown managed to make Dad feel suspicious that *he* should have made the reservations, that he should have handled everything.

We stayed at the Gotham Hotel. The reservations had been made and everything was in order. There was a TV in our room, but all the stations had signed off, and with the audition at ten o'clock, we weren't going to get to stay up any later anyway. Dad put us right to bed, locked the door, and went out. Jermaine and I were too tired to even talk.

We were all up on time the next morning; Dad saw to that. But, in truth, we were just as excited as he was and hopped out of bed when he called us. The audition was unusual for us because we hadn't played in many places where they expected us to be professional. We knew it

was going to be difficult to judge whether we were doing well. We were used to audience response whether we were competing or just performing at a club, but Dad had told us the longer we stayed, the more they wanted to hear.

We climbed into the VW, after cereal and milk at the coffee shop. I noticed they offered grits on the menu, so I knew there were a lot of Southern people who stayed there. We had never been to the South then and wanted to visit Mom's part of the country someday. We wanted to have a sense of our roots and those of other black people, especially after what had happened to Dr. King. I remember so well the day he died. Everyone was torn up. We didn't rehearse that night. I went to Kingdom Hall with Mom and some of the others. People were crying like they had lost a member of their own family. Even the men who were usually pretty unemotional were unable to control their grief. I was too young to grasp the full tragedy of the situation, but when I look back on that day now, it makes me want to cry—for Dr. King, for his family, and for all of us.

Jermaine was the first to spot the studio, which was known as Hitsville, U.S.A. It looked kind of run-down, which was not what I'd expected. We wondered who we might see,

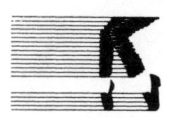

who might be there making a record that day. Dad had coached us to let him do all the talking. Our job was to perform like we'd never performed before. And that was asking a lot, because we always put everything into each performance, but we knew what he meant.

There were a lot of people waiting inside, but Dad said the password and a man in a shirt and tie came out to meet us. He knew each of our names, which astounded us. He asked us to leave our coats there and follow him. The other people just stared through us like we were ghosts. I wondered who they were and what their stories were. Had they traveled far? Had they been here day after day hoping to get in without an appointment?

When we entered the studio, one of the Motown guys was adjusting a movie camera. There was an area set up with instruments and microphones. Dad disappeared into one of the sound booths to talk to someone. I tried to pretend that I was at the Fox Theater, on the rising stage, and this was just business as usual. I decided, looking around, that if I ever built my own studio, I'd get a mike like the one they had at the Apollo, which rose out of the floor. I nearly fell on my face once running down those basement steps while trying to find out where it went when it slowly disappeared beneath the stage floor.

The last song we sang was "Who's Lovin' You." When

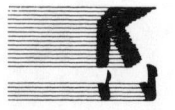

it ended, no one applauded or said a word. I couldn't stand not knowing, so I blurted, "How was that?" Jermaine shushed me. The older guys who were backing us up were laughing about something. I looked at them out of the corner of my eye. "Jackson Jive, huh?" one of them called out with a big grin on his face. I was confused. I think my brothers were too.

The man who had led us back said, "Thanks for coming up." We looked at Dad's face for some indication, but he didn't seem pleased or disappointed. It was still daylight out when we left. We took I-94 back to Gary, subdued, knowing there was homework to do for class tomorrow, wondering if that was all there was to that.

CHAPTER TWO

THE PROMISED LAND

We were jubilant when we learned we had passed the Motown audition. I remember Berry Gordy sitting us all down and saying that we were going to make history together. "I'm gonna make you the biggest thing in the world," he said, "and you're gonna be written about in history books." He really said that to us. We were leaning forward, listening to him, and saying, "Okay! Okay!" I'll never forget that. We were all over at his house, and it was like a fairy tale come true listening to this powerful, talented man tell us we were going to be very big. "Your first record will be a number one, your second record will be a number one, and so will your third record. Three number one records in a row. You'll hit the charts just as

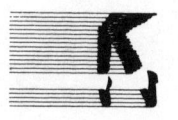

Diana Ross and the Supremes did." This was almost un-heard of in those days, but he was right; we turned around and did just that. Three in a row.

So Diana didn't find us first, but I don't think we'll ever be able to repay Diana properly for all she did for us in those days. When we finally moved to Southern Califor-nia, we actually lived with Diana and stayed with her for more than a year on a part-time basis. Some of us lived with Berry Gordy and some of us with Diana, and then we would switch. She was so wonderful, mothering us and making us feel right at home. She really helped take care of us for at least a year and a half while my parents closed up the Gary house and looked for a house we could all live in here in California. It was great for us because Berry and Diana lived on the same street in Beverly Hills. We could walk up to Berry's house and then go back to Diana's. Most of the time I'd spend the day at Diana's and the night at Berry's. This was an important period in my life because Diana loved art and encouraged me to appreci-ate it too. She took the time to educate me about it. We'd go out almost every day, just the two of us, and buy pencils and paint. When we weren't drawing or painting, we'd go to museums. She introduced me to the works of the great artists like Michelangelo and Degas and that was the start of my lifelong interest in art. She really taught me a great

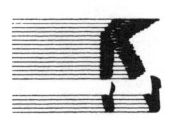

deal. It was so new to me and so exciting. It was really different from what I was used to doing, which was living and breathing music, rehearsing day in and day out. You wouldn't think a big star like Diana would take the time to teach a kid to paint, to give him an education in art, but she did and I loved her for it. I still do. I'm crazy about her. She was my mother, my lover, and my sister all combined in one amazing person.

Those were truly wild days for me and my brothers. When we flew to California from Chicago, it was like being in another country, another world. To come from our part of Indiana, which is so urban and often bleak, and to land in Southern California was like having the world transformed into a wonderful dream. I was uncontrollable back then. I was all over the place—Disneyland, Sunset Strip, the beach. My brothers loved it too, and we got into everything, like kids who had just visited a candy store for the first time. We were awestruck by California; trees had oranges and leaves on them in the middle of winter. There were palm trees and beautiful sunsets, and the weather was so warm. Every day was special. I would be doing something that was fun and wouldn't want it to end, but then I'd realize there was something else to do later that was going to be just as enjoyable and that I could look forward to just as much. Those were heady days.

69

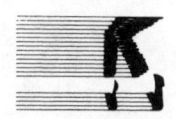

One of the best parts of being there was meeting all the big Motown stars who had emigrated to California along with Berry Gordy after he moved from Detroit. I remember when I first shook Smokey Robinson's hand. It was like shaking hands with a king. My eyes lit up with stars, and I remember telling my mother that his hand felt as if it was layered with soft pillows. You don't think about the little impressions people walk away with when you're a star yourself, but the fans do. At least, I know I did. I mean, I walked around saying, "His hand is *so soft.*" When I think about it now, it sounds silly, but it made a big impression on me. I had shaken Smokey Robinson's hand. There are so many artists and musicians and writers I admire. When I was young, the people I watched were the *real* showmen—James Brown, Sammy Davis, Jr., Fred Astaire, Gene Kelly. A great showman touches everybody; that's the real test of greatness and these men have it. Like Michelangelo's work, it touches you, I don't care who you are. I am always excited when I get a chance to meet someone whose work has affected me in some way. Maybe I've read a book that has touched me deeply or made me think about things that I haven't focused on before. A certain song or style of singing can excite me or move me and become a favorite that I'll never tire of hearing. A picture or a painting can reveal a universe. In

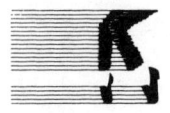

the same vein, an actor's performance or a collective performance can transform me.

In those days Motown had never recorded a kids' group. In fact the only child singer they had ever produced was Stevie Wonder. So Motown was determined that if they were going to promote kids, they'd promote the kind of kids who were good at more than just singing and dancing. They wanted people to like us because of who we were, not just because of our records. They wanted us to set an example by sticking to our schoolwork and being friendly to our fans, reporters, and everyone who came into contact with us. This wasn't hard for us because our mother had raised us to be polite and considerate. It was second nature. Our only problem with schoolwork was that once we became well known, we couldn't *go* to school because people would come into our classrooms through the windows, looking for an autograph or a picture. I was trying to keep up with my classes and not be the cause of disruptions, but it finally became impossible and we were given tutors to teach us at home.

During this period a lady named Suzanne de Passe was having a great effect on our lives. She worked for Motown, and it was she who trained us religiously once we moved to L.A. She also became a manager for the Jackson 5. We lived with her occasionally, ate with her,

and even played with her. We were a rowdy, high-spirited bunch, and she was young herself and full of fun. She really contributed a lot toward the shaping of the Jackson 5, and I'll never be able to thank her enough for all she did.

I remember Suzanne showing us these charcoal sketches of the five of us. In each sketch we had a different hairstyle. In another set of color drawings we were all pictured in different clothes that could be switched around like Colorforms. After we all decided on the hairstyles, they took us to a barber so he could make us match up with our pictures. Then, after she showed us the clothes, we went down to a wardrobe department where they gave us outfits to try on. They'd see us in one set of clothes, decide the clothes weren't right, and we'd all go back to the Colorforms to "try on" some more.

We had classes in manners and grammar. They gave us a list of questions, and they said they were the kinds of questions that we could expect people to ask us. We were always being asked about our interests and our hometown and how we liked singing together. Fans and reporters alike wanted to know how old we each were when we started performing. It was hard to have your life turn into public property, even if you appreciated that people were interested in you because of your music.

One of the many photo sessions we did with Motown.

The Motown people tested us on the answers to questions we hadn't heard from anyone yet. They tested us on grammar. And table manners. When we were ready, they brought us in for the last alterations on our sleeves and the trimming of our new Afros.

After all that there was a new song to learn called "I Want You Back." The song had a story behind it that we found out about little by little. It was written by someone from Chicago named Freddie Perren. He had been Jerry Butler's pianist when we opened for Jerry in a Chicago nightclub. He had felt sorry for these little kids the club owner had hired, figuring the club couldn't afford to get anyone else. His opinion changed dramatically when he saw us perform.

As it turned out, "I Want You Back" was originally called "I Want to Be Free" and was written for Gladys Knight. Freddie had even thought that Berry might go over Gladys's head and give the song to the Supremes. Instead, he mentioned to Jerry that he'd just signed this group of kids from Gary, Indiana. Freddie put two and two together, realized it was us, and decided to trust fate.

When we were learning the Steeltown songs back in Gary, Tito and Jermaine had to pay special attention because they were responsible for playing on those records. When they heard the demo for "I Want You Back," they

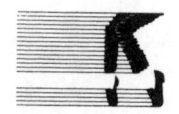

listened to the guitar and bass parts, but Dad explained that Motown didn't expect them to play on our records; the rhythm track would be taken care of before we put our vocals down. But he reminded them that this would put more pressure on them to keep up their practice independently, because we'd have to duplicate those songs in front of our fans. In the meantime, all of us had lyrics and cues to learn.

The guys looking after us in the singing department were Freddy Perrin and Bobby Taylor and Deke Richards, who, along with Hal Davis and another Motown guy named "Fonce" Mizell, were part of the team that wrote and produced our first singles. Together these guys were called "The Corporation." We went over to Richards's apartment to rehearse, and he was impressed that we had prepared so well. He didn't have to do much tinkering with the vocal arrangement he'd worked out, and he thought that while we were still hot, we should go right to the studio and cut our parts. The following afternoon we went to the studio. We were all so happy with what we got that we took our rough mix over to Berry Gordy. It was still midafternoon when we arrived at his studio. We figured that once Berry heard it, we'd be home in time for supper.

But it was one in the morning when I finally slumped

in the back seat of Richards's car, bobbing and steadying my head all the way home to fight off sleep. Gordy hadn't liked the song we did. We went over every part again, and when we did, Gordy figured out what changes he had to make in the arrangement. He was trying new things with us, like a school chorus master who has everyone singing their part as if they're singing alone, even if you can't hear him or her distinctly for the crowd. After he was through rehearsing us as a group, and he had reworked the music, he took me aside, one on one, to explain my part. He told me exactly what he wanted and how he wanted me to help him get it. Then he explained everything to Freddie Perren, who was going to record it. Berry was brilliant in this area. Right after the single was released, we went in to cut an album. We were particularly impressed with the "I Want You Back" session then because that one song took more time (and tape) than all the other songs on the record combined. That's the way Motown did things in those days because Berry insisted on perfection and attention to detail. I'll never forget his persistence. This was his genius. Then and later, I observed every moment of the sessions where Berry was present and never forgot what I learned. To this day I use the same principles. Berry was my teacher and a great one. He could identify the little elements that would make a song *great* rather than just

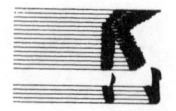

good. It was like magic, as if Berry was sprinkling pixie dust over everything.

For me and my brothers, recording for Motown was an exciting experience. Our team of writers shaped our music by being with us as we recorded it over and over, molding and sculpting a song until it was just perfect. We would cut a track over and over for *weeks* until we got it just as they wanted it. And I could see while they were doing it that it was getting better and better. They would change words, arrangements, rhythms, everything. Berry gave them the freedom to work this way because of his own perfectionist nature. I guess if they hadn't been doing it, he would have. Berry had such a knack. He'd just walk into the room where we were working and tell me what to do and he'd be right. It was amazing.

When "I Want You Back" was released in November 1969, it sold two million copies in six weeks and went to number one. Our next single, "ABC," came out in March 1970 and sold two million records in three weeks. I still like the part where I say, "Siddown, girl! I think I loove you! No, get up, girl, *show me what you can do!*" When our third single, "The Love You Save," went to number one in June of 1970, Berry's promise came true.

When our next single, "I'll Be There," was also a big hit in the fall of that year, we realized we might even

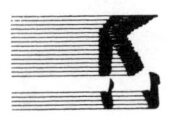

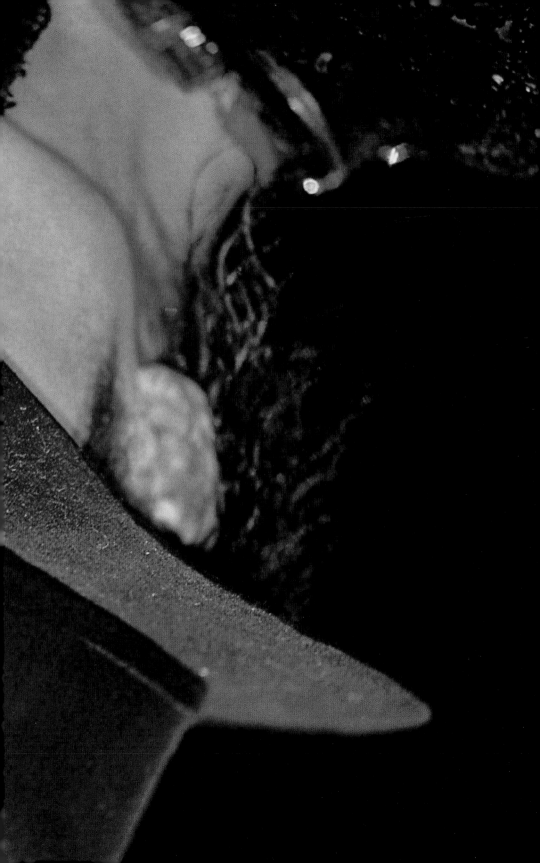

surpass Berry's expectations and be able to pay him back for all the effort he had made for us.

My brothers and I—our whole family—were very proud. We had created a new sound for a new decade. It was the first time in recording history that a bunch of kids had made so many hit records. The Jackson 5 had never had much competition from kids our own age. In the amateur days there was a kids' group called the Five Stairsteps that we used to see. They were good, but they didn't seem to have the strong family unit that we did, and sadly they broke up. After "ABC" hit the charts in such a big way, we started seeing other groups that record companies were grooming to ride the bandwagon we had built. I enjoyed all these groups: the Partridge Family, the Osmonds, the DeFranco Family. The Osmonds were already around, but they were doing a much different style of music, like barbershop harmony and crooning. As soon as we hit, they and the other groups got into soul real fast. We didn't mind. Competition, as we knew, was healthy. Our own relatives thought "One Bad Apple" was us. I remember being so little that they had a special apple crate for me to stand on with my name on it so I could reach the microphone. Microphones didn't go down far enough for kids my age. So many of my childhood years went by that way, with me standing on that apple box

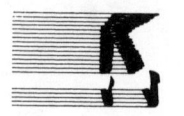

APRIL 29, 1971
No. 81
50c UK 15 NP

ROLLING STONE

Why does this eleven year-old stay up past his bedtime?

Michael Jackson and his six gold records

The Murder of Ruben Salazar
by Hunter S. Thompson

singing my heart out while other kids were outside play-ing.

As I said before, in those early days "The Corpora-tion" at Motown produced and shaped all our music. I remember lots of times when I felt the song should be sung one way and the producers felt it should be sung another way. But for a long time I was very obedient and wouldn't say anything about it. Finally it reached a point where I got fed up with being told exactly how to sing. This was in 1972 when I was fourteen years old, around the time of the song "Lookin' Through the Windows." They wanted me to sing a certain way, and I knew they were wrong. No matter what age you are, if you *have* it and you *know* it, then people should listen to you. I was furious with our producers and very upset. So I called Berry Gordy and complained. I said that they had always told me how to sing, and I had agreed all this time, but now they were getting too . . . mechanical.

So he came into the studio and told them to let me do what I wanted to do. I think he told them to let me be more free or something. And after that, I started adding a lot of vocal twists that they really ended up loving. I'd do a lot of ad-libbing, like twisting words or adding some edge to them.

When Berry was in the studio with us, he would al-

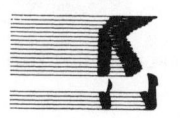

By this time the microphone had become a natural extension of my hand.

ways add something that was right. He'd go from studio to studio, checking on different aspects of people's work, often adding elements that made the records better. Walt Disney used to do the same thing; he'd go check on his various artists and say, "Well, this character should be more outgoing." I always knew when Berry was enjoying something I was doing in the studio, because he has this habit of rolling his tongue in his cheek when he's pleased by something. If things were really going well, he'd punch the air like the ex-professional boxer he is.

My three favorite songs from those days are "Never Can Say Goodbye," "I'll Be There," and "ABC." I'll never forget the first time I heard "ABC." I thought it was *so* good. I remember feeling this eagerness to sing that song, to get in the studio and really make it *work* for us.

We were still rehearsing daily and working hard— some things didn't change—but we were grateful to be where we were. There were so many people pulling for us, and we were so determined ourselves that it seemed anything could happen.

Once "I Want You Back" came out, everyone at Motown prepared us for success. Diana loved it and presented us at a big-name Hollywood discotheque, where she had us playing in a comfortable party atmosphere like at Berry's. Following directly on the heels of Diana's

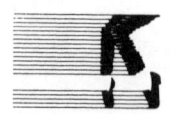

event came an invitation to play at the "Miss Black America" telecast. Being on the show would enable us to give people a preview of our record *and* our show. After we got the invitation, my brothers and I remembered our disappointment at not getting to go to New York to do our first TV show because Motown had called. Now we were going to do our first TV show *and* we were with Motown. Life was very good. Diana, of course, put the cherry on top. She was going to host "The Hollywood Palace," a big Saturday night show; it would be her last appearance with the Supremes and the first major exposure for us. This meant a lot to Motown, because by then they had decided that our new album would be called "Diana Ross Presents the Jackson 5." Never before had a superstar like Diana passed the torch to a bunch of kids. Motown, Diana, and five kids from Gary, Indiana, were all pretty excited. By then "I Want You Back" had come out, and Berry was proven right again; all the stations that played Sly and the Beatles were playing us, too.

As I mentioned earlier, we didn't work as hard on the album as we did on the single, but we had fun trying out all sorts of songs—from "Who's Lovin' You," the old Miracles' song we were doing in the talent show days, to "Zip-A-Dee-Doo-Dah."

We did songs on that album that appealed to a wide

audience—kids, teenagers, and grownups—and we all felt
that was a reason for its big success. We knew that "The
Hollywood Palace" had a live audience, a sophisticated
Hollywood crowd, and we were concerned; but we had
them from the first note. There was an orchestra in the
pit, so that was the first time I heard *all* of "I Want You
Back" performed live because I wasn't there when they
recorded the strings for the album. Doing that show made
us feel like kings, the way winning the citywide show in
Gary had.

Selecting the right songs for us to do was going to be a
real challenge now that we weren't depending on other
people's hits to win a crowd. The Corporation guys and
Hal Davis were put to work writing songs especially for
us, as well as producing them. Berry didn't want to have
to bail us all out again. So even after our first singles hit
number one on the charts, we were busy with the follow-
ups.

"I Want You Back" could have been sung by a grown-
up, but "ABC" and "The Love You Save" were written for
our young voices, with parts for Jermaine as well as me—
another bow to the Sly sound, which rotated singers
around the stage. The Corporation had also written those
songs with dance routines in mind: the steps our fans did
at parties as well as those we did on stage. The verses were

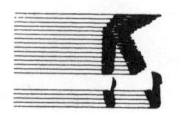

tongue-twisting, and that's why they were split up between Jermaine and me.

Neither of those records could have happened without "I Want You Back." We were adding and subtracting
ideas in the arrangements from that one mother lode of a
song, but the public seemed to want everything we were
doing. We later made two more records in the vein,
"Mama's Pearl" and "Sugar Daddy," which reminded me
of my own schoolyard days: "While I'm giving you the
candy, *he's* getting all your love!" We added one new
wrinkle when Jermaine and I sang harmony together,
which always got an enthusiastic response when we did it
from the same mike on stage.

The pros have told us that no group had a better start
than we did. Ever.

"I'll Be There" was our real breakthrough song; it was the
one that said, "We're here to stay." It was number one for
five weeks, which is *very* unusual. That's a long time for a
song and the song was one of my favorites of all the songs
we've ever done. How I loved the words: "You and I must
make a pact, we must bring salvation back . . ." Willie
Hutch and Berry Gordy didn't seem like people who'd
write like that. They were always kidding around with us
when we weren't in the studio. But that song grabbed me

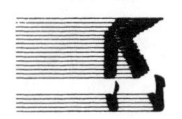

from the moment I heard the demo. I didn't even know what a harpsichord was until that record's opening notes were played for us. The song was produced thanks to the genius of Hal Davis, assisted by Suzy Ikeda, my other half who stood next to me song after song, making sure I put the right emotion and feeling and heart into the composition. It was a serious song, but we threw in a fun part when I sang "Just look over your shoulder, honey!" Without the honey, that's right out of the Four Tops' great song "Reach Out, I'll Be There." So we were feeling more and more like a part of Motown's history as well as its future.

Originally the plan was for me to sing all the bouncy stuff and Jermaine to do the ballads. But though Jermaine's voice at seventeen was more mature, ballads were more my love, if not really my style—yet. That was our fourth straight number one as a group, and a lot of people liked Jermaine's song "I Found That Girl," the B-side of "The Love You Save," just as much as the hits.

We worked those songs into one big medley, with plenty of room for dancing, and we went back to that medley when we performed on all kinds of TV shows. For instance, we played on "The Ed Sullivan Show" three different times. Motown always told us what to say in interviews back then, but Mr. Sullivan was one of the people who drew us out and made us feel comfortable.

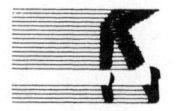

Looking back, I wouldn't say Motown was putting us in any kind of straitjacket or turning us into robots, even though I wouldn't have done it that way myself; and if I had children, I wouldn't tell them what to say. The Motown people were doing something with us that hadn't been done before, and who was to say what was the right way to handle that sort of stuff?

Reporters would ask us all kinds of questions, and the Motown people would be standing by to help us out or monitor the questions if need be. We wouldn't have dreamed of trying anything that would embarrass them. I guess they were worried about the possibility of our sounding militant the way people were often doing in those days. Maybe they were worried after they gave us those Afros that they had created little Frankensteins. Once a reporter asked a Black Power question and the Motown person told him we didn't think about that stuff because we were a "commercial product." It sounded weird, but we winked and gave the power salute when we left, which seemed to thrill the guy.

We even had a reunion with Don Cornelius on his "Soul Train" show. He had been a local disc jockey during our Chicago days, so we all knew one another from that time. We enjoyed watching his show and picked up ideas

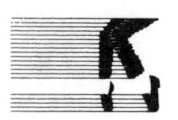

from those dancers who were from our part of the country.

The crazy days of the big Jackson 5 tours began right after the successes we had with our records. It started with a big arena tour in the fall of 1970; we played huge halls like Madison Square Garden and the Los Angeles Forum. When "Never Can Say Goodbye" was a big hit in 1971, we played forty-five cities that summer, followed by fifty more cities later that year.

I recall most of that time as a period of extreme closeness with my brothers. We have always been a very loyal and affectionate group. We clowned around, goofed off a lot together, and played outrageous pranks on each other and the people who worked with us. We never got too rowdy—no TVs sailed out of our hotel windows, but a lot of water was spilled on various heads. We were mostly trying to conquer the boredom we felt from being so long on the road. When you're bored on tour, you tend to do anything to cheer yourself up. Here we were, cramped up in these hotel rooms, unable to go anywhere because of the mobs of screaming girls outside, and we wanted to have some fun. I wish we could have captured some of the stuff we did on film, especially some of the wild pranks. We'd all wait until our security manager, Bill Bray, was

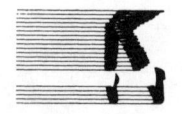

asleep. Then we'd stage insane fast-walk races in the hallways, pillow fights, tag-team wrestling matches, shaving cream wars, you name it. We were nuts. We'd drop balloons and paper bags full of water off hotel balconies and watch them explode. Then we'd die laughing. We threw stuff at each other and spent hours on the phone making fake calls and ordering immense room service meals that were delivered to the rooms of strangers. Anyone who walked into one of our bedrooms had a ninety percent chance of being drenched by a bucket of water propped over the doors.

When we'd arrive in a new city, we'd try to do all the sightseeing we could. We traveled with a wonderful tutor, Rose Fine, who taught us a great deal and made sure we did our lessons. It was Rose who instilled in me a love of books and literature that sustains me today. I read everything I could get my hands on. New cities meant new places to shop. We loved to shop, especially in bookstores and department stores, but as our fame spread our fans transformed casual shopping trips into hand-to-hand combat. Being mobbed by near hysterical girls was one of the most terrifying experiences for me in those days. I mean, it was *rough.* We'd decide to run into some department store to see what they had, and the fans would find out we were there and would demolish the place, just tear it up.

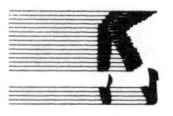

Counters would get knocked over, glass would break, the cash registers would be toppled. All we had wanted to do was look at some clothes! When those mob scenes broke out, all the craziness and adulation and notoriety became more than we could handle. If you haven't witnessed a scene like that, you can't imagine what it's like. Those girls were *serious.* They still are. They don't realize they might hurt you because they're acting out of love. They mean well, but I can testify that it *hurts* to be mobbed. You feel as if you're going to suffocate or be dismembered. There are a thousand hands grabbing at you. One girl is twisting your wrist this way while another girl is pulling your watch off. They grab your hair and pull it hard, and it hurts like fire. You fall against things and the scrapes are horrible. I still wear the scars, and I can remember in which city I got each of them. Early on, I learned how to run through crowds of thrashing girls outside of theaters, hotels, and airports. It's important to remember to shield your eyes with your hands because girls can forget they have nails during such emotional confrontations. I know the fans mean well and I love them for their enthusiasm and support, but crowd scenes *are* scary.

The wildest mob scene I ever witnessed happened the first time we went to England. We were in the air over the Atlantic when the pilot announced that he had just

been told there were ten thousand kids waiting for us at Heathrow Airport. We couldn't believe it. We were excited, but if we could have turned around and flown home, we might have. We knew this was going to be something, but since there wasn't enough fuel to go back, we flew on. When we landed, we could see that the fans had literally taken over the whole airport. It was wild to be mobbed like that. My brothers and I felt fortunate to make it out of the airport alive that day.

I wouldn't trade my memories of those days with my brothers for anything. I often wish I could relive those days. We were like the seven dwarfs: each of us was different, each had his own personality. Jackie was the athlete and the worrier. Tito was the strong, compassionate father figure. He was totally into cars and loved putting them together and tearing them apart. Jermaine was the one I was closest to when we were growing up. He was funny and easygoing, and was constantly fooling around. It was Jermaine who put all those buckets of cold water on the doors of our hotel rooms. Marlon was and is one of the most determined people I've ever met. He, too, was a real joker and prankster. He used to be the one who'd always get in trouble in the early days because he'd be out of step or miss a note, but that was far from true later.

Bill Cosby gives us the rules of love and baseball.

The diversity of my brothers' personalities and the closeness we felt were what kept me going during those gruelling days of constant touring. Everybody helped everybody. Jackie and Tito would keep us from going too far with our pranks. They'd seem to have us under control, and then Jermaine and Marlon would shout, "Let's go crazy!!"

I really miss all that. In the early days we were together all the time. We'd go to amusement parks or ride horses or watch movies. We did everything together. As soon as someone said, "I'm going swimming," we'd all yell, "Me too!"

The separation from my brothers started much later, when they began to get married. An understandable change occurred as each of them became closest to his wife and *they* became a family unit unto themselves. A part of me wanted us to stay as we were—brothers who were also best friends—but change is inevitable and always good in one sense or another. We still love each other's company. We still have a great time when we're together. But the various paths our lives have taken won't allow us the freedom to enjoy one another's company as much as we did.

In those days, touring with the Jackson 5, I always shared a room with Jermaine. He and I were close, both

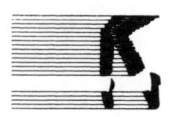

onstage and off, and shared a lot of the same interests. Since Jermaine was also the brother most intrigued by the girls who wanted to get at him, he and I would get into mischief on the road.

I think our father decided early on that he had to keep a more watchful eye on us than on our other brothers. He would usually take the room next to ours, which meant he could come in to check on us anytime through the connecting doors. I really despised this arrangement, not only because he could monitor our misbehavior, but also because he used to do the meanest things to us. Jermaine and I would be sleeping, exhausted after a show, and my father would bring a bunch of girls into the room; we'd wake up and they'd be standing there, looking at us, giggling.

Because show business and my career were my life, the biggest personal struggle I had to face during those teenage years did not involve the recording studios or my stage performance. In those days, the biggest struggle was right there in my mirror. To a great degree, my identity as a person was tied to my identity as a celebrity.

My appearance began to really change when I was about fourteen. I grew quite a bit in height. People who didn't know me would come into a room expecting to be introduced to cute little Michael Jackson and they'd walk

right past me. I would say, "I'm Michael," and they would look doubtful. Michael was a cute little kid; I was a gangly adolescent heading toward five feet ten inches. I was not the person they expected or even wanted to see. Adolescence is hard enough, but imagine having your own natural insecurities about the changes your body is undergoing heightened by the negative reactions of others. They seemed so surprised that I could change, that my body was undergoing the same natural change everyone's does.

It was tough. Everyone had called me cute for a long time, but along with all the other changes, my skin broke out in a terrible case of acne. I looked in the mirror one morning and it was like, "OH NO!" I seemed to have a pimple for every oil gland. And the more I was bothered by it, the worse it got. I didn't realize it then, but my diet of greasy processed food didn't help either.

I became subconsciously scarred by this experience with my skin. I got very shy and became embarrassed to meet people because my complexion was so bad. It really seemed that the more I looked in the mirror, the worse the pimples got. My appearance began to depress me. So I know that a case of acne can have a devastating effect on a person. The effect on me was so bad that it messed up my whole personality. I couldn't look at people when I talked to them. I'd look down, or away. I felt I didn't have any-

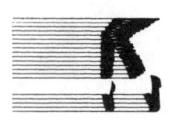

thing to be proud of and I didn't even want to go out. I didn't do anything.

My brother Marlon would be covered with pimples and he wouldn't care but I didn't want to see anybody and I didn't want anyone to see my skin in that shape. It makes you wonder about what makes us the way we are, that two brothers could be so different.

I still had our hit records to be proud of, and once I hit the stage, I didn't think about anything else. All that worry was gone.

But once I came offstage, there was that mirror to face again.

Eventually, things changed. I started feeling differently about my condition. I've learned to change how I think and learned to feel better about myself. Most important, I changed my diet. That was the key.

In the fall of 1971 I cut my first solo record, "Got to Be There." It was wonderful working on that record and it became one of my favorites. It was Berry Gordy's idea that I should do a solo recording, and so I became one of the first people in a Motown group to really step out. Berry also said he thought I should record my own album. Years later, when I did, I realized he was right.

There was a small conflict during that era that was typical of the struggles I went through as a young singer.

When you're young and have ideas, people often think you're just being childish and silly. We were on tour in 1972, the year "Got to Be There" became a big hit. One night I said to our road manager, "Before I sing that song, let me go offstage and grab that little hat I wore for the picture on the album cover. If the audience sees me wearing that hat, they'll go crazy."

He thought it was the most ridiculous idea he had ever heard. I was not allowed to do it because I was young, and *they* all thought it was a dumb idea. Not long after that incident, Donny Osmond began wearing a very similar hat all over the country and people *loved* it. I felt good about my instincts; I had thought it would work. I had seen Marvin Gaye wear a hat when he sang "Let's Get It On," and people went bananas. They knew what was coming when Marvin put that hat on. It added excitement and communicated something to the audience that allowed them to become more involved with the show.

I was already a devoted fan of film and animation by the time "The Jackson Five" Saturday morning cartoon show started appearing over network television in 1971. Diana Ross had enhanced my appreciation of animation when she taught me to draw, but being a cartoon character pushed me over the brink into a full-time love of the

movies and the kind of animated motion pictures pioneered by Walt Disney. I have such admiration for Mr. Disney and what he accomplished with the help of so many talented artists. When I think about the joy he and his company have brought to millions of children—and adults—the world over, I am in awe.

I loved being a cartoon. It was so much fun to get up on Saturday mornings to watch cartoons and look forward to seeing ourselves on the screen. It was like a fantasy come true for all of us.

My first real involvement with films came when I sang the title song for the movie *Ben* in 1972.

Ben meant a lot to me. Nothing had ever excited me as much as going to the studio to put my voice on film. I had a great time. Later, when the movie came out, I'd go to the theater and wait until the end when the credits would flash on, and it would say, " 'Ben' sung by Michael Jackson." I was really impressed by that. I loved the song and loved the story. Actually, the story was a lot like *E.T.* It was about a boy who befriended a rat. People didn't understand the boy's love for this little creature. He was dying of some disease and his only true friend was Ben, the leader of the rats in the city where they lived. A lot of people thought the movie was a bit odd, but I was not one

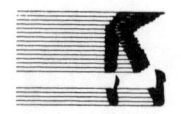

of them. The song went to number one and is still a favorite of mine. I have always loved animals and I enjoy reading about them and seeing movies in which they're featured.

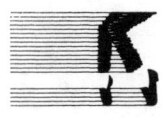

CHAPTER THREE

DANCING MACHINE

The media write weird stuff about me all the time. The distortion of the truth bothers me. I usually don't read a lot of what is printed, although I often hear about it.

I don't understand why they feel the need to make up things about me. I suppose if there's nothing scandalous to report, it's necessary to make things interesting. I take some small pride in thinking that I've come out pretty well, all things considered. A lot of children in the entertainment business ended up doing drugs and destroying themselves: Frankie Lymon, Bobbie Driscoll, any of a number of child stars. And I can understand their turning to drugs, considering the enormous stresses put upon

them at a young age. It's a difficult life. Very few manage to maintain any semblance of a normal childhood.

I myself have never even tried drugs—no marijuana, no cocaine, nothing. I mean, I haven't even *tried* these things.

Forget it.

This isn't to say we were never tempted. We were musicians doing business during an era when drug use was common. I don't mean to be judgmental—it's not even a moral issue for me—but I've seen drugs destroy too many lives to think they're anything to fool with. I'm certainly no angel, and I may have my own bad habits, but drugs aren't among them.

By the time *Ben* came out, we knew that we were going to go around the world. American soul music had become as popular in other countries as blue jeans and hamburgers. We were invited to become a part of that big world, and in 1972 we began our first overseas tour with a visit to England. Though we'd never been there before or appeared on British television, people knew all the words to our songs. They even had wide scarves with our pictures on them and "Jackson 5" written in big broad letters. The theaters were smaller than the ones we were used to playing in the United States, but the enthusiasm from the

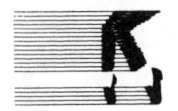

crowds was very gratifying as we'd finish each song. They didn't scream *during* the songs the way crowds did back home, so people over there could actually tell how good Tito was getting on the guitar, because they could hear him.

We took Randy along because we wanted to give him the experience and allow him to see what was going on. He wasn't officially part of our act, but stayed in the background with bongos. He had his own Jackson 5 outfit, so when we introduced him, people cheered. The next time we came back, Randy would be a part of the group. I had been the bongo player before Randy, and Marlon had played them before me, so it had become almost a tradition to break the new guy in on those crazy little drums.

We had three years of hits behind us when we toured Europe that first time, so there was enough to please both the kids who followed our music and the Queen of England, whom we met at a Royal Command Performance. That was very exciting for us. I had seen photographs of other groups, like the Beatles, meeting the Queen after command performances, but I never dreamed we'd get the chance to play for her.

England was our jumping-off point, and it was different from any place we'd been before, but the farther we traveled, the more exotic the world looked. We saw the

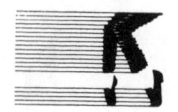

great museums of Paris and the beautiful mountains of Switzerland. Europe was an education in the roots of Western culture and, in a way, a preparation for visiting Eastern countries that were more spiritual. I was very impressed that the people there didn't value material things as much as they did animals and nature. For instance, China and Japan were places that helped me grow because these countries made me understand there was more to life than the things you could hold in your hand or see with your eyes. And in all of these countries, the people had heard of us and liked our music.

Australia and New Zealand, our next stops, were English-speaking, but we met people who were still living in tribes in the outback. They greeted us as brothers even though they didn't speak our language. If I'd ever needed proof that all men could be brothers, I certainly had it during that tour.

And then there was Africa. We had read up on Africa because our tutor, Miss Fine, had prepared special lessons on the customs and history of each country we visited. We didn't get to see the prettier parts of Africa, but the ocean and the shore and the people were unbelievably beautiful near the coast where we were. We went to a game reserve one day and observed animals roaming wild. The music was eye-opening too. The rhythms were phenomenal.

The Royal Command Performance remains one of the greatest
honors of my life.

When we first came off the plane, it was dawn and there was a long line of Africans dancing in their native costumes, with drums and shakers. They were dancing all around, welcoming us. They were really into it. Boy, it was something. What a perfect way to welcome us to Africa. I'll never forget that.

And the craftspeople in the marketplace were incredible. People were making things as we watched and selling other things. I remember one man who made beautiful wood carvings. He'd ask you what you wanted and you'd say, "A man's face," and he'd take a piece from a tree trunk, slice it, and create this remarkable face. You could watch him do it right before your eyes. I'd just sit there and watch people step up to ask him to make something for them and he'd do this whole thing over and over.

It was a visit to Senegal that made us realize how fortunate we were and how our African heritage had helped to make us what we were. We visited an old, abandoned slave camp at Gore Island and we were so moved. The African people had given us gifts of courage and endurance that we couldn't hope to repay.

I guess if Motown could have had us age the way they wanted us to, they would have wanted Jackie to stay the age he was when we became a headline act and have each

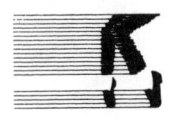

of us catch up with him—although I think they'd have wanted to keep me a year or so younger, so I could still be a child star. That may sound nonsensical, but it really wasn't much more farfetched than the way they were continuing to mold us, keeping us from being a real group with its own internal direction and ideas. We were growing up and we were expanding creatively. We had so many ideas we wanted to try out, but they were convinced that we shouldn't fool with a successful formula. At least they didn't drop us as soon as my voice changed, as some said they might.

It got to the point that it seemed there were more guys in the booth than there were on the studio floor at any given time. They all seemed to be bumping into one another, giving advice and monitoring our music.

Our loyal fans stuck with us on records like "I Am Love" and "Skywriter." These songs were musically ambitious pop recordings, with sophisticated string arrangements, but they weren't right for us. Sure, we couldn't do "ABC" all our lives—that was the last thing we wanted—but even the older fans thought "ABC" had more going for it, and that was hard for us to live with. During the mid-seventies we were in danger of becoming an oldies act, and I wasn't even eighteen yet.

When Jermaine married Hazel Gordy, our boss's

daughter, people were winking at us, saying that we'd
always be looked after. Indeed, when "Get It Together"
came out in 1973, it got the same treatment from Berry
that "I Want You Back" had gotten. It was our biggest hit
in two years, though you could have said it was more like a
bone transplant than the spanking little baby that our first
hit was. Nevertheless, "Get It Together" had good, tough
low harmony, a sharper wah-wah guitar, and strings that
buzzed like fireflies. Radio stations liked it, but not as
much as the new dance clubs called discos did. Motown
picked up on this and brought back Hal Davis from The
Corporation days to really put the juice into "Dancing
Machine." The Jackson 5 were no longer just the backup
group for the 101 Strings or whatever.

Motown had come a long way from the early days
when you could find good studio musicians supplement-
ing their session pay with bowling alley gigs. A new sophistication turned up in the music on "Dancing Machine." That song had the best horn part we'd worked
with yet and a "bubble machine" in the break, made out
of synthesizer noise, that kept the song from going completely out of style. Disco music had its detractors, but to
us it seemed our rite of passage into the adult world.

I loved "Dancing Machine," loved the groove and the
feel of that song. When it came out in 1974, I was deter-

mined to find a dance move that would enhance the song and make it more exciting to perform—and, I hoped, more exciting to watch.

So when we sang "Dancing Machine" on "Soul Train," I did a street-style dance move called the Robot. That performance was a lesson to me in the power of television. Overnight, "Dancing Machine" rose to the top of the charts, and within a few days it seemed that every kid in the United States was doing the Robot. I had never seen anything like it.

Motown and the Jackson 5 could agree on one thing: As our act grew, our audience should too. We had two re-cruits coming up: Randy had already toured with us, and Janet was showing talent with her singing and dancing lessons. We couldn't put Randy and Janet into our old lineup any more than we could put square pegs into round holes. I wouldn't insult their considerable talent by saying that show business was so in their blood that they just took their places automatically, as if we'd reserved a spot for them. They worked hard and earned their places in the group. They didn't join us because they ate meals with us and shared our old toys.

If you just went by blood, I'd have as much crane operator in me as singer. You can't measure these things.

Dad worked us hard and kept certain goals in sight while spinning dreams at night.

Just as disco might have seemed like a very unlikely place for a kids' group to become a grown-up act, Las Vegas, with its showcase theaters, wasn't exactly the family atmosphere that Motown had originally groomed us for, but we decided to play there just the same. There wasn't much to do in Las Vegas if you didn't gamble, but we thought of the theaters in the city as just big clubs with the club hours and clientele of our Gary and South Side Chicago days—except for the tourists. Tourist crowds were a good thing for us, since they knew our old hits and would watch our skits and listen to new songs without getting restless. It was great to see the delight on their faces when little Janet came out in her Mae West costume for a number or two.

We had performed skits before, in a 1971 TV special called *Goin' Back to Indiana,* which celebrated our Gary homecoming the first time we all decided to return. Our records had become hits all over the world since we'd seen our hometown last.

It was even more fun to do skits with nine of us, instead of just five, plus whatever guests happened to appear with us. Our expanded lineup was a dream come true for Dad. Looking back, I know the Las Vegas shows

were an experience I'll never recapture. We didn't have the high-pressure concert crowd wanting all our hit songs and nothing more. We were temporarily freed from the pressures of having to keep up with what everyone else was doing. We had a ballad or two in every show to break in my "new voice." At fifteen, I was having to think about things like that.

There were people from CBS Television at our Las Vegas shows and they approached us about doing a variety show for the upcoming summer. We were very interested and pleased that we were being recognized as more than just a "Motown group." Over time, this distinction would not be lost on us. Because we had creative control over our Las Vegas revue, it was harder for us to return to our lack of freedom in recording and writing music once we got back to Los Angeles. We'd always intended to grow and develop in the musical field. That was our bread and butter, and we felt we were being held back. Sometimes I felt we were being treated as if we still lived in Berry Gordy's house—and with Jermaine now a son-in-law, our frustration was only heightened.

By the time we began putting our own act together, there were signs that other Motown institutions were changing. Marvin Gaye took charge of his own music and produced his masterpiece album, *What's Goin' On.*

113

Stevie Wonder was learning more about electronic keyboards than the experienced studio hired guns—they
were coming to him for advice. One of our last great
memories from our Motown days is of Stevie leading us in
chanting to back up his tough, controversial song "You
Haven't Done Nothin'." Though Stevie and Marvin were
still in the Motown camp, they had fought for—and won—
the right to make their own records, and even to publish
their own songs. Motown hadn't even budged with us. To
them we were still kids, even if they weren't dressing us
and "protecting" us any longer.

Our problems with Motown began around 1974,
when we told them in no uncertain terms that we wanted
to write and produce our own songs. Basically, we didn't
like the way our music sounded at the time. We had a
strong competitive urge and we felt we were in danger of
being eclipsed by other groups who were creating a more
contemporary sound.

Motown said, "No, you can't write your own songs;
you've got to have songwriters and producers." They not
only refused to grant our requests, they told us it was
taboo to even mention that we wanted to do our own
music. I really got discouraged and began to seriously
dislike all the material Motown was feeding us. Eventu-

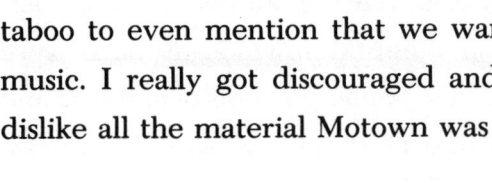

ally I became so disappointed and upset that I wanted to leave Motown behind.

When I feel that something is not right, I have to speak up. I know most people don't think of me as tough or strong-willed, but that's just because they don't know me. Eventually my brothers and I reached a point with Motown where we were miserable but no one was saying anything. My brothers didn't say anything. My father didn't say anything. So it was up to me to arrange a meeting with Berry Gordy and talk to him. I was the one who had to say that we—the Jackson 5—were going to leave Motown. I went over to see him, face to face, and it was one of the most difficult things I've ever done. If I had been the only one of us who was unhappy, I might have kept my mouth shut, but there had been so much talk at home about how unhappy we *all* were that I went in and talked to him and told him how we felt. I told him I was unhappy.

Remember, I love Berry Gordy. I think he's a genius, a brilliant man who's one of the giants of the music business. I have nothing but respect for him, but that day I was a lion. I complained that we weren't allowed any freedom to write songs and produce. He told me that he still thought we needed outside producers to make hit records.

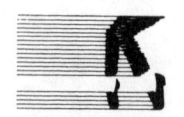

But I knew better. Berry was talking out of anger. That was a difficult meeting, but we're friends again, and he's still like a father to me—very proud of me and happy about my success. No matter what, I will always love Berry because he taught me some of the most valuable things I've learned in my life. He's the man who told the Jackson 5 they would become a part of history, and that is exactly what happened. Motown has done so much for so many people over the years. I feel we're fortunate to have been one of the groups Berry personally introduced to the public and I owe enormous thanks to this man. My life would have been very different without him. We all felt that Motown started us, supporting our professional careers. We all felt our roots were there, and we all wished we could stay. We were grateful for everything they had done for us, but change is inevitable. I'm a person of the present, and I have to ask, How are things going now? What's happening now? What's going to happen in the future that could affect what has happened in the past?

It's important for artists always to maintain control of their lives and work. There's been a big problem in the past with artists being taken advantage of. I've learned that a person *can* prevent that from happening by standing up for what he or she believes is right, without con-

cern for the consequences. We could have stayed with Motown; but if we had, we'd probably be an oldies act.

I knew it was time for change, so we followed our instincts, and we won when we decided to try for a fresh start with another label, Epic.

We were relieved that we had finally made our feelings clear and cut the ties that were binding us, but we were also really devastated when Jermaine decided to stay with Motown. He was Berry's son-in-law and his situation was more complicated than ours. He thought it was more important for him to stay than to leave, and Jermaine always did as his conscience told him, so he left the group.

I clearly remember the first show we did without him, because it was so painful for me. Since my earliest days on the stage—and even in our rehearsals in our Gary living room—Jermaine stood at my left with his bass. I *depended* on being next to Jermaine. And when I did that first show without him there, with no one next to me, I felt totally naked onstage for the first time in my life. So we worked harder to compensate for the loss of one of our shining stars, Jermaine. I remember that show well because we got three standing ovations. We worked *hard*.

When Jermaine left the group, Marlon had a chance to take his place and he really shone onstage. My brother

117

Randy officially took my place as bongo player and the baby of the band.

Around the time that Jermaine left, things were further complicated for us because of the fact that we were doing a stupid summer replacement TV series. It was a dumb move to agree to do that show and I hated every minute of it.

I had loved the old "Jackson Five" cartoon show. I used to wake up early on Saturday mornings and say, "I'm a cartoon!" But I hated doing this television show because I felt it would hurt our recording career rather than help it. I think a TV series is the worst thing an artist who has a recording career can do. I kept saying, "But this is gonna hurt our record sales." And others said, "No, it's gonna help them."

They were totally wrong. We had to dress in ridiculous outfits and perform stupid comedy routines to canned laughter. It was all so fake. We didn't have time to learn or master anything about television. We had to create three dance numbers a day, trying to meet a deadline. The Nielsen ratings controlled our lives from week to week. I'd never do it again. It's a dead-end road. What happens is partly psychological. You are in people's homes every week and they begin to feel they know you too well. You're doing all this silly comedy to canned laughter and

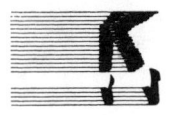

Berry was closely involved in everything we did, including our appearance
on the Diana Ross TV Special in 1971.

your music begins to recede into the background. When you try to get serious again and pick up your career where you left off, you can't because you're overexposed. People are thinking of you as the guys who do the silly, crazy routines. One week you're Santa Claus, the next week you're Prince Charming, another week you're a rabbit. It's crazy, because you lose your identity in the business; the rocker image you had is gone. I'm not a comedian. I'm not a show host. I'm a musician. That's why I've turned down offers to host the Grammy Awards and the American Music Awards. Is it really entertaining for me to get up there and crack a few weak jokes and force people to laugh because I'm Michael Jackson, when I know in my heart that I'm not funny?

After our TV show I can remember doing theaters-in-the-round where the stage didn't revolve because if they had turned it, we would have been singing to some empty seats. I learned something from that experience and I was the one who refused to renew our contract with the network for another season. I just told my father and brothers that I thought it was a big mistake, and they understood my point of view. I had actually had a lot of misgivings about the show *before* we started taping it, but I ended up agreeing to give it a try because everyone thought it would be a great experience and very good for us.

The problem with TV is that everything must be crammed into a little space of time. You don't have time to perfect anything. Schedules—tight schedules—rule your life. If you're not happy with something, you just forget it and move on to the next routine. I'm a perfectionist by nature. I like things to be the best they can be. I want people to hear or watch something I've done and feel that I've given it everything I've got. I feel I owe an audience that courtesy. On the show our sets were sloppy, the lighting was often poor, and our choreography was *rushed.* Somehow, the show was a big hit. There was a popular show on opposite us and we beat them out in the Nielsens. CBS really wanted to keep us, but I knew that show was a mistake. As it turned out, it did hurt our record sales and it took us a while to recover from the damage. When you know something's wrong for you, you have to make difficult decisions and trust your instincts.

I rarely did TV after that; the *Motown 25* special is the only show that comes to mind. Berry asked me to be on that show and I kept trying to say no, but he finally talked me into it. I told him I wanted to do "Billie Jean" even though it would be the only non-Motown song on the show, and he readily agreed. "Billie Jean" was number one at the time. My brothers and I really rehearsed for the show. I choreographed our routines, so I was pretty

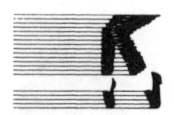

wrapped up in those numbers, but I had a good notion of what I wanted to do with "Billie Jean." I had a sense that the routine had worked itself out in my mind while I was busy with other things. I asked someone to rent or buy me a black fedora—a spy hat—and the day of the show I began putting the routine together. I'll never forget that night, because when I opened my eyes at the end, people were on their feet applauding. I was overwhelmed by the reaction. It felt so good.

Our only "break" during the Motown-to-Epic switch was the TV show. While that was all going on, we heard that Epic had Kenny Gamble and Leon Huff working on demos for us. We were told we'd be recording in Philadelphia after our shows were all done.

If there was anyone who stood to gain the most from switching labels, it was Randy, who was now part of the Five. But now that he finally *was* one of us, we were no longer known as the Jackson 5. Motown said that the group's name was the company's registered trademark, and that we couldn't use it when we left. That was hardball, of course, so we called ourselves the Jacksons from that time on.

Dad had met with the Philly guys while negotiations were going on with Epic. We'd always had great respect for the records that Gamble and Huff had overseen,

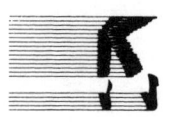

records like "Backstabbers" by the O'Jays, "If You Don't Know Me by Now," by Harold Melvin and the Blue Notes (featuring Teddy Pendergrass), and "When Will I See You Again," by the Three Degrees, along with many other hits. They told Dad they'd been watching us, and they said they wouldn't mess with our singing. Dad mentioned that we were hoping to have a song or two of our own included in the new album, and they promised to give them a fair hearing.

We'd gotten to talk with Kenny and Leon and their team of people, which included Leon McFadden and John Whitehead. They showed what they could do for themselves when they made "Ain't No Stoppin' Us Now" in 1979. Dexter Wanzel was also a part of this team. Kenny Gamble and Leon Huff are such pros. I actually got a chance to watch them create as they presented songs to us and that helped my songwriting a lot. Just watching Huff play the piano while Gamble sang taught me more about the anatomy of a song than anything else. Kenny Gamble is a master melody man. He made me pay closer attention to the melody because of watching him create. And I would watch, too. I'd sit there like a hawk, observing every decision, listening to every note. They'd come to us in our hotel and play a whole album's worth of music for us. That's the way we'd be introduced to the songs they

had chosen for our album—aside from the two songs we were writing ourselves. It was an amazing thing to be present for.

We had cut some demos of our songs at home during our breaks from shooting, but we decided to wait on those —we felt there was no sense putting a gun to anyone's head. We knew that Philly had a lot to offer us, so we'd save our surprise for them later.

Our two songs, "Blues Away" and "Style of Life," were two hard secrets to keep at the time because we were so proud of them. "Style of Life" was a jam that Tito directed, and it was in keeping with the nightclub groove that "Dancing Machine" got us into, but we kept it a little leaner and meaner than Motown would have cut it.

"Blues Away" was one of my first songs, and though I don't sing it any more, I'm not embarrassed to hear it. I couldn't have gone on in this business if I had ended up hating my own records after all that work. It's a light song about overcoming a deep depression—I was going for the Jackie Wilson "Lonely Teardrops" way of laughing on the outside to stop the churning inside.

When we saw the cover art for *The Jacksons* album, the first we cut for Epic, we were surprised to see that we all looked alike. Even Tito looked skinny! I had my "crown"

Afro then, so I didn't stick out so much, I guess. Still, once we performed our new songs like "Enjoy Yourself" and "Show You the Way to Go," people knew I was still second from the left, right out front. Randy took Tito's old spot on my far right, and Tito moved into the old place Jermaine had. It took a long time for me to feel comfortable with that, as I've mentioned, though it was through no fault of Tito's.

Those two singles were fun records—"Enjoy Yourself" was great for dancing. It had rhythm guitar and horns that I really liked. It was also a number one record. For my taste, I leaned a little more toward "Show You the Way to Go" because it showed what good regard the Epic people had for our singing. We were all over that record and it was the best one we did. I loved the high hat and strings fluttering alongside us like birds' wings. I'm surprised that song in particular wasn't a bigger hit.

127

Though we couldn't spell it out, we kind of hinted about our situation in a song called "Living Together," which Kenny and Leon chose with us in mind. "If we're going to stick together, we've got to be a family. Have yourself a real good time, but don't you know it's getting late." The strings pointed and thrust like they did in "Backstabbers," but that was a Jacksons' message, even if it wasn't in the Jacksons' style—yet.

Gamble and Huff had written enough songs for another album, but we knew from experience that while they were doing what they did best, we were losing some of our identity. We were honored to be a part of the Philly family, but that wasn't enough for us. We were determined to do all of the things we had wanted to do for so many years. That's why we had to go back into our Encino studio and work together again as a family.

Going Places, our second album for Epic, was different from our first. There were more songs with messages and not as many dance songs. We knew that the message to promote peace and let music take over was a good one, but again it was more like the old O'Jays' "Love Train" and not really our style.

Still, maybe it wasn't a bad thing that there was no big pop hit on *Going Places* because it made "Different Kind of Lady" an obvious choice for club play. It was positioned in the middle of side one, so there were two Gamble and Huff songs sandwiching it, and our song stood out like a ball of fire. That was a real band cooking, with the Philly horns giving it one exclamation point after another, just as we'd hoped. That's the feel we were trying for when we were making demos with our old friend Bobby Taylor before going to Epic. Kenny and Leon put the finishing

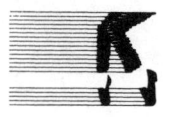

touches on it, the icing, but on this one we'd baked the cake ourselves.

After *Going Places* was in the stores, Dad asked me to accompany him to a meeting with Ron Alexenburg. Ron signed us for CBS, and he really believed in us. We wanted to convince him that we were ready now to take charge of our own music. We felt that CBS had evidence of what we could do on our own, so we stated our case, explaining that we'd originally wanted Bobby Taylor to work with us. Bobby had stuck with us through all those years, and we had thought he'd be a fine producer for us. Epic wanted Gamble and Huff because they had the track record, but maybe they were the wrong jockeys or we were the wrong horses for them, because we were letting them down in the sales department through no fault of our own. We had a strong work ethic that backed up everything we did.

Mr. Alexenburg was certainly used to dealing with performers, although I'm sure that among his business friends he could be just as cutting about musicians as we musicians could be when we were swapping our own stories among ourselves. But Dad and I were on the same wavelength when it came to the business side of music. People who make music and people who sell records are not natural enemies. I care as much about what I do as a

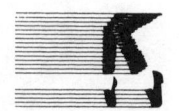

classical musician, and I want what I do to reach the widest possible audience. The record people care about their artists, and they want to reach the widest market. As we sat in the CBS boardroom eating a nicely catered lunch, we told Mr. Alexenburg that Epic had done its best, and it wasn't good enough. We felt we could do better, that our reputation was worth putting on the line.

When we left that skyscraper known as Black Rock, Dad and I didn't say much to each other. The ride back to the hotel was a silent one, with each of us thinking our own thoughts. There wasn't much to add to what we had already said. Our whole lives had been leading to that single, important confrontation, however civilized and aboveboard it was. Maybe Ron Alexenburg has had reason to smile over the years when he remembers that day.

When that meeting took place at CBS headquarters in New York, I was only nineteen years old. I was carrying a heavy burden for nineteen. My family was relying on me more and more as far as business and creative decisions were concerned, and I was so worried about trying to do the right thing for them; but I also had an opportunity to do something I'd wanted to do all my life—act in a film. Ironically the old Motown connection was paying a late dividend.

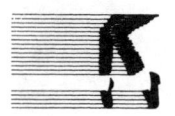

Motown had bought the rights to film the Broadway show known as *The Wiz* even as we were leaving the company. *The Wiz* was an updated, black-oriented version of the great movie *The Wizard of Oz,* which I had always loved. I remember that when I was a kid *The Wizard of Oz* was shown on television once a year and always on a Sunday night. Kids today can't imagine what a big event that was for all of us because they've grown up with videocassettes and the expanded viewing that cable provides.

I had seen the Broadway show too, which was certainly no letdown. I swear I saw it six or seven times. I later became very friendly with the star of the show, Stephanie Mills, the Broadway Dorothy. I told her then, and I've always believed since, that it was a tragedy that her performance in the play could not have been preserved on film. I cried time after time. As much as I like the Broadway stage, I don't think I'd want to play on it myself. When you give a performance, whether on record or on film, you want to be able to judge what you've done, to measure yourself and try to improve. You can't do that in an untaped or unrecorded performance. It makes me sad to think of all the great actors who have played roles we would give anything to see, but they're lost to us because they couldn't be, or simply weren't, recorded.

If I had been tempted to go onstage, it would probably have been to work with Stephanie, although her performances were so moving that I might have cried right
there in front of the audience. Motown bought *The Wiz*
for one reason, and as far as I was concerned, it was the
best reason possible: Diana Ross.

Diana was close to Berry Gordy and had her loyalties
to him and to Motown, but she did not forget us just
because our records now had a different label on them.
We had been in touch throughout the changes, and she
had even met up with us in Las Vegas, where she gave us
tips during our run there. Diana was going to play Dorothy, and since it was the only part that was definitely cast,
she encouraged me to audition. She also assured me that
Motown would not keep me from getting a part just to
spite me or my family. She would make sure of that if she
had to, but she didn't think she'd have to.

She didn't. It was Berry Gordy who said he hoped I'd
audition for *The Wiz*. I was very fortunate he felt that
way, because I was bitten by the acting bug during that
experience. I said to myself, *this* is what I'm interested in
doing when I have a chance—this is it. When you make a
film, you're capturing something elusive and you're stopping time. The people, their performances, the story become a thing that can be shared by people all over the

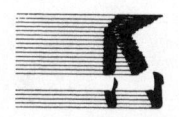

world for generations and generations. Imagine never having seen *Captains Courageous* or *To Kill a Mockingbird*! Making movies is exciting work. It's such a team effort and it's also a lot of fun. Someday soon I plan to devote a lot of my time to making films.

I auditioned for the part of the Scarecrow because I thought his character best fit my style. I was too bouncy for the Tin Man and too light for the Lion, so I had a definite goal, and I tried to put a lot of thought into my reading and dancing for the part. When I got the call back from the director, Sidney Lumet, I felt so proud but also a little scared. The process of making a film was new to me, and I was going to have to let go of my responsibilities to my family and my music for months. I had visited New York, where we were shooting, to get the feel for Harlem that *The Wiz*'s story called for, but I had never lived there. I was surprised by how quickly I got used to the lifestyle. I enjoyed meeting a whole group of people I'd always heard about on the other coast but had never laid eyes on.

Making *The Wiz* was an education for me on so many levels. As a recording artist I already felt like an old pro, but the film world was completely new to me. I watched as closely as I could and learned a lot.

During this period in my life, I was searching, both consciously and unconsciously. I was feeling some stress

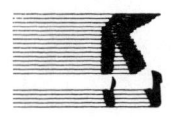

and anxiety about what I wanted to do with my life now that I was an adult. I was analyzing my options and preparing to make decisions that could have a lot of repercussions. Being on the set of *The Wiz* was like being in a big school. My complexion was still a mess during the filming of the movie, so I found myself really enjoying the makeup. It was an amazing makeup job. Mine took five hours to do, six days a week; we didn't shoot on Sundays. We finally got it down to four hours flat after doing it long enough. The other people who were being made up were amazed that I didn't mind sitting there having this done for such long periods of time. They hated it, but I enjoyed having the stuff put on my face. When I was transformed into the Scarecrow, it was the most wonderful thing in the world. I got to be somebody else and escape through my character. Kids would come visit the set, and I'd have such fun playing with them and responding to them as the Scarecrow.

135

I'd always pictured myself doing something very elegant in the movies, but it was my experience with the makeup and costume and prop people in New York that made me realize another aspect of how wonderful film-making could be. I had always loved the Charlie Chaplin movies, and no one ever saw him doing anything overtly elegant in the silent movie days. I wanted something of

the quality of his characters in my Scarecrow. I loved everything about the costume, from the coil legs to the tomato nose to the fright wig. I even kept the orange and white sweater that came with it and used it in a picture session years later.

The film had marvelous, very complicated dance numbers, and learning them was no problem. But that in itself became an unexpected problem with my costars.

Ever since I was a very little boy, I've been able to watch somebody do a dance step and then immediately know how to do it. Another person might have to be taken through the movement step by step and told to count and put this leg here and the hip to the right. When your hip goes to the left, put your neck over there . . . that sort of thing. But if I see it, I can do it.

When we were doing *The Wiz*, I was being instructed in the choreography along with my costars—the Tin Man, the Lion, and Diana Ross—and they were getting mad at me. I couldn't figure out what was wrong until Diana took me aside and told me that I was embarrassing her. I just stared at her. Embarrassing Diana Ross? Me? She said she knew I wasn't aware of it, but I was learning the dances much too quickly. It was embarrassing for her and the others, who just couldn't learn steps as soon as they saw the choreographer do them. She said he'd show us some-

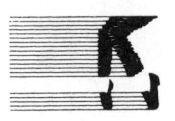

thing and I'd just go out there and do it. When he asked the others to do it, it took them longer to learn. We laughed about it, but I tried to make the ease with which I learned my steps less obvious.

I also learned that there could be a slightly vicious side to the business of making a movie. Often when I was in front of the camera, trying to do a serious scene, one of the other characters would start making faces at me, trying to crack me up. I had always been drilled in serious professionalism and preparedness and therefore I thought it was a pretty mean thing to do. This actor would know that I had important lines to say that day, yet he would make these really crazy faces to distract me. I felt it was more than inconsiderate and unfair.

Much later Marlon Brando would tell me that people used to do that to him all the time.

The problems on the set were really few and far between and it was great working with Diana so closely. She's such a beautiful, talented woman. Doing this movie together was very special for me. I love her very much. I have always loved her very much.

The whole *Wiz* period was a time of stress and anxiety, even though I was enjoying myself. I remember July 4 of that year very well, because I was on the beach at my

brother Jermaine's house, about half a block away along the waterfront. I was messing around in the surf, and all of a sudden I couldn't breathe. No air. Nothing. I asked myself what's wrong? I tried not to panic, but I ran back to the house to find Jermaine, who took me to the hospital. It was wild. A blood vessel had burst in my lung. It has never reoccurred, although I used to feel little pinches and jerks in there that were probably my imagination. I later learned that this condition was related to pleurisy. It was suggested by my doctor that I try to take things a little slower, but my schedule would not permit it. Hard work continued to be the name of the game.

As much as I liked the old *Wizard of Oz,* this new script, which differed from the Broadway production in scope rather than spirit, asked more questions than the original movie and answered them too. The atmosphere of the old movie was that of a magic kingdom sort of fairy tale. Our movie, on the other hand, had sets based on realities that kids could identify with, like schoolyards, subway stations, and the real neighborhood that our Dorothy came from. I still enjoy seeing *The Wiz* and reliving the experience. I am especially fond of the scene where Diana asks, "What am I afraid of? Don't know what I'm made of . . ." because I've felt that way many times, even during the good

moments of my life. She sings about overcoming fear and walking straight and tall. She knows and the audience knows that no threat of danger can hold her back.

My character had plenty to say and to learn. I was propped up on my pole with a bunch of crows laughing at me, while I sang "You Can't Win." The song was about humiliation and helplessness—something that so many people have felt at one time or another—and the feeling that there are people out there who don't actively hold you back as much as they work quietly on your insecurities so that you hold *yourself* back. The script was clever and showed me pulling bits of information and quotations out of my straw while not really knowing how to use them. My straw contained all the answers, but I didn't know the questions.

The great difference between the two *Wizard* movies was that all the answers are given to Dorothy by the Good Witch and by her friends in Oz in the original, while in our version Dorothy comes to her own conclusions. Her loyalty to her three friends and her courage in fighting Elvina in that amazing sweatshop scene make Dorothy a memorable character. Diana's singing and dancing and acting have stayed with me ever since. She was a perfect Dorothy. After the evil witch had been defeated, the sheer joy of our dancing took over. To dance with Diana in

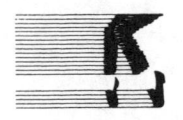

that movie was like an abridged version of my own story —my knock-kneed walk and "bigfoot" spin were me in my early days; our tabletop dance in the sweatshop scene was where we were right then. Everything was onward and upward. When I told my brothers and father I had gotten this part, they thought it might be too much for me, but the opposite was true. *The Wiz* gave me new inspiration and strength. The question became what to do with those things. How could I best harness them?

As I was asking myself what I wanted to do next, another man and I were traveling parallel paths that would converge on the set of *The Wiz*. We were in Brooklyn rehearsing one day, and we were reading our parts out loud to one another. I had thought that learning lines would be the most difficult thing I'd ever do, but I was pleasantly surprised. Everyone had been kind, assuring me that it was easier than I thought. And it was.

We were doing the crows' scene that day. The other guys wouldn't even have their heads visible in this scene because they'd be in crow costumes. They seemed to know their parts backward and forward. I'd studied mine too, but I hadn't said them aloud more than once or twice.

The directions called for me to pull a piece of paper from my straw and read it. It was a quote. The author's

name, Socrates, was printed at the end. I had read Socrates, but I had never pronounced his name, so I said, "Sohcrates," because that's the way I had always assumed it was pronounced. There was a moment's silence before I heard someone whisper, "Soc-ruh-teeze." I looked over at this man I vaguely recognized. He was not one of the actors, but he seemed to belong there. I remember thinking he looked very self-confident and had a friendly face.

I smiled, a little embarrassed at having mispronounced the name, and thanked him for his help. His face was naggingly familiar, and I was suddenly sure that I had met him before. He confirmed my suspicions by extending his hand.

"Quincy Jones. I'm doing the score."

CHAPTER
FOUR

ME AND Q

had actually first met Quincy Jones in Los Angeles when I was about twelve years old. Quincy later told me that at the time Sammy Davis, Jr., had said to him, "This kid is gonna be the next biggest thing since sliced bread." Something like that, anyway, and Quincy said, "Oh yeah?" I was little at the time, but I vaguely remember Sammy Davis introducing me to Q.

Our friendship really began to blossom on the set of *The Wiz,* and it developed into a father-and-son relationship. After *The Wiz* I called him and said, "Look, I'm going to do an album—do you think you could recommend some producers?"

I wasn't hinting. My question was a naïve but honest

one. We talked about music for a while, and, after coming up with some names and some half-hearted hemming and hawing, he said, "Why don't you let me do it?"

I really hadn't thought of it. It sounded to him as if I was hinting, but I wasn't. I just didn't think he would be that interested in my music. So I stammered something like, "Oh sure, great idea. I never thought about that."

Quincy still kids me about it.

Anyway, we immediately began to plan the album that became *Off the Wall.*

My brothers and I decided to form our own production company, and we began thinking about names to call it.

You don't find many articles about peacocks in the newspaper, but around this time I found the only one that mattered. I had always thought peacocks were beautiful and had admired one that Berry Gordy had at one of his homes. So when I read the article, which had an accompanying picture of a peacock, and revealed a great deal about the bird's characteristics, I was excited. I thought I might have found the image we were looking for. It was an in-depth piece, a little dry in places, but interesting. The writer said that the peacock's full plumage would explode only when it was in love, and then all the colors would shine—all the colors of the rainbow on one body.

I was immediately taken with that beautiful image and the meaning behind it. That bird's plumage conveyed the message I was looking for to explain the Jacksons and our intense devotion to one another, as well as our multifaceted interests. My brothers liked the idea, so we called our new company Peacock Productions, to sidestep the trap of relying too heavily on the Jackson name. Our first world tour had focused our interest in uniting people of all races through music. Some people we knew wondered what we meant when we talked about uniting all the races through music—after all, we were black musicians. Our answer was "music is color-blind." We saw that every night, especially in Europe and the other parts of the world we had visited. The people we met there loved our music. It didn't matter to them what color our skin was or which country we called home.

We wanted to form our own production company because we wanted to grow and establish ourselves as a new presence in the music world, not just as singers and dancers, but as writers, composers, arrangers, producers, and even publishers. We were interested in so many things, and we needed an umbrella company to keep track of our projects. CBS had agreed to let us produce our own album—the last two albums had sold well, but "Different Kind of Lady" showed a potential that they

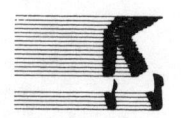

agreed was worth letting us develop. They did have one condition for us: they assigned an A&R man, Bobby Colomby, who used to be with Blood, Sweat, and Tears, to check in with us from time to time to see how we were doing and to see if we needed any help. We knew that the five of us needed some outside musicians to get the best possible sound, and we were weak in two areas: the keyboard and arranging sides of things. We had been faithfully adding all the new technology to our Encino studio without really having a mastery of it. Greg Phillinganes was young for a studio pro, but that was a plus as far as we were concerned because we wanted someone who would be more open to newer ways of doing things than the seasoned veterans we had encountered over the years.

He came to Encino to do preproduction work, and we all took turns surprising each other. Our mutual preconceptions just dissolved. It was a great thing to watch. As we sketched out our new songs for him, we told him that we liked the vocal tracks that Philly International always put a premium on, but when the mix came out, we always seemed to be fighting someone else's wall of sound, all those strings and cymbals. We wanted to sound cleaner and more funky, with a flintier bass and sharper horn parts. With his beautiful rhythm arrangements, Greg put into musical form what we were sketch-

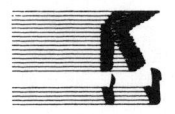

ing for him and then some. We felt he was reading our minds.

A Bobby Colomby recruit who came to work with us then was Paulinho de Costa, whom we worried about because it seemed to us that Randy was being told he couldn't handle all the percussion by himself. But Paulinho brought with him the Brazilian samba tradition of adapting and improvising on primitive and often home-made instruments. When de Costa's sound joined forces with Randy's more conventional approach, we seemed to have the whole world covered.

Artistically speaking we were caught between a rock and a hard place. We had worked with the smartest, hippest pop people in the world at Motown and Philly International, and we would have been fools to discount the things we'd absorbed from them, yet we couldn't be imitators. Fortunately we got a running start with a song that Bobby Colomby brought us called "Blame It on the Boogie." It was an up-tempo, finger-poppin'-time song that was a good vehicle for the band approach we wanted to cultivate. I had fun slurring the chorus: "Blame It on the Boogie" could be sung in one breath without putting my lips together. We had a little fun with the credits on the inner sleeve of the record; "Blame It on the Boogie" was written by three guys from England, including one

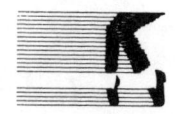

named Michael Jackson. It was a startling coincidence. As it turned out, writing disco songs was a natural for me because I was used to having dance breaks incorporated into all the major songs I was asked to sing.

There was a lot of uncertainty and excitement about our future. We were going through a lot of creative and personal changes—our music, the family dynamics, our desires and goals. All of this made me think more seriously about how I was spending my life, especially in relation to other people my age. I had always shouldered a lot of responsibility, but it suddenly seemed that everyone wanted a piece of me. There wasn't that much to go around, and I needed to be responsible to myself. I had to take stock of my life and figure out what people wanted from me and to whom I was going to give wholly. It was a hard thing for me to do, but I had to learn to be wary of some of the people around me. God was at the top of my list of priorities, and my mother and father and brothers and sisters followed. I was reminded of that old song by Clarence Carter called "Patches," where the oldest son is asked to take care of the farm after his father dies and his mother tells him she's depending on him. Well, we weren't sharecroppers and I wasn't the oldest, but those were slim shoulders on which to place such burdens. For some reason I always found it very difficult to say no to my

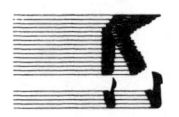

family and the other people I loved. I would be asked to do something or take care of something and I would agree, even if I worried that it might be more than I could handle.

I felt under a great deal of stress and I was often emotional. Stress can be a terrible thing; you can't keep your emotions bottled up for long. There were a lot of people at this time who wondered just how committed I was to music after learning of my newfound interest in movies after being in one. It was hinted that my decision to audition had come at a bad time for the new band setup. It seemed, to outsiders, to come just as we were about to get started. But of course it worked out just fine.

"That's What You Get for Being Polite" was my way of letting on that I knew I wasn't living in an ivory tower and that I had insecurities and doubts just as all older teenagers do. I was worried that the world and all it had to offer could be passing me by even as I tried to get on top of my field.

There was a Gamble and Huff song called "Dreamer" on the first Epic album which had this theme, and as I was learning it, I felt they could have written it with me in mind. I have always been a dreamer. I set goals for myself. I look at things and try to imagine what is possible and then hope to surpass those boundaries.

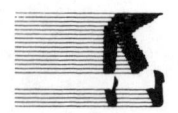

In 1979 I turned twenty-one years old and began to take full control of my career. My father's personal management contract with me ran out around this time, and although it was a hard decision, the contract was not renewed.

Trying to fire your dad is not easy.

But I just didn't like the way certain things were being handled. Mixing family and business can be a delicate situation. It can be great or it can be awful; it depends on the relationships. Even at the best of times it's a hard thing to do.

Did it change the relationship between me and my father? I don't know if it did in his heart, but it certainly didn't in mine. It was a move I knew I had to make because at the time I was beginning to feel that I was working for *him* rather than that he was working for *me.* And on the creative side we are of two completely different minds. He would come up with ideas that I would totally disagree with because they weren't right for me. All I wanted was control over my own life. And I took it. I had to do it. Everyone comes to that point, sooner or later, and I had been in the business for a long time. I was pretty experienced for twenty-one—a fifteen-year veteran.

We were eager to take the *Destiny* band and concept on the road, but I got hoarse from too many shows, too much singing. When we had to cancel some performances, no one held it against me, but I felt as if I was holding my brothers back after the great job they had done while we worked together to get us all back on track. We made some makeshift adjustments in order to ease the strain on my throat. Marlon took over for me in some passages that required holding long notes. "Shake Your Body (Down to the Ground)," our set piece on the album, turned out to be a lifesaver for us onstage because we already had a good jam in the studio to build on. It was frustrating to have finally realized our dream of having our own music as the showpiece, rather than the novelty song, and not being able to give it our very best shot. It wasn't long, however, before our time would come.

In looking back, I realize I was more patient than perhaps my brothers wanted me to be. As we were remixing *Destiny,* it occurred to me that we had "left out" some things that I hadn't talked to my brothers about because I wasn't sure they'd be as interested in them as I was. Epic had arranged in the contract that they would handle any solo album I might decide to do. Perhaps they were hedging their bets; if the Jacksons couldn't make their new sound work, they could try to turn me into something

With Berry Gordy and Suzanne de Passe

Working on *The E. T. Storybook* with Q and Steven Spielberg.

they could mold for the rest of my life. That might seem like a suspicious way of thinking, but I knew from experience that money people always want to know what is going on and what can happen and how to recoup their investment. It seemed logical for them to think that way. In the light of what's happened since, I wonder about those thoughts I had, but they were real at the time.

Destiny was our biggest success as an album, and we knew we had really reached the point where people bought your record because they knew you were good and knew you'd give them your very best on every song and every album. I wanted my first solo album to be the best it could be.

I didn't want *Off the Wall* to sound like outtakes from *Destiny.* That's why I wanted to hire an outside producer who wouldn't come to this project with any preconceived notions about how it should sound. I also needed someone with a good ear to help me choose material because I didn't have enough time to write two sides of songs I'd be proud of. I knew the public expected more than two good singles on an album, especially in the discos with their extended cuts, and I wanted the fans to feel satisfied.

These are all reasons why Quincy proved to be the best producer I could have asked for. Quincy Jones's

friends called him "Q" for short because of a love he has for barbecue. Later, after we'd finished *Off the Wall*, he invited me to a concert of his orchestral music at the Hollywood Bowl, but I was so shy at the time that I stood in the wings to watch the show as I had as a child. He said he expected more from me than that, and we've been trying to live up to each other's standards ever since.

That day I called to ask his advice about a producer, he started talking about people in the business—who I could work with and who I'd have trouble with. He knew track records, who was booked, who'd be too lax, who'd put the "pedal to the metal." He knew Los Angeles better than Mayor Bradley, and that's how he kept up with what was going on. As a jazz arranger, orchestrator, and film composer, someone people thought was on the outside looking in as far as pop music was concerned, he was an invaluable guide. I was so glad that my outside source was a good friend who also happened to be *the* perfect choice for a producer. He had a world of talent to choose from among his contacts, and he was a good listener, as well as a brilliant man.

The *Off the Wall* album was originally going to be called *Girlfriend*. Paul and Linda McCartney wrote a song of that title with me in mind before they ever met me.

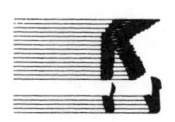

Paul McCartney always tells people this story about me calling him and saying we should write some hit songs together.

But that's not exactly how we first met.

I saw Paul for the first time at a party on the *Queen Mary,* which is docked in Long Beach. His daughter Heather got my number from someone and gave me a call to invite me to this big party. She liked our music and we got to talking. Much later, when his Wings over America tour was completed, Paul and his family were in Los Angeles. They invited me to a party at the Harold Lloyd estate. Paul McCartney and I first met at that party. We shook hands amid a huge crowd of people, and he said, "You know, I've written a song for you." I was very surprised and thanked him. And he started singing "Girlfriend" to me at this party.

So we exchanged phone numbers and promised to get together soon, but different projects and life just got in the way for both of us and we didn't talk again for a couple of years. He ended up putting the song on his own album *London Town.*

The strangest thing happened when we were making *Off the Wall;* Quincy walked up to me one day and said, "Michael, I've got a song that's perfect for you." He played "Girlfriend" for me, not realizing, of course, that

157

Paul had written it for me originally. When I told him, he was astonished and pleased. We recorded it soon after and put it on the album. It was an incredible coincidence.

Quincy and I talked about *Off the Wall* and carefully planned the kind of sound we wanted. When he asked me what I most wanted to have happen in the studio, I told him, we've got to make it sound different from the Jacksons. Hard words to spit out, considering how hard we'd worked to *become* the Jacksons, but Quincy knew what I meant, and together we created an album that reflected our goal. "Rock with You," the big hit single, was the sort of thing I was aiming for. It was perfect for me to sing, and move to. Rod Temperton, whom Quincy had known because of his work with the group Heatwave on "Boogie Nights," had written the song with a more relentless, get-down arrangement in mind, but Quincy softened the attack and slipped in a synthesizer that sounded like a conch shell's insides on a beach. Q and I were both very fond of Rod's work, and we eventually asked him to work on stylizing three of his songs for me, including the title cut. Rod was a kindred spirit in many ways. Like me, he felt more at home singing and writing about the night life than actually going out and living it. It always surprises me when people assume that something an artist has created is based on a true experience or reflects his or her

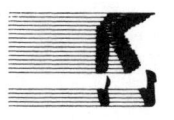

own lifestyle. Often nothing could be farther from the truth. I know I draw on my experiences at times, but I also hear and read things that trigger an idea for a song. An artist's imagination is his greatest tool. It can create a mood or feeling that people want to have, as well as transport you to a different place altogether.

In the studio Quincy allowed the arrangers and musicians quite a bit of freedom to express themselves, perhaps with the exception of the orchestral arrangements, which are his forte. I brought Greg Phillinganes, a member of the *Destiny* team, over to "run the floor" on numbers that he and I had worked on together in Encino, while the studio people were being lined up for the date. In addition to Greg, Paulinho da Costa was back on percussion and Randy made a cameo appearance on "Don't Stop Till You Get Enough."

Quincy is amazing and doesn't just pick yes-men to do his bidding. I have been around professionals all my life, and I can tell who is trying to keep up, who can create, and who is capable of crossing swords once in a while in a constructive way without losing sight of the shared goal. We had Louis "Thunder Thumbs" Johnson, who had worked with Quincy on the Brothers Johnson albums. We also had an all-star team of Wah Wah Watson, Marlo Henderson, David Williams, and Larry Carlton

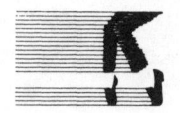

from the Crusaders playing guitar on the album. George Duke, Phil Upchurch, and Richard Heath were picked from the cream of the jazz/funk crop, and yet they never let on that maybe this music was a little different from what they were used to. Quincy and I had a good working relationship, so we shared responsibilities and consulted with one another constantly.

The Brothers Johnson notwithstanding, Quincy hadn't done much dance music before *Off the Wall,* so on "Don't Stop Till You Get Enough," "Working Day and Night," and "Get on the Floor" Greg and I worked together to build a thicker wall of sound in Quincy's studio. "Get on the Floor," though it wasn't a single, was particularly satisfying because Louis Johnson gave me a smooth-enough bottom to ride in the verses and let me come back stronger and stronger with each chorus. Bruce Swedien, Quincy's engineer, put the final touches on that mix, and I still get pleasure out of hearing it.

"Working Day and Night" was Paulinho's showcase, with my background vocals hurrying to keep up with his grab bag of toys. Greg set up a prepared electric piano with the timbre of a perfect acoustic one, to knock out any lingering echo. The lyrical theme was similar to "The Things I Do for You" from *Destiny,* but since this was a

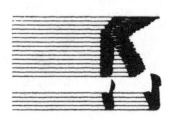

refinement of something I'd said earlier, I wanted to keep it simple and let the music put the song over the top.

"Don't Stop Till You Get Enough" had a spoken intro over bass, partly to build up tension and surprise people with the swirling strings and percussion. It was also unusual because of my vocal arrangement. On that cut I sing in overdubs as a kind of group. I wrote myself a high part, one that my solo voice couldn't carry on its own, to fit in with the music I was hearing in my head, so I let the arrangement take over from the singing. Q's fade at the end was amazing, with guitars chopping like kalimbas, the African thumb pianos. That song means a lot to me because it was the first song I wrote as a whole. "Don't Stop Till You Get Enough" was my first big chance, and it went straight to number one. It was the song that won me my first Grammy. Quincy had the confidence in me to encourage me to go into the studio by myself, which I appreciated. Then he added strings, which put icing on the cake.

The ballads were what made *Off the Wall* a Michael Jackson album. I'd done ballads with the brothers, but they had never been too enthusiastic about them and did them more as a concession to me than anything else. *Off the Wall* had, in addition to "Girlfriend," a slippery, engaging melody called "I Can't Help It" which was memo-

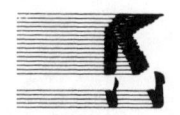

rable and great fun to sing but a little quirkier than a gentle song like, say, "Rock with You."

Two of the biggest hits were "Off the Wall" and "Rock with You." You know, so much up-tempo dance music is threatening, but I liked the coaxing, the gentleness, taking a shy girl and letting her shed her fears rather than forcing them out of her. On *Off the Wall* I went back to a high-pitched voice, but "Rock with You" called for a more natural sound. I felt that if you were having a party, those two songs would get people in the door, and the harder boogie songs would send everyone home in a good mood. And then there was "She's Out of My Life." Maybe that was too personal for a party.

It was for me. Sometimes it's hard for me to look my dates in the eye even if I know them well. My dating and relationships with girls have not had the happy ending I've been looking for. Something always seems to get in the way. The things I share with millions of people aren't the sort of things you share with one. Many girls want to know what makes me tick—why I live the way I live or do the things I do—trying to get inside my head. They want to rescue me from loneliness, but they do it in such a way that they give me the impression they want to share my loneliness, which I wouldn't wish on anybody, because I believe I'm one of the loneliest people in the world.

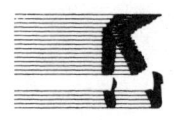

"She's Out of My Life" is about knowing that the barriers that have separated me from others are temptingly low and seemingly easy to jump over and yet they remain standing while what I really desire disappears from my sight. Tom Bahler composed a beautiful bridge, which seemed right out of an old Broadway musical. In reality, such problems are not so easily resolved and the song presents this fact, that the problem is not overcome. We couldn't put this cut at the beginning or the end of the record, because it would have been such a downer. That's why when Stevie's song comes on afterward, so gently and tentatively, as if it was opening a door that had been bolted shut, I still go, "Whew." By the time Rod's "Burn This Disco Out" closes the record, the trance is broken.

But I got too wrapped up in "She's Out of My Life." In this case, the story's true—I cried at the end of a take, because the words suddenly had such a strong effect on me. I had been letting so much build up inside me. I was twenty-one years old, and I was so rich in some experiences while being poor in moments of true joy. Sometimes I imagine that my life experience is like an image in one of those trick mirrors in the circus, fat in one part and thin to the point of disappearing in another. I was worried that would show up on "She's Out of My Life," but if it

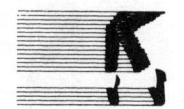

touched people's heartstrings, knowing that would make me feel less lonely.

When I got emotional after that take, the only people with me were Q and Bruce Swedien. I remember burying my face in my hands and hearing only the hum of the machinery as my sobs echoed in the room. Later I apologized, but they said there was no need.

Making *Off the Wall* was one of the most difficult periods of my life, despite the eventual success it enjoyed. I had very few close friends at the time and felt very isolated. I was so lonely that I used to walk through my neighborhood hoping I'd run into somebody I could talk to and perhaps become friends with. I wanted to meet people who didn't know who I was. I wanted to run into somebody who would be my friend because they liked me and needed a friend too, not because I was who I am. I wanted to meet *anybody* in the neighborhood—the neighborhood kids, anybody.

Success definitely brings on loneliness. It's true. People think you're lucky, that you have everything. They think you can go anywhere and do anything, but that's not the point. One hungers for the basic stuff.

I've learned to cope better with these things now and I don't get nearly as depressed as I used to.

I didn't really have any girlfriends when I was in school. There were girls I thought were cute, but I found it so difficult to approach them. I was too embarrassed—I don't know why—it was just crazy. There was one girl who was a good friend to me. I liked her, but I was too embarrassed to tell her.

My first real date was with Tatum O'Neal. We met at a club on Sunset Strip called On the Rox. We exchanged phone numbers and called each other often. I talked to her for hours: from the road, from the studio, from home. On our first date we went to a party at Hugh Hefner's Playboy Mansion and had a great time. She had held my hand for the first time that night at On the Rox. When we met, I was sitting at this table and all of a sudden I felt this soft hand reach over and grab mine. It was Tatum. This probably wouldn't mean a lot to other people, but it was serious stuff to me. *She touched me.* That's how I felt about it. In the past, girls had always touched me on tour; grabbing at me and screaming, behind a wall of security guards. But this was different, this was one-on-one, and that's always the best.

Ours developed into a real close relationship. I fell in love with her (and she with me) and we were very close for a long time. Eventually the relationship transcended

into a good friendship. We still talk now and then, and I guess you'd have to say she was my first love—after Diana.

When I heard Diana Ross was getting married, I was happy for her because I knew it would make her very joyous. Still, it was hard for me, because I had to walk around pretending to be overwhelmed that Diana was getting married to this man I'd never met. I wanted her to be happy, but I have to admit that I was a bit hurt and a little jealous because I've always loved Diana and always will.

Another love was Brooke Shields. We were romantically serious for a while. There have been a lot of wonderful women in my life, women whose names wouldn't mean anything to the readers of this book, and it would be unfair to discuss them because they are not celebrities and are unaccustomed to having their names in print. I value my privacy and therefore I respect theirs as well.

Liza Minelli is a person whose friendship I'll always cherish. She's like my show business sister. We get together and talk about the business; it comes out of our pores. We both eat, sleep, and drink various moves and songs and dance. We have the best time together. I love her.

Right after we finished *Off the Wall*, I plunged into making the *Triumph* album with my brothers. We wanted

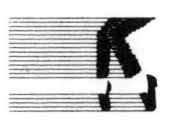

to combine the best of both albums for our tour. "Can You Feel It?" was the first cut on the album, and it had the closest thing to a rock feel that the Jacksons had ever done. It wasn't really dance music either. We had it in mind for the video that opened our tour, kind of like our own *Also Sprach Zarathustra,* the *2001* theme. Jackie and I had thought of combining the band sound with a gospel/children's choir feel. That was a nod to Gamble and Huff, in a way, because the song was a celebration of love taking over, cleansing the sins of the world. Randy's singing is so good, even if his range is not all he'd like it to be. His breathing and phrasing kept me pumped up on my toes when we sang it. There was a bright foghorn-type keyboard that I worked on for hours, going over it and over it again, until I got it the way I wanted it. We had six minutes, and I don't think it was one second too long.

"Lovely One" was an extension of "Shake Your Body Down to the Ground," with that lighter *Off the Wall* sound injected. I tried out a newer, more ethereal voice on Jackie's "Your Ways," with the keyboards adding a faraway quality. Paulinho brought out all the artillery: triangles, skulls, gongs. This song's about a strange girl who is the way she is and there's nothing I can do about it, other than enjoy it when I can.

"Everybody" is more playful than the *Off the Wall*

dance tunes, with Mike McKinney propelling it like a plane turning and bearing down. The background vocals suggest "Get on the Floor's" influence, but Quincy's sound is deeper, like you're in the eye of the storm—our sound was more like going up the glass elevator to the top floor while looking down, rising effortlessly.

"Time Waits for No One" was written by Jackie and Randy with my voice and style in mind. They knew they were trying to keep up with the *Off the Wall* songwriters and they did a very good job. "Give It Up" gave everyone a chance to sing, Marlon in particular. We strayed from the band sound on those tracks, perhaps sinking back into that Philly trap of letting the arrangement overwhelm us. "Walk Right Now" and "Wondering Who" were closer to the *Destiny* sound, but for the most part they were suffering from too many cooks and not enough broth.

There was one exception: "Heartbreak Hotel." I swear that was a phrase that came out of my head and I wasn't thinking of any other song when I wrote it. The record company printed it on the cover as "This Place Hotel," because of the Elvis Presley connection. As important as he was to music, black as well as white, he just wasn't an influence on me. I guess he was too early for me. Maybe it was timing more than anything else. By the time our song had come out, people thought that if I kept living

in seclusion the way I was, I might die the way he did. The parallels aren't there as far as I'm concerned and I was never much for scare tactics. Still, the way Elvis destroyed himself interests me, because I don't ever want to walk those grounds myself.

LaToya was asked to contribute the scream that opens the song—not the most auspicious start to a recording career, I'll admit, but she was just getting her feet wet in the studio. She has made some good records since and is quite accomplished. The scream was the kind that normally shatters a bad dream, but our intention was to have the dream only begin, to make the listener wonder whether it was a dream or reality. That was the effect I think we got. The three female backup singers were amused when they were doing the scary backup effects that I wanted, until they actually heard them in the mix.

"Heartbreak Hotel" was the most ambitious song I had composed. I think I worked on a number of levels: You could dance to it, sing along with it, get scared by it, and just listen. I had to tack on a slow piano and cello coda that ended on a positive note to reassure the listener; there's no point in trying to scare someone if there isn't something to bring the person back safe and sound from where you've taken them. "Heartbreak Hotel" had revenge in it and I am fascinated by the concept of revenge.

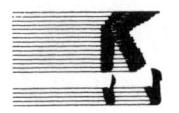

EARTHBREAK HOTEL

s and Music by MICHAEL JACKSON   Recorded by THE JACKSONS on Epic Records

MICHAEL   TITO   RANDY   JACKIE   MARLON

Photography: Francesco Scavullo

It's something I can't understand. The idea of making someone "pay" for something they've done to you or that you imagine they've done to you is totally alien to me. The setup showed my own fears and for the time being helped quell them. There were so many sharks in this business looking for blood in the water.

If this song, and later "Billie Jean," seemed to cast women in an unfavorable light, it was not meant to be taken as a personal statement. Needless to say, I love the interaction between the sexes; it is a natural part of life and I love women. I just think that when sex is used as a form of blackmail or power, it's a repugnant use of one of God's gifts.

Triumph gave us that final burst of energy we needed to put together a perfect show, with no marginal material. We began rehearsing with our touring band, which included bass player Mike McKinney. David Williams would travel with us too, but he was now a permanent member of the band.

The upcoming tour was going to be a big undertaking. We had special effects arranged for us by the great magician Doug Henning. I wanted to disappear completely in a puff of smoke right after "Don't Stop." He had to coordinate the special effects with the Showco people

who controlled the whole setup. I was happy to talk with him while we walked through the routine. It seemed almost unfair for him to give me his secrets, and apart from the money I wasn't offering him anything he could make use of in return. I felt a little embarrassed about that, yet I really wanted our show to be great and I knew Henning's contribution would be spectacular. We were competing with bands like Earth, Wind, and Fire and the Commodores for the position of top band in the country, and we knew there were people who felt that the Jackson brothers had been around for ten years and were finished.

I had worked hard on the concept for the set for the upcoming tour. It had the feel of *Close Encounters* behind it. I was trying to make the statement that there was life and meaning beyond space and time and the peacock had burst forth ever brighter and ever prouder. I wanted our film to reflect this idea, too.

My pride in the rhythms, the technical advances, and the success of *Off the Wall* was offset by the jolt I got when the Grammy nominations were announced for 1979. Although *Off the Wall* had been one of the most popular records of the year, it received only one nomination: Best R&B Vocal Performance. I remember where I was when I

got the news. I felt ignored by my peers and it hurt. People told me later that it surprised the industry too.

I was disappointed and then I got excited thinking about the album to come. I said to myself, "Wait until next time"—they won't be able to ignore the next album. I watched the ceremony on television and it was nice to win in my category, but I was still upset by what I perceived as the rejection of my peers. I just kept thinking, "Next time, next time." In many ways an artist is his work. It's difficult to separate the two. I think I can be brutally objective about my work as I create it, and if something doesn't work, I can feel it, but when I turn in a finished album—or song—you can be sure that I've given it every ounce of energy and God-given talent that I have. *Off the Wall* was well received by my fans and I think that's why the Grammy nominations hurt. That experience lit a fire in my soul. All I could think of was the next album and what I would do with it. I wanted it to be truly great.

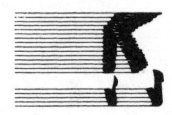

CHAPTER FIVE

THE MOONWALK

Off *the Wall* was released in August 1979, the same month I turned twenty-one and took control of my own affairs, and it was definitely one of the major landmarks of my life. It meant a great deal to me, because its eventual success proved beyond a shadow of a doubt that a former "child star" could mature into a recording artist with contemporary appeal. *Off the Wall* also went a step beyond the dance grooves we had cooked up. When we started the project, Quincy and I talked about how important it was to capture passion and strong feelings in a recorded performance. I still think that's what we achieved on the ballad "She's Out of My Life," and to a lesser extent on "Rock with You."

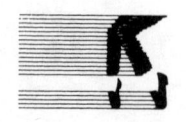

Looking back, I can view the whole tapestry and see how *Off the Wall* prepared me for the work we would do on the album that became *Thriller.* Quincy, Rod Temperton, and many of the musicians who played on *Off the Wall* would help me realize a dream that I had had for a long time. *Off the Wall* had sold almost six million copies in this country, but I wanted to make an album that would be even bigger. Ever since I was a little boy, I had dreamed of creating the biggest-selling record of all time. I remember going swimming as a child and making a wish before I jumped into the pool. Remember, I grew up knowing the industry, understanding goals, and being told what was and was not possible. I wanted to do something special. I'd stretch my arms out, as if I were sending my thoughts right up into space. I'd make my wish, then I'd dive into the water. I'd say to myself, "This is my dream. This is my wish," every time before I'd dive into the water.

I believe in wishes and in a person's ability to make a wish come true. I really do. Whenever I saw a sunset, I would quietly make my secret wish right before the sun tucked under the western horizon and disappeared. It would seem as if the sun had taken my wish with it. I'd make it right before that last speck of light vanished. And

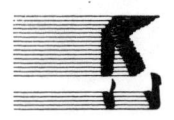

a wish is more than a wish, it's a goal. It's something your conscious and subconscious can help make reality.

I remember being in the studio once with Quincy and Rod Temperton while we were working on *Thriller.* I was playing a pinball machine and one of them asked me, "If this album doesn't do as well as *Off the Wall,* will you be disappointed?"

I remember feeling upset—hurt that the question was even raised. I told them *Thriller* had to do better than *Off the Wall.* I admitted that I wanted this album to be the biggest-selling album of all time.

They started laughing. It was a seemingly unrealistic thing to want.

There were times during the *Thriller* project when I would get emotional or upset because I couldn't get the people working with me to see what I saw. That still happens to me sometimes. Often people just don't see what I see. They have too much doubt. You can't do your best when you're doubting yourself. If you don't believe in yourself, who will? Just doing as well as you did last time is not good enough. I think of it as the "Try to get what you can" mentality. It doesn't require you to stretch, to grow. I don't believe in that.

I believe we are powerful, but we don't use our minds to full capacity. Your mind is powerful enough to help you

181

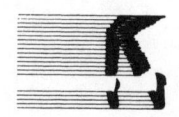

Beginning of the world tour, 1987.

attain whatever you want. I *knew* what we could do with that record. We had a great team there, a lot of talent and good ideas, and I knew we could do anything. The success of *Thriller* transformed many of my dreams into reality. It did become the biggest-selling album of all time, and that fact appeared on the cover of *The Guinness Book of World Records.*

Making the *Thriller* album was very hard work, but it's true that you only get out of something what you put into it. I'm a perfectionist; I'll work until I drop. And I worked so hard on that album. It helped that Quincy showed great confidence in what we were doing during those sessions. I guess I had proved myself to him during our work on *Off the Wall.* He listened to what I had to say and helped me accomplish what I had hoped to on that album, but he showed even more faith in me during the making of *Thriller.* He realized I had the confidence and experience I needed to make that record and at times he wasn't in the studio with us for that reason. I'm really very self-confident when it comes to my work. When I take on a project, I believe in it 100 percent. I really put my soul into it. I'd die for it. That's how I am.

Quincy is brilliant at balancing out an album, creating the right mix of up-tempo numbers and slow ones. We started out working with Rod Temperton on songs for the

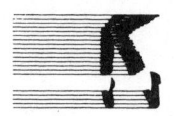

Thriller album, which was originally called *Starlight.* I was writing songs myself while Quincy was listening to other people's songs, hoping to find just the right ones for the album. He's good at knowing what I'll like and what will work for me. We both share the same philosophy about making albums; we don't believe in B-sides or album songs. Every song should be able to stand on its own as a single, and we always push for this.

I had finished some songs of my own, but I didn't give them to Quincy until I saw what had come in from other writers. The first song I had was "Startin' Something," which I had written when we were doing *Off the Wall* but had never given to Quincy for that album. Sometimes I have a song I've written that I really like and I just can't bring myself to present it. While we were making *Thriller,* I even held on to "Beat It" for a long time before I played it for Quincy. He kept telling me that we needed a great rock song for the album. He'd say, "Come on, where is it? I *know* you got it." I like my songs but initially I'm shy about playing them for people, because I'm afraid they *won't* like them and that's a painful experience.

He finally convinced me to let him hear what I had. I brought out "Beat It" and played it for him and he went crazy. I felt on top of the world.

When we were about to start work on *Thriller,* I

185

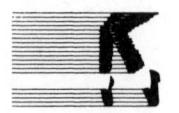

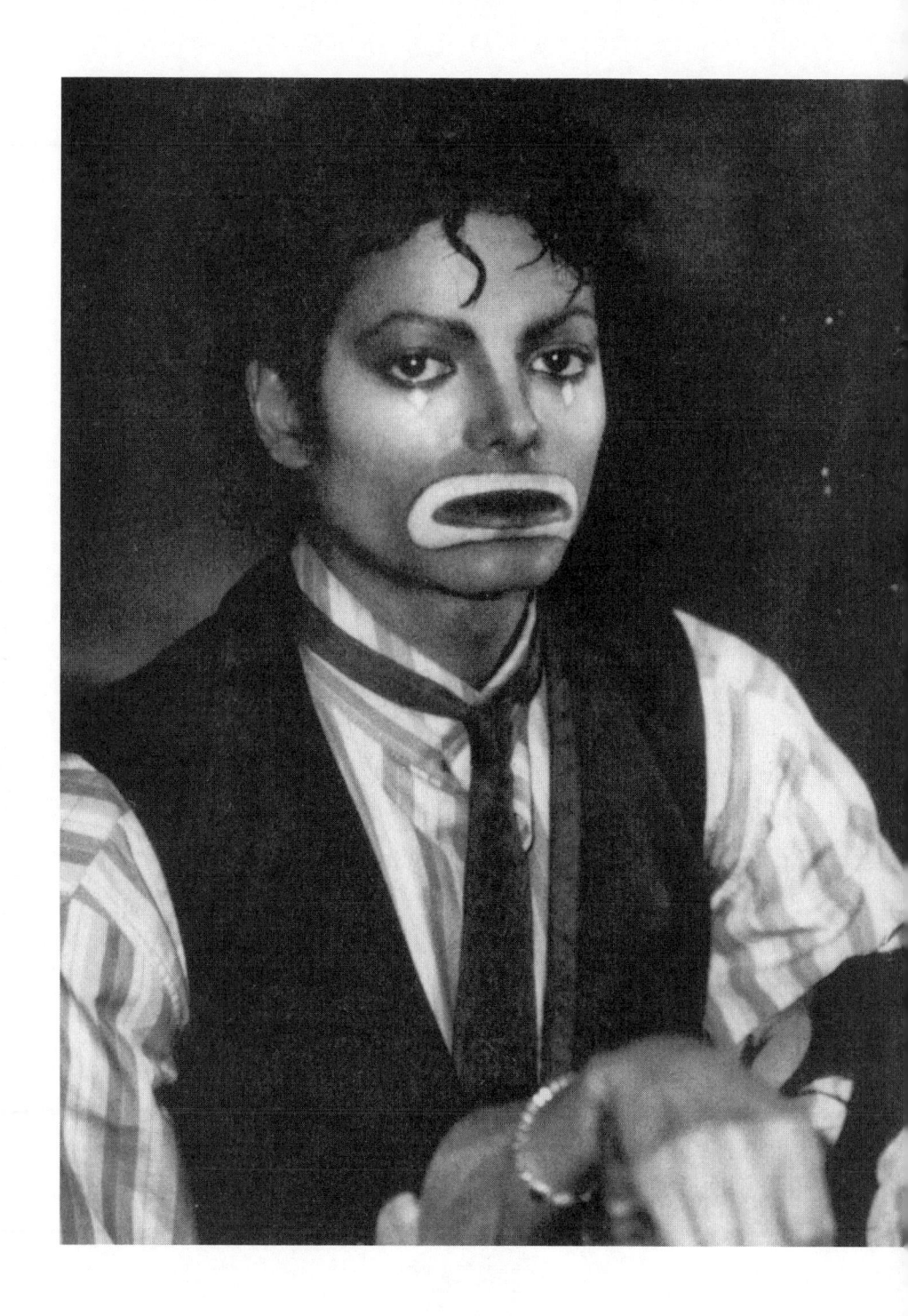

With my sister LaToya in the "Say Say Say" video.

called Paul McCartney in London and this time I did say, "Let's get together and write some hits." Our collaboration produced "Say Say Say" and "The Girl Is Mine."

Quincy and I eventually chose "The Girl Is Mine" as the obvious first single from *Thriller*. We really didn't have much choice. When you have two strong names like that together on a song, it has to come out first or it gets played to death and overexposed. We had to get it out of the way.

When I approached Paul, I wanted to repay the favor he had done me in contributing "Girlfriend" to *Off the Wall*. I wrote "The Girl Is Mine," which I knew would be right for his voice and mine working together, and we also did work on "Say Say Say," which we would finish up later with George Martin, the great Beatles producer.

"Say Say Say" was coauthored by Paul, a man who could play all the instruments in the studio and score every part, and a kid, me, who couldn't. Yet we worked together as equals and enjoyed ourselves. Paul never had to carry me in that studio. The collaboration was also a real step forward for me in terms of confidence, because there was no Quincy Jones watching over me to correct my mistakes. Paul and I shared the same idea of how a pop song should work and it was a real treat to work with him. I feel that ever since John Lennon's death he has had to

live up to expectations people had no right to hang on him; Paul McCartney has given so much to this industry and to his fans.

Eventually, I would buy the ATV music publishing catalogue, which included many of the great Lennon-McCartney songs. But most people don't know that it was Paul who introduced me to the idea of getting involved in music publishing. I was staying with Paul and Linda at their house in the country when Paul told me about his own involvement in music publishing. He handed me a little book with *MPL* printed on the cover. He smiled as I opened it, because he knew I was going to find the contents exciting. It contained a list of all the songs Paul owns and he'd been buying the rights to songs for a long time. I had never given the idea of buying songs any thought before. When the ATV music publishing catalogue, which contains many Lennon-McCartney songs, went on sale, I decided to put in a bid.

I consider myself a musician who is incidentally a businessman, and Paul and I had both learned the hard way about business and the importance of publishing and royalties and the dignity of songwriting. Songwriting should be treated as the lifeblood of popular music. The creative process doesn't involve time clocks or quota systems, it involves inspiration and the willingness to follow

through. When I was sued by someone I had never heard of for "The Girl Is Mine," I was quite willing to stand on my reputation. I stated that many of my ideas come in dreams, which some people thought was a convenient cop-out, but it's true. Our industry is so lawyer-heavy that getting sued for something you didn't do seems to be as much a part of the initiation process as winning amateur night used to be.

"Not My Lover" was a title we almost used for "Billie Jean" because Q had some objections to calling the song "Billie Jean," my original title. He felt people might immediately think of Billie Jean King, the tennis player.

A lot of people have asked me about that song, and the answer is very simple. It's just a case of a girl who says that I'm the father of her child and I'm pleading my innocence because "the kid is not my son."

There was never a real "Billie Jean." (Except for the ones who came after the song.) The girl in the song is a composite of people we've been plagued by over the years. This kind of thing has happened to some of my brothers and I used to be really amazed by it. I couldn't understand how these girls could say they were carrying someone's child when it wasn't true. I can't imagine lying about something like that. Even today there are girls who

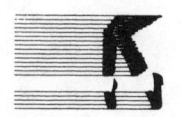

come to the gate at our house and say the strangest things, like, "Oh, I'm Michael's wife," or "I'm just dropping off the keys to our apartment." I remember one girl who used to drive us completely crazy. I really think that she believed in her mind that she belonged with me. There was another girl who claimed I had gone to bed with her, and she made threats. There've been a couple of serious scuffles at the gate on Hayvenhurst, and they can get dangerous. People yell into the intercom that Jesus sent them to speak with me and God told them to come— unusual and unsettling things.

A musician knows hit material. It has to feel right. Everything has to feel in place. It fulfills you and it makes you feel good. You know it when you hear it. That's how I felt about "Billie Jean." I knew it was going to be big while I was writing it. I was really absorbed in that song. One day during a break in a recording session I was riding down the Ventura Freeway with Nelson Hayes, who was working with me at the time. "Billie Jean" was going around in my head and that's all I was thinking about. We were getting off the freeway when a kid on a motorcycle pulls up to us and says, "Your car's on fire." Suddenly we noticed the smoke and pulled over and the whole bottom of the Rolls-Royce was on fire. That kid probably saved our lives. If the car had exploded, we could have been killed.

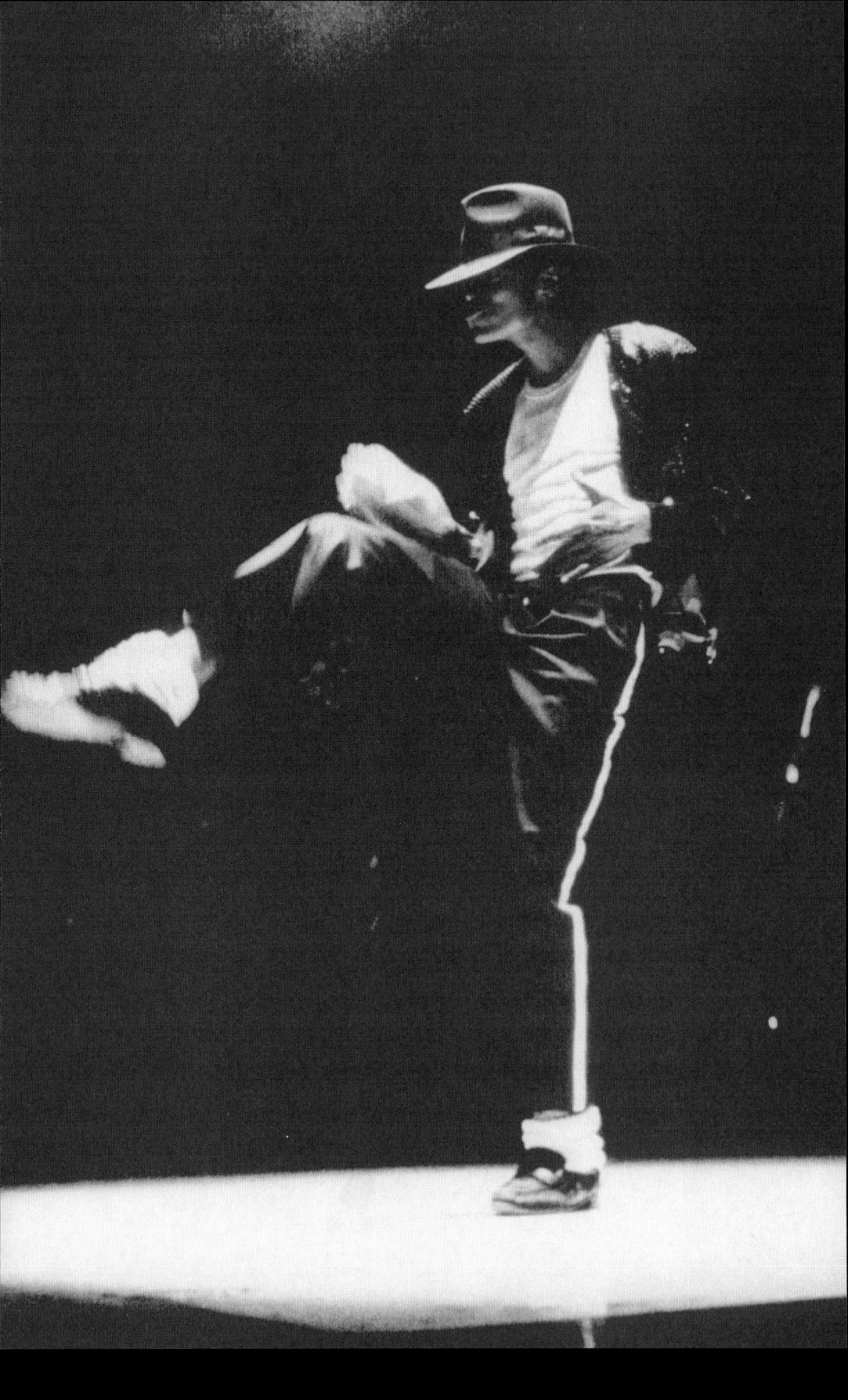

But I was so absorbed by this tune floating in my head that I didn't even focus on the awful possibilities until later. Even while we were getting help and finding an alternate way to get where we were going, I was silently composing additional material, that's how involved I was with "Billie Jean."

Before I wrote "Beat It," I had been thinking I wanted to write the type of rock song that I would go out and buy, but also something totally different from the rock music I was hearing on Top 40 radio at the time.

"Beat It" was written with school kids in mind. I've always loved creating pieces that will appeal to kids. It's fun to write for them and know what they like because they're a very demanding audience. You can't fool them. They are still the audience that's most important to me, because I really care about them. If they like it, it's a hit, no matter what the charts say.

The lyrics of "Beat It" express something I would do if I were in trouble. Its message—that we should abhor violence—is something I believe deeply. It tells kids to be smart and avoid trouble. I don't mean to say you should turn the other cheek while someone kicks in your teeth, but, unless your back is against the wall and you have absolutely no choice, just get away before violence breaks

out. If you fight and get killed, you've gained nothing and lost everything. You're the loser, and so are the people who love you. That's what "Beat It" is supposed to get across. To me true bravery is settling differences without a fight and having the wisdom to make that solution possible.

When Q called Eddie Van Halen, he thought it was a crank call. Because of the bad connection, Eddie was convinced that the voice on the other end was a fake. After being told to get lost, Q simply dialed the number again. Eddie agreed to play the session for us and gave us an incredible guitar solo on "Beat It."

The newest members of our team were the band Toto, who had the hit records "Rosanna" and "Africa." They had been well known as individual session musicians before they came together as a group. Because of their experience, they knew both sides of studio work, when to be independent, and when to be cooperative and follow the producer's lead. Steve Porcaro had worked on *Off the Wall* during a break as keyboardist for Toto. This time he brought his band mates with him. Musicologists know that the band's leader David Paich is the son of Marty Paich, who worked on Ray Charles' great records like "I Can't Stop Loving You."

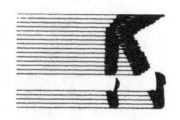

I love "Pretty Young Thing," which was written by Quincy and James Ingram. "Don't Stop Till You Get Enough" had whetted my appetite for the spoken intro, partly because I didn't think my speaking voice was something my singing needed to hide. I have always had a soft speaking voice. I haven't cultivated it or chemically altered it: that's me—take it or leave it. Imagine what it must be like to be criticized for something about yourself that is natural and God given. Imagine the hurt of having untruths spread by the press, of having people wonder if you're telling the truth—defending yourself because someone decided it would make good copy and would force you to deny what they said, thus creating another story. I've tried not to answer such ridiculous charges in the past because that dignifies them and the people who make them. Remember, the press is a business: Newspapers and magazines are in business to make money— sometimes at the expense of accuracy, fairness, and even the truth.

Anyway, in the intro to "Pretty Young Thing," I sounded a bit more confident than I had on the last album. I liked the "code" in the lyrics, and "tenderoni" and "sugar fly" were fun rock 'n' roll-type words that you couldn't find in the dictionary. I got Janet and LaToya into the studio for this one, and they produced the "real"

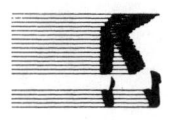

backup vocals. James Ingram and I programmed an electronic device called a Vocoder, which gave out that E.T. voice.

"Human Nature" was the song the Toto guys brought to Q, and he and I both agreed that the song had the prettiest melody we'd heard in a long time, even more than "Africa." It's music with wings. People asked me about the lyrics: "Why does he do me that way . . . I like loving this way . . ." People often think the lyrics you're singing have some special personal significance for you, which often isn't true. It is important to reach people, to move them. Sometimes one can do this with the mosaic of the music melody arrangement and lyrics, sometimes it is the intellectual content of the lyrics. I was asked a lot of questions about "Muscles," the song I wrote and produced for Diana Ross. That song fulfilled a lifelong dream of returning some of the many favors she's done for me. I have always loved Diana and looked up to her. Muscles, by the way, is the name of my snake.

"The Lady in My Life" was one of the most difficult tracks to cut. We were used to doing a lot of takes in order to get a vocal as nearly perfect as possible, but Quincy wasn't satisfied with my work on that song, even after literally dozens of takes. Finally he took me aside late one session and told me he wanted me to beg. That's what he

said. He wanted me to go back to the studio and literally *beg* for it. So I went back in and had them turn off the studio lights and close the curtain between the studio and the control room so I wouldn't feel self-conscious. Q started the tape and I begged. The result is what you hear in the grooves.

Eventually we came under tremendous pressure from our record company to finish *Thriller.* When a record company rushes you, they really rush you, and they were rushing us hard on *Thriller.* They said it had to be ready on a certain date, do or die.

So we went through a period where we were breaking our backs to get the album done by their deadline. There were a lot of compromises made on the mixes of various tracks, and on whether certain tracks were even going to be on the record. We cut so many corners that we almost lost the whole album.

When we finally listened to the tracks we were going to hand in, *Thriller* sounded so crappy to me that tears came to my eyes. We had been under enormous pressure because while we were trying to finish *Thriller* we also had been working on *The E.T. Storybook,* and there had been deadline pressure on that as well. All these people were fighting back and forth with each other, and we

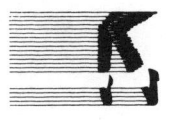

came to realize that the sad truth was that the mixes of *Thriller* didn't work.

We sat there in the studio, Westlake Studio in Hollywood, and listened to the whole album. I felt devastated. All this pent-up emotion came out. I got angry and left the room. I told my people, "That's it, we're not releasing it. Call CBS and tell them they are not getting this album. We are *not* releasing it."

Because I knew it was wrong. If we hadn't stopped the process and examined what we were doing, the record would have been terrible. It never would have been reviewed the way it was because, as we learned, you can ruin a great album in the mix. It's like taking a great movie and ruining it in the editing. You simply have to take your time.

Some things can't be rushed.

There was a bit of yelling and screaming from the record people, but in the end they were smart and understood. They knew too; it was just that I was the first to say it. Finally I realized I had to do the whole thing—mix the entire album—all over again.

We took a couple of days off, drew a deep breath, and stepped back. Then we came to it fresh, cleaned our ears out, and began to mix two songs a week. When it was done

199

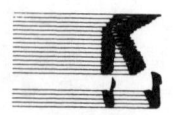

—boom—it hit us hard. CBS could hear the difference too. *Thriller* was a tough project.

It felt so good when we finished. I was so excited I couldn't wait for it to come out. When we finished, there wasn't any kind of celebration that I can recall. We didn't go out to a disco or anything. We just rested. I prefer just being with people I really like anyway. That's my way of celebrating.

The three videos that came out of *Thriller*—"Billie Jean," "Beat It," and "Thriller"—were all part of my original concept for the album. I was determined to present this music as visually as possible. At the time I would look at what people were doing with video, and I couldn't understand why so much of it seemed so primitive and weak. I saw kids watching and accepting boring videos because they had no alternatives. My goal is to do the best I can in every area, so why work hard on an album and then produce a terrible video? I wanted something that would *glue* you to the set, something you'd want to watch over and over. The idea from the beginning was to give people quality. So I wanted to be a pioneer in this relatively new medium and make the best short music movies we could make. I don't even like to call them videos. On the set I explained that we were doing a *film,* and that was how I

Jermaine joins the Jacksons on stage for the first time since the Jackson 5 days. A very special evening. Motown 25, 1983.

approached it. I wanted the most talented people in the business—the best cinematographer, the best director, the best lighting people we could get. We weren't shooting on videotape; it was 35-mm film. We were serious.

For the first video, "Billie Jean," I interviewed several directors, looking for someone who seemed really unique. Most of them didn't present me with anything that was truly innovative. At the same time I was trying to think bigger, the record company was giving me a problem on the budget. So I ended up paying for "Beat It" and "Thriller" because I didn't want to argue with anybody about money. I own both of those films myself as a result.

"Billie Jean" was done with CBS's money—about $250,000. At the time that was a lot of money for a video, but it really pleased me that they believed in me that much. Steve Baron, who directed "Billie Jean," had very imaginative ideas, although he didn't agree at first that there should be dancing in it. I felt that people wanted to see dancing. It was great to dance for the video. That freeze-frame where I go on my toes was spontaneous; so were many of the other moves.

"Billie Jean's" video made a big impression on the MTV audience and was a huge hit.

"Beat It" was directed by Bob Giraldi, who had done a lot of commercials. I remember being in England when

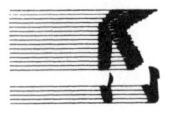

it was decided that "Beat It" would be the next single released from *Thriller,* and we had to choose a director for the video.

I felt "Beat It" should be interpreted literally, the way it was written, one gang against another on tough urban streets. It had to be *rough.* That's what "Beat It" was about.

When I got back to L.A., I saw Bob Giraldi's demo reel and knew that he was the director I wanted for "Beat It." I loved the way he told a story in his work, so I talked with him about "Beat It." We went over things, my ideas and his ideas, and that's how it was created. We played with the storyboard and molded it and sculpted it.

I had street gangs on my mind when I wrote "Beat It," so we rounded up some of the toughest gangs in Los Angeles and put them to work on the video. It turned out to be a good idea, and a great experience for me. We had some rough kids on that set, tough kids, and they hadn't been to wardrobe. Those guys in the pool room in the first scene were serious; they were not actors. That stuff was real.

Now I hadn't been around really tough people all that much, and these guys were more than a little intimidating at first. But we had security around and were ready for anything that might happen. Of course we soon realized

203

we didn't need any of this, that the gang members were mostly humble, sweet, and kind in their dealings with us. We fed them during breaks, and they all cleaned up and put their trays away. I came to realize that the whole thing about being bad and tough is that it's done for recognition. All along these guys had wanted to be seen and respected, and now we were going to put them on TV. They *loved* it. "Hey, look at me, I'm somebody!" And I think that's really why many of the gangs act the way they do. They're rebels, but rebels who want attention and respect. Like all of us, they just want to be seen. And I gave them that chance. For a few days at least they were stars.

They were so wonderful to me—polite, quiet, supportive. After the dance numbers they'd compliment my work, and I could tell they really meant it. They wanted a lot of autographs and frequently stood around my trailer. Whatever they wanted, I gave them: photographs, autographs, tickets for the Victory tour, anything. They were a nice bunch of guys.

The truth of that experience came out on the screen. The "Beat It" video was menacing, and you could *feel* those people's emotions. You felt the experience of the streets and the reality of their lives. You look at "Beat It" and know those kids are tough. They were being them-

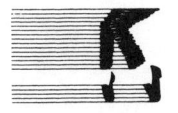

selves, and it came across. It was nothing like actors acting; it was as far from that as possible. They were being
themselves; that feeling you got was *their* spirit.

I've always wondered if they got the same message
from the song that I did.

When *Thriller* first came out, the record company assumed it would sell a couple of million copies. In general
record companies never believe a new album will do considerably better than the last one you did. They figure you
either got lucky last time or the number you last sold is the
size of your audience. They usually just ship a couple of
million out to the stores to cover the sales in case you get
lucky again.

That's how it usually works, but I wanted to alter
their attitude with *Thriller.*

One of the people who helped me with *Thriller* was
Frank Dileo. Frank was vice president for promotion at
Epic when I met him. Along with Ron Weisner and Fred
DeMann, Frank was responsible for turning my dream for
Thriller into a reality. Frank heard parts of *Thriller* for the
first time at Westlake Studio in Hollywood, where much of
the album was recorded. He was there with Freddie
DeMann, one of my managers, and Quincy and I played
them "Beat It" and a little bit of "Thriller," which we

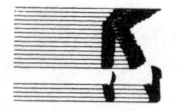

Frank Dileo and I clown around for the camera.

At John Branca and Julia McArthur's wedding with Little Richard, who
performed the ceremony.

were still working on. They were very impressed, and we started to talk seriously about how to "break" this album wide open.

Frank really worked hard and proved to be my right hand during the years ahead. His brilliant understanding of the recording industry proved invaluable. For instance, we released "Beat It" as a single while "Billie Jean" was still at number one. CBS screamed, "You're crazy. This will kill 'Billie Jean.'" But Frank told them not to worry, that both songs would be number one and both would be in the Top 10 at the same time. They were.

By the spring of 1983 it was clear that the album was going to go crazy. Over the top. Every time they released another single, sales of the album would go even higher.

Then the "Beat It" video took off.

On May 16, 1983, I performed "Billie Jean" on a network telecast in honor of Motown's twenty-fifth anniversary. Almost fifty million people saw that show. After that, many things changed.

The *Motown 25* show had actually been taped a month earlier, in April. The whole title was *Motown 25: Yesterday, Today, and Forever,* and I'm forced to admit I had to be talked into doing it. I'm glad I did because the show

eventually produced some of the happiest and proudest moments of my life.

As I mentioned earlier, I said no to the idea at first. I had been asked to appear as a member of the Jacksons and then to do a dance number on my own. But none of us were Motown artists any longer. There were lengthy debates between me and my managers, Weisner and DeMann. I thought about how much Berry Gordy had done for me and the group, but I told my managers and Motown that I didn't want to go on TV. My whole attitude toward TV is fairly negative. Eventually Berry came to see me to discuss it. I was editing "Beat It" at the Motown studio, and someone must have told him I was in the building. He came down to the studio and talked to me about it at length. I said, "Okay, but if I do it, I want to do 'Billie Jean.' " It would have been the only non-Motown song in the whole show. He told me that's what he wanted me to do anyway. So we agreed to do a Jacksons' medley, which would include Jermaine. We were all thrilled.

So I gathered my brothers and rehearsed them for this show. I really worked them, and it felt nice, a bit like the old days of the Jackson 5. I choreographed them and rehearsed them for *days* at our house in Encino, videotaping every rehearsal so we could watch it later. Jermaine and Marlon also made their contributions. Next we went

208

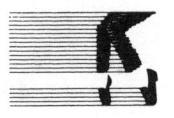

to Motown in Pasadena for rehearsals. We did our act and, even though we reserved our energy and never went all out at rehearsal, all the people there were clapping and coming around and watching us. Then I did my "Billie Jean" rehearsal. I just walked through it because as yet I had nothing planned. I hadn't had time because I was so busy rehearsing the group.

The next day I called my management office and said, "Please order me a spy's hat, like a cool fedora—something that a secret agent would wear." I wanted something sinister and special, a real slouchy kind of hat. I still didn't have a very good idea of what I was going to do with "Billie Jean."

During the *Thriller* sessions, I had found a black jacket, and I said, "You know, someday I'm going to wear this to perform. It was so perfect and so show business that I wore it on *Motown 25.*

But the night before the taping, I still had no idea what I was going to do with my solo number. So I went down to the kitchen of our house and played "Billie Jean." Loud. I was in there by myself, the night before the show, and I pretty much stood there and let the song tell me what to do. I kind of let the dance create itself. I really let it *talk* to me; I heard the beat come in, and I took this spy's hat and started to pose and step, letting the "Billie Jean"

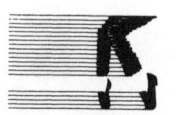

rhythm create the movements. I felt almost compelled to let it create itself. I couldn't help it. And that—being able to "step back" and let the dance come through—was a lot of fun.

I had also been practicing certain steps and movements, although most of the performance was actually spontaneous. I had been practicing the Moonwalk for some time, and it dawned on me in our kitchen that I would finally do the Moonwalk in public on *Motown 25.*

Now the Moonwalk was already out on the street by this time, but I enhanced it a little when I did it. It was born as a break-dance step, a "popping" type of thing that black kids had created dancing on street corners in the ghetto. Black people are truly innovative dancers; they create many of the new dances, pure and simple. So I said, "This is my chance to do it," and I did it. These three kids taught it to me. They gave me the basics—and I had been doing it a lot in private. I had practiced it together with certain other steps. All I was really sure of was that on the bridge to "Billie Jean" I was going to walk backward and forward at the same time, like walking on the moon.

On the day of the taping, Motown was running behind schedule. Late. So I went off and rehearsed by myself. By then I had my spy hat. My brothers wanted to know what the hat was for, but I told them they'd have to

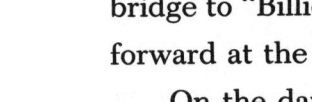

210

wait and see. But I did ask Nelson Hayes for a favor.
"Nelson—after I do the set with my brothers and the
lights go down, sneak the hat out to me in the dark. I'll be
in the corner, next to the wings, talking to the audience,
but you sneak that hat back there and put it in my hand in
the dark."

So after my brothers and I finished performing, I
walked over to the side of the stage and said, "You're
beautiful! I'd like to say those were the good old days;
those were magic moments with all my brothers, including Jermaine. But what I really like"—and Nelson is
sneaking the hat into my hand—"are the newer songs." I
turned around and grabbed the hat and went into "Billie
Jean," into that heavy rhythm; I could tell that people in
the audience were really enjoying my performance. My
brothers told me they were crowding the wings watching
me with their mouths open, and my parents and sisters
were out there in the audience. But I just remember
opening my eyes at the end of the thing and seeing this
sea of people standing up, applauding. And I felt so many
conflicting emotions. I knew I had done my best and felt
good, so good. But at the same time I felt disappointed in
myself. I had planned to do one really long spin and to
stop on my toes, suspended for a moment, but I didn't stay
on my toes as long as I wanted. I did the spin and I landed

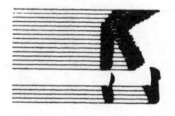

on one toe. I wanted to just stay there, just *freeze* there, but it didn't work quite as I'd planned.

When I got backstage, the people back there were congratulating me. I was still disappointed about the spin. I had been concentrating so hard and I'm such a perfectionist. At the same time I knew this was one of the happiest moments of my life. I knew that for the first time my brothers had really gotten a chance to watch me and see what I was doing, how I was evolving. After the performance, each of them hugged and kissed me backstage. They had never done that before, and I felt happy for all of us. It was so wonderful when they kissed me like that. I loved it! I mean, we hug all the time. My whole family embraces a lot, except for my father. He's the only one who doesn't. Whenever the rest of us see each other, we embrace, but when they all kissed me that night, I felt as if I had been blessed by them.

The performance was still gnawing at me, and I wasn't satisfied until a little boy came up to me backstage. He was about ten years old and was wearing a tuxedo. He looked up at me with stars in his eyes, frozen where he stood, and said, "Man, who ever taught you to dance like that?"

I kind of laughed and said, "Practice, I guess." And this boy was looking at me, awestruck. I walked away, and

for the first time that evening I felt really good about what I had accomplished that night. I said to myself, I must have done really well because children are honest. When that kid said what he did, I really felt that I *had* done a good job. I was so moved by the whole experience that I went right home and wrote down everything which had happened that night. My entry ended with my encounter with the child.

The day after the *Motown 25* show, Fred Astaire called me on the telephone. He said—these are his exact words—"You're a hell of a mover. Man, you really put them on their asses last night." That's what Fred Astaire said to me. I thanked him. Then he said, "You're an angry dancer. I'm the same way. I used to do the same thing with my cane."

I had met him once or twice in the past, but this was the first time he had ever called me. He went on to say, "I watched the special last night; I taped it and I watched it again this morning. You're a *hell* of a mover."

It was the greatest compliment I had ever received in my life, and the only one I had ever wanted to believe. For Fred Astaire to tell me that meant more to me than anything. Later my performance was nominated for an Emmy Award in a musical category, but I lost to Leontyne Price. It didn't matter. Fred Astaire had told me things I

My friend Fred Astaire.

would never forget—*that* was my reward. Later he invited me to his house, and there were more compliments from him until I really blushed. He went over my "Billie Jean" performance, step by step. The great choreographer Hermes Pan, who had choreographed Fred's dances in the movies, came over, and I showed them how to Moonwalk and demonstrated some other steps that really interested them.

Not long after that Gene Kelly came by my house to visit and also said he liked my dancing. It was a fantastic experience, that show, because I felt I had been inducted into an informal fraternity of dancers, and I felt so honored because these were the people I most admired in the world.

Right after *Motown 25* my family read a lot of stuff in the press about my being "the new Sinatra" and as "exciting as Elvis"—that kind of thing. It was very nice to hear, but I knew the press could be so fickle. One week they love you, and the next week they act like you're rubbish.

Later I gave the glittery black jacket I wore on *Motown 25* to Sammy Davis as a present. He said he was going to do a takeoff of me on stage, and I said, "Here, you want to wear this when you do it?" He was so happy. I love Sammy. He's such a fine man and a real showman. One of the best.

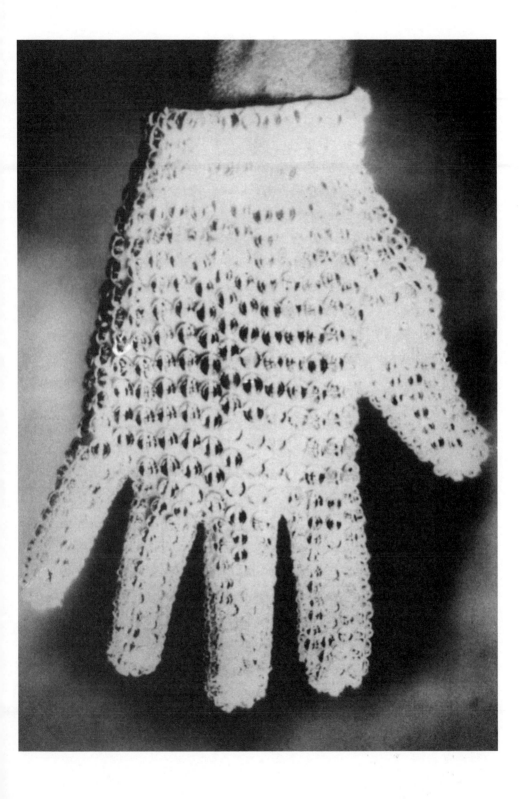

I had been wearing a single glove for years before *Thriller.* I felt that one glove was cool. Wearing two gloves seemed so ordinary, but a single glove was different and was definitely a look. But I've long believed that thinking too much about your look is one of the biggest mistakes you can make, because an artist should let his style evolve naturally, spontaneously. You can't *think* about these things; you have to *feel* your way into them.

I actually had been wearing the glove for a long time, but it hadn't gotten a lot of attention until all of a sudden it hit with *Thriller* in 1983. I was wearing it on some of the old tours back in the 1970s, and I wore one glove during the *Off the Wall* tour and on the cover of the live album that came out afterward.

It's so show business that one glove. I love wearing it. Once, by coincidence, I wore a black glove to the American Music Awards ceremony, which happened to fall on Martin Luther King, Jr.'s birthday. Funny how things happen sometimes.

I admit that I love starting trends, but I never thought wearing white socks was going to catch on. Not too long ago it was considered extremely square to wear white socks. It was cool in the 1950s, but in the '60s and '70s you

wouldn't be caught dead in white socks. It was too square to even consider—for most people.

But I never stopped wearing them. Ever. My brothers would call me a dip, but I didn't care. My brother Jermaine would get upset and call my mother, "Mother, Michael's wearing his white socks again. Can't you do something? Talk to him." He would complain bitterly. They'd all tell me I was a goofball. But I still wore my white socks, and now it's cool again. Those white socks must have caught on just to spite Jermaine. I get tickled when I think about it. After *Thriller* came out, it even became okay to wear your pants high around your ankles again.

My attitude is if fashion says it's forbidden, I'm going to do it.

When I'm at home, I don't like to dress up. I wear anything that's handy. I used to spend days in my pajamas. I like flannel shirts, old sweaters and slacks, simple clothes.

When I go out, I dress up in sharper, brighter, more tailored clothes, but around the house and in the studio anything goes. I don't wear much jewelry—usually none —because it gets in my way. Occasionally people give me gifts of jewelry and I treasure them for the sentiment, but usually I just put them away somewhere. Some of it has been stolen. Jackie Gleason gave me a beautiful ring. He

219

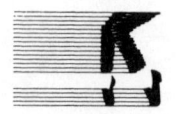

took it off his finger and gave it to me. It was stolen and I miss it, but it doesn't really bother me because the gesture meant more than anything else, and that can't be taken from me. The ring was just a material thing.

What really makes me happy, what I love is performing and creating. I really don't care about all the material trappings. I love to put my soul into something and have people accept it and like it. That's a wonderful feeling.

I appreciate art for that reason. I'm a great admirer of Michelangelo and of how he poured his soul into his work. He knew in his heart that one day he would die, but that the work he did would live on. You can tell he painted the ceiling of the Sistine Chapel with all his soul. At one point he even destroyed it and did it over because he wanted it to be perfect. He said, "If the wine is sour, pour it out."

I can look at a painting and lose myself. It pulls you in, all the pathos and drama. It communicates with you. You can sense what the artist was feeling. I feel the same way about photography. A poignant or strong photograph can speak volumes.

As I said earlier, there were many changes in my life in the aftermath of *Motown 25*. We were told that forty-seven million people watched that show, and apparently many of them went out and bought *Thriller*. By the fall of

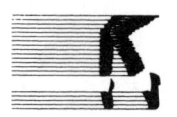

A visit to the White House.

1983 the album had sold eight million copies, eclipsing, by far, CBS's expectations for the successor to *Off the Wall.* At that point Frank Dileo said he'd like to see us produce another video or short film.

It was clear to us that the next single and video should be "Thriller," a long track that had plenty of material for a brilliant director to play with. As soon as the decision was made, I knew who I wanted to have direct it. The year before I had seen a horror film called *An American Were-wolf in London,* and I knew that the man who made it, John Landis, would be perfect for "Thriller," since our concept for the video featured the same kind of transformations that happened to his character.

So we contacted John Landis and asked him to direct. He agreed and submitted his budget, and we went to work. The technical details of this film were so awesome that I soon got a call from John Branca, my attorney and one of my closest and most valued advisers. John had been working with me ever since the *Off the Wall* days; in fact he even helped me out by donning many hats and functioning in several capacities when I had no manager after *Thriller* was released. He's one of those extremely talented, capable men who can do anything. Anyway, John was in a panic because it had become obvious to him that the original budget for the "Thriller" video was going to

With Ola Ray in the "Thriller" video.

double. I was paying for this project myself, so the money for the budget overruns was coming out of my pocket.

But at this point John came up with a great idea. He suggested we make a separate video, financed by somebody else, about the making of the "Thriller" video. It seemed odd that no one had ever done this before. We felt sure it would be an interesting documentary, and at the same time it would help pay for our doubled budget. It didn't take John long to put this deal together. He got MTV and the Showtime cable network to put up the cash, and Vestron released the video after "Thriller" aired.

The success of *The Making of Thriller* was a bit of a shock to all of us. In its cassette form it sold about a million copies by itself. Even now, it holds the record as the best-selling music video of all time.

The "Thriller" film was ready in late 1983. We released it in February and it made its debut on MTV. Epic released "Thriller" as a single and sales of the album went crazy. According to statistics, the "Thriller" film and the release of the single resulted in fourteen million additional album and tape sales within a six-month period. At one point in 1984, we were selling a million records a week.

I'm still stunned by this response. By the time we finally closed down the *Thriller* campaign a year later, the

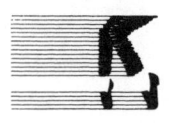

album was at the thirty-two million mark. Today sales are at forty million. A dream come true.

During this period I changed my management as well. My contract with Weisner and DeMann had expired in early 1983. My father was no longer representing me and I was looking at various people. One day I was at the Beverly Hills Hotel, visiting Frank Dileo, and I asked him if he had any interest in leaving Epic and managing my career.

Frank asked me to think about it some more and if I was certain to call him back on Friday.

Needless to say, I called back.

The success of *Thriller* really hit me in 1984, when the album received a gratifying number of nominations for the American Music Awards and the Grammy Awards. I remember feeling an overwhelming rush of jubilation. I was whooping with joy and dancing around the house, screaming. When the album was certified as the best-selling album of all time, I couldn't believe it. Quincy Jones was yelling, "Bust open the champagne!" We were all in a state. Man! What a feeling! To work so hard on something, to give so much and to succeed! Everyone involved with *Thriller* was floating on air. It was wonderful.

I imagined that I felt like a long-distance runner must

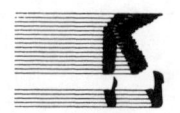

Some of the many awards I've been honored to receive.

feel when breaking the tape at the finish line. I would think of an athlete, running as hard and as fast as he can. Finally he gets close to the finish line and his chest hits that ribbon and the crowd is soaring with him. And I'm not even into sports!

But I identify with that person because I know how hard he's trained and I know how much that moment means to him. Perhaps a whole life has been devoted to this endeavor, this one moment. And then he wins. That's the realization of a dream. That's powerful stuff. I can share that feeling because I know.

One of the side effects of the *Thriller* period was to make me weary of constantly being in the public eye. Because of this, I resolved to lead a quieter, more private life. I was still quite shy about my appearance. You must remember that I had been a child star and when you grow up under that kind of scrutiny people don't want you to change, to get older and look different. When I first became well known, I had a lot of baby fat and a very round, chubby face. That roundness stayed with me until several years ago when I changed my diet and stopped eating beef, chicken, pork, and fish, as well as certain fattening foods. I just wanted to look better, live better, and be healthier. Gradually, as I lost weight, my face took on its present

227

In Florida at Barry Gibb's house.

shape and the press started accusing me of surgically altering my appearance, beyond the nose job I freely admitted I had, like many performers and film stars. They would take an old picture from adolescence or high school, and compare it to a current photograph. In the old picture my face would be round and pudgy. I'd have an Afro, and the picture would be badly lit. The new picture would show a much older, more mature face. I've got a different hairstyle and a different nose. Also, the photographer's lighting is excellent in the recent photographs. It's really not fair to make such comparisons. They have said I had bone surgery done on my face. It seems strange to me that people would jump to that conclusion and I thought it was very unfair.

Judy Garland and Jean Harlow and many others have had their noses done. My problem is that as a child star people got used to seeing me look one way.

I'd like to set the record straight right now. I have never had my cheeks altered or my eyes altered. I have not had my lips thinned, nor have I had dermabrasion or a skin peel. All of these charges are ridiculous. If they were true, I would say so, but they aren't. I have had my nose altered twice and I recently added a cleft to my chin, but that is it. Period. I don't care what anyone else says—it's my face and I know.

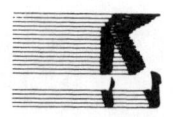

I'm a vegetarian now and I'm so much thinner. I've been on a strict diet for *years*. I feel better than I ever have, healthier and more energetic. I don't understand why the press is so interested in speculating about my appearance anyway. What does my face have to do with my music or my dancing?

The other day a man asked me if I was happy. And I answered, "I don't think I'm ever totally happy." I'm one of the hardest people to satisfy, but at the same time, I'm aware of how much I have to be thankful for and I am truly appreciative that I have my health and the love of my family and friends.

I'm also easily embarrassed. The night I won eight American Music Awards, I accepted them wearing my shades on the network broadcast. Katharine Hepburn called me up and congratulated me, but she gave me a hard time because of the sunglasses. "Your fans want to see your eyes," she scolded me. "You're cheating them." The following month, February 1984, at the Grammy show, *Thriller* had walked off with seven Grammy Awards and looked like it was going to win an eighth. All evening I had been going up to the podium and collecting awards with my sunglasses on. Finally, when *Thriller* won for

Best Album, I went up to accept it, took off my glasses, and stared into the camera. "Katharine Hepburn," I said, "this is for you." I knew she was watching and she was.

You have to have some fun.

CHAPTER

SIX

ALL YOU NEED
IS LOVE

I had planned to spend most of 1984 working on some movie ideas I had, but those plans got sidetracked. First, in January, I was burned on the set of a Pepsi commercial I was shooting with my brothers.

The reason for the fire was stupidity, pure and simple. We were shooting at night and I was supposed to come down a staircase with magnesium flash bombs going off on either side of me and just behind me. It seemed so simple. I was to walk down the stairs and these bombs would blow up behind me. We did several takes that were wonderfully timed. The lightning effects from the bombs were great. Only later did I find out that these bombs were only two feet away from either side of my head, which was a

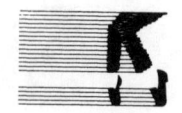

total disregard of the safety regulations. I was supposed to stand in the middle of a magnesium explosion, two feet on either side.

Then Bob Giraldi, the director, came to me and said, "Michael, you're going down too early. We want to *see* you up there, up on the stairs. When the lights come on, we want to reveal that you're there, so *wait.*"

So I waited, the bombs went off on either side of my head, and the sparks set my hair on fire. I was dancing down this ramp and turning around, spinning, not knowing I was on fire. Suddenly I felt my hands reflexively going to my head in an attempt to smother the flames. I fell down and just tried to shake the flames out. Jermaine turned around and saw me on the ground, just after the explosions had gone off, and he thought I had been shot by someone in the crowd—because we were shooting in front of a big audience. That's what it looked like to him.

Miko Brando, who works for me, was the first person to reach me. After that, it was chaos. It was crazy. No film could properly capture the drama of what went on that night. The crowd was screaming. Someone shouted, "Get some ice!" There were frantic running sounds. People were yelling, "Oh no!" The emergency truck came up and before they put me in I saw the Pepsi executives huddled together in a corner, looking terrified. I remem-

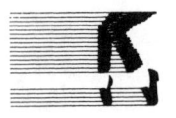

ber the medical people putting me on a cot and the guys from Pepsi were so scared they couldn't even bring themselves to check on me.

Meanwhile, I was kind of detached, despite the terrible pain. I was watching all the drama unfold. Later they told me I was in shock, but I remember enjoying the ride to the hospital because I never thought I'd ride in an ambulance with the sirens wailing. It was one of those things I had always wanted to do when I was growing up. When we got there, they told me there were news crews outside, so I asked for my glove. There's a famous shot of me waving from the stretcher with my glove on.

Later one of the doctors told me that it was a miracle I was alive. One of the firemen had mentioned that in most cases your clothes catch on fire, in which case your whole face can be disfigured or you can die. That's it. I had third-degree burns on the back of my head that almost went through to my skull, so I had a lot of problems with it, but I was very lucky.

What we now know is that the incident created a lot of publicity for the commercial. They sold more Pepsi than ever before. And they came back to me later and offered me the biggest commercial endorsement fee in history. It was so unprecedented that it went into *The Guinness Book of World Records.* Pepsi and I worked

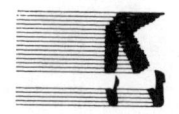

together on another commercial, called "The Kid," and I gave them problems by limiting the shots of me because I felt the shots they were asking for didn't work well. Later, when the commercial was a success, they told me I had been right.

I still remember how scared those Pepsi executives looked the night of the fire. They thought that my getting burned would leave a bad taste in the mouth of every kid in America who drank Pepsi. They knew I could have sued them and I could have, but I was real nice about it. Real nice. They gave me $1,500,000 which I immediately donated to the Michael Jackson Burn Center. I wanted to do something because I was so moved by the other burn patients I met while I was in the hospital.

Then there was the Victory tour. I did fifty-five shows with my brothers over the course of five months.

I didn't want to go on the Victory tour and I fought against it. I felt the wisest thing for me would be *not* to do the tour, but my brothers wanted to do it and I did it for them. So I told myself that since I was committed to doing this, I might as well put my soul into it.

When it came down to the actual tour, I was outvoted on a number of issues, but you don't think when you're onstage, you just deliver. My goal for the Victory tour was to give each performance everything I could. I hoped

people might come to see me who didn't even like me. I hoped they might hear about the show and want to see what's going on. I wanted incredible word-of-mouth response to the show so a wide range of people would come and see us. Word of mouth is the best publicity. Nothing beats it. If someone I trust comes to me and tells me something is great, I'm sold.

I felt very powerful in those days of Victory. I felt on top of the world. I felt determined. That tour was like: "We're a mountain. We've come to share our music with you. We have something we want to tell you." At the beginning of the show, we rose out of the stage and came down these stairs. The opening was dramatic and bright and captured the whole feeling of the show. When the lights came on and they saw us, the roof would come off the place.

239

It was a nice feeling, playing with my brothers again. It gave us a chance to relive our days as the Jackson 5 and the Jacksons. We were all together again. Jermaine had come back and we were riding a wave of popularity. It was the biggest tour any group had ever done, in huge outdoor stadiums. But I was disappointed with the tour from the beginning. I had wanted to move the world like it had never been moved. I wanted to present something that would make people say, "Wow! That's wonderful!"

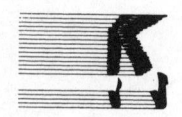

The response we got *was* wonderful and the fans were great, but I became unhappy with our show. I didn't have the time or the opportunity to perfect it the way I wanted to. I was disappointed in the staging of "Billie Jean." I wanted it to be so much more than it was. I didn't like the lighting and I never got my steps quite the way I wanted them. It killed me to have to accept these things and settle for doing it the way I did.

There've been times right before a show when certain things were bothering me—business or personal problems. I would think, "I don't know how to go through with this. I don't know how I'm going to get through the show. I can't perform like this."

But once I get to the side of the stage, something happens. The rhythm starts and the lights hit me and the problems disappear. This has happened so many times. The thrill of performing just takes over. It's like God saying, "Yes, you can. Yes, you can. Just wait. Wait till you hear this. Wait till you see this." And the backbeat gets in my backbone and it vibrates and it just takes me. Sometimes I almost lose control and the musicians say, "What is he doing?" and they start following me. You change the whole schedule of a piece. You stop and you just take over from scratch and do a whole other thing. The song takes you in another direction.

There was a part of the show on the Victory tour where I was doing this scatting theme and the audience was repeating what I said. I'd say, "Da, de, da, de" and they'd say, "Da, de, da, de." There've been times when I've done that and they would start stomping. And when the whole audience is doing that, it sounds like an earthquake. Oh! It's a great feeling to be able to do that with all those people—whole stadiums—and they're all doing the same thing you're doing. It's the greatest feeling in the world. You look out in the audience and see toddlers and teens and grandparents and people in their twenties and thirties. Everybody is swaying, their hands are up, and they're all singing. You ask that the house lights come on and you see their faces and you say, "Hold hands" and they hold hands and you say, "Stand up" or "Clap" and they do. They're enjoying themselves and they'll do whatever you tell them. They love it and it's so beautiful—all the races of people are together doing this. At times like that I say, "Look around you. Look at yourselves. Look. Look around you. Look at what you have done." Oh, it's so beautiful. Very powerful. Those are great moments.

The Victory tour was my first chance to be exposed to the Michael Jackson fans since *Thriller* had come out two years earlier. There were some strange reactions. I'd bump into people in hallways and they'd go, "Naw, that

can't be him. He wouldn't be here." I was baffled and I'd ask myself, "Why wouldn't I? I'm on earth *somewhere.* I've got to be somewhere at any given time. Why not here?" Some fans imagine you to be almost an illusion, this thing that doesn't exist. When they see you, they feel it's a miracle or something. I've had fans ask me if I use the bathroom. I mean, it gets embarrassing. They just lose touch with the fact that you're like them because they get so excited. But I can understand it because I'd feel the same way if, for instance, I could have met Walt Disney or Charlie Chaplin.

Kansas City opened the tour. It was Victory's first night. We were walking by the hotel pool in the evening and Frank Dileo lost his balance and fell in. People saw this and started to get excited. Some of us were kind of embarrassed, but I was laughing. He wasn't hurt and he looked *so* surprised. We jumped over a low wall and found ourselves on the street without any security. People didn't seem to be able to believe that we were just walking around on the street like that. They gave us a wide berth.

Later when we returned to the hotel, Bill Bray, who has headed my security team since I was a child, just shook his head and laughed as we recounted our adventures.

Bill is very careful and immensely professional in his

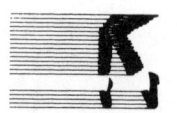

job, but he doesn't worry about things after the fact. He travels with me everywhere and occasionally he's my only companion on short trips. I can't imagine life without Bill; he's warm and funny and absolutely in love with life. He's a great man.

When the tour was in Washington, D.C., I was out on our hotel balcony with Frank, who has a great sense of humor and enjoys playing pranks himself. We were teasing one another and I started pulling $100 bills from his pockets and throwing them to people who were walking down below. This almost caused a riot. He was trying to stop me, but we were both laughing. It reminded me of the pranks my brothers and I used to pull on tour. Frank sent our security people downstairs to try and find any undiscovered money in the bushes.

In Jacksonville, the local police almost killed us in a traffic accident during the four-block drive from the hotel to the stadium. Later, in another part of Florida, when the old tour boredom set in that I described earlier, I played a little trick on Frank. I asked him to come up to my suite and when he came in I offered him some watermelon, which was lying on a table across the room. Frank went over to pick up a piece and tripped over my boa constrictor, Muscles, who was on the road with me. Muscles is

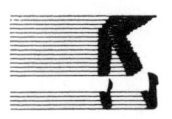

Having fun with Bill Bray.

harmless, but Frank hates snakes and proceeded to scream and yell. I started chasing him around the room with the boa. Frank got the upper hand, however. He panicked, ran from the room, and grabbed the security guard's gun. He was going to shoot Muscles, but the guard calmed him down. Later he said all he could think of was: "I've got to get that snake." I've found that a lot of tough men are afraid of snakes.

We were locked in hotels all over America, just like in the old days. Me and Jermaine or me and Randy would get up to our old tricks, taking buckets of water and pouring them off hotel balconies onto people eating in the atriums far below. We were up so high the water was just mist by the time it reached them. It was just like the old days, bored in the hotels, locked away from fans for our own protection, unable to go anywhere without massive security.

But there were a lot of days that were fun too. We had a lot of time off on that tour and we got to take five little vacations to Disney World. Once, when we were staying in the hotel there, an amazing thing happened. I'll never forget it. I was on a balcony where we could see a big area. There were all these people. It was so crowded that people were bumping into each other. Someone in that

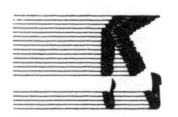

crowd recognized me and started screaming my name. Thousands of people began chanting, "Michael! Michael!" and it was echoing all over the park. The chanting continued until finally it was so loud that if I hadn't acknowledged it, it would have been rude. As soon as I did, everybody started screaming. I said, "Oh, this is so beautiful. I've got it so good." All the work I'd put in on *Thriller*, my crying and believing in my dreams and working on those songs and falling asleep near the microphone stand because I was so tired, all of it was repaid by this display of affection.

I've seen times where I'd walk into a theater to see a play and everybody would just start applauding. Just because they're glad that I happen to be there. At moments like that, I feel so honored and so happy. It makes all the work seem worthwhile.

249

The Victory tour was originally going to be called "The Final Curtain" because we all realized it was going to be the last tour we did together. But we decided not to put the emphasis on that.

I enjoyed the tour. I knew it would be a long road; in the end, it was probably too long. The best part of it for me was seeing the children in the audience. Every night there would be a number of them who had gotten all

dressed up. They were so excited. I was truly inspired by the kids on that tour, kids of all ethnic groups and ages. It's been my dream since I was a child to somehow unite people of the world through love and music. I still get goose bumps when I hear the Beatles sing "All You Need Is Love." I've always wished that song could be an anthem for the world.

I loved the shows we did in Miami and all the time we spent there. Colorado was great too. We got to spend some time relaxing up at the Caribou Ranch. And New York was really something, as it always is. Emmanuel Lewis came to the show, as did Yoko, Sean Lennon, Brooke, a lot of good friends. Thinking back, the offstage moments stand out for me as much as the concerts themselves. I found I could lose myself in some of those shows. I remember swinging my jackets around and slinging them into the audience. The wardrobe people would get annoyed at me and I'd say honestly, "I'm sorry but I can't help it. I can't control myself. Something takes over and I *know* I shouldn't do it, but you just can't control it. There's a spirit of joy and communion that gets inside you and you want to just let it all out."

We were on the Victory tour when we learned that my sister Janet had gotten married. Everybody was afraid to tell me because I am so close to Janet. I was shocked. I

252

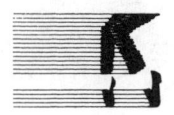

feel very protective of her. Quincy Jones's little daughter was the one to break the news to me.

I've always enjoyed a wonderfully close relationship with all three of my beautiful sisters. LaToya is really a wonderful person. She's very easy to be around, but she can be funny, too. You go in her room and you can't sit on the couch, you can't sit on the bed, you can't walk on the carpet. This is the truth. She will run you out of her room. She wants everything to be perfect in there. I say, "You *have* to walk on the carpet sometimes," but she doesn't want prints on it. If you cough at the table, she covers her plate. If you sneeze, forget it. That's how she is. Mother says she used to be that way herself.

Janet, on the other hand, was always a tomboy. She has been my best friend in the family for the longest time. That's why it killed me to see her go off and get married. We did everything together. We shared the same interests, the same sense of humor. When we were younger, we'd get up on "free" mornings and write out a whole schedule for the day. Usually it would read something like this: GET UP, FEED THE ANIMALS, HAVE BREAKFAST, WATCH SOME CARTOONS, GO TO THE MOVIES, GO TO A RESTAURANT, GO TO ANOTHER MOVIE, GO HOME AND GO SWIMMING. That was our idea of a great day. In the eve-

ning, we'd look back at the list and think about all the fun we'd had.

It was great being with Janet because we didn't have to worry that one of us wouldn't like something. We liked the same things. We'd sometimes read to each other. She was like my twin.

LaToya and I are very different, on the other hand. She won't even feed the animals; the smell alone drives her away. And forget going to the movies. She doesn't understand what I see in *Star Wars* or *Close Encounters* or *Jaws*. Our tastes in films are miles apart.

When Janet was around and I wasn't working on something, we'd be inseparable. But I knew we'd eventually develop separate interests and attachments. It was inevitable.

Her marriage didn't last long, unfortunately, but now she's happy again. I do think that marriage can be a wonderful thing if it's right for the two people involved. I believe in love—very much so—how can you not believe after you've experienced it? I believe in relationships. One day I know I'll find the right woman and get married myself. I often look forward to having children; in fact, it would be nice to have a big family, since I come from such a large one myself. In my fantasy about having a large family, I imagine myself with thirteen children.

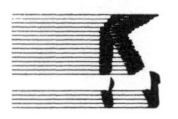

I can't resist babies. In China, 1987.

Right now, my work still takes up most of my time and most of my emotional life. I work all the time. I love creating and coming up with new projects. As for the future, *Que sera, sera.* Time will tell. It would be hard for me to be that dependent on somebody else, but I can imagine it if I try. There's so much I want to do and so much work to be done.

I can't help but pick up on some of the criticism leveled at me at times. Journalists seem willing to say anything to sell a paper. They say I've had my eyes widened, that I want to look more white. More white? What kind of statement is that? I didn't invent plastic surgery. It's been around for a long time. A lot of very fine, very nice people have had plastic surgery. No one writes about their surgery and levies such criticism at them. It's not fair. Most of what they print is a fabrication. It's enough to make you want to ask, "What happened to truth? Did it go out of style?"

In the end, the most important thing is to be true to yourself and those you love and work hard. I mean, work like there's no tomorrow. Train. Strive. I mean, really train and cultivate your talent to the highest degree. Be the best at what you do. Get to know more about your field than anybody alive. Use the tools of your trade, if it's books or a floor to dance on or a body of water to swim in.

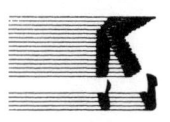

Whatever it is, it's yours. That's what I've always tried to remember. I thought about it a lot on the Victory tour.

In the end, I felt I touched a lot of people on the Victory tour. Not exactly in the way I wanted to, but I felt that would happen later, when I was off on my own, performing and making movies. I donated all my performance money to charity, including funds for the burn center that helped me after the fire on the Pepsi set. We donated more than four million dollars that year. For me, that was what the Victory tour was all about—giving back.

After my experiences with the Victory tour, I started making my career decisions with more care than ever. I had learned a lesson on an earlier tour, which I remembered vividly during the difficulties with Victory.

We did a tour years ago with this guy who ripped us off, but he taught me something. He said, "Listen, all these people work for *you*. You don't work for *them*. You are paying them."

He kept telling me that. Finally I began to understand what he meant. It was an entirely new concept for me because at Motown everything was done for us. Other people made our decisions. I've been mentally scarred by that experience. "You've got to wear this. You've got to do these songs. You are going here. You are going to do this

interview and that TV show." That's how it went. We couldn't say anything. When he told me I was in control, I finally woke up. I realized he was right.

Despite everything, I owe that guy a debt of gratitude.

Captain Eo came about because the Disney Studios wanted me to come up with a new ride for the parks. They said they didn't care what I did, as long as it was something creative. I had this big meeting with them, and during the course of the afternoon I told them that Walt Disney was a hero of mine and that I was very interested in Disney's history and philosophy. I wanted to do something with them that Mr. Disney himself would have approved. I had read a number of books about Walt Disney and his creative empire, and it was very important to me to do things as he would have.

In the end, they asked me to do a movie and I agreed. I told them I would like to work with George Lucas and Steven Spielberg. It turned out Steven was busy, so George brought in Francis Ford Coppola and that was the *Captain Eo* team.

I flew up to San Francisco a couple of times to visit George at his place, Skywalker Ranch, and gradually we came up with a scenario for a short film that would incor-

porate every recent advance in 3-D technology. *Captain Eo* would look and feel like the audience was in a spaceship, along for the ride.

Captain Eo is about transformation and the way music can help to change the world. George came up with the name Captain Eo. (*Eo* is Greek for "dawn.") The story is about a young guy who goes on a mission to this miserable planet run by an evil queen. He is entrusted with the responsibility of bringing the inhabitants light and beauty. It's a great celebration of good over evil.

Working on *Captain Eo* reinforced all the positive feelings I've had about working in film and made me realize more than ever that movies are where my future path probably lies. I love the movies and have since I was real little. For two hours you can be transported to another place. Films can take you anywhere. That's what I like. I can sit down and say, "Okay, nothing else exists right now. Take me to a place that's wonderful and make me forget about my pressures and my worries and day-to-day schedule."

I also love to be in front of a 35 mm camera. I used to hear my brothers say, "I'll be glad when this shoot is over," and I couldn't understand why they weren't enjoying it. I would be watching, trying to learn, seeing what the director was trying to get, what the light man was

259

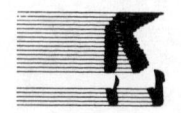

doing. I wanted to know where the light was coming from and why the director was doing a scene so many times. I enjoyed hearing about the changes being made in the script. It's all part of what I consider my ongoing education in films. Pioneering new ideas is so exciting to me and the movie industry seems to be suffering right now from a dearth of ideas; so many people are doing the same things. The big studios remind me of the way Motown was acting when we were having disagreements with them: They want easy answers, they want their people to do formula stuff—sure bets—only the public gets bored, of course. So many of them are doing the same old corny stuff. George Lucas and Steven Spielberg are exceptions.

I'm going to try to make some changes. I'm going to try to change things around someday.

Marlon Brando has become a very close and trusted friend of mine. I can't tell you how much he's taught me. We sit and talk for hours. He has told me a great deal about the movies. He is such a wonderful actor and he has worked with so many giants in the industry—from other actors to cameramen. He has a respect for the artistic value of filmmaking that leaves me in awe. He's like a father to me.

So these days movies are my number one dream, but I have a lot of other dreams too.

In early 1985 we cut "We Are the World" at an all-night all-star recording session that was held after the ceremony for the American Music Awards. I wrote the song with Lionel Richie after seeing the appalling news footage of starving people in Ethiopia and the Sudan.

Around that time, I used to ask my sister Janet to follow me into a room with interesting acoustics, like a closet or the bathroom, and I'd sing to her, just a note, a rhythm of a note. It wouldn't be a lyric or anything; I'd just hum from the bottom of my throat. I'd say, "Janet, what do you see? What do you see when you hear this sound?" And this time she said, "Dying children in Africa."

"You're right. That's what I was dictating from my soul."

And she said, "You're talking about Africa. You're talking about dying children." That's where "We Are the World" came from. We'd go in a dark room and I'd sing notes to her. To my mind, that's what singers should be able to do. We should be able to perform and be effective, even if it's in a dark room. We've lost a lot because of TV. You should be able to move people without all that advanced technology, without pictures, using only sound.

I've been performing for as long as I can remember. I know a lot of secrets, a lot of things like that.

I think that "We Are the World" is a very spiritual song, but spiritual in a special sense. I was proud to be a part of that song and to be one of the musicians there that night. We were united by our desire to make a difference. It made the world a better place for us and it made a difference to the starving people we wanted to help.

We collected some Grammy Awards and began to hear easy-listening versions of "We Are the World" in elevators along with "Billie Jean." Since first writing it, I had thought that song should be sung by children. When I finally heard children singing it on producer George Duke's version, I almost cried. It's the *best* version I've heard.

After "We Are the World," I again decided to retreat from public view. For two and a half years I devoted most of my time to recording the follow-up to *Thriller,* the album that came to be titled *Bad.*

Why did it take so long to make *Bad?* The answer is that Quincy and I decided that this album should be as close to perfect as humanly possible. A perfectionist has to take his time; he shapes and he molds and he sculpts that thing until it's perfect. He can't let it go before he's satisfied; he can't.

If it's not right, you throw it away and do it over. You

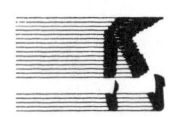

work that thing till it's just right. When it's as perfect as you can make it, you put it out there. Really, you've got to get it to where it's just right; that's the secret. That's the difference between a number thirty record and a number one record that stays number one for weeks. It's got to be good. If it is, it stays up there and the whole world wonders when it's going to come down.

I have a hard time explaining how Quincy Jones and I work together on making an album. What I do is, I write the songs and do the music and then Quincy brings out the best in me. That's the only way I can explain it. Quincy will listen and make changes. He'll say, "Michael, you should put a change in there," and I'll write a change. And he'll guide me on and help me create and help me invent and work on new sounds, new kinds of music.

And we fight. During the *Bad* sessions we disagreed on some things. If we struggle at all, it's about new stuff, the latest technology. I'll say, "Quincy, you know, music changes all the time." I want the latest drum sounds that people are doing. I want to go beyond the latest thing. And then we go ahead and make the best record that we can.

We don't ever try to pander to the fans. We just try to play on the quality of the song. People will not buy junk.

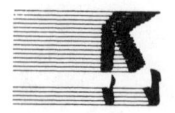

They'll only buy what they like. If you take all the trouble to get in your car, go to the record store, and put your money on the counter, you've got to really like what you're going to buy. You don't say, "I'll put a country song on here for the country market, a rock song for that market," and so on. I feel close to all different styles of music. I love some rock songs and some country songs and some pop and all the old rock 'n' roll records.

We did go after a rock type of song with "Beat It." We got Eddie Van Halen to play guitar because we knew he'd do the best job. Albums should be for all races, all tastes in music.

In the end, many songs kind of create themselves. You just say, "This is it. This is how it's going to be." Of course, not every song is going to have a great dance tempo. It's like "Rock with You" isn't a great dance tempo. It was meant for the old dance the Rock. But it's not a "Don't Stop" or "Working Day and Night" rhythm or a "Startin' Something" type of thing—something you can play with on the dance floor and get sweaty, working out to.

We worked on *Bad* for a long time. Years. In the end, it was worth it because we were satisfied with what we had achieved, but it was difficult too. There was a lot of tension because we felt we were competing with our-

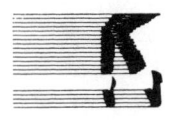

selves. It's very hard to create something when you feel like you're in competition with yourself because no matter how you look at it, people are always going to compare *Bad* to *Thriller*. You can always say, "Aw, forget *Thriller*," but no one ever will.

I think I have a slight advantage in all of this because I always do my best work under pressure.

"Bad" is a song about the street. It's about this kid from a bad neighborhood who gets to go away to a private school. He comes back to the old neighborhood when he's on a break from school and the kids from the neighborhood start giving him trouble. He sings, "I'm bad, you're bad, who's bad, who's the best?" He's saying when you're strong and good, *then* you're bad.

"Man in the Mirror" is a great message. I love that song. If John Lennon was alive, he could really relate to that song because it says that if you want to make the world a better place, you have to work on yourself and change first. It's the same thing Kennedy was talking about when he said, "Ask not what your country can do for you; ask what you can do for your country." If you want to make the world a better place, take a look at yourself and make a change. Start with the man in the

mirror. Start with yourself. Don't be looking at all the other things. Start with *you.*

That's the truth. That's what Martin Luther King meant and Gandhi too. That's what I believe.

Several people have asked me if I had anybody in mind when I wrote "Can't Stop Loving You." And I say that I didn't, really. I was thinking of somebody while I was singing it, but not while I was writing it.

I wrote all the songs on *Bad* except for two, "Man in the Mirror," which Siedah Garrett wrote with George Ballard, and "Just Good Friends," which is by these two writers who wrote "What's Love Got to Do with It" for Tina Turner. We needed a duet for me and Stevie Wonder to sing and they had this song; I don't even think they intended for it to be a duet. They wrote it for me, but I knew it would be perfect for me and Stevie to sing together.

"Another Part of Me" was one of the earliest songs written for *Bad* and made its public debut at the end of *Captain Eo* when the captain says good-bye. "Speed Demon" is a machine song. "The Way You Make Me Feel" and "Smooth Criminal" are simply the grooves I was in at the time. That's how I would put it.

"Leave Me Alone" is a track that appears only on the

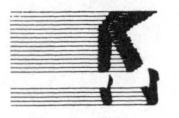

In the subway, New York City, 1987, filming "Bad."

compact disc of *Bad*. I worked hard on the song, stacking vocals on top of each other like layers of clouds. I'm sending a simple message here: "Leave me alone." The song is about a relationship between a guy and a girl. But what I'm really saying to people who are bothering me is: *"Leave me alone."*

The pressure of success does funny things to people. A lot of people become successful very quickly and it's an instant occurrence in their lives. Some of these people, whose success might be a one-shot thing, don't know how to handle what happens to them.

I look at fame from a different perspective, since I've been in this business for so long now. I've learned that the way to survive as your own person is to shun personal publicity and keep a low profile as much as possible. I guess it's good in some ways and bad in others.

The hardest part is having no privacy. I remember when we were filming "Thriller," Jackie Onassis and Shaye Areheart came to California to discuss this book. There were photographers in the trees, everywhere. It was not possible for us to do anything without it being noticed and reported.

The price of fame can be a heavy one. Is the price you pay worth it? Consider that you really have *no* privacy. You can't really do anything unless special arrangements

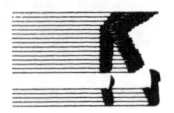

are made. The media prints whatever you say. They report whatever you do. They know what you buy, which movies you see, you name it. If I go to a public library, they print the titles of the books I check out. In Florida once, they printed my whole schedule in the paper; everything I did from ten in the morning until six at night. "After he did this, he did that, and after he did that, he went there, then he went door to door, and then he . . ."

I remember thinking to myself, "What if I were trying to do something that I didn't happen to *want* reported in the paper?" All of this is the price of fame.

I think my image gets distorted in the public's mind. They don't get a clear or full picture of what I'm like, despite the press coverage I mentioned early. Mistruths are printed as fact, in some cases, and frequently only half of a story will be told. The part that doesn't get printed is often the part that would make the printed part less sensational by shedding light on the facts. As a result, I think some people don't think I'm a person who determines what's happening with his career. Nothing could be further from the truth.

I've been accused of being obsessed with my privacy and it's true that I am. People stare at you when you're famous. They're observing you and that's understandable, but it's not always easy. If you were to ask me why I wear

sunglasses in public as often as I do, I'd tell you it's because I simply don't like to have to constantly look everyone in the eye. It's a way of concealing just a bit of myself. After I had my wisdom teeth pulled, the dentist gave me a surgical mask to wear home to keep out germs. I loved that mask. It was great—much better than sunglasses—and I had fun wearing it around for a while. There's so little privacy in my life that concealing a little bit of me is a way to give myself a break from all that. It may be considered strange, I know, but I like my privacy.

I can't answer whether or not I like being famous, but I do love achieving goals. I love not only reaching a mark I've set for myself but exceeding it. Doing more than I thought I could, that's a great feeling. There's nothing like it. I think it's so important to set goals for yourself. It gives you an idea of where you want to go and how you want to get there. If you don't aim for something, you'll never know whether you could have hit the mark.

I've always joked that I didn't ask to sing and dance, but it's true. When I open my mouth, music comes out. I'm honored that I have this ability. I thank God for it every day. I try to cultivate what He gave me. I feel I'm compelled to do what I do.

There are so many things all around us to be thankful for. Wasn't it Robert Frost who wrote about the world a

My nephew Taj and I have some real fun.

Arriving in Sydney, Australia, holding a gift from a young fan.

person can see in a leaf? I think that's true. That's what I love about being with kids. They notice everything. They aren't jaded. They get excited by things we've forgotten to get excited about any more. They are so natural too, so unself-conscious. I love being around them. There always seems to be a bunch of kids over at the house and they're always welcome. They energize me—just being around them. They look at everything with such fresh eyes, such open minds. That's part of what makes kids so creative. They don't worry about the rules. The picture doesn't have to be in the center of the piece of paper. The sky doesn't have to be blue. They are accepting of people too. The only demand they make is to be treated fairly—and to be loved. I think that's what we all want.

I would like to think that I'm an inspiration for the children I meet. I want kids to like my music. Their approval means more to me than anyone else's. It's always the kids who know which song is going to be a hit. You see kids who can't even talk yet, but they've got a little rhythm going. It's funny. But they're a tough audience. In fact, they're the toughest audience. There have been so many parents who have come to me and told me that their baby knows "Beat It" or loves "Thriller." George Lucas told me his daughter's first words were "Michael Jackson." I felt on top of the world when he told me that.

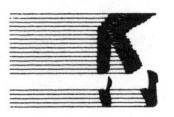

I spend a lot of free time—in California and when I'm traveling—visiting children's hospitals. It makes me so happy to be able to brighten those kids' day by just showing up and talking with them, listening to what they have to say and making them feel better. It's so sad for children to have to get sick. More than anyone else, kids don't deserve that. They often can't even understand what's wrong with them. It makes my heart twist. When I'm with them, I just want to hug them and make it all better for them. Sometimes sick children will visit me at home or in my hotel rooms on the road. A parent will get in touch with me and ask if their child can visit with me for a few minutes. Sometimes when I'm with them I feel like I understand better what my mother must have gone through with her polio. Life is too precious and too short not to reach out and touch the people we can.

You know, when I was going through that bad period with my skin and my adolescent growth spurts, it was kids who never let me down. They were the only ones who accepted the fact that I was no longer little Michael and that I was really the same person inside, even if you didn't recognize me. I've never forgotten that. Kids are great. If I were living for no other reason than to help and please kids, that would be enough for me. They're amazing people. Amazing.

275

Between breaks in filming *Smooth Criminal* with Sean Lennon, Brandon Adams, and Kelly Parker.

I am a person who is very much in control of his life. I have a team of exceptional people working for me and they do an excellent job of presenting me with the facts that keep me up-to-date on everything that's going on at MJJ Productions so that I can know the options and make the decisions. As far as my creativity is concerned, that's my domain and I enjoy that aspect of my life as much or more than any other.

I think I have a goody-goody image in the press and I hate that, but it's hard to fight because I don't normally talk about myself. I am a shy person. It's true. I don't like giving interviews or appearing on talk shows. When Doubleday approached me about doing this book, I was interested in being able to talk about how I feel in a book that would be mine—my words and my voice. I hope it will help clear up some misconceptions.

Everybody has many facets to them and I'm no different. When I'm in public, I often feel shy and reserved. Obviously, I feel differently away from the glare of cameras and staring people. My friends, my close associates, know there's another Michael that I find it difficult to present in the outlandish "public" situations I often find myself in.

It's different when I'm onstage, however. When I perform, I lose myself. I'm in total control of that stage. I don't think about anything. I know what I want to do from the moment I step out there and I love every minute of it. I'm actually relaxed onstage. Totally relaxed. It's nice. I feel relaxed in the studio too. I know whether something *feels* right. If it doesn't, I know how to fix it. Everything has to be in place and if it is you feel good, you feel fulfilled. People used to underestimate my ability as a songwriter. They didn't think of me as a songwriter, so when I started coming up with songs, they'd look at me like: "Who *really* wrote that?" I don't know what they must have thought—that I had someone back in the garage who was writing them for me? But time cleared up those misconceptions. You always have to prove yourself to people and so many of them don't want to believe. I've heard tales of Walt Disney going from studio to studio when he first started out, trying to sell his work unsuccessfully and being turned down. When he was finally given a chance, everyone thought he was the greatest thing that ever happened.

Sometimes when you're treated unfairly it makes you stronger and more determined. Slavery was a terrible thing, but when black people in America finally got out

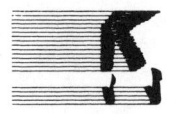

from under that crushing system, they were *stronger.* They knew what it was to have your spirit crippled by people who are controlling your life. They were never going to let that happen again. I admire that kind of strength. People who have it take a stand and put their blood and soul into what they believe.

People often ask me what I'm like. I hope this book will answer some of those questions, but these things might help too. My favorite music is an eclectic mix. For example, I love classical music. I'm crazy about Debussy. *Prelude to the Afternoon of a Faun* and *Clair de Lune.* And Prokofiev. I could listen to *Peter and the Wolf* over and over and over again. Copland is one of my all-time favorite composers. You can recognize his distinctive brass sounds right away. *Billy the Kid* is fabulous. I listen to a lot of Tchaikovsky. The *Nutcracker Suite* is a favorite. I have a large collection of show tunes also—Irving Berlin, Johnny Mercer, Lerner and Loewe, Harold Arlen, Rodgers and Hammerstein, and the great Holland-Dozier-Holland. I really admire those guys.

I like Mexican food very much. I'm a vegetarian, so fortunately fresh fruits and vegetables are a favorite of mine.

I love toys and gadgets. I like to see the latest things

manufacturers have come out with. If there's something really wonderful, I'll buy one.

I'm crazy about monkeys, especially chimps. My chimp Bubbles is a constant delight. I really enjoy taking him with me on trips or excursions. He's a wonderful distraction and a *great* pet.

I love Elizabeth Taylor. I'm inspired by her bravery. She has been through so much and she is a survivor. That lady has been through a lot and she's walked out of it on two feet. I identify with her very strongly because of our experiences as child stars. When we first started talking on the phone, she told me she felt as if she had known me for years. I felt the same way.

Katharine Hepburn is a dear friend too. I was afraid to meet her at first. We talked for a while when I first arrived for a stay on the set of *On Golden Pond*, where I was Jane Fonda's guest. She invited me to have dinner with her the next night. I felt very fortunate. Since then, we have visited one another and remained close. Remember, it was Katharine Hepburn who got me to remove my sunglasses at the Grammy Awards. She's a big influence on me. She's another strong person and a private person.

I believe performers should try to be strong as an example to their audiences. It's staggering what a person

can do if they only try. If you're under pressure, play off that pressure and use it to advantage to make whatever you're doing better. Performers owe it to people to be strong and fair.

Often in the past performers have been tragic figures. A lot of the truly great people have suffered or died because of pressure and drugs, especially liquor. It's so sad. You feel cheated as a fan that you didn't get to watch them evolve as they grew older. One can't help wondering what performances Marilyn Monroe would have put in or what Jimi Hendrix might have done in the 1980s.

A lot of celebrities say they don't want their children to go into show business. I can understand their feelings, but I don't agree with them. If I had a son or daughter, I'd say, "By all means, be my guest. Step right in there. If you want to do it, do it."

To me, nothing is more important than making people happy, giving them a release from their problems and worries, helping to lighten their load. I want them to walk away from a performance I've done, saying, "That was great. I want to go back again. I had a great time." To me, that's what it's all about. That's wonderful. That's why I don't understand when some celebrities say they don't want their kids in the business.

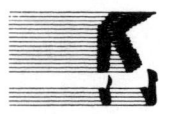

I think they say that because they've been hurt themselves. I can understand that. I've been there too.

—Michael Jackson
Encino, California
1988

What one wishes is to be touched by truth and to be able to interpret that truth so that one may use what one is feeling and experiencing, be it despair or joy, in a way that will add meaning to one's life and will hopefully touch others as well.

This is art in its highest form. Those moments of enlightenment are what I continue to live for.

—*Michael Jackson*

Jacqueline Kennedy Onassis and Shaye Areheart were
Michael Jackson's editors at Doubleday Publishing Company,
which published Moonwalk *in 1988.*

Michael Jackson had an infectious laugh and a wonderful sense
of humor. When Jacqueline Kennedy Onassis and I visited him
for the first time at his home in Encino in 1983, he was a gra-
cious and charming host. Waiting with him to say hello were
his mother, Katherine, and his sisters, La Toya and Janet,
looking as young and fresh as high school students. Michael
was dressed in what I would come to regard as his everyday
attire—black loafers, white socks, black slacks, a white (or
sometimes blue) oxford long-sleeved shirt over a white T-
shirt. He was sweet and funny and a little shy, but it was
obvious that he was honored to have Jackie in his home and
pleased that she and I wanted him to write a book.

We talked and nibbled on the spread of food Mrs. Jackson had put out for us, and then Michael asked if we'd like
a tour of the house and the grounds. We saw his trophies
and plaques, the gold records and many photographs of

Michael with people like Fred Astaire, James Brown, and Elizabeth Taylor, and, well, seemingly anyone who was famous in America in 1983. Michael had impeccable manners and he wasn't in the least boastful about any of this, but you could tell he was proud—a little boy from Gary, Indiana, had managed all of this!

The last room we toured had a very large glass terrarium with a lid on it. It was on a low table, and it was hard to see what was inside. Jackie and I were looking around, admiring some very beautiful birds in cages, oblivious to what Michael was up to, when suddenly he turned from the terrarium and said with a sweet smile, "Here, Shaye, you want to hold Muscles?" Languishing across his outstretched hands was a very pretty boa constrictor. I took it. It felt like damp silk and, much to my surprise, began to move sideways, so that I was in danger of dropping it. I exclaimed to that effect, and Michael protectively retrieved his snake with a look of abject disappointment on his face. It was only much later, when he teased me about it, that I realized he was hoping—wildly hoping—for a shriek from me and, maybe, a hysterical dash out of the room. He was a kid at heart—then and always.

Michael was making the music video for his song "Thriller" while we were in Los Angeles, and he invited us to come see what he was up to. We went out to the studio the next day and met John Landis, who was directing the video, and saw the set, which was riddled with the holes that the ghouls would emerge from. Michael and John began joking about

the insurance mess they would be in if we got hurt, and suddenly we were being ushered to Michael's trailer, where we began to talk about what the book could and should be. He was a very visual person and he thought he might like it to be a coffee-table picture book with a lot of text. We weren't set on a particular format so we were open to discussing anything and everything. It was then that Michael asked Jackie if she would be willing to write a foreword to the book once it was completed, and she agreed. We went back to New York with a book deal in hand, and the adventure began in earnest.

Over the four years that I intermittently worked and traveled with Michael while he was creating his book, *Moonwalk,* I saw his delight in the world, his fresh perspective on what most of us would call reality. Michael was an artist, and artists are not like us; they don't want to work in an office, to live conventionally, to never ruffle feathers.

Michael lived music, he breathed music. While walking down the stairs or riding in a car, he would open his mouth and a bit of a song he was working on, or a melody that was running through his head, would rise to the listener's ears, and all within hearing range would feel quite amazed to be in the company of someone who was so obviously a musical genius.

Michael, we all know, was deprived of a childhood, and it

haunted him and kept him in "Neverland." He realized how important and special childhood was, even as those of us who were lucky enough to have one did not. He had lived in the land of the grown-ups for too many years, and he saw with wonder and a growing uneasiness that adults frequently live in a treacherous world of brutality, backbiting, and fear. Having been introduced to it too soon, Michael never wanted to live that way. He was deprived of many of the most basic aspects of childhood, and so instead of playing and goofing off, he worked. He traveled from nightclub to nightclub, from venue to venue, from a hundred inebriated people in a smoke-filled room to the *Ed Sullivan Show*. This was no childhood; this was hard work, and pressure on the shoulders of a little boy with a gorgeous voice and the electric stage persona of someone five times his age.

When he was old enough and financially secure enough, Michael Jackson created his own world, a place where there was peace and kindness, where every candy imaginable was available in dispensers that don't take money, where a movie theater with popcorn and soda pop sat excitingly empty, the projectionist waiting to hear your wishes, a place where chimps dressed in sailor suits and fun was the only accepted currency. Michael loved being in the company of children, because, as he told me many times, "Children don't lie to you. Children are pure and innocent and good. Being with children is like being blessed, like being with angels."

Jackie and I asked Michael to write about his life, because

even at the age he was when we initiated the project, he had spent almost twenty years in show business. He was a great performer, a singer, a songwriter, and a dancer whom Fred Astaire admired. What did this amazing young man have to say, what stories did he want to tell, what had he experienced? As it turned out, Michael had been in the public's eye for so long that he had become very protective of those things his fans could not see, did not know. He had been written about at every stage of his life. Facts had been telegraphed, as had falsehoods. He liked the idea that he could set the record straight in his own book, in his own words, but, too, there was an overriding desire to leave some things for himself and for those people he loved the most.

On our second trip to L.A. to see Michael, we brought along the designer J.C. Suares and a hodgepodge of art supplies and big sheets of drawing paper. We stood around Michael's huge dining room table and he talked about what he'd like the book to be. Michael, who loved to draw, and J.C. sketched out pages, and we all talked about the endless possibilities.

Eventually, *Moonwalk* became the book you are holding in your hands—a smaller size but filled with some of Michael's favorite images, and a drawing of himself and a signature that he did for us on a blank sheet of paper so we could use it as part of the title page. He loved his fans and liked the idea that everyone who owned the book would feel as if they had a signed copy.

Michael had an amazing eye. It was he who dreamed up the white glove, the bits of white tape on his fingertips, the uniforms. It was he who thought that marching down steps with dozens of blue-suited policemen would look cool, that running through the streets with hundreds of men in uniforms would be dramatic and thrilling for the viewer. He sought out the best talent to work with and he oversaw every aspect of his music videos, which he actually thought of as short films and always referred to as short films.

I was with him a few times when people would come to the house to try to get his approval on merchandise they wanted to create. He wanted it to be of the finest quality, to be worth the money people would pay; he wanted it to last. He was a perfectionist. Look again at the music videos; really look at every detail, note the care taken with every shot, every outfit, the lighting. His hand was in everything, his unerring eye was always the final arbiter.

I wish I could say he gave the same attention to his book. While he loved books and carried them with him wherever he went, creating one was just not as exciting as finding the right note or step or guitarist, so the writing of this book took a long time. Still, he wanted *Moonwalk* to happen or it would not have. He gave me amazing access. After one writer who was helping him was unable to capture what he wanted, he suggested to Jackie that maybe I could come out to L.A. and ask him questions, and he would record the answers. The tapes could be transcribed, and he could read them and

add material or be inspired by one story to tell another. I had never interviewed anyone. I was clumsy at the task, but he was easy to work with and forgiving. We spent many after-noons talking in his private sitting room and library off the second floor of the house in Encino with the tape recorder running.

It was a pleasant, wood-paneled room with floor-to-ceiling bookshelves and a fireplace. Usually, we'd sit in front of a fire, Michael stretched out on a sofa, me cross-legged on the floor worrying with the tape recorder. All I had to do was get him started, and he would tell story after story about his family and his childhood, about what it felt like when Motown finally called and Berry Gordy and Diana Ross en-tered his life. He talked and talked, and then we would get the tapes transcribed. Michael would read the transcriptions and fiddle with them and so would I.

In the evenings, we would sometimes see a movie in the screening room. I remember him taking his friend and advi-sor Karen Langford and me to the L.A. County Children's Museum, which they kept open for us after hours. We ex-hausted ourselves leaping against Velcro walls, standing in front of spinning lights, and throwing ourselves into pools of plastic balls. On the way home, he asked his driver to pull over somewhere near the intersection of Hollywood and Vine and jumped from the car to dance on his star on the Hollywood Walk of Fame, singing some perfect little bit of a song before leaping back in, and off we went into the night.

It was exhilarating to be in his presence. He was exciting and funny and brilliant.

A few years passed this way—I had a full-time job back in New York at Doubleday Publishing Company and Michael was busy making videos, writing songs, and recording his next album. Finally, a real writer was given all of the material we had amassed and quickly shaped it into a narrative. When Stephen Davis turned in the final manuscript, Michael had left on the Asia portion of his *Bad* tour. Our CEO, Alberto Vitale, wanted to get the book done as soon as possible—after all, it had been almost four years. I explained that Michael was in Japan and we'd have to wait months for him to return from this portion of the world tour so that he could read and approve everything.

"So go," he said to me. "To Japan?" I asked, shocked. "Why not?" he answered with his signature brevity. So I called Michael's people and asked if I could join him on tour to go over the final draft of *Moonwalk*. Michael said okay but suggested I meet him in Australia, where his schedule would be slightly less hectic than in Japan. He was going to Melbourne first and then on to Sydney and Brisbane. I would join him in Melbourne and stay as long as it took to get what I needed.

It was in Melbourne that I got to see Michael in concert for the first time. He was an electric performer, and I saw this again and again as we traveled and he did show after show. The crowds were huge and mad for him. I wasn't on tour with him anywhere else, but I can promise you that Australians loved Michael Jackson!

We could work together on the book only on the nights that he didn't have a performance. I had brought two copies of the manuscript with me from New York. The first night we got together, I asked Michael how he wanted to work. I suggested that he could read a page while I read the same page, and he could give me any corrections that he might have. He just stared at me with a bemused look on his face. So I said, "Or I could read it to you, and you could stop me whenever you want to make changes." He grinned and said, "That's a much better idea! Read it to me."

So for two weeks in early November 1987, in Melbourne and Sydney—when Michael had the time—I sat at one end of his bed in jeans and he sat at the other in Chinese red silk pajamas, and I read every word of *Moonwalk* as he patiently corrected mistakes and added material, more near the end. When the last page was turned and we were done, we celebrated, and I took the final manuscript and flew back to America.

I saw him in December in L.A. when he got home from the tour, and we discussed what should be on the cover and how the book should be advertised and promoted. He had made it clear that he wasn't willing to do any appearances, TV or radio, but he did suggest that I could be the one to talk about the making of the book when it came out, and I did a little.

Then, without warning, Michael had a crisis of faith about the book shortly before we were to go to press. His lawyer, close advisor, and friend John Branca, who had been involved

with the making of the book in so many wonderful ways, called me at Doubleday to break the news. I was stunned. The book was completely done—introduction, photos, designed cover—everything was set to go to the printer. Jackie and I were very pleased with the way it had turned out, but now Michael had changed his mind.

For about a week, he and John and Karen and all of us at Doubleday struggled with this dilemma. I think he suddenly felt terribly exposed. He had never said so much about himself and his family and his life. He had never done a book before, and books are powerful. Once the words are printed, they are there forever. Would people like it? Had he revealed too much? Would he feel comfortable having the world know his feelings and thoughts? Eventually, he calmed down and let it go, and we started the presses.

Moonwalk instantly became a #1 *New York Times* bestseller and a bestseller around the world. The year was 1988 and Michael was very happy and proud of the attention the book was receiving and so, of course, were we.

I hope you have enjoyed *Moonwalk* and that you feel like you know the real Michael Jackson now, because he was an extraordinary man. I have never met anyone like him, and I doubt I ever will.

Shaye Areheart
New York City
2009